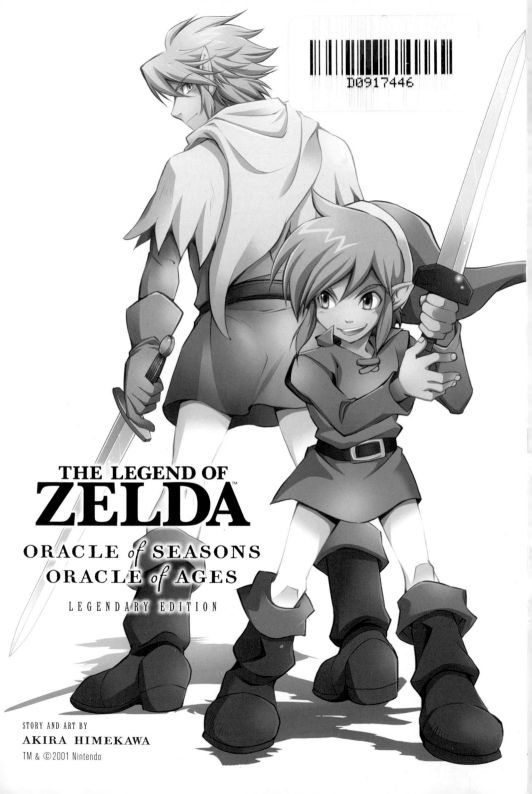

THE LEGEND OF
ZELDA™

ORACLE *of* SEASONS
ORACLE *of* AGES

LEGENDARY EDITION

STORY AND ART BY
AKIRA HIMEKAWA

TM & ©2001 Nintendo

D0917446

THE LEGEND OF ZELDA™

ORACLE *of* SEASONS
ORACLE *of* AGES
LEGENDARY EDITION

ORACLE OF AGES

ALL NEW BONUS STORY

THE LEGEND OF ZELDA: ORACLE OF SEASONS SHORT EDITION

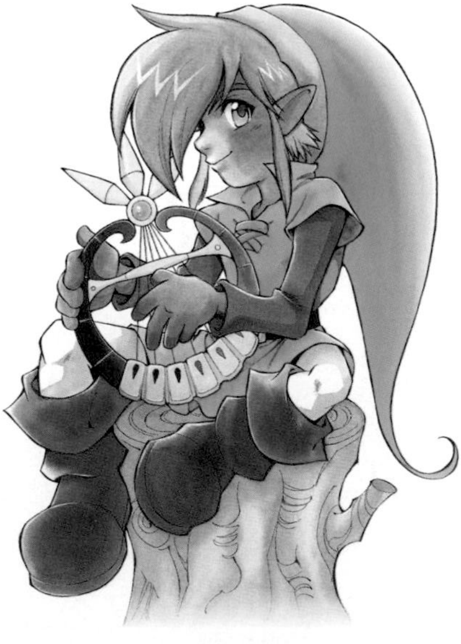

CONTENTS

ORACLE OF SEASONS

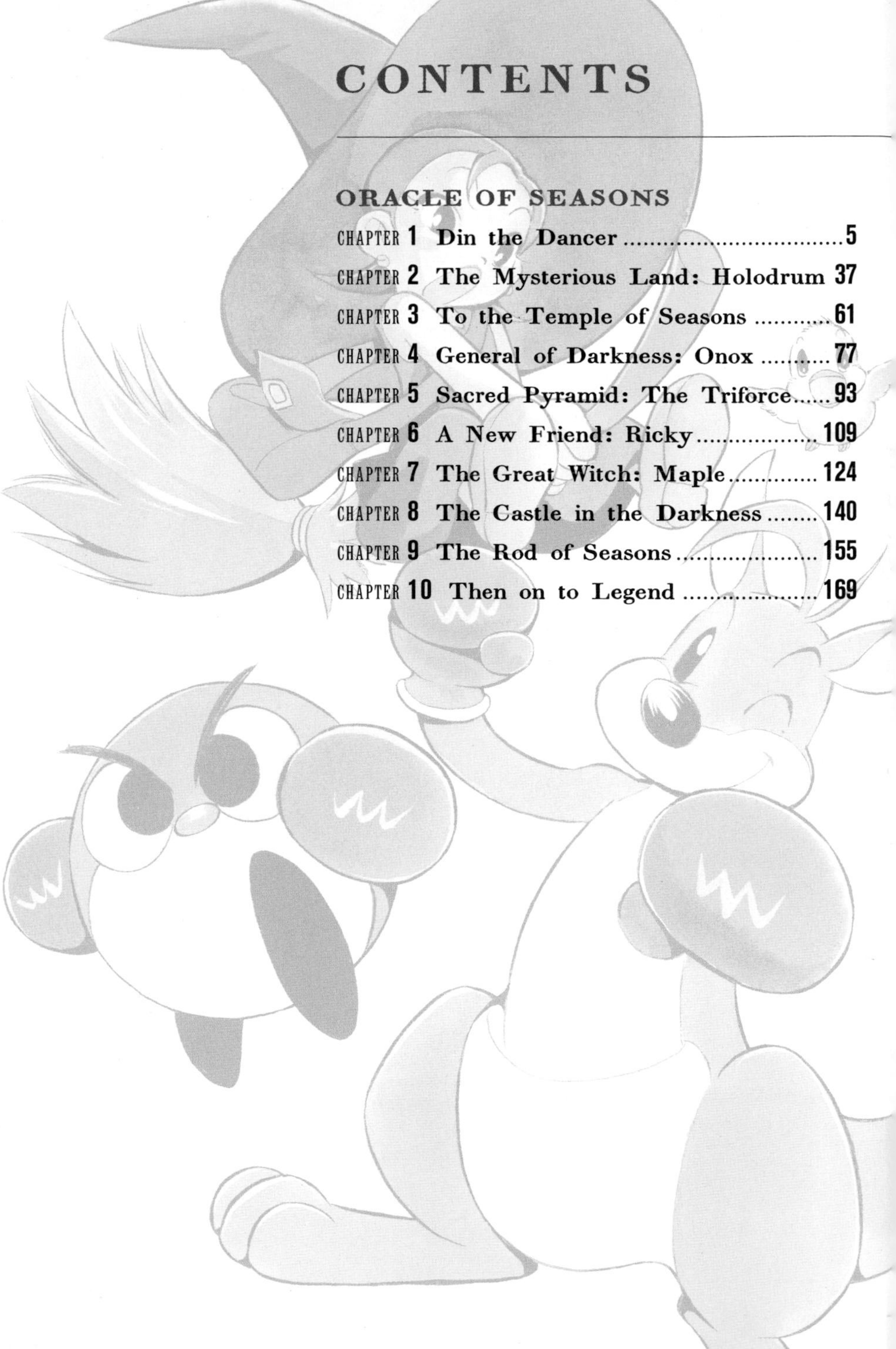

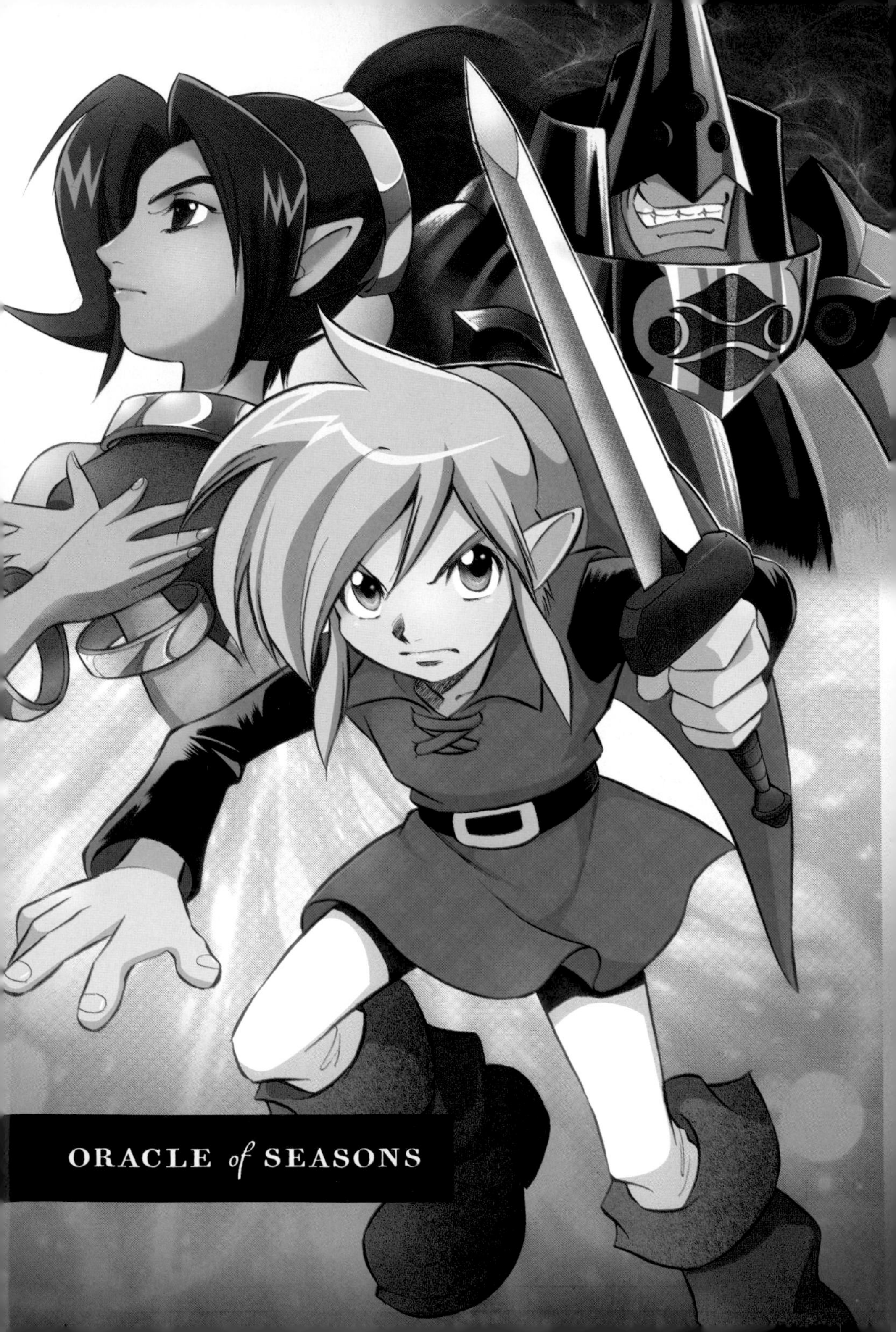
ORACLE of SEASONS

CHAPTER 1
DIN THE DANCER

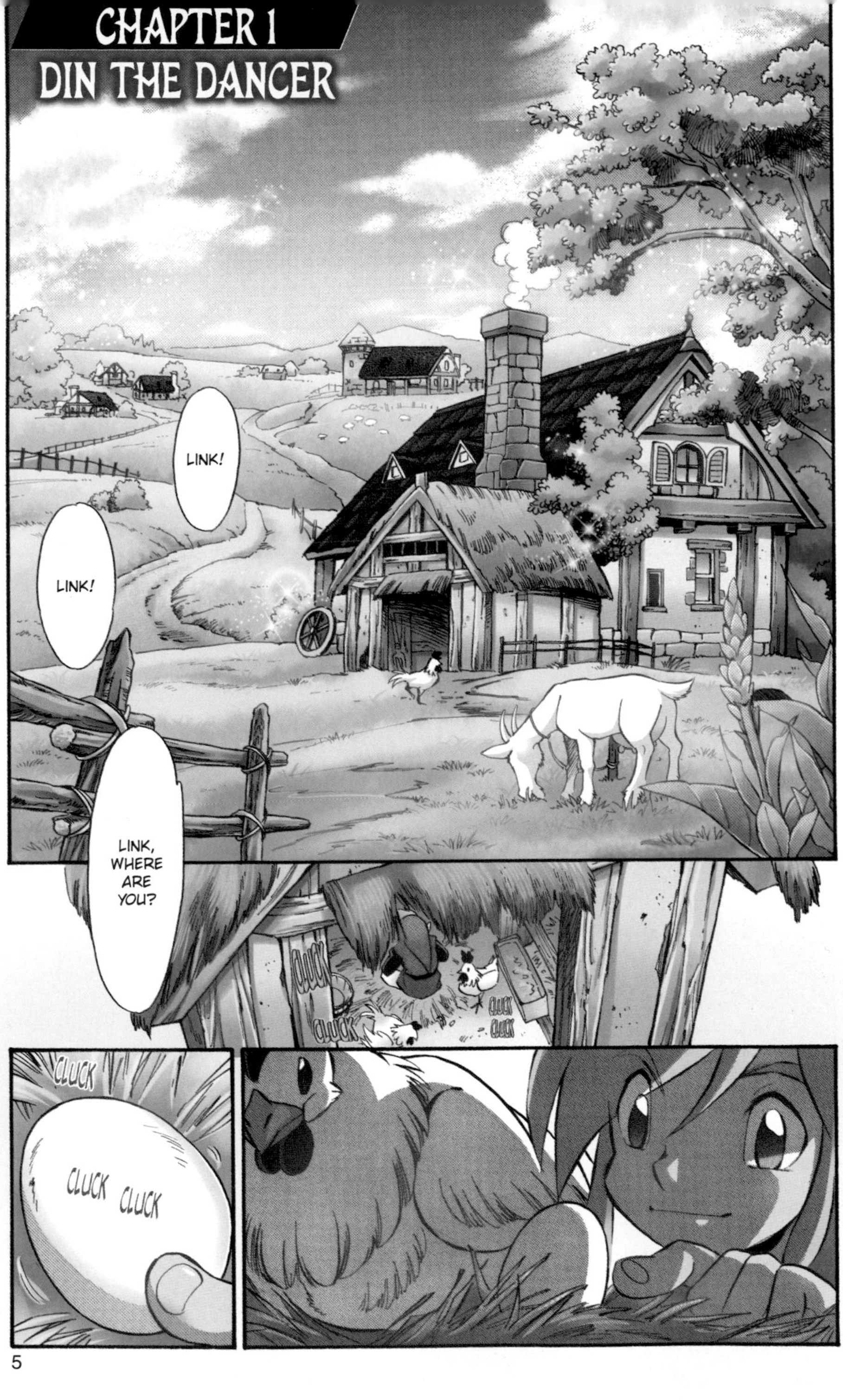

LINK!
LINK!
LINK, WHERE ARE YOU?
CLUCK
CLUCK CLUCK
CLUCK
CLUCK
CLUCK CLUCK

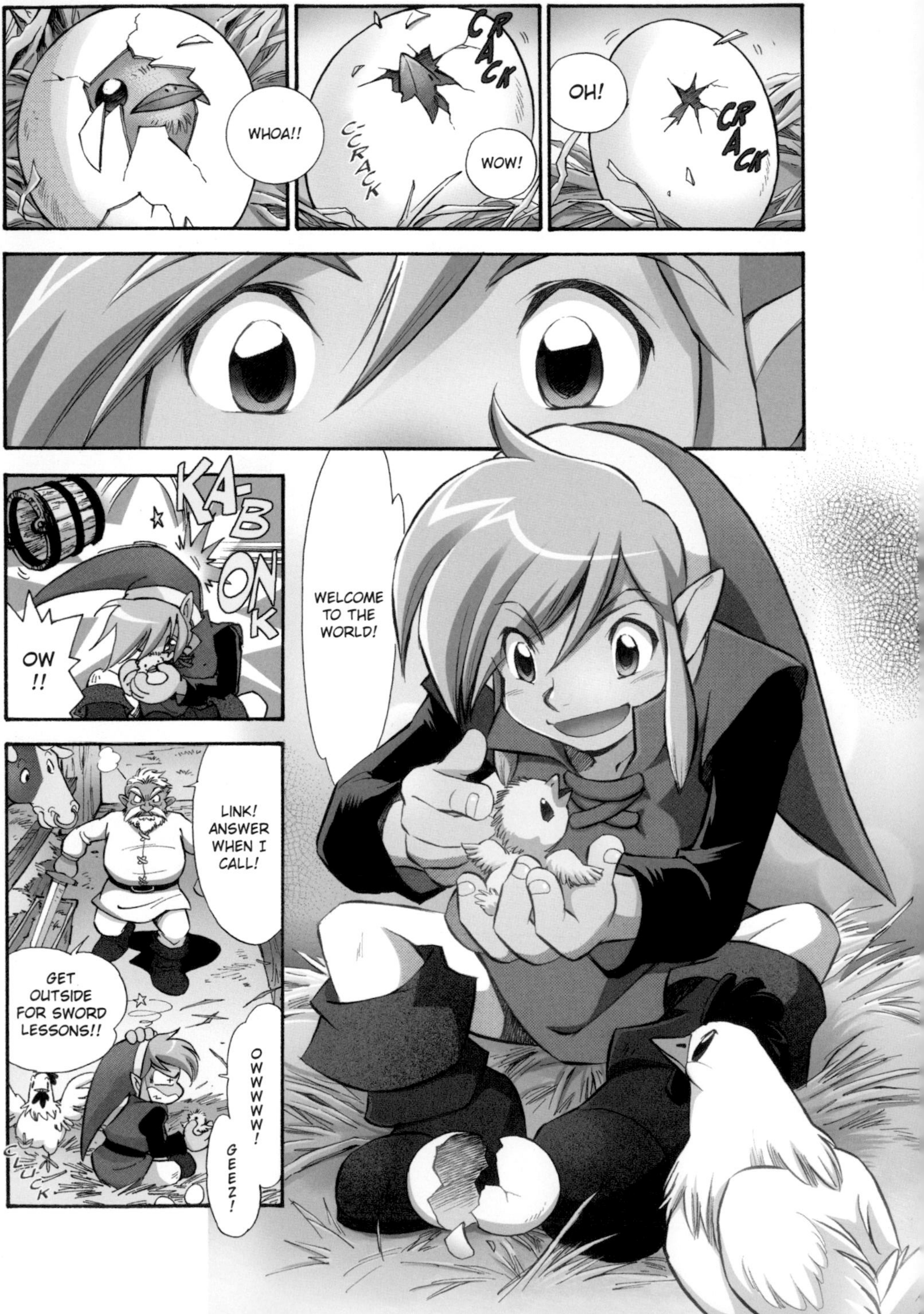

OH!
CRACK
CRACK
WOW!
C-CRACK
WHOA!!
WELCOME TO THE WORLD!
KA-BONK
OW!!
LINK! ANSWER WHEN I CALL!
GET OUTSIDE FOR SWORD LESSONS!!
OWWWWWW! GEEZ!
CLUCK

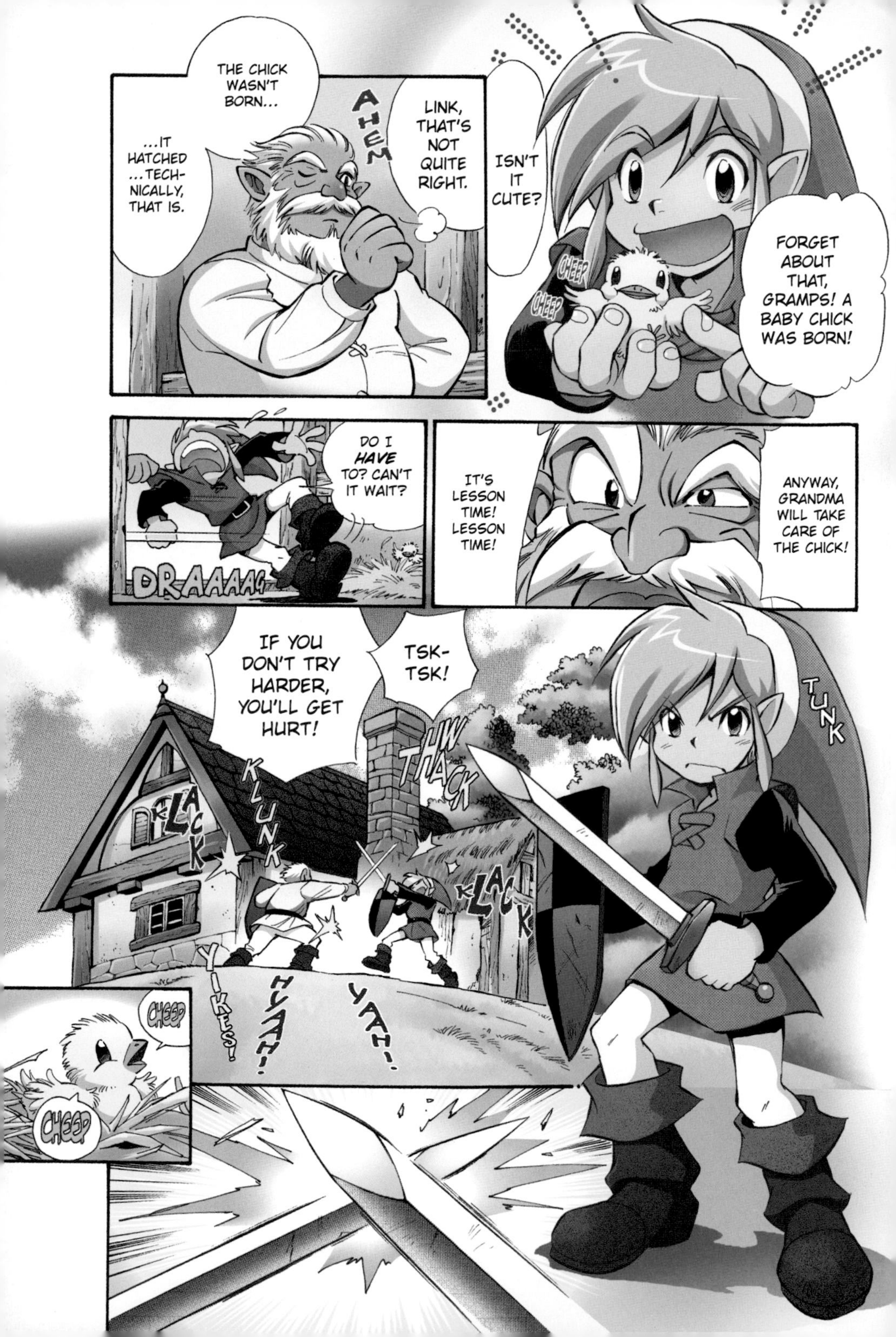
FORGET ABOUT THAT, GRAMPS! A BABY CHICK WAS BORN!
CHEEP
CHEEP
ISN'T IT CUTE?
LINK, THAT'S NOT QUITE RIGHT.
AHEM
THE CHICK WASN'T BORN...
...IT HATCHED ...TECHNICALLY, THAT IS.
ANYWAY, GRANDMA WILL TAKE CARE OF THE CHICK!
IT'S LESSON TIME! LESSON TIME!
DO I *HAVE* TO? CAN'T IT WAIT?
DRAAAAG
TSK-TSK!
IF YOU DON'T TRY HARDER, YOU'LL GET HURT!
TUNK
THWACK
KLUNK
KLACK
KLACK
YAH!
HYAH!
YIKES!
CHEEP
CHEEP

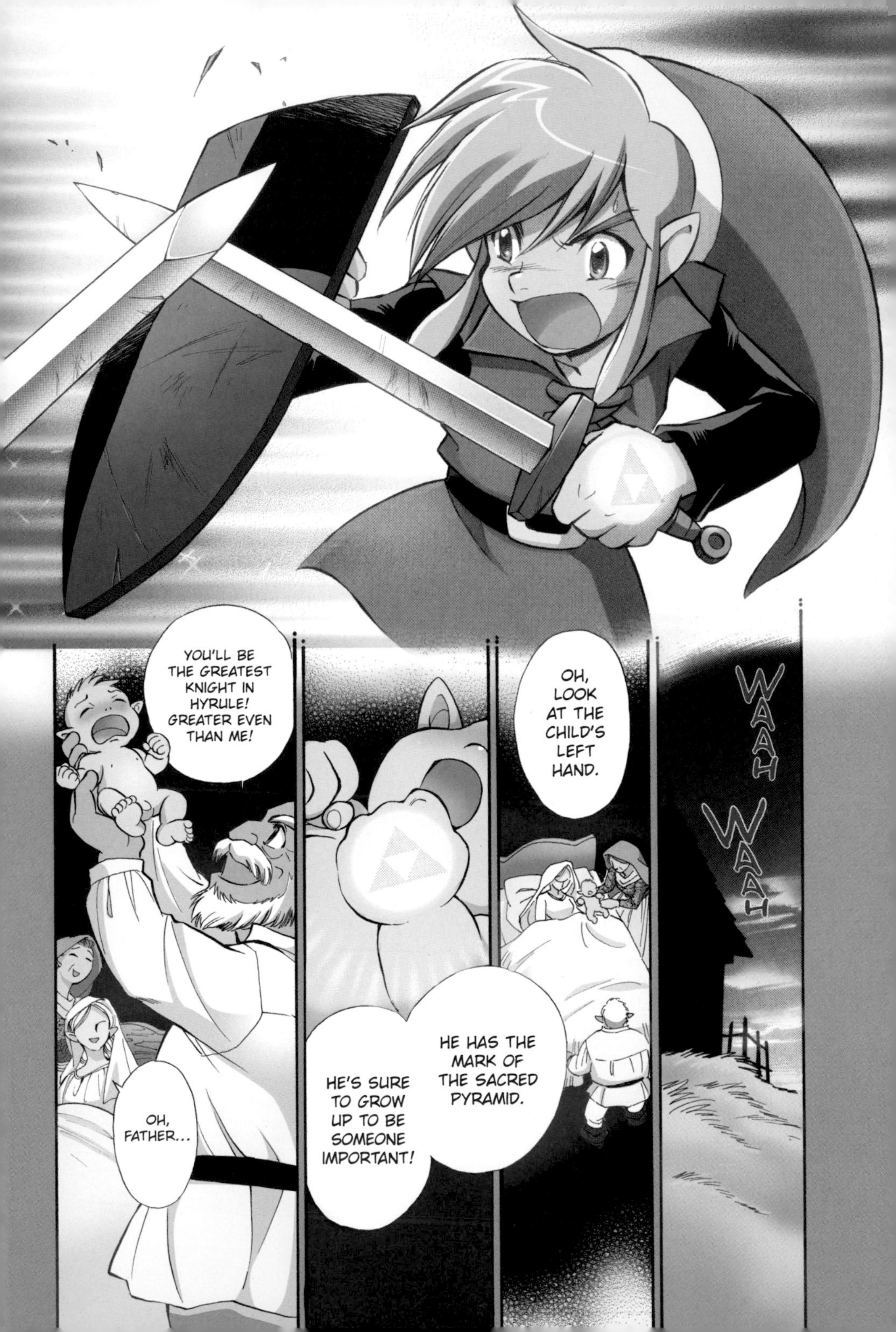
WAAH WAAAH
OH, LOOK AT THE CHILD'S LEFT HAND.
HE HAS THE MARK OF THE SACRED PYRAMID.
HE'S SURE TO GROW UP TO BE SOMEONE IMPORTANT!
YOU'LL BE THE GREATEST KNIGHT IN HYRULE! GREATER EVEN THAN ME!
OH, FATHER...

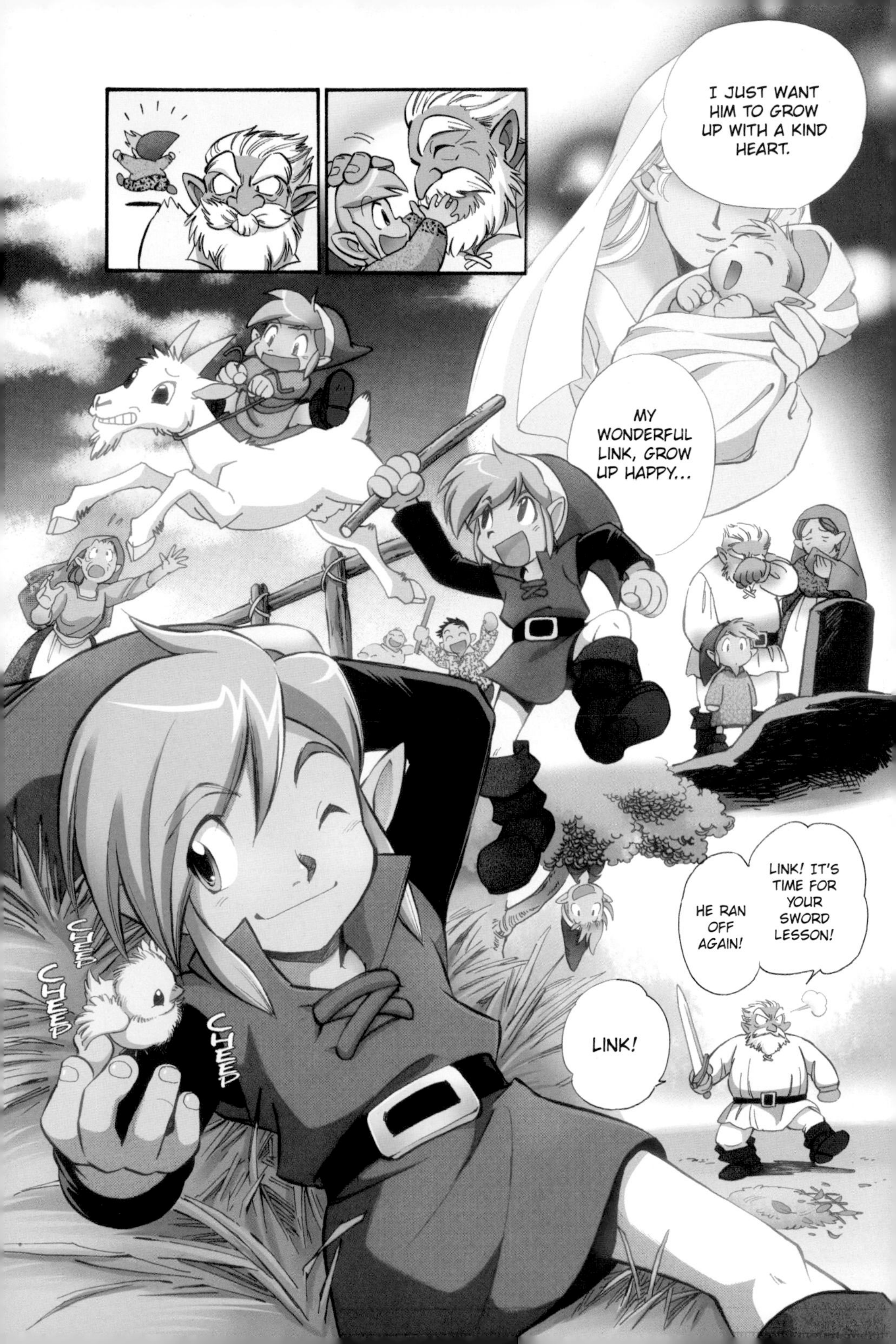
I JUST WANT HIM TO GROW UP WITH A KIND HEART.
MY WONDERFUL LINK, GROW UP HAPPY...
LINK! IT'S TIME FOR YOUR SWORD LESSON!
HE RAN OFF AGAIN!
LINK!
CHEEP
CHEEP
CHEEP
CHEEP

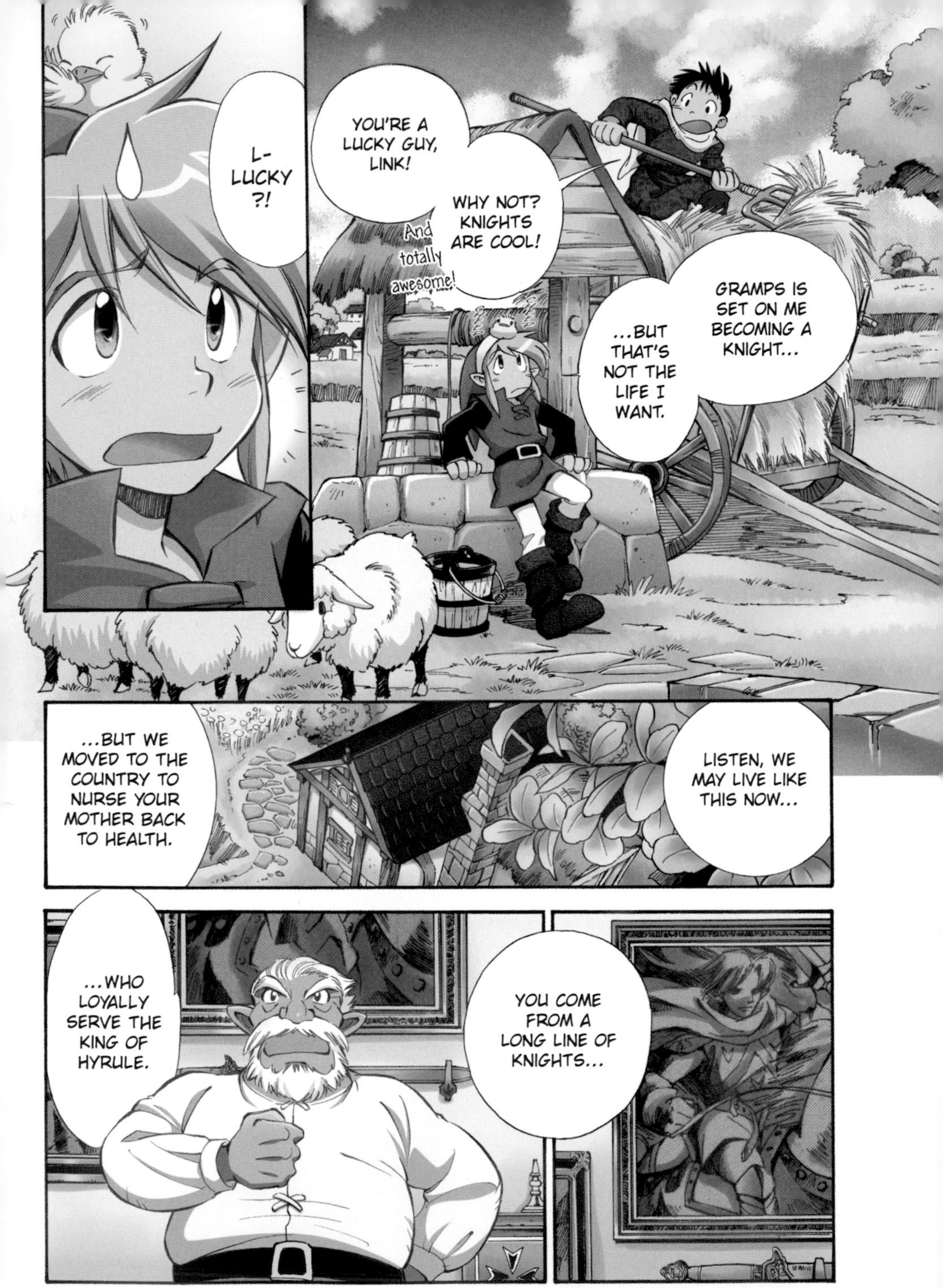
GRAMPS IS SET ON ME BECOMING A KNIGHT...
...BUT THAT'S NOT THE LIFE I WANT.
YOU'RE A LUCKY GUY, LINK!
L-LUCKY ?!
WHY NOT? KNIGHTS ARE COOL!
And totally awesome!
LISTEN, WE MAY LIVE LIKE THIS NOW...
...BUT WE MOVED TO THE COUNTRY TO NURSE YOUR MOTHER BACK TO HEALTH.
YOU COME FROM A LONG LINE OF KNIGHTS...
...WHO LOYALLY SERVE THE KING OF HYRULE.

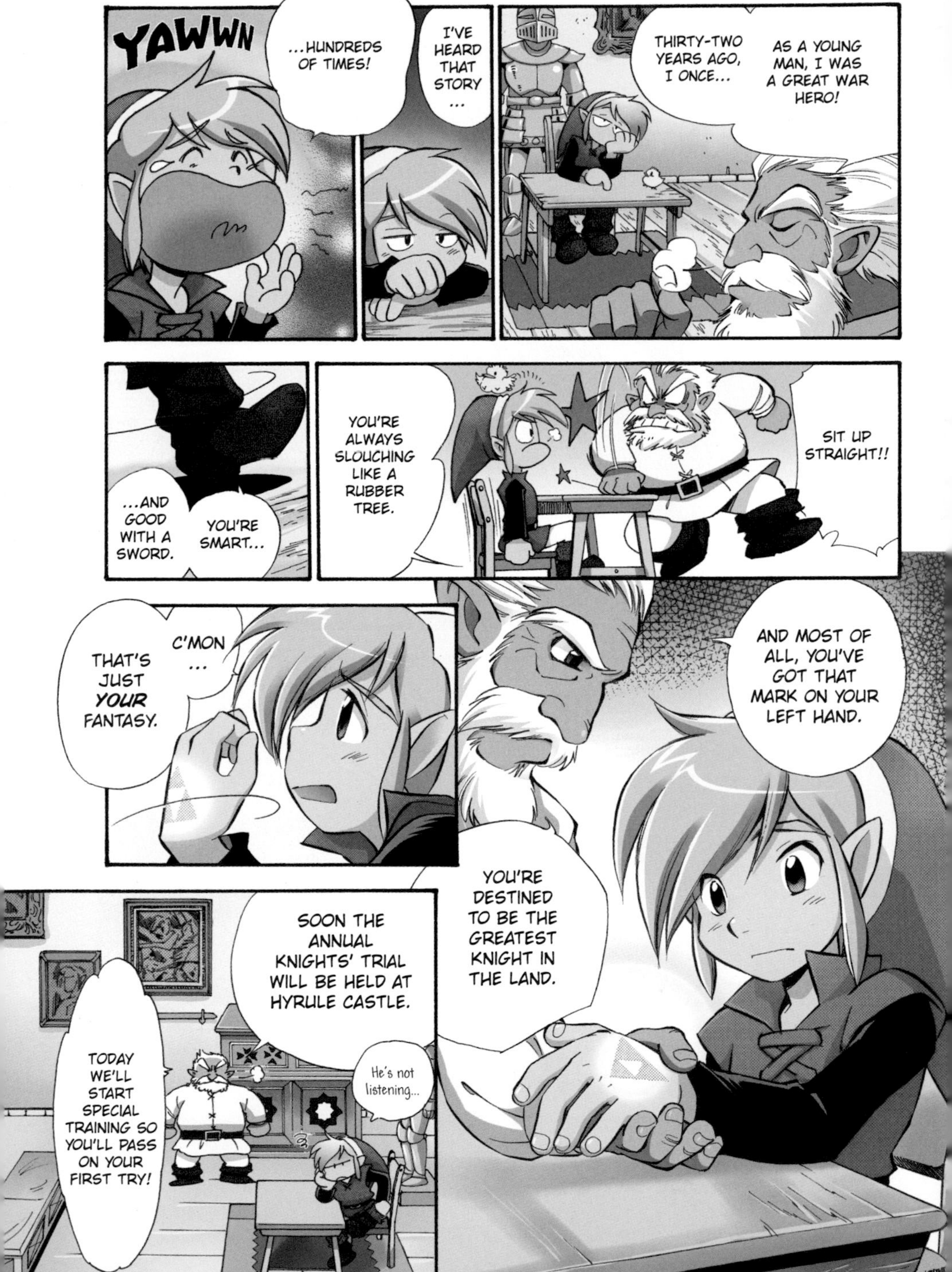
AS A YOUNG MAN, I WAS A GREAT WAR HERO!
THIRTY-TWO YEARS AGO, I ONCE...
I'VE HEARD THAT STORY ...
...HUNDREDS OF TIMES!
YAWWN
SIT UP STRAIGHT!!
YOU'RE ALWAYS SLOUCHING LIKE A RUBBER TREE.
YOU'RE SMART...
...AND GOOD WITH A SWORD.
AND MOST OF ALL, YOU'VE GOT THAT MARK ON YOUR LEFT HAND.
YOU'RE DESTINED TO BE THE GREATEST KNIGHT IN THE LAND.
C'MON ...
THAT'S JUST *YOUR* FANTASY.
SOON THE ANNUAL KNIGHTS' TRIAL WILL BE HELD AT HYRULE CASTLE.
TODAY WE'LL START SPECIAL TRAINING SO YOU'LL PASS ON YOUR FIRST TRY!
He's not listening...

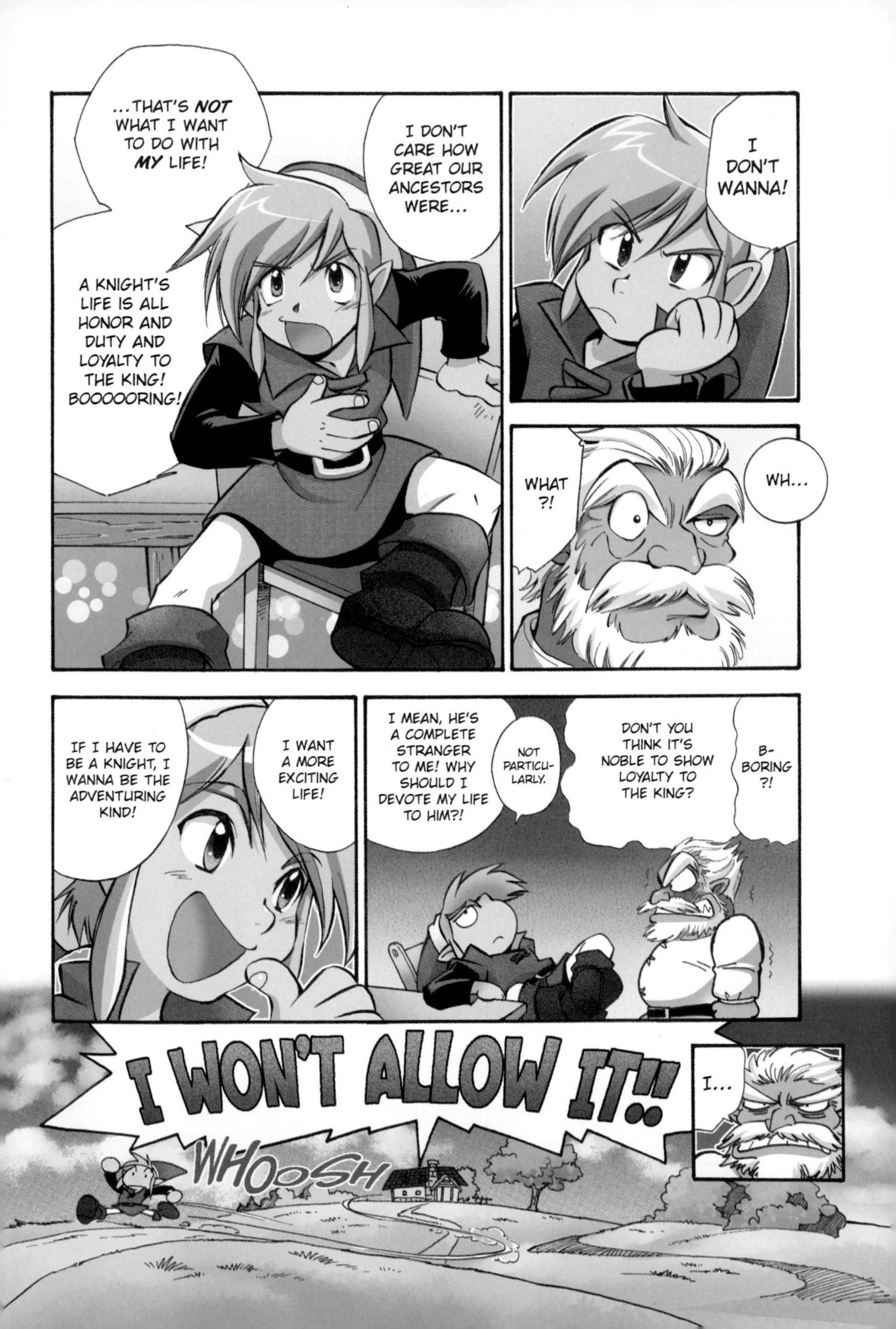
I DON'T WANNA!
WH...
WHAT ?!
I DON'T CARE HOW GREAT OUR ANCESTORS WERE...
...THAT'S NOT WHAT I WANT TO DO WITH MY LIFE!
A KNIGHT'S LIFE IS ALL HONOR AND DUTY AND LOYALTY TO THE KING! BOOOOORING!
B-BORING ?!
DON'T YOU THINK IT'S NOBLE TO SHOW LOYALTY TO THE KING?
NOT PARTICULARLY.
I MEAN, HE'S A COMPLETE STRANGER TO ME! WHY SHOULD I DEVOTE MY LIFE TO HIM?!
I WANT A MORE EXCITING LIFE!
IF I HAVE TO BE A KNIGHT, I WANNA BE THE ADVENTURING KIND!
I...
I WON'T ALLOW IT!!
WHOOSH

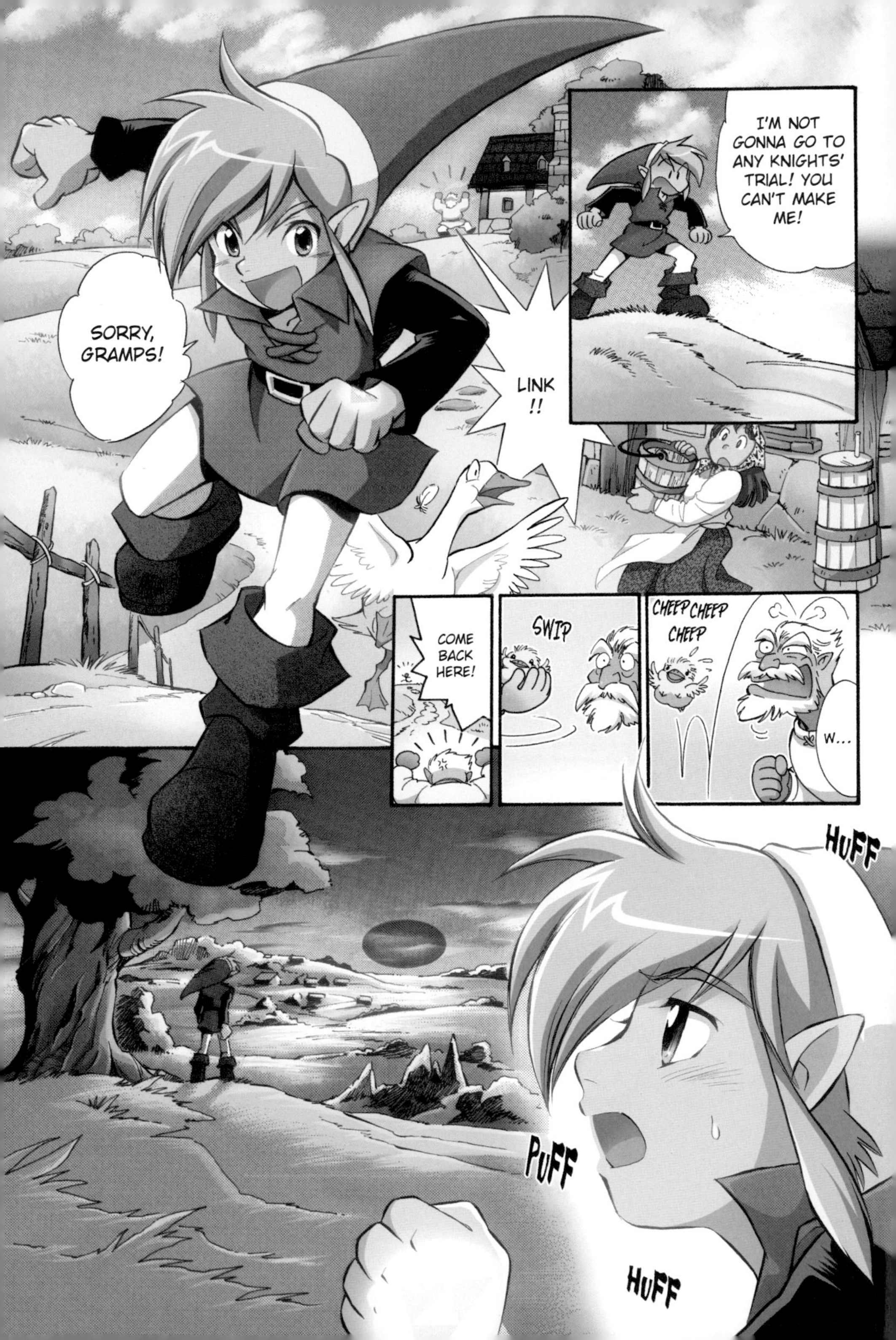
I'M NOT GONNA GO TO ANY KNIGHTS' TRIAL! YOU CAN'T MAKE ME!
LINK !!
SORRY, GRAMPS!
CHEEP CHEEP CHEEP
W...
SWIP
COME BACK HERE!
HUFF
PUFF
HUFF

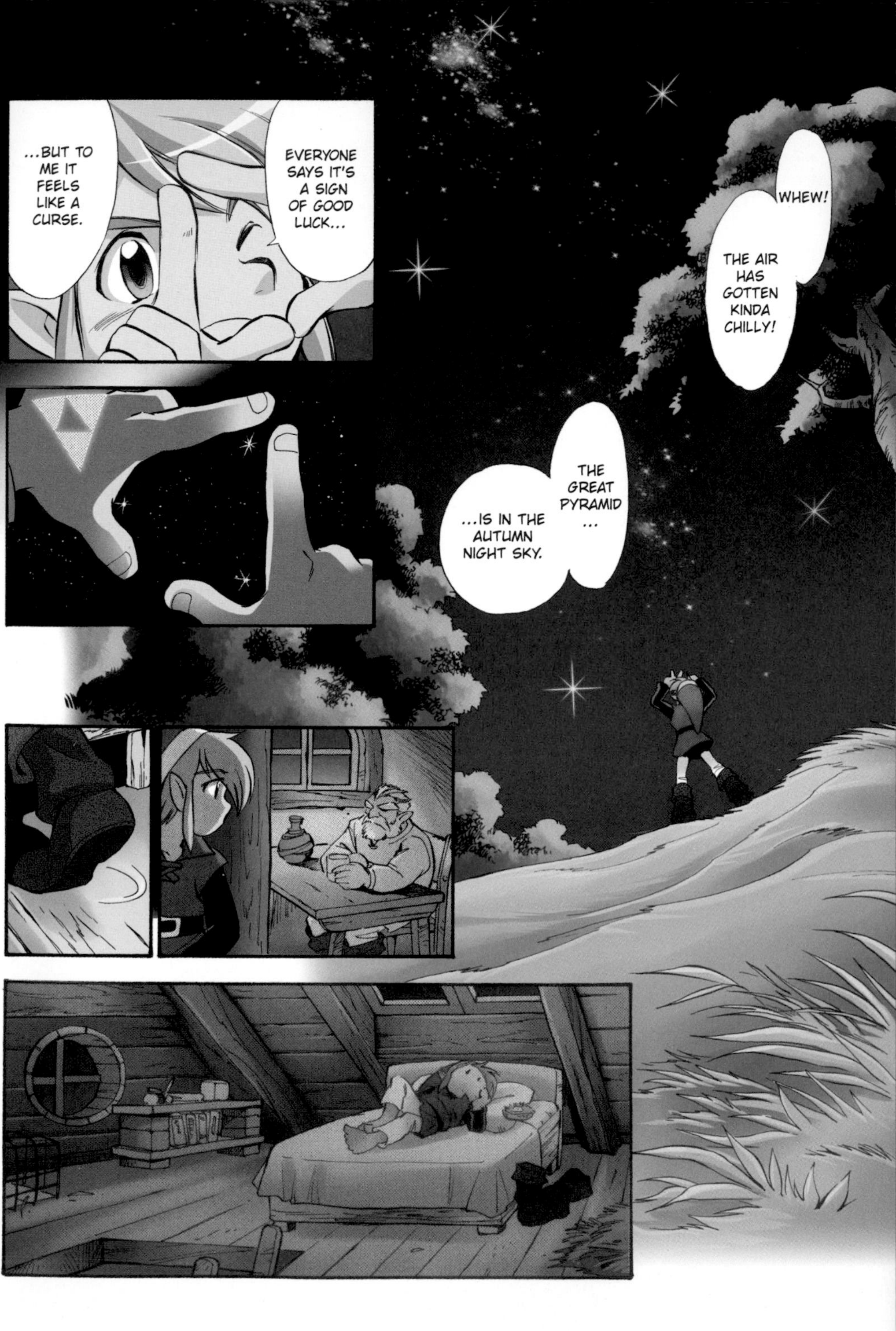
WHEW!
THE AIR HAS GOTTEN KINDA CHILLY!
THE GREAT PYRAMID ...
...IS IN THE AUTUMN NIGHT SKY.
EVERYONE SAYS IT'S A SIGN OF GOOD LUCK...
...BUT TO ME IT FEELS LIKE A CURSE.

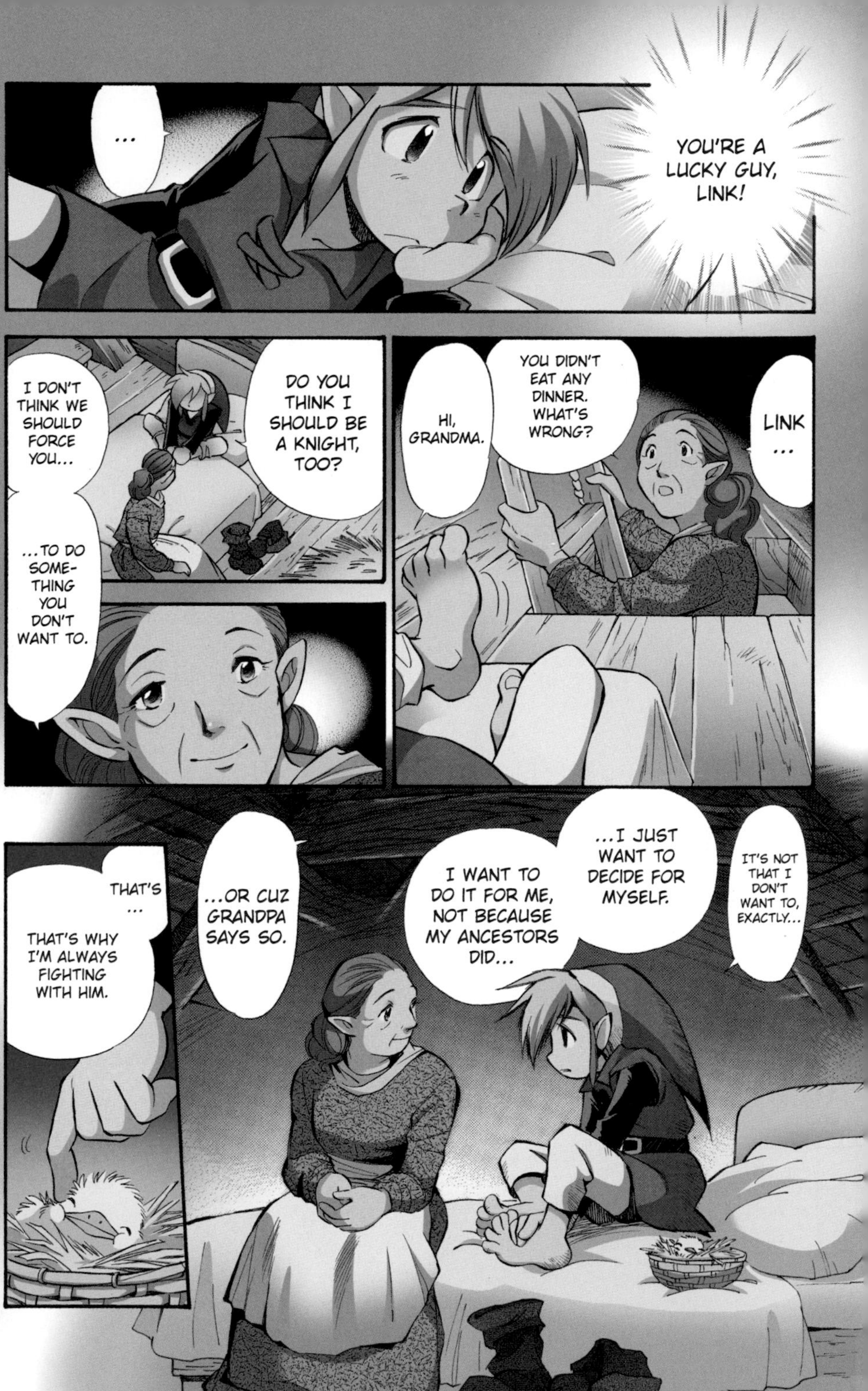
YOU'RE A LUCKY GUY, LINK!
...
LINK...
YOU DIDN'T EAT ANY DINNER. WHAT'S WRONG?
HI, GRANDMA.
DO YOU THINK I SHOULD BE A KNIGHT, TOO?
I DON'T THINK WE SHOULD FORCE YOU...
...TO DO SOMETHING YOU DON'T WANT TO.
IT'S NOT THAT I DON'T WANT TO, EXACTLY...
...I JUST WANT TO DECIDE FOR MYSELF.
I WANT TO DO IT FOR ME, NOT BECAUSE MY ANCESTORS DID...
...OR CUZ GRANDPA SAYS SO.
THAT'S ...
THAT'S WHY I'M ALWAYS FIGHTING WITH HIM.

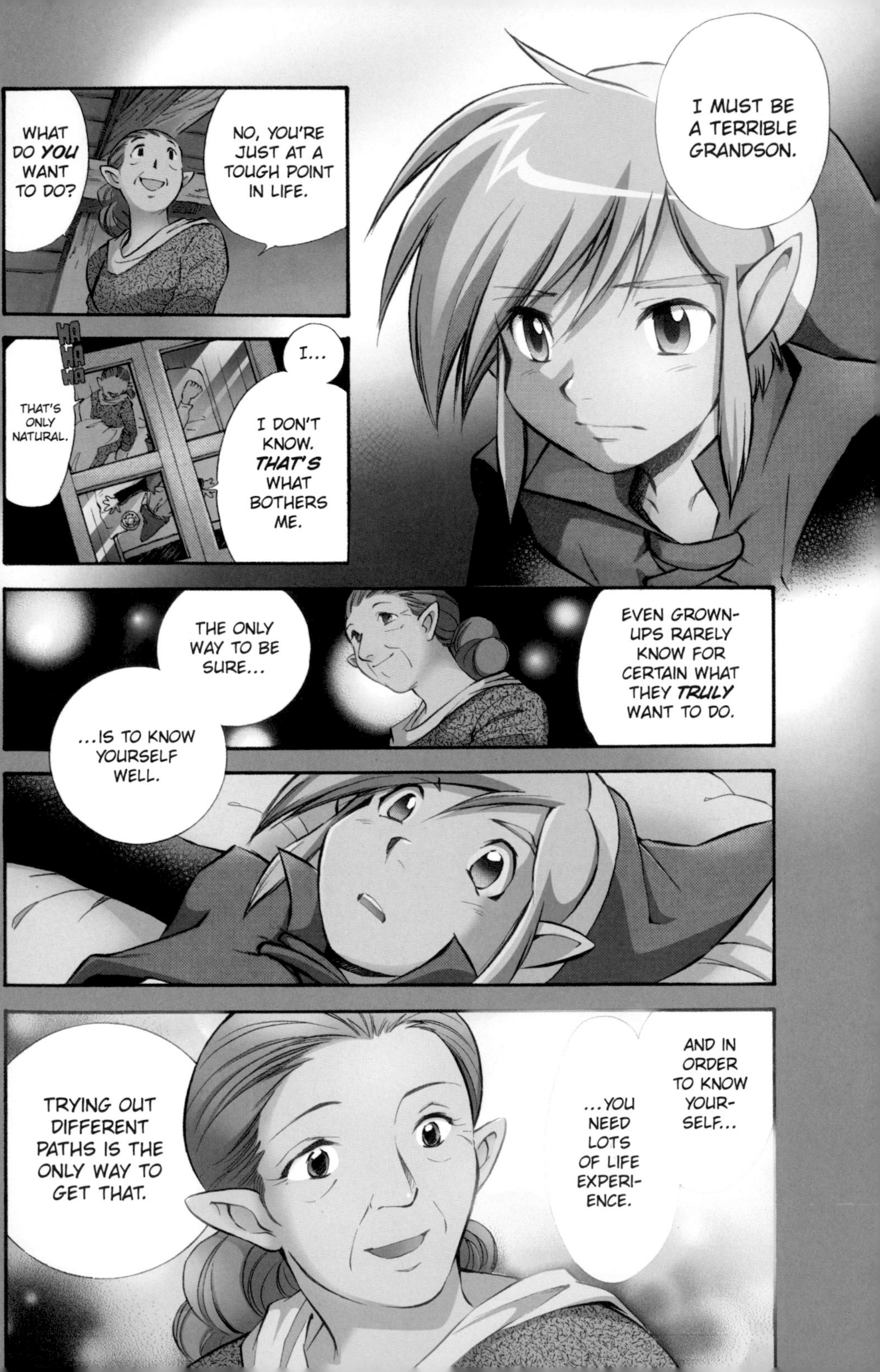
I MUST BE A TERRIBLE GRANDSON.
NO, YOU'RE JUST AT A TOUGH POINT IN LIFE.
WHAT DO *YOU* WANT TO DO?
I...
I DON'T KNOW. ***THAT'S*** WHAT BOTHERS ME.
HA HA HA
THAT'S ONLY NATURAL.
EVEN GROWN-UPS RARELY KNOW FOR CERTAIN WHAT THEY ***TRULY*** WANT TO DO.
THE ONLY WAY TO BE SURE...
...IS TO KNOW YOURSELF WELL.
AND IN ORDER TO KNOW YOURSELF...
...YOU NEED LOTS OF LIFE EXPERIENCE.
TRYING OUT DIFFERENT PATHS IS THE ONLY WAY TO GET THAT.

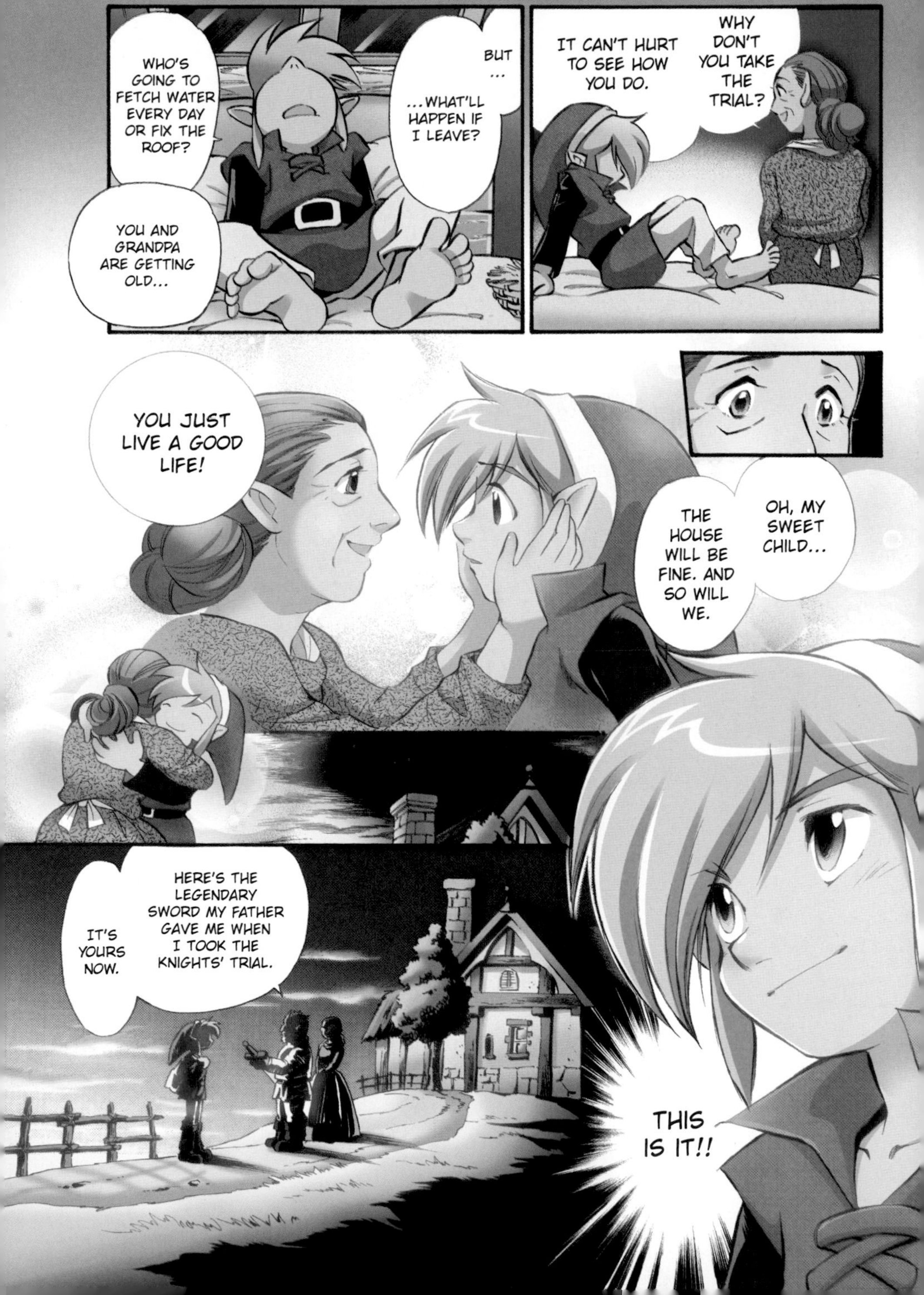
WHY DON'T YOU TAKE THE TRIAL?
IT CAN'T HURT TO SEE HOW YOU DO.
BUT...
...WHAT'LL HAPPEN IF I LEAVE?
WHO'S GOING TO FETCH WATER EVERY DAY OR FIX THE ROOF?
YOU AND GRANDPA ARE GETTING OLD...
OH, MY SWEET CHILD...
THE HOUSE WILL BE FINE. AND SO WILL WE.
YOU JUST LIVE A GOOD LIFE!
HERE'S THE LEGENDARY SWORD MY FATHER GAVE ME WHEN I TOOK THE KNIGHTS' TRIAL.
IT'S YOURS NOW.
THIS IS IT!!

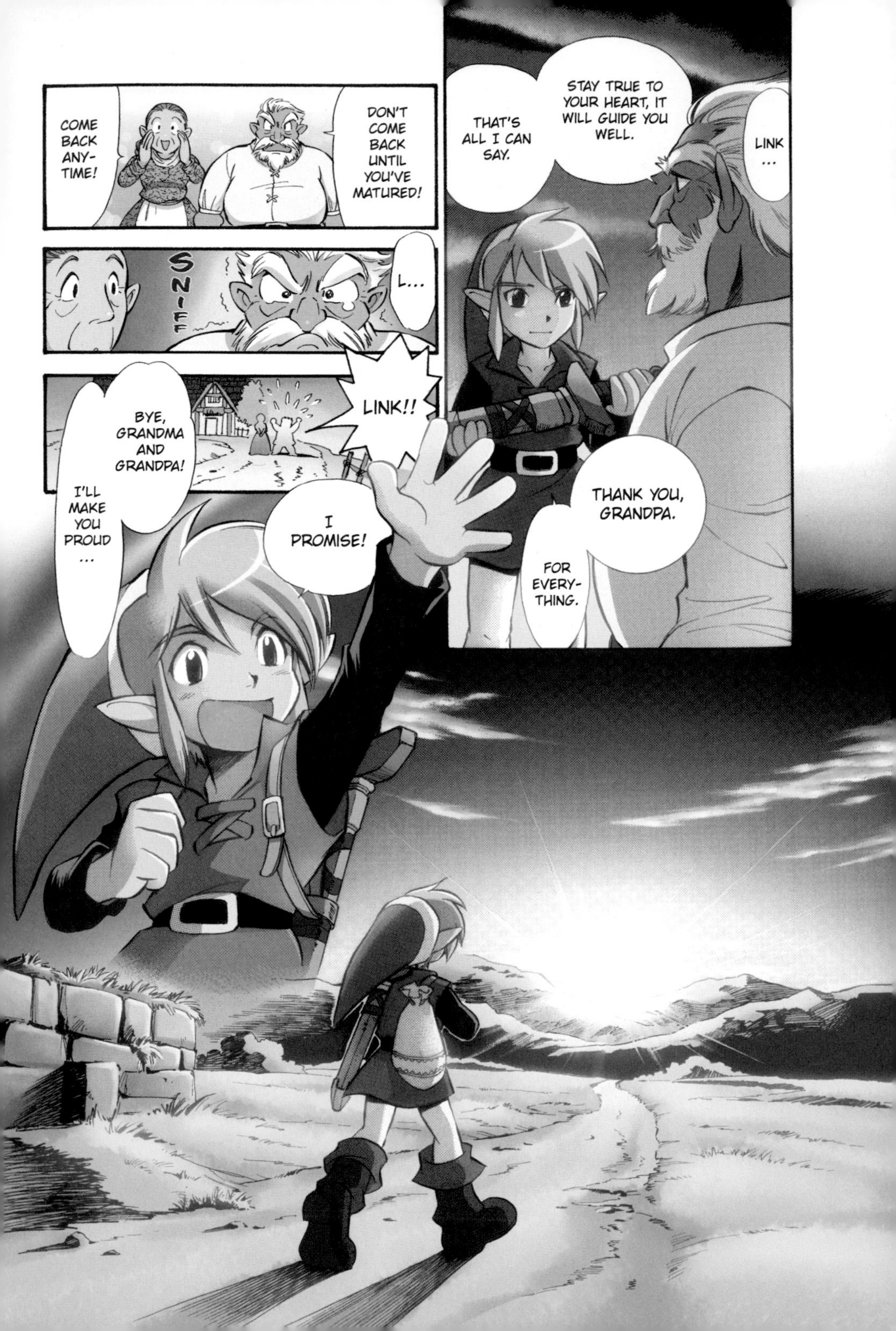
LINK ...
STAY TRUE TO YOUR HEART, IT WILL GUIDE YOU WELL.
THAT'S ALL I CAN SAY.
THANK YOU, GRANDPA.
FOR EVERY-THING.
DON'T COME BACK UNTIL YOU'VE MATURED!
COME BACK ANY-TIME!
L...
SNIFF
LINK!!
BYE, GRANDMA AND GRANDPA!
I PROMISE!
I'LL MAKE YOU PROUD ...

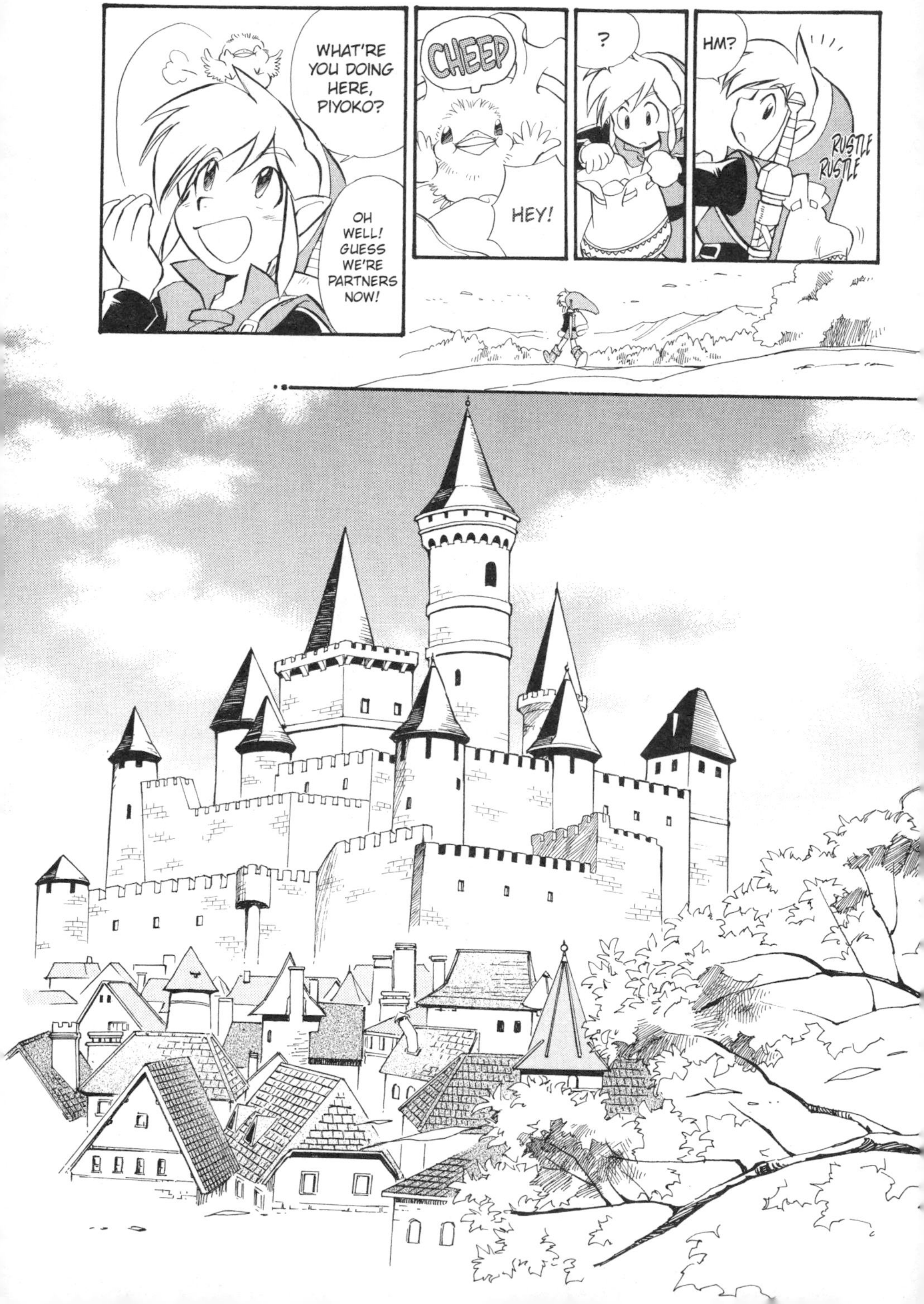
HM?
RUSTLE RUSTLE
?
CHEEP
HEY!
WHAT'RE YOU DOING HERE, PIYOKO?
OH WELL! GUESS WE'RE PARTNERS NOW!

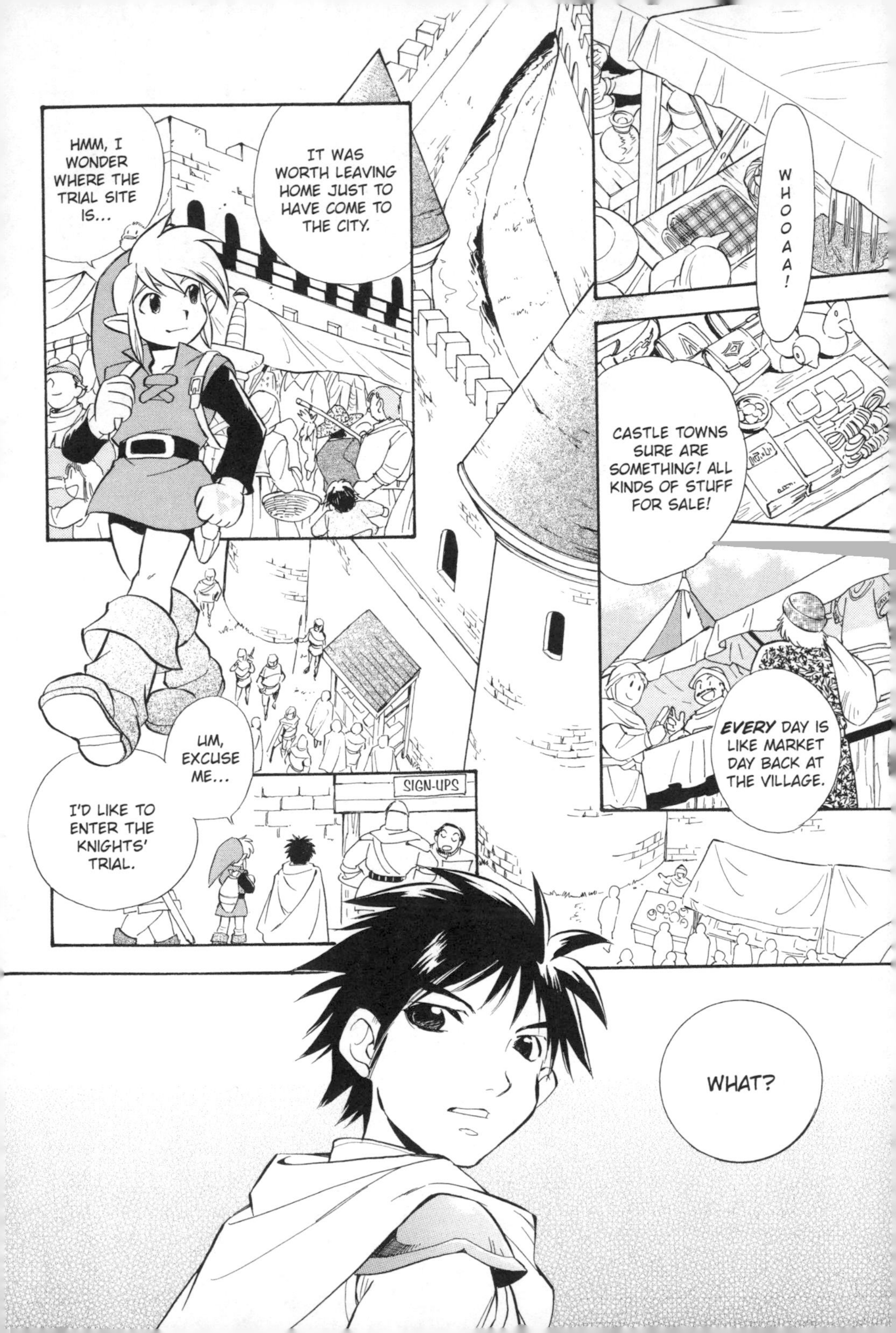
WHOOOAA!
CASTLE TOWNS SURE ARE SOMETHING! ALL KINDS OF STUFF FOR SALE!
EVERY DAY IS LIKE MARKET DAY BACK AT THE VILLAGE.
IT WAS WORTH LEAVING HOME JUST TO HAVE COME TO THE CITY.
HMM, I WONDER WHERE THE TRIAL SITE IS…
SIGN-UPS
UM, EXCUSE ME…
I'D LIKE TO ENTER THE KNIGHTS' TRIAL.
WHAT?

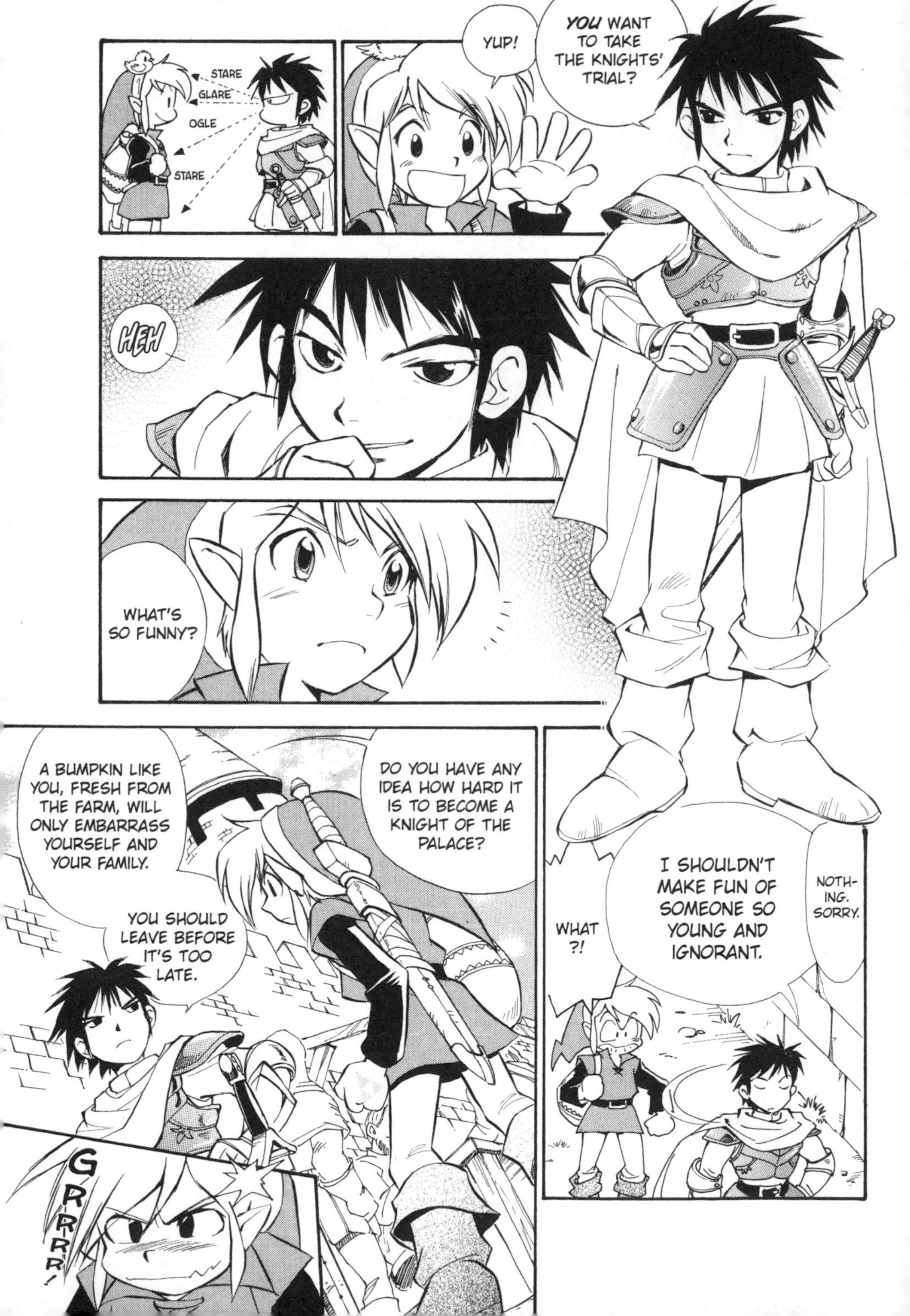

YOU WANT TO TAKE THE KNIGHTS' TRIAL?
YUP!
STARE
GLARE
OGLE
STARE
HEH
WHAT'S SO FUNNY?
I SHOULDN'T MAKE FUN OF SOMEONE SO YOUNG AND IGNORANT.
WHAT ?!
NOTH-ING. SORRY.
DO YOU HAVE ANY IDEA HOW HARD IT IS TO BECOME A KNIGHT OF THE PALACE?
A BUMPKIN LIKE YOU, FRESH FROM THE FARM, WILL ONLY EMBARRASS YOURSELF AND YOUR FAMILY.
YOU SHOULD LEAVE BEFORE IT'S TOO LATE.
GRRRR!

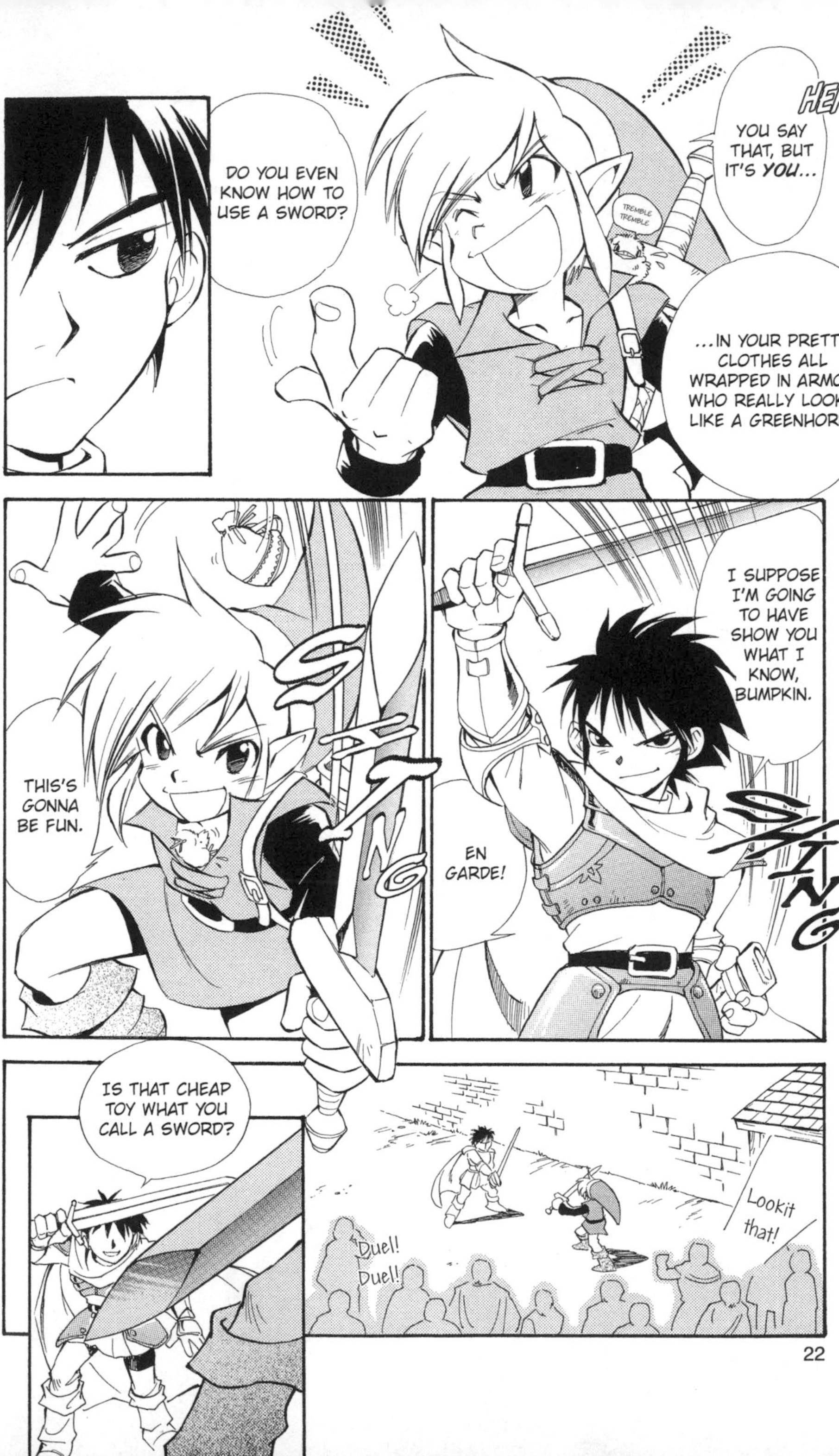

DO YOU EVEN KNOW HOW TO USE A SWORD?
HEH
YOU SAY THAT, BUT IT'S *YOU*...
TREMBLE TREMBLE
...IN YOUR PRETTY CLOTHES ALL WRAPPED IN ARMOR WHO REALLY LOOKS LIKE A GREENHORN!
I SUPPOSE I'M GOING TO HAVE SHOW YOU WHAT I KNOW, BUMPKIN.
SHING
EN GARDE!
SHING
THIS'S GONNA BE FUN.
Lookit that!
Duel! Duel!
IS THAT CHEAP TOY WHAT YOU CALL A SWORD?

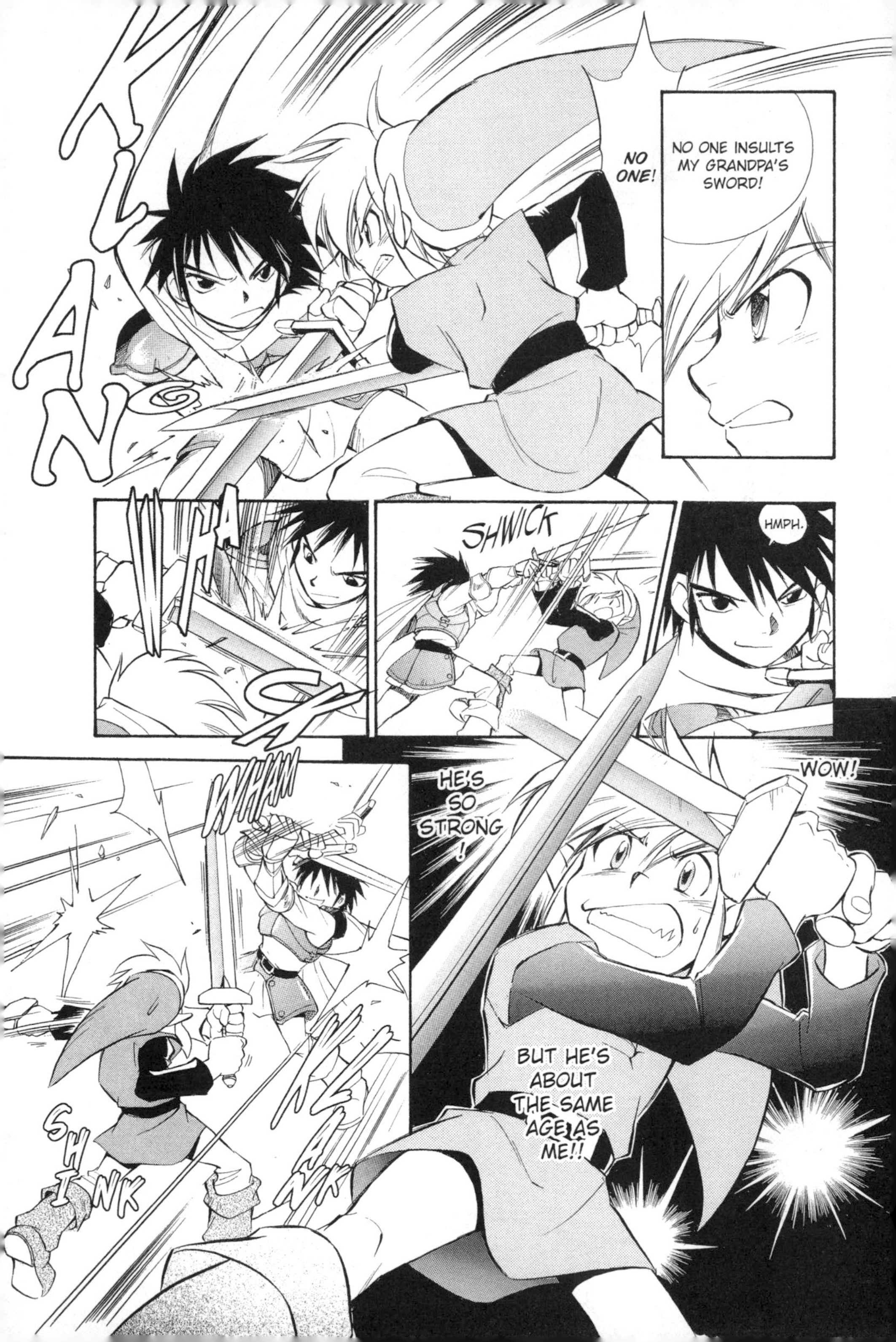
NO ONE INSULTS MY GRANDPA'S SWORD!
NO ONE!
KLANG
HMPH.
SHWICK
WHACK
WOW!
HE'S SO STRONG!
BUT HE'S ABOUT THE SAME AGE AS ME!!
WHAM
SHINK

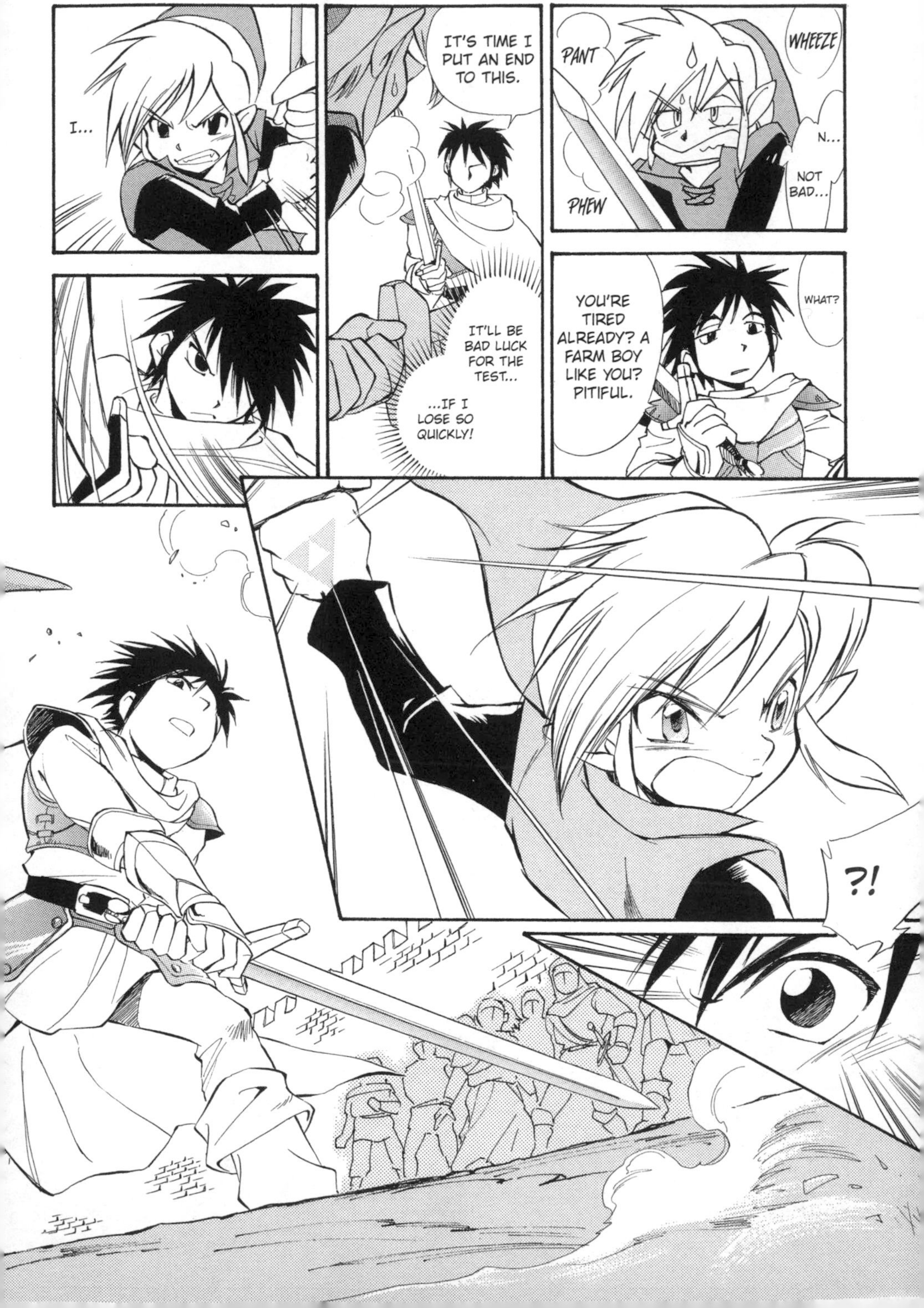
WHEEZE
PANT
N...
NOT BAD...
PHEW
YOU'RE TIRED ALREADY? A FARM BOY LIKE YOU? PITIFUL.
WHAT?
IT'S TIME I PUT AN END TO THIS.
IT'LL BE BAD LUCK FOR THE TEST...
...IF I LOSE SO QUICKLY!
I...
?!

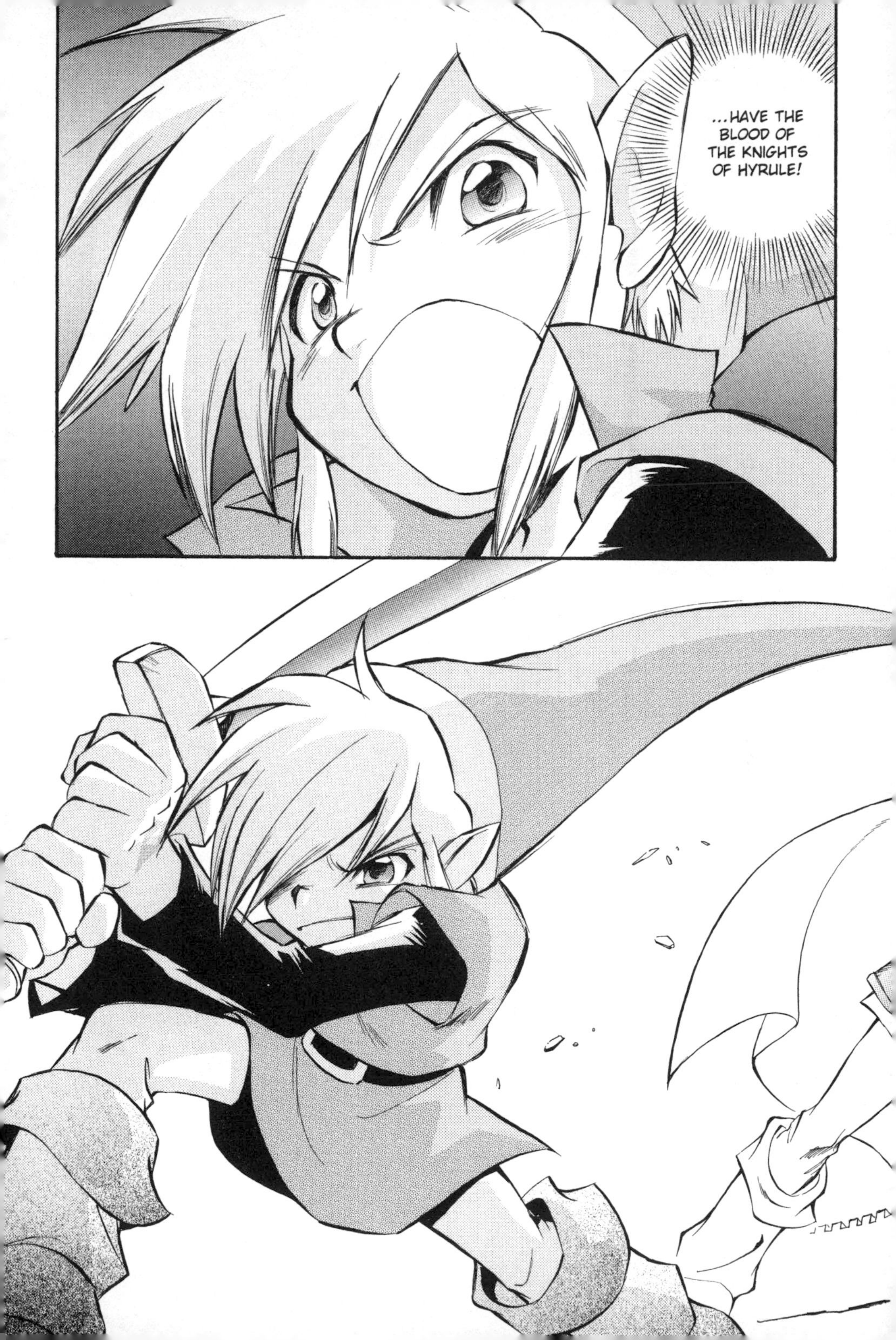
...HAVE THE BLOOD OF THE KNIGHTS OF HYRULE!

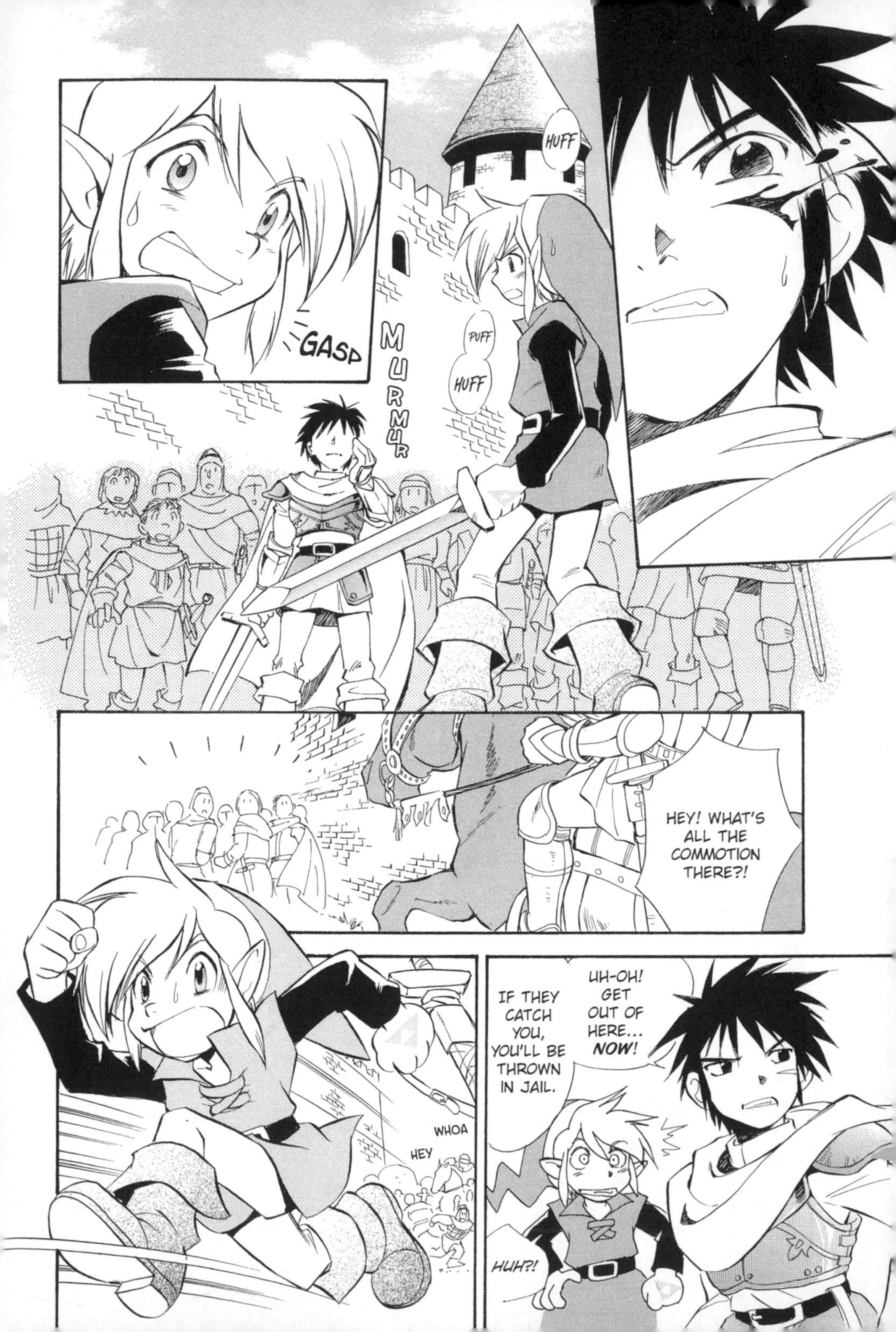
HUFF
PUFF
HUFF
MURMUR
GASP
HEY! WHAT'S ALL THE COMMOTION THERE?!
UH-OH! GET OUT OF HERE... **NOW**!
IF THEY CATCH YOU, YOU'LL BE THROWN IN JAIL.
HUH?!
WHOA
HEY

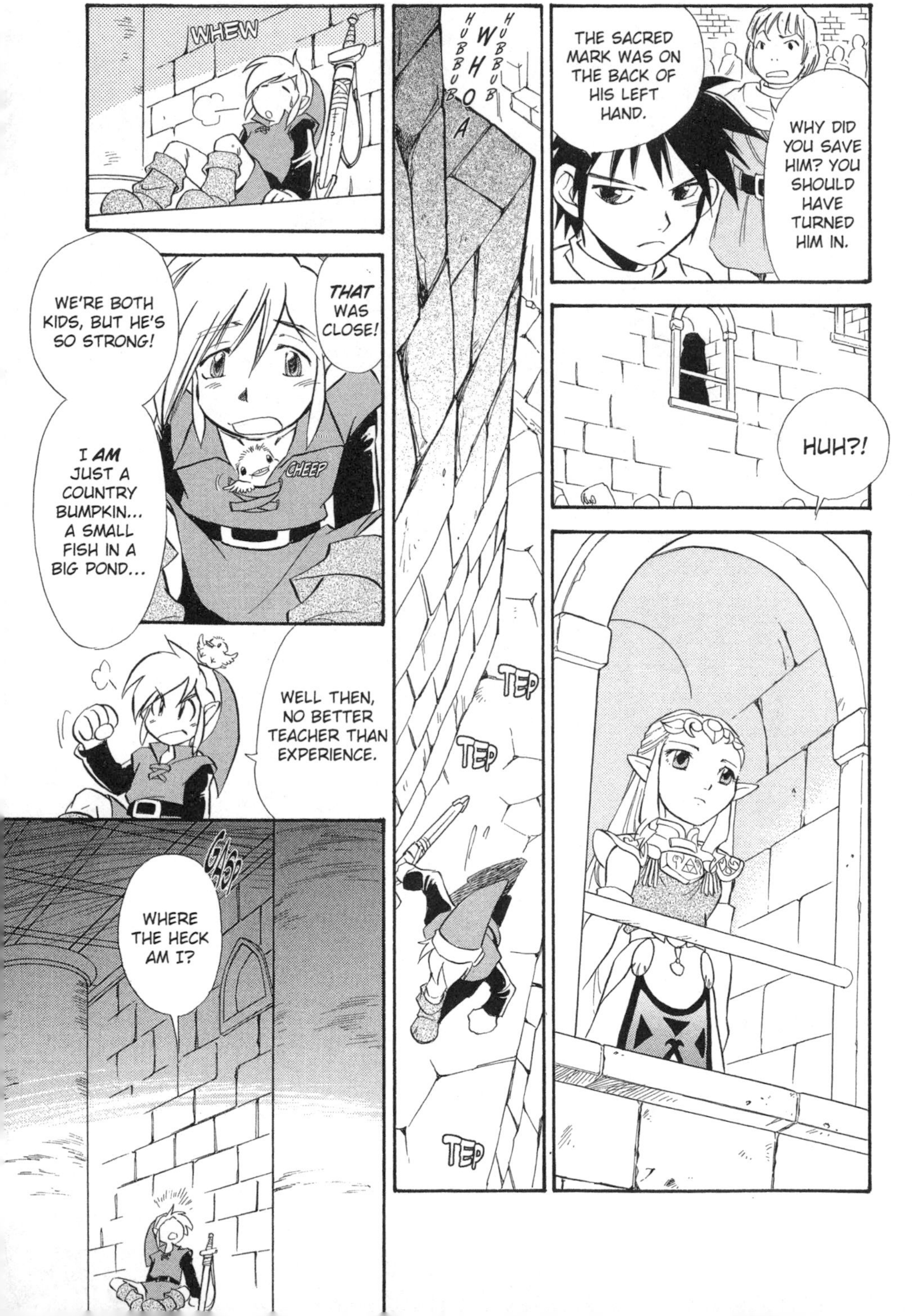

WHY DID YOU SAVE HIM? YOU SHOULD HAVE TURNED HIM IN.
THE SACRED MARK WAS ON THE BACK OF HIS LEFT HAND.
HUH?!
HUBBUB
WHOA
HUBBUB
TEP
TEP
TEP
WHEW
THAT WAS CLOSE!
WE'RE BOTH KIDS, BUT HE'S SO STRONG!
CHEEP
I AM JUST A COUNTRY BUMPKIN... A SMALL FISH IN A BIG POND...
WELL THEN, NO BETTER TEACHER THAN EXPERIENCE.
GASP
WHERE THE HECK AM I?

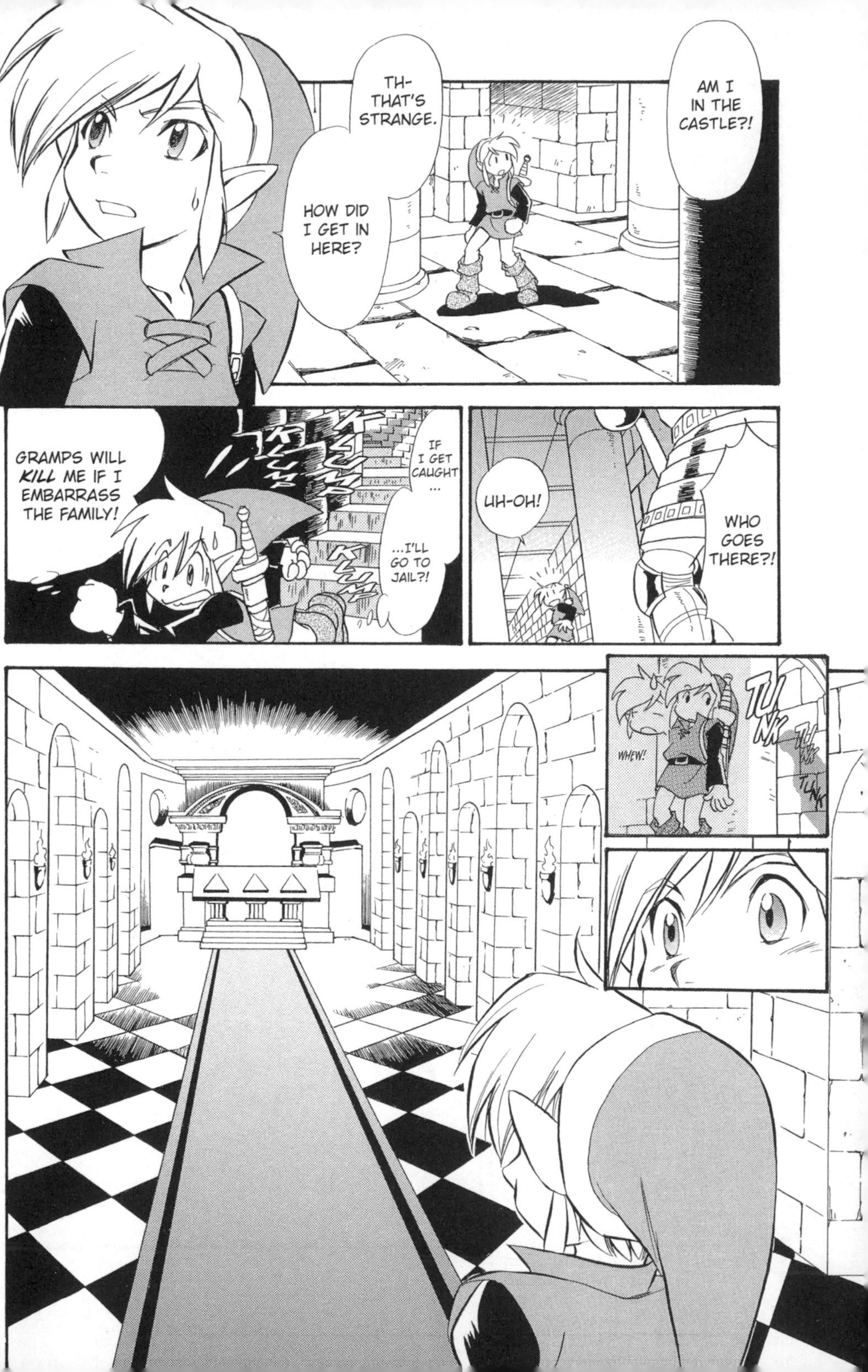
AM I IN THE CASTLE?!
TH- THAT'S STRANGE.
HOW DID I GET IN HERE?
WHO GOES THERE?!
UH-OH!
KLUMP KLUMP
IF I GET CAUGHT ...
KLUMP KLUMP
...I'LL GO TO JAIL?!
GRAMPS WILL *KILL* ME IF I EMBARRASS THE FAMILY!
TUNK TUNK TUNK
WHEW!

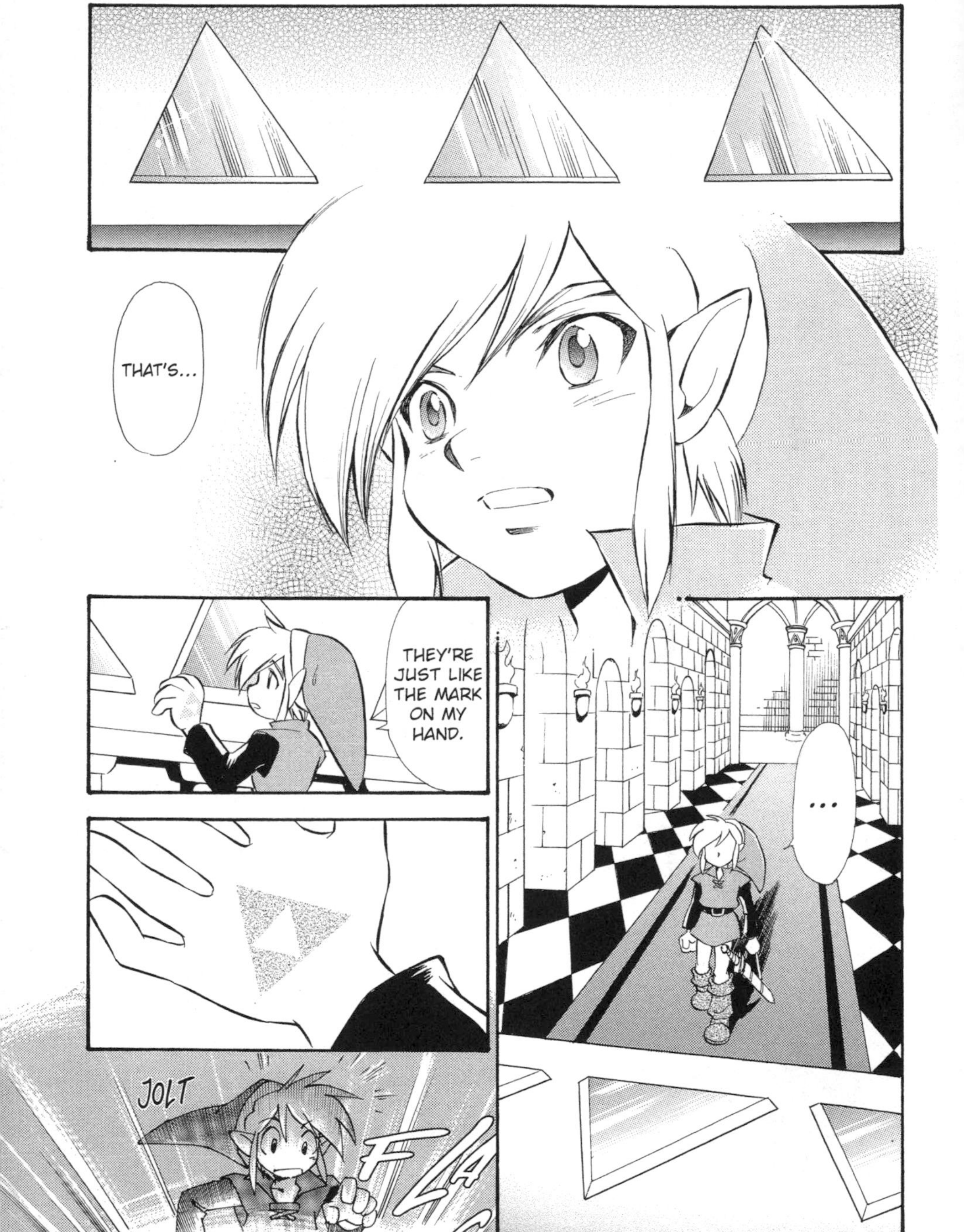
THAT'S...
...
THEY'RE JUST LIKE THE MARK ON MY HAND.
JOLT
FLASH

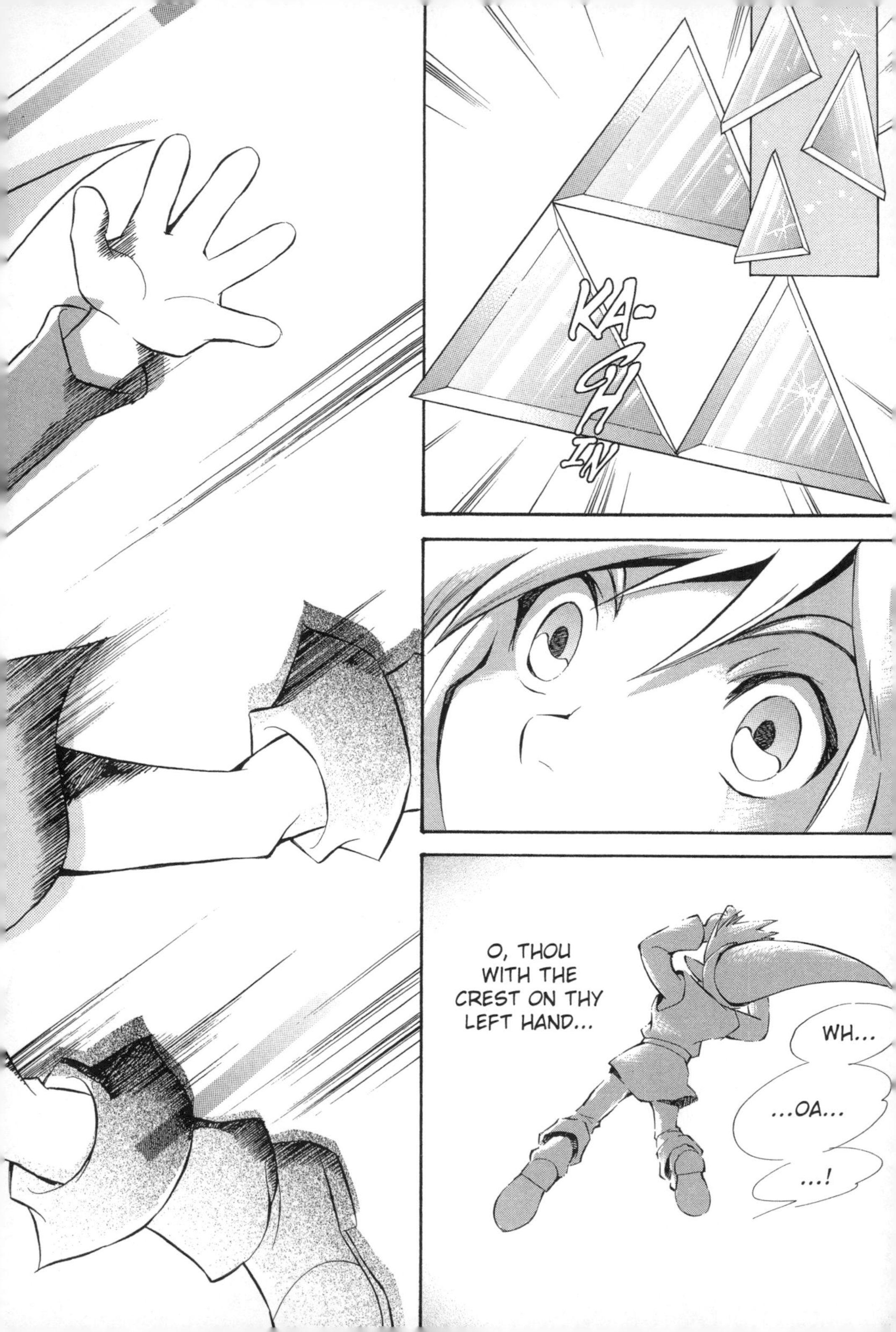
KA-CHIN
O, THOU WITH THE CREST ON THY LEFT HAND...
WH...
...OA...
...!

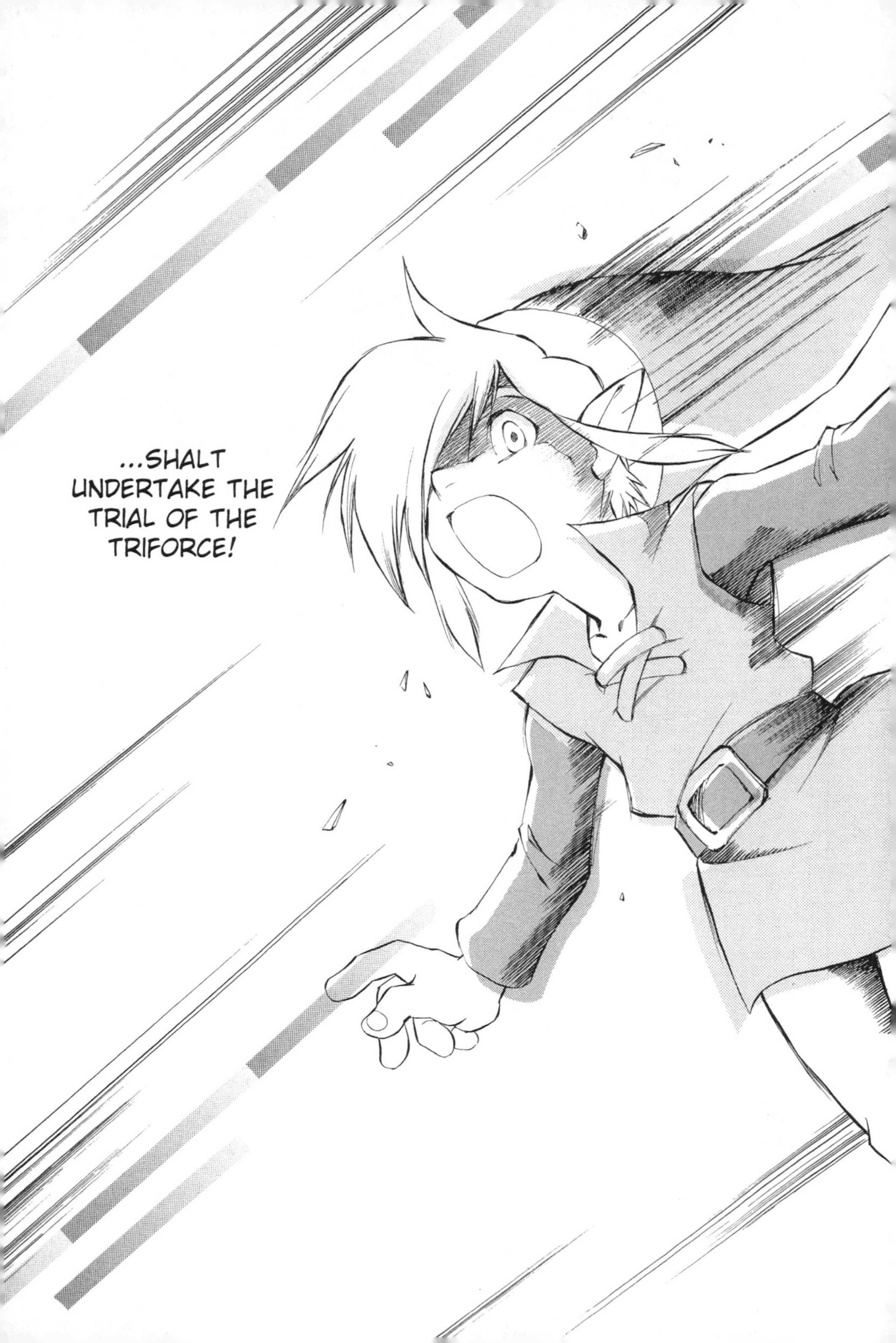
...SHALT UNDERTAKE THE TRIAL OF THE TRIFORCE!

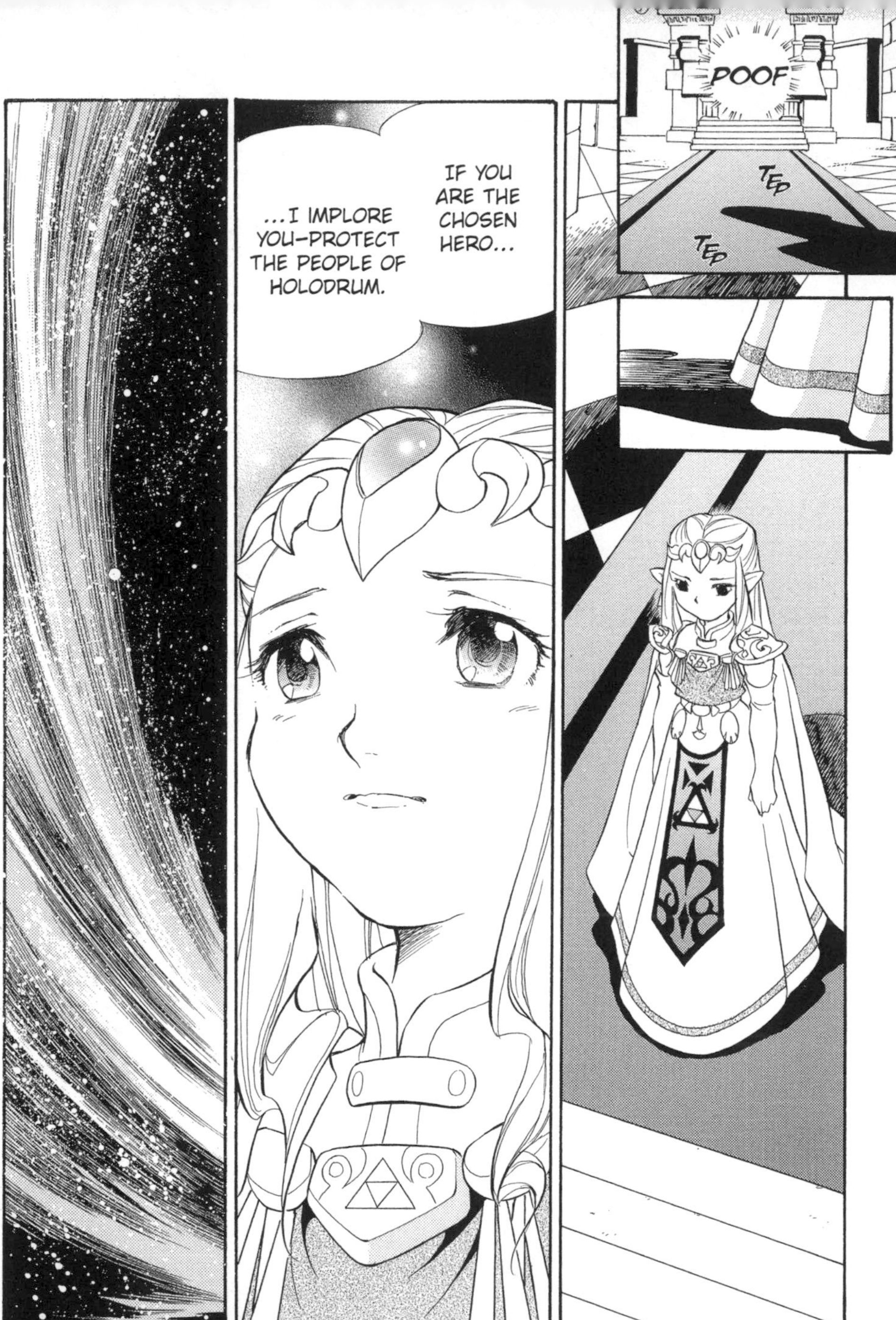
POOF
TEP
TEP
IF YOU ARE THE CHOSEN HERO...
...I IMPLORE YOU—PROTECT THE PEOPLE OF HOLODRUM.

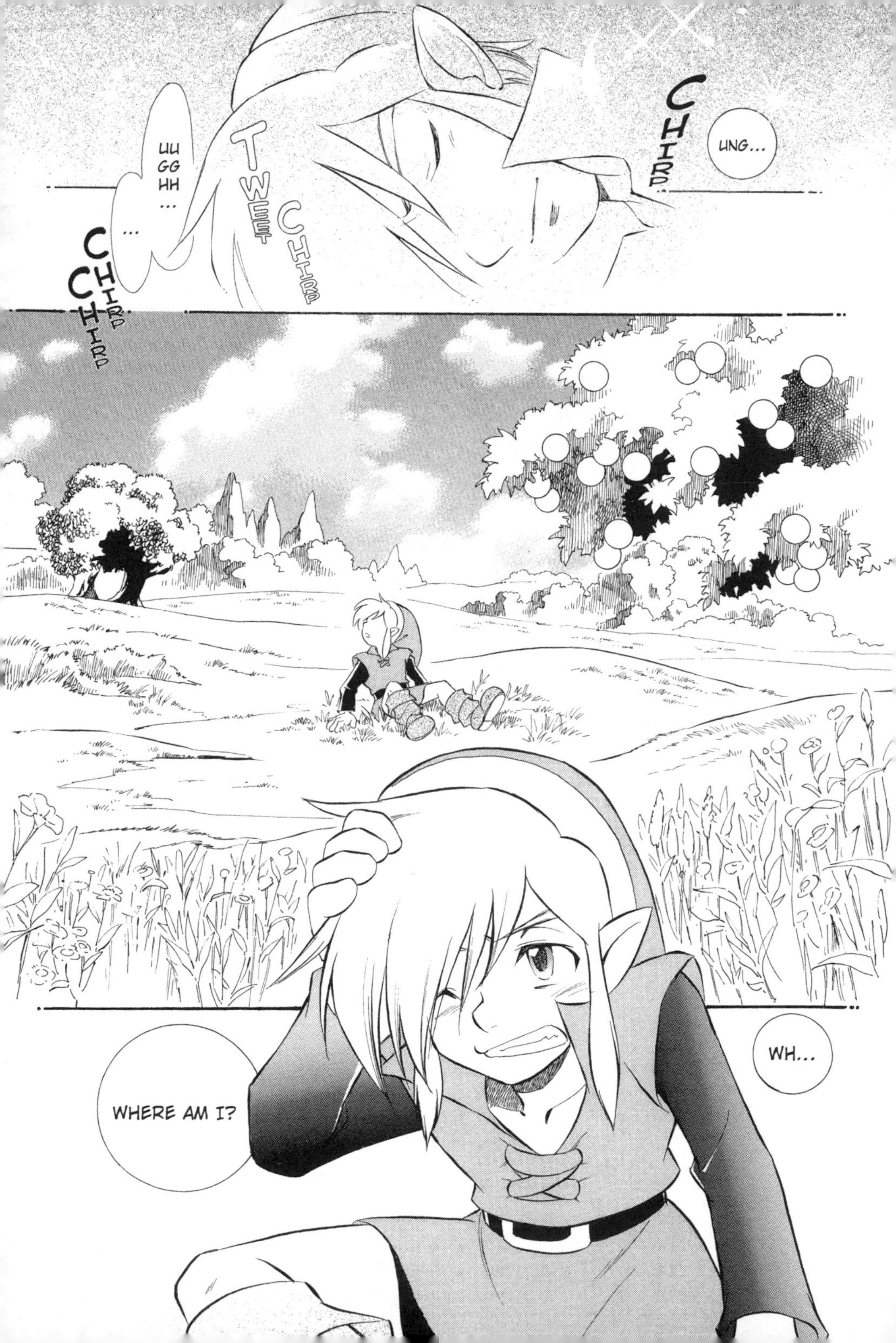
UNG...
CHIRP
CHIRP
TWEET
UUGGHH...
...
CHIRP
CHIRP
WH...
WHERE AM I?

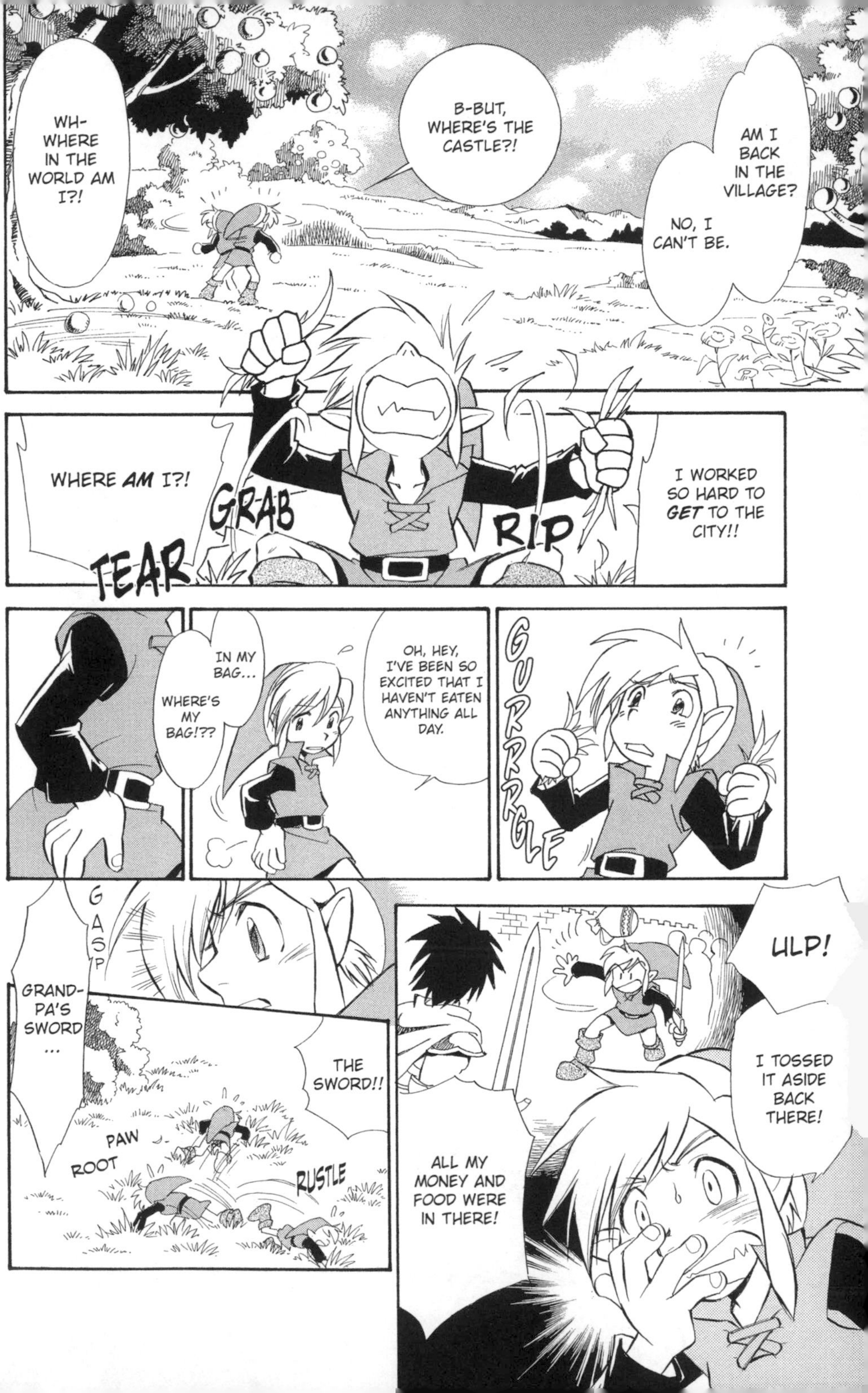
AM I BACK IN THE VILLAGE?
NO, I CAN'T BE.
B-BUT, WHERE'S THE CASTLE?!
WH- WHERE IN THE WORLD AM I?!
I WORKED SO HARD TO *GET* TO THE CITY!!
RIP
GRAB
WHERE *AM* I?!
TEAR
GURRRGLE
OH, HEY, I'VE BEEN SO EXCITED THAT I HAVEN'T EATEN ANYTHING ALL DAY.
IN MY BAG...
WHERE'S MY BAG!??
ULP!
I TOSSED IT ASIDE BACK THERE!
ALL MY MONEY AND FOOD WERE IN THERE!
GASP
THE SWORD!!
GRAND-PA'S SWORD ...
RUSTLE
PAW
ROOT

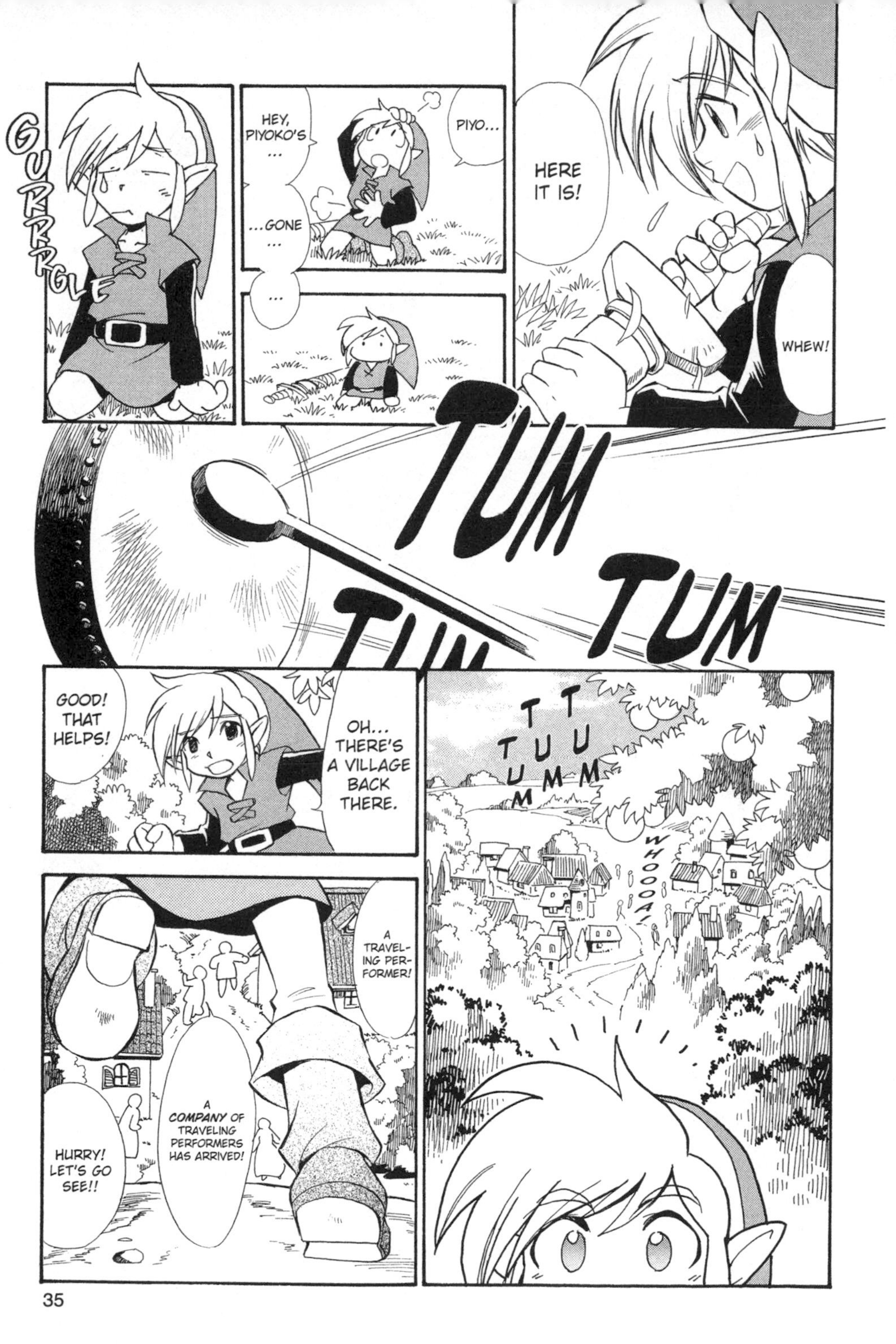
HERE IT IS!
WHEW!
PIYO...
HEY, PIYOKO'S ...
...GONE ...
...
GURRRGLE
TUM
TUM
TUM TUM TUM
WHOOOA!
OH... THERE'S A VILLAGE BACK THERE.
GOOD! THAT HELPS!
A TRAVELING PERFORMER!
A *COMPANY* OF TRAVELING PERFORMERS HAS ARRIVED!
HURRY! LET'S GO SEE!!

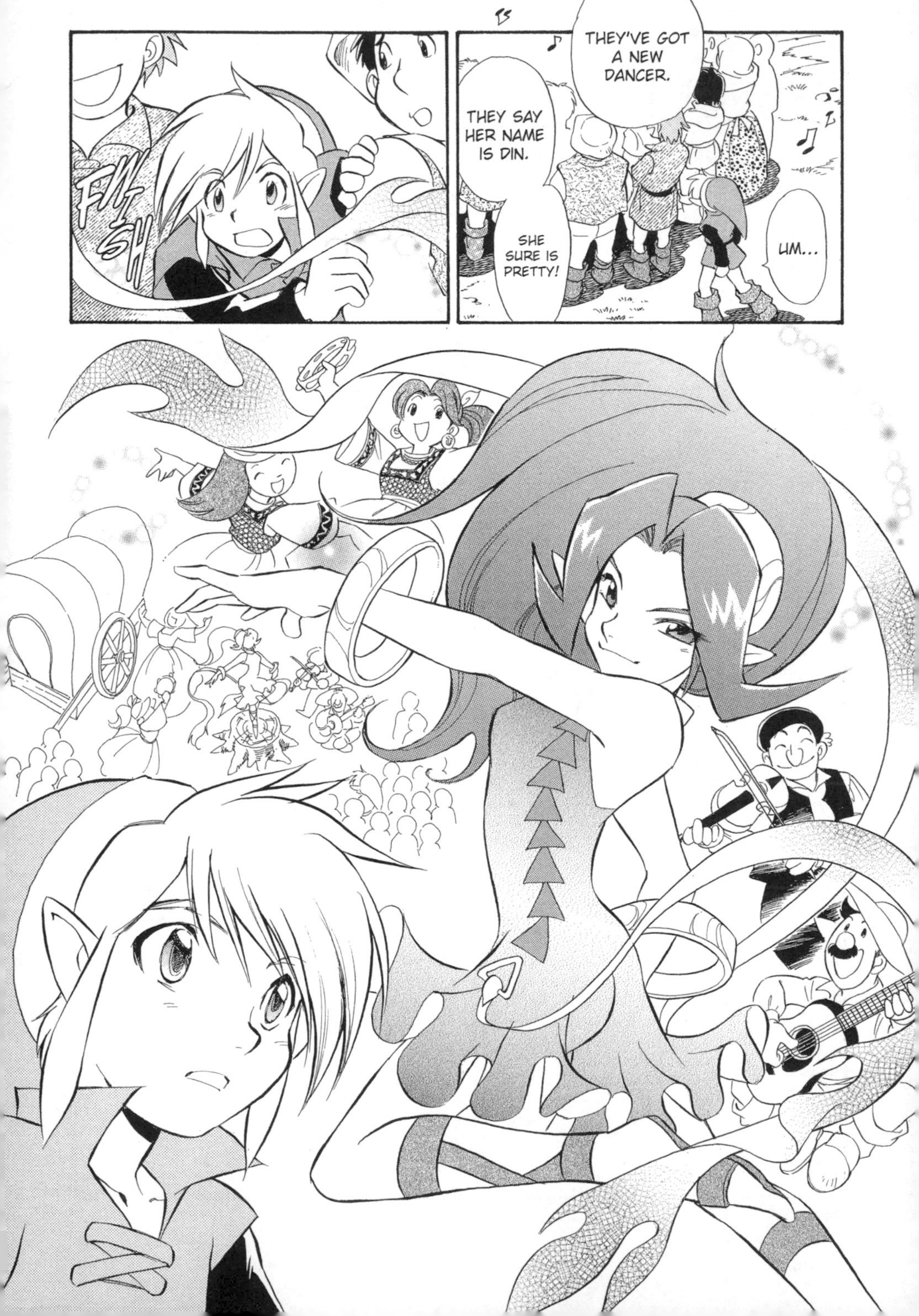
THEY'VE GOT A NEW DANCER.
THEY SAY HER NAME IS DIN.
SHE SURE IS PRETTY!
UM...
FWISH

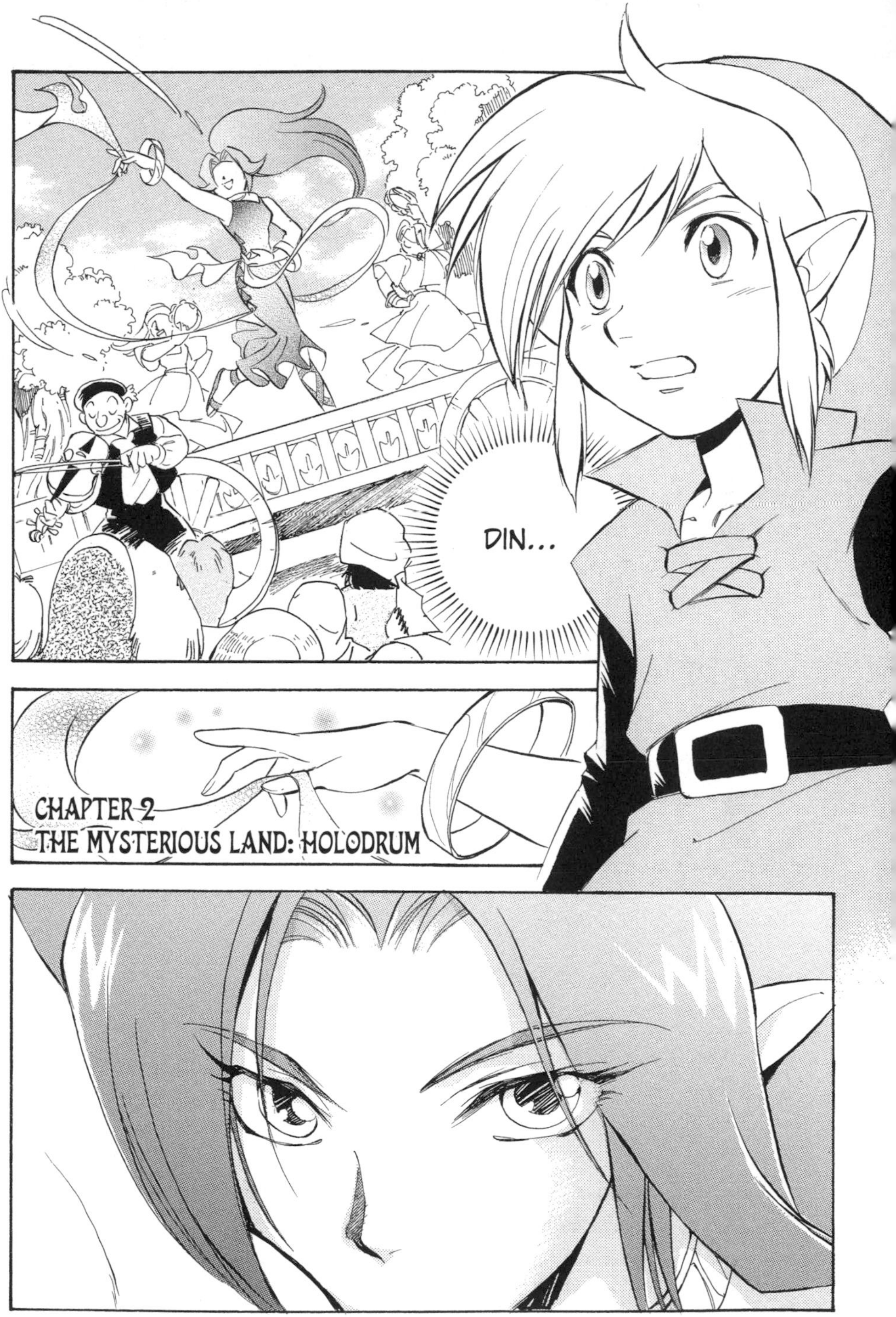
DIN...
CHAPTER 2
THE MYSTERIOUS LAND: HOLODRUM

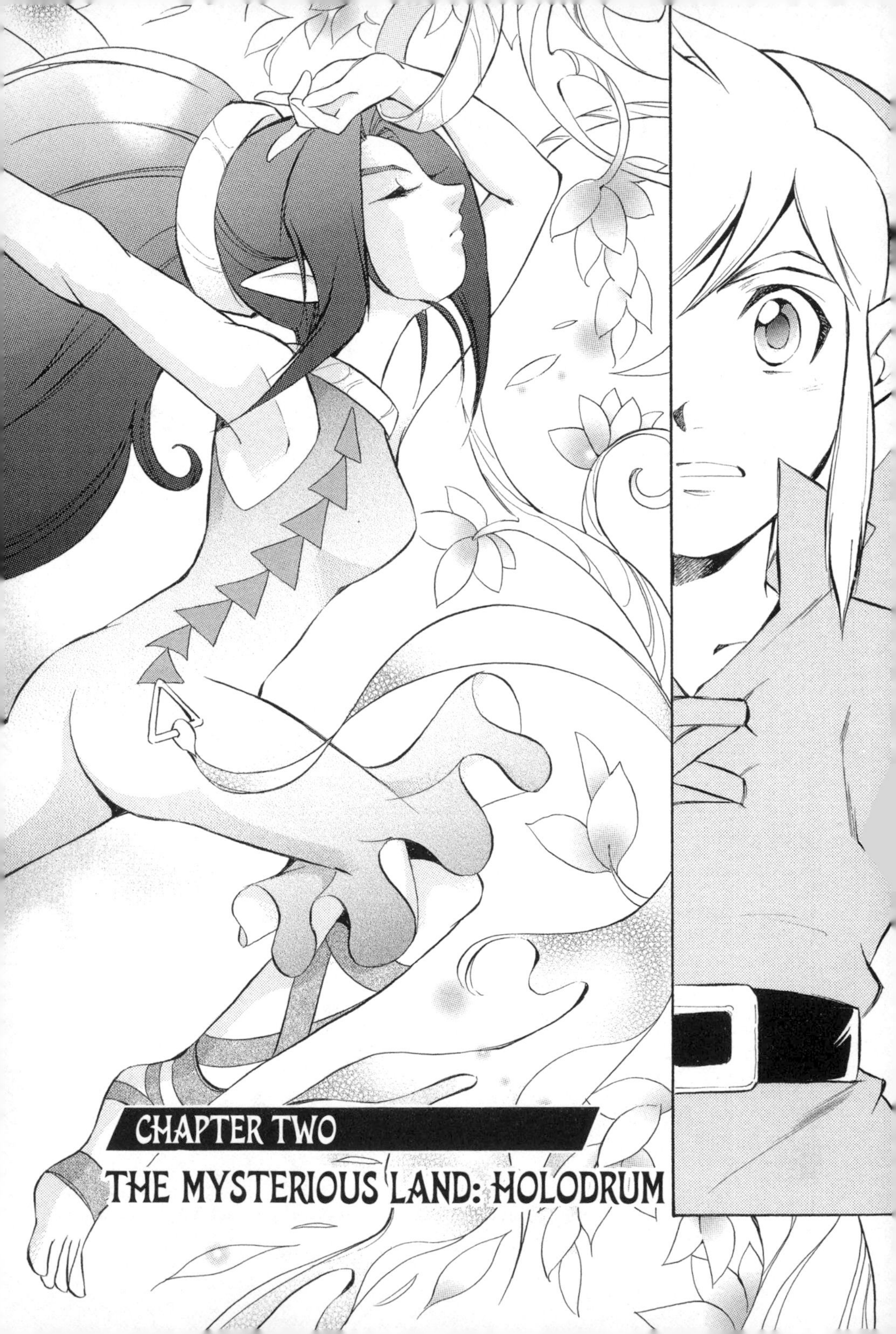
CHAPTER TWO
THE MYSTERIOUS LAND: HOLODRUM

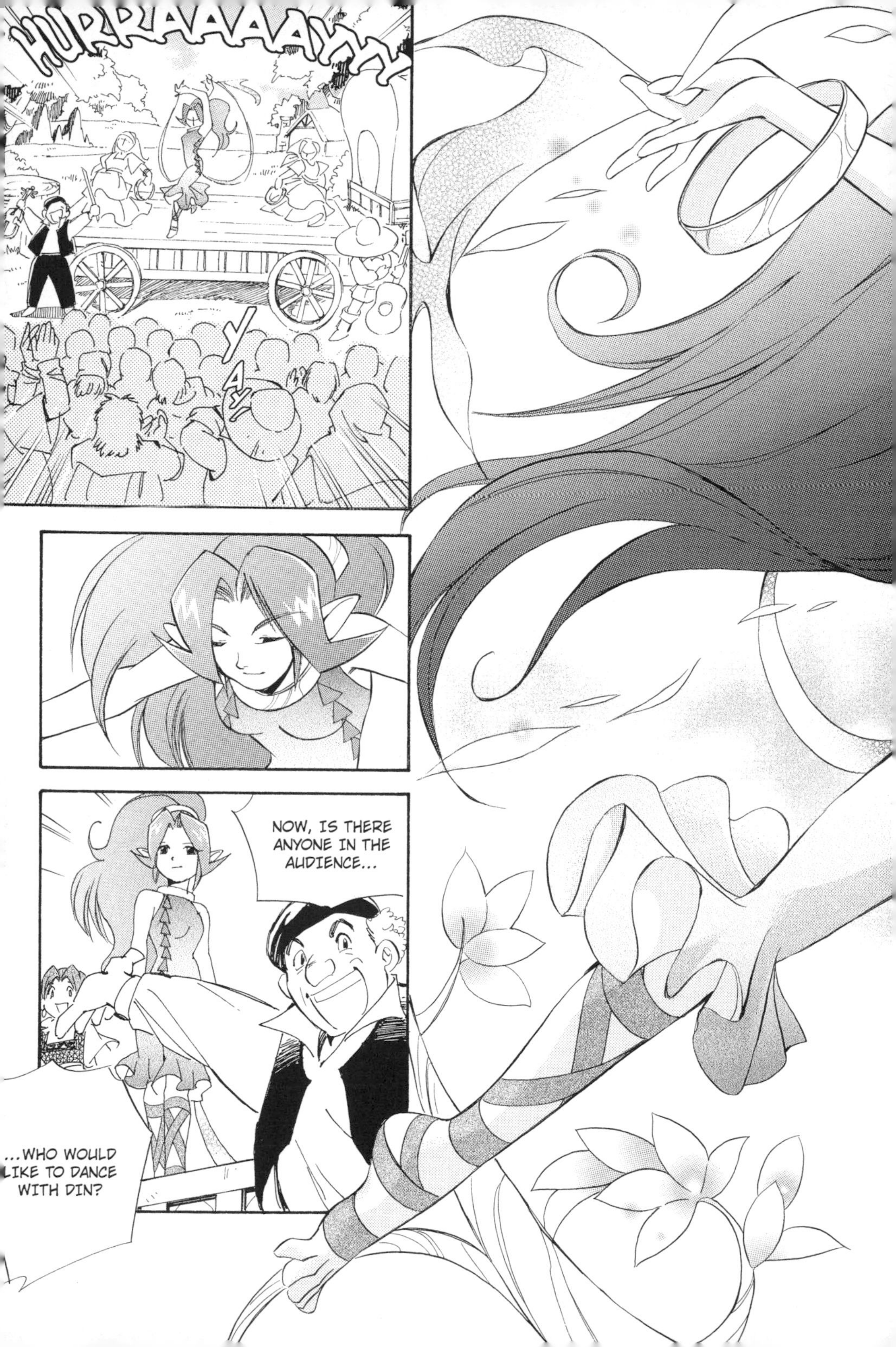
HURRAAAAYYY
YAY!
NOW, IS THERE ANYONE IN THE AUDIENCE...
...WHO WOULD LIKE TO DANCE WITH DIN?

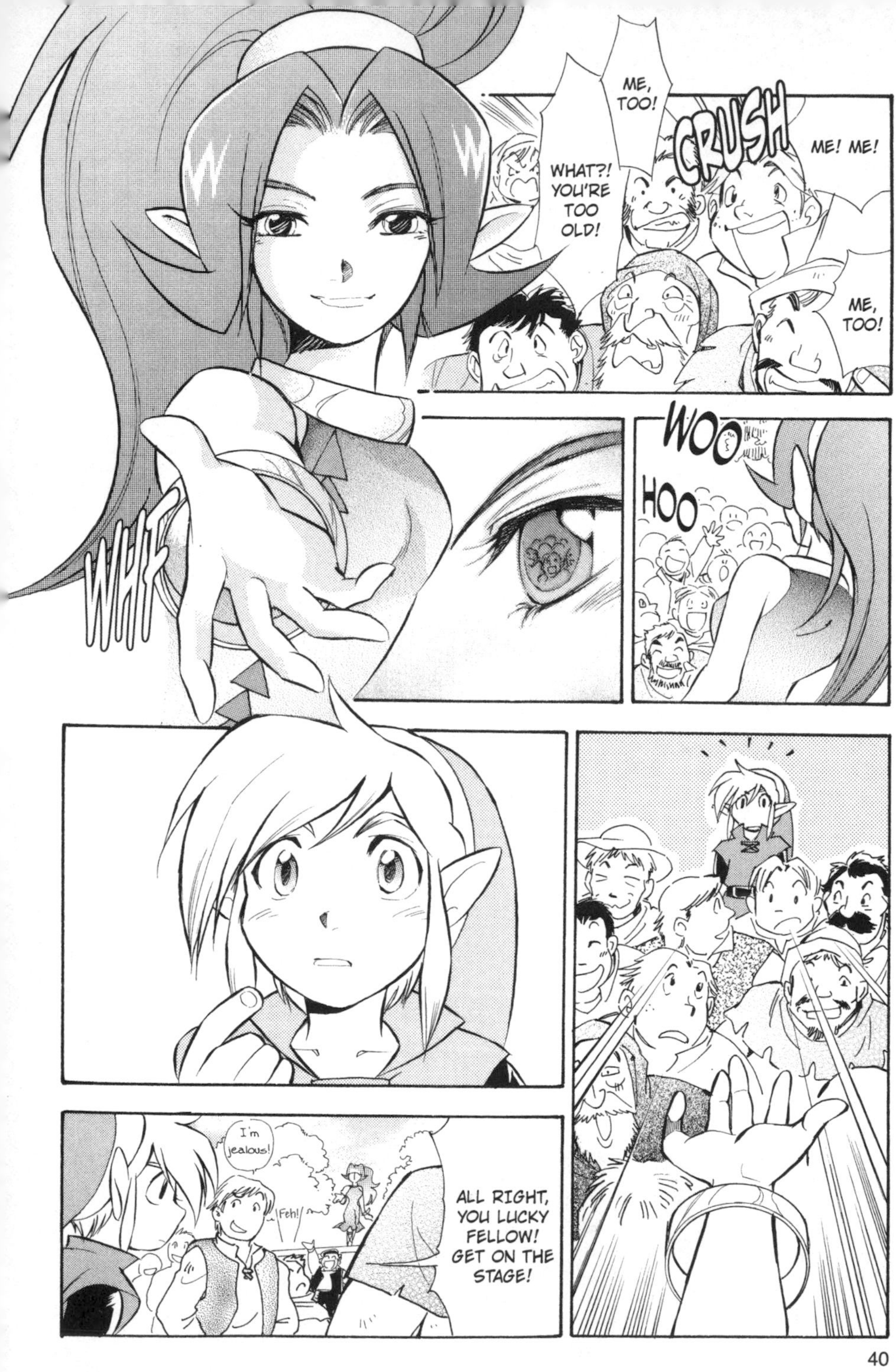

ME! ME!
CRUSH
ME, TOO!
WHAT?! YOU'RE TOO OLD!
ME, TOO!
WOO
HOO
WHIF
ALL RIGHT, YOU LUCKY FELLOW! GET ON THE STAGE!
I'm jealous!
Feh!

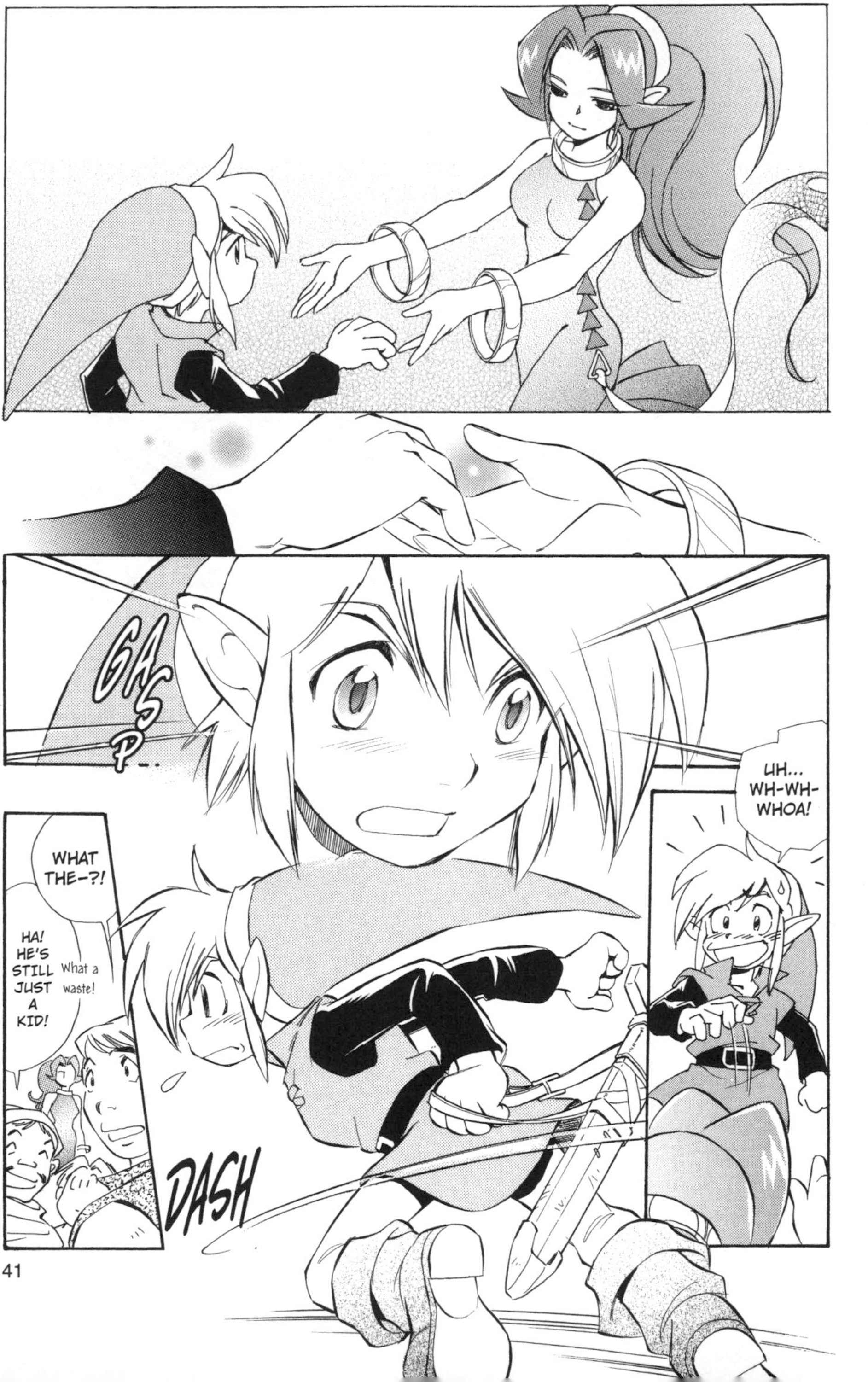
GASP...
UH... WH-WH-WHOA!
WHAT THE-?!
HA! HE'S STILL JUST A KID!
What a waste!
DASH

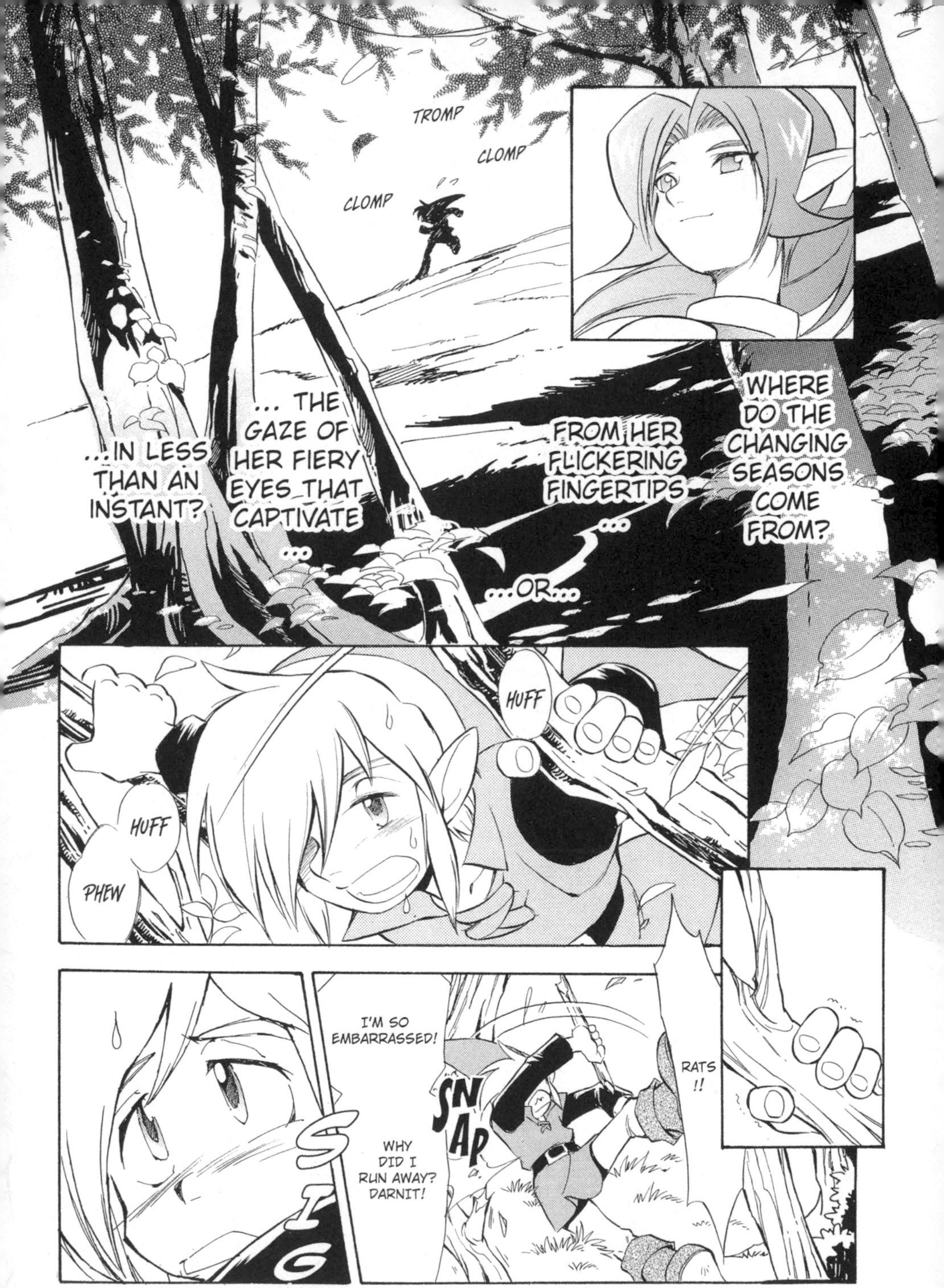
TROMP
CLOMP
CLOMP
WHERE DO THE CHANGING SEASONS COME FROM?
FROM HER FLICKERING FINGERTIPS ...
...OR...
... THE GAZE OF HER FIERY EYES THAT CAPTIVATE ...
...IN LESS THAN AN INSTANT?
HUFF
HUFF
PHEW
RATS !!
I'M SO EMBARRASSED!
WHY DID I RUN AWAY? DARNIT!
SNAP
SIGH

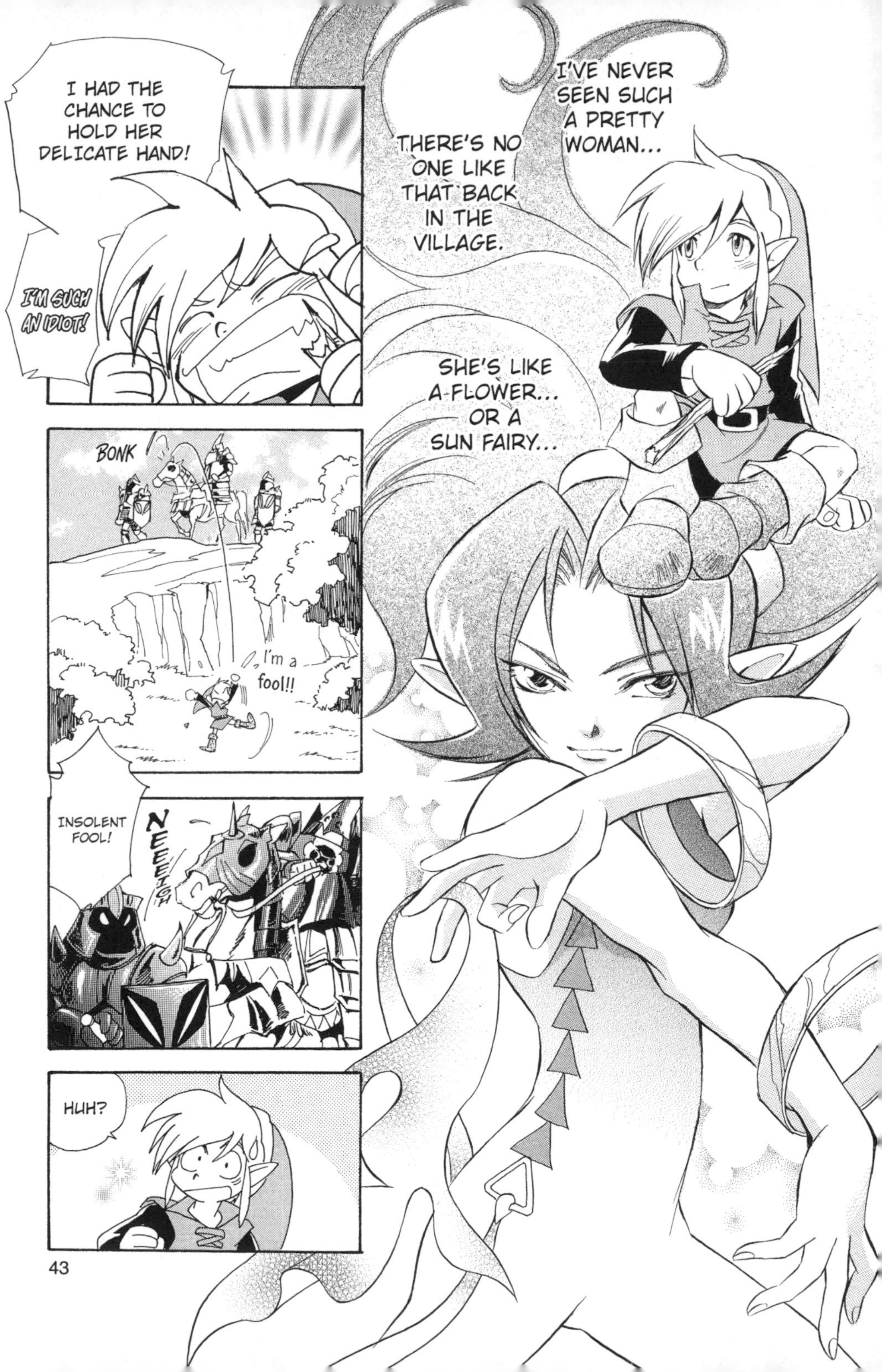
I'VE NEVER SEEN SUCH A PRETTY WOMAN...
THERE'S NO ONE LIKE THAT BACK IN THE VILLAGE.
SHE'S LIKE A FLOWER... OR A SUN FAIRY...
I HAD THE CHANCE TO HOLD HER DELICATE HAND!
I'M SUCH AN IDIOT!
BONK
I'm a fool!!
NEEEEIGH
INSOLENT FOOL!
HUH?

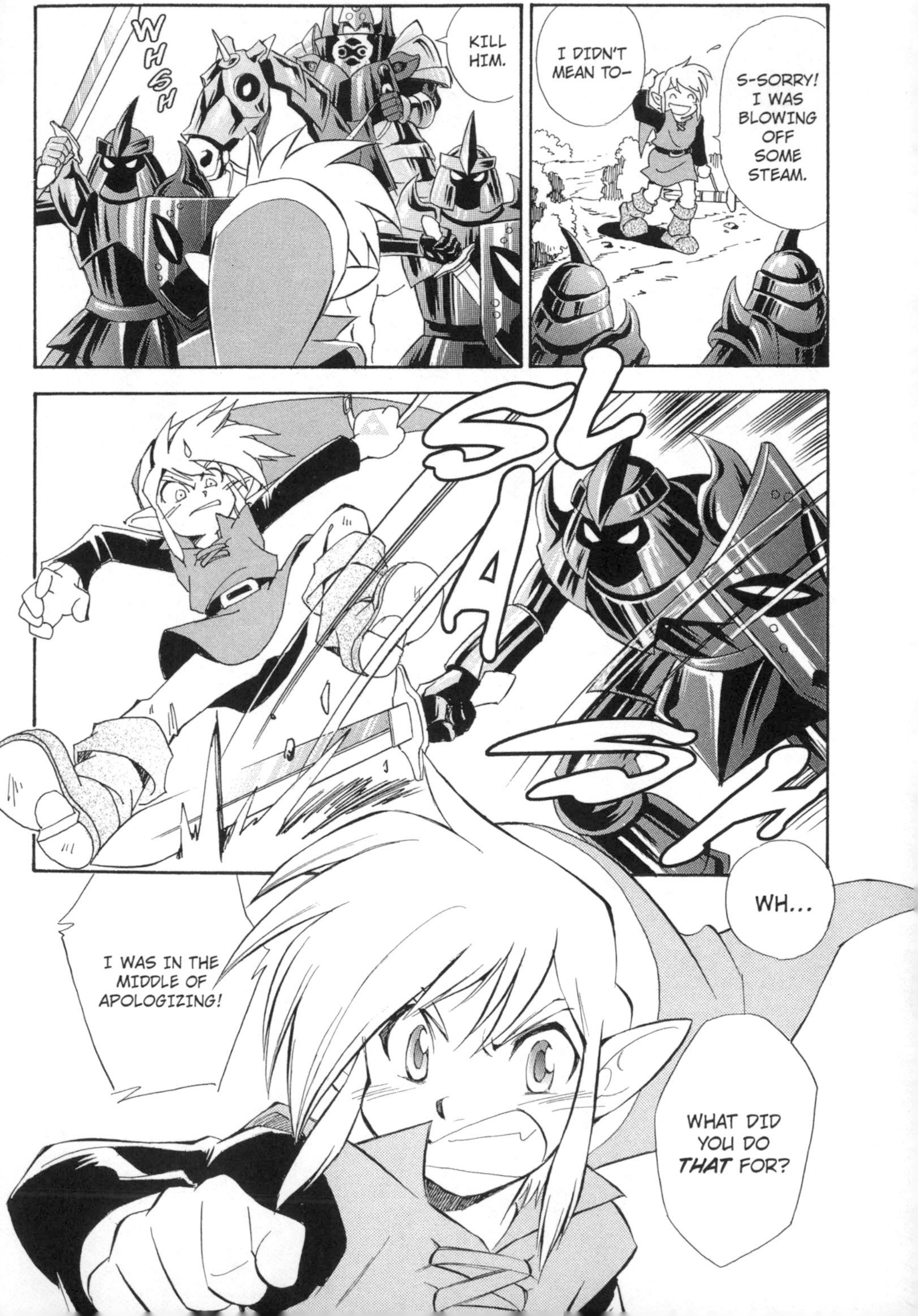
S-SORRY! I WAS BLOWING OFF SOME STEAM.
I DIDN'T MEAN TO–
KILL HIM.
WHSH
SLASH
WH...
WHAT DID YOU DO *THAT* FOR?
I WAS IN THE MIDDLE OF APOLOGIZING!

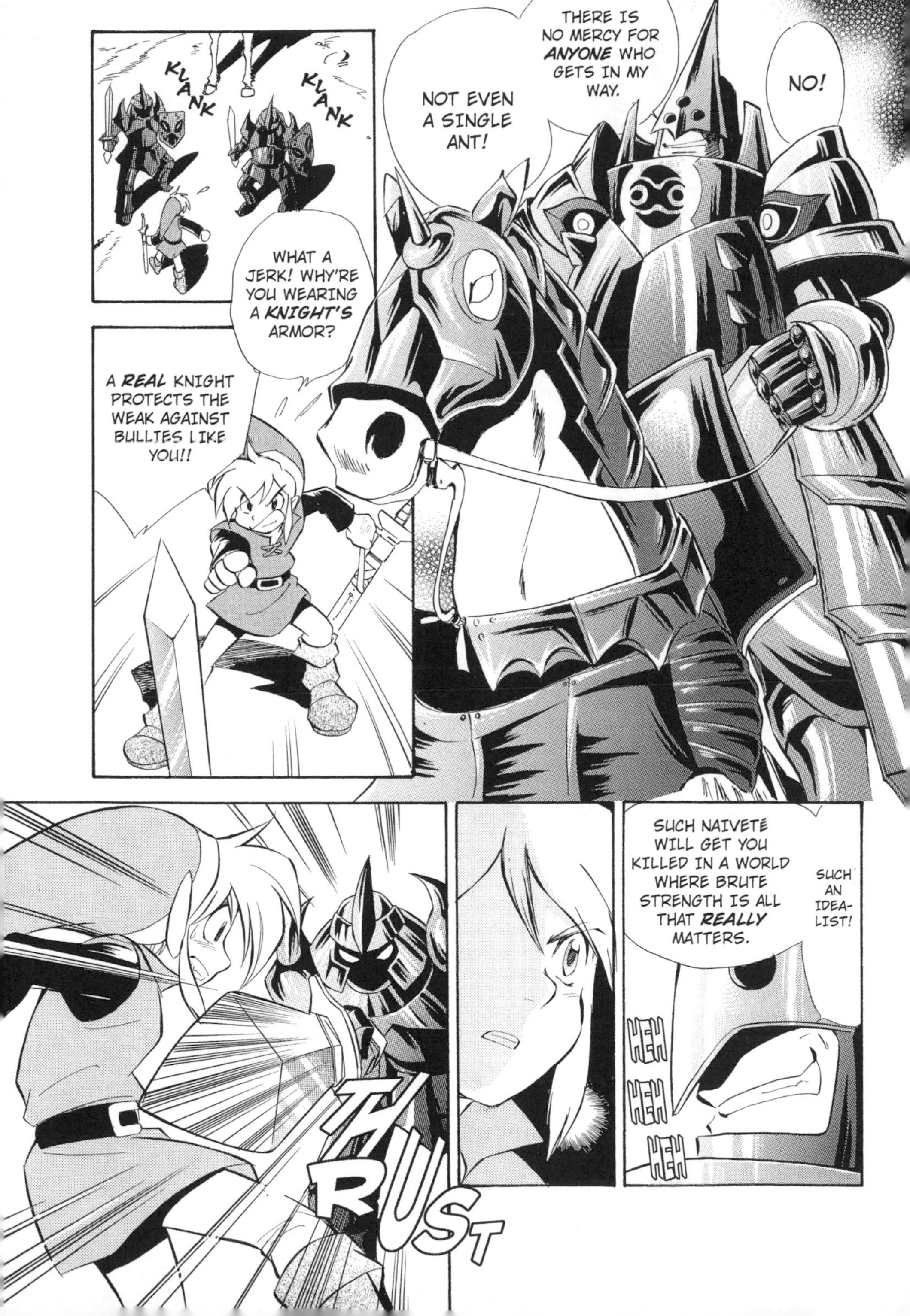
NO!
THERE IS NO MERCY FOR ANYONE WHO GETS IN MY WAY.
NOT EVEN A SINGLE ANT!
KLANK
KLANK
WHAT A JERK! WHY'RE YOU WEARING A KNIGHT'S ARMOR?
A REAL KNIGHT PROTECTS THE WEAK AGAINST BULLTES LIKE YOU!!
SUCH AN IDEA-LIST!
SUCH NAIVETÉ WILL GET YOU KILLED IN A WORLD WHERE BRUTE STRENGTH IS ALL THAT REALLY MATTERS.
HEH
HEH
HEH
THRUST

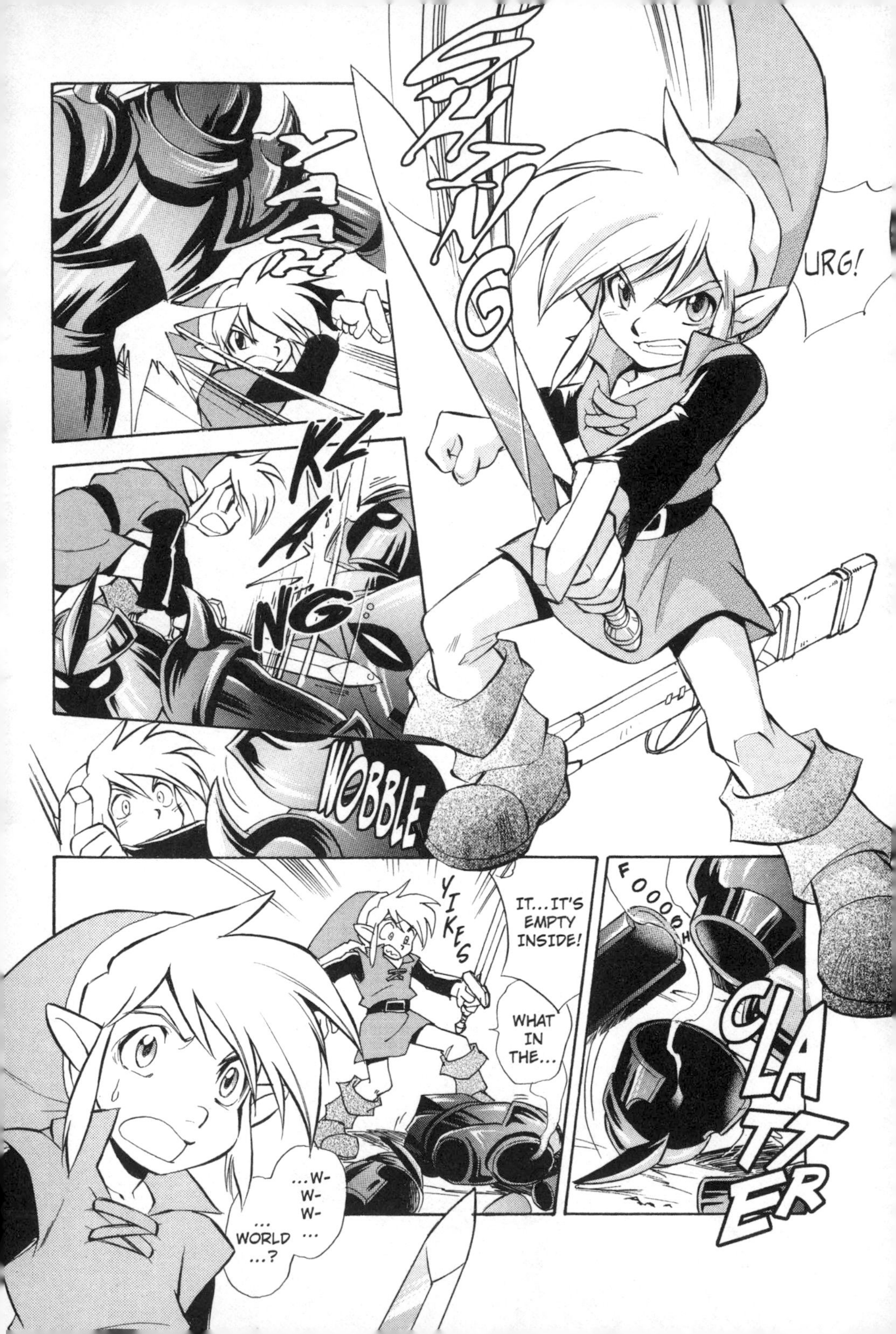
SHING
URG!
YAAH
KLANG
WOBBLE
FOOOOOH
CLATTER
IT...IT'S EMPTY INSIDE!
YIKES
WHAT IN THE...
...W- W- W- ... WORLD ...?

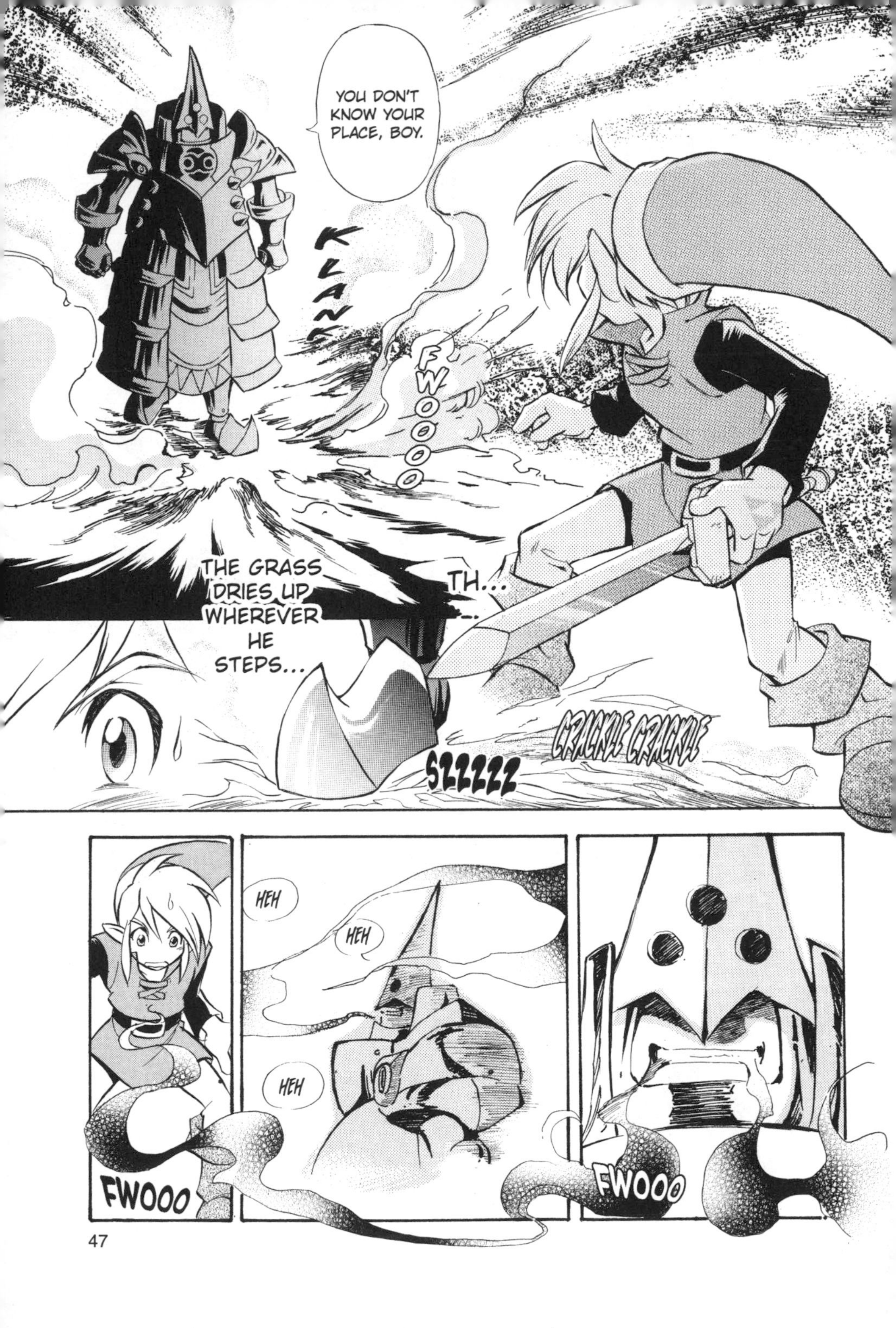
YOU DON'T KNOW YOUR PLACE, BOY.
KLANK
FWOOOOO
TH...
THE GRASS DRIES UP WHEREVER HE STEPS...
CRACKLE CRACKLE
SZZZZZ
FWOOO
HEH
HEH
HEH
FWOOO

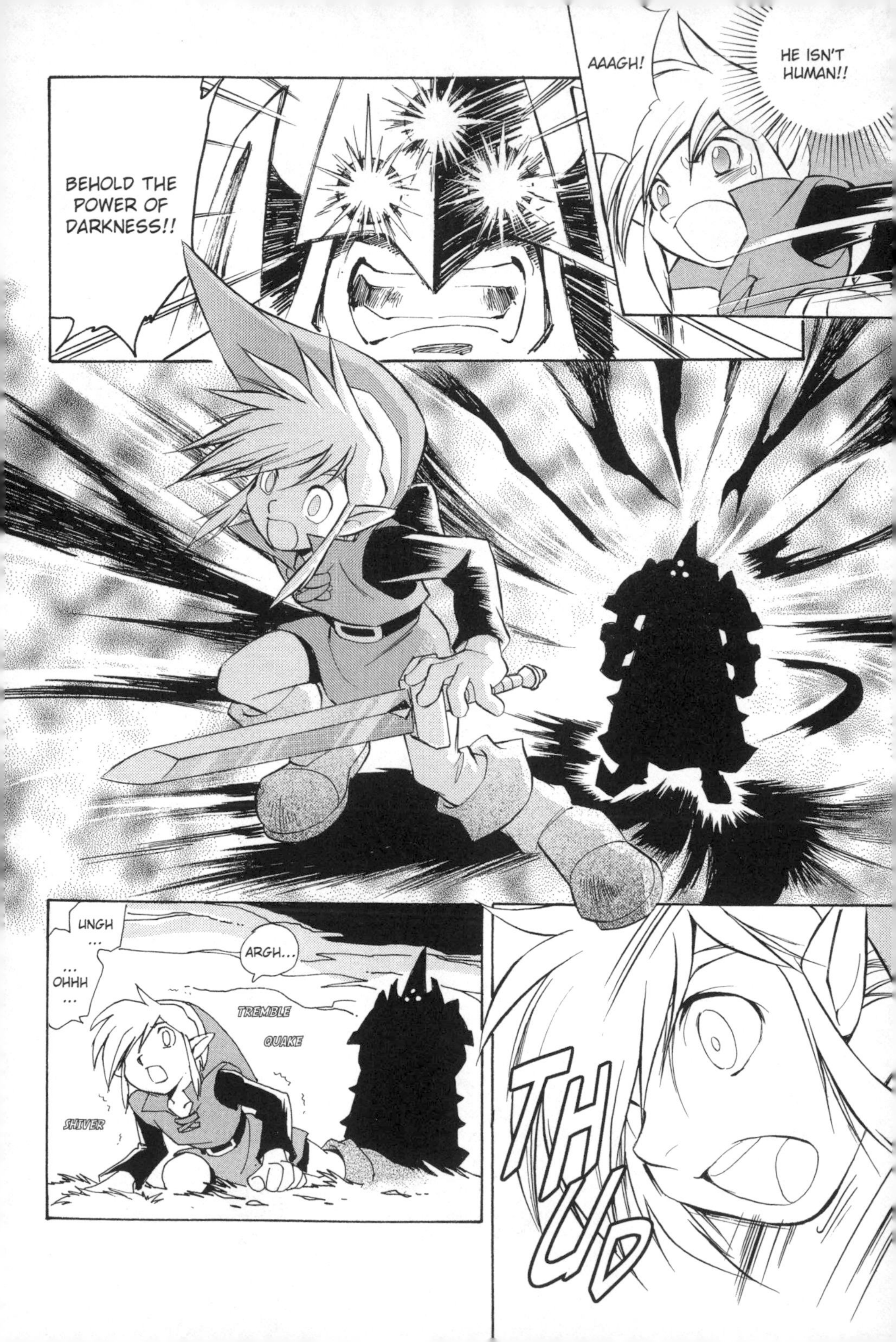
HE ISN'T HUMAN!!
AAAGH!
BEHOLD THE POWER OF DARKNESS!!
THUD
ARGH...
UNGH ...
... OHHH ...
TREMBLE
QUAKE
SHIVER

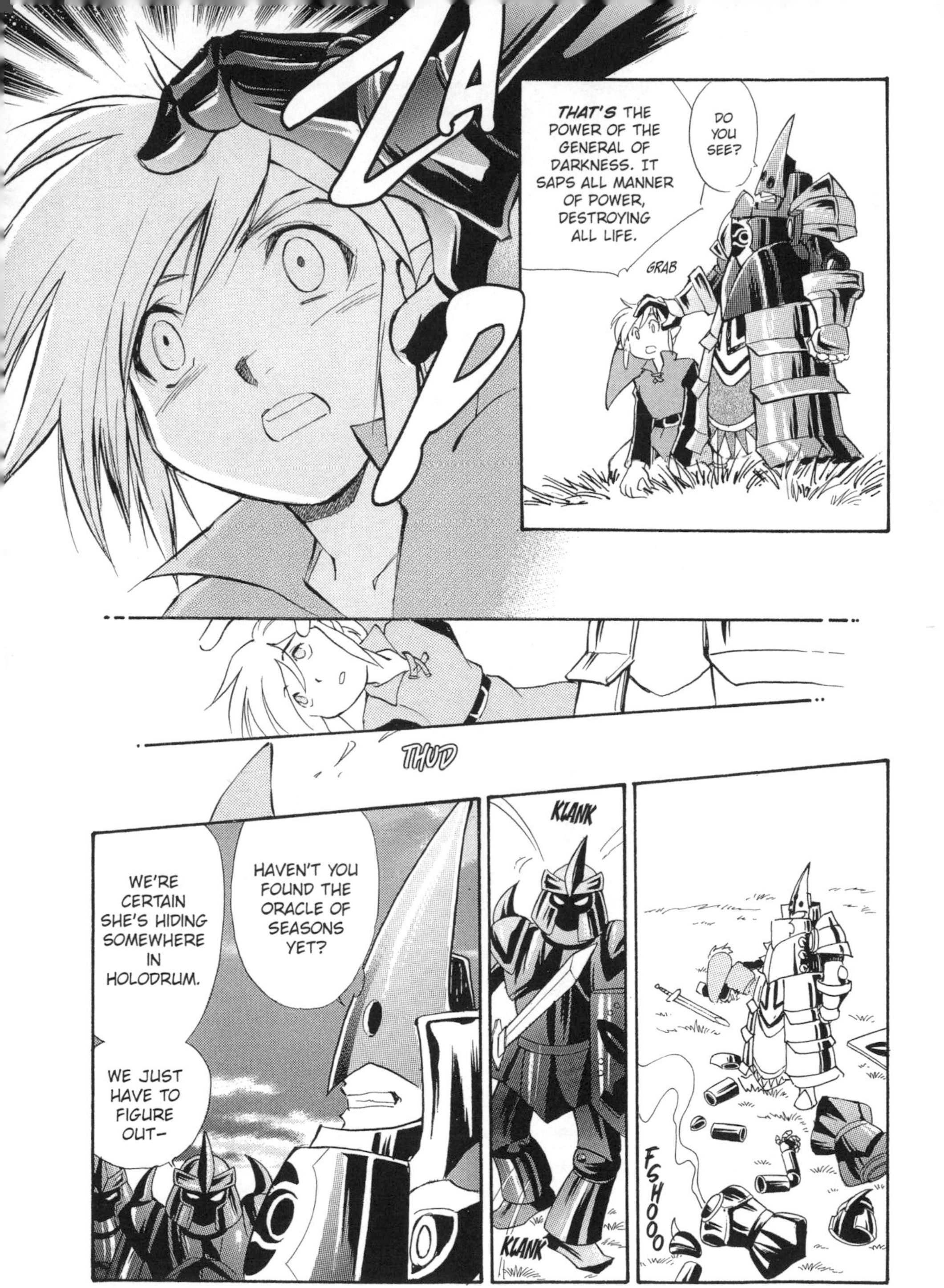
DO YOU SEE?
THAT'S THE POWER OF THE GENERAL OF DARKNESS. IT SAPS ALL MANNER OF POWER, DESTROYING ALL LIFE.
GRAB
ZAP
THUD
FSHOOO
KLANK
KLANK
HAVEN'T YOU FOUND THE ORACLE OF SEASONS YET?
WE'RE CERTAIN SHE'S HIDING SOMEWHERE IN HOLODRUM.
WE JUST HAVE TO FIGURE OUT-

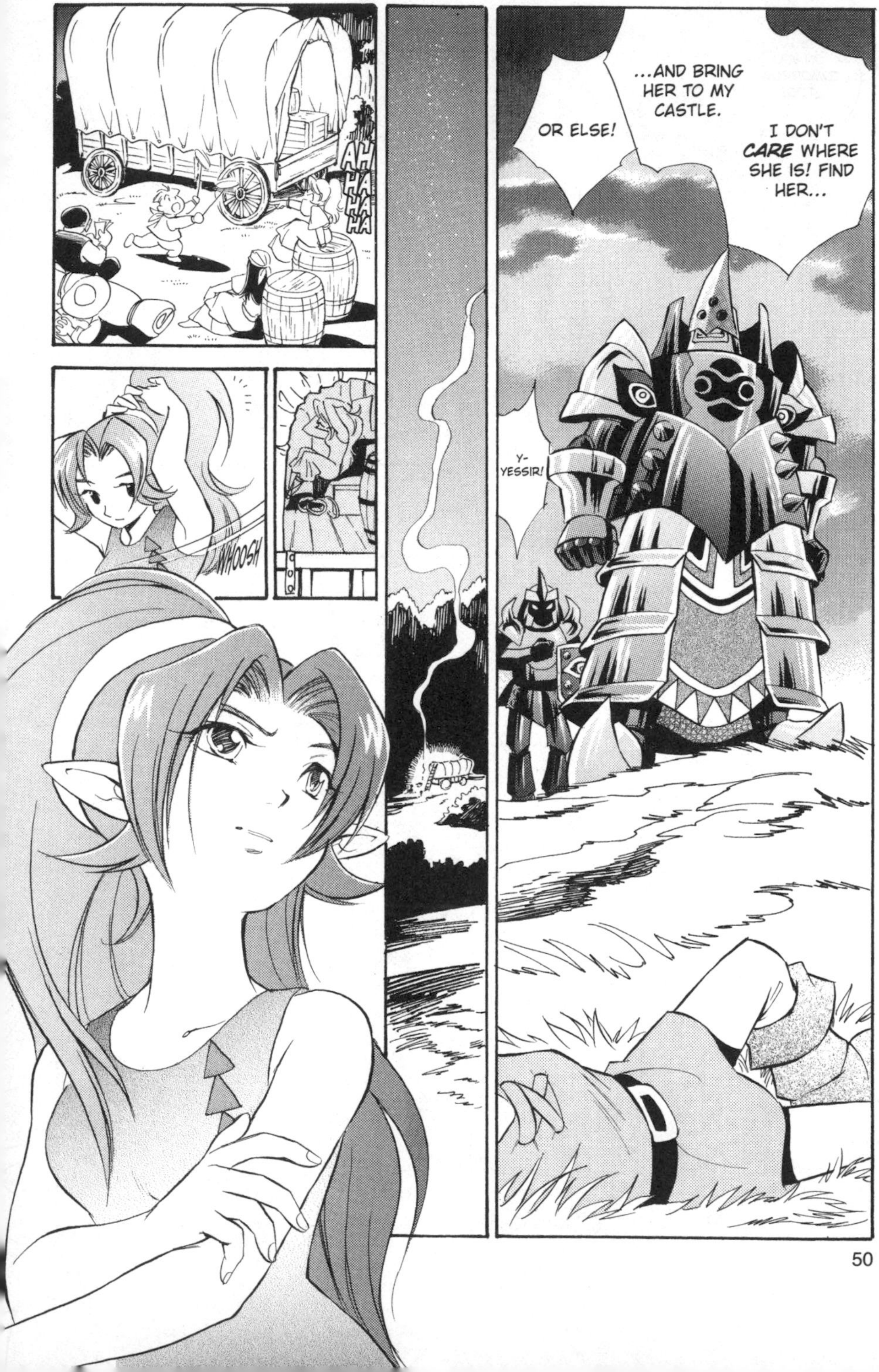
I DON'T **CARE** WHERE SHE IS! FIND HER...
...AND BRING HER TO MY CASTLE.
OR ELSE!
Y-YESSIR!
AH HA HA HA
WHOOSH

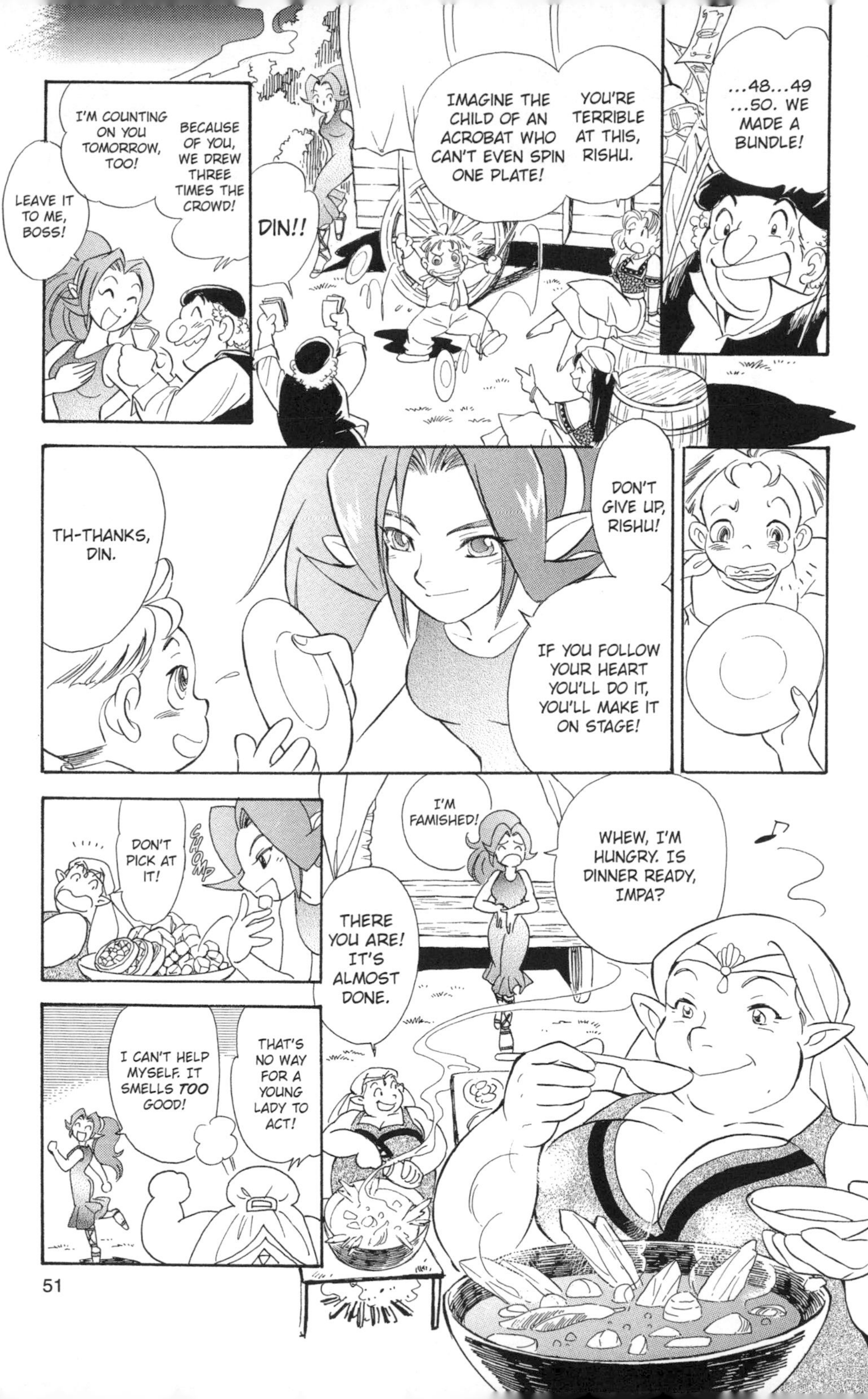
...48...49 ...50. WE MADE A BUNDLE!
YOU'RE TERRIBLE AT THIS, RISHU.
IMAGINE THE CHILD OF AN ACROBAT WHO CAN'T EVEN SPIN ONE PLATE!
DIN!!
BECAUSE OF YOU, WE DREW THREE TIMES THE CROWD!
I'M COUNTING ON YOU TOMORROW, TOO!
LEAVE IT TO ME, BOSS!
DON'T GIVE UP, RISHU!
IF YOU FOLLOW YOUR HEART YOU'LL DO IT, YOU'LL MAKE IT ON STAGE!
TH-THANKS, DIN.
WHEW, I'M HUNGRY. IS DINNER READY, IMPA?
I'M FAMISHED!
THERE YOU ARE! IT'S ALMOST DONE.
CHOMP
DON'T PICK AT IT!
THAT'S NO WAY FOR A YOUNG LADY TO ACT!
I CAN'T HELP MYSELF. IT SMELLS *TOO* GOOD!

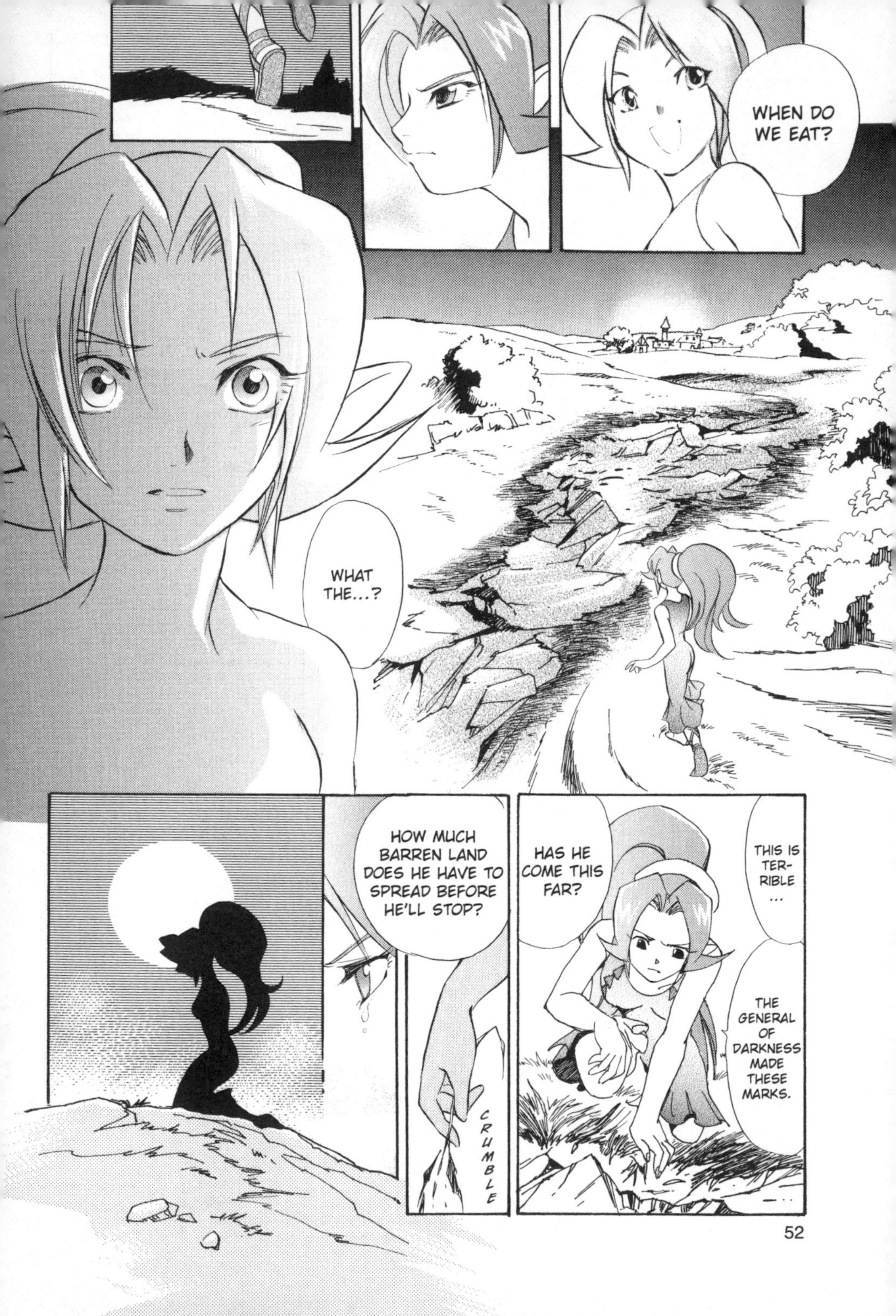
WHEN DO WE EAT?
WHAT THE...?
THIS IS TERRIBLE...
HAS HE COME THIS FAR?
THE GENERAL OF DARKNESS MADE THESE MARKS.
—...
HOW MUCH BARREN LAND DOES HE HAVE TO SPREAD BEFORE HE'LL STOP?
CRUMBLE

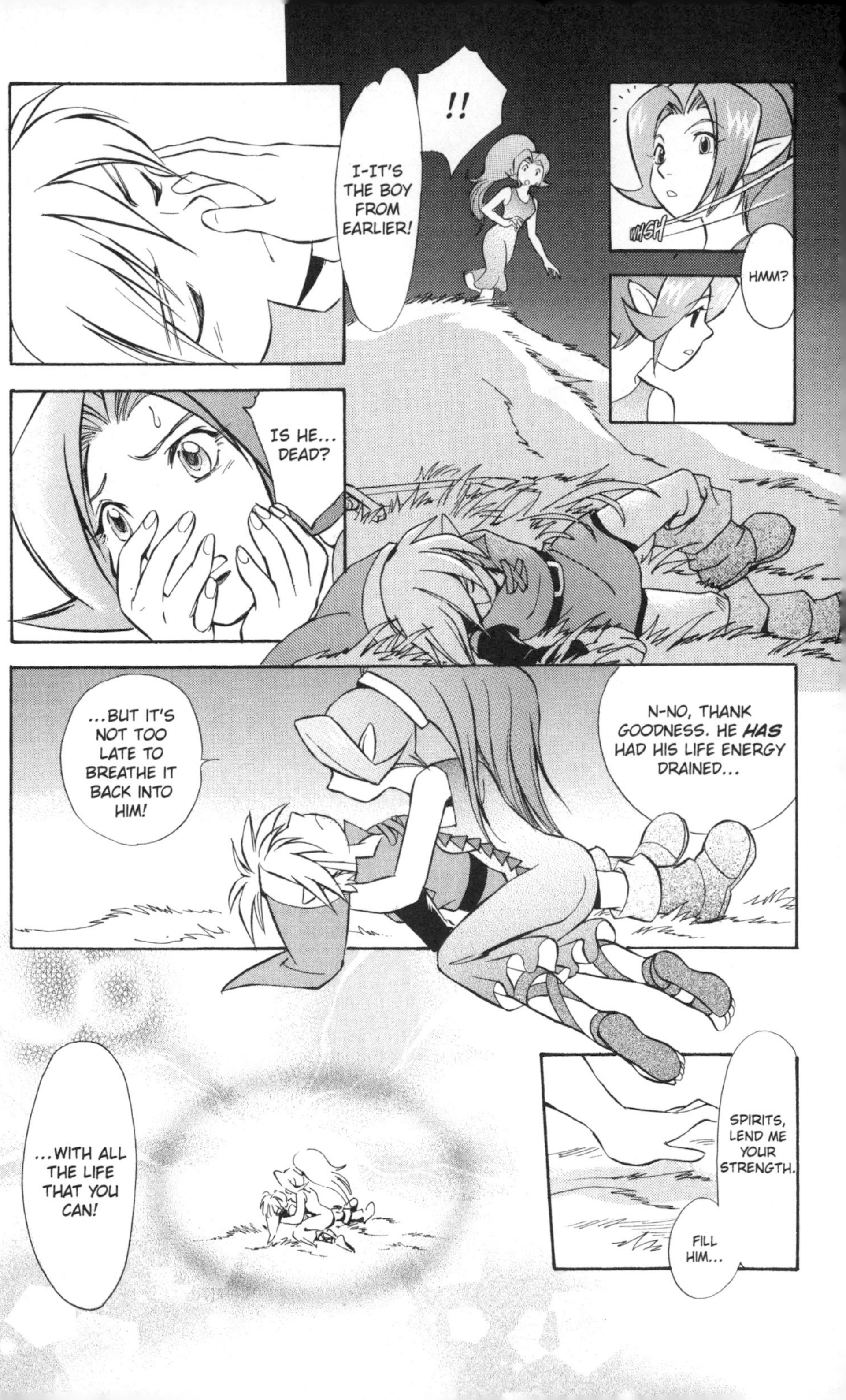
WHSH
HMM?
!!
I-IT'S THE BOY FROM EARLIER!
IS HE... DEAD?
N-NO, THANK GOODNESS. HE **HAS** HAD HIS LIFE ENERGY DRAINED...
...BUT IT'S NOT TOO LATE TO BREATHE IT BACK INTO HIM!
SPIRITS, LEND ME YOUR STRENGTH.
FILL HIM...
...WITH ALL THE LIFE THAT YOU CAN!

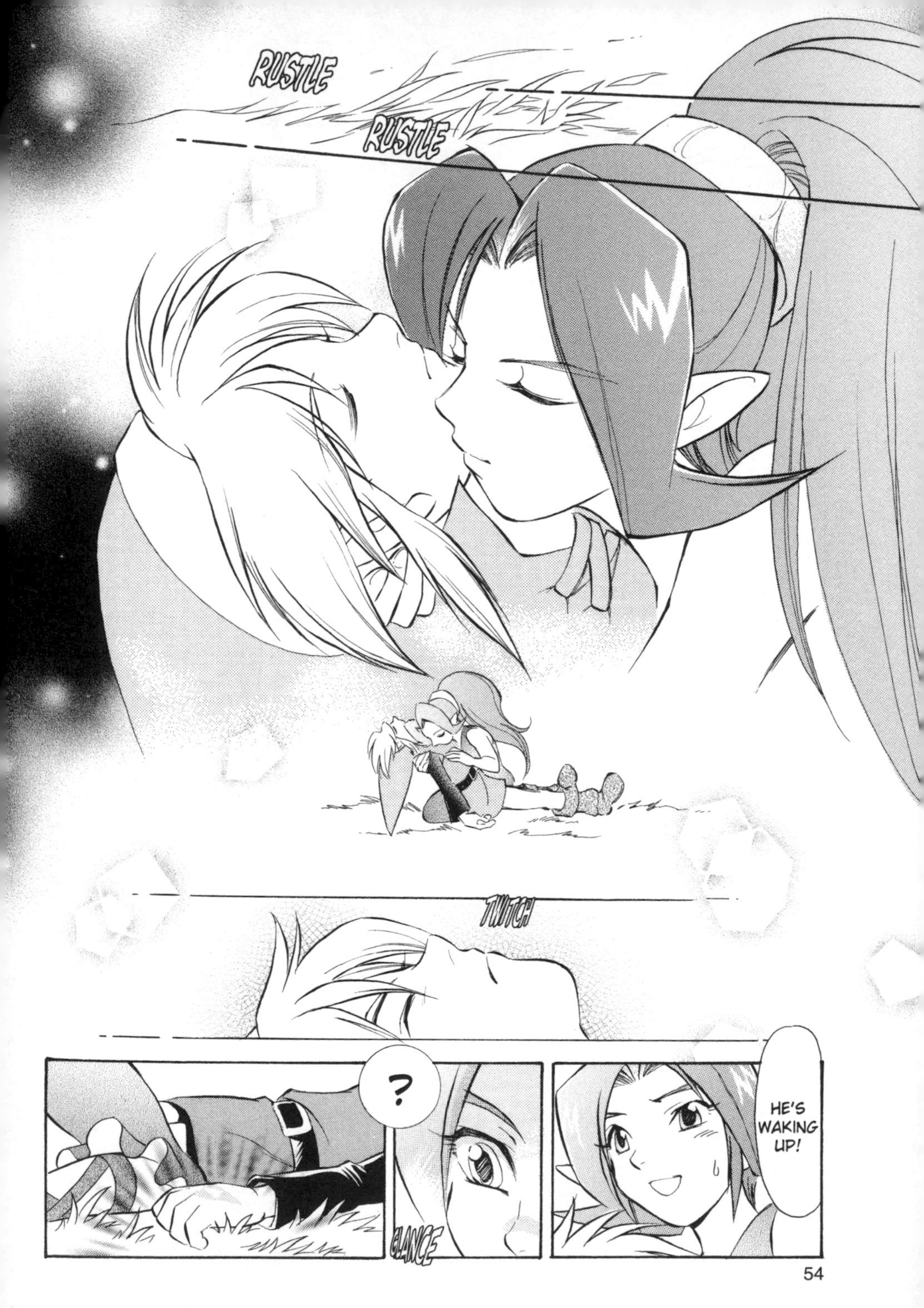
RUSTLE
RUSTLE
TWITCH
HE'S WAKING UP!
?
GLANCE

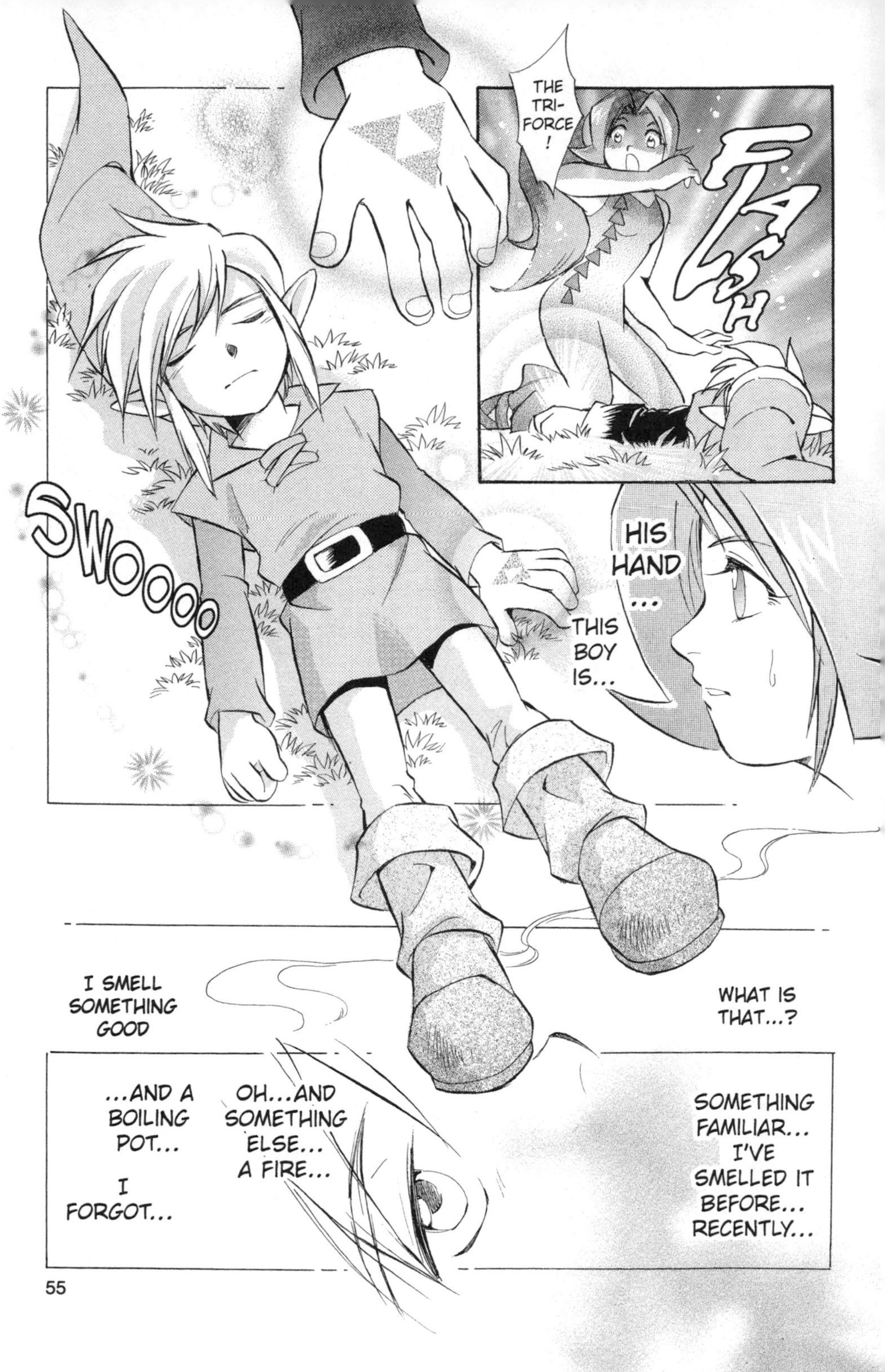
THE TRI-FORCE!
FLASH
HIS HAND...
THIS BOY IS...
SWOOOO
WHAT IS THAT...?
I SMELL SOMETHING GOOD
SOMETHING FAMILIAR... I'VE SMELLED IT BEFORE... RECENTLY...
OH...AND SOMETHING ELSE... A FIRE...
...AND A BOILING POT...
I FORGOT...

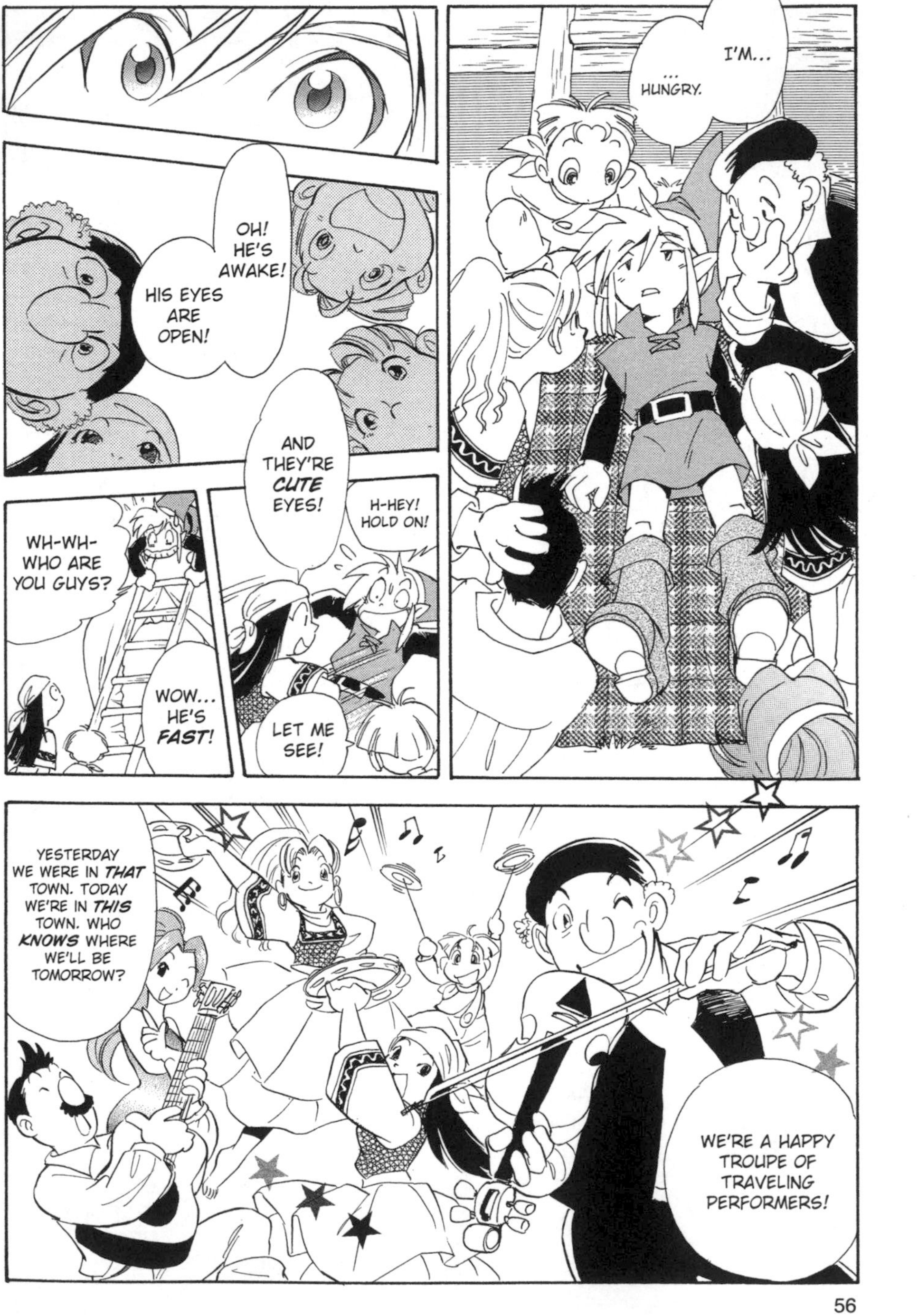
I'M...
...HUNGRY.
OH! HE'S AWAKE!
HIS EYES ARE OPEN!
AND THEY'RE **CUTE** EYES!
H-HEY! HOLD ON!
LET ME SEE!
WH-WH-WHO ARE YOU GUYS?
WOW... HE'S **FAST**!
YESTERDAY WE WERE IN **THAT** TOWN. TODAY WE'RE IN **THIS** TOWN. WHO **KNOWS** WHERE WE'LL BE TOMORROW?
WE'RE A HAPPY TROUPE OF TRAVELING PERFORMERS!

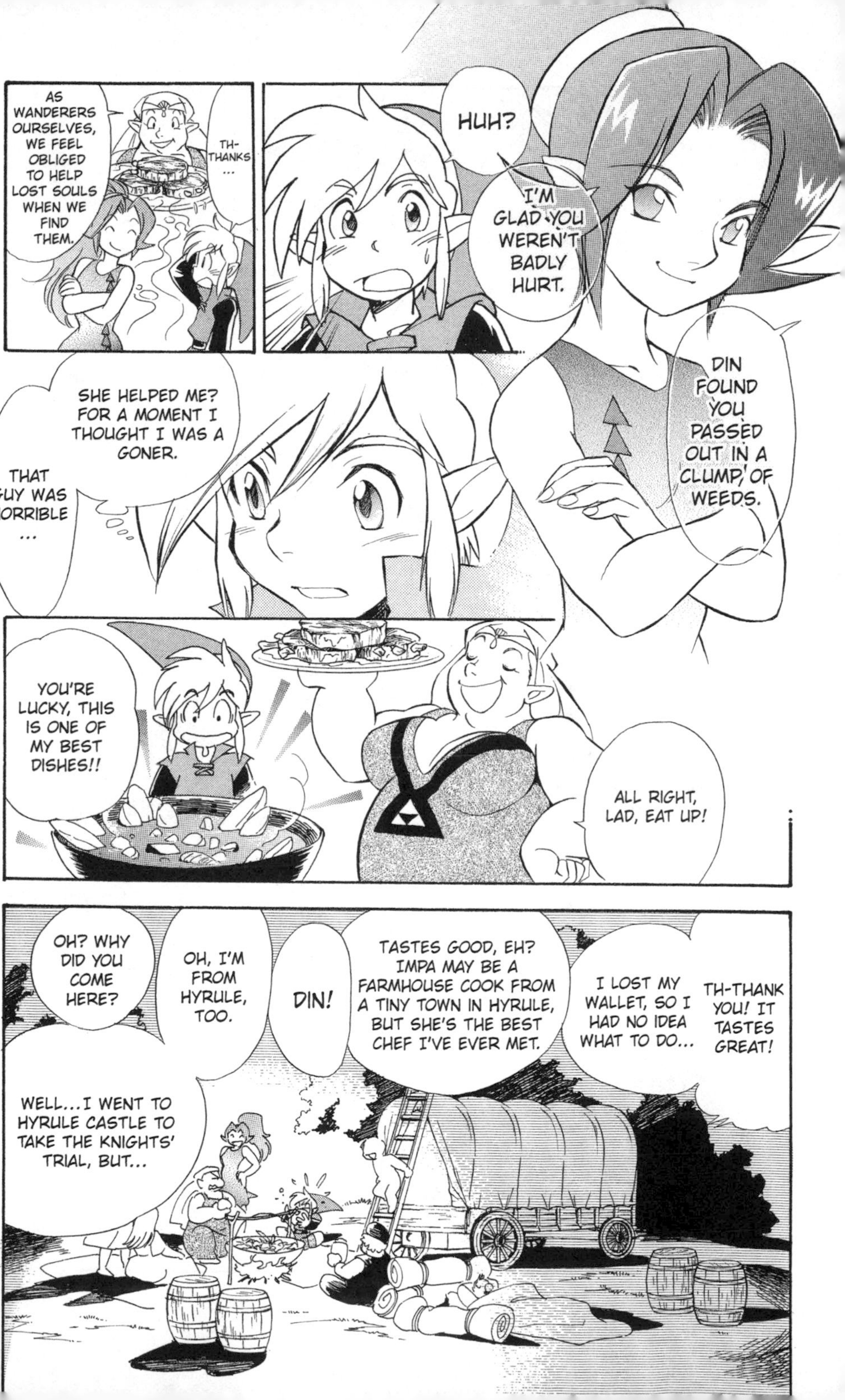
HUH?
I'M GLAD YOU WEREN'T BADLY HURT.
DIN FOUND YOU PASSED OUT IN A CLUMP OF WEEDS.
SHE HELPED ME? FOR A MOMENT I THOUGHT I WAS A GONER.
THAT GUY WAS HORRIBLE...
AS WANDERERS OURSELVES, WE FEEL OBLIGED TO HELP LOST SOULS WHEN WE FIND THEM.
TH-THANKS...
ALL RIGHT, LAD, EAT UP!
YOU'RE LUCKY, THIS IS ONE OF MY BEST DISHES!!
TH-THANK YOU! IT TASTES GREAT!
I LOST MY WALLET, SO I HAD NO IDEA WHAT TO DO...
TASTES GOOD, EH? IMPA MAY BE A FARMHOUSE COOK FROM A TINY TOWN IN HYRULE, BUT SHE'S THE BEST CHEF I'VE EVER MET.
DIN!
OH, I'M FROM HYRULE, TOO.
OH? WHY DID YOU COME HERE?
WELL...I WENT TO HYRULE CASTLE TO TAKE THE KNIGHTS' TRIAL, BUT...

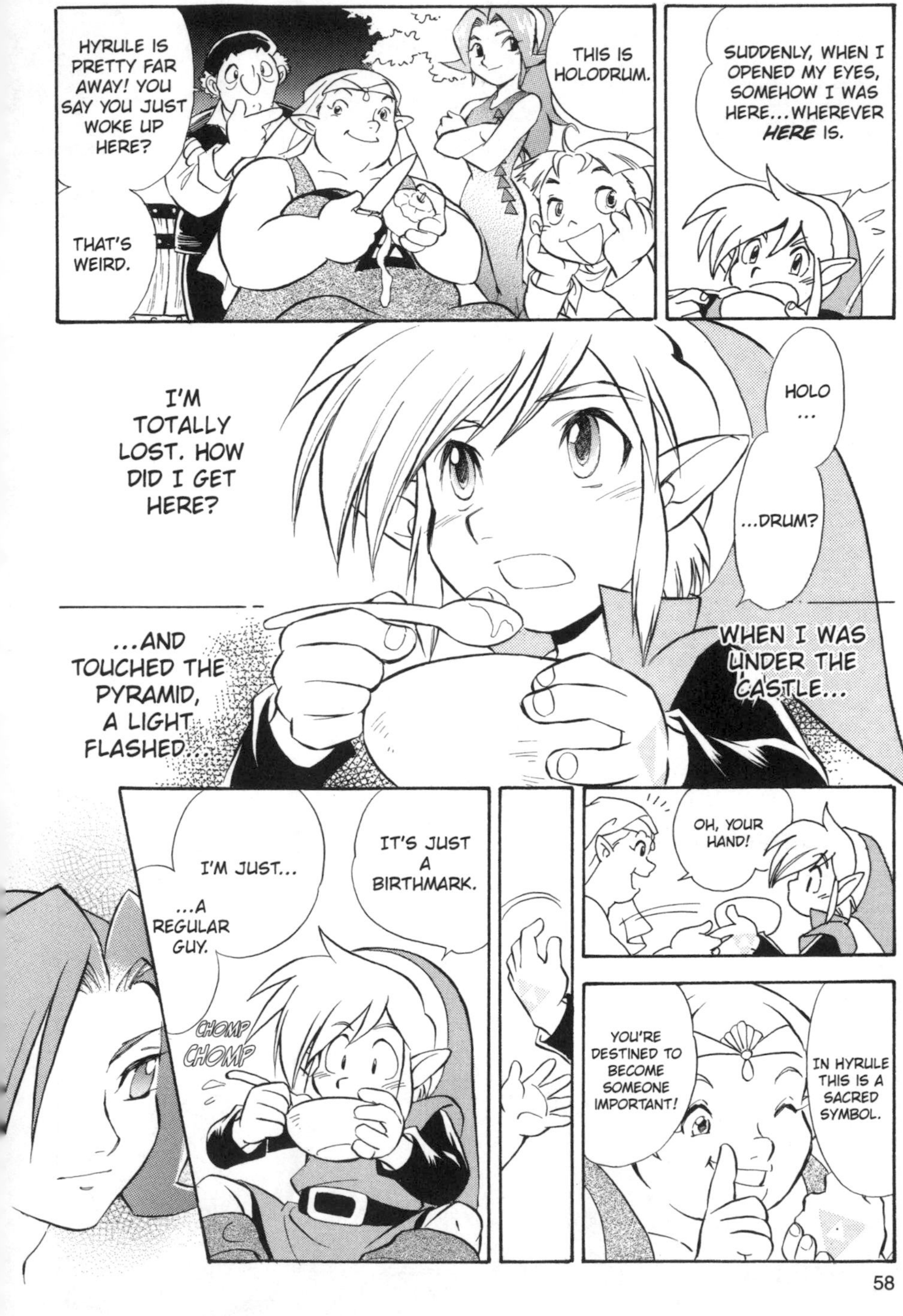
SUDDENLY, WHEN I OPENED MY EYES, SOMEHOW I WAS HERE...WHEREVER **HERE** IS.
THIS IS HOLODRUM.
HYRULE IS PRETTY FAR AWAY! YOU SAY YOU JUST WOKE UP HERE?
THAT'S WEIRD.
HOLO ...
...DRUM?
I'M TOTALLY LOST. HOW DID I GET HERE?
WHEN I WAS UNDER THE CASTLE...
...AND TOUCHED THE PYRAMID, A LIGHT FLASHED...
OH, YOUR HAND!
IN HYRULE THIS IS A SACRED SYMBOL.
YOU'RE DESTINED TO BECOME SOMEONE IMPORTANT!
IT'S JUST A BIRTHMARK.
I'M JUST...
...A REGULAR GUY.
CHOMP CHOMP

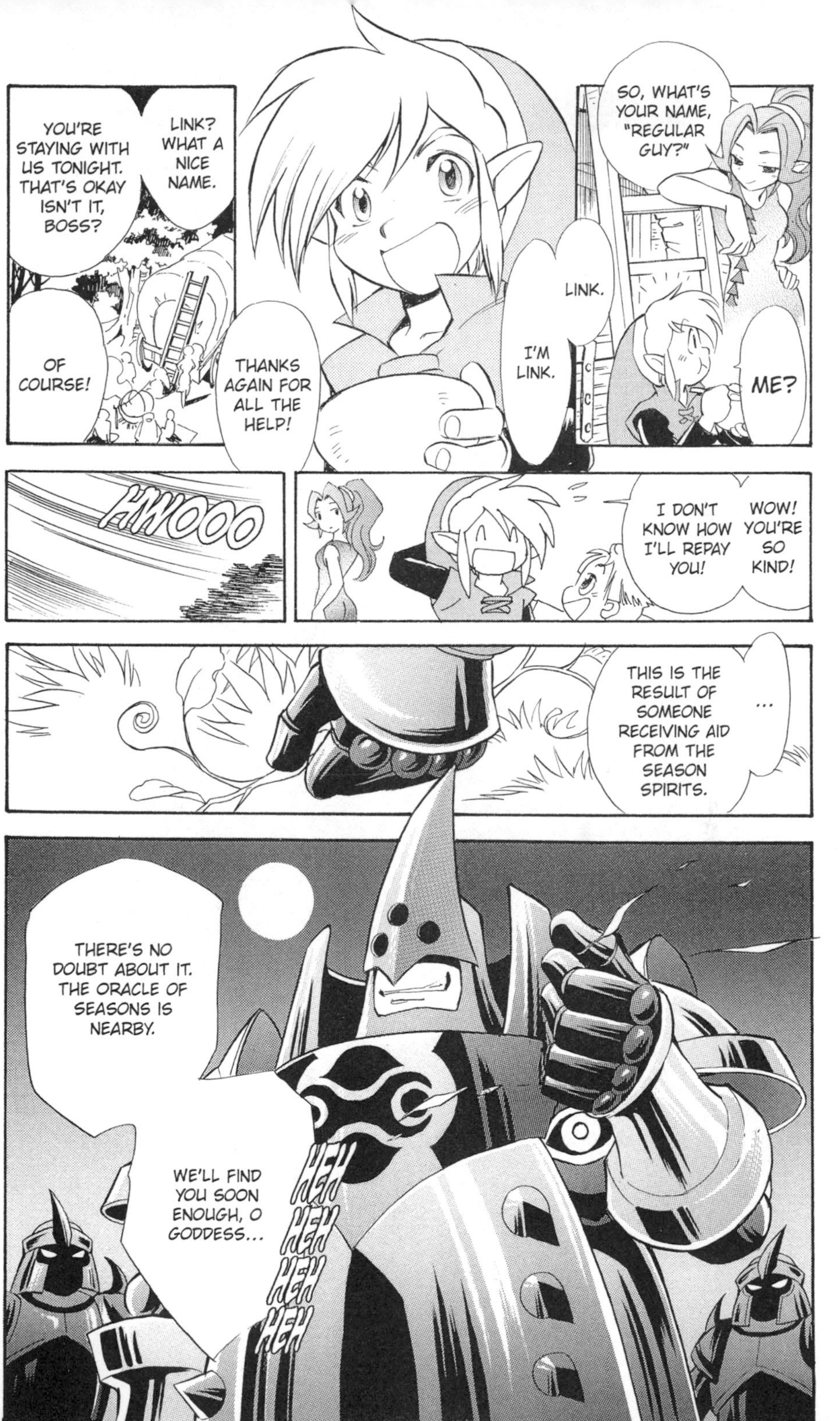

SO, WHAT'S YOUR NAME, "REGULAR GUY?"
ME?
LINK.
I'M LINK.
THANKS AGAIN FOR ALL THE HELP!
LINK? WHAT A NICE NAME.
YOU'RE STAYING WITH US TONIGHT. THAT'S OKAY ISN'T IT, BOSS?
OF COURSE!
WOW! YOU'RE SO KIND!
I DON'T KNOW HOW I'LL REPAY YOU!
HWOOO
...
THIS IS THE RESULT OF SOMEONE RECEIVING AID FROM THE SEASON SPIRITS.
THERE'S NO DOUBT ABOUT IT. THE ORACLE OF SEASONS IS NEARBY.
HEH HEH HEH HEH HEH
WE'LL FIND YOU SOON ENOUGH, O GODDESS...

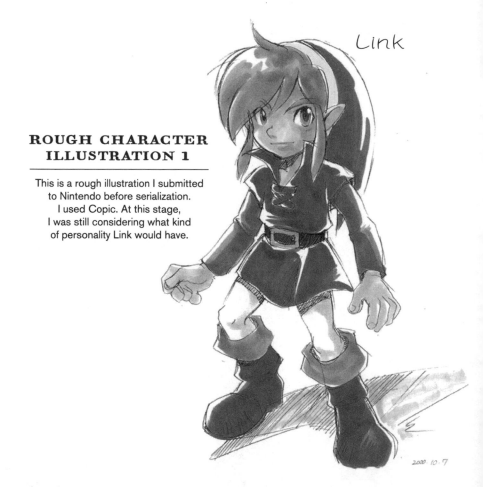

Link

ROUGH CHARACTER
ILLUSTRATION 1

This is a rough illustration I submitted
to Nintendo before serialization.
I used Copic. At this stage,
I was still considering what kind
of personality Link would have.

CHAPTER 3
TO THE TEMPLE OF SEASONS

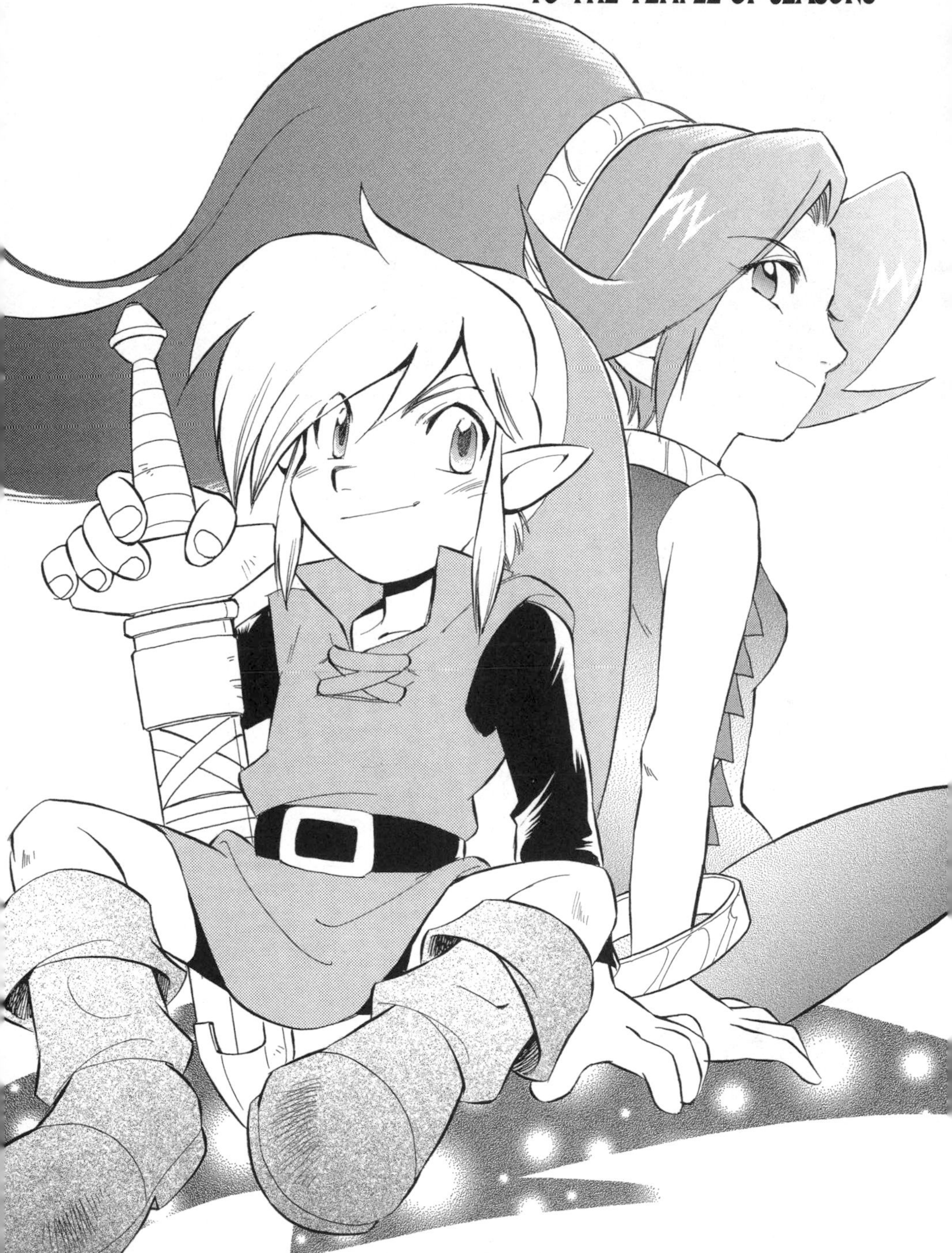

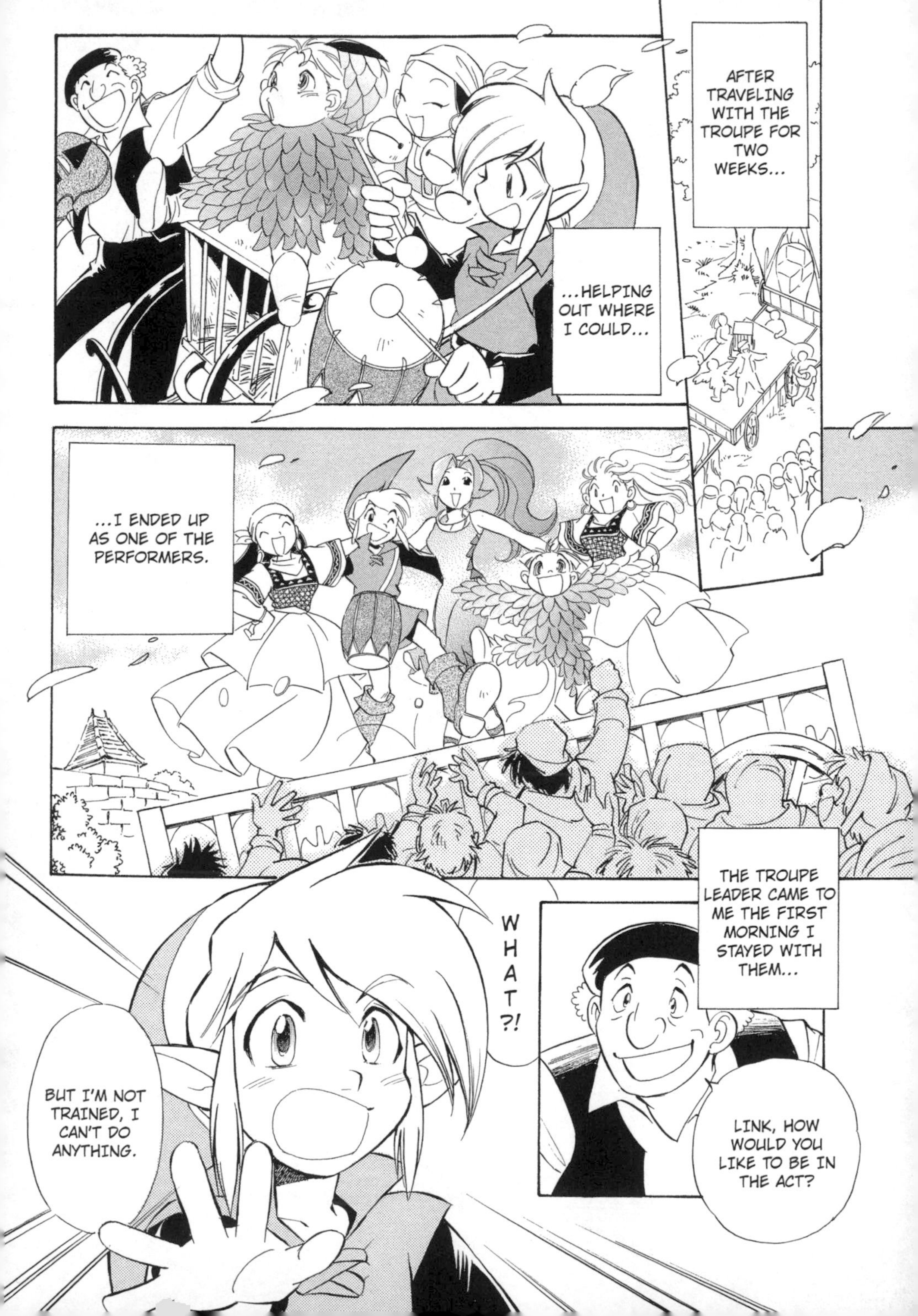
AFTER TRAVELING WITH THE TROUPE FOR TWO WEEKS...
...HELPING OUT WHERE I COULD...
...I ENDED UP AS ONE OF THE PERFORMERS.
THE TROUPE LEADER CAME TO ME THE FIRST MORNING I STAYED WITH THEM...
LINK, HOW WOULD YOU LIKE TO BE IN THE ACT?
WHAT?!
BUT I'M NOT TRAINED, I CAN'T DO ANYTHING.

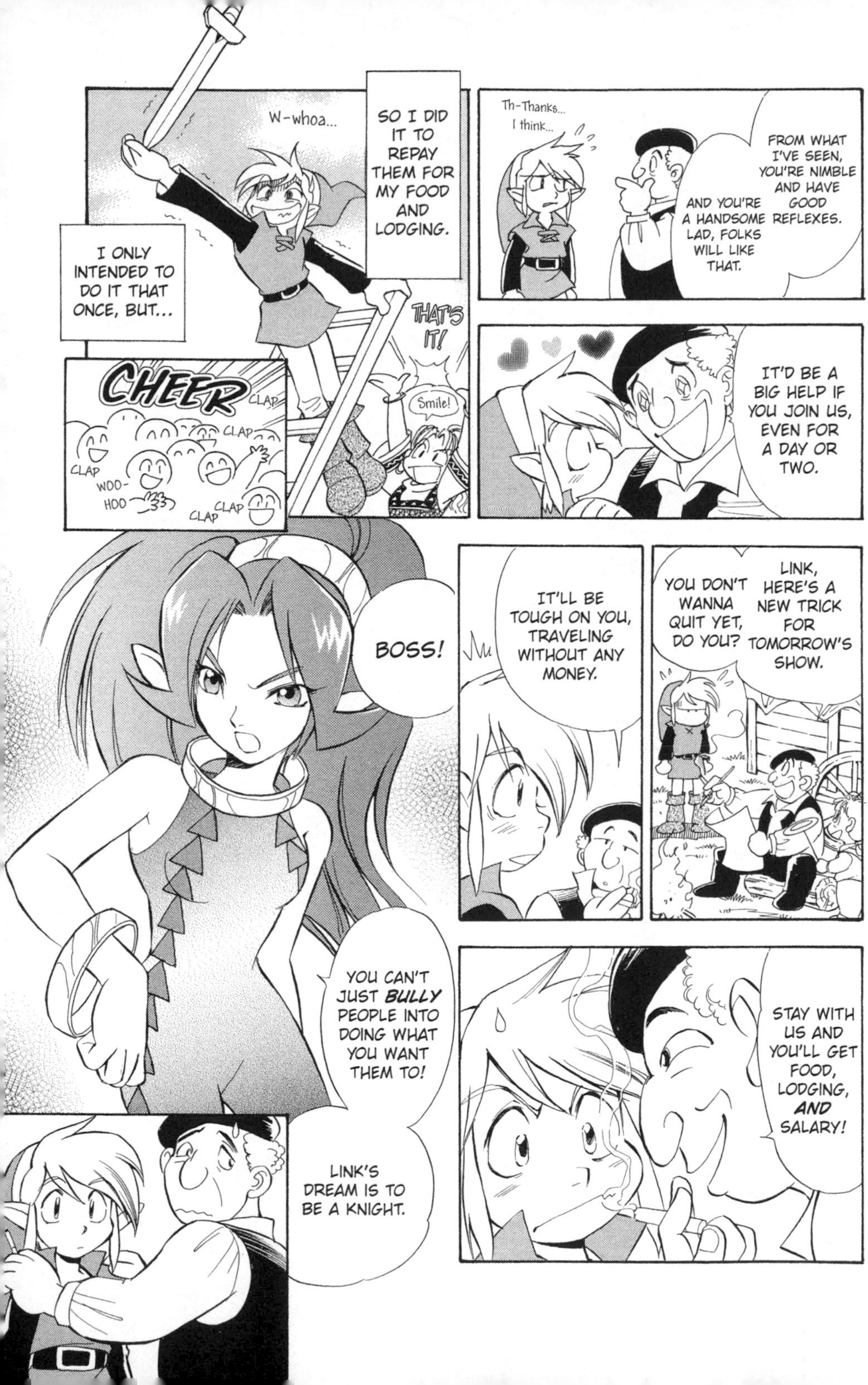

FROM WHAT I'VE SEEN, YOU'RE NIMBLE AND HAVE GOOD REFLEXES.
AND YOU'RE A HANDSOME LAD, FOLKS WILL LIKE THAT.
Th-Thanks... I think...
SO I DID IT TO REPAY THEM FOR MY FOOD AND LODGING.
W-whoa...
I ONLY INTENDED TO DO IT THAT ONCE, BUT...
THAT'S IT!
Smile!
IT'D BE A BIG HELP IF YOU JOIN US, EVEN FOR A DAY OR TWO.
CHEER
CLAP
CLAP
CLAP
WOO-HOO
CLAP
CLAP
LINK, HERE'S A NEW TRICK FOR TOMORROW'S SHOW.
YOU DON'T WANNA QUIT YET, DO YOU?
IT'LL BE TOUGH ON YOU, TRAVELING WITHOUT ANY MONEY.
STAY WITH US AND YOU'LL GET FOOD, LODGING, AND SALARY!
BOSS!
YOU CAN'T JUST BULLY PEOPLE INTO DOING WHAT YOU WANT THEM TO!
LINK'S DREAM IS TO BE A KNIGHT.

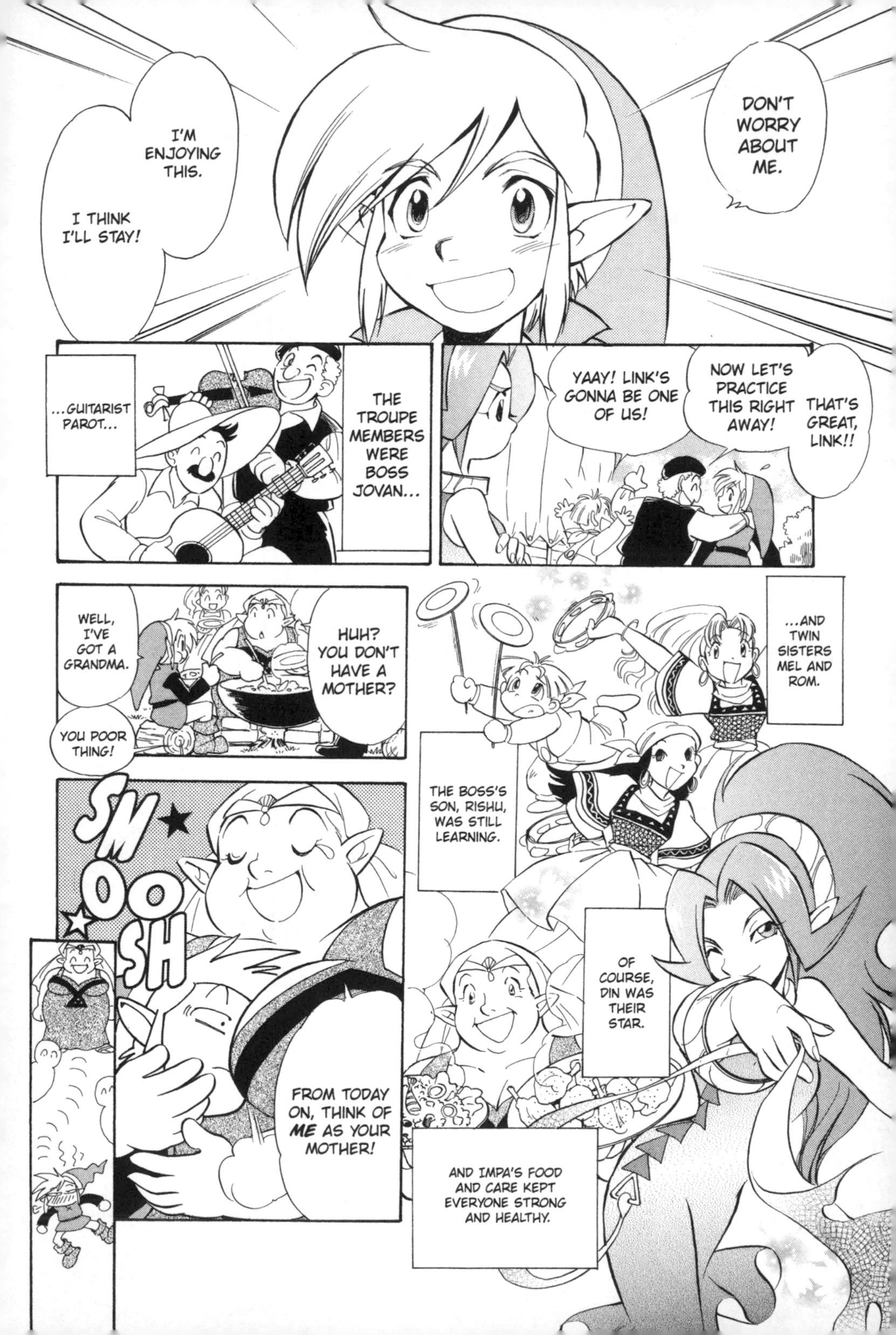
DON'T WORRY ABOUT ME.
I'M ENJOYING THIS.
I THINK I'LL STAY!
THAT'S GREAT, LINK!!
NOW LET'S PRACTICE THIS RIGHT AWAY!
YAAY! LINK'S GONNA BE ONE OF US!
THE TROUPE MEMBERS WERE BOSS JOVAN...
...GUITARIST PAROT...
...AND TWIN SISTERS MEL AND ROM.
THE BOSS'S SON, RISHU, WAS STILL LEARNING.
OF COURSE, DIN WAS THEIR STAR.
AND IMPA'S FOOD AND CARE KEPT EVERYONE STRONG AND HEALTHY.
HUH? YOU DON'T HAVE A MOTHER?
WELL, I'VE GOT A GRANDMA.
YOU POOR THING!
SMOOSH
FROM TODAY ON, THINK OF ***ME*** AS YOUR MOTHER!

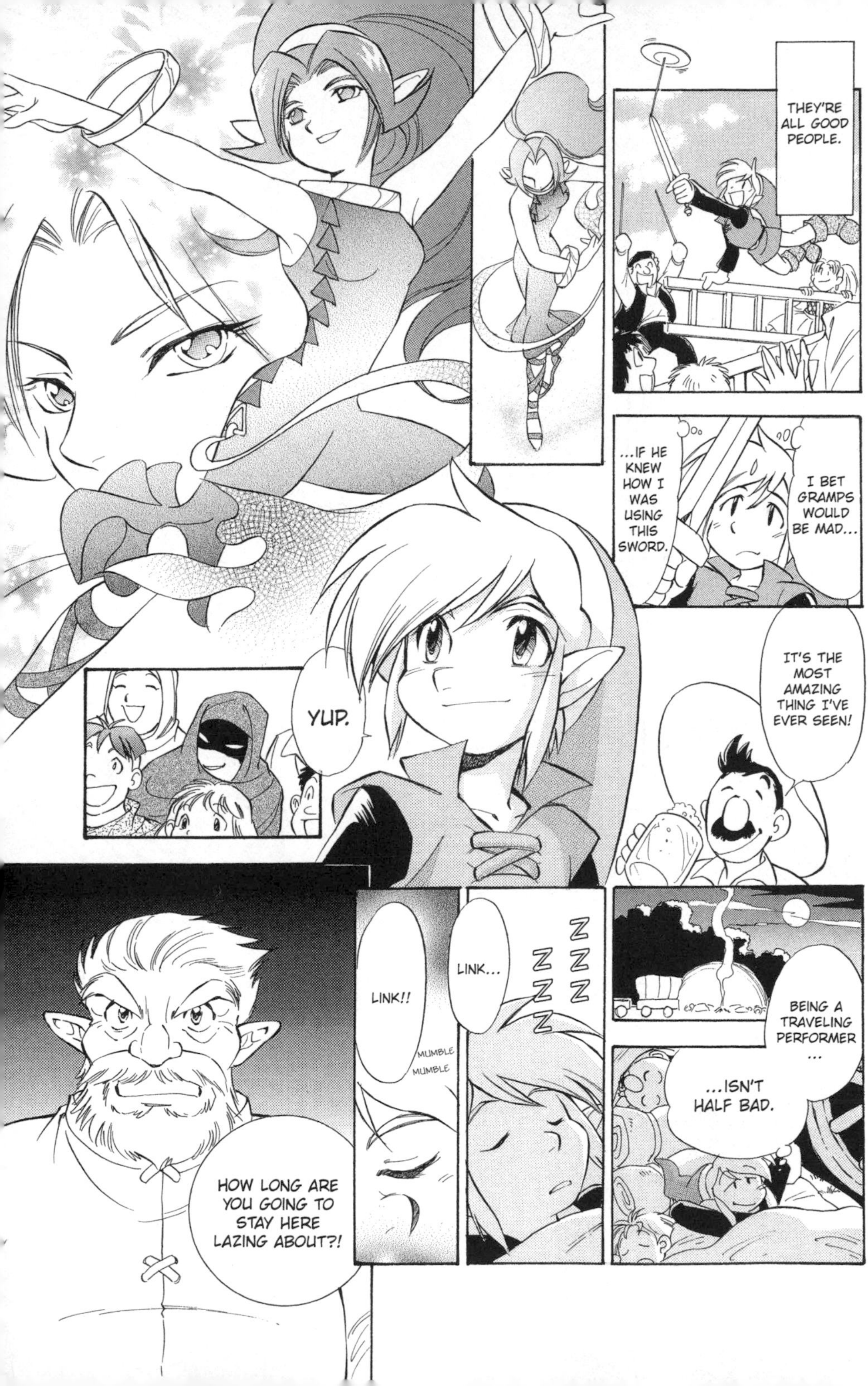
THEY'RE ALL GOOD PEOPLE.
I BET GRAMPS WOULD BE MAD...
...IF HE KNEW HOW I WAS USING THIS SWORD.
IT'S THE MOST AMAZING THING I'VE EVER SEEN!
YUP.
BEING A TRAVELING PERFORMER ...
...ISN'T HALF BAD.
Z Z Z Z Z Z
LINK...
LINK!!
MUMBLE MUMBLE
HOW LONG ARE YOU GOING TO STAY HERE LAZING ABOUT?!

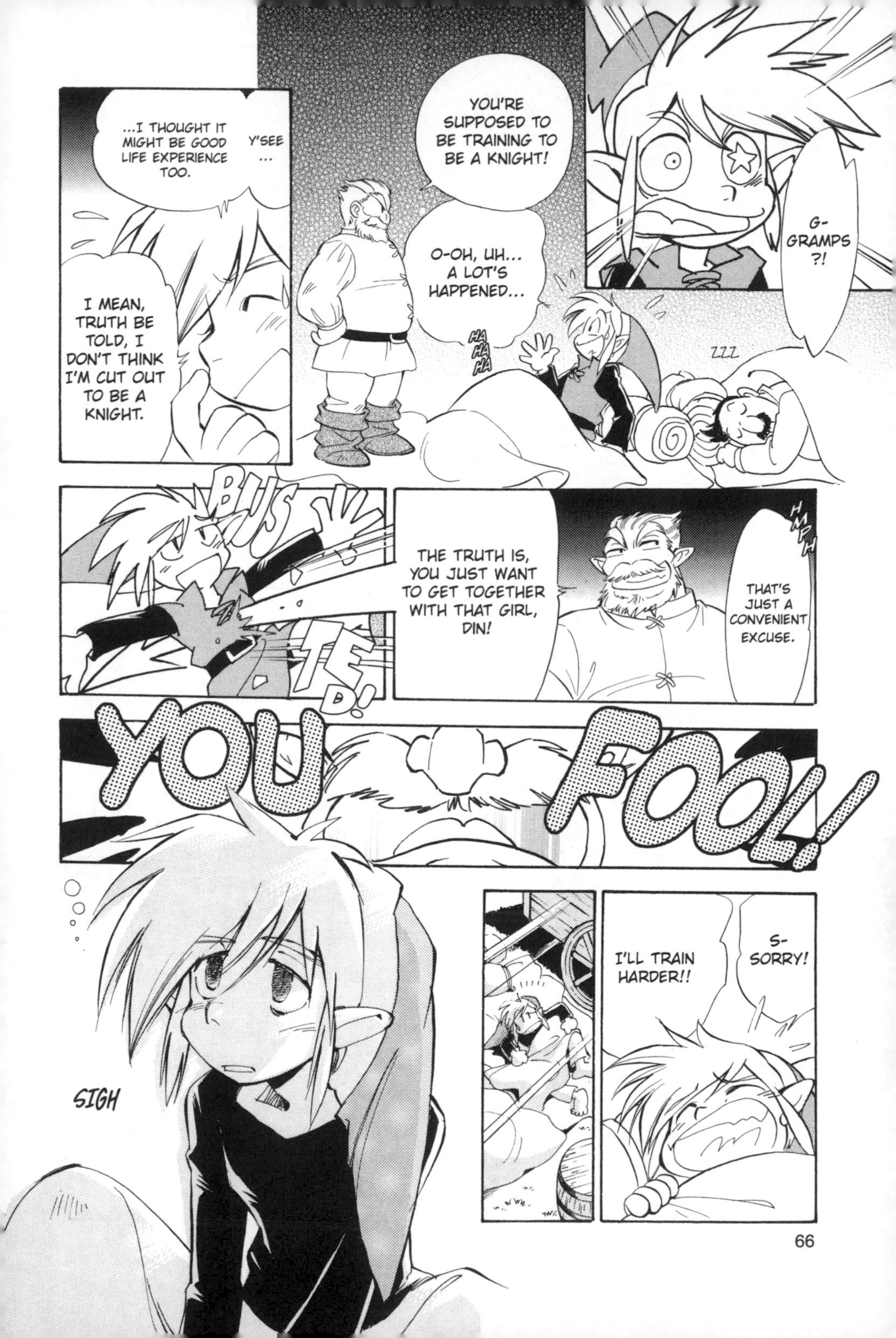
G-GRAMPS?!
YOU'RE SUPPOSED TO BE TRAINING TO BE A KNIGHT!
O-OH, UH... A LOT'S HAPPENED...
HA HA HA
ZZZ
Y'SEE ...
...I THOUGHT IT MIGHT BE GOOD LIFE EXPERIENCE TOO.
I MEAN, TRUTH BE TOLD, I DON'T THINK I'M CUT OUT TO BE A KNIGHT.
HMPH
THAT'S JUST A CONVENIENT EXCUSE.
THE TRUTH IS, YOU JUST WANT TO GET TOGETHER WITH THAT GIRL, DIN!
BUSTED!
YOU FOOL!!
S-SORRY!
I'LL TRAIN HARDER!!
SIGH

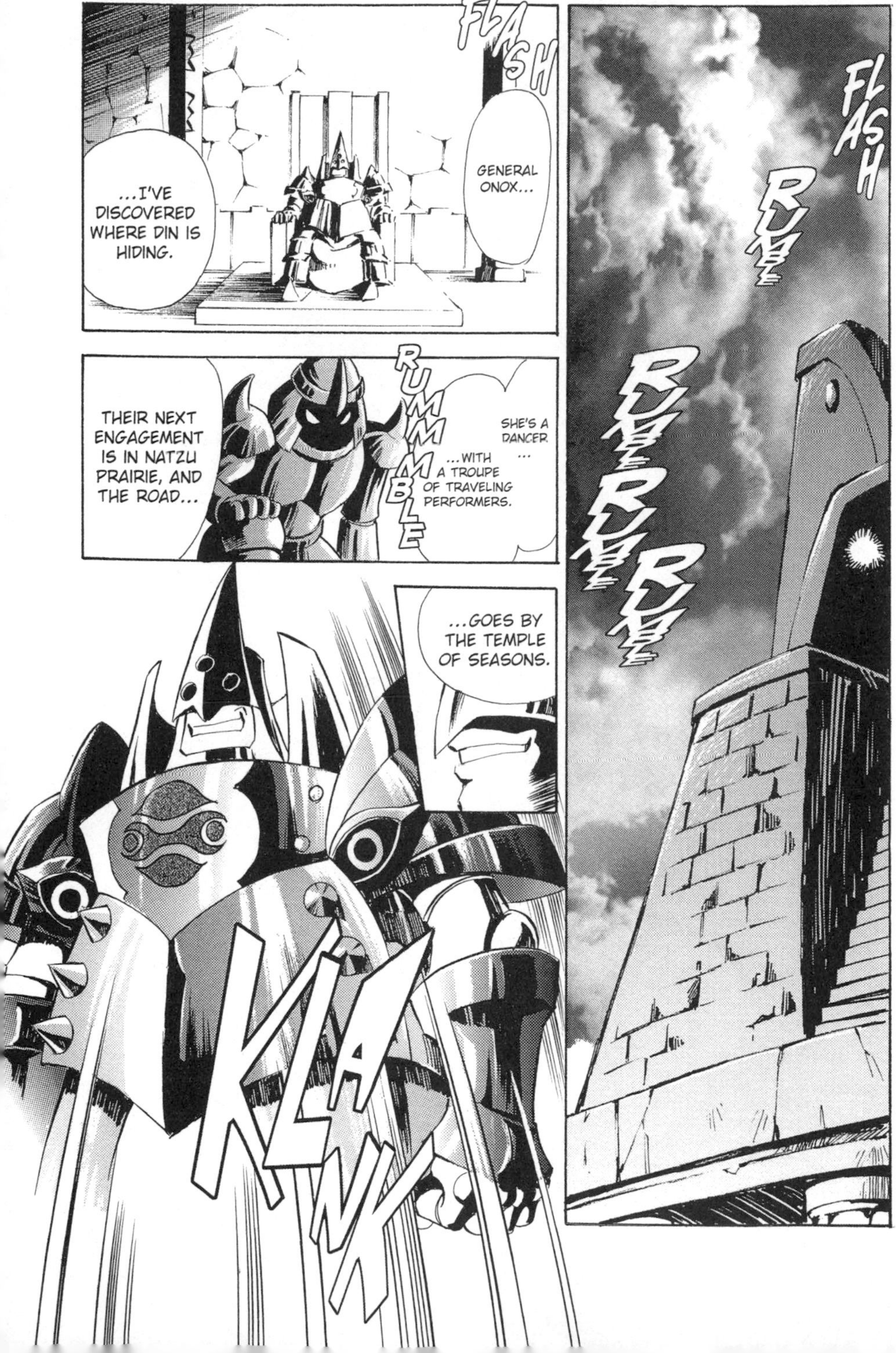
FLASH
RUMBLE
RUMBLE
RUMBLE
RUMBLE
FLASH
GENERAL ONOX...
...I'VE DISCOVERED WHERE DIN IS HIDING.
RUMMMMBLE
SHE'S A DANCER. ...
...WITH A TROUPE OF TRAVELING PERFORMERS.
THEIR NEXT ENGAGEMENT IS IN NATZU PRAIRIE, AND THE ROAD...
...GOES BY THE TEMPLE OF SEASONS.
KLANK

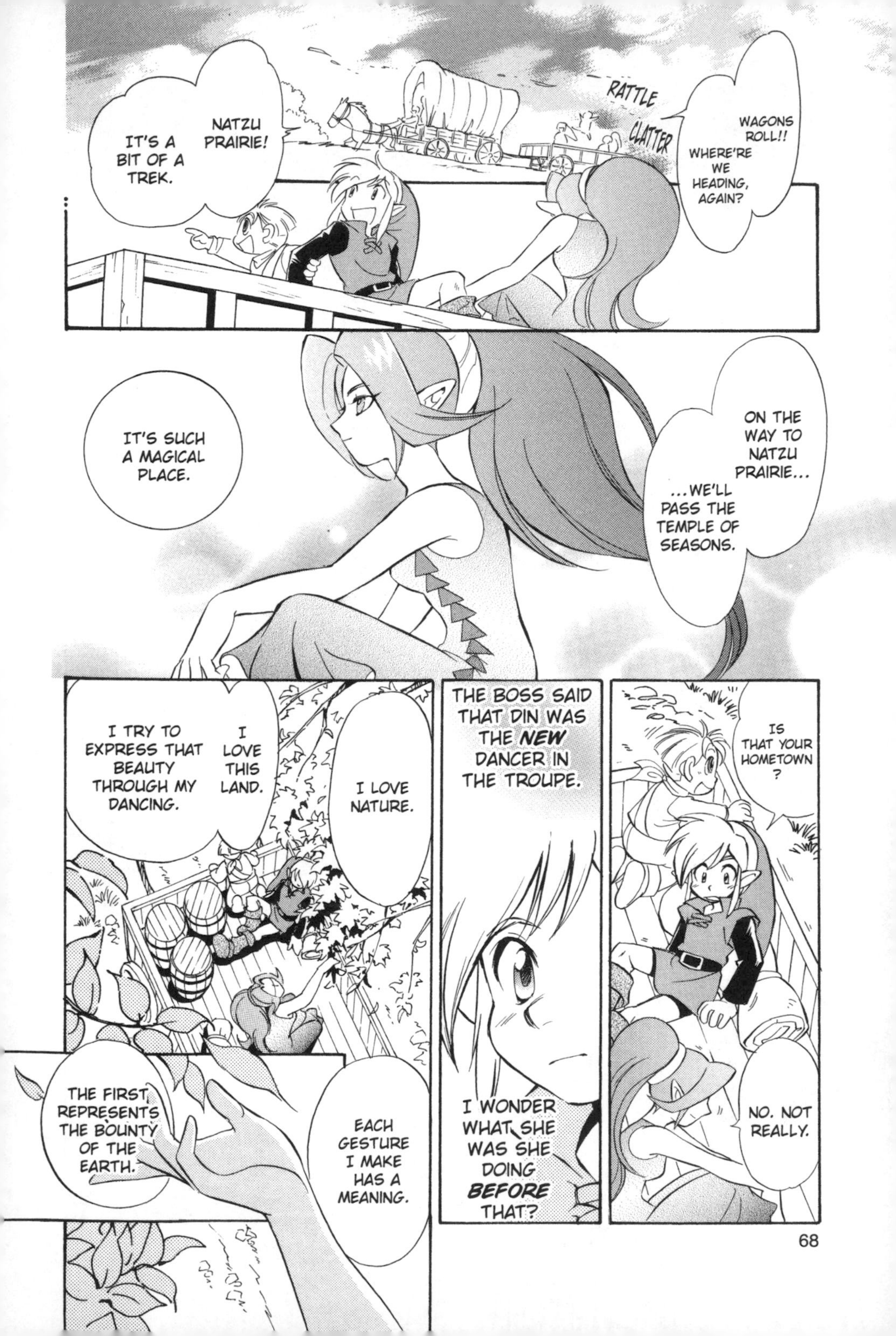
WAGONS ROLL!! WHERE'RE WE HEADING, AGAIN?
RATTLE
CLATTER
NATZU PRAIRIE!
IT'S A BIT OF A TREK.
ON THE WAY TO NATZU PRAIRIE...
...WE'LL PASS THE TEMPLE OF SEASONS.
IT'S SUCH A MAGICAL PLACE.
IS THAT YOUR HOMETOWN?
NO. NOT REALLY.
THE BOSS SAID THAT DIN WAS THE NEW DANCER IN THE TROUPE.
I WONDER WHAT SHE WAS SHE DOING BEFORE THAT?
I LOVE NATURE.
I LOVE THIS LAND.
I TRY TO EXPRESS THAT BEAUTY THROUGH MY DANCING.
EACH GESTURE I MAKE HAS A MEANING.
THE FIRST REPRESENTS THE BOUNTY OF THE EARTH.

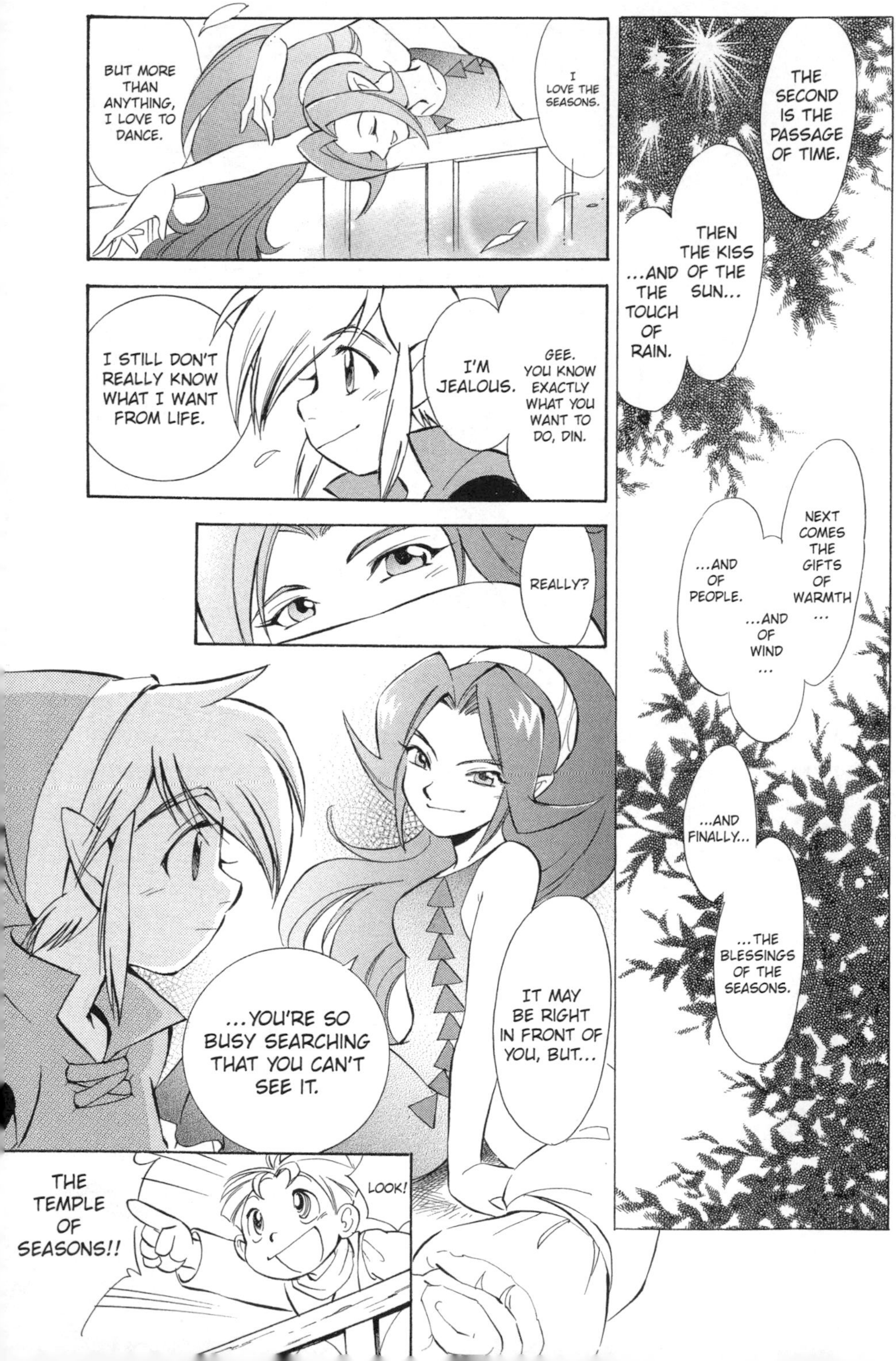
THE SECOND IS THE PASSAGE OF TIME.
THEN THE KISS OF THE SUN...
...AND THE TOUCH OF RAIN.
NEXT COMES THE GIFTS OF WARMTH...
...AND OF WIND...
...AND OF PEOPLE.
...AND FINALLY...
...THE BLESSINGS OF THE SEASONS.
I LOVE THE SEASONS.
BUT MORE THAN ANYTHING, I LOVE TO DANCE.
GEE. YOU KNOW EXACTLY WHAT YOU WANT TO DO, DIN.
I'M JEALOUS.
I STILL DON'T REALLY KNOW WHAT I WANT FROM LIFE.
REALLY?
IT MAY BE RIGHT IN FRONT OF YOU, BUT...
...YOU'RE SO BUSY SEARCHING THAT YOU CAN'T SEE IT.
LOOK!
THE TEMPLE OF SEASONS!!

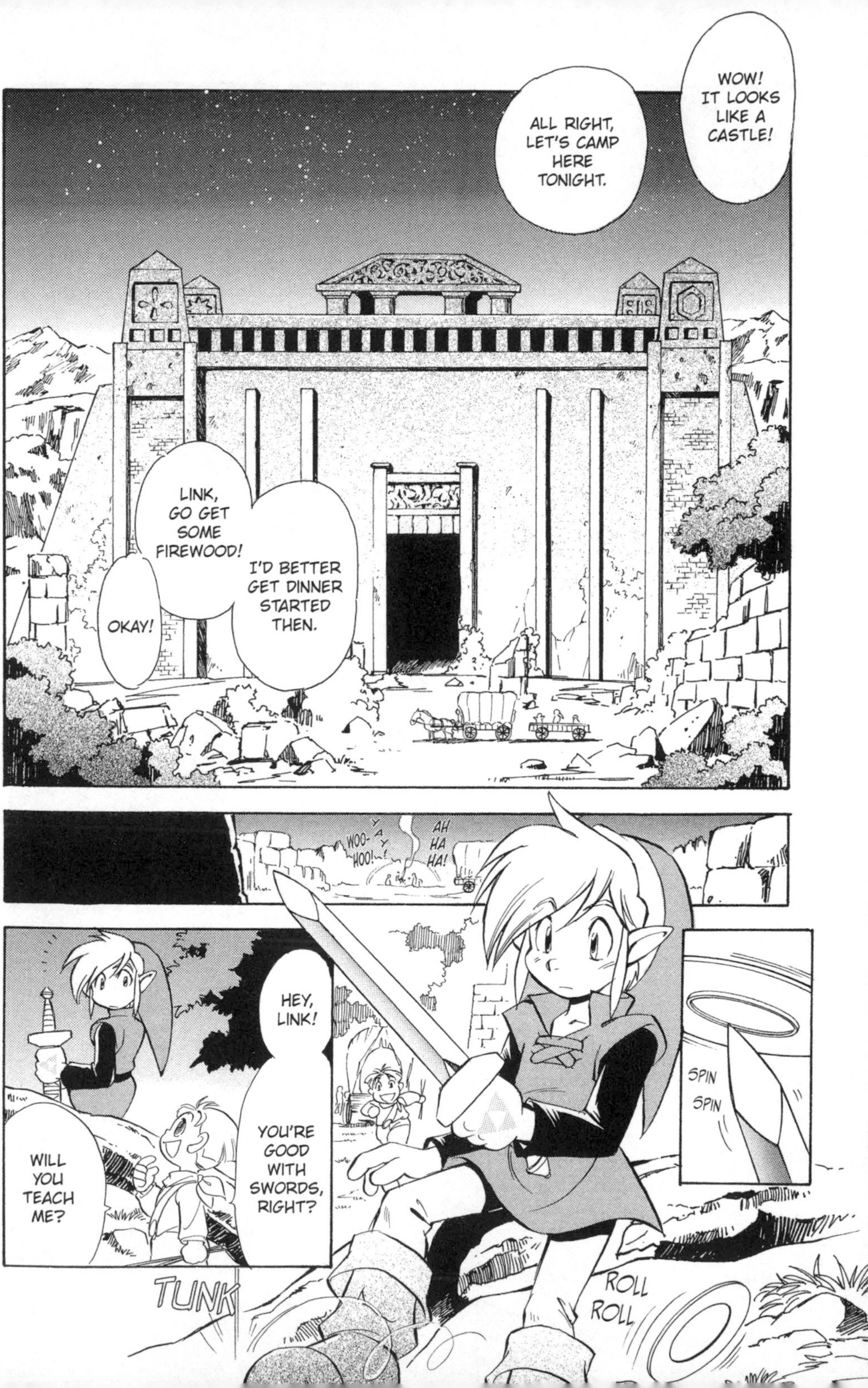
WOW! IT LOOKS LIKE A CASTLE!
ALL RIGHT, LET'S CAMP HERE TONIGHT.
I'D BETTER GET DINNER STARTED THEN.
LINK, GO GET SOME FIREWOOD!
OKAY!
AH HA HA!
YAY!
WOO-HOO!
SPIN SPIN
ROLL ROLL
TUNK
HEY, LINK!
YOU'RE GOOD WITH SWORDS, RIGHT?
WILL YOU TEACH ME?

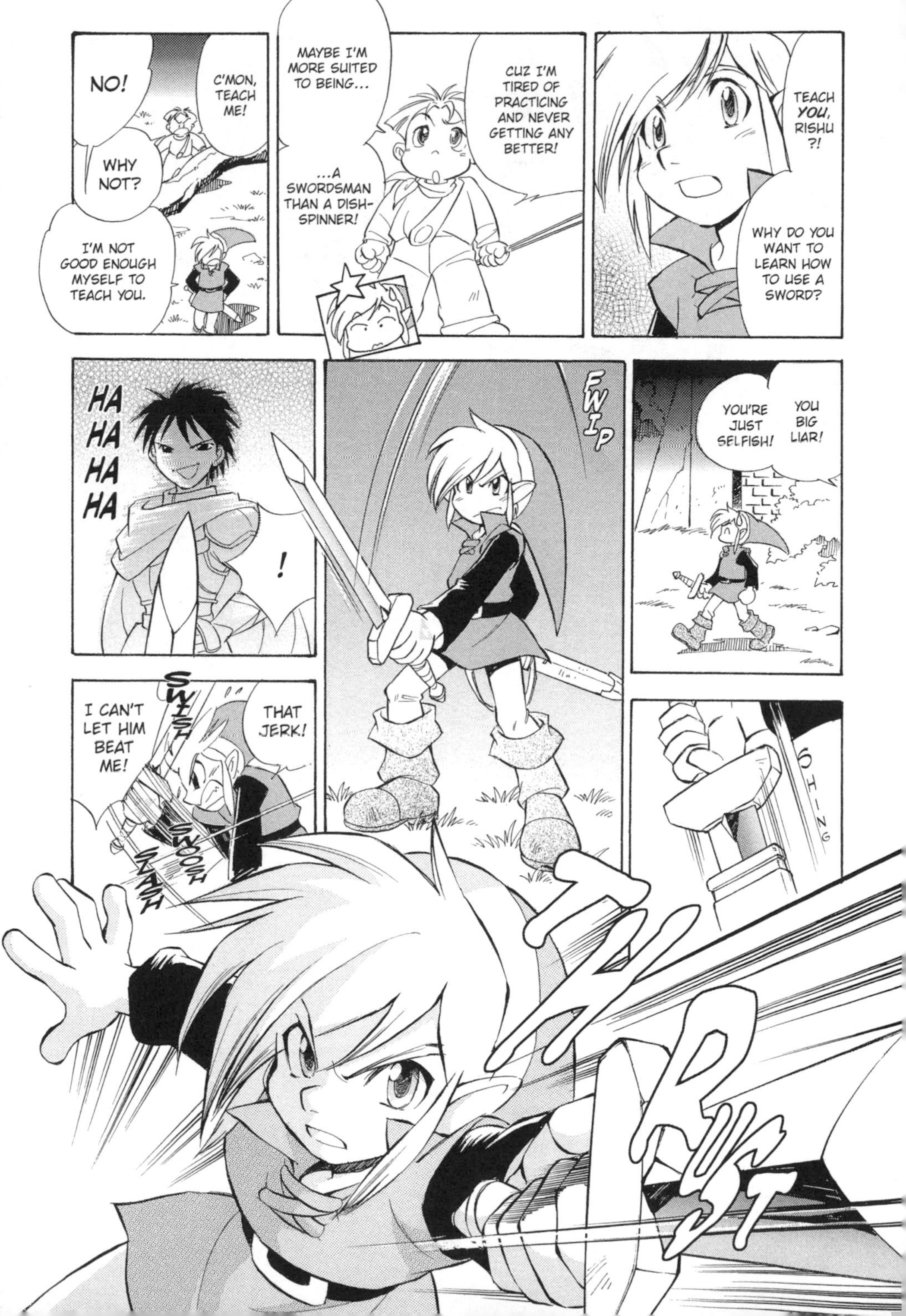
TEACH YOU, RISHU?!
WHY DO YOU WANT TO LEARN HOW TO USE A SWORD?
CUZ I'M TIRED OF PRACTICING AND NEVER GETTING ANY BETTER!
MAYBE I'M MORE SUITED TO BEING...
...A SWORDSMAN THAN A DISH-SPINNER!
C'MON, TEACH ME!
NO!
WHY NOT?
I'M NOT GOOD ENOUGH MYSELF TO TEACH YOU.
YOU BIG LIAR!
YOU'RE JUST SELFISH!
SHING
FWIP
HA HA HA HA
!
THAT JERK!
I CAN'T LET HIM BEAT ME!
SWISH
SWOOSH
SLASH
THRUST

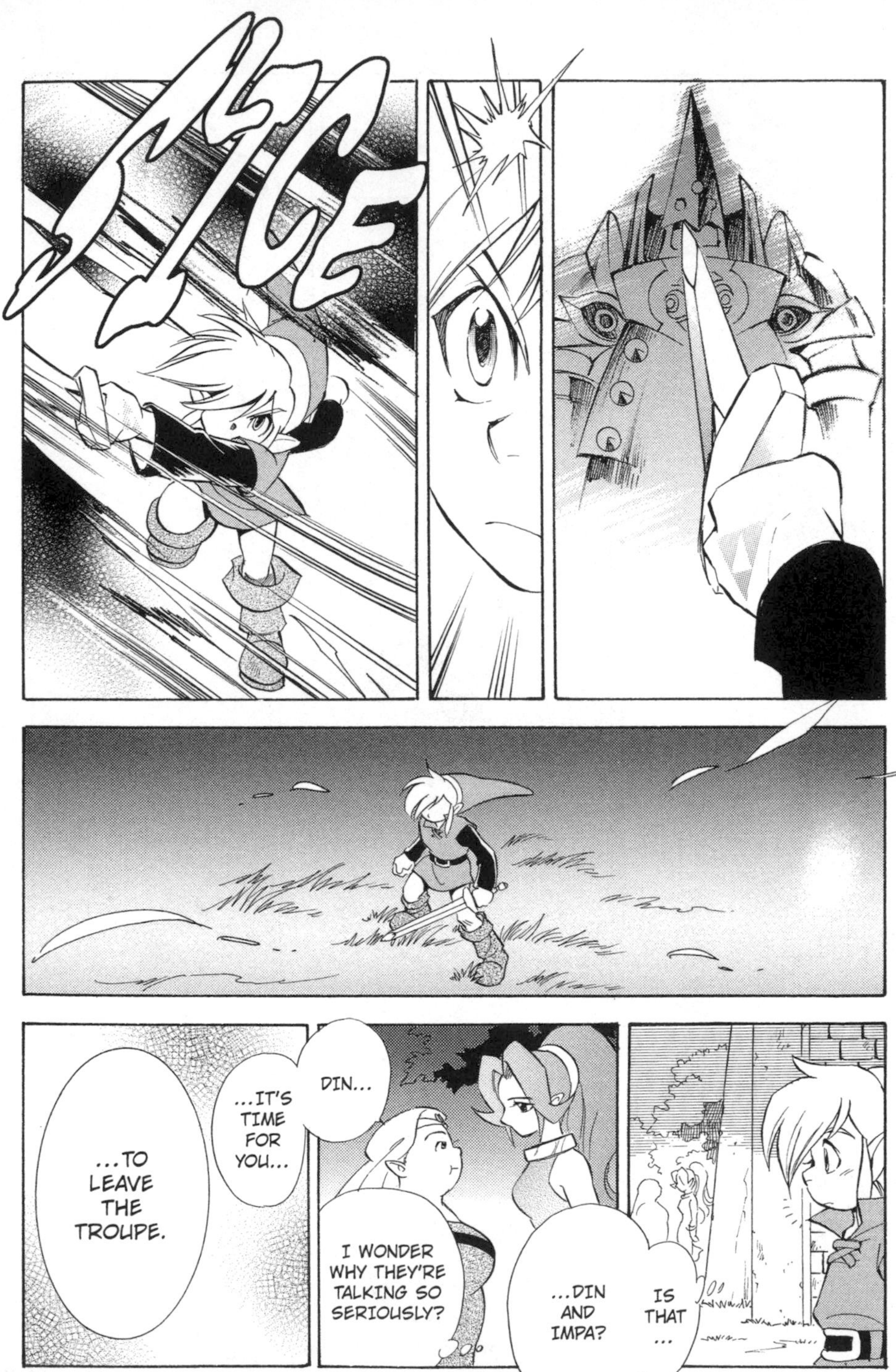
IS THAT ...
...DIN AND IMPA?
DIN...
...IT'S TIME FOR YOU...
I WONDER WHY THEY'RE TALKING SO SERIOUSLY?
...TO LEAVE THE TROUPE.

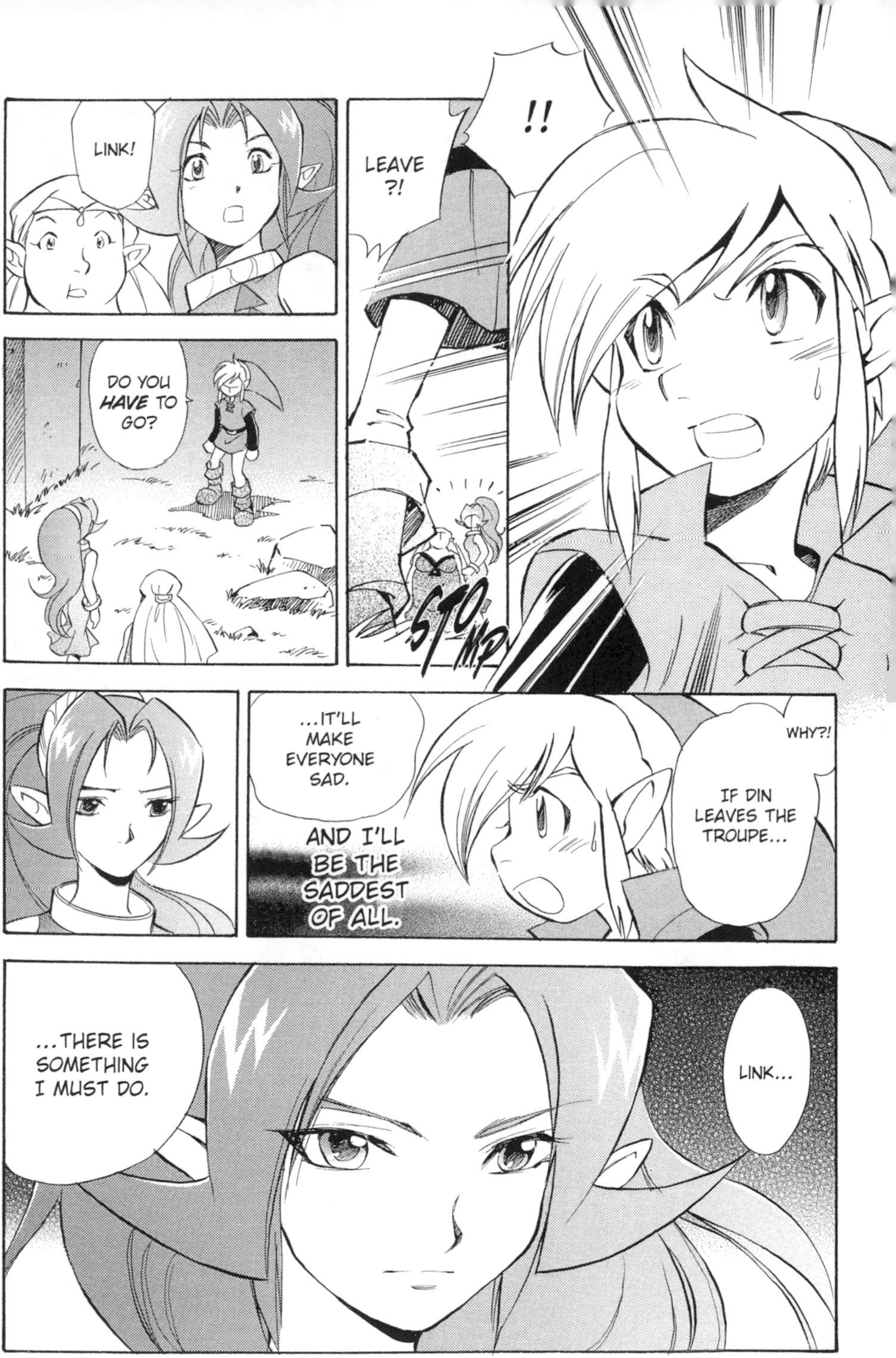
!!
LEAVE ?!
STOMP
LINK!
DO YOU HAVE TO GO?
WHY?!
IF DIN LEAVES THE TROUPE...
...IT'LL MAKE EVERYONE SAD.
AND I'LL BE THE SADDEST OF ALL.
LINK...
...THERE IS SOMETHING I MUST DO.

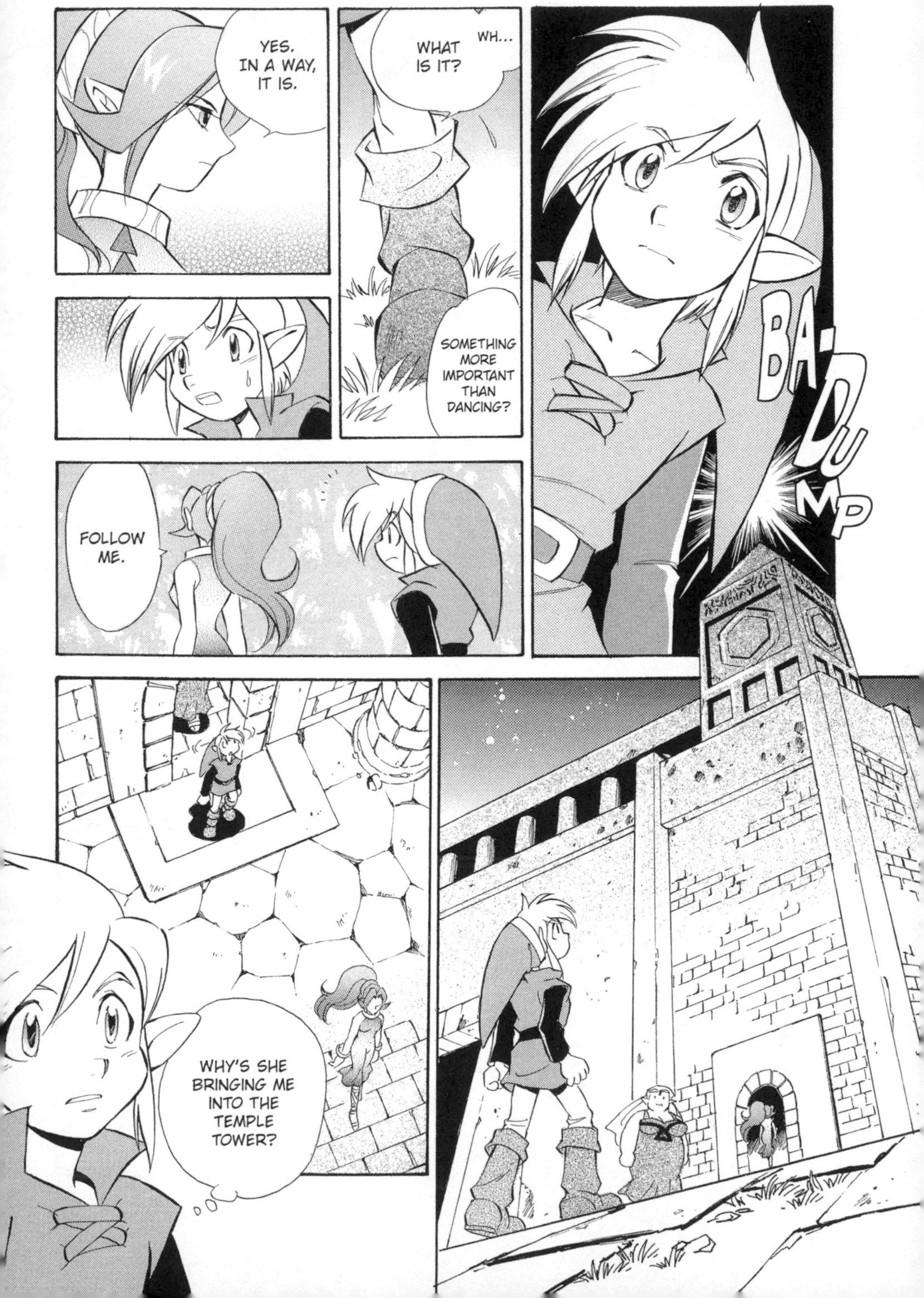
BA-DUMP
WH...
WHAT IS IT?
SOMETHING MORE IMPORTANT THAN DANCING?
YES. IN A WAY, IT IS.
FOLLOW ME.
WHY'S SHE BRINGING ME INTO THE TEMPLE TOWER?

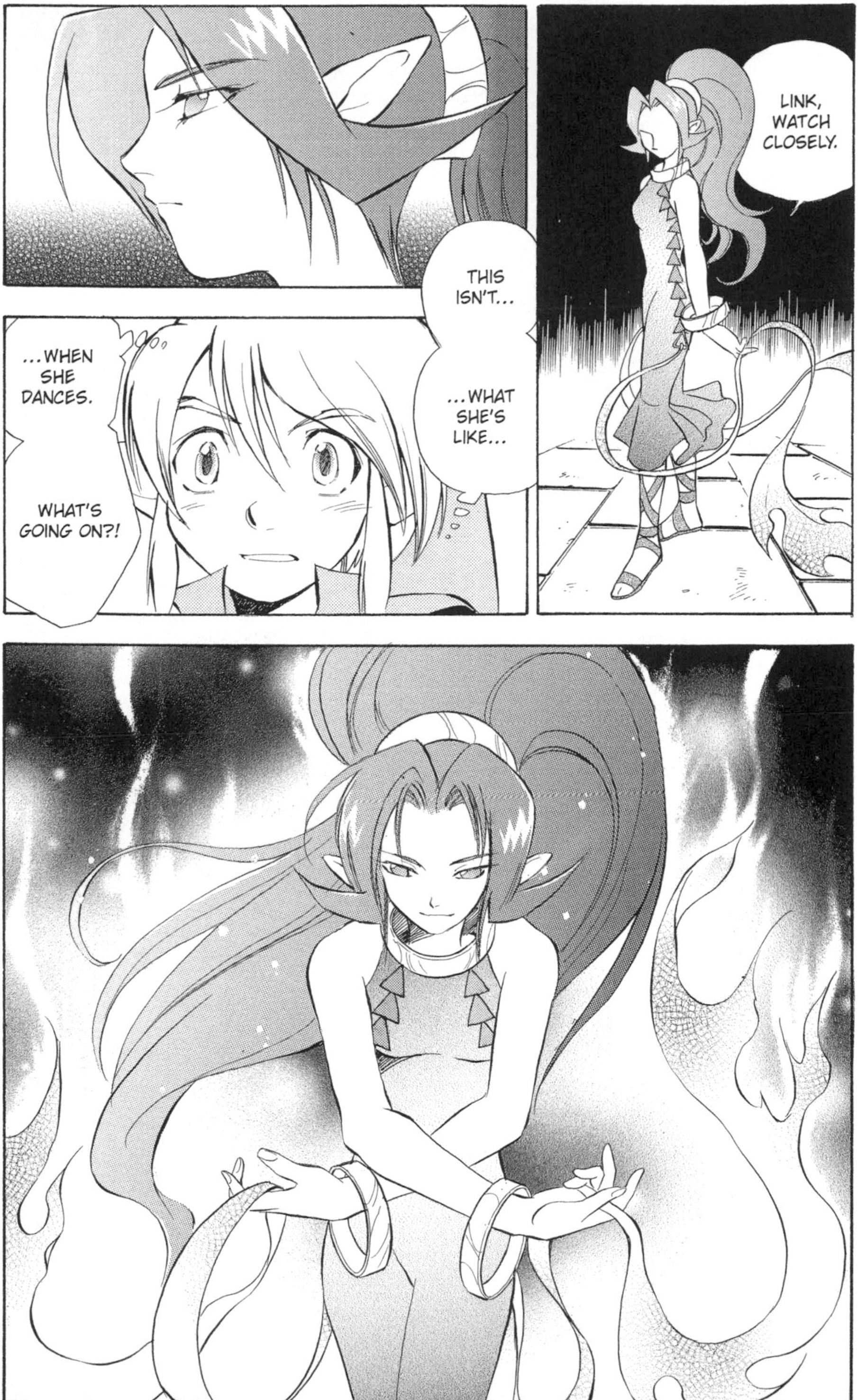
LINK, WATCH CLOSELY.
THIS ISN'T...
...WHAT SHE'S LIKE...
...WHEN SHE DANCES.
WHAT'S GOING ON?!

ROUGH CHARACTER
ILLUSTRATION 2

Link is just a normal guy—
but in a good way. He's
sentimental and mischievous,
but he turns into a reliable
hero in times of trouble.
It's fun drawing his
various emotions.

2000 10·7

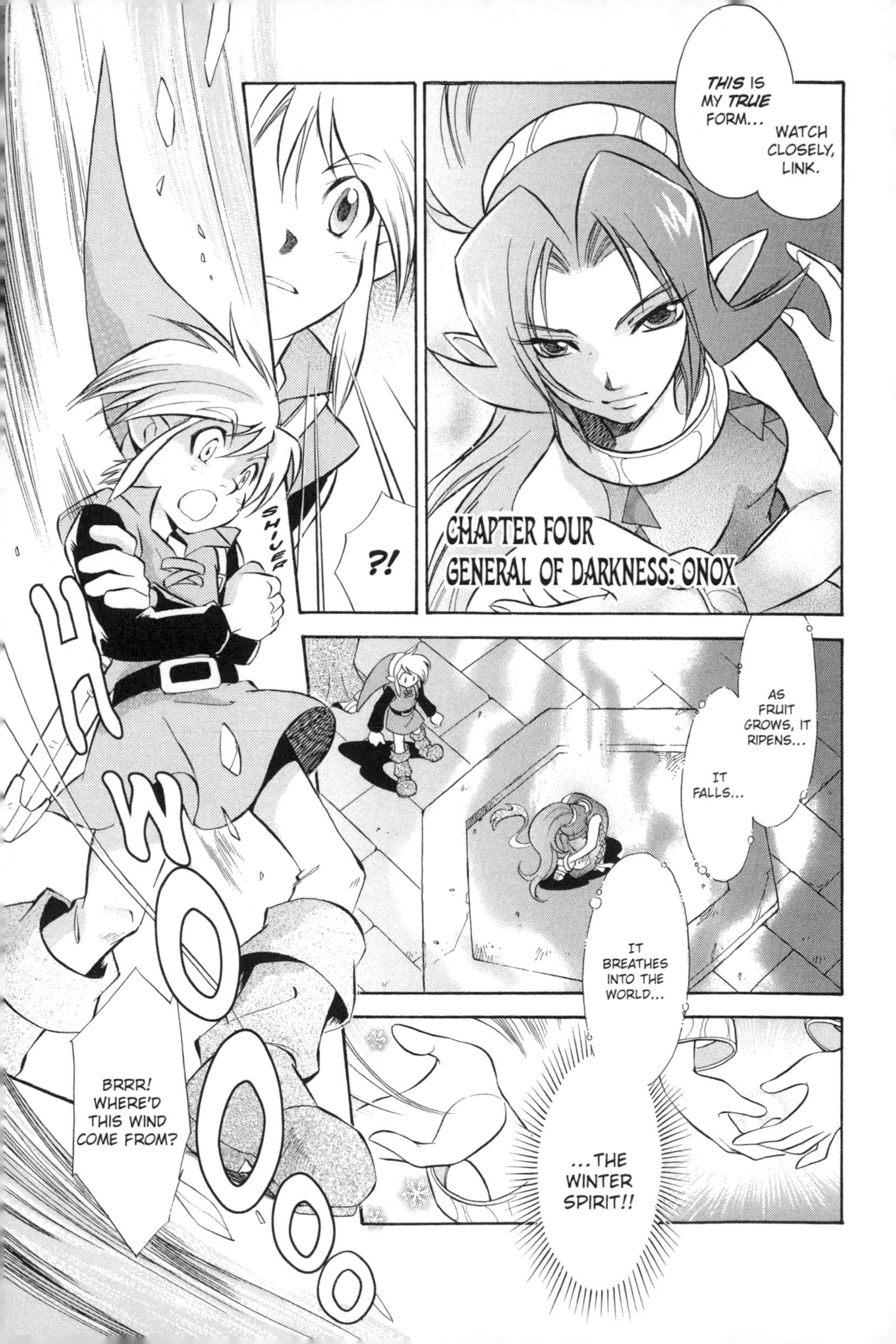

THIS IS MY TRUE FORM...
WATCH CLOSELY, LINK.
CHAPTER FOUR
GENERAL OF DARKNESS: ONOX
?!
AS FRUIT GROWS, IT RIPENS...
IT FALLS...
IT BREATHES INTO THE WORLD...
...THE WINTER SPIRIT!!
SHIVER
HWOOOOOOO
BRRR! WHERE'D THIS WIND COME FROM?

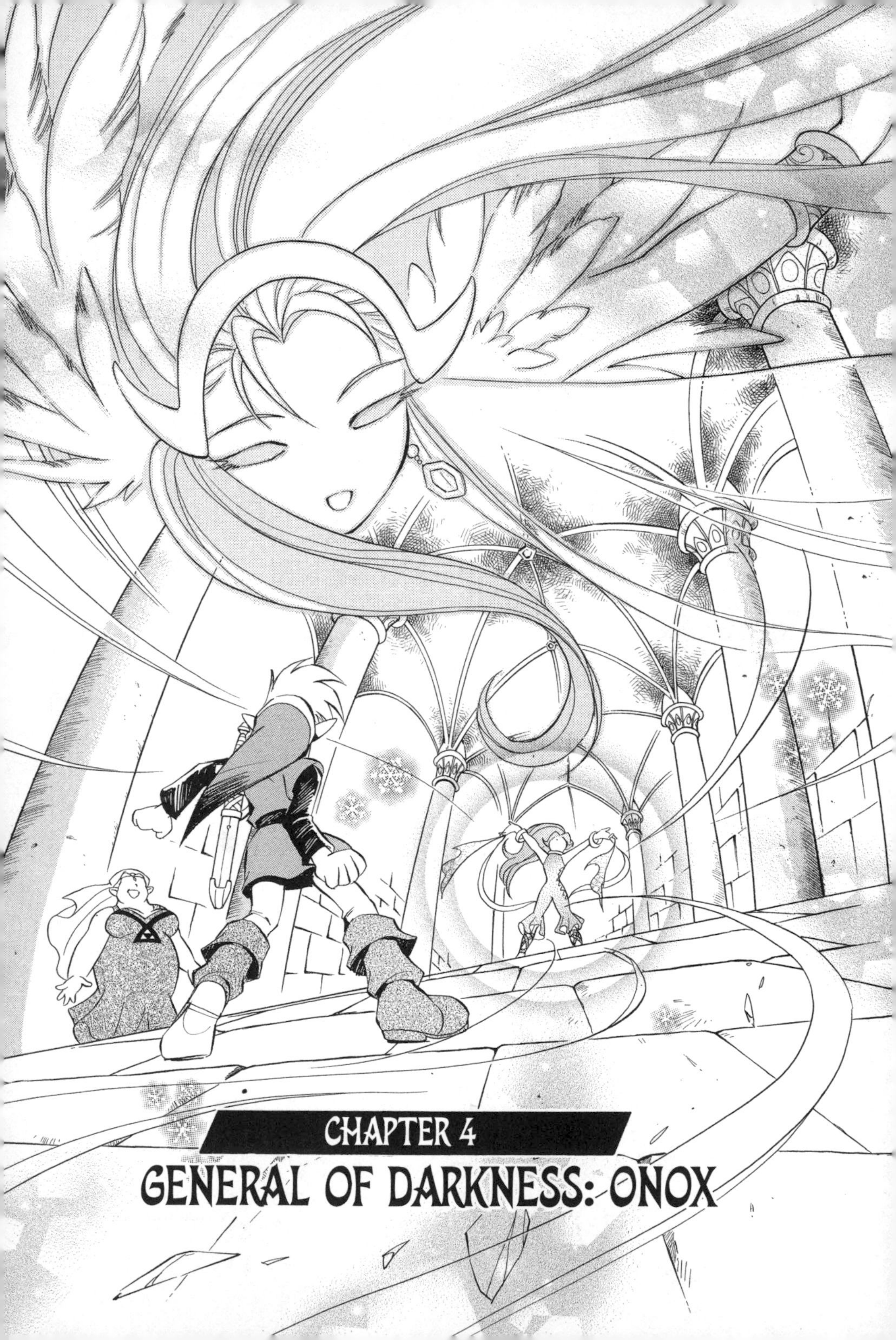

CHAPTER 4

GENERAL OF DARKNESS: ONOX

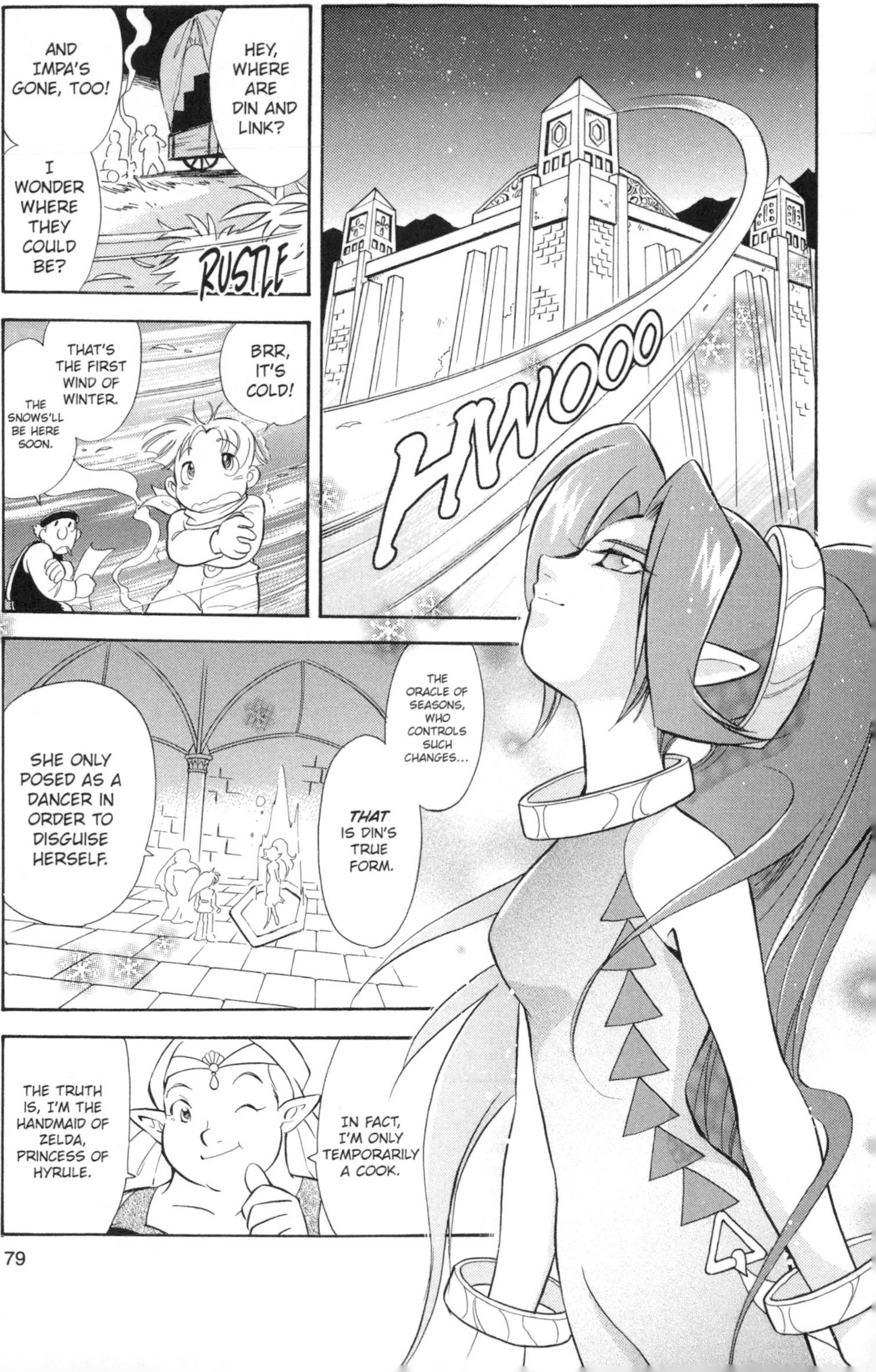
HWOOO
HEY, WHERE ARE DIN AND LINK?
AND IMPA'S GONE, TOO!
I WONDER WHERE THEY COULD BE?
RUSTLE
BRR, IT'S COLD!
THAT'S THE FIRST WIND OF WINTER.
THE SNOWS'LL BE HERE SOON.
THE ORACLE OF SEASONS, WHO CONTROLS SUCH CHANGES...
THAT IS DIN'S TRUE FORM.
SHE ONLY POSED AS A DANCER IN ORDER TO DISGUISE HERSELF.
IN FACT, I'M ONLY TEMPORARILY A COOK.
THE TRUTH IS, I'M THE HANDMAID OF ZELDA, PRINCESS OF HYRULE.

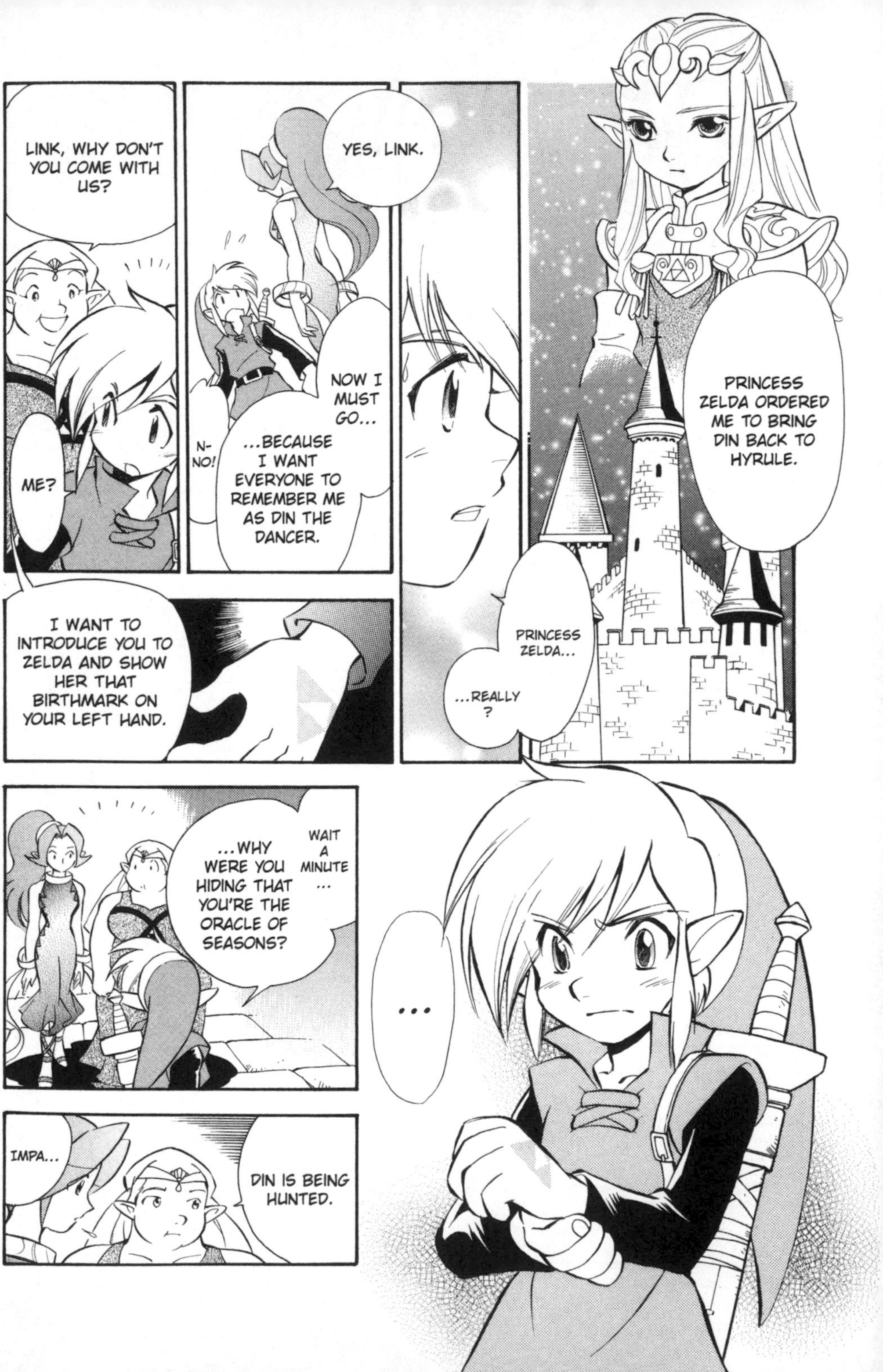
PRINCESS ZELDA ORDERED ME TO BRING DIN BACK TO HYRULE.
PRINCESS ZELDA...
...REALLY ?
YES, LINK.
NOW I MUST GO...
...BECAUSE I WANT EVERYONE TO REMEMBER ME AS DIN THE DANCER.
N-NO!
LINK, WHY DON'T YOU COME WITH US?
ME?
I WANT TO INTRODUCE YOU TO ZELDA AND SHOW HER THAT BIRTHMARK ON YOUR LEFT HAND.
...
WAIT A MINUTE...
...WHY WERE YOU HIDING THAT YOU'RE THE ORACLE OF SEASONS?
DIN IS BEING HUNTED.
IMPA...

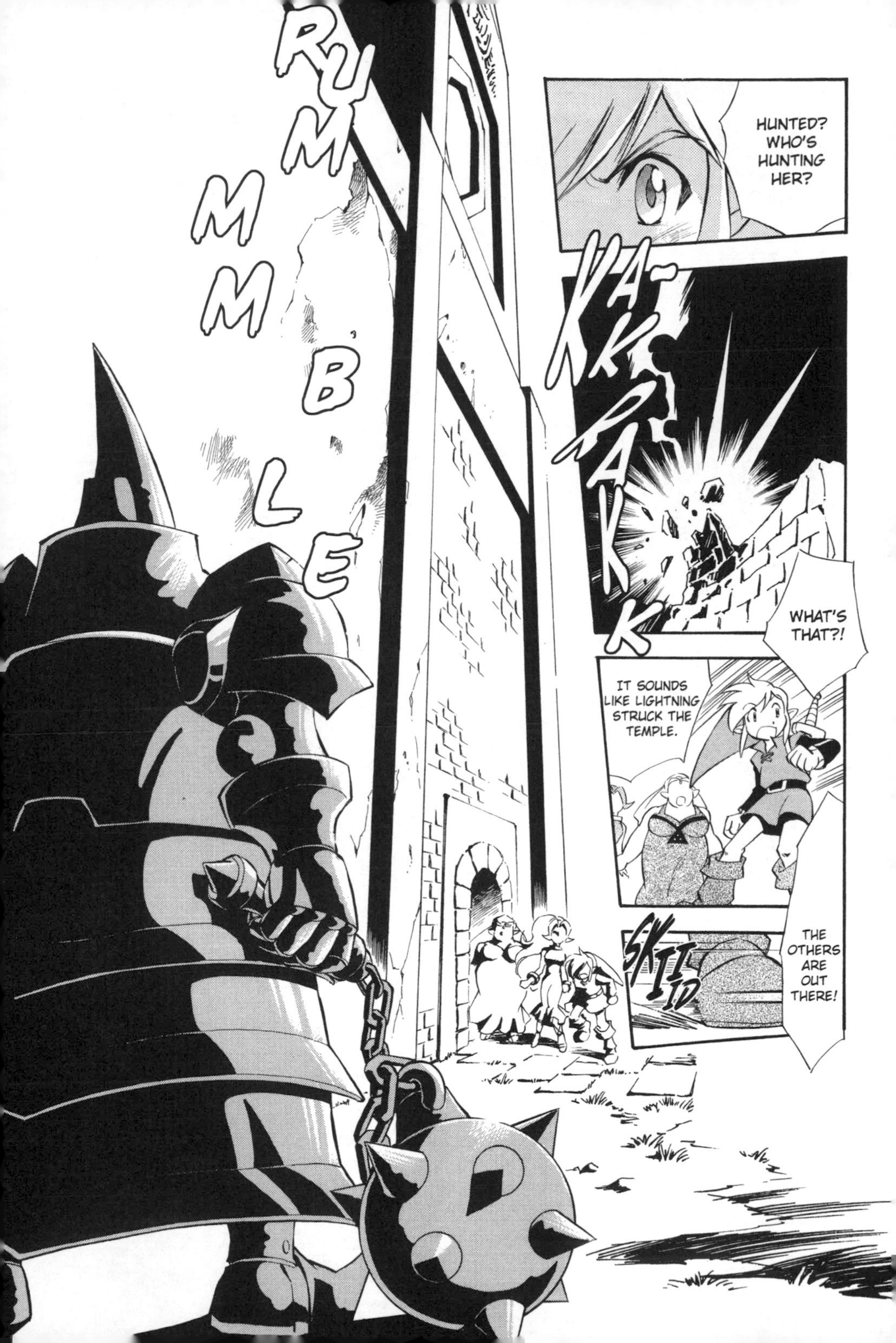
HUNTED? WHO'S HUNTING HER?
KA-KRAKK
WHAT'S THAT?!
IT SOUNDS LIKE LIGHTNING STRUCK THE TEMPLE.
SKIID
THE OTHERS ARE OUT THERE!
RUMMMBLE

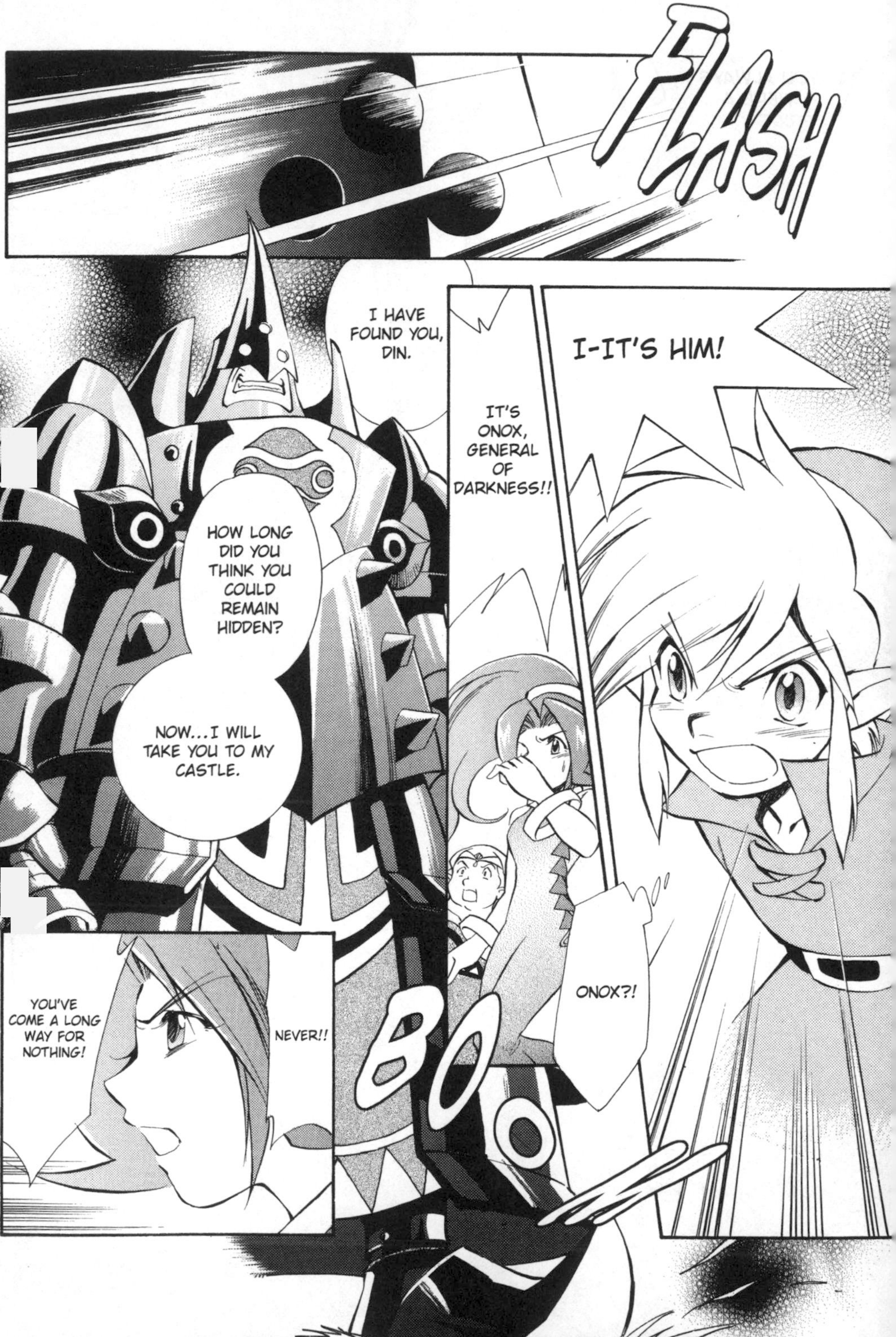
FLASH
I HAVE FOUND YOU, DIN.
I-IT'S HIM!
IT'S ONOX, GENERAL OF DARKNESS!!
ONOX?!
HOW LONG DID YOU THINK YOU COULD REMAIN HIDDEN?
NOW...I WILL TAKE YOU TO MY CASTLE.
NEVER!!
YOU'VE COME A LONG WAY FOR NOTHING!
BOO

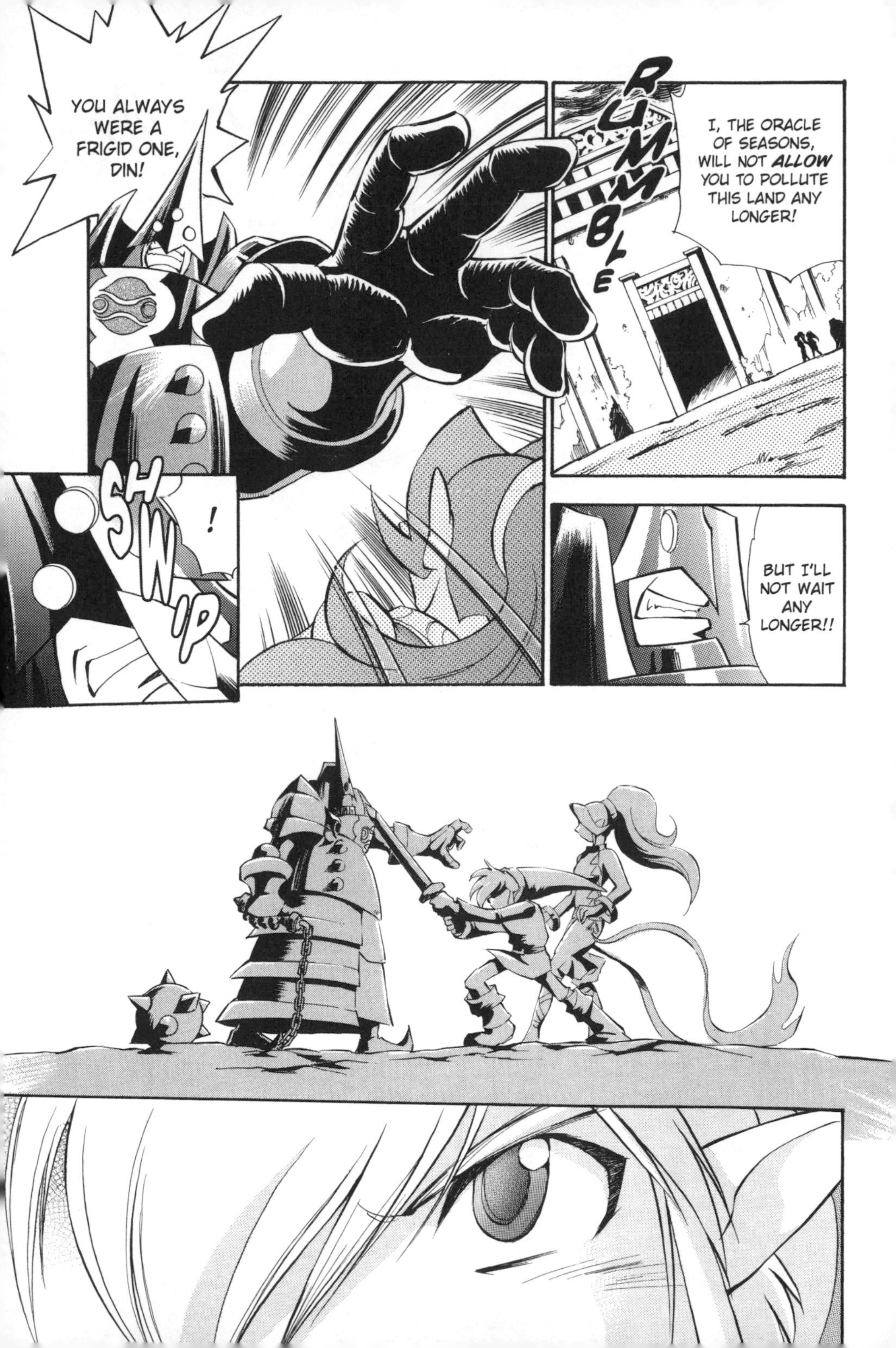
RUMMBLE
I, THE ORACLE OF SEASONS, WILL NOT *ALLOW* YOU TO POLLUTE THIS LAND ANY LONGER!
YOU ALWAYS WERE A FRIGID ONE, DIN!
BUT I'LL NOT WAIT ANY LONGER!!
SHWIP
!

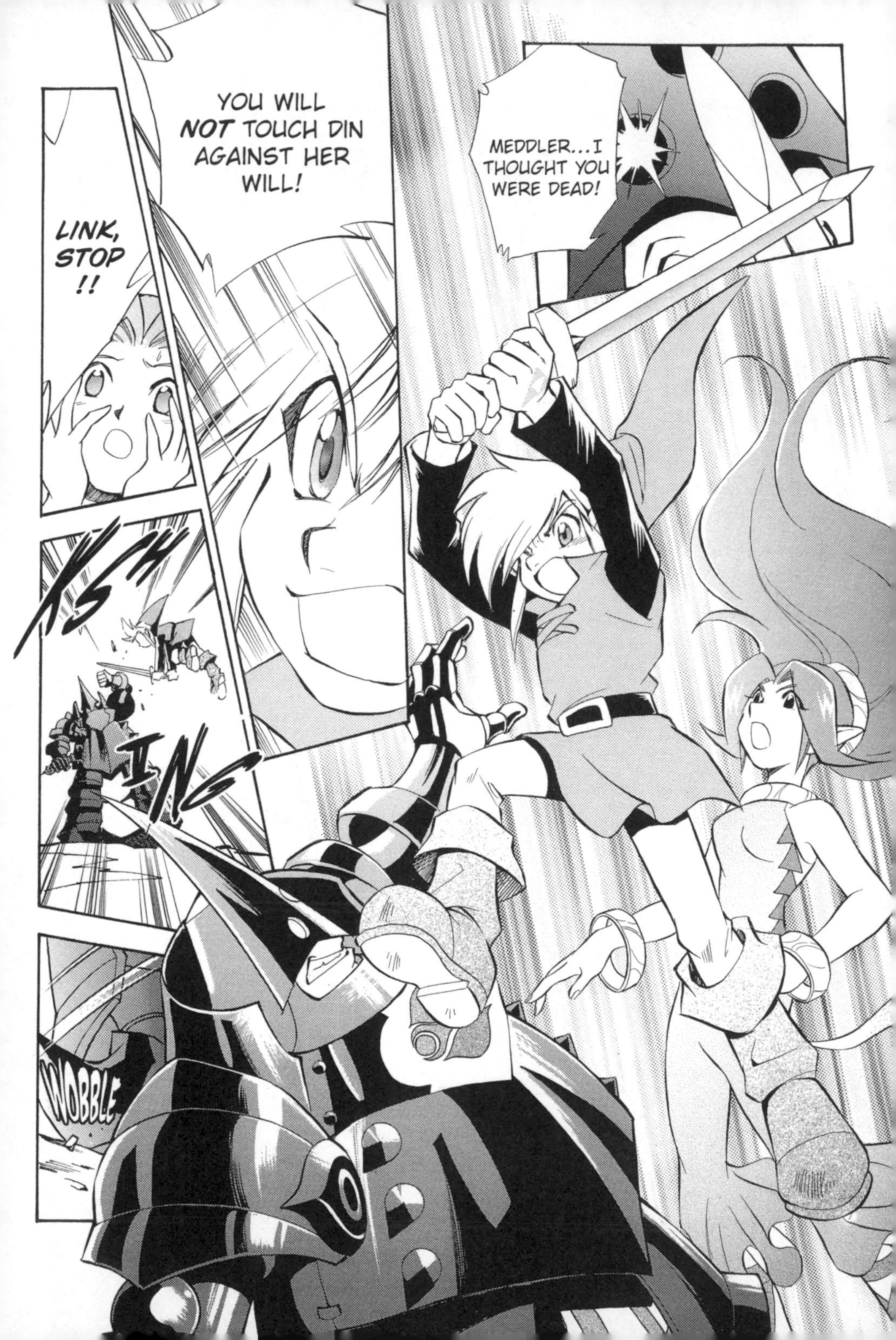
MEDDLER...I THOUGHT YOU WERE DEAD!
YOU WILL NOT TOUCH DIN AGAINST HER WILL!
LINK, STOP!!
KSHING
WOBBLE

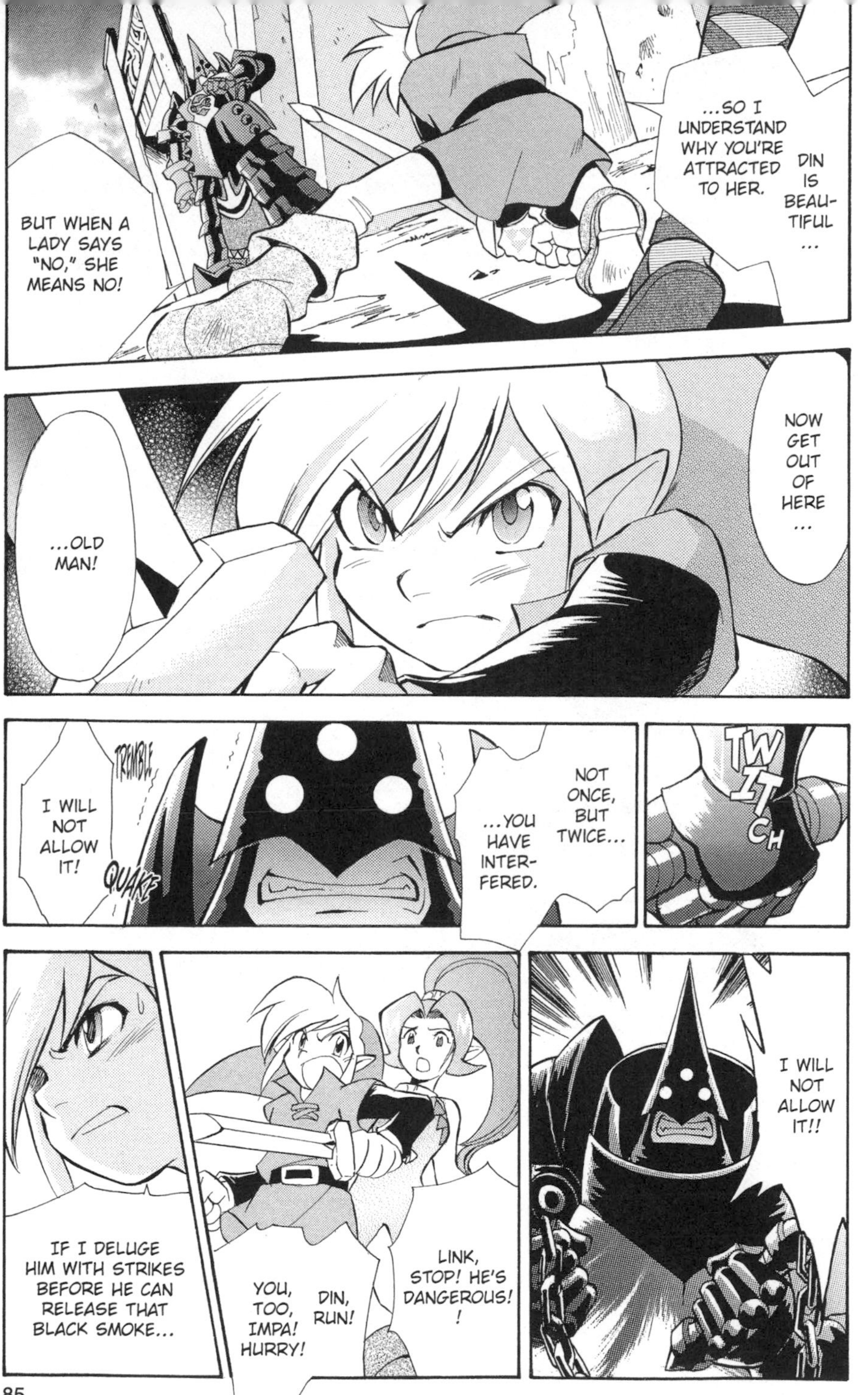
DIN IS BEAUTIFUL...
...SO I UNDERSTAND WHY YOU'RE ATTRACTED TO HER.
BUT WHEN A LADY SAYS "NO," SHE MEANS NO!
NOW GET OUT OF HERE...
...OLD MAN!
TWITCH
NOT ONCE, BUT TWICE...
...YOU HAVE INTERFERED.
TREMBLE
I WILL NOT ALLOW IT!
QUAKE
I WILL NOT ALLOW IT!!
LINK, STOP! HE'S DANGEROUS!!
DIN, RUN!
YOU, TOO, IMPA! HURRY!
IF I DELUGE HIM WITH STRIKES BEFORE HE CAN RELEASE THAT BLACK SMOKE...

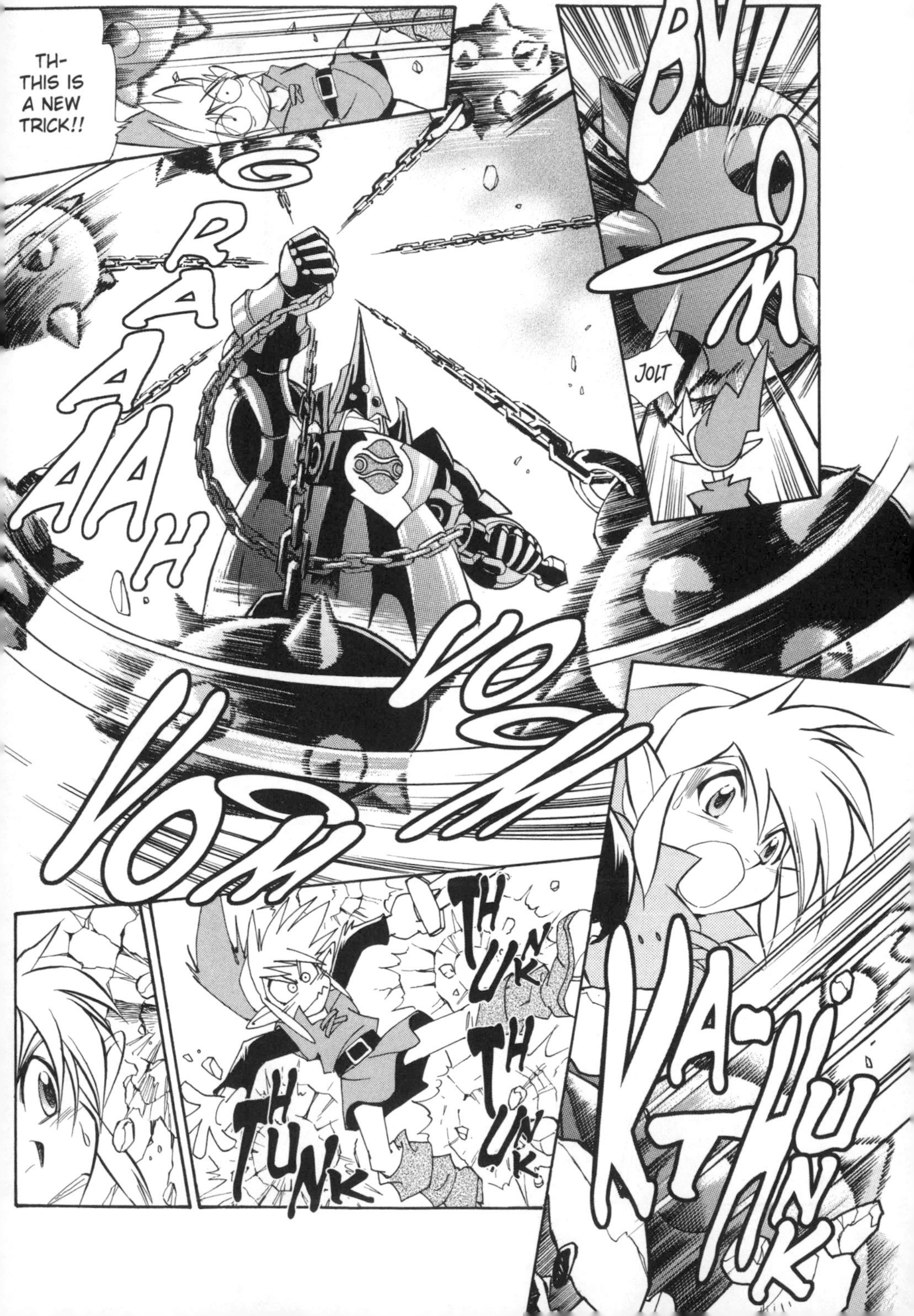
BUOOM
JOLT
TH-
THIS IS
A NEW
TRICK!!
GRAAAAH
VOOM
VOOM
KA-CHUNK
THUNK
THUNK
THUNK

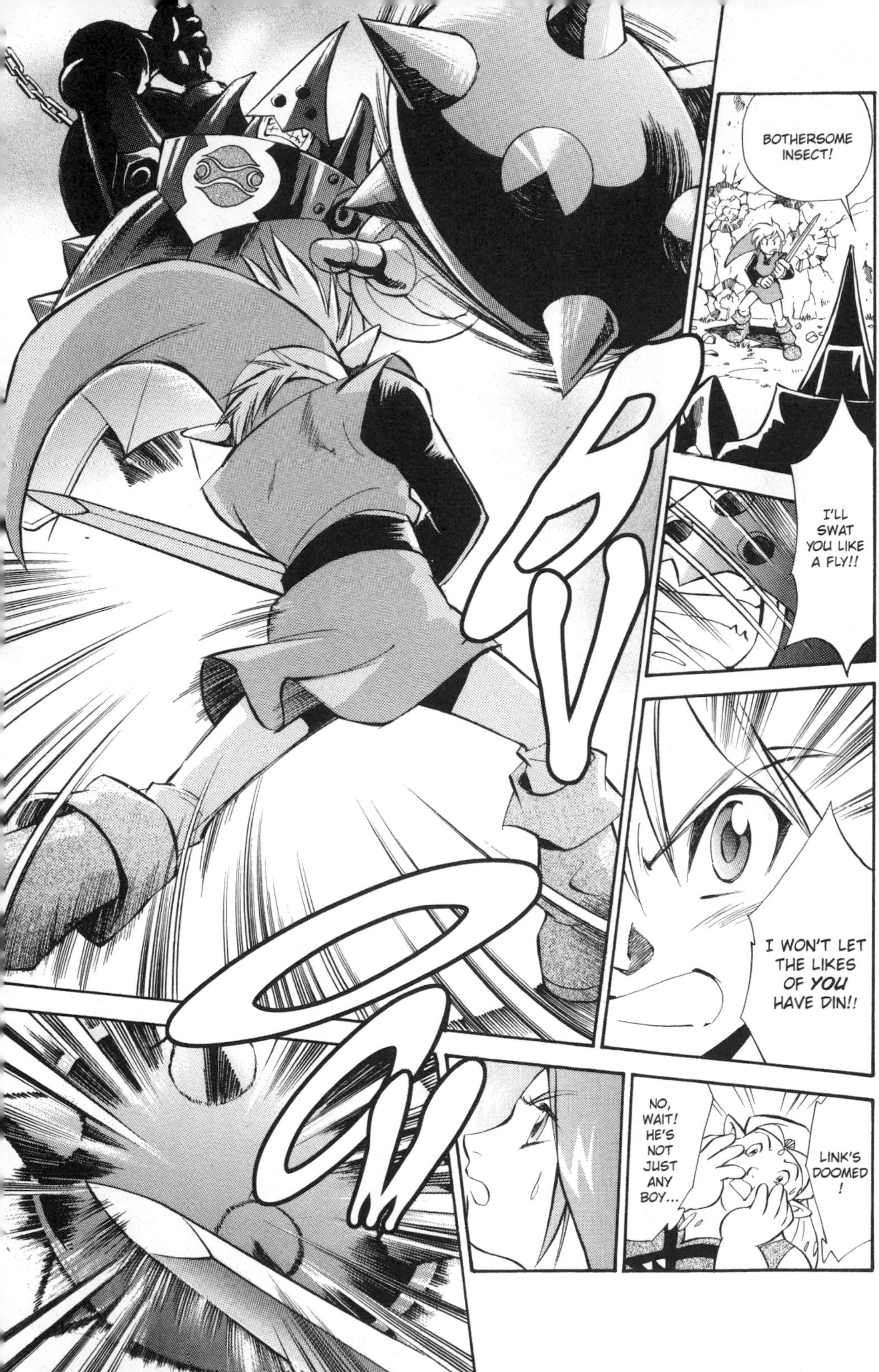
BOTHERSOME INSECT!
I'LL SWAT YOU LIKE A FLY!!
I WON'T LET THE LIKES OF *YOU* HAVE DIN!!
LINK'S DOOMED!
NO, WAIT! HE'S NOT JUST ANY BOY...

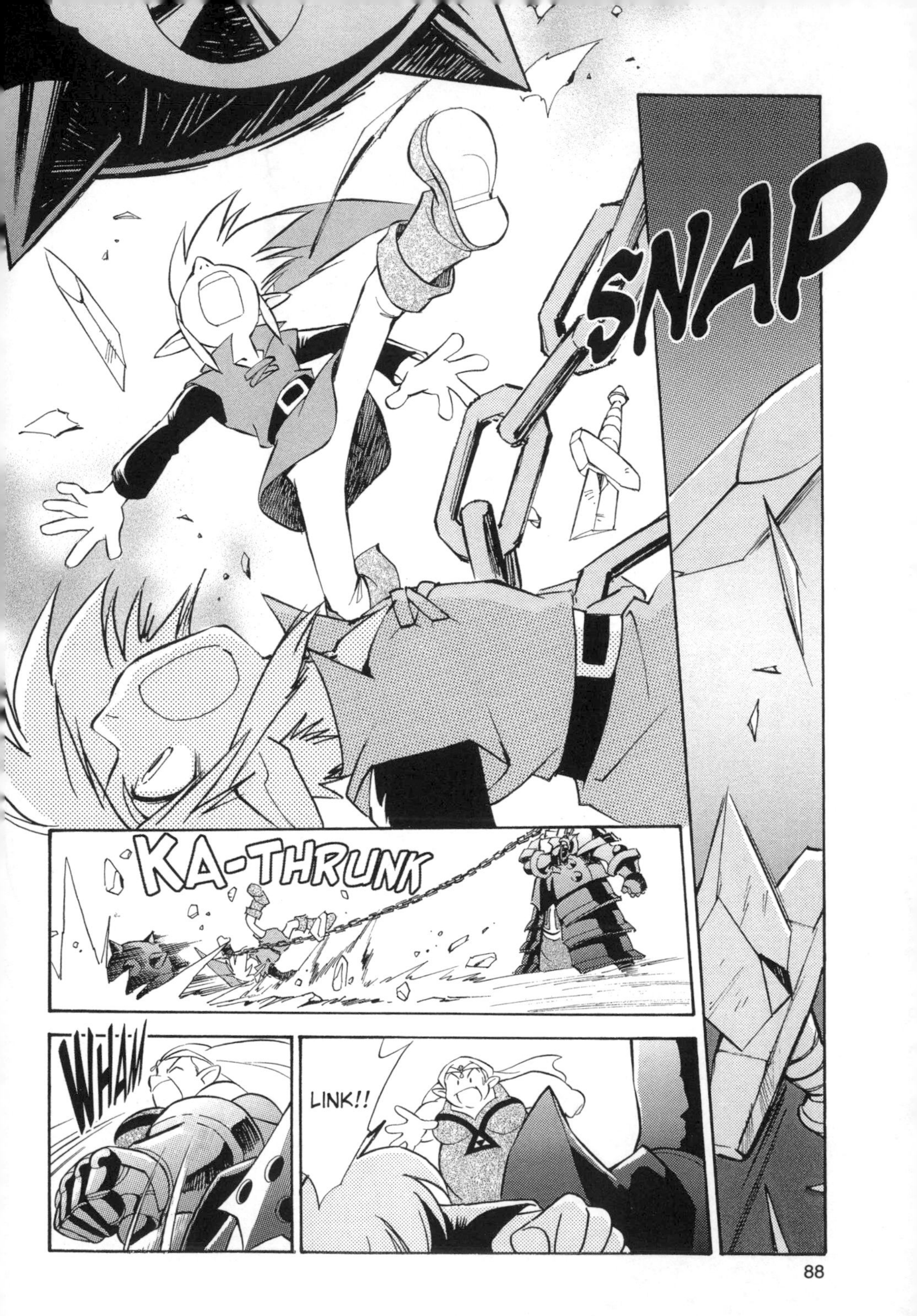
SNAP
KA-THRUNK
LINK!!
WHAM

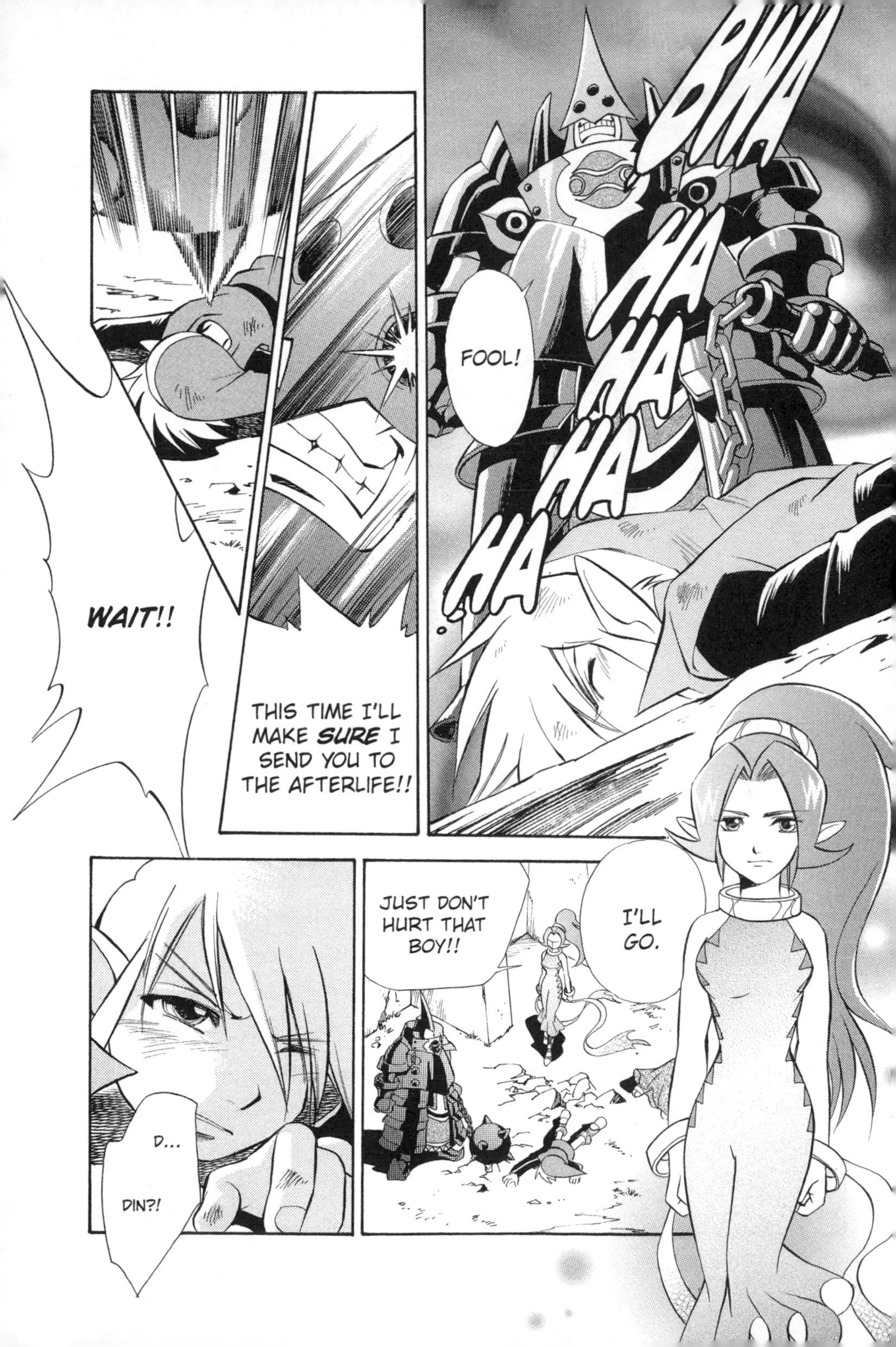
BWAHAHAHAHA
FOOL!
THIS TIME I'LL MAKE ***SURE*** I SEND YOU TO THE AFTERLIFE!!
WAIT!!
I'LL GO.
JUST DON'T HURT THAT BOY!!
D...
DIN?!

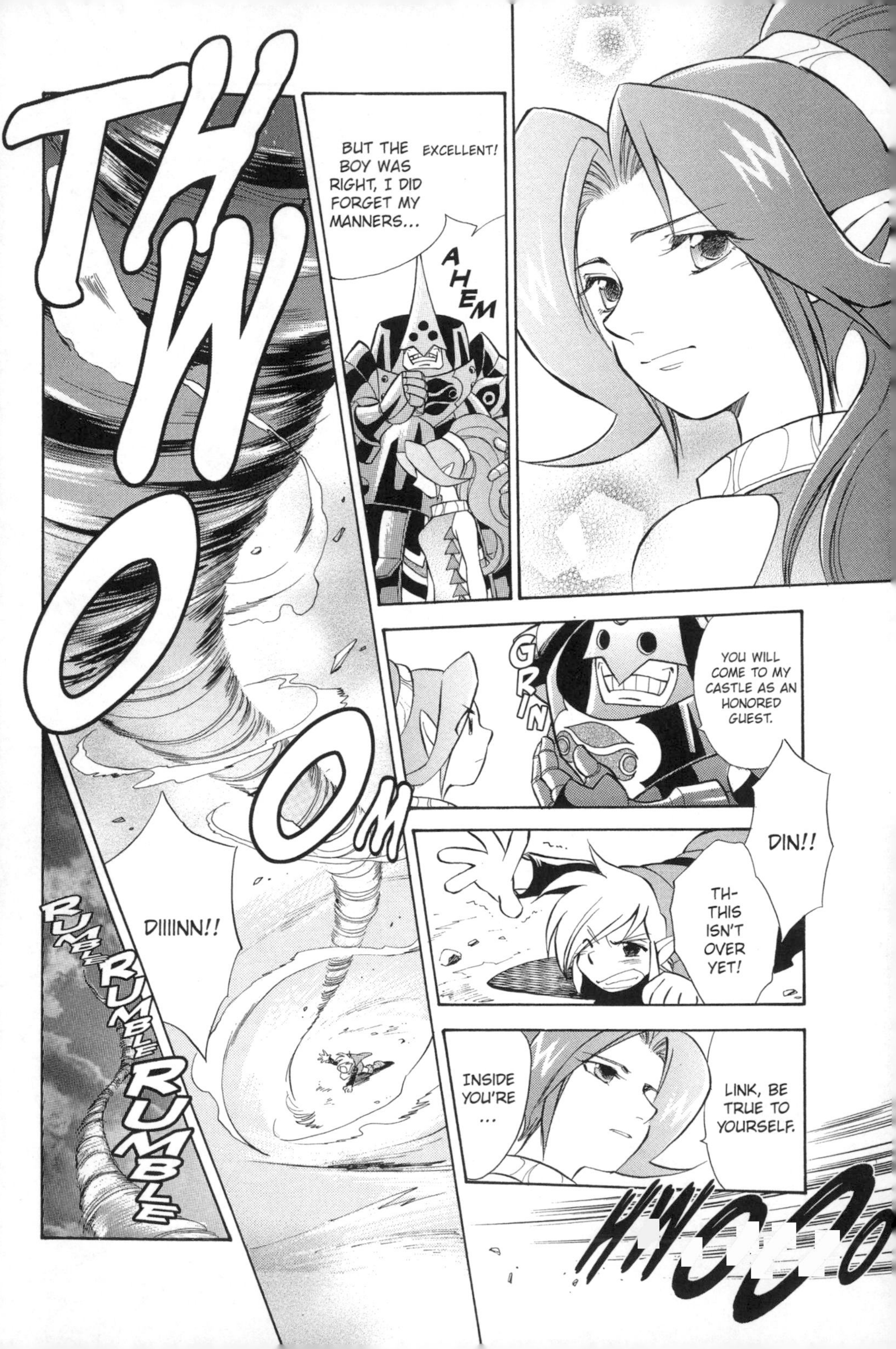

EXCELLENT!
BUT THE BOY WAS RIGHT, I DID FORGET MY MANNERS...
AHEM
YOU WILL COME TO MY CASTLE AS AN HONORED GUEST.
GRIN
DIN!!
TH-THIS ISN'T OVER YET!
LINK, BE TRUE TO YOURSELF.
INSIDE YOU'RE ...
HWOOOO
THWOOOM
DIIIINN!!
RUMBLE RUMBLE RUMBLE

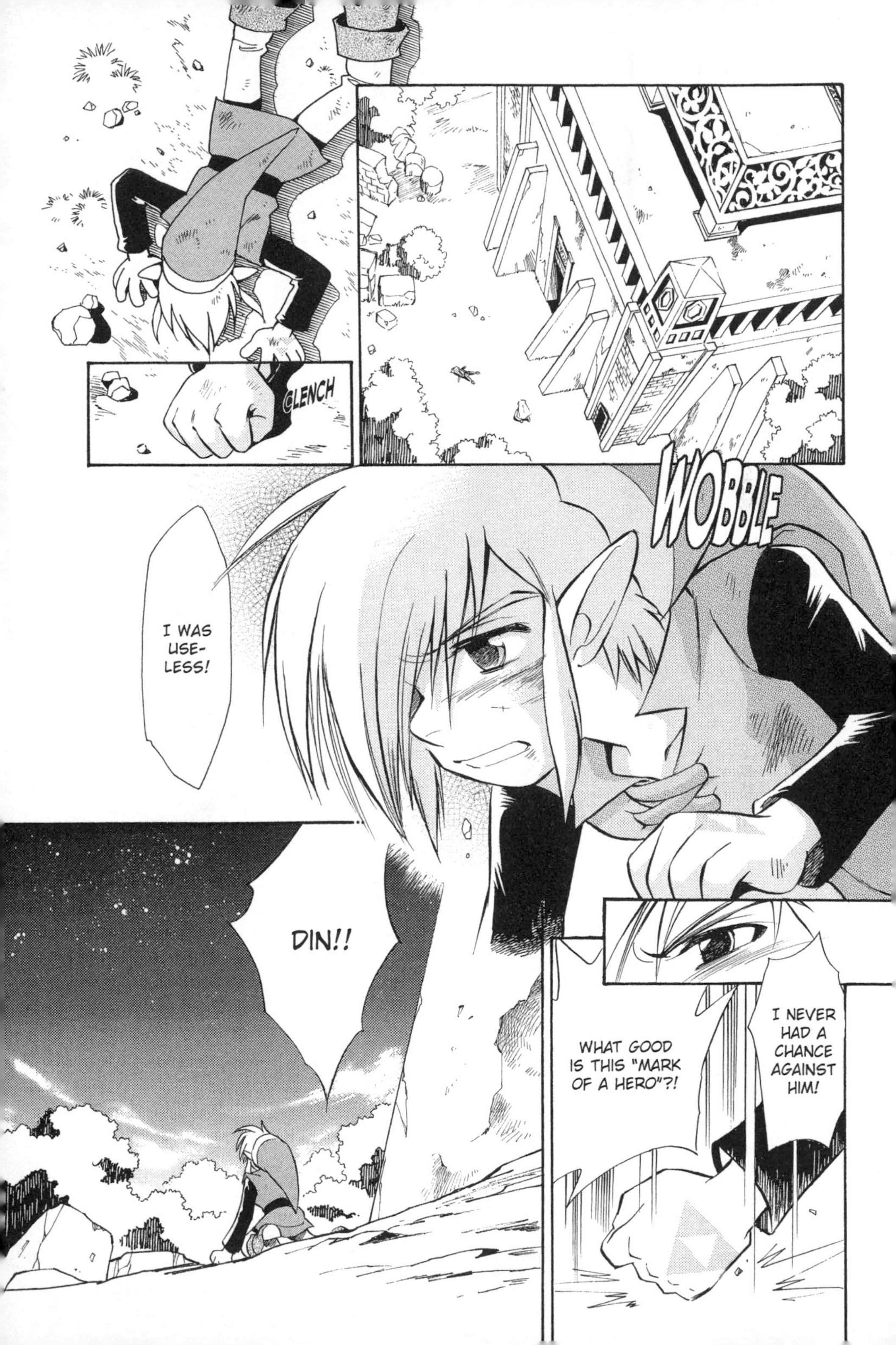
CLENCH
WOBBLE
I WAS USE-LESS!
I NEVER HAD A CHANCE AGAINST HIM!
WHAT GOOD IS THIS "MARK OF A HERO"?!
DIN!!

ROUGH CHARACTER
ILLUSTRATION 3

Din, the Oracle of Seasons. Her costume
as a dancer is red, so I imagined her as
a passionate girl with expressive eyes.

Din

2000·10·11

CHAPTER 5
SACRED PYRAMID: THE TRIFORCE

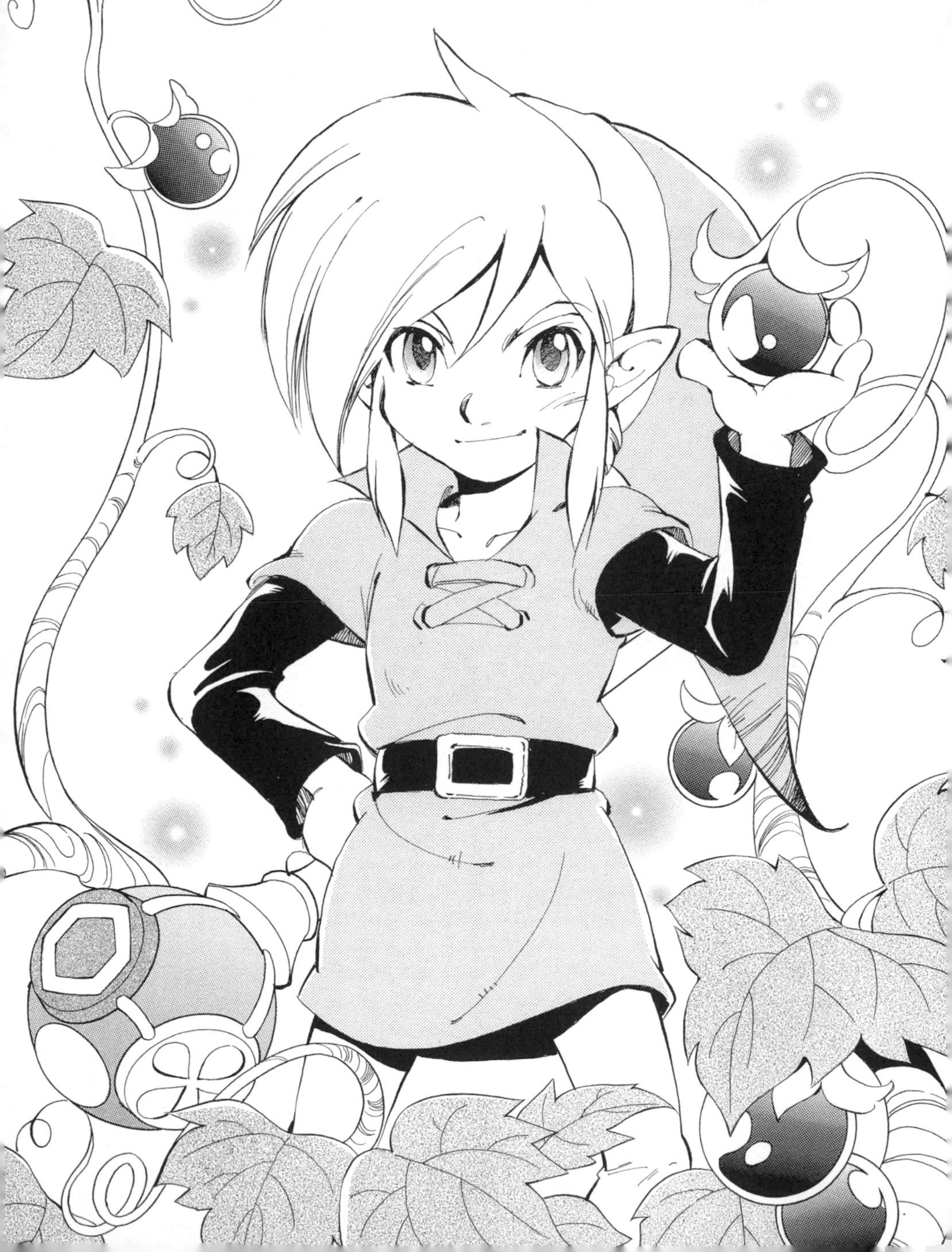

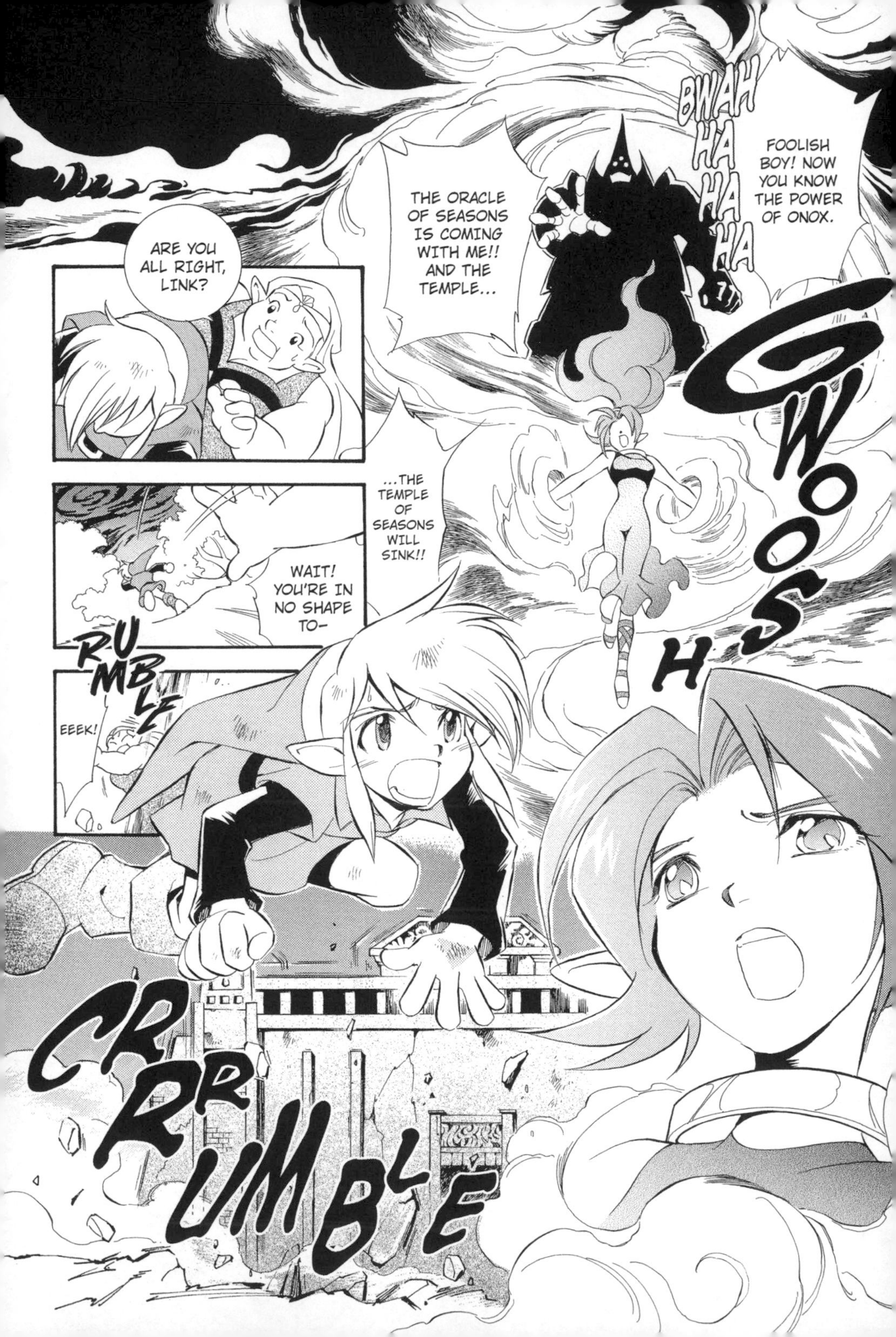
BWAH HA HA HA HA
FOOLISH BOY! NOW YOU KNOW THE POWER OF ONOX.
THE ORACLE OF SEASONS IS COMING WITH ME!! AND THE TEMPLE...
...THE TEMPLE OF SEASONS WILL SINK!!
GWOOSH
ARE YOU ALL RIGHT, LINK?
WAIT! YOU'RE IN NO SHAPE TO-
RUMBLE
EEEK!
CRRRUMBLE

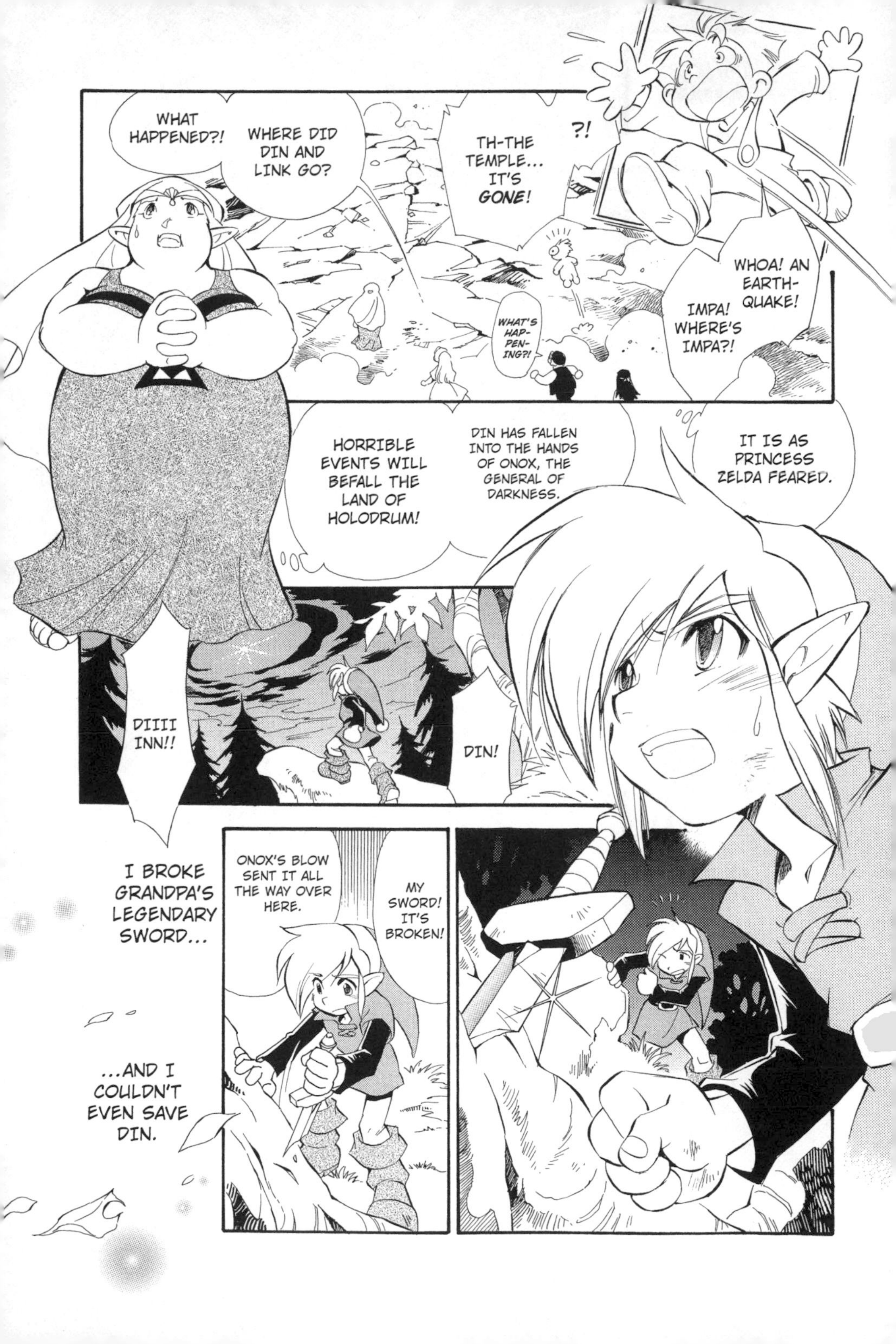
?!
TH-THE TEMPLE... IT'S GONE!
WHOA! AN EARTH-QUAKE!
IMPA! WHERE'S IMPA?!
WHERE DID DIN AND LINK GO?
WHAT HAPPENED?!
WHAT'S HAP-PEN-ING?!
IT IS AS PRINCESS ZELDA FEARED.
DIN HAS FALLEN INTO THE HANDS OF ONOX, THE GENERAL OF DARKNESS.
HORRIBLE EVENTS WILL BEFALL THE LAND OF HOLODRUM!
DIN!
DIIII INN!!
MY SWORD! IT'S BROKEN!
ONOX'S BLOW SENT IT ALL THE WAY OVER HERE.
I BROKE GRANDPA'S LEGENDARY SWORD...
...AND I COULDN'T EVEN SAVE DIN.

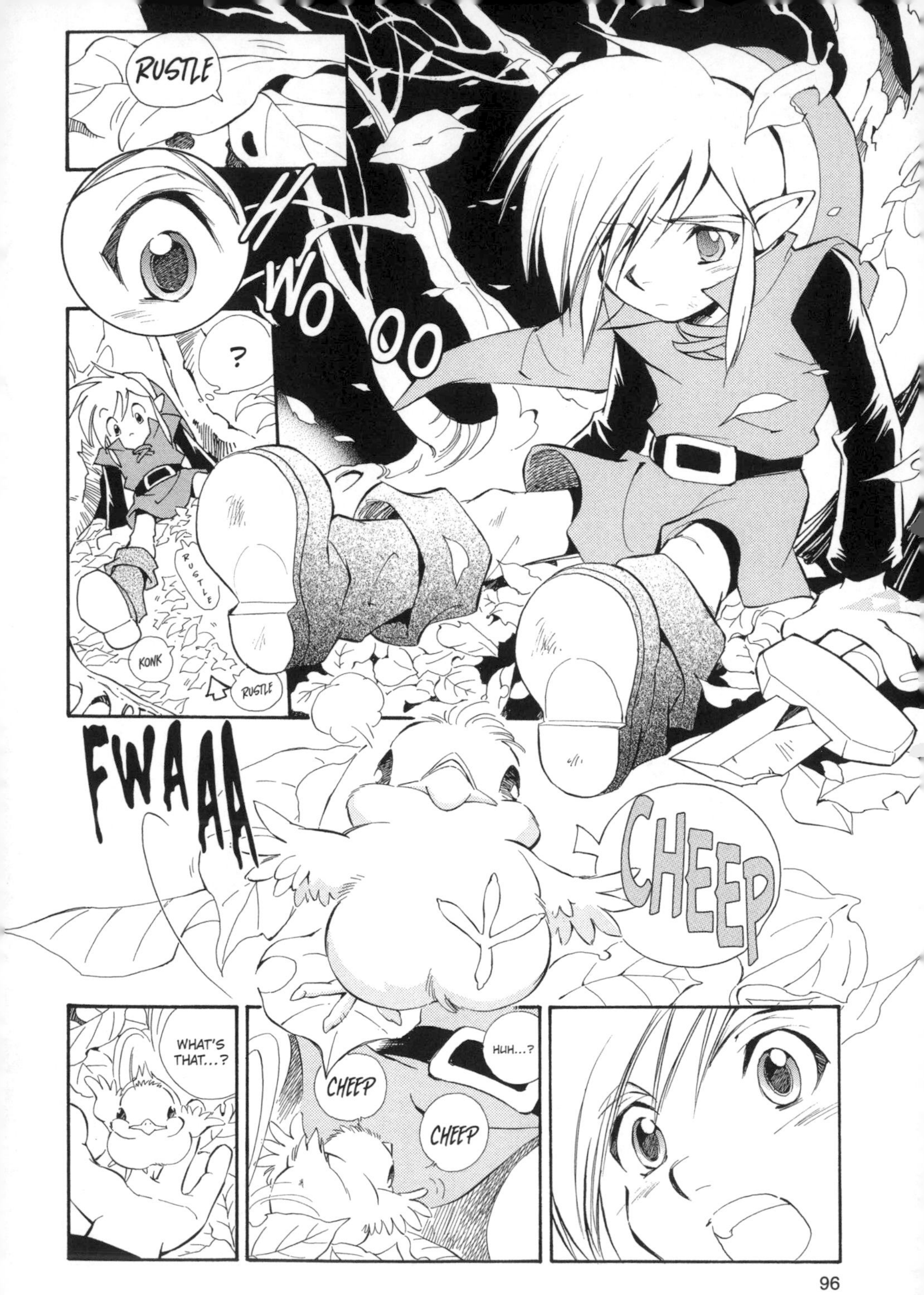
HWOOO
RUSTLE
?
RUSTLE
KONK
RUSTLE
FWAAA
CHEEP
HUH...?
CHEEP
CHEEP
WHAT'S THAT...?

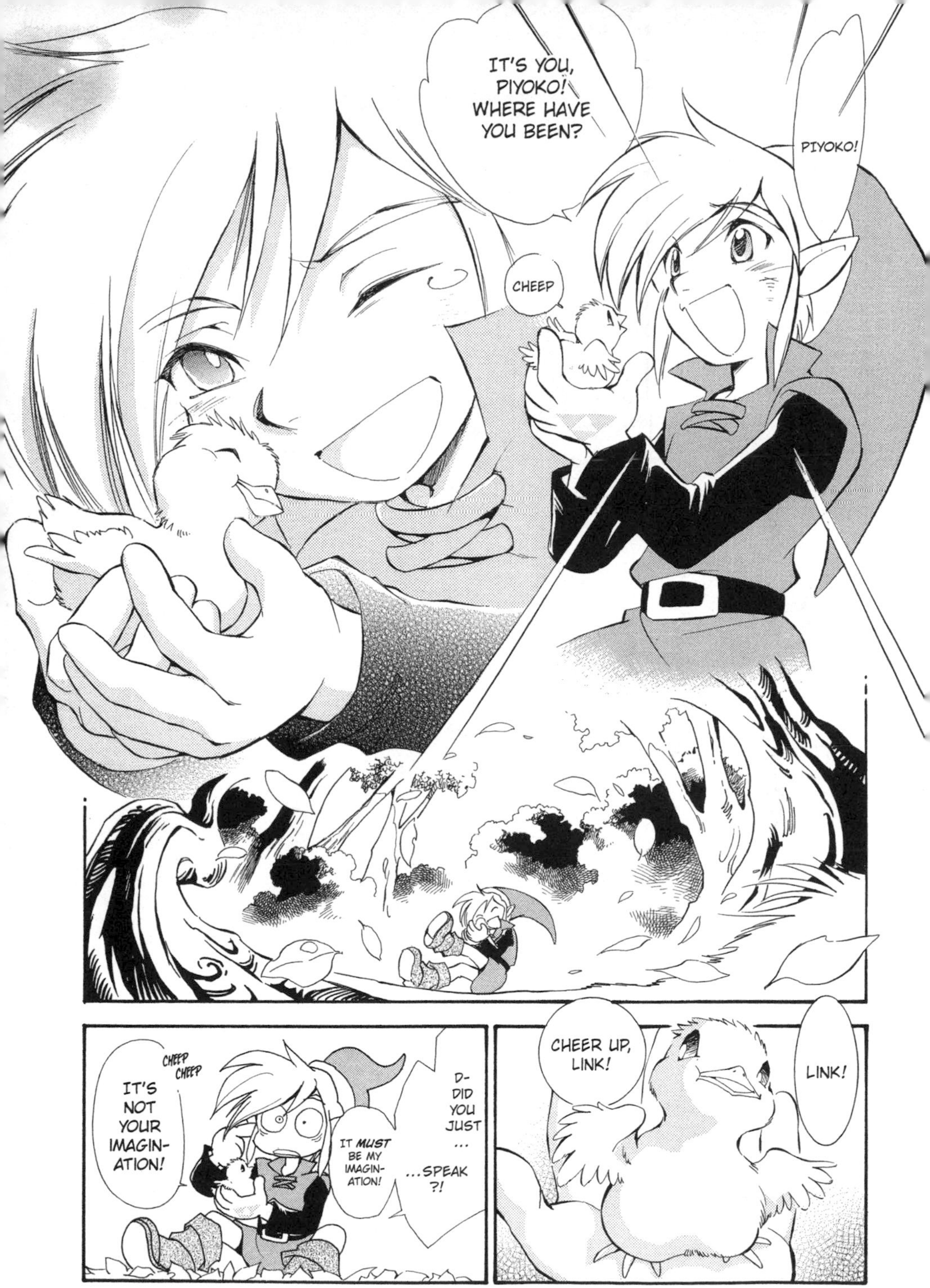
PIYOKO!
IT'S YOU, PIYOKO! WHERE HAVE YOU BEEN?
CHEEP
LINK!
CHEER UP, LINK!
D-DID YOU JUST ...
...SPEAK?!
IT *MUST* BE MY IMAGIN-ATION!
CHEEP CHEEP
IT'S NOT YOUR IMAGIN-ATION!

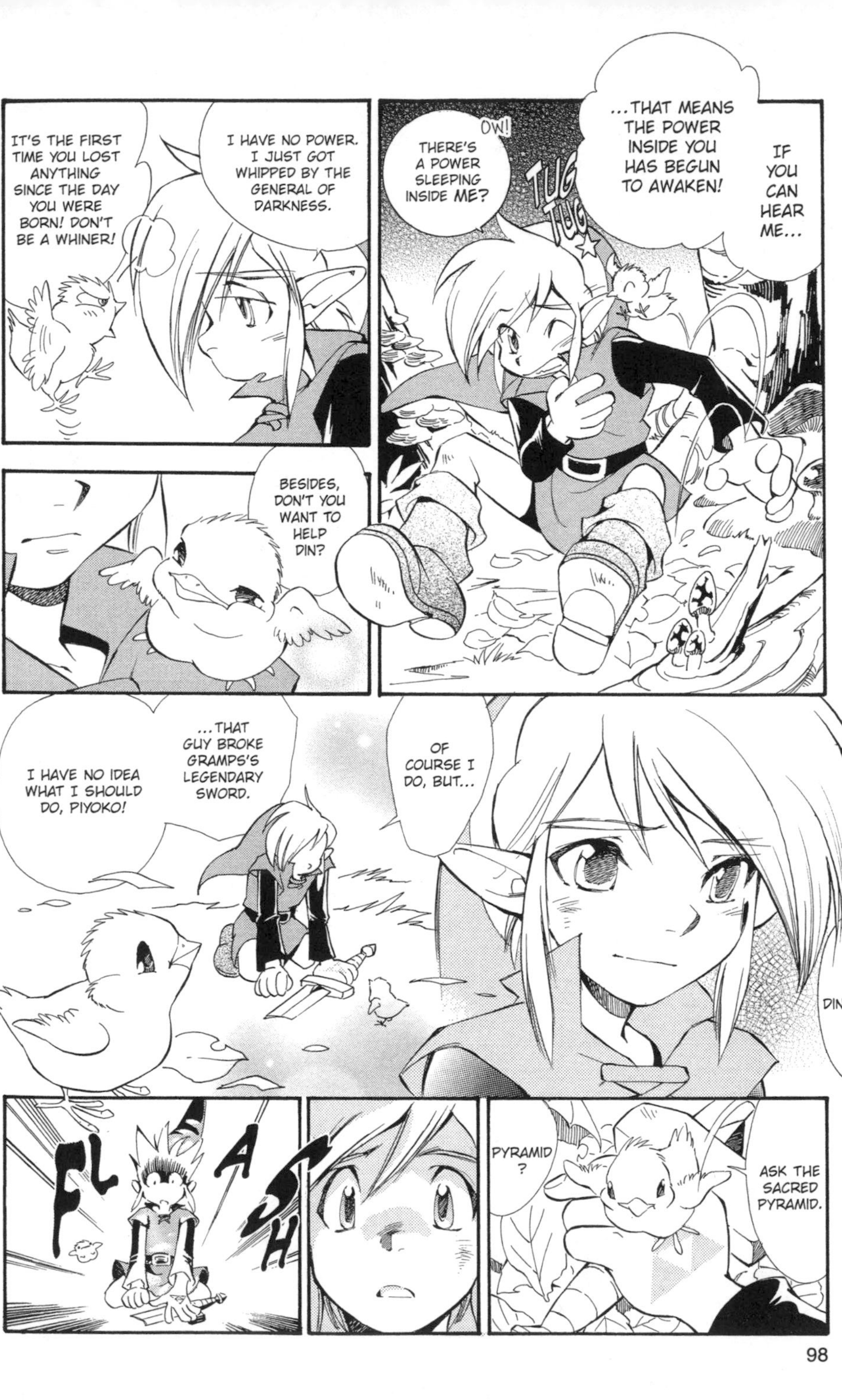
IF YOU CAN HEAR ME...
...THAT MEANS THE POWER INSIDE YOU HAS BEGUN TO AWAKEN!
TUG TUG
OW!
THERE'S A POWER SLEEPING INSIDE ME?
I HAVE NO POWER. I JUST GOT WHIPPED BY THE GENERAL OF DARKNESS.
IT'S THE FIRST TIME YOU LOST ANYTHING SINCE THE DAY YOU WERE BORN! DON'T BE A WHINER!
BESIDES, DON'T YOU WANT TO HELP DIN?
DIN...
OF COURSE I DO, BUT...
...THAT GUY BROKE GRAMPS'S LEGENDARY SWORD.
I HAVE NO IDEA WHAT I SHOULD DO, PIYOKO!
ASK THE SACRED PYRAMID.
PYRAMID?
FLASH

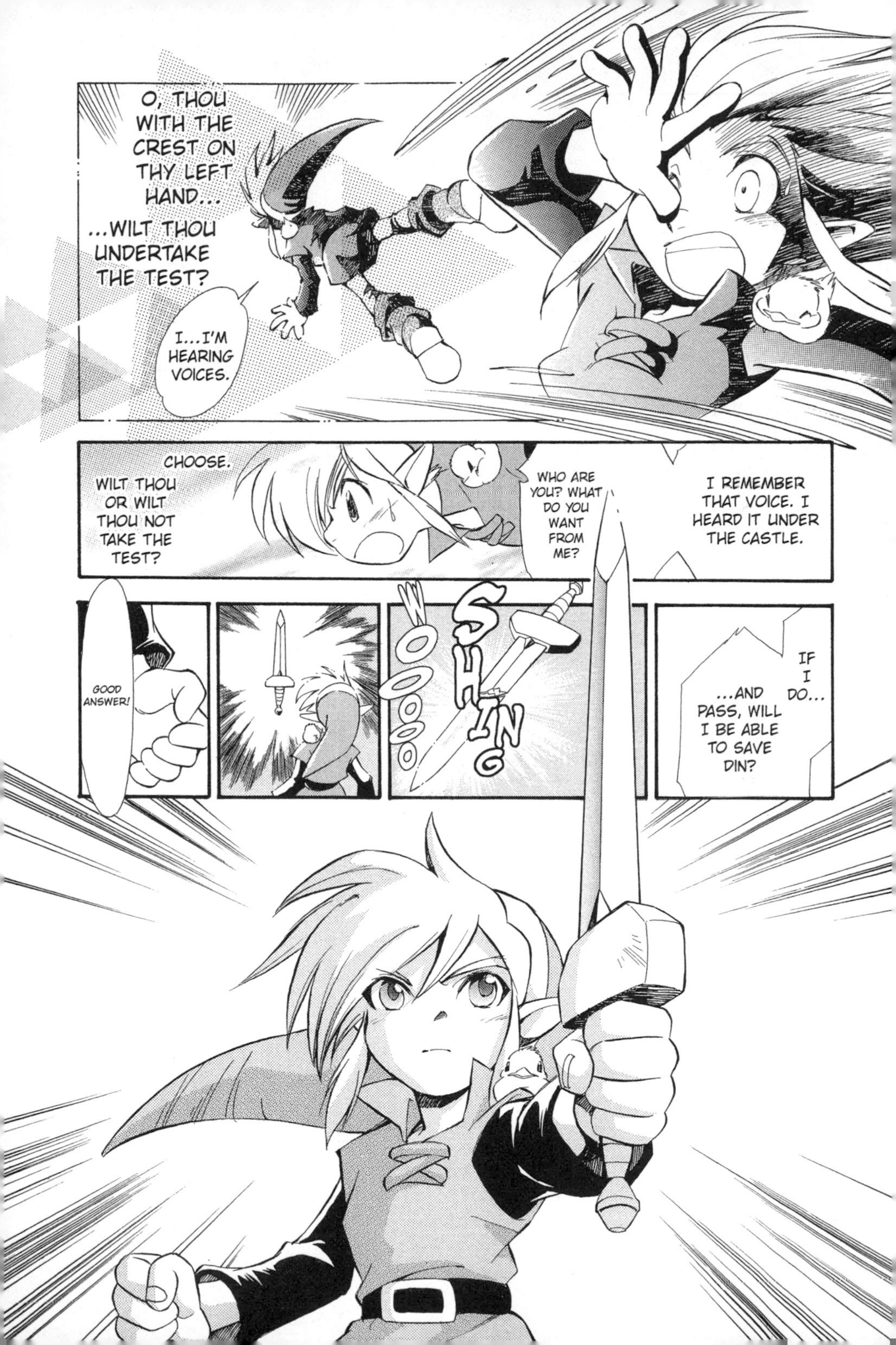
O, THOU WITH THE CREST ON THY LEFT HAND...
...WILT THOU UNDERTAKE THE TEST?
I...I'M HEARING VOICES.
I REMEMBER THAT VOICE. I HEARD IT UNDER THE CASTLE.
WHO ARE YOU? WHAT DO YOU WANT FROM ME?
CHOOSE.
WILT THOU OR WILT THOU NOT TAKE THE TEST?
IF I DO...
...AND PASS, WILL I BE ABLE TO SAVE DIN?
SHING
WOOOOO
GOOD ANSWER!

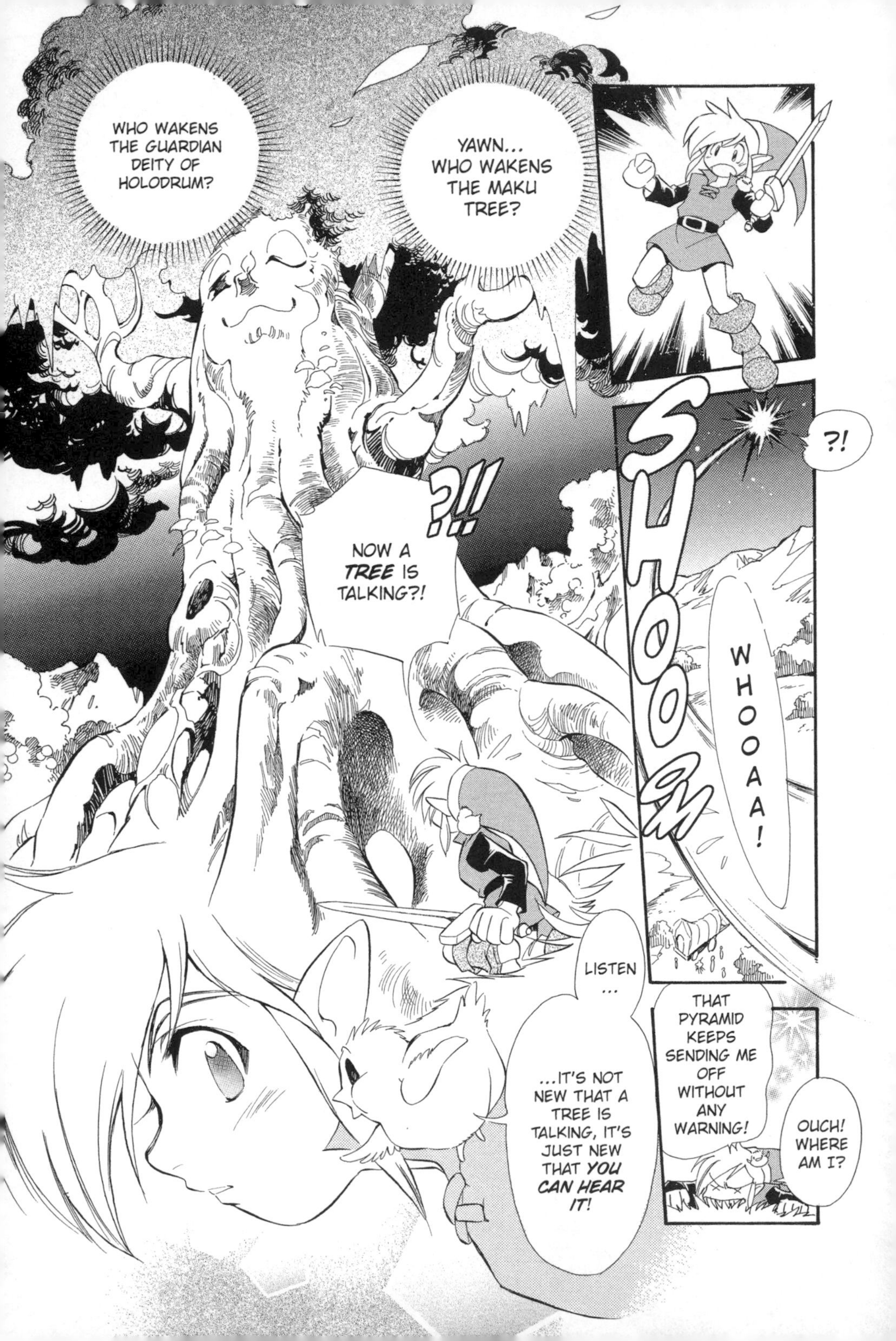
?!
SHOOOM
WHOOAA!
OUCH! WHERE AM I?
THAT PYRAMID KEEPS SENDING ME OFF WITHOUT ANY WARNING!
YAWN... WHO WAKENS THE MAKU TREE?
WHO WAKENS THE GUARDIAN DEITY OF HOLODRUM?
?!!
NOW A *TREE* IS TALKING?!
LISTEN...
...IT'S NOT NEW THAT A TREE IS TALKING, IT'S JUST NEW THAT *YOU CAN HEAR IT!*

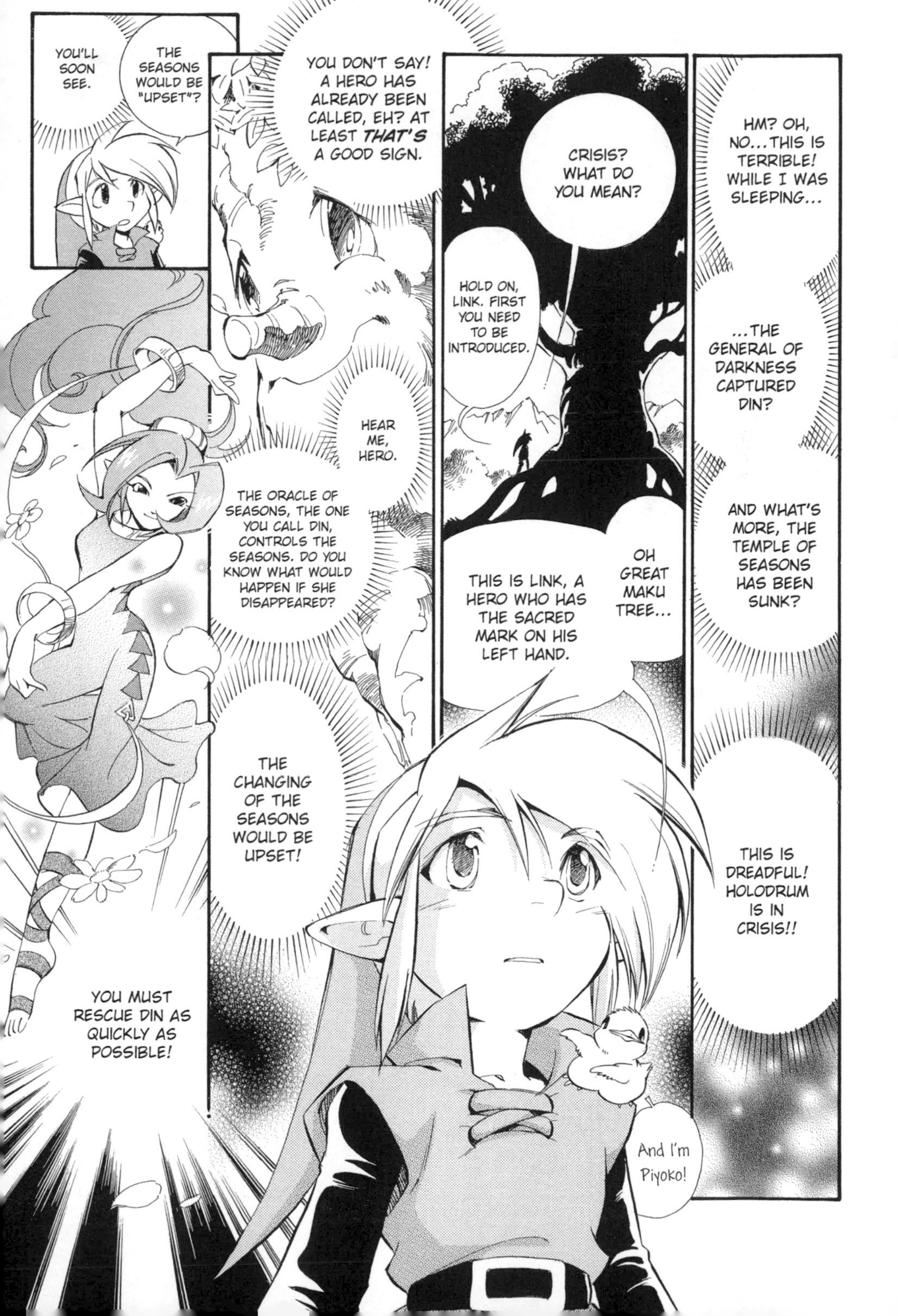
HM? OH, NO...THIS IS TERRIBLE! WHILE I WAS SLEEPING...
...THE GENERAL OF DARKNESS CAPTURED DIN?
AND WHAT'S MORE, THE TEMPLE OF SEASONS HAS BEEN SUNK?
THIS IS DREADFUL! HOLODRUM IS IN CRISIS!!
CRISIS? WHAT DO YOU MEAN?
HOLD ON, LINK. FIRST YOU NEED TO BE INTRODUCED.
OH GREAT MAKU TREE...
THIS IS LINK, A HERO WHO HAS THE SACRED MARK ON HIS LEFT HAND.
And I'm Piyoko!
YOU DON'T SAY! A HERO HAS ALREADY BEEN CALLED, EH? AT LEAST THAT'S A GOOD SIGN.
HEAR ME, HERO.
THE ORACLE OF SEASONS, THE ONE YOU CALL DIN, CONTROLS THE SEASONS. DO YOU KNOW WHAT WOULD HAPPEN IF SHE DISAPPEARED?
THE CHANGING OF THE SEASONS WOULD BE UPSET!
THE SEASONS WOULD BE "UPSET"?
YOU'LL SOON SEE.
YOU MUST RESCUE DIN AS QUICKLY AS POSSIBLE!

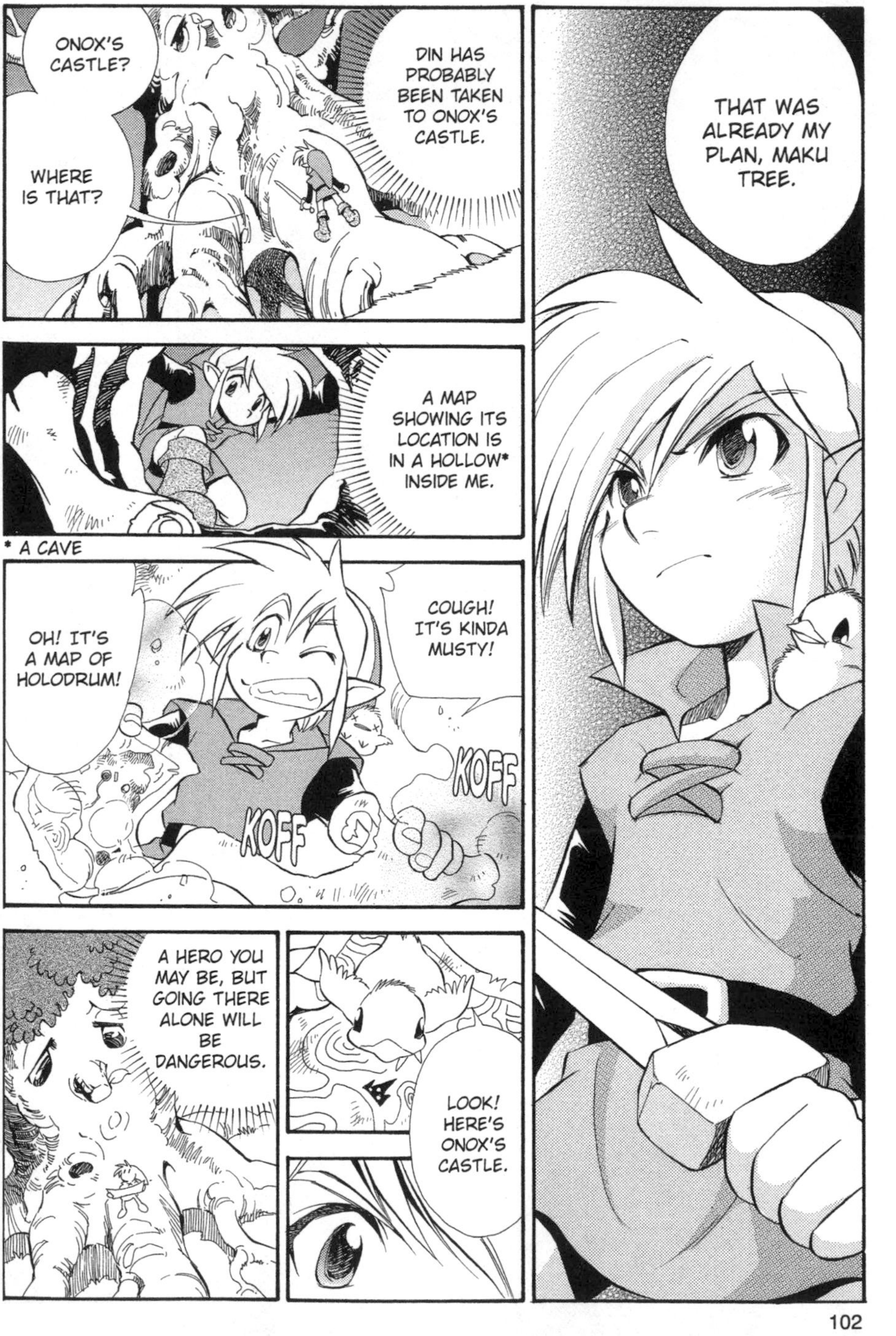
THAT WAS ALREADY MY PLAN, MAKU TREE.
DIN HAS PROBABLY BEEN TAKEN TO ONOX'S CASTLE.
ONOX'S CASTLE?
WHERE IS THAT?
A MAP SHOWING ITS LOCATION IS IN A HOLLOW* INSIDE ME.
* A CAVE
COUGH! IT'S KINDA MUSTY!
KOFF
KOFF
OH! IT'S A MAP OF HOLODRUM!
LOOK! HERE'S ONOX'S CASTLE.
A HERO YOU MAY BE, BUT GOING THERE ALONE WILL BE DANGEROUS.

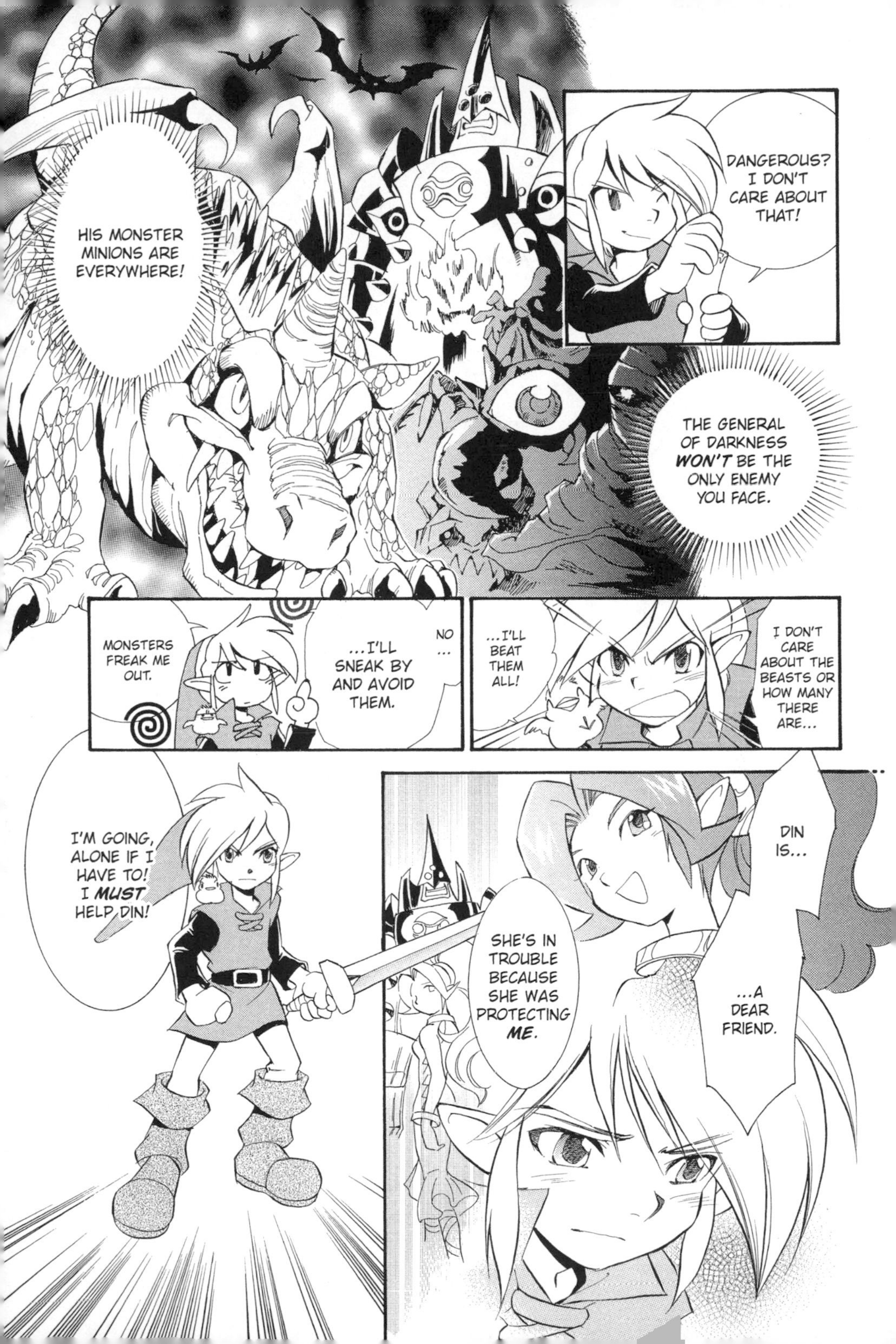
DANGEROUS? I DON'T CARE ABOUT THAT!
THE GENERAL OF DARKNESS WON'T BE THE ONLY ENEMY YOU FACE.
HIS MONSTER MINIONS ARE EVERYWHERE!
I DON'T CARE ABOUT THE BEASTS OR HOW MANY THERE ARE...
...I'LL BEAT THEM ALL!
NO...
...I'LL SNEAK BY AND AVOID THEM.
MONSTERS FREAK ME OUT.
DIN IS...
...A DEAR FRIEND.
SHE'S IN TROUBLE BECAUSE SHE WAS PROTECTING ME.
I'M GOING, ALONE IF I HAVE TO! I MUST HELP DIN!

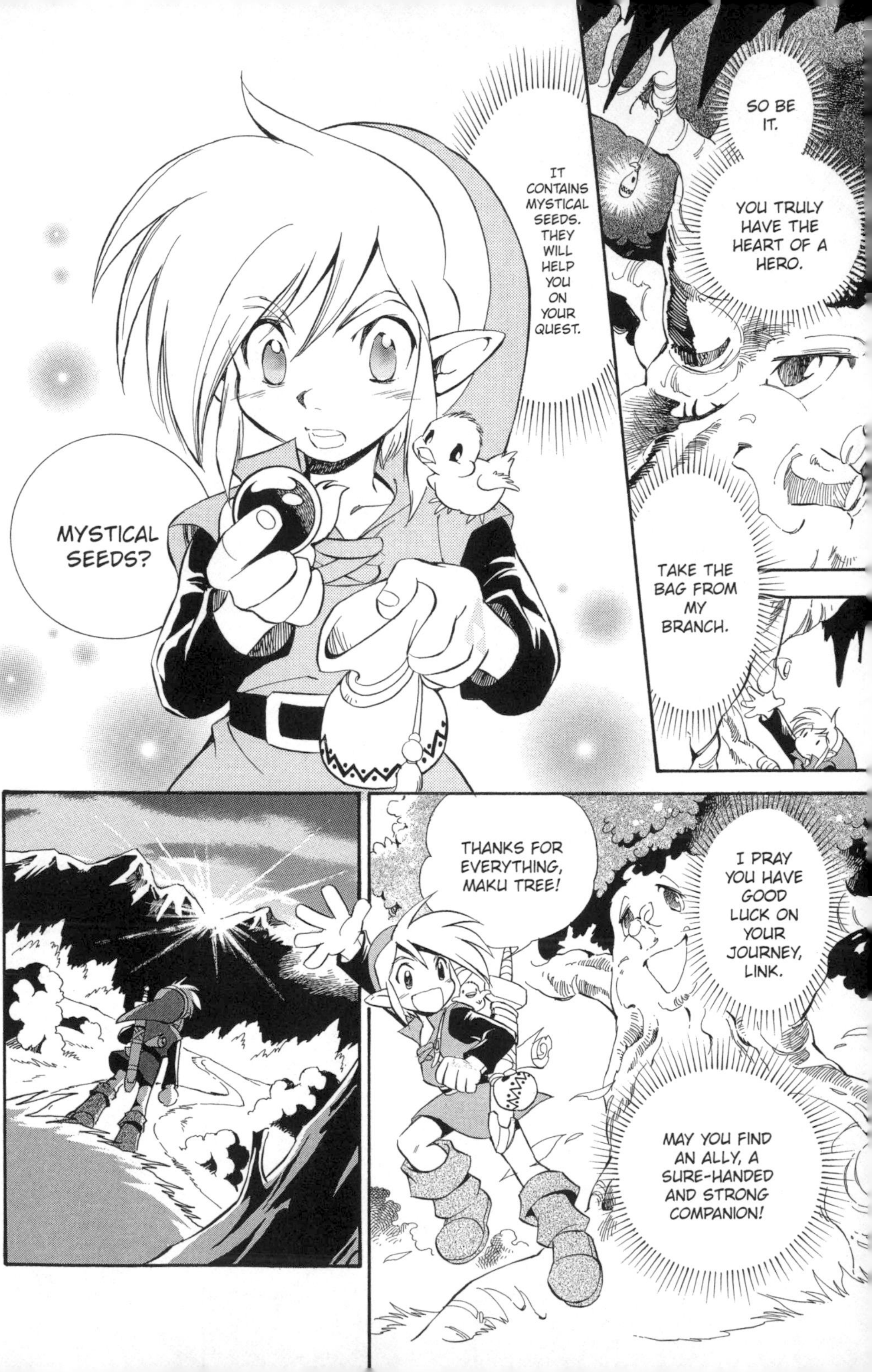
SO BE IT.
YOU TRULY HAVE THE HEART OF A HERO.
TAKE THE BAG FROM MY BRANCH.
IT CONTAINS MYSTICAL SEEDS. THEY WILL HELP YOU ON YOUR QUEST.
MYSTICAL SEEDS?
I PRAY YOU HAVE GOOD LUCK ON YOUR JOURNEY, LINK.
THANKS FOR EVERYTHING, MAKU TREE!
MAY YOU FIND AN ALLY, A SURE-HANDED AND STRONG COMPANION!

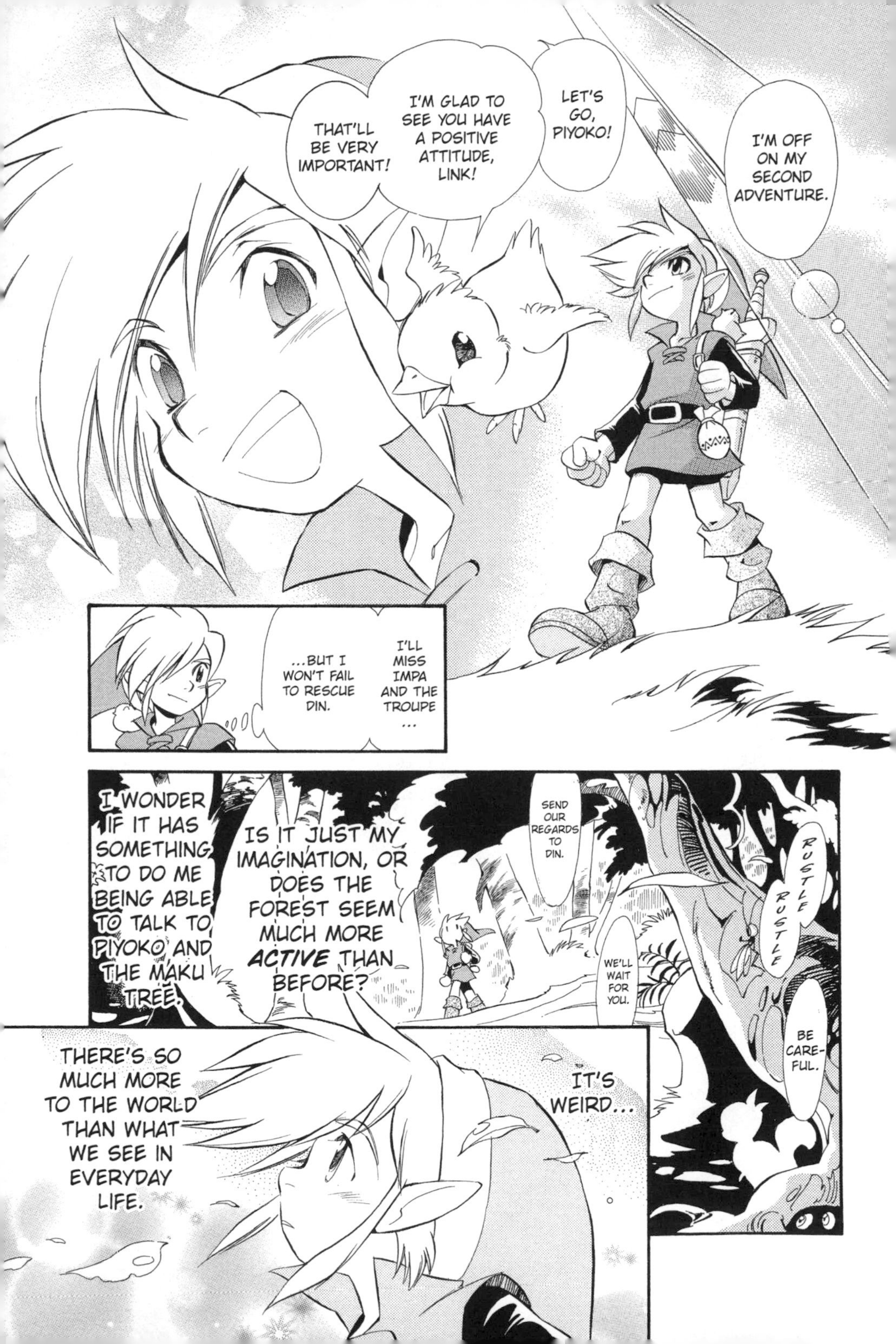
I'M OFF ON MY SECOND ADVENTURE.
LET'S GO, PIYOKO!
I'M GLAD TO SEE YOU HAVE A POSITIVE ATTITUDE, LINK!
THAT'LL BE VERY IMPORTANT!
I'LL MISS IMPA AND THE TROUPE ...
...BUT I WON'T FAIL TO RESCUE DIN.
RUSTLE RUSTLE
SEND OUR REGARDS TO DIN.
WE'LL WAIT FOR YOU.
BE CARE-FUL.
IS IT JUST MY IMAGINATION, OR DOES THE FOREST SEEM MUCH MORE ACTIVE THAN BEFORE?
I WONDER IF IT HAS SOMETHING TO DO ME BEING ABLE TO TALK TO PIYOKO AND THE MAKU TREE.
IT'S WEIRD...
THERE'S SO MUCH MORE TO THE WORLD THAN WHAT WE SEE IN EVERYDAY LIFE.

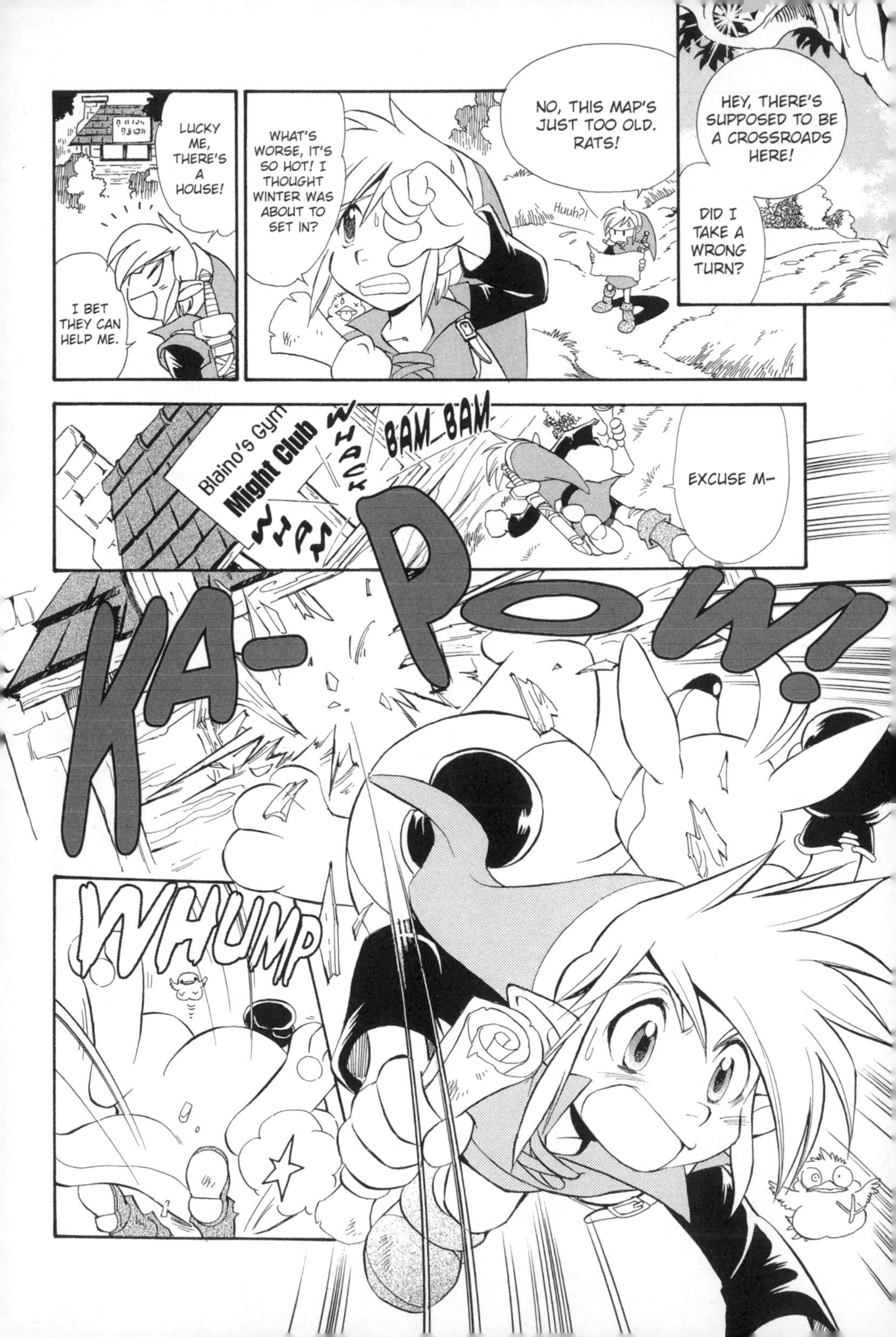
HEY, THERE'S SUPPOSED TO BE A CROSSROADS HERE!
DID I TAKE A WRONG TURN?
Huuh?!
NO, THIS MAP'S JUST TOO OLD. RATS!
WHAT'S WORSE, IT'S SO HOT! I THOUGHT WINTER WAS ABOUT TO SET IN?
LUCKY ME, THERE'S A HOUSE!
I BET THEY CAN HELP ME.
EXCUSE M-
BAM BAM
WHACK
Blaino's Gym
Might Club
KA-POW!
WHUMP

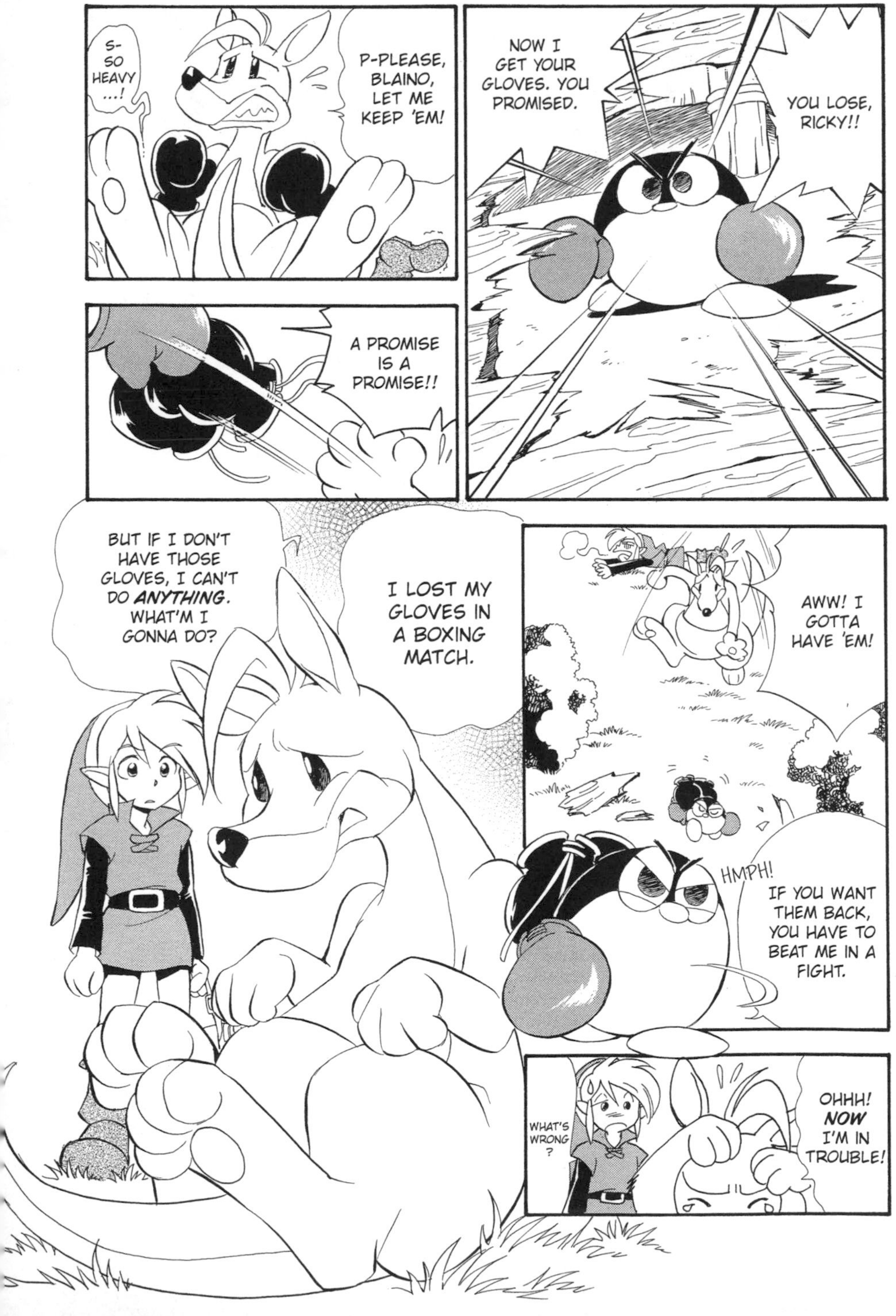
YOU LOSE, RICKY!!
NOW I GET YOUR GLOVES. YOU PROMISED.
P-PLEASE, BLAINO, LET ME KEEP 'EM!
S-SO HEAVY ...!
A PROMISE IS A PROMISE!!
AWW! I GOTTA HAVE 'EM!
HMPH!
IF YOU WANT THEM BACK, YOU HAVE TO BEAT ME IN A FIGHT.
OHHH! ***NOW*** I'M IN TROUBLE!
WHAT'S WRONG ?
I LOST MY GLOVES IN A BOXING MATCH.
BUT IF I DON'T HAVE THOSE GLOVES, I CAN'T DO ***ANYTHING***. WHAT'M I GONNA DO?

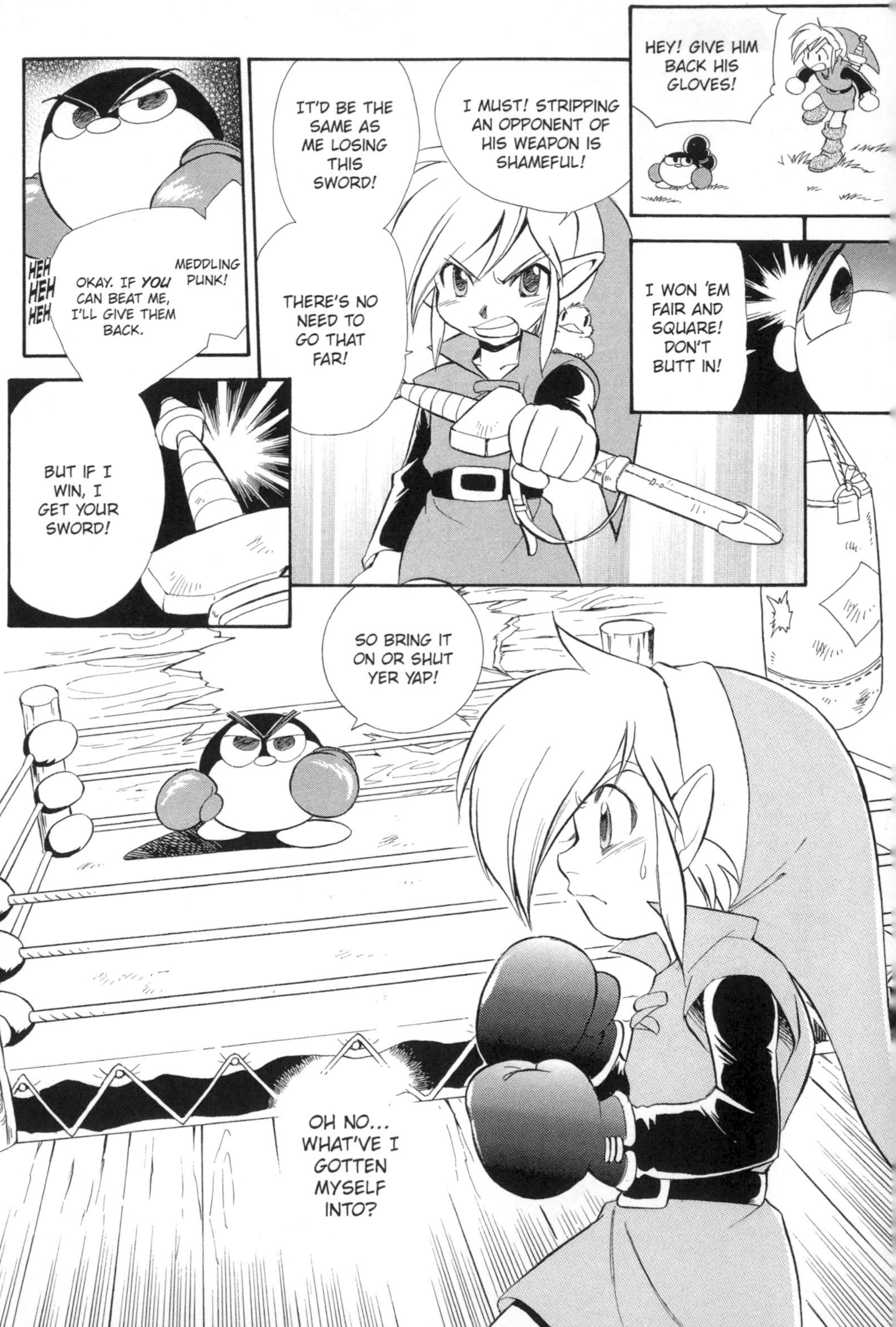
HEY! GIVE HIM BACK HIS GLOVES!
I WON 'EM FAIR AND SQUARE! DON'T BUTT IN!
I MUST! STRIPPING AN OPPONENT OF HIS WEAPON IS SHAMEFUL!
IT'D BE THE SAME AS ME LOSING THIS SWORD!
THERE'S NO NEED TO GO THAT FAR!
HEH HEH HEH
MEDDLING PUNK!
OKAY. IF *YOU* CAN BEAT ME, I'LL GIVE THEM BACK.
BUT IF I WIN, I GET YOUR SWORD!
SO BRING IT ON OR SHUT YER YAP!
OH NO... WHAT'VE I GOTTEN MYSELF INTO?

CHAPTER 6
A NEW FRIEND: RICKY

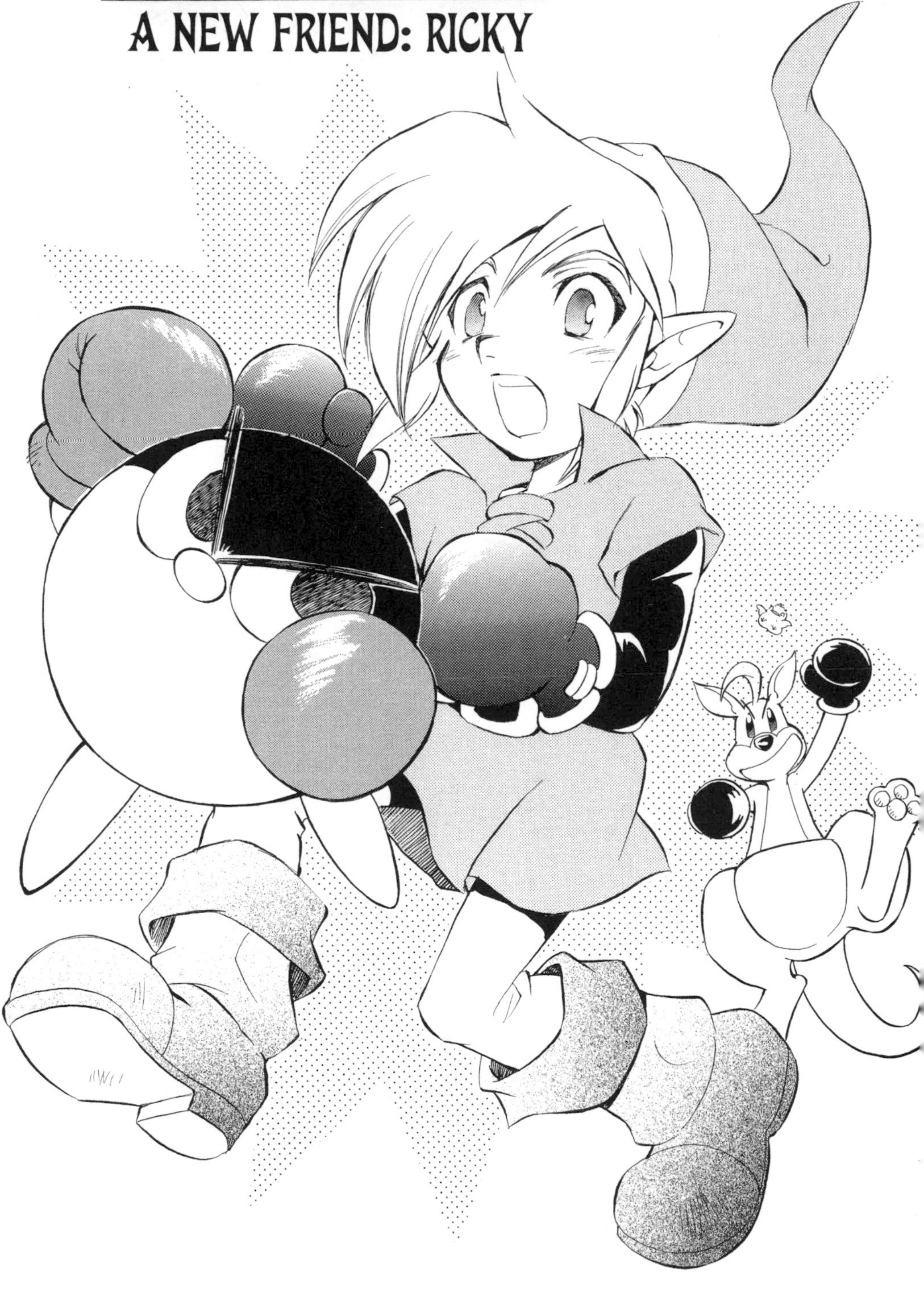

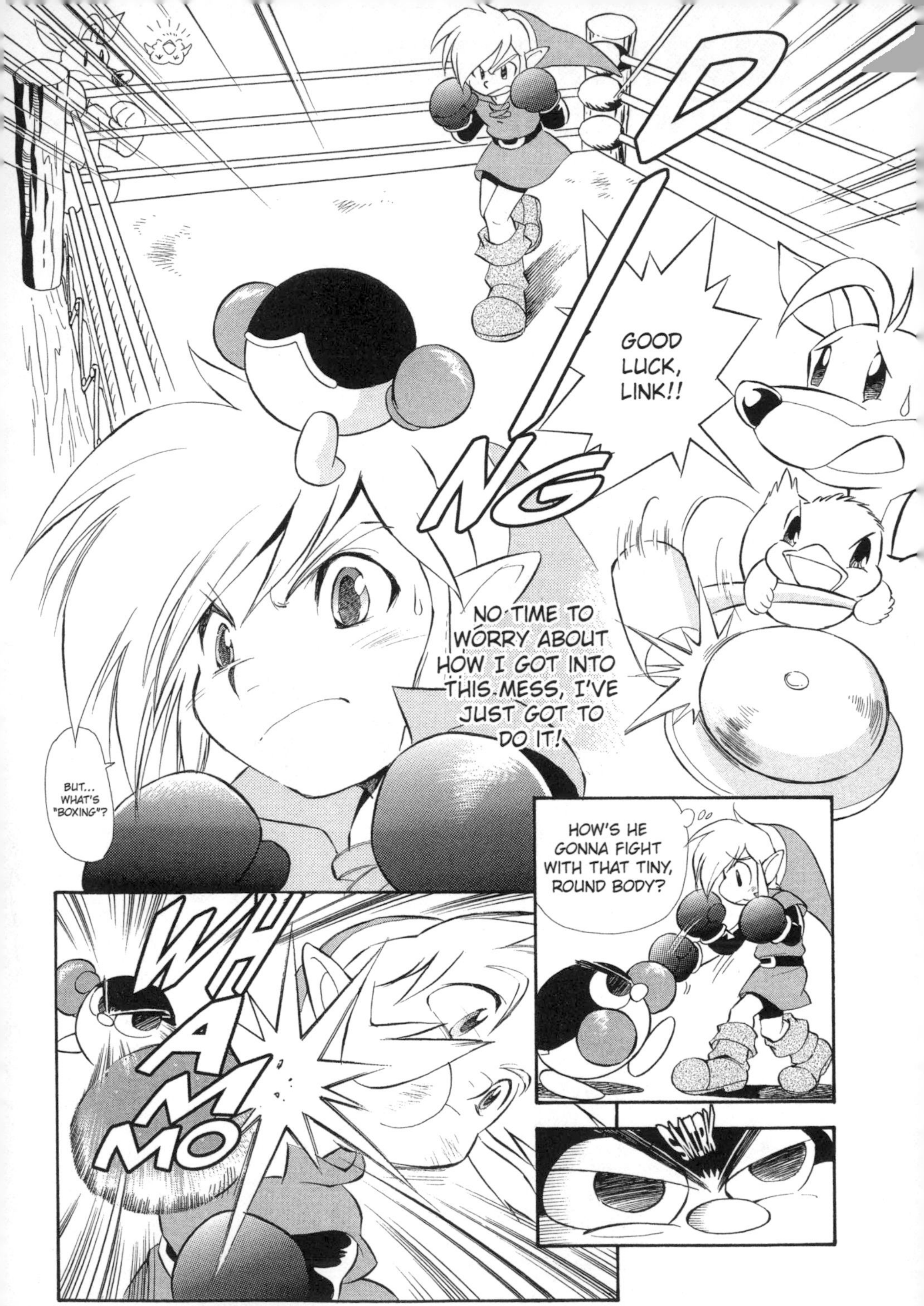
DING
GOOD LUCK, LINK!!
NO TIME TO WORRY ABOUT HOW I GOT INTO THIS MESS, I'VE JUST GOT TO DO IT!
BUT... WHAT'S "BOXING"?
HOW'S HE GONNA FIGHT WITH THAT TINY, ROUND BODY?
WHAMMO

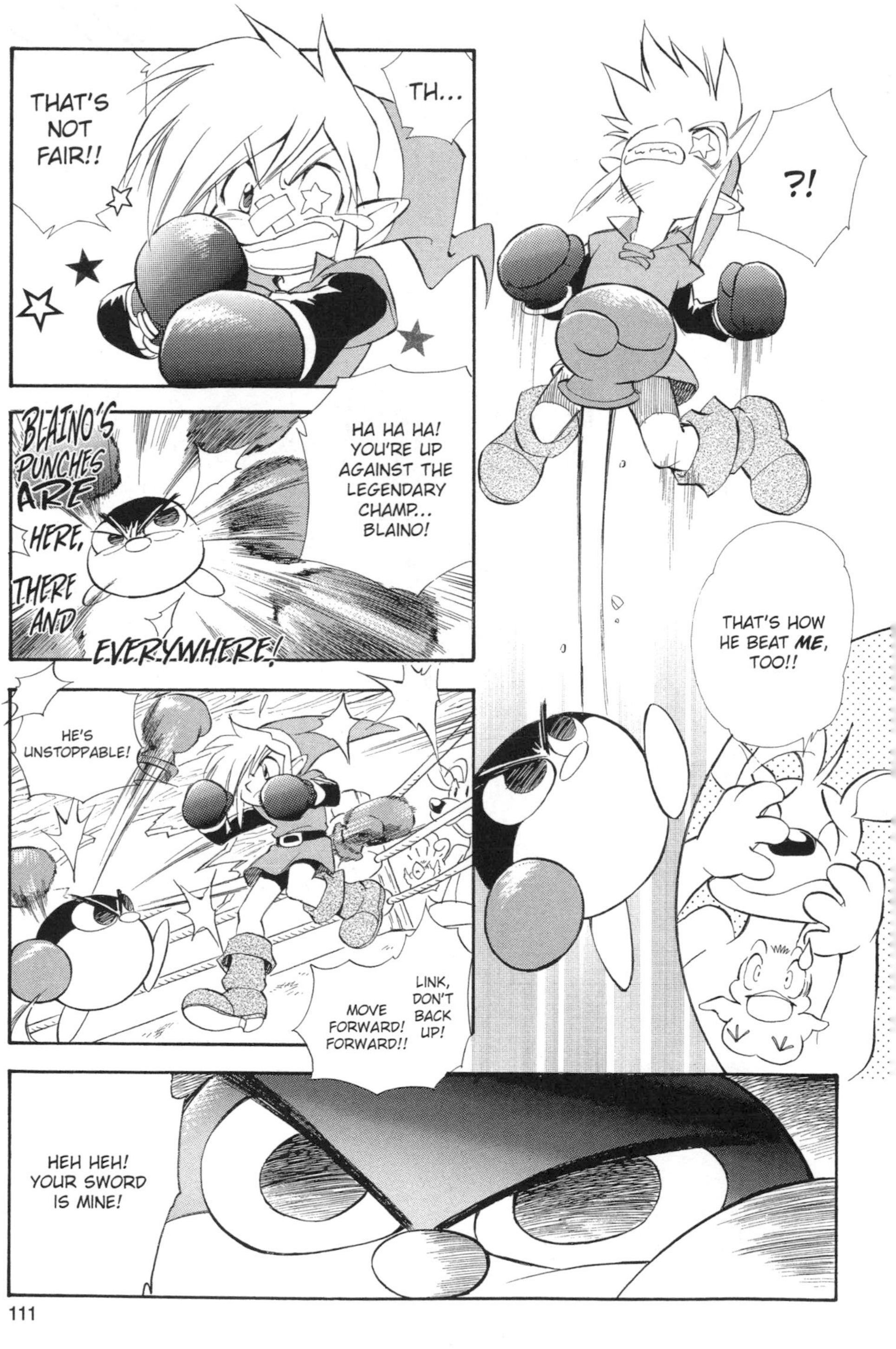
?!
THAT'S HOW HE BEAT ME, TOO!!
TH...
THAT'S NOT FAIR!!
HA HA HA! YOU'RE UP AGAINST THE LEGENDARY CHAMP... BLAINO!
BLAINO'S PUNCHES ARE HERE, THERE AND EVERYWHERE!
LINK, DON'T BACK UP!
MOVE FORWARD! FORWARD!!
HE'S UNSTOPPABLE!
HEH HEH! YOUR SWORD IS MINE!

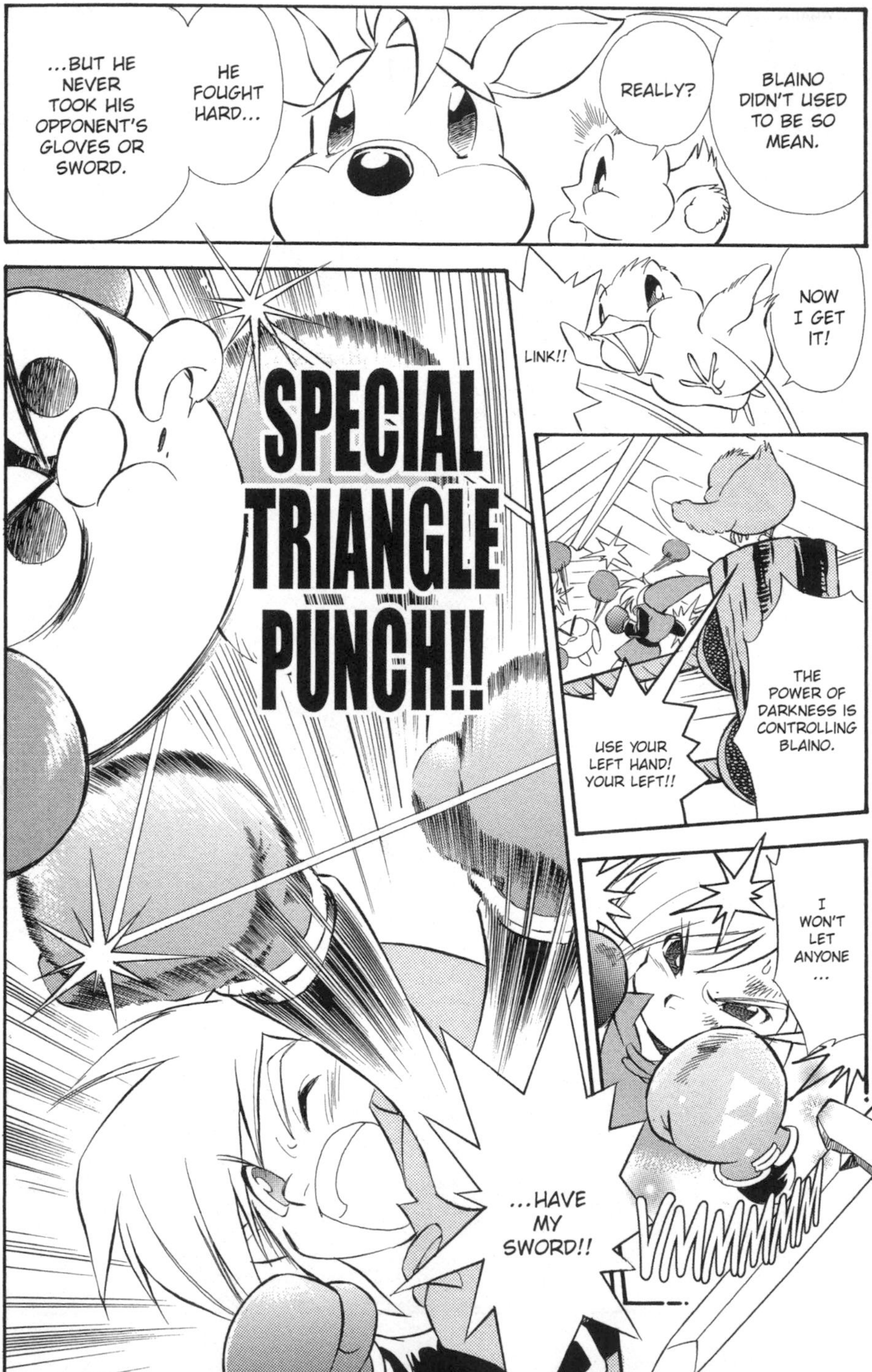
BLAINO DIDN'T USED TO BE SO MEAN.
REALLY?
HE FOUGHT HARD...
...BUT HE NEVER TOOK HIS OPPONENT'S GLOVES OR SWORD.
NOW I GET IT!
LINK!!
THE POWER OF DARKNESS IS CONTROLLING BLAINO.
USE YOUR LEFT HAND! YOUR LEFT!!
I WON'T LET ANYONE ...
...HAVE MY SWORD!!
VMMMMMM
SPECIAL TRIANGLE PUNCH!!

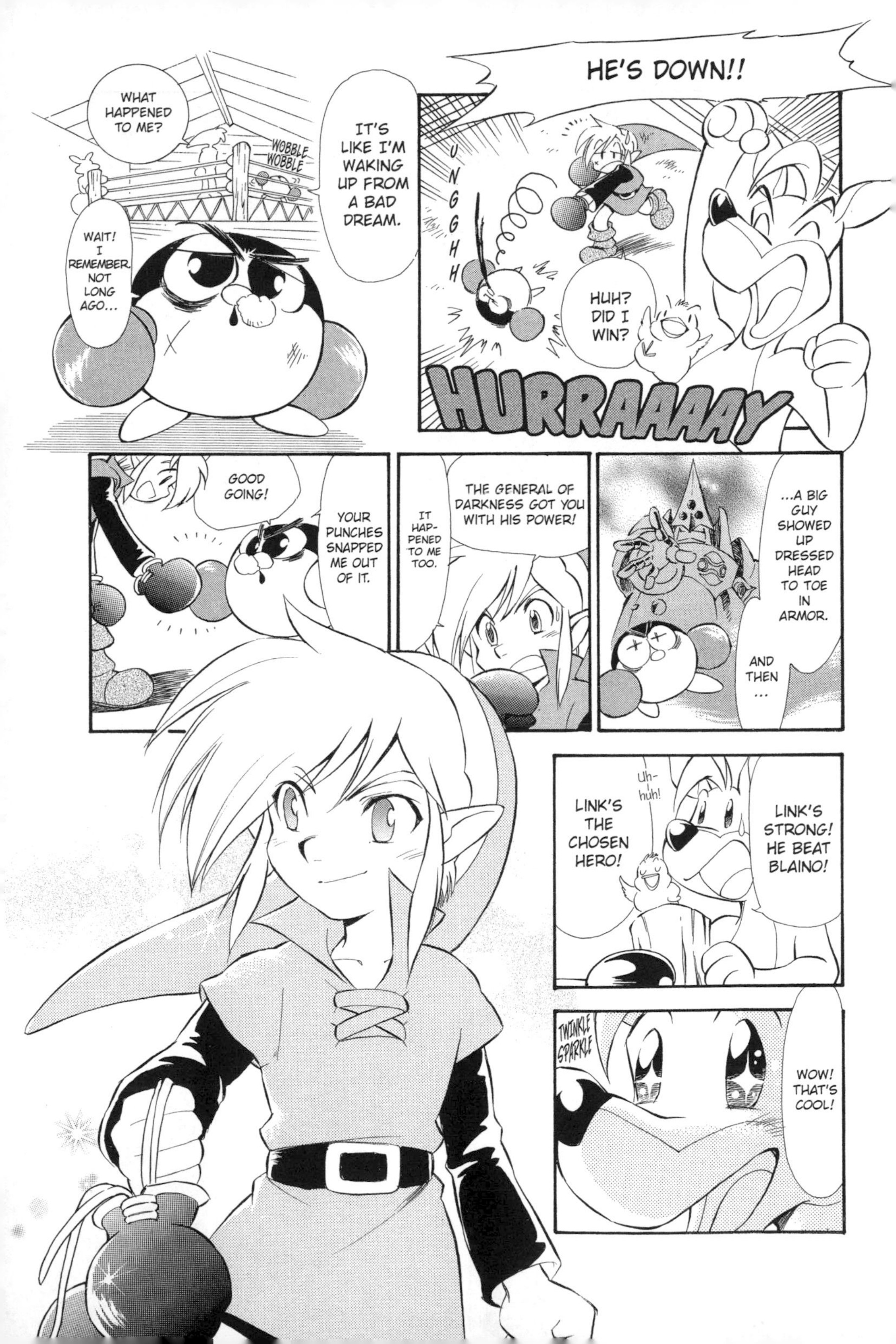
HE'S DOWN!!
UNGGHH
HUH? DID I WIN?
HURRAAAAY
WHAT HAPPENED TO ME?
IT'S LIKE I'M WAKING UP FROM A BAD DREAM.
WOBBLE WOBBLE
WAIT! I REMEMBER NOT LONG AGO...
...A BIG GUY SHOWED UP DRESSED HEAD TO TOE IN ARMOR.
AND THEN...
THE GENERAL OF DARKNESS GOT YOU WITH HIS POWER!
IT HAPPENED TO ME TOO.
YOUR PUNCHES SNAPPED ME OUT OF IT.
GOOD GOING!
LINK'S STRONG! HE BEAT BLAINO!
Uh-huh!
LINK'S THE CHOSEN HERO!
WOW! THAT'S COOL!
TWINKLE SPARKLE

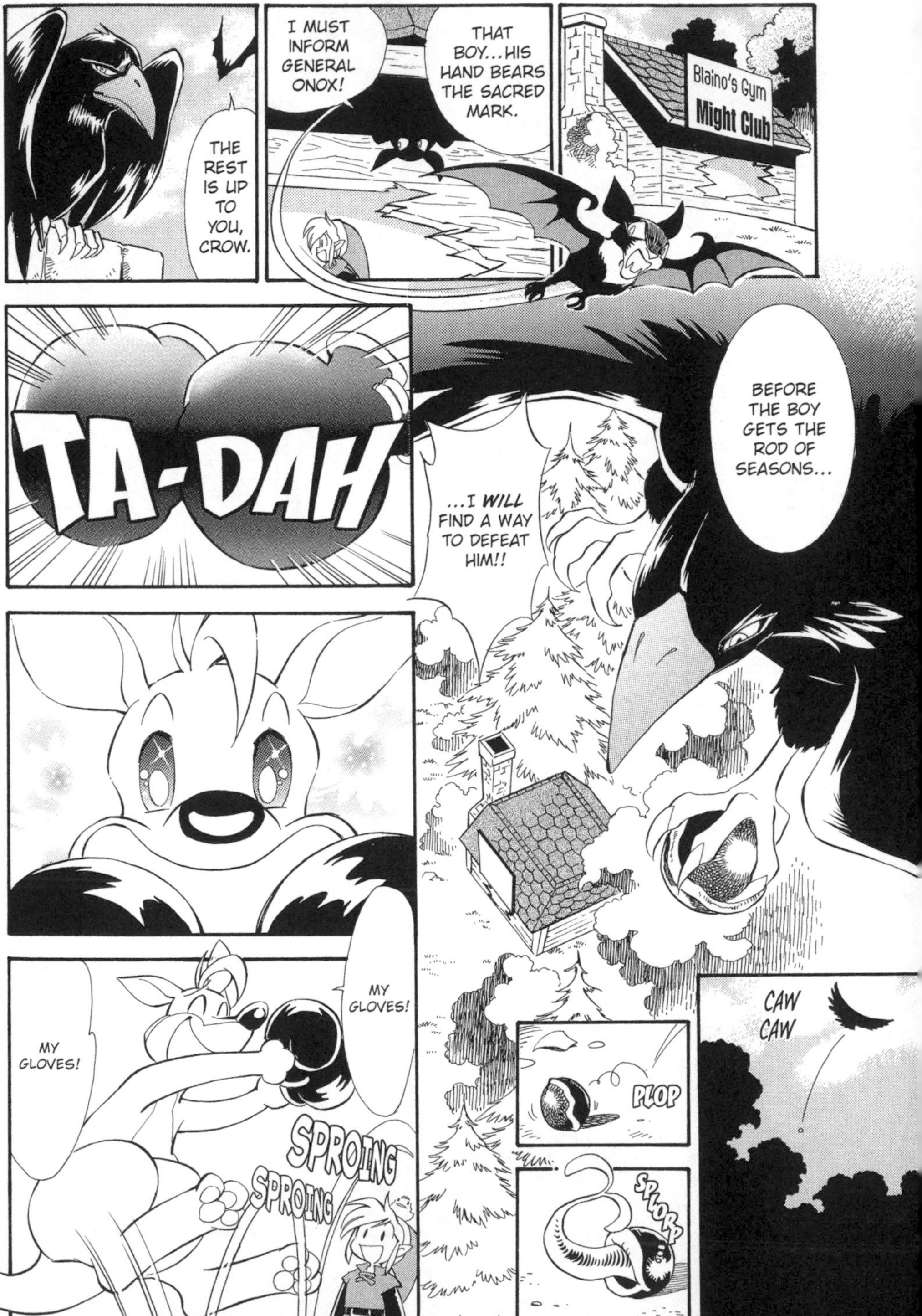
Blaino's Gym
Might Club
THAT BOY...HIS HAND BEARS THE SACRED MARK.
I MUST INFORM GENERAL ONOX!
THE REST IS UP TO YOU, CROW.
BEFORE THE BOY GETS THE ROD OF SEASONS...
...I *WILL* FIND A WAY TO DEFEAT HIM!!
CAW CAW
PLOP
SPLORP
TA-DAH
MY GLOVES!
MY GLOVES!
SPROING
SPROING

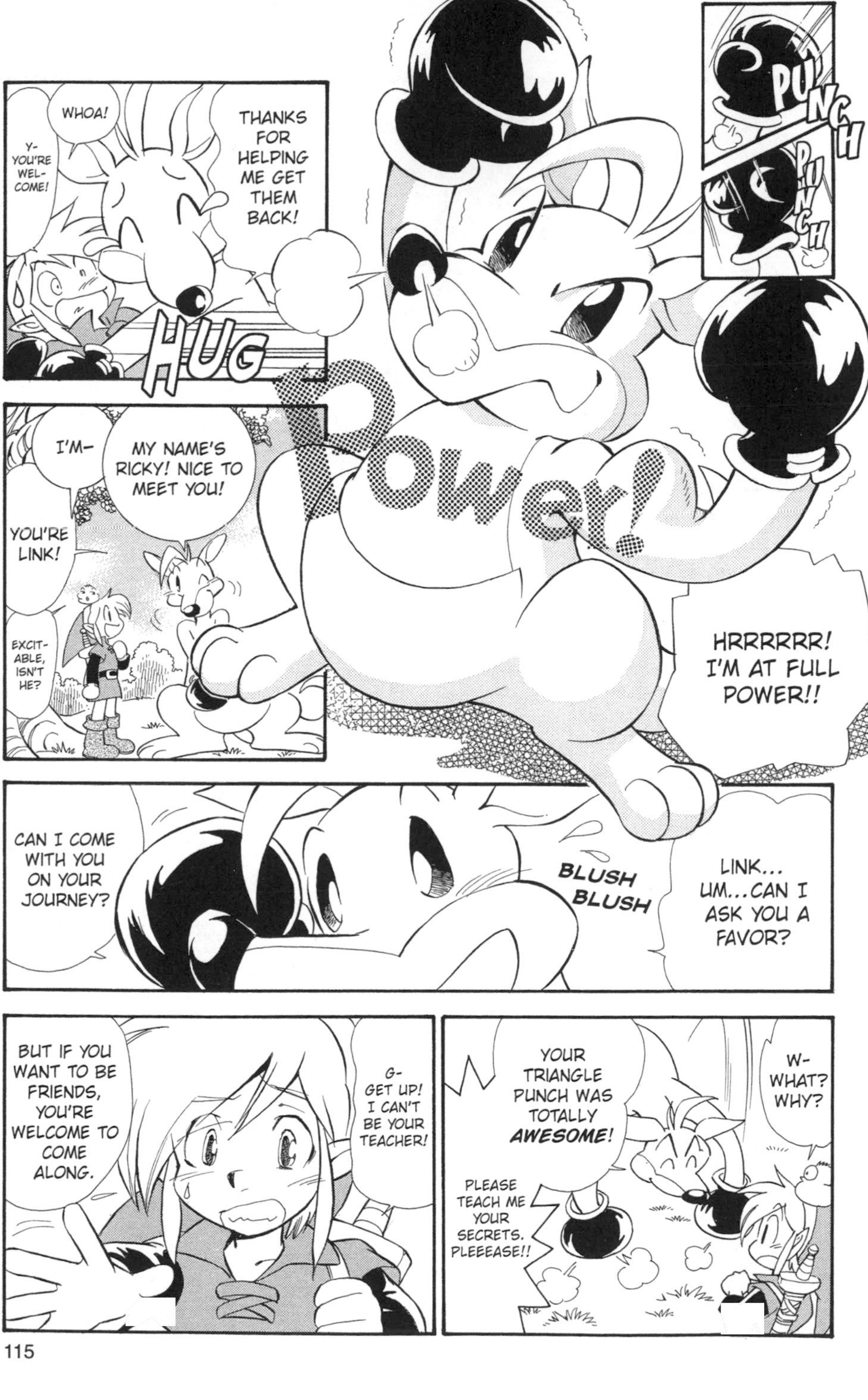
PUNCH
PUNCH
Power!
HRRRRRR! I'M AT FULL POWER!!
THANKS FOR HELPING ME GET THEM BACK!
WHOA!
Y-YOU'RE WEL-COME!
HUG
MY NAME'S RICKY! NICE TO MEET YOU!
I'M—
YOU'RE LINK!
EXCITABLE, ISN'T HE?
LINK... UM...CAN I ASK YOU A FAVOR?
BLUSH BLUSH
CAN I COME WITH YOU ON YOUR JOURNEY?
W-WHAT? WHY?
YOUR TRIANGLE PUNCH WAS TOTALLY **AWESOME**!
PLEASE TEACH ME YOUR SECRETS. PLEEEASE!!
G-GET UP! I CAN'T BE YOUR TEACHER!
BUT IF YOU WANT TO BE FRIENDS, YOU'RE WELCOME TO COME ALONG.

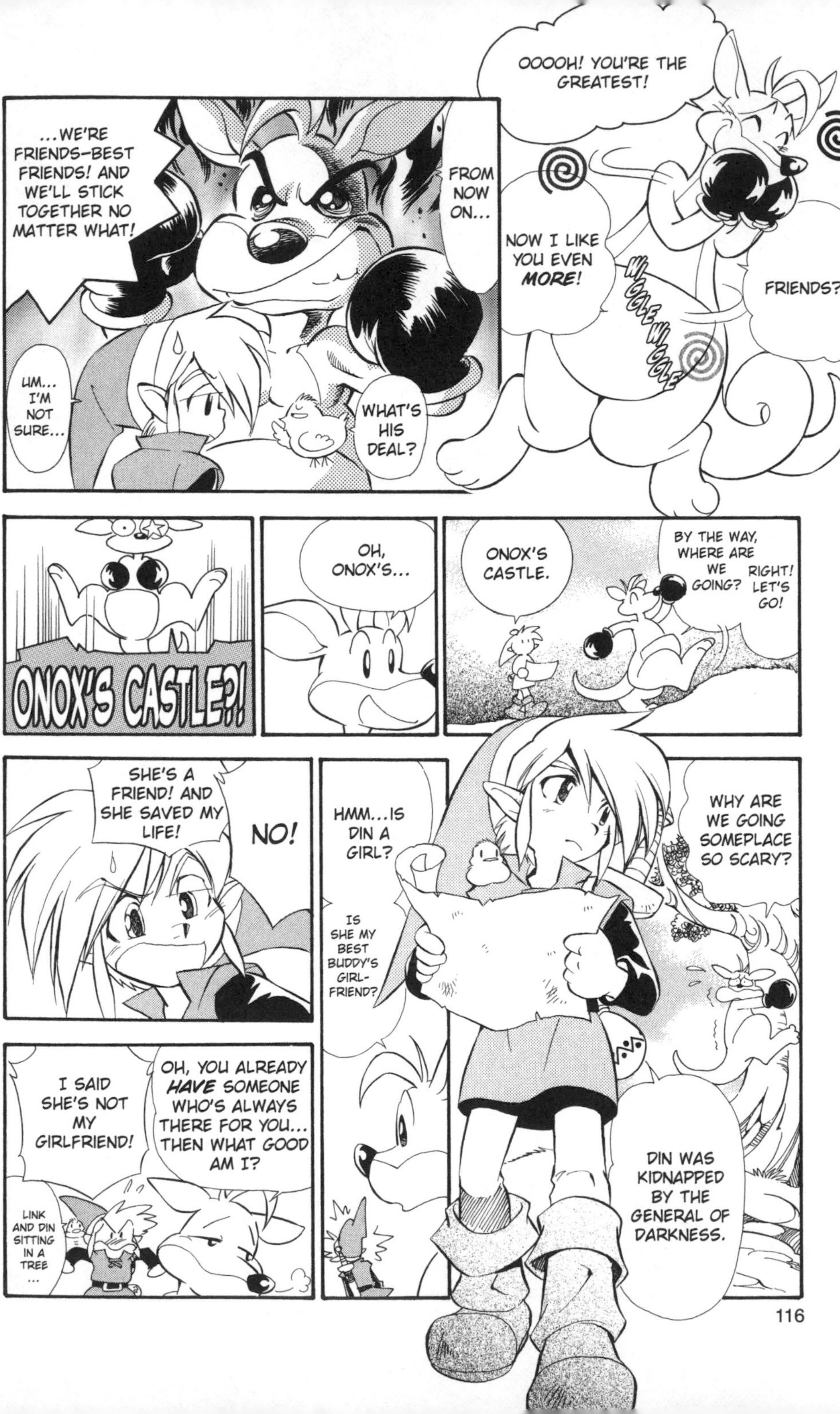
OOOOH! YOU'RE THE GREATEST!
FRIENDS?!
WIGGLE WIGGLE
NOW I LIKE YOU EVEN ***MORE***!
FROM NOW ON...
...WE'RE FRIENDS—BEST FRIENDS! AND WE'LL STICK TOGETHER NO MATTER WHAT!
WHAT'S HIS DEAL?
UM... I'M NOT SURE...
BY THE WAY, WHERE ARE WE GOING?
ONOX'S CASTLE.
RIGHT! LET'S GO!
OH, ONOX'S...
ONOX'S CASTLE?!
WHY ARE WE GOING SOMEPLACE SO SCARY?
DIN WAS KIDNAPPED BY THE GENERAL OF DARKNESS.
HMM...IS DIN A GIRL?
IS SHE MY BEST BUDDY'S GIRLFRIEND?
NO!
SHE'S A FRIEND! AND SHE SAVED MY LIFE!
OH, YOU ALREADY ***HAVE*** SOMEONE WHO'S ALWAYS THERE FOR YOU... THEN WHAT GOOD AM I?
I SAID SHE'S NOT MY GIRLFRIEND!
LINK AND DIN SITTING IN A TREE ...

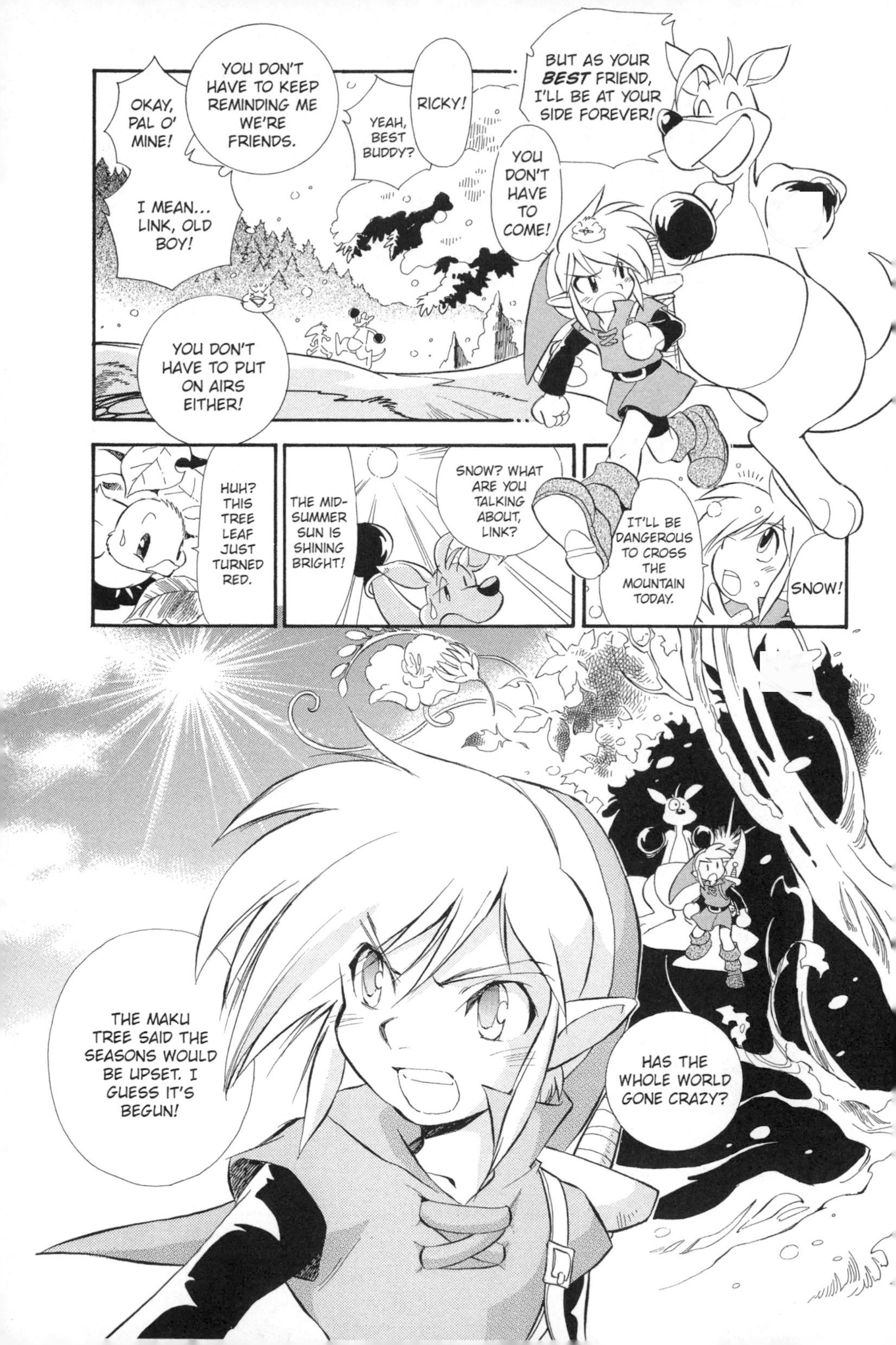
BUT AS YOUR **BEST** FRIEND, I'LL BE AT YOUR SIDE FOREVER!
YOU DON'T HAVE TO COME!
RICKY!
YEAH, BEST BUDDY?
YOU DON'T HAVE TO KEEP REMINDING ME WE'RE FRIENDS.
OKAY, PAL O' MINE!
I MEAN... LINK, OLD BOY!
YOU DON'T HAVE TO PUT ON AIRS EITHER!
SNOW!
IT'LL BE DANGEROUS TO CROSS THE MOUNTAIN TODAY.
SNOW? WHAT ARE YOU TALKING ABOUT, LINK?
THE MID-SUMMER SUN IS SHINING BRIGHT!
HUH? THIS TREE LEAF JUST TURNED RED.
HAS THE WHOLE WORLD GONE CRAZY?
THE MAKU TREE SAID THE SEASONS WOULD BE UPSET. I GUESS IT'S BEGUN!

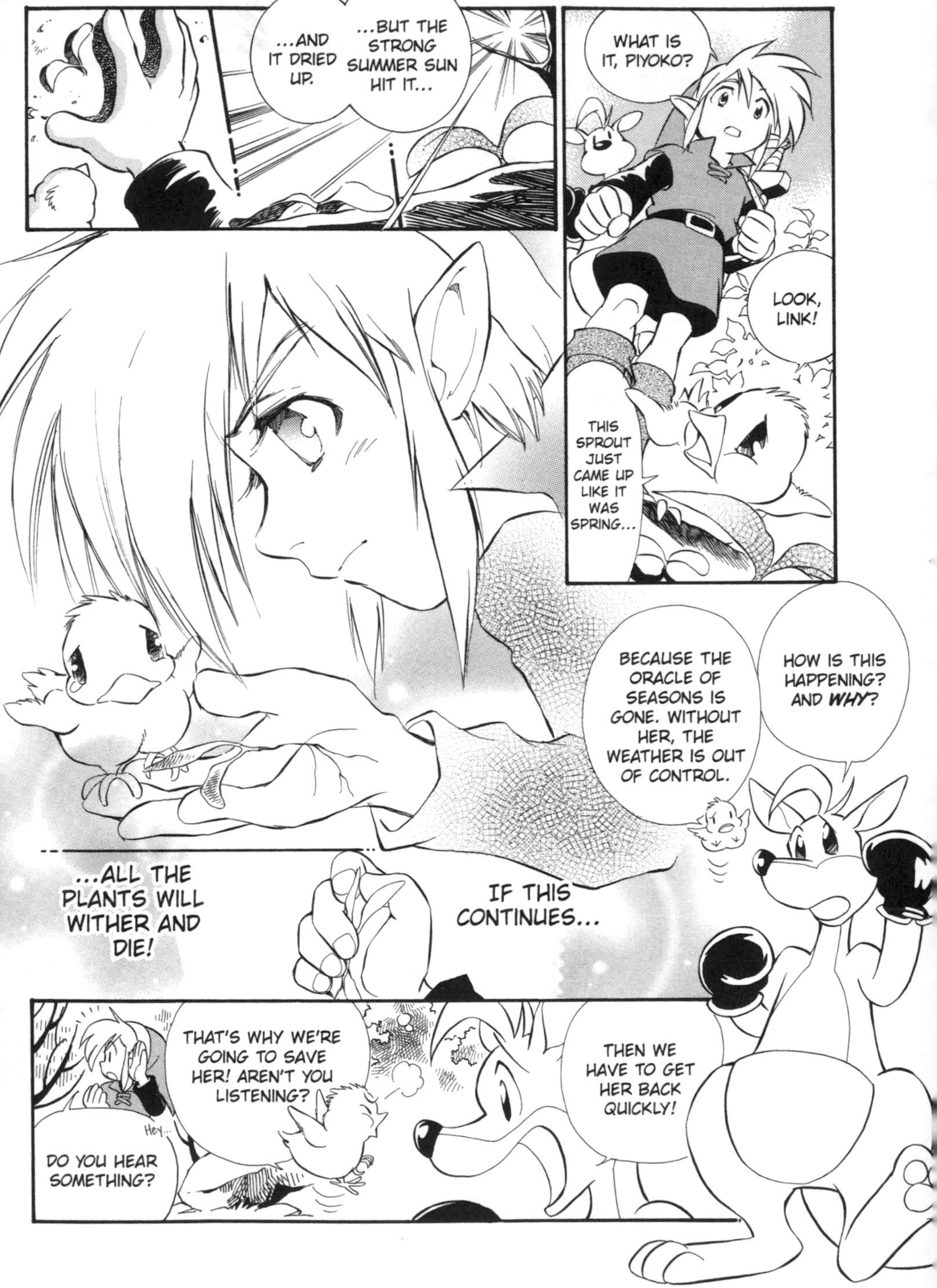
WHAT IS IT, PIYOKO?
LOOK, LINK!
THIS SPROUT JUST CAME UP LIKE IT WAS SPRING...
...BUT THE STRONG SUMMER SUN HIT IT...
...AND IT DRIED UP.
HOW IS THIS HAPPENING? AND *WHY*?
BECAUSE THE ORACLE OF SEASONS IS GONE. WITHOUT HER, THE WEATHER IS OUT OF CONTROL.
IF THIS CONTINUES...
...ALL THE PLANTS WILL WITHER AND DIE!
THEN WE HAVE TO GET HER BACK QUICKLY!
THAT'S WHY WE'RE GOING TO SAVE HER! AREN'T YOU LISTENING?
Hey...
DO YOU HEAR SOMETHING?

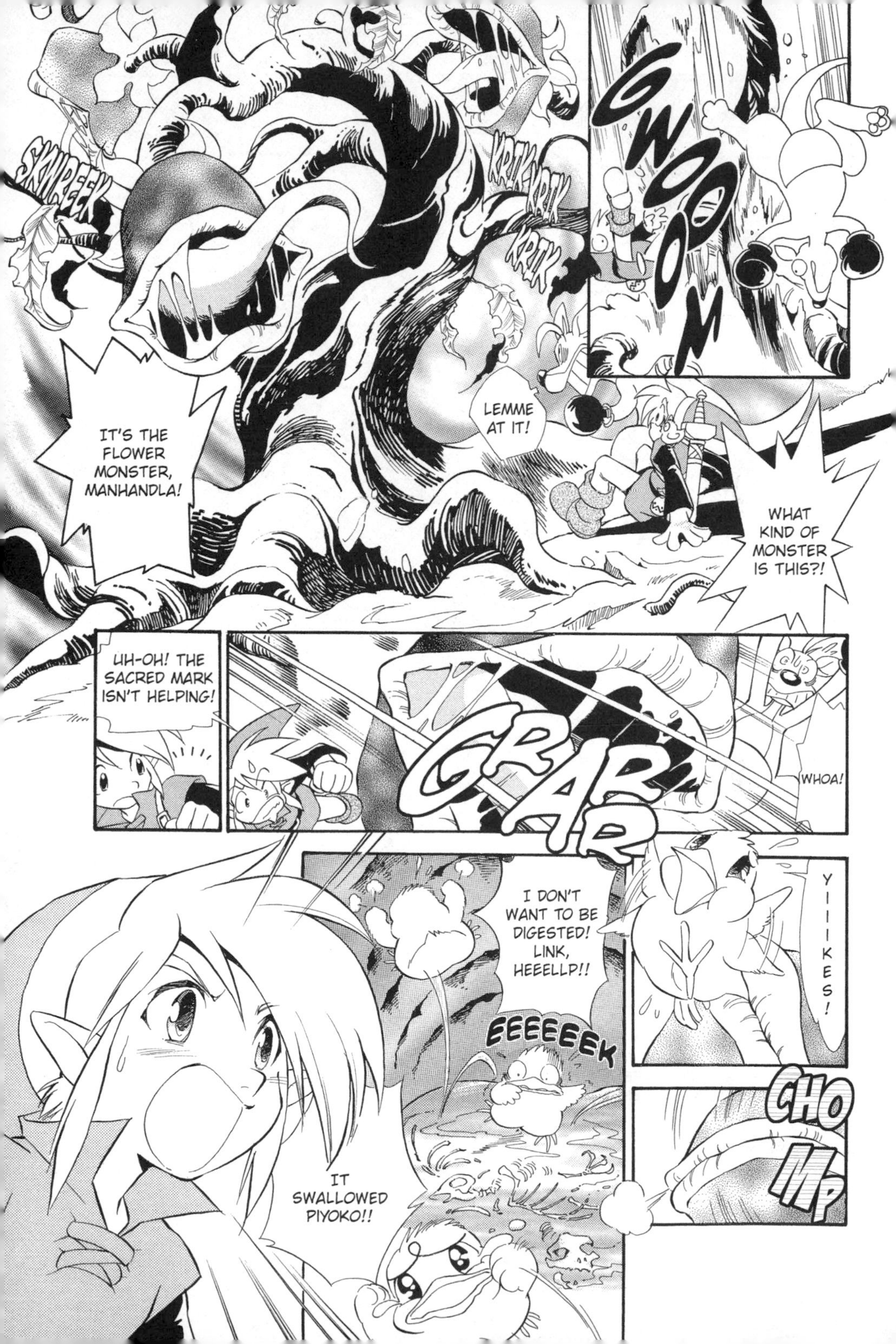
GWOOOOM
KRIK KRIK KRIK
SKWREEK
LEMME AT IT!
WHAT KIND OF MONSTER IS THIS?!
IT'S THE FLOWER MONSTER, MANHANDLA!
WHOA!
GRAR
UH-OH! THE SACRED MARK ISN'T HELPING!
YIIIKES!
CHOMP
I DON'T WANT TO BE DIGESTED! LINK, HEEELLP!!
EEEEEEK
IT SWALLOWED PIYOKO!!

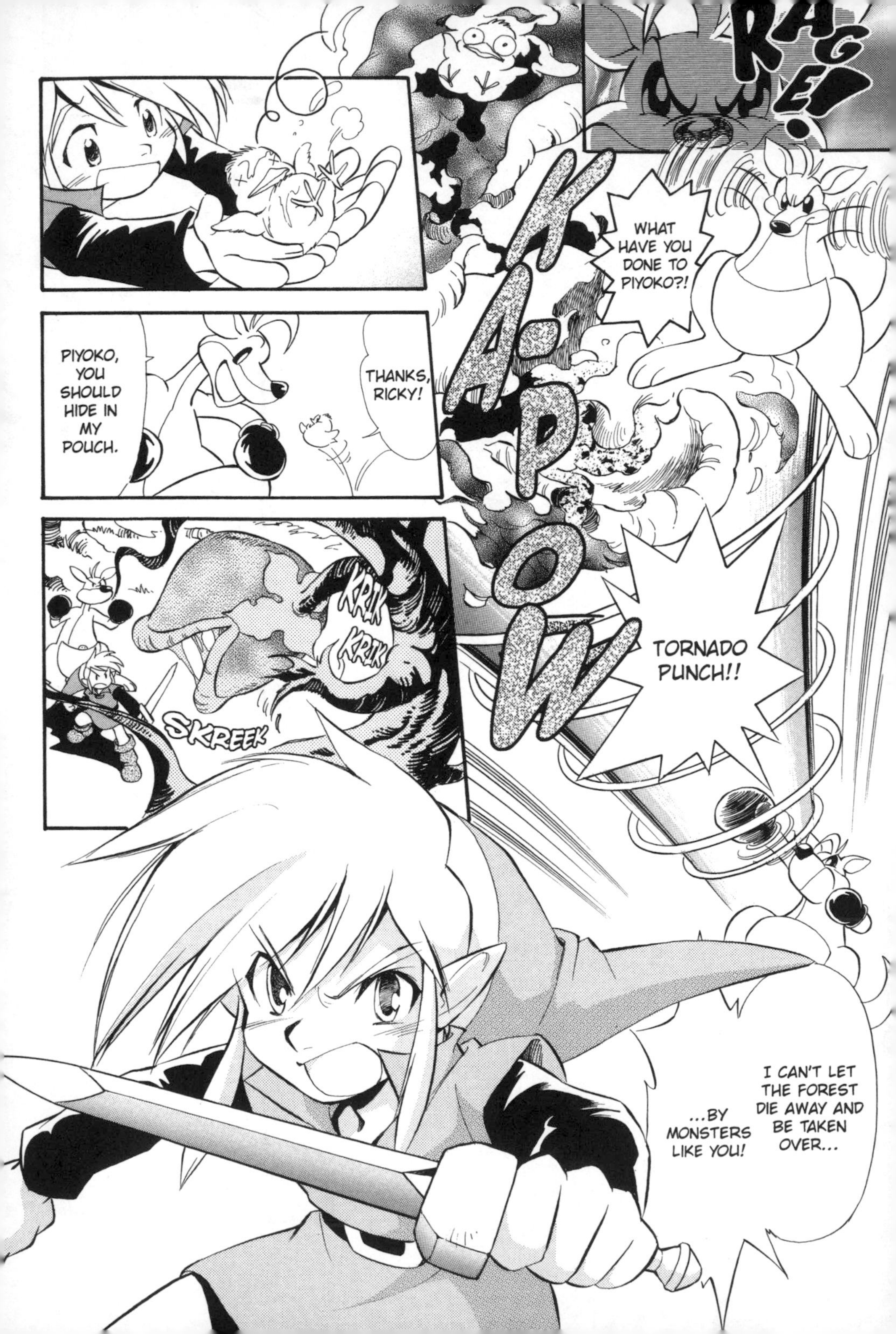
RAGE!
KA-POW!
WHAT HAVE YOU DONE TO PIYOKO?!
TORNADO PUNCH!!
THANKS, RICKY!
PIYOKO, YOU SHOULD HIDE IN MY POUCH.
KRIK KRIK
SKREEK
I CAN'T LET THE FOREST DIE AWAY AND BE TAKEN OVER...
...BY MONSTERS LIKE YOU!

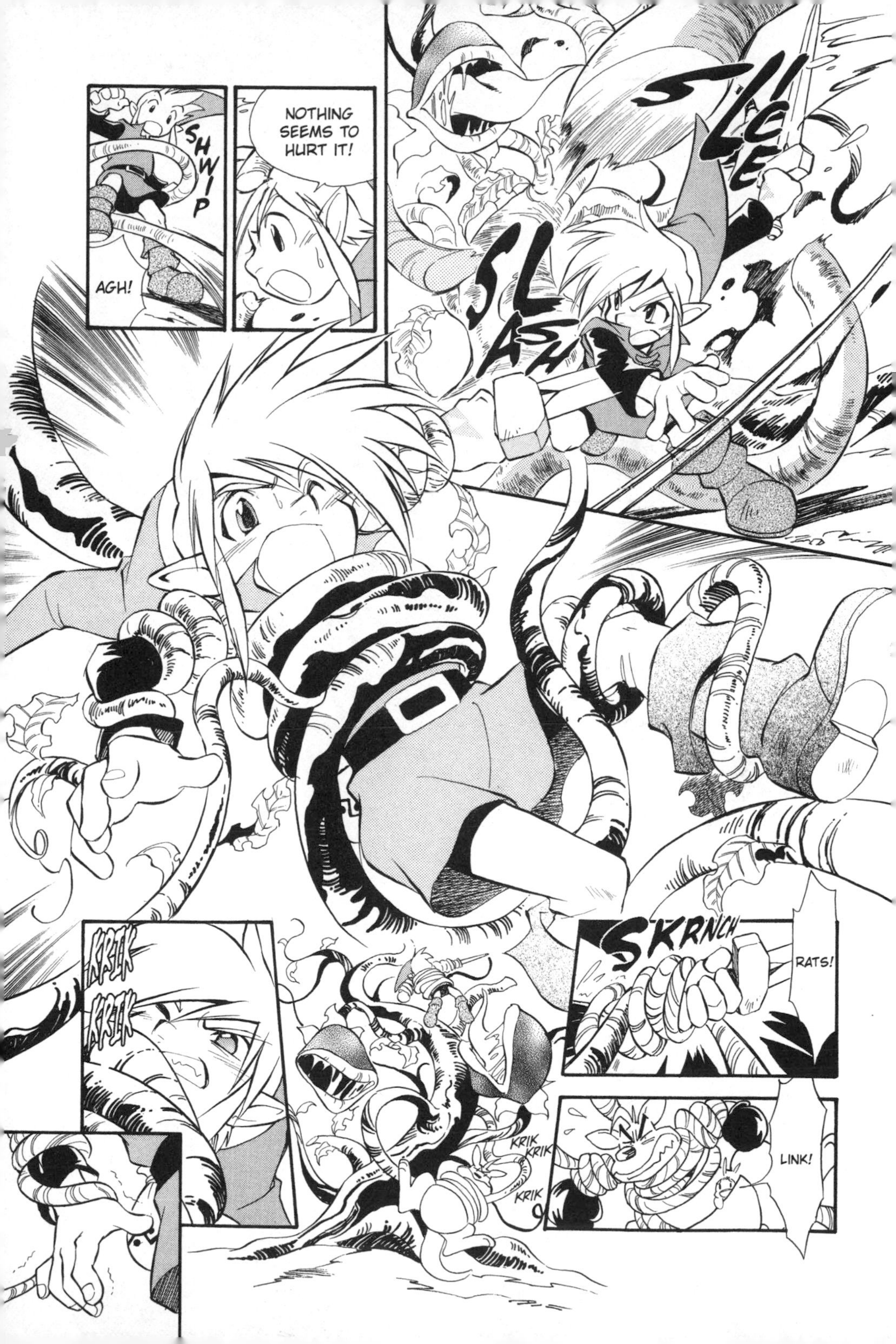
SLICE
SLASH
NOTHING SEEMS TO HURT IT!
SHWIP
AGH!
SKRNCH
RATS!
LINK!
KRIK KRIK KRIK
KRIK KRIK

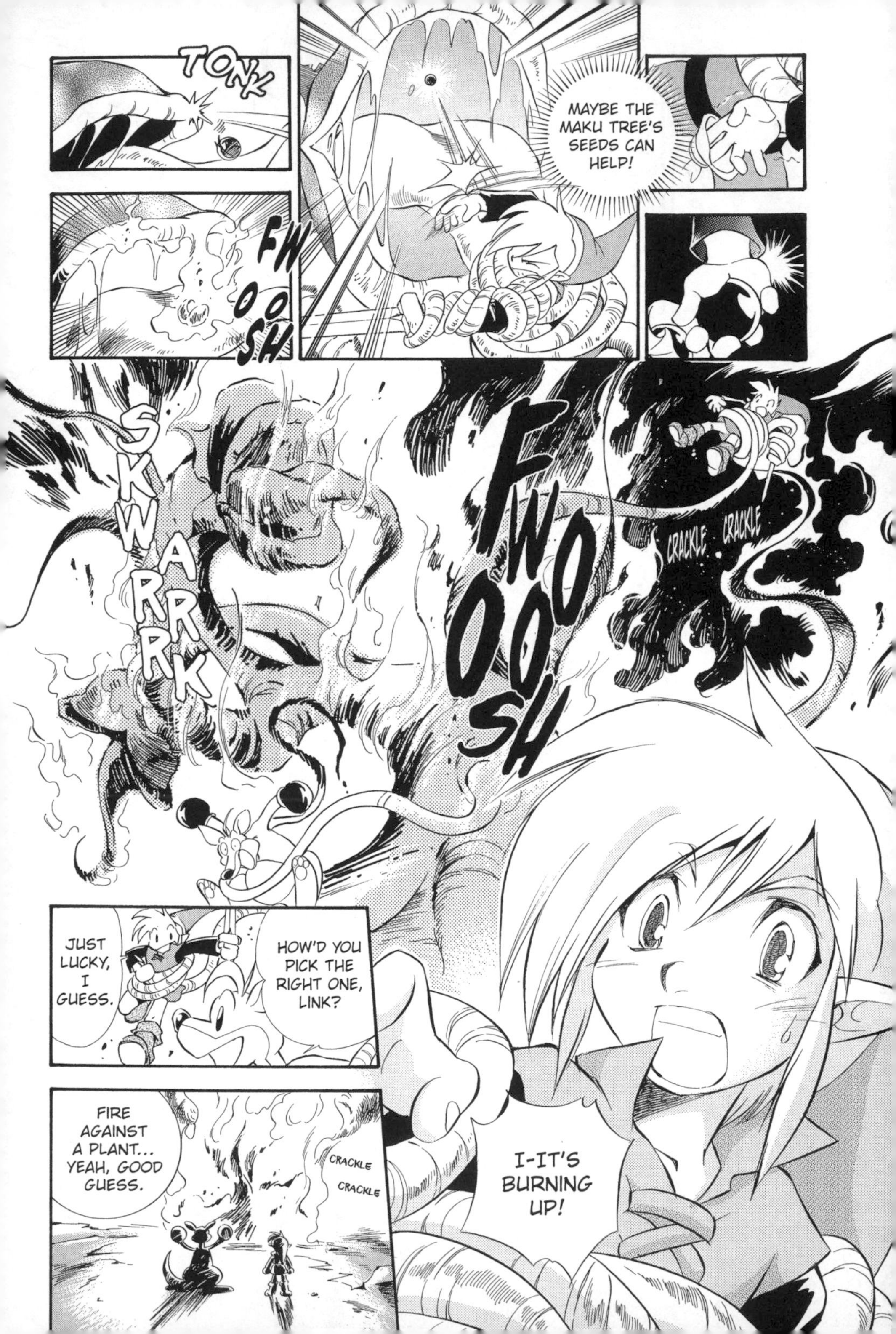
MAYBE THE MAKU TREE'S SEEDS CAN HELP!
TONK
FWOOSH
SKWARRRRK
FWOOOOSH
CRACKLE CRACKLE
I-IT'S BURNING UP!
HOW'D YOU PICK THE RIGHT ONE, LINK?
JUST LUCKY, I GUESS.
FIRE AGAINST A PLANT... YEAH, GOOD GUESS.
CRACKLE
CRACKLE

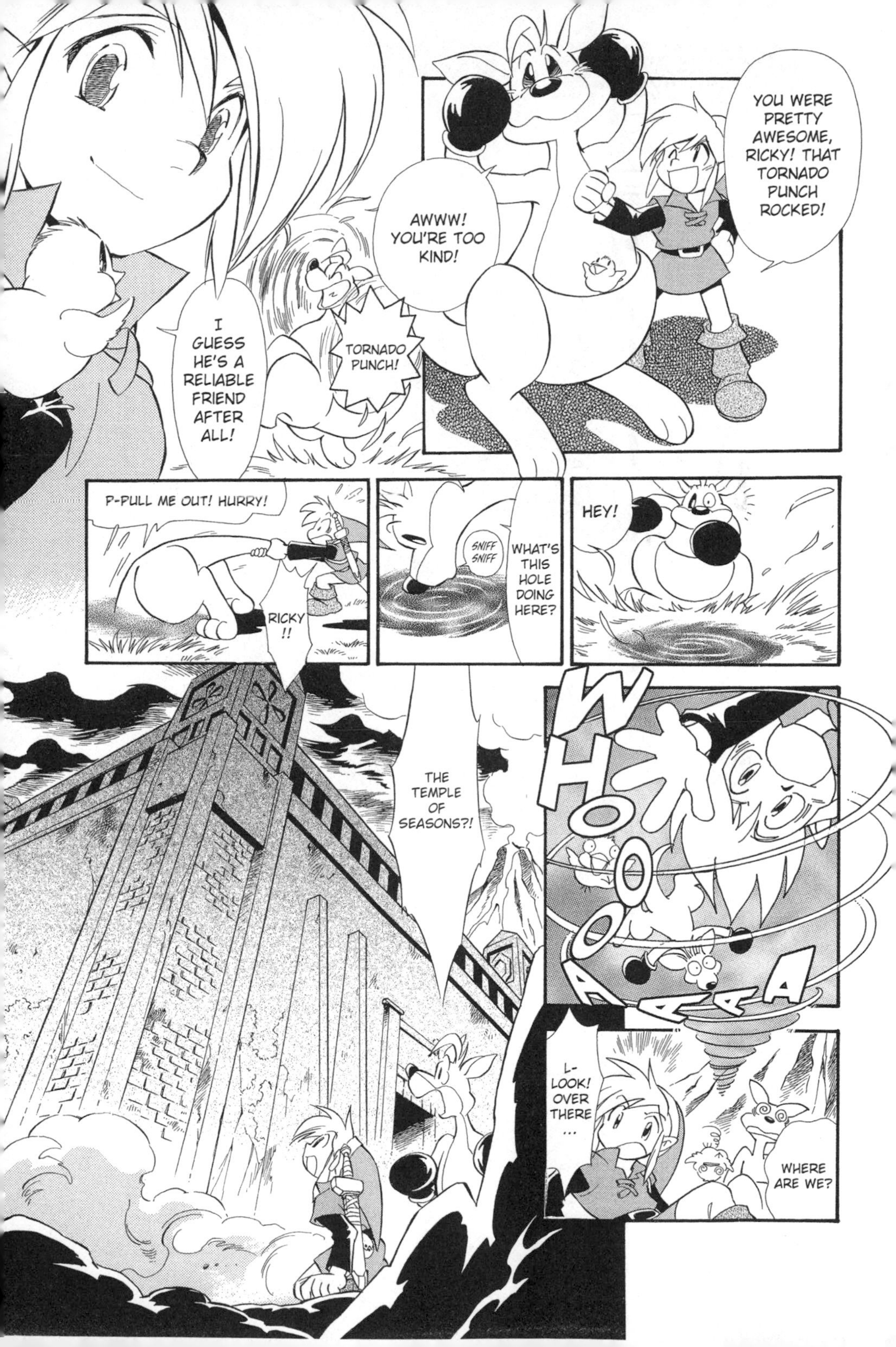
YOU WERE PRETTY AWESOME, RICKY! THAT TORNADO PUNCH ROCKED!
AWWW! YOU'RE TOO KIND!
TORNADO PUNCH!
I GUESS HE'S A RELIABLE FRIEND AFTER ALL!
HEY!
SNIFF SNIFF
WHAT'S THIS HOLE DOING HERE?
P-PULL ME OUT! HURRY!
RICKY!!
WHOOOOAAAA
WHERE ARE WE?
L-LOOK! OVER THERE...
THE TEMPLE OF SEASONS?!

CHAPTER 7
THE GREAT WITCH: MAPLE

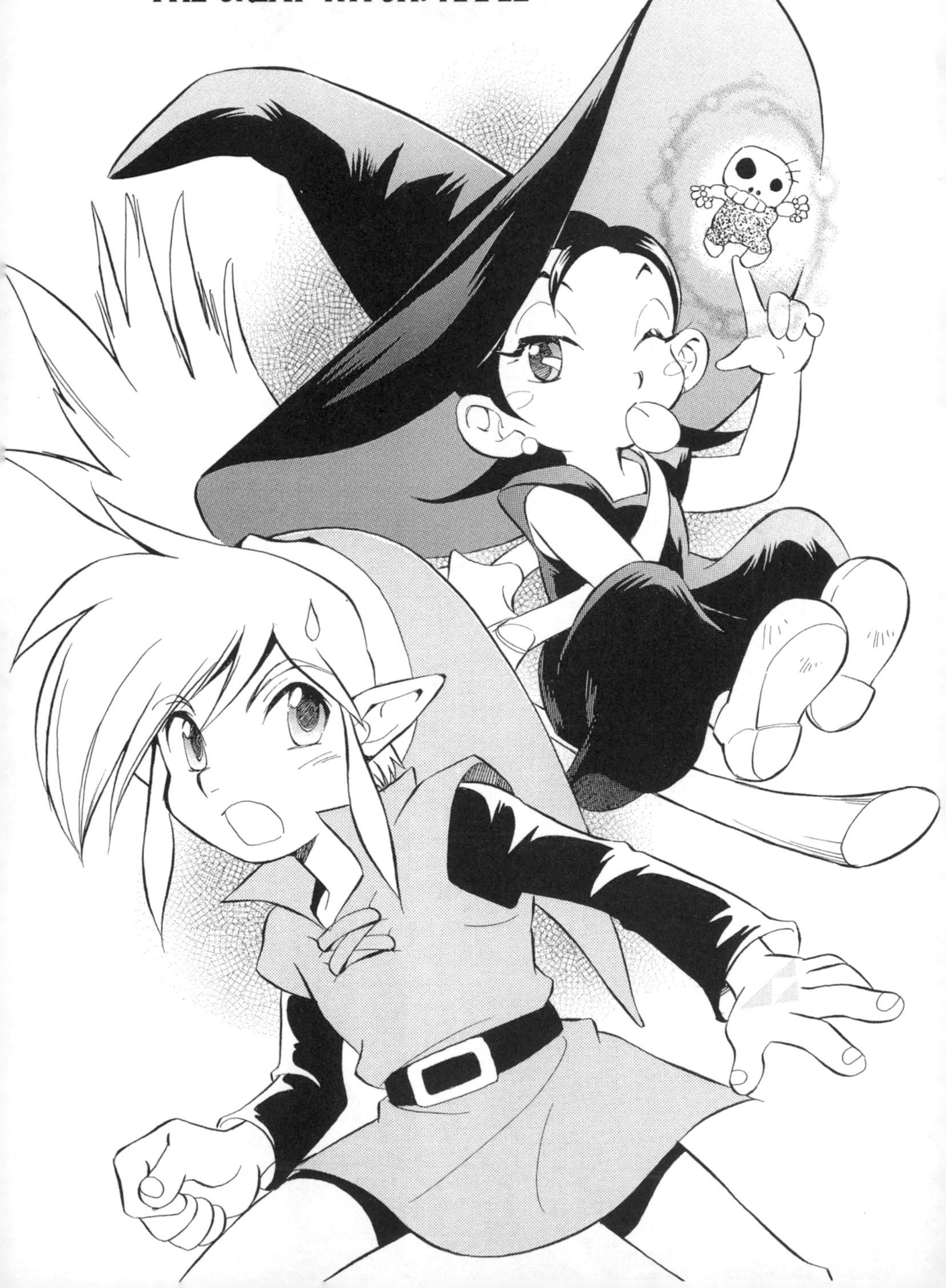

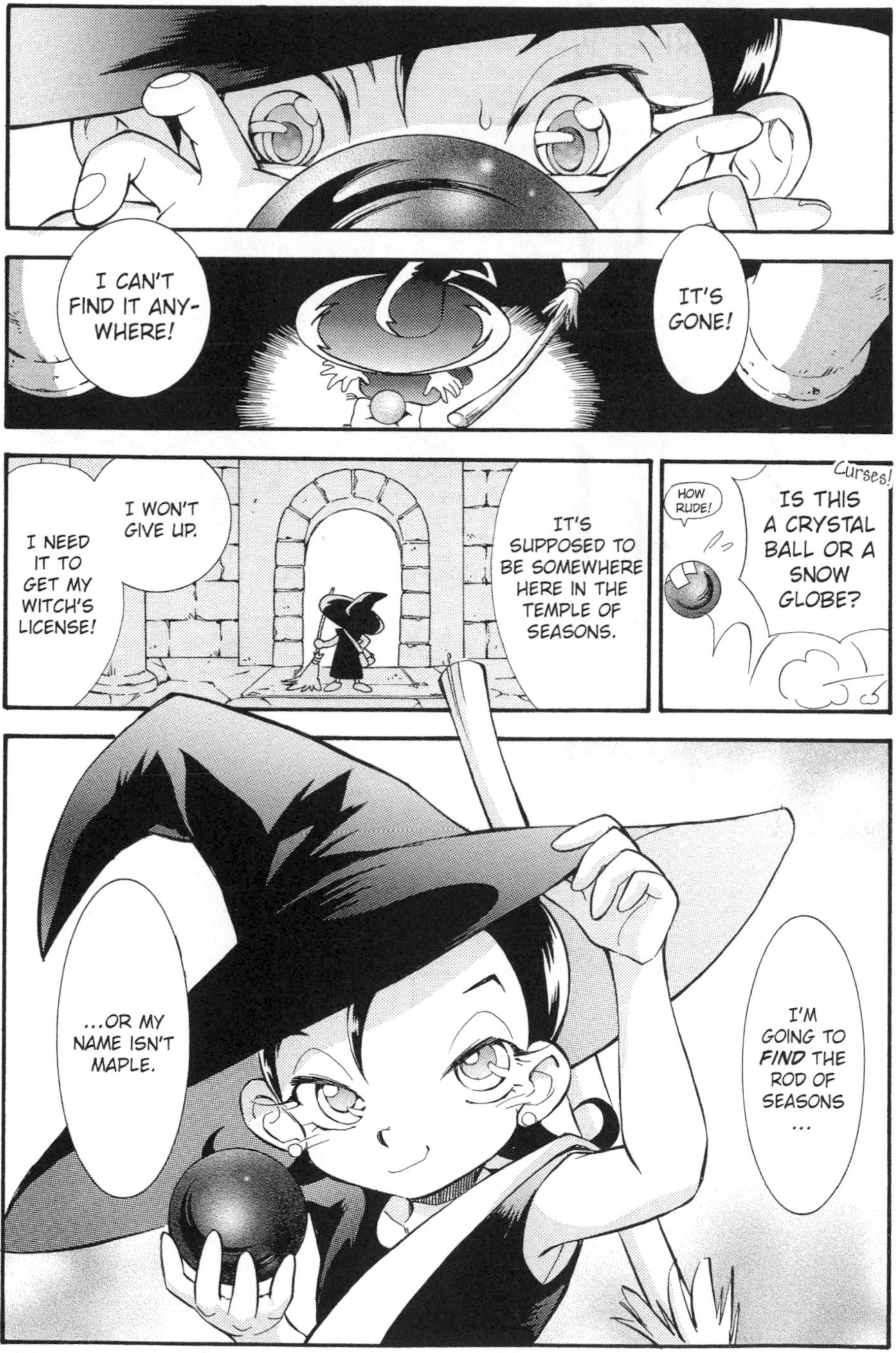
IT'S GONE!
I CAN'T FIND IT ANY-WHERE!
Curses!
IS THIS A CRYSTAL BALL OR A SNOW GLOBE?
HOW RUDE!
IT'S SUPPOSED TO BE SOMEWHERE HERE IN THE TEMPLE OF SEASONS.
I WON'T GIVE UP.
I NEED IT TO GET MY WITCH'S LICENSE!
I'M GOING TO *FIND* THE ROD OF SEASONS...
...OR MY NAME ISN'T MAPLE.

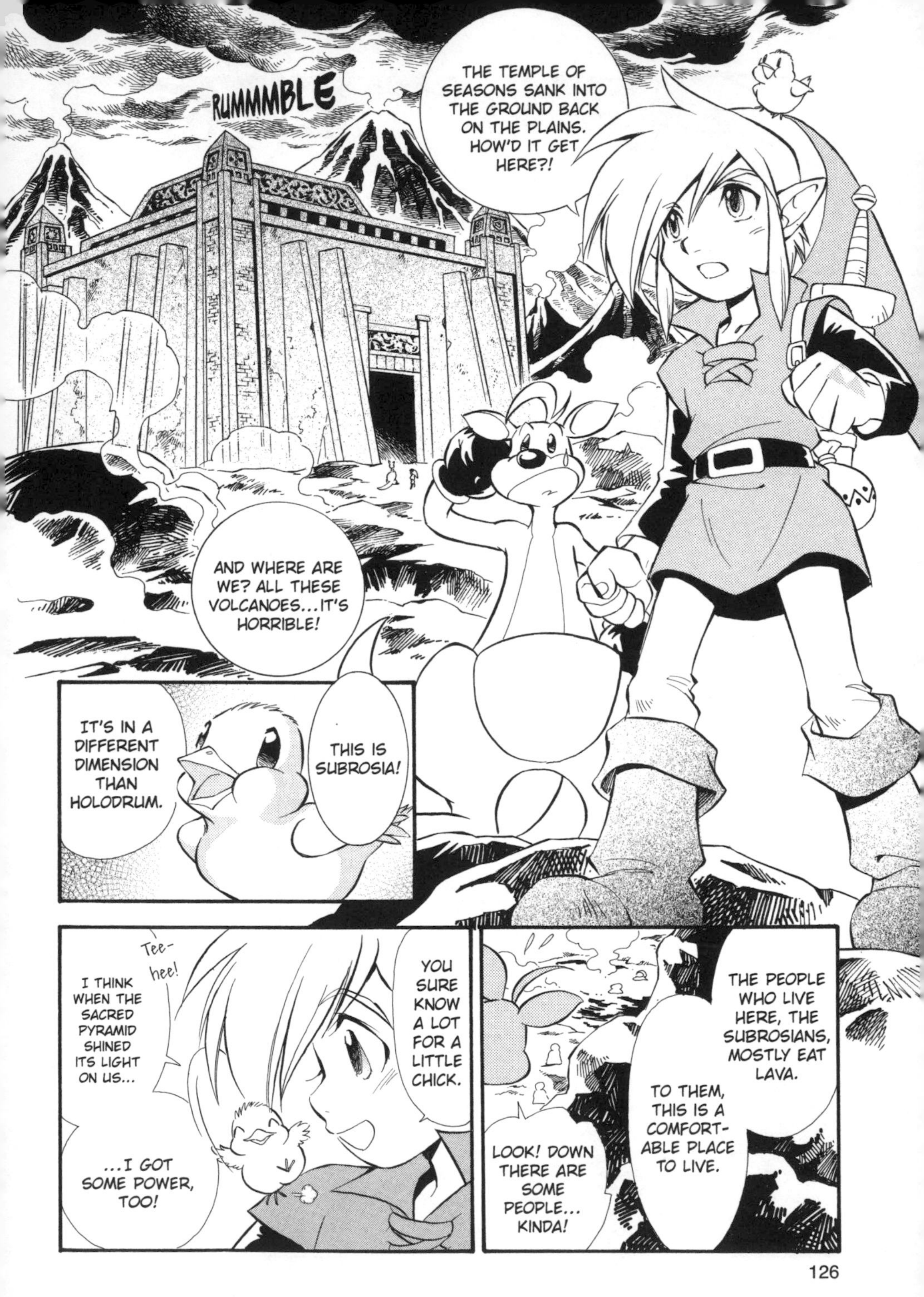
THE TEMPLE OF SEASONS SANK INTO THE GROUND BACK ON THE PLAINS. HOW'D IT GET HERE?!
RUMMMBLE
AND WHERE ARE WE? ALL THESE VOLCANOES...IT'S HORRIBLE!
THIS IS SUBROSIA!
IT'S IN A DIFFERENT DIMENSION THAN HOLODRUM.
THE PEOPLE WHO LIVE HERE, THE SUBROSIANS, MOSTLY EAT LAVA.
TO THEM, THIS IS A COMFORT-ABLE PLACE TO LIVE.
LOOK! DOWN THERE ARE SOME PEOPLE... KINDA!
YOU SURE KNOW A LOT FOR A LITTLE CHICK.
Tee-hee!
I THINK WHEN THE SACRED PYRAMID SHINED ITS LIGHT ON US...
...I GOT SOME POWER, TOO!

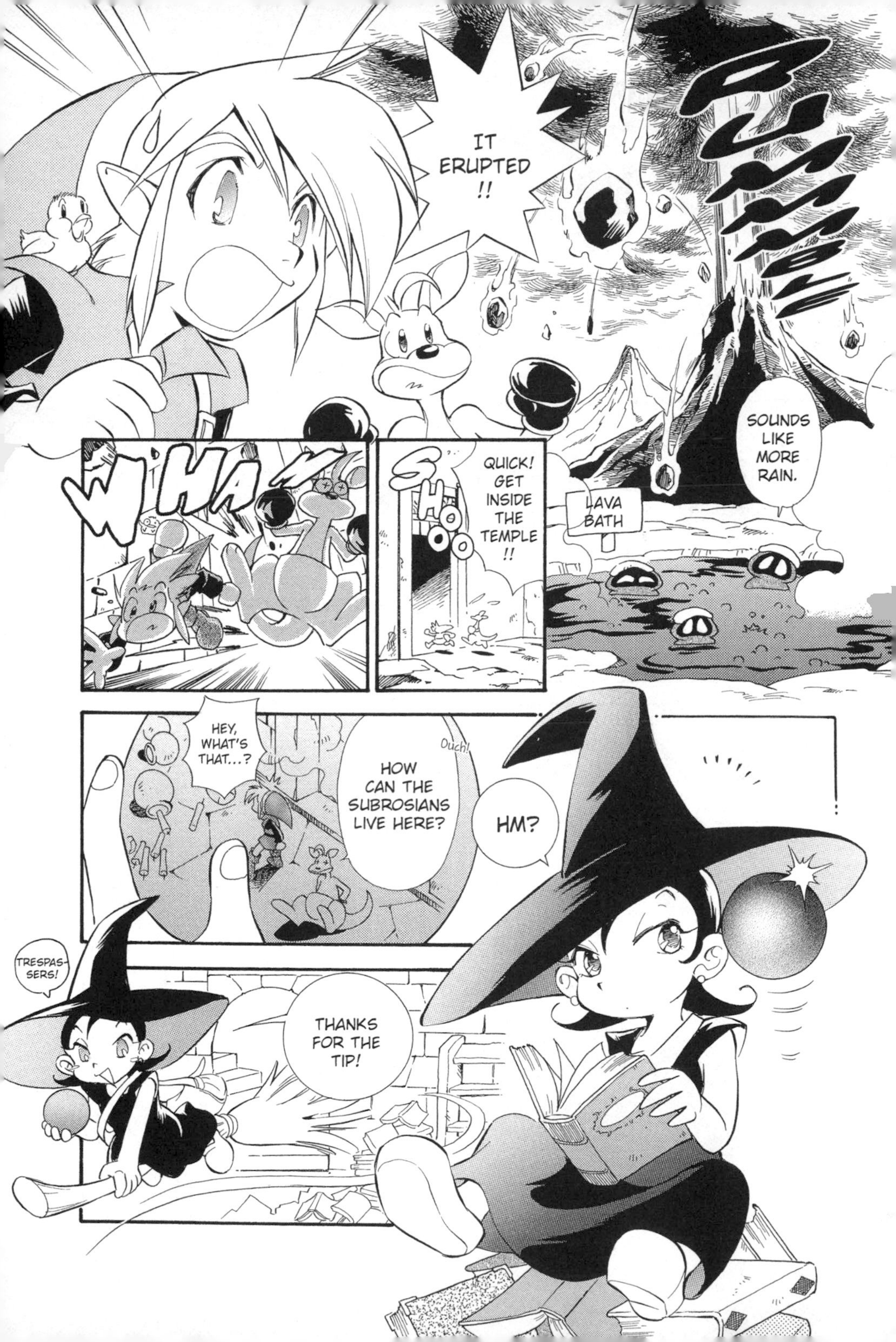
IT ERUPTED!!
SOUNDS LIKE MORE RAIN.
LAVA BATH
QUICK! GET INSIDE THE TEMPLE!!
SHOOO
WHAM
HM?
HOW CAN THE SUBROSIANS LIVE HERE?
Ouch!
HEY, WHAT'S THAT...?
THANKS FOR THE TIP!
TRESPASSERS!

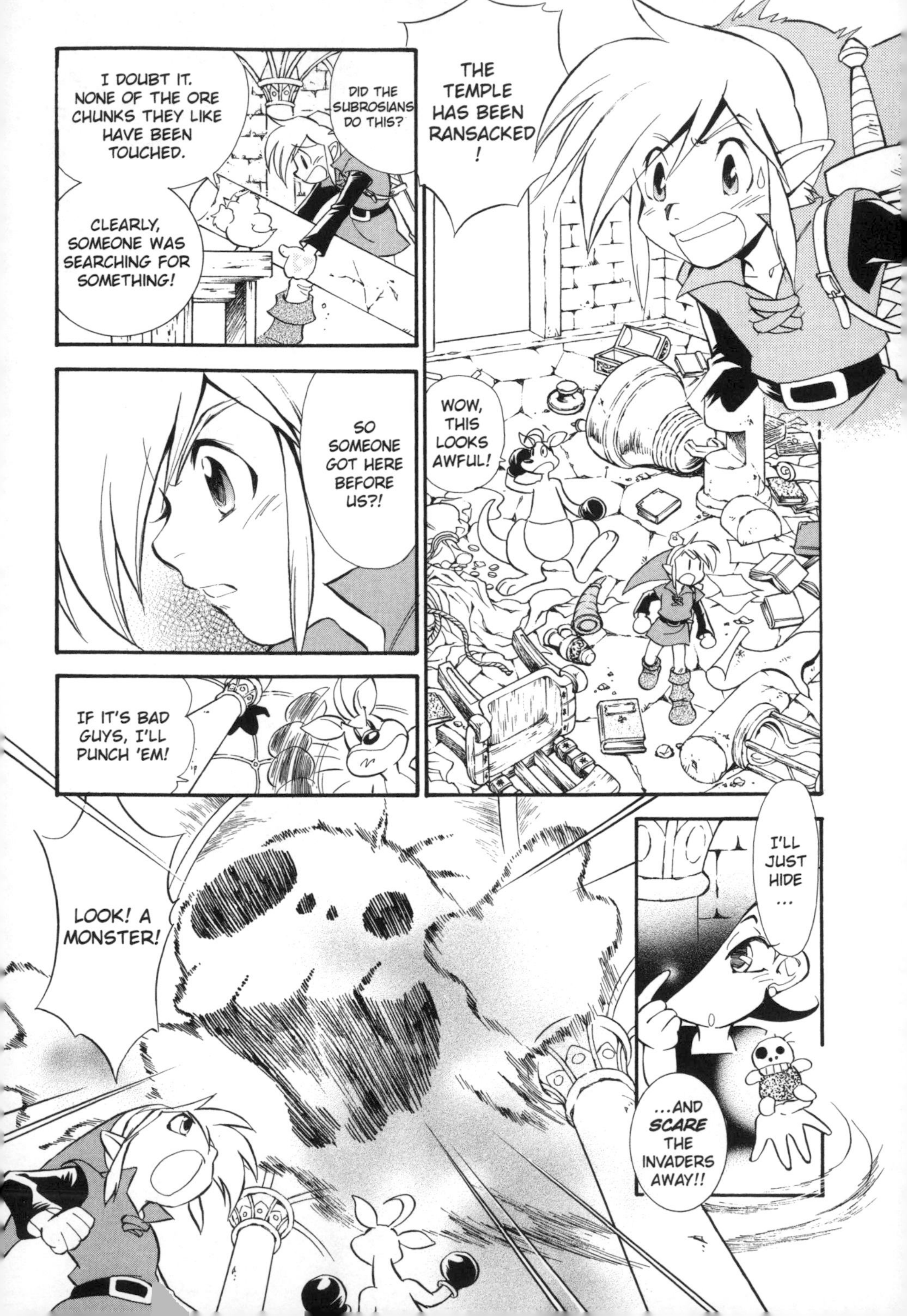
THE TEMPLE HAS BEEN RANSACKED!
WOW, THIS LOOKS AWFUL!
DID THE SUBROSIANS DO THIS?
I DOUBT IT. NONE OF THE ORE CHUNKS THEY LIKE HAVE BEEN TOUCHED.
CLEARLY, SOMEONE WAS SEARCHING FOR SOMETHING!
SO SOMEONE GOT HERE BEFORE US?!
IF IT'S BAD GUYS, I'LL PUNCH 'EM!
I'LL JUST HIDE...
...AND SCARE THE INVADERS AWAY!!
LOOK! A MONSTER!

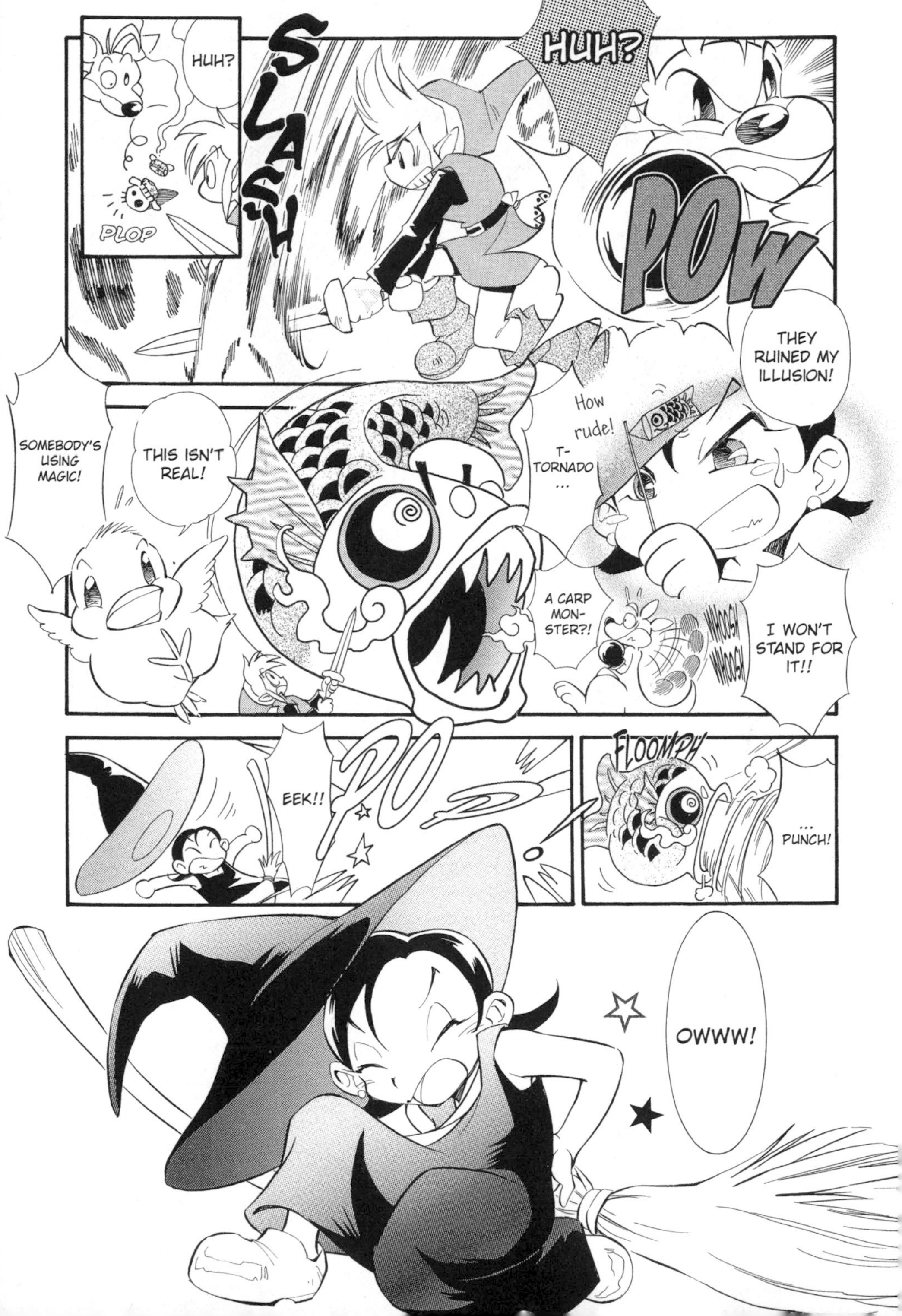

HUH?
POW
SLASH
HUH?
PLOP
THEY RUINED MY ILLUSION!
How rude!
T-TORNADO ...
WHOOSH WHOOSH
I WON'T STAND FOR IT!!
A CARP MON-STER?!
THIS ISN'T REAL!
SOMEBODY'S USING MAGIC!
FLOOMPH
... PUNCH!
EEK!!
OWWW!

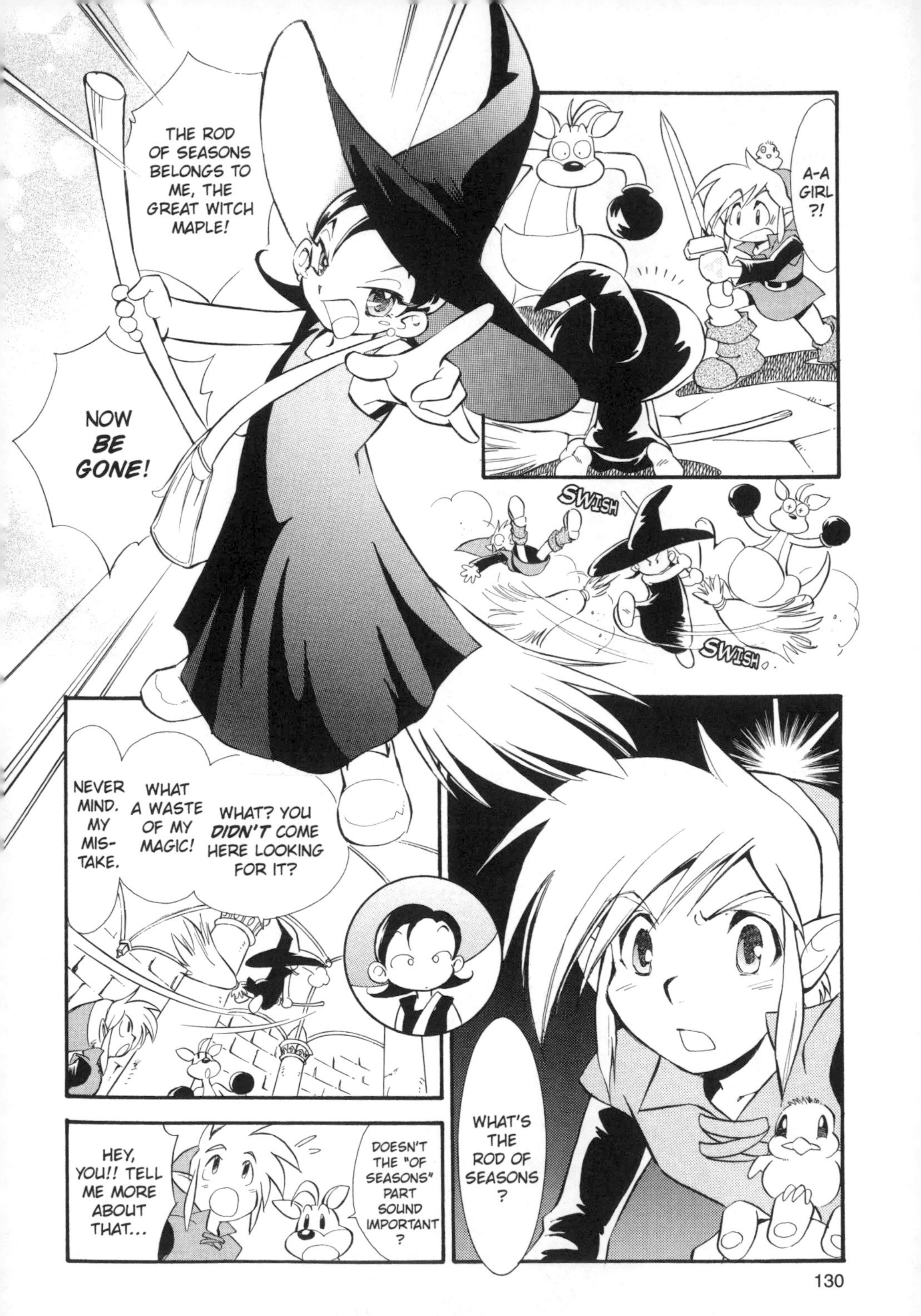
A-A GIRL ?!
THE ROD OF SEASONS BELONGS TO ME, THE GREAT WITCH MAPLE!
NOW *BE GONE*!
SWISH
SWISH
WHAT'S THE ROD OF SEASONS ?
WHAT? YOU *DIDN'T* COME HERE LOOKING FOR IT?
WHAT A WASTE OF MY MAGIC!
NEVER MIND. MY MIS-TAKE.
DOESN'T THE "OF SEASONS" PART SOUND IMPORTANT ?
HEY, YOU!! TELL ME MORE ABOUT THAT...

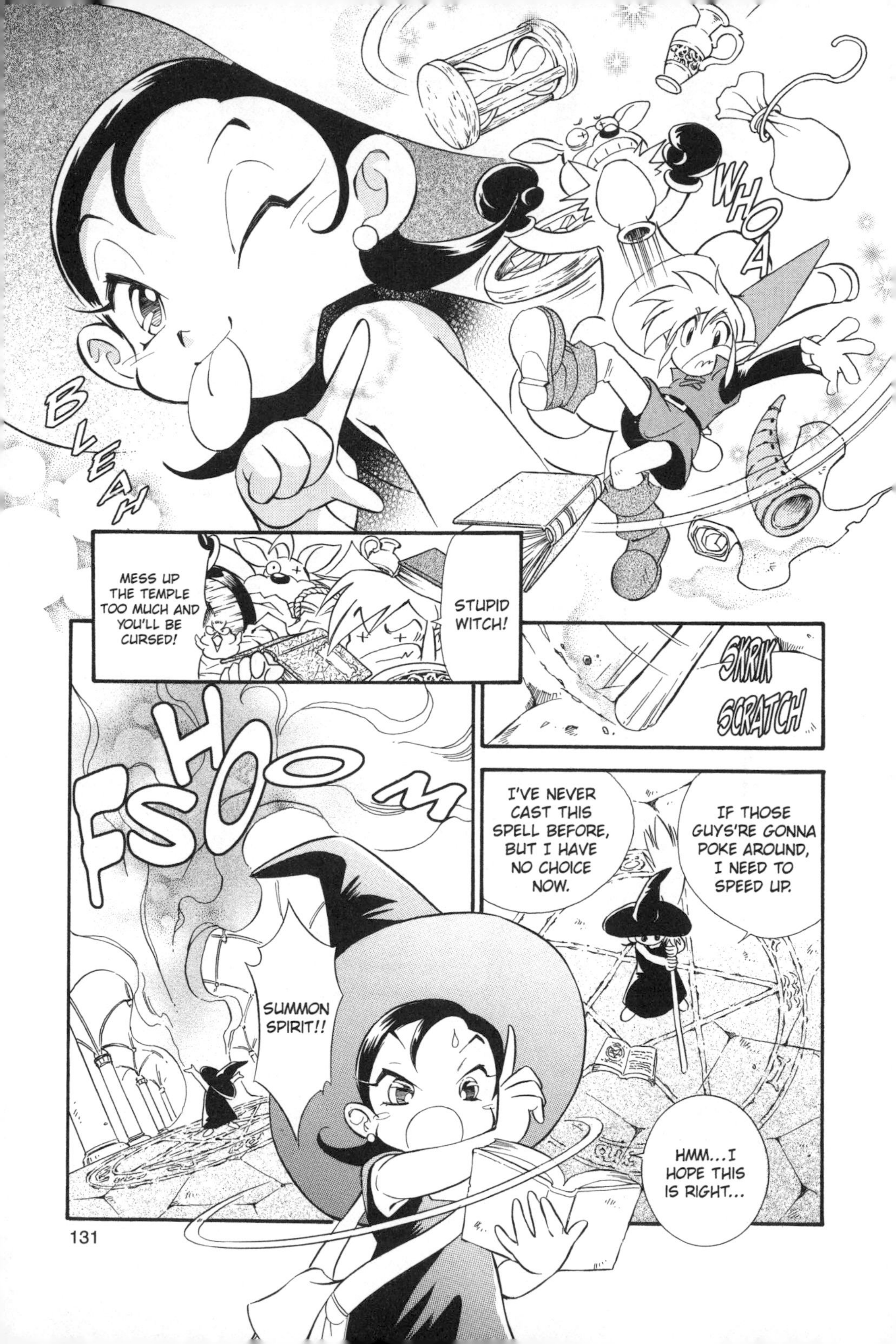
WHOA
BLEAH
STUPID WITCH!
MESS UP THE TEMPLE TOO MUCH AND YOU'LL BE CURSED!
SKRIK SCRATCH
IF THOSE GUYS'RE GONNA POKE AROUND, I NEED TO SPEED UP.
I'VE NEVER CAST THIS SPELL BEFORE, BUT I HAVE NO CHOICE NOW.
HMM...I HOPE THIS IS RIGHT...
FSHOOM
SUMMON SPIRIT!!

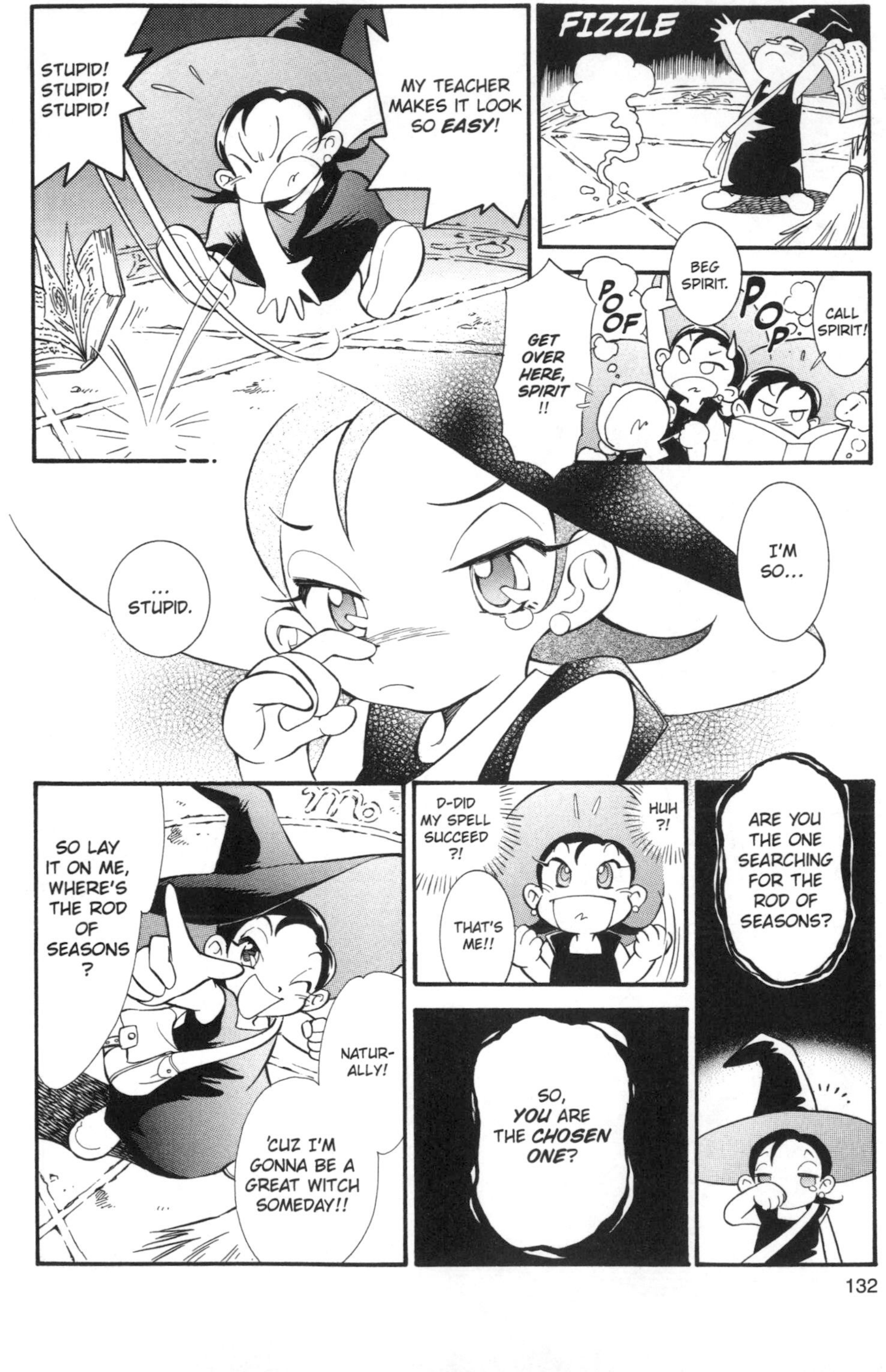
FIZZLE
CALL SPIRIT!
POP
BEG SPIRIT.
POOF
GET OVER HERE, SPIRIT!!
MY TEACHER MAKES IT LOOK SO EASY!
STUPID! STUPID! STUPID!
I'M SO...
... STUPID.
ARE YOU THE ONE SEARCHING FOR THE ROD OF SEASONS?
HUH?!
D-DID MY SPELL SUCCEED?!
THAT'S ME!!
SO, YOU ARE THE CHOSEN ONE?
SO LAY IT ON ME, WHERE'S THE ROD OF SEASONS?
NATUR-ALLY!
'CUZ I'M GONNA BE A GREAT WITCH SOMEDAY!!

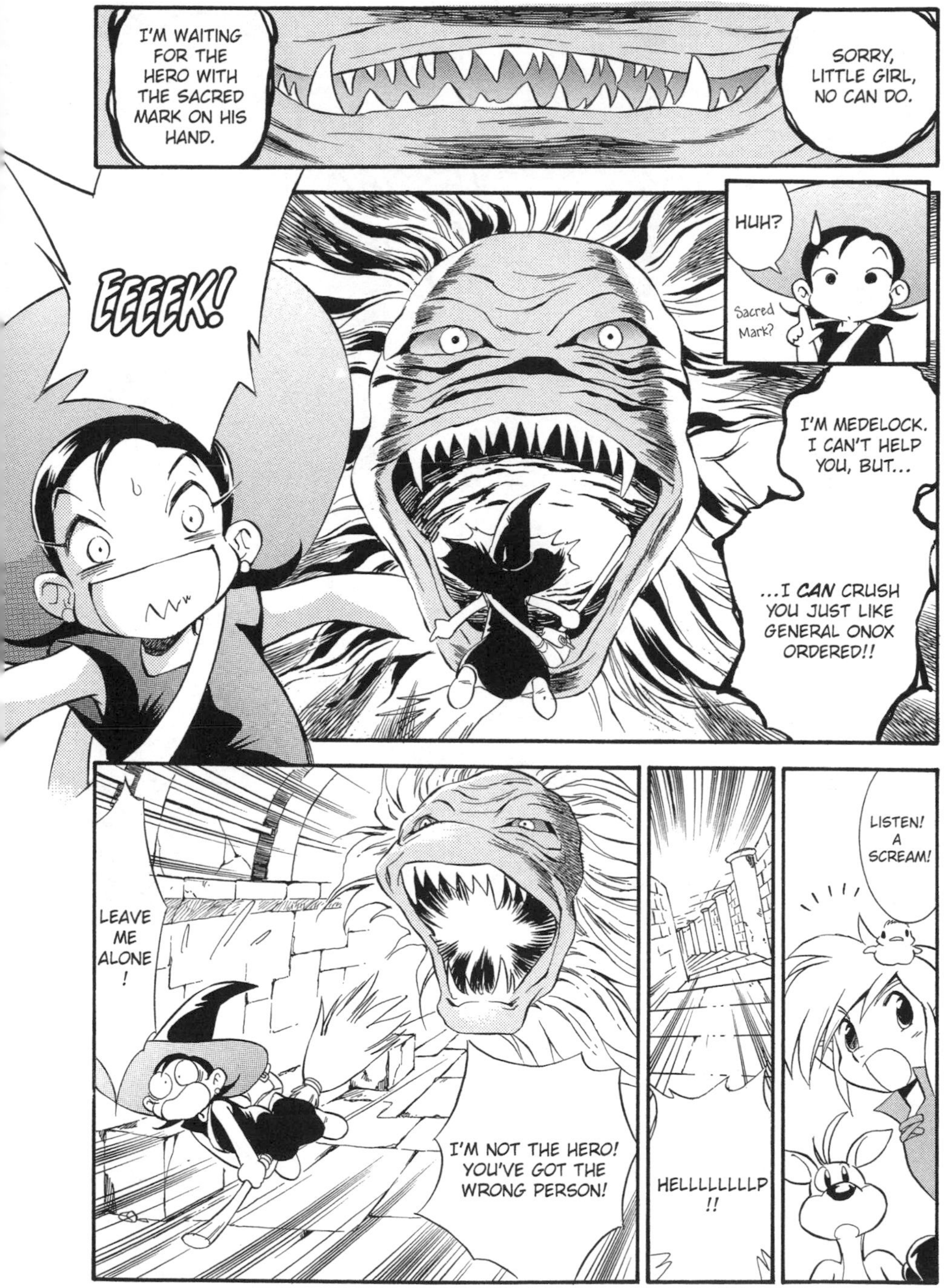
I'M WAITING FOR THE HERO WITH THE SACRED MARK ON HIS HAND.
SORRY, LITTLE GIRL, NO CAN DO.
HUH?
Sacred Mark?
I'M MEDELOCK. I CAN'T HELP YOU, BUT...
...I *CAN* CRUSH YOU JUST LIKE GENERAL ONOX ORDERED!!
EEEEK!
LISTEN! A SCREAM!
HELLLLLLLLP!!
LEAVE ME ALONE!
I'M NOT THE HERO! YOU'VE GOT THE WRONG PERSON!

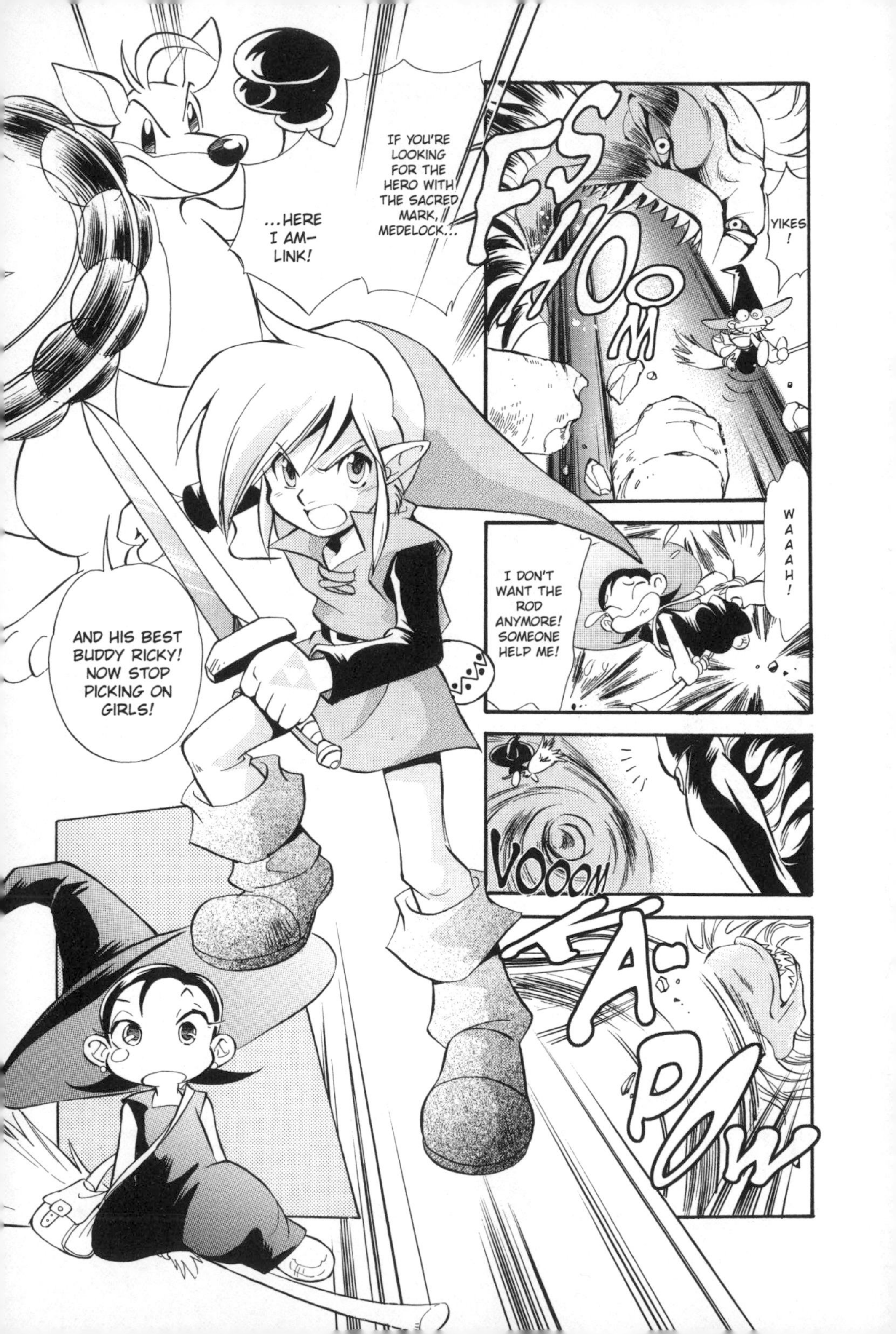
YIKES!
FSHOOM
WAAAAH!
I DON'T WANT THE ROD ANYMORE! SOMEONE HELP ME!
VOOOM
KAPOW
IF YOU'RE LOOKING FOR THE HERO WITH THE SACRED MARK, MEDELOCK...
...HERE I AM—LINK!
AND HIS BEST BUDDY RICKY! NOW STOP PICKING ON GIRLS!

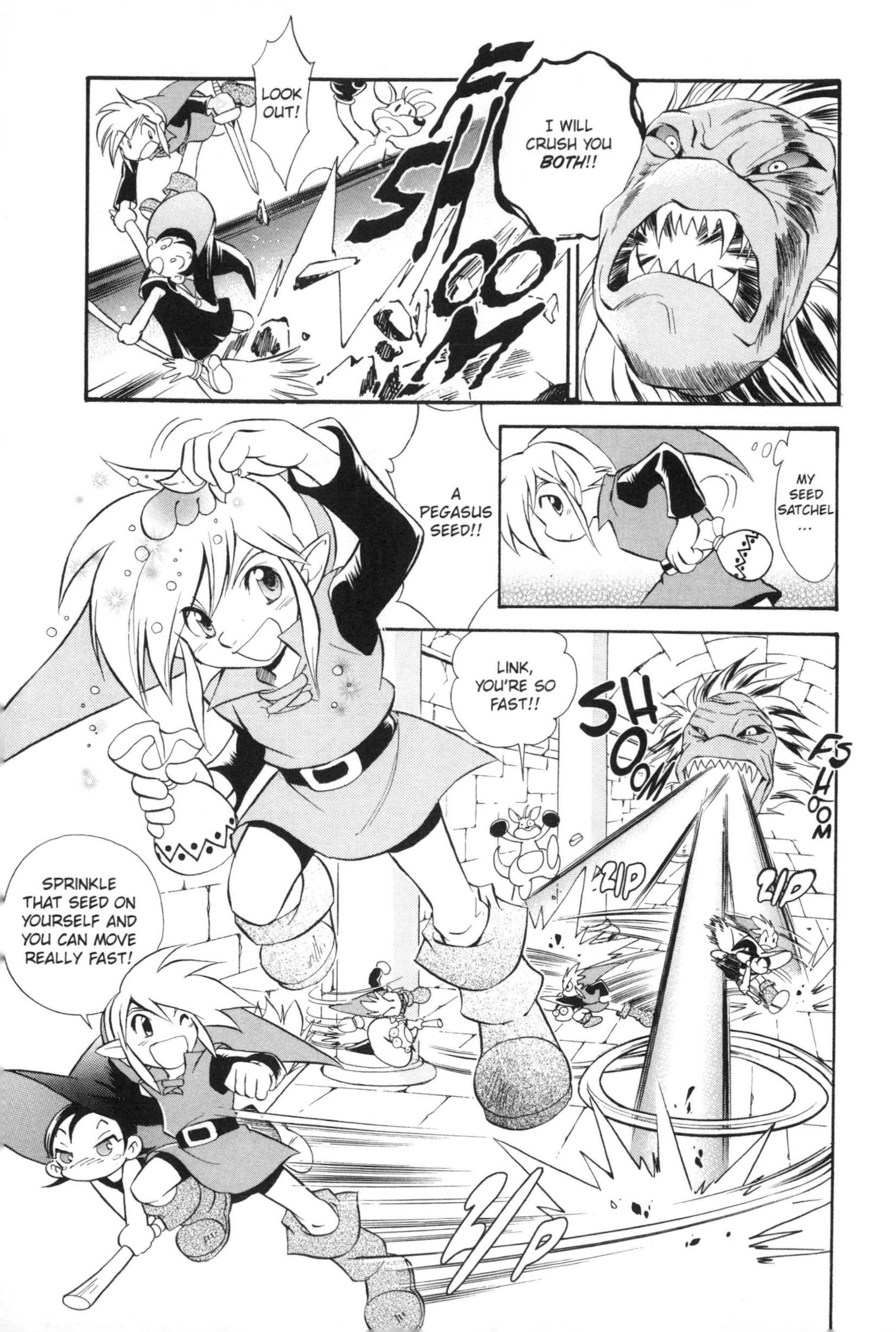
I WILL CRUSH YOU BOTH!!
SHOOM
LOOK OUT!
MY SEED SATCHEL ...
A PEGASUS SEED!!
FSHOOM
SHOOM
LINK, YOU'RE SO FAST!!
ZIP
ZIP
SPRINKLE THAT SEED ON YOURSELF AND YOU CAN MOVE REALLY FAST!
ZIP

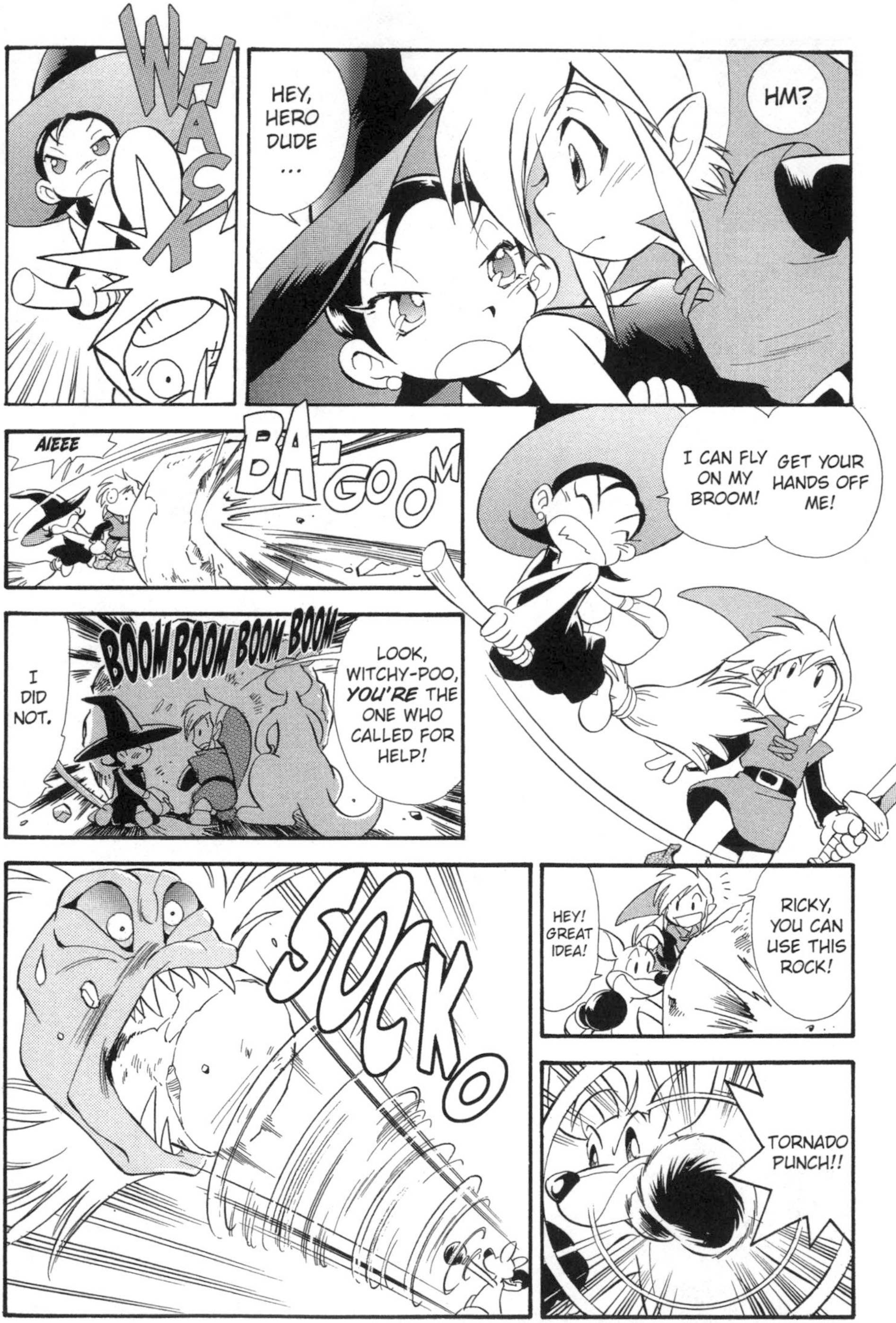
HEY, HERO DUDE ...
HM?
WHACK
GET YOUR HANDS OFF ME!
I CAN FLY ON MY BROOM!
BA-GOOOM
AIEEE
BOOM BOOM BOOM BOOM
LOOK, WITCHY-POO, *YOU'RE* THE ONE WHO CALLED FOR HELP!
I DID NOT.
RICKY, YOU CAN USE THIS ROCK!
HEY! GREAT IDEA!
TORNADO PUNCH!!
SOCKO

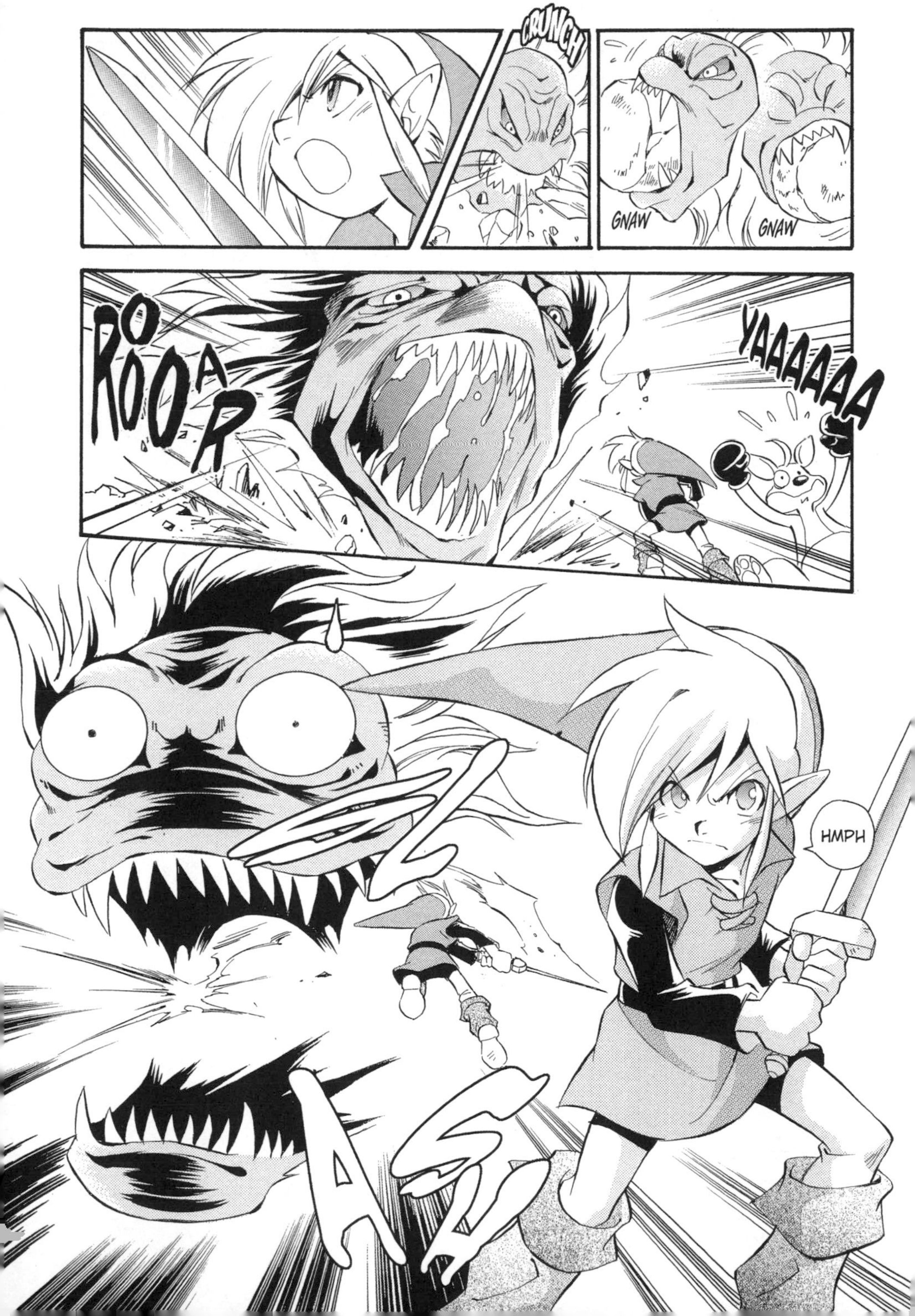
GNAW
GNAW
CRUNCH
YAAAAAA
ROOOAR
HMPH

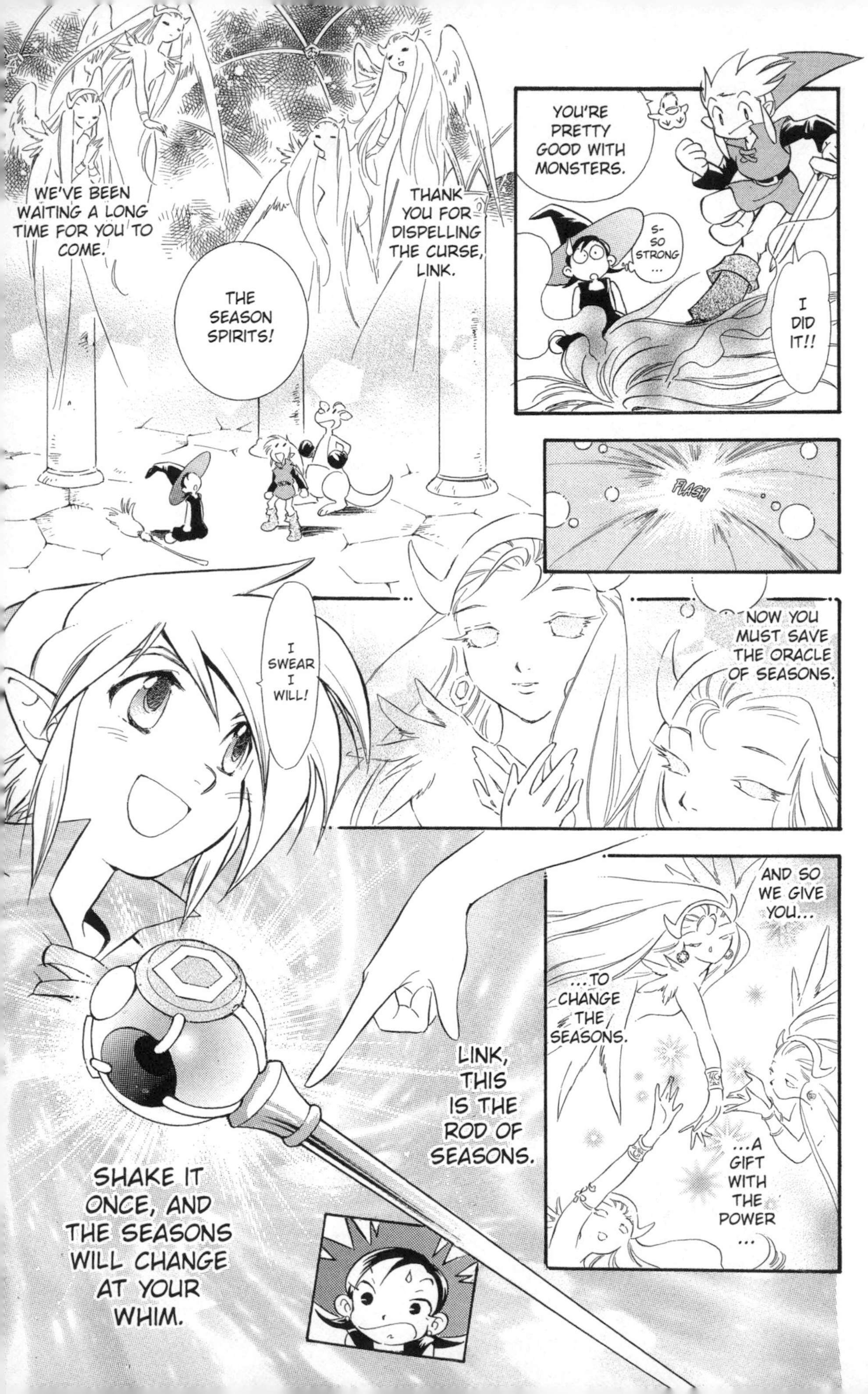

I DID IT!!
S-SO STRONG...
YOU'RE PRETTY GOOD WITH MONSTERS.
FLASH
THANK YOU FOR DISPELLING THE CURSE, LINK.
WE'VE BEEN WAITING A LONG TIME FOR YOU TO COME.
THE SEASON SPIRITS!
NOW YOU MUST SAVE THE ORACLE OF SEASONS.
I SWEAR I WILL!
AND SO WE GIVE YOU...
...A GIFT WITH THE POWER...
...TO CHANGE THE SEASONS.
LINK, THIS IS THE ROD OF SEASONS.
SHAKE IT ONCE, AND THE SEASONS WILL CHANGE AT YOUR WHIM.

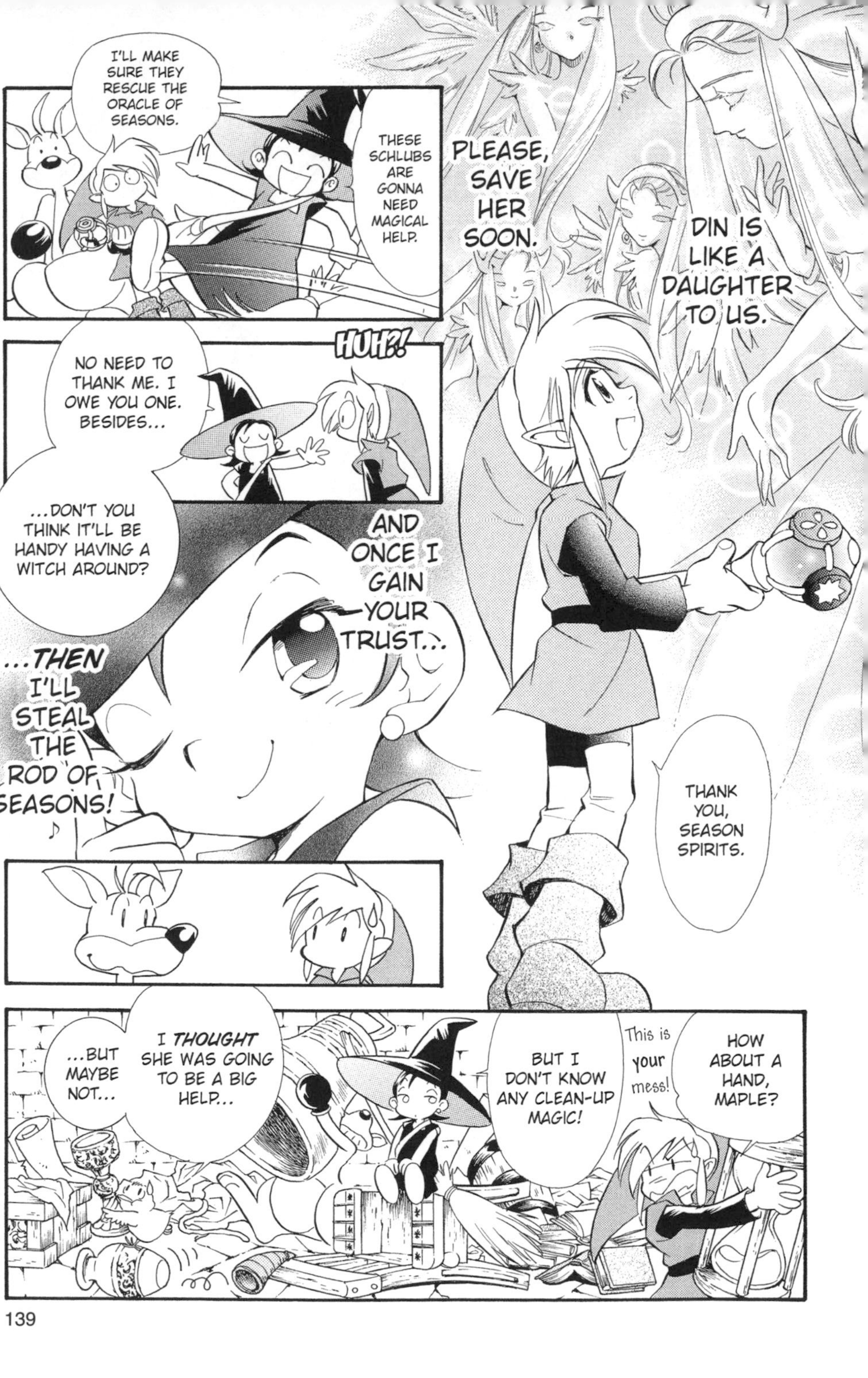
PLEASE, SAVE HER SOON.
DIN IS LIKE A DAUGHTER TO US.
THANK YOU, SEASON SPIRITS.
I'LL MAKE SURE THEY RESCUE THE ORACLE OF SEASONS.
THESE SCHLUBS ARE GONNA NEED MAGICAL HELP.
HUH?!
NO NEED TO THANK ME. I OWE YOU ONE. BESIDES...
...DON'T YOU THINK IT'LL BE HANDY HAVING A WITCH AROUND?
AND ONCE I GAIN YOUR TRUST...
...THEN I'LL STEAL THE ROD OF SEASONS! ♪
HOW ABOUT A HAND, MAPLE?
This is your mess!
BUT I DON'T KNOW ANY CLEAN-UP MAGIC!
I THOUGHT SHE WAS GOING TO BE A BIG HELP...
...BUT MAYBE NOT...

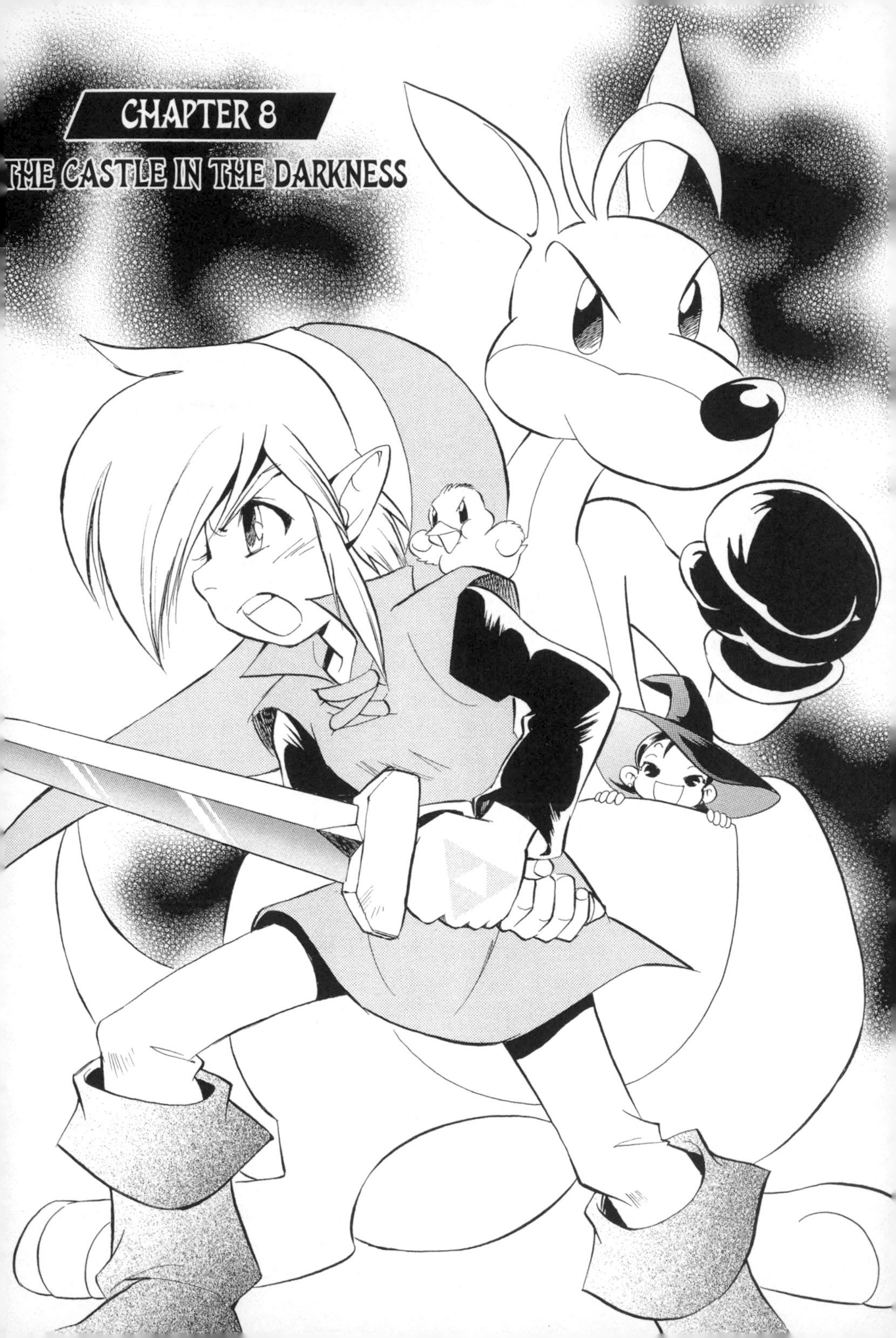
CHAPTER 8
THE CASTLE IN THE DARKNESS

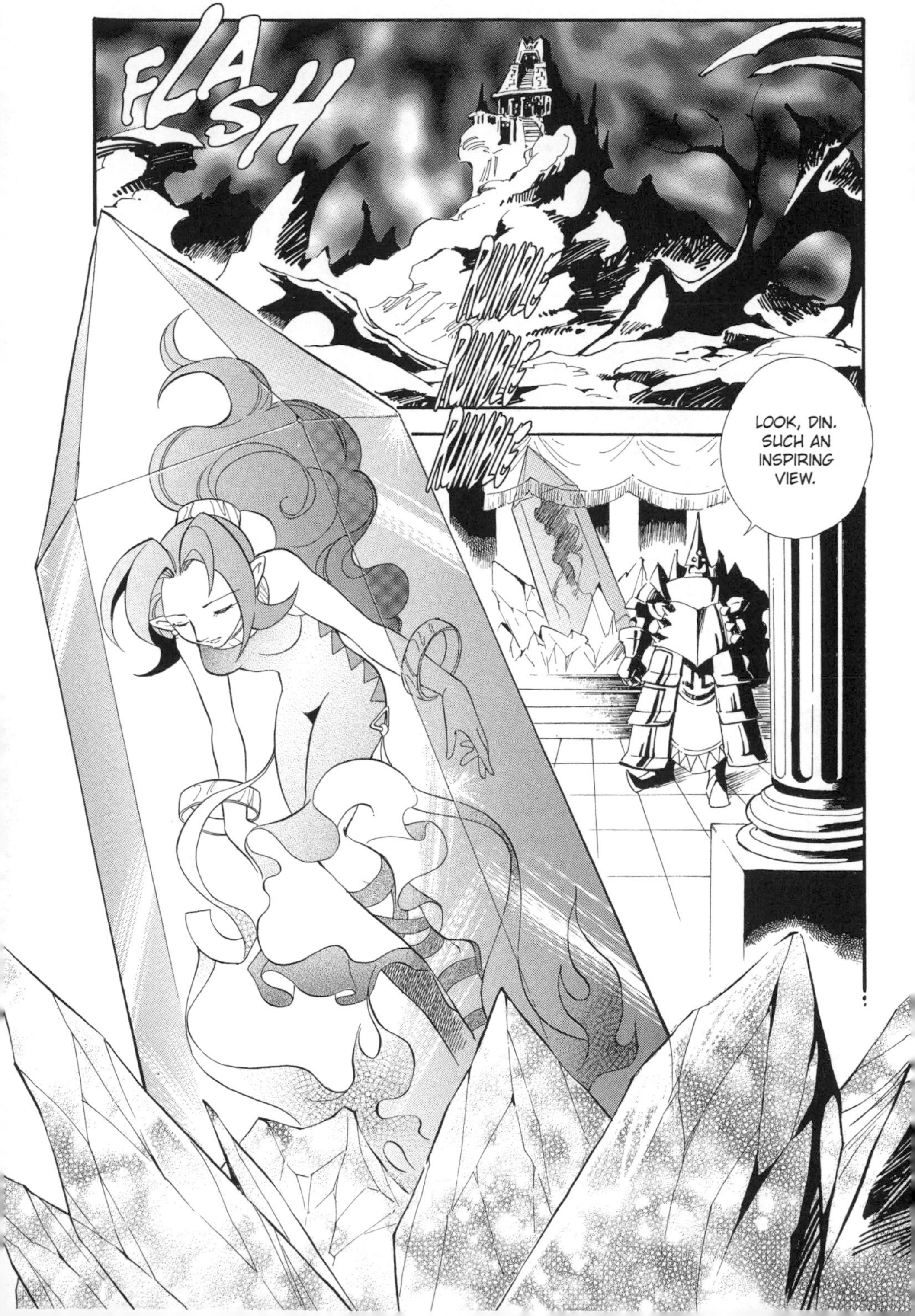
FLASH
RUMBLE... RUMBLE RUMBLE
LOOK, DIN. SUCH AN INSPIRING VIEW.

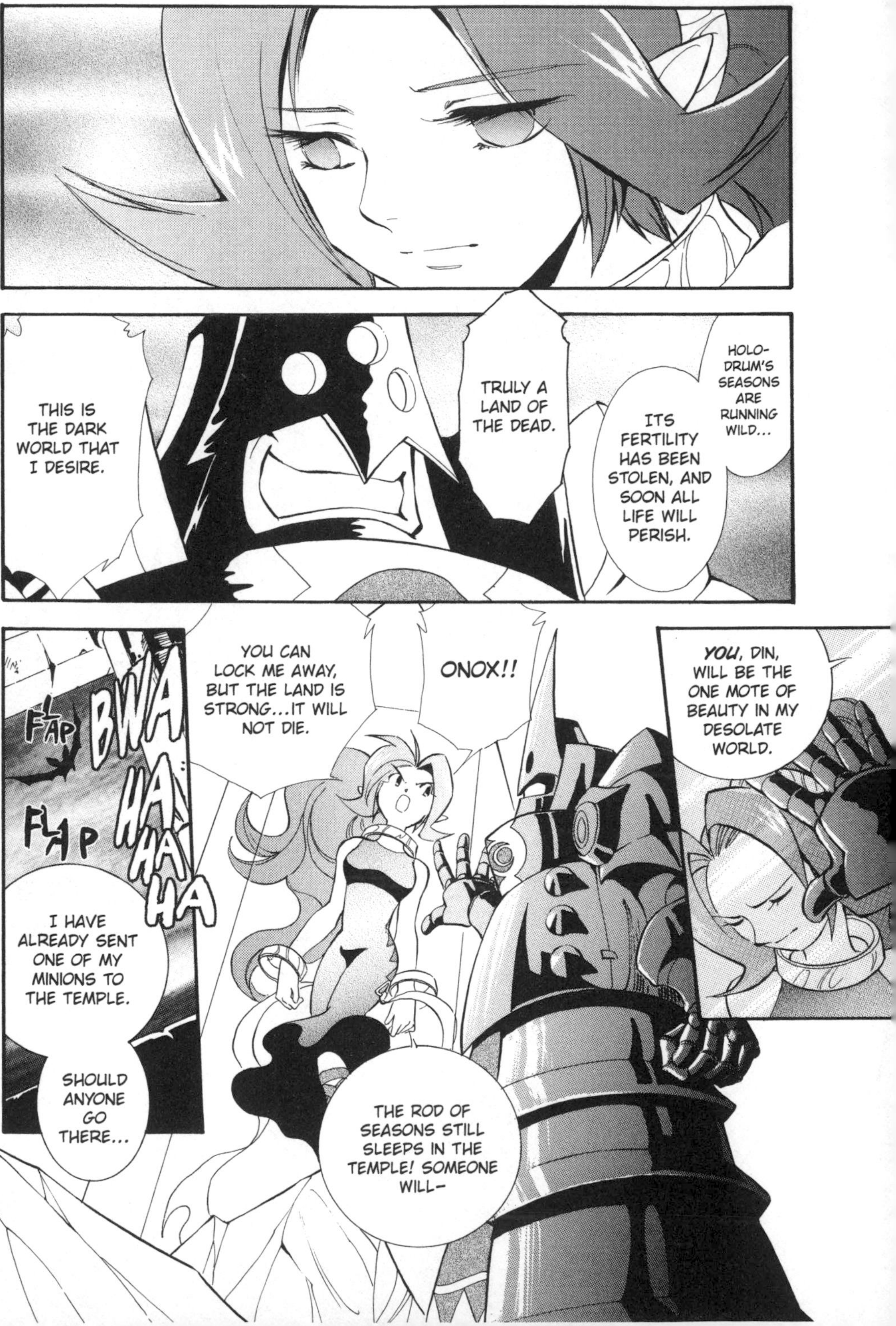
HOLO-DRUM'S SEASONS ARE RUNNING WILD...
ITS FERTILITY HAS BEEN STOLEN, AND SOON ALL LIFE WILL PERISH.
TRULY A LAND OF THE DEAD.
THIS IS THE DARK WORLD THAT I DESIRE.
YOU, DIN, WILL BE THE ONE MOTE OF BEAUTY IN MY DESOLATE WORLD.
ONOX!!
YOU CAN LOCK ME AWAY, BUT THE LAND IS STRONG...IT WILL NOT DIE.
THE ROD OF SEASONS STILL SLEEPS IN THE TEMPLE! SOMEONE WILL–
I HAVE ALREADY SENT ONE OF MY MINIONS TO THE TEMPLE.
SHOULD ANYONE GO THERE...
BWA HA HA HA HA
FLAP
FLAP

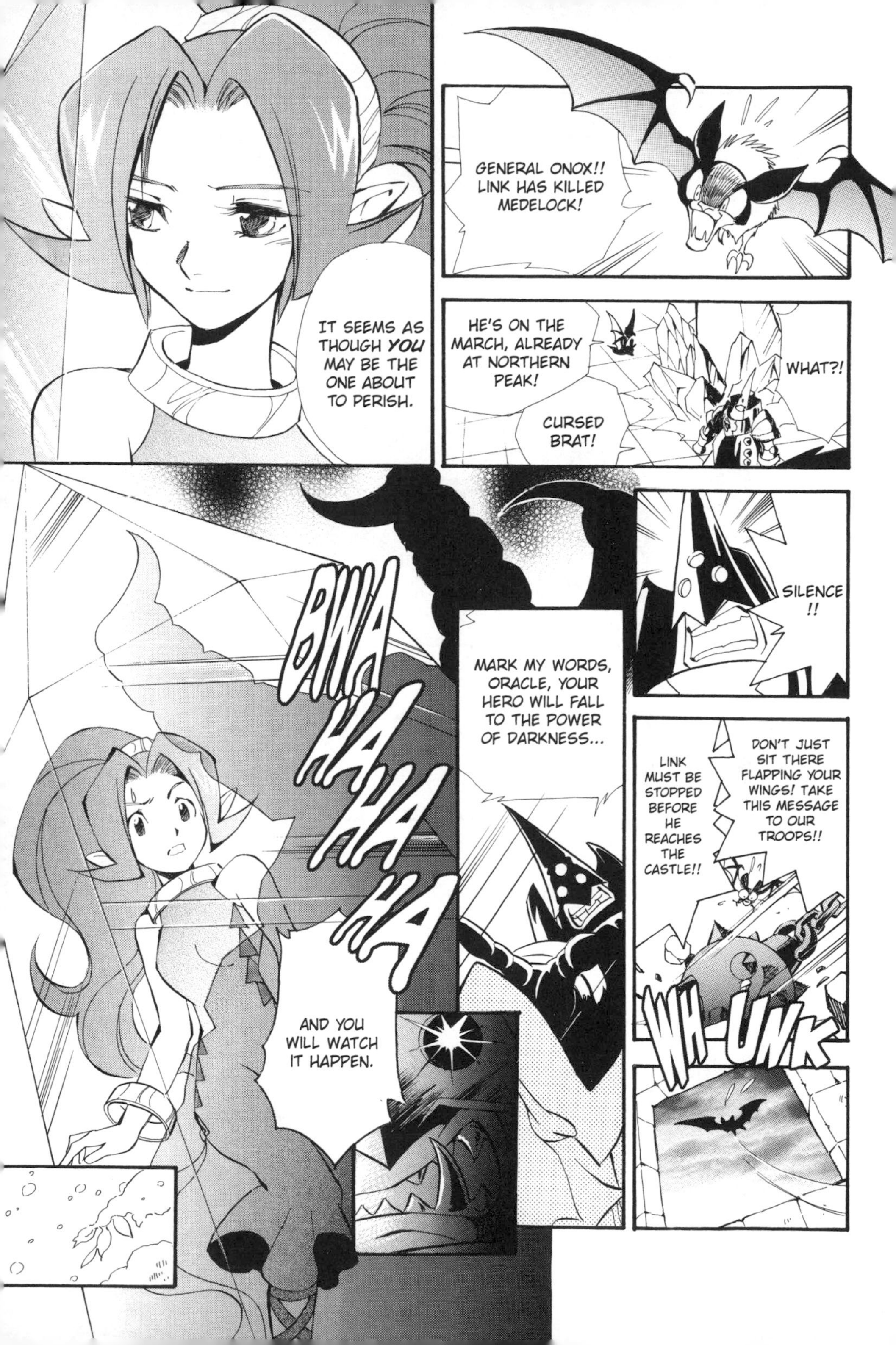
GENERAL ONOX!! LINK HAS KILLED MEDELOCK!
HE'S ON THE MARCH, ALREADY AT NORTHERN PEAK!
WHAT?!
CURSED BRAT!
IT SEEMS AS THOUGH *YOU* MAY BE THE ONE ABOUT TO PERISH.
SILENCE!!
DON'T JUST SIT THERE FLAPPING YOUR WINGS! TAKE THIS MESSAGE TO OUR TROOPS!!
LINK MUST BE STOPPED BEFORE HE REACHES THE CASTLE!!
WH-UNK
MARK MY WORDS, ORACLE, YOUR HERO WILL FALL TO THE POWER OF DARKNESS...
BWA HA HA HA HA
AND YOU WILL WATCH IT HAPPEN.

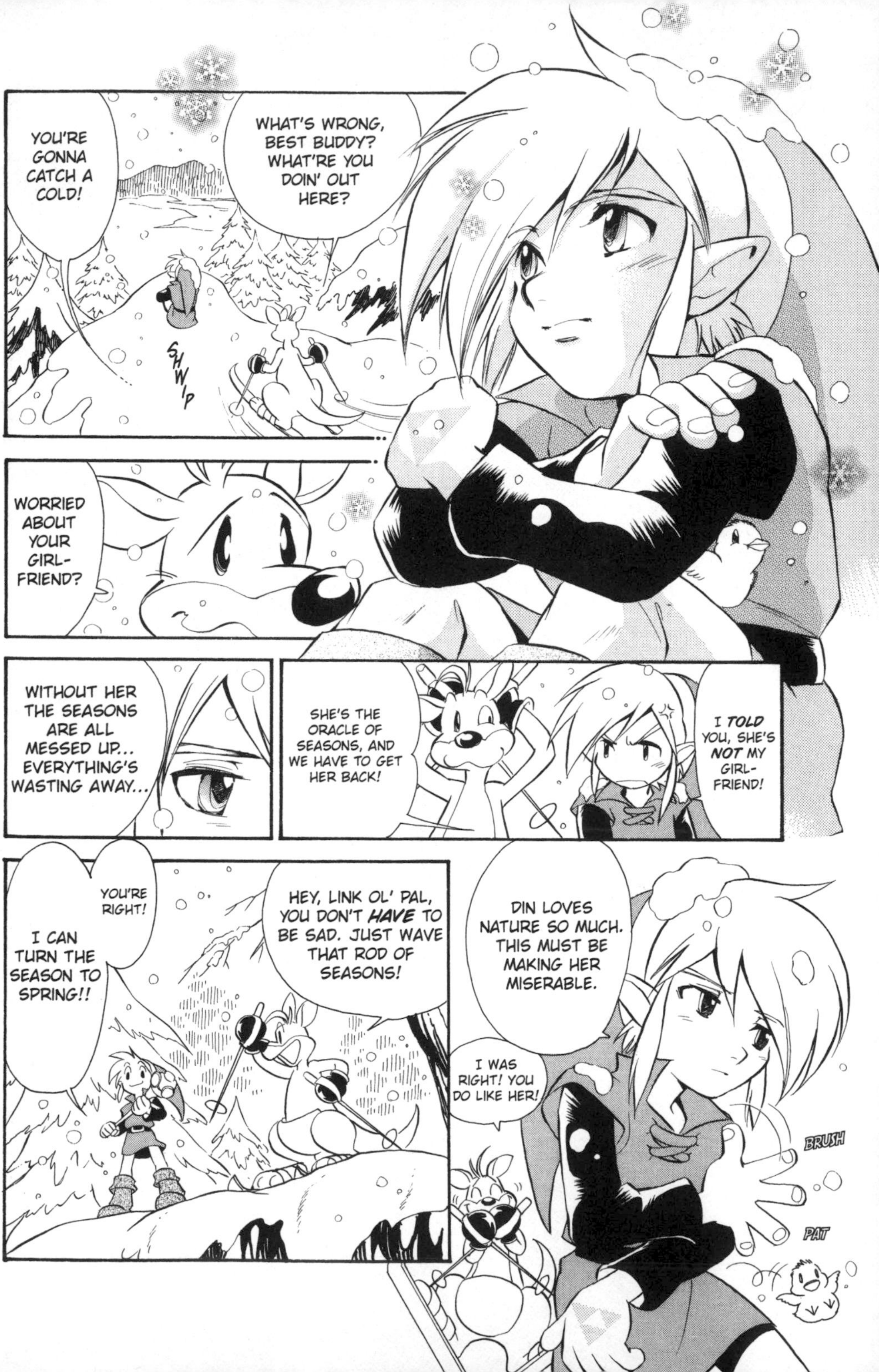

WHAT'S WRONG, BEST BUDDY? WHAT'RE YOU DOIN' OUT HERE?
YOU'RE GONNA CATCH A COLD!
SHWIP
WORRIED ABOUT YOUR GIRL-FRIEND?
I *TOLD* YOU, SHE'S *NOT* MY GIRL-FRIEND!
SHE'S THE ORACLE OF SEASONS, AND WE HAVE TO GET HER BACK!
WITHOUT HER THE SEASONS ARE ALL MESSED UP... EVERYTHING'S WASTING AWAY...
DIN LOVES NATURE SO MUCH. THIS MUST BE MAKING HER MISERABLE.
BRUSH
I WAS RIGHT! YOU DO LIKE HER!
PAT
HEY, LINK OL' PAL, YOU DON'T *HAVE* TO BE SAD. JUST WAVE THAT ROD OF SEASONS!
YOU'RE RIGHT!
I CAN TURN THE SEASON TO SPRING!!

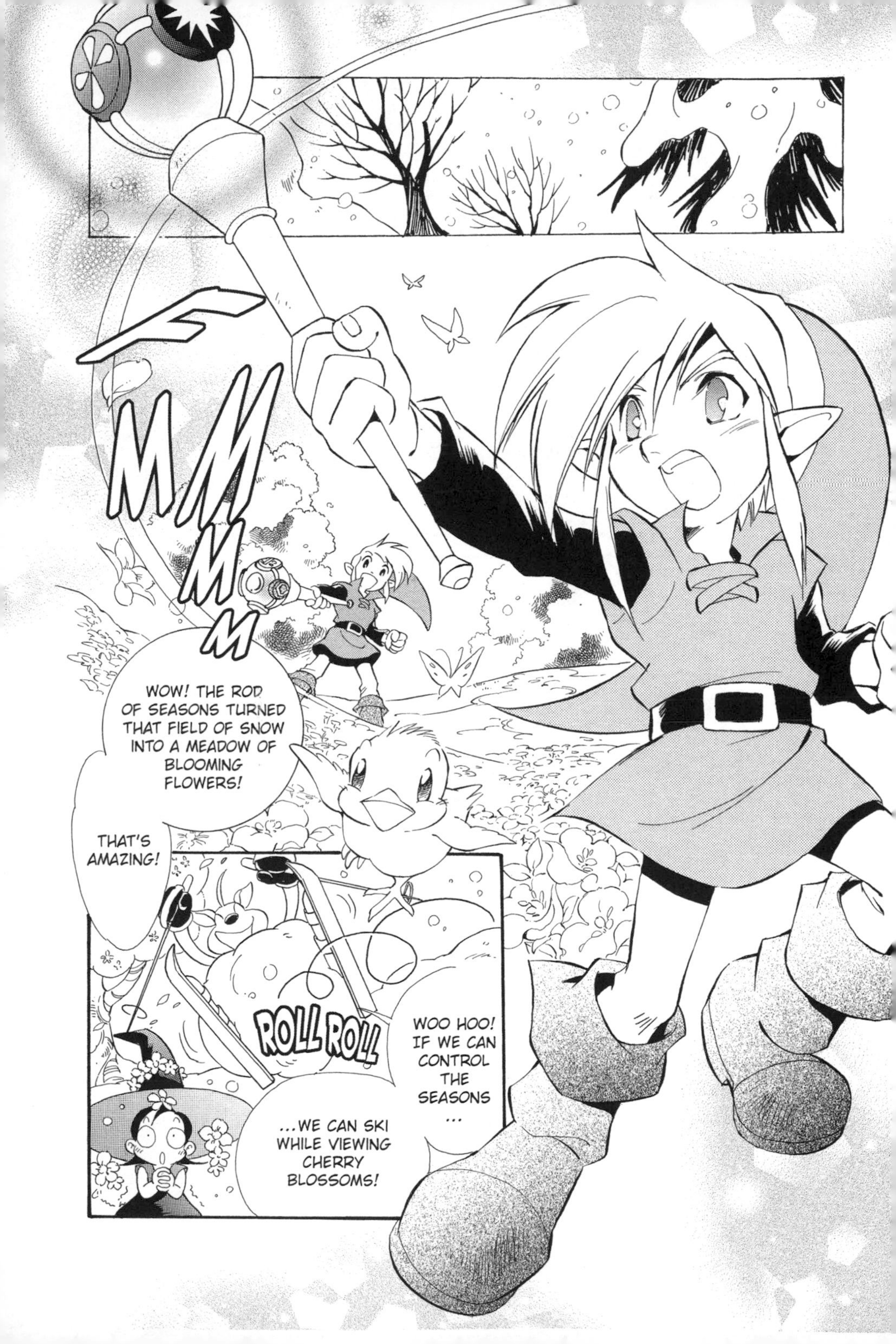
FMMMMM
WOW! THE ROD OF SEASONS TURNED THAT FIELD OF SNOW INTO A MEADOW OF BLOOMING FLOWERS!
THAT'S AMAZING!
WOO HOO! IF WE CAN CONTROL THE SEASONS ...
ROLL ROLL
...WE CAN SKI WHILE VIEWING CHERRY BLOSSOMS!

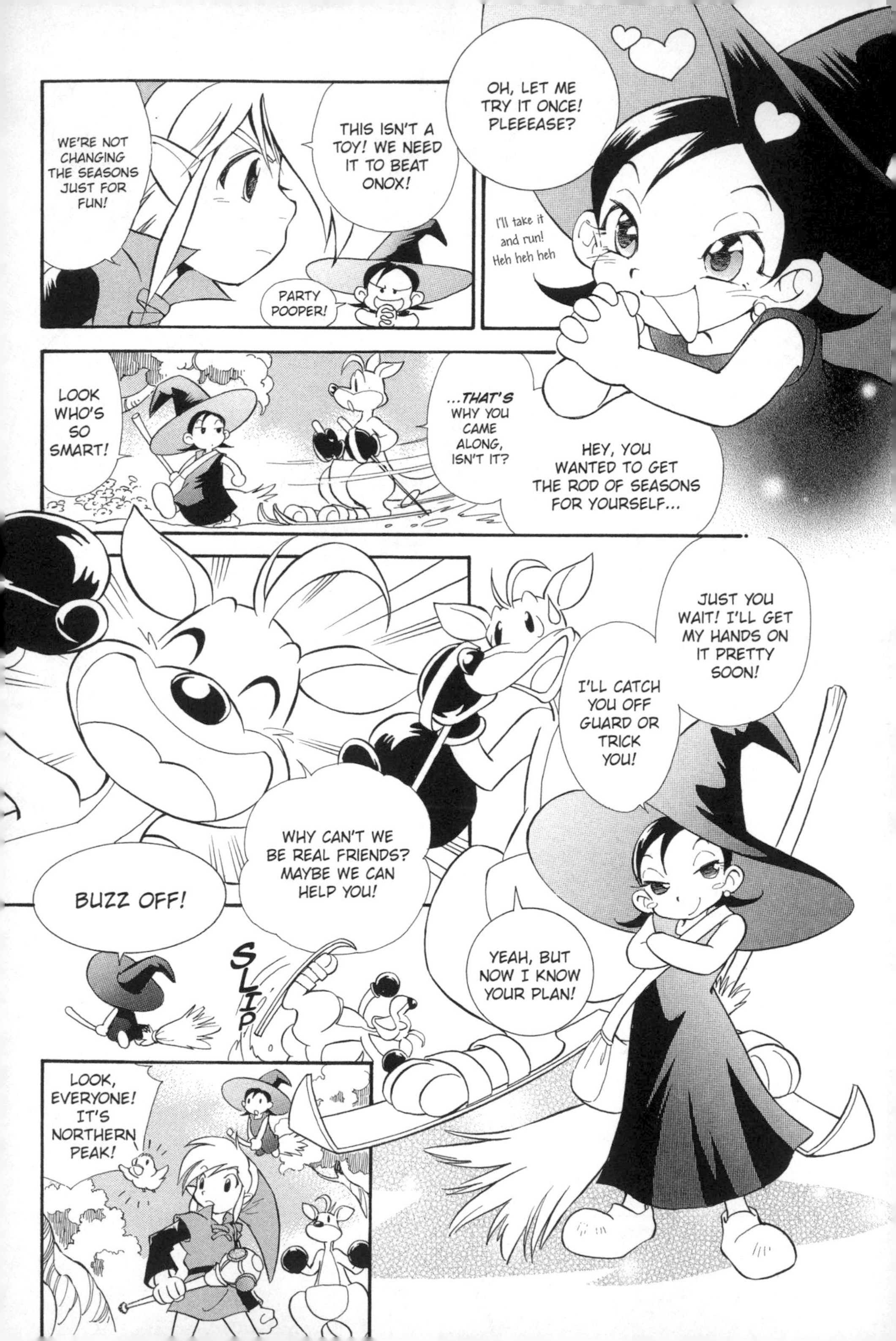
OH, LET ME TRY IT ONCE! PLEEEASE?
I'll take it and run! Heh heh heh
THIS ISN'T A TOY! WE NEED IT TO BEAT ONOX!
WE'RE NOT CHANGING THE SEASONS JUST FOR FUN!
PARTY POOPER!
HEY, YOU WANTED TO GET THE ROD OF SEASONS FOR YOURSELF...
...*THAT'S* WHY YOU CAME ALONG, ISN'T IT?
LOOK WHO'S SO SMART!
JUST YOU WAIT! I'LL GET MY HANDS ON IT PRETTY SOON!
I'LL CATCH YOU OFF GUARD OR TRICK YOU!
YEAH, BUT NOW I KNOW YOUR PLAN!
WHY CAN'T WE BE REAL FRIENDS? MAYBE WE CAN HELP YOU!
BUZZ OFF!
SLIP
LOOK, EVERYONE! IT'S NORTHERN PEAK!

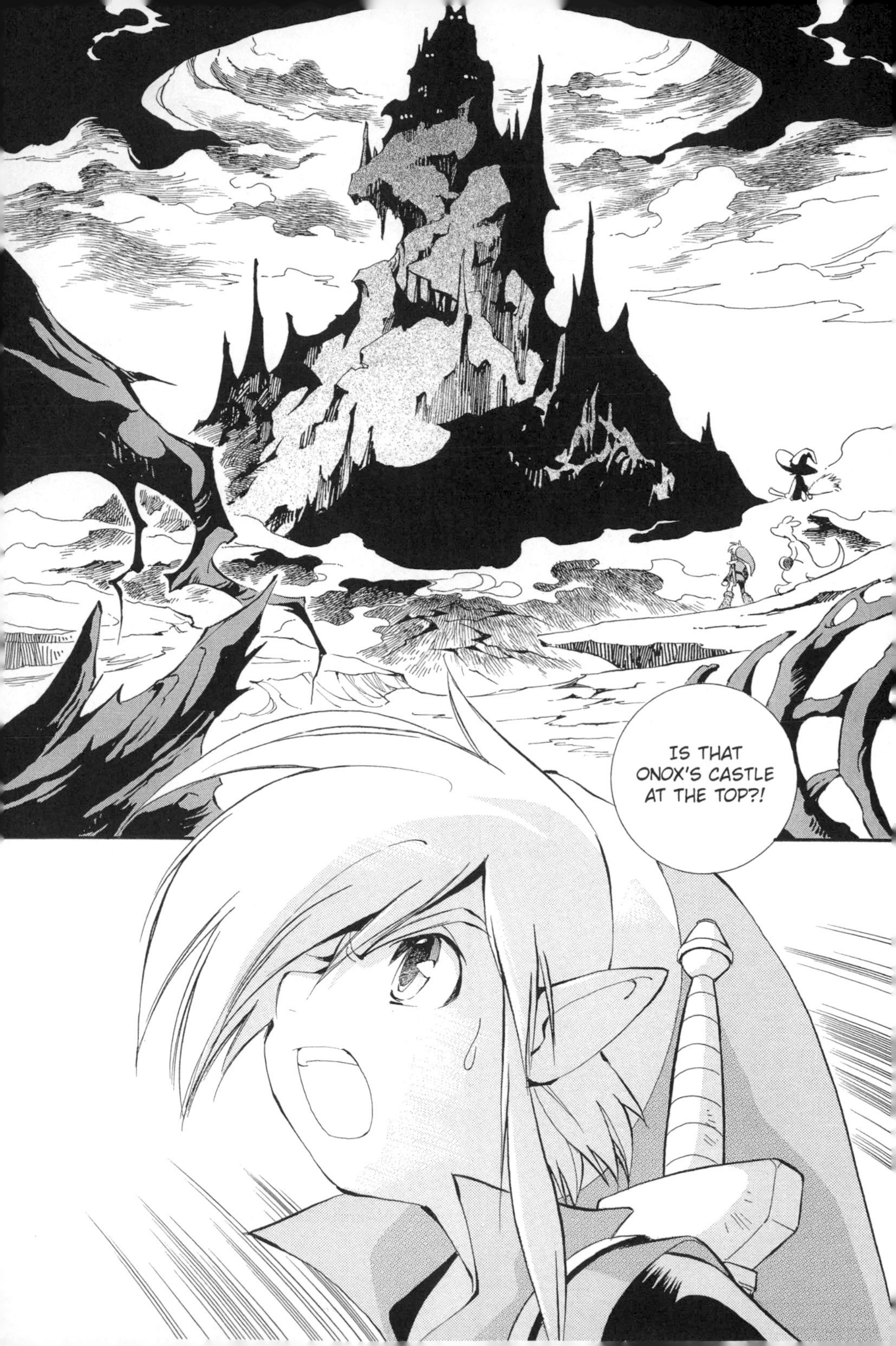
IS THAT ONOX'S CASTLE AT THE TOP?!

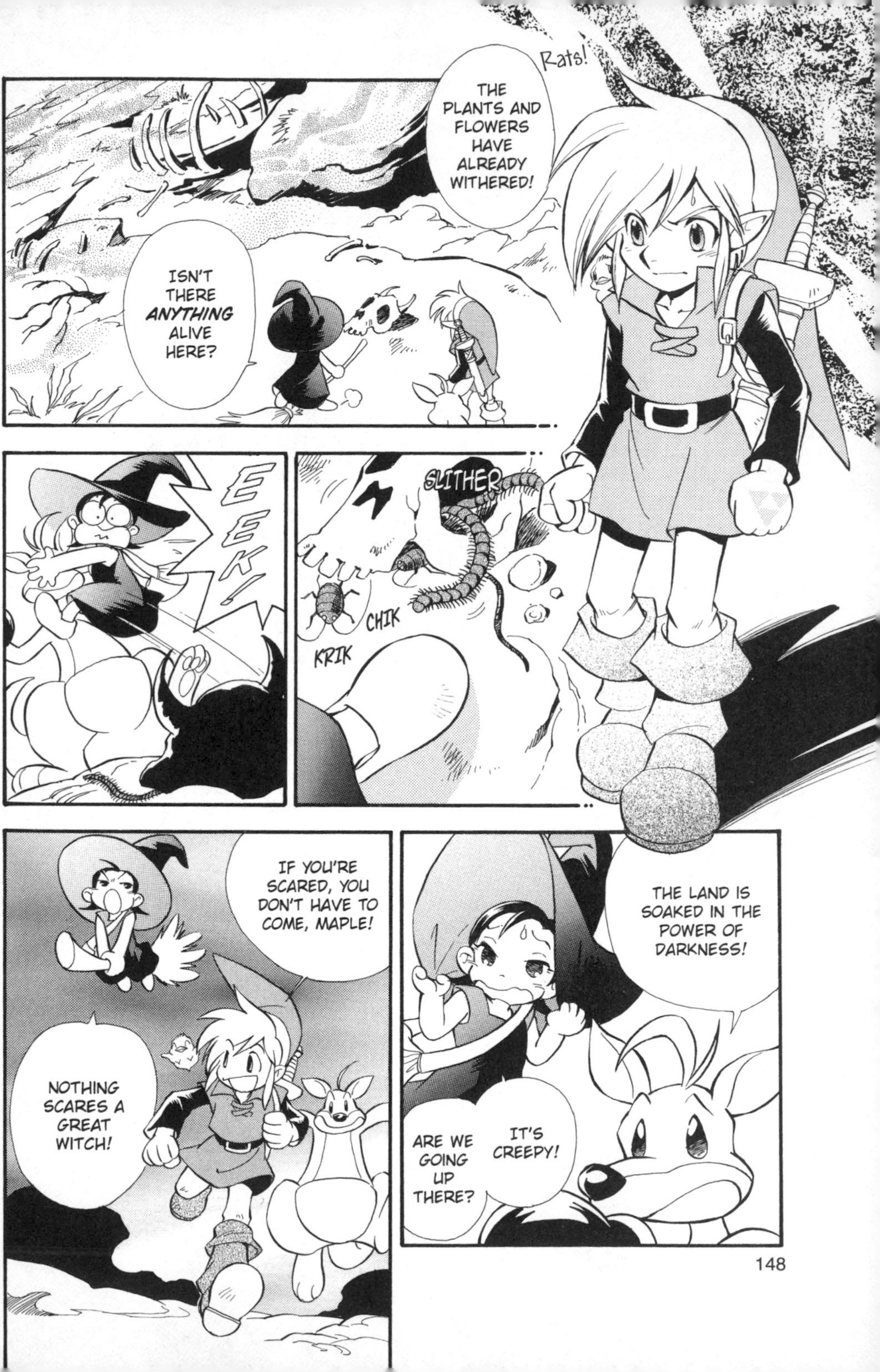
Rats!
THE PLANTS AND FLOWERS HAVE ALREADY WITHERED!
ISN'T THERE *ANYTHING* ALIVE HERE?
SLITHER
CHIK
KRIK
EEEK!
THE LAND IS SOAKED IN THE POWER OF DARKNESS!
IT'S CREEPY!
ARE WE GOING UP THERE?
IF YOU'RE SCARED, YOU DON'T HAVE TO COME, MAPLE!
NOTHING SCARES A GREAT WITCH!

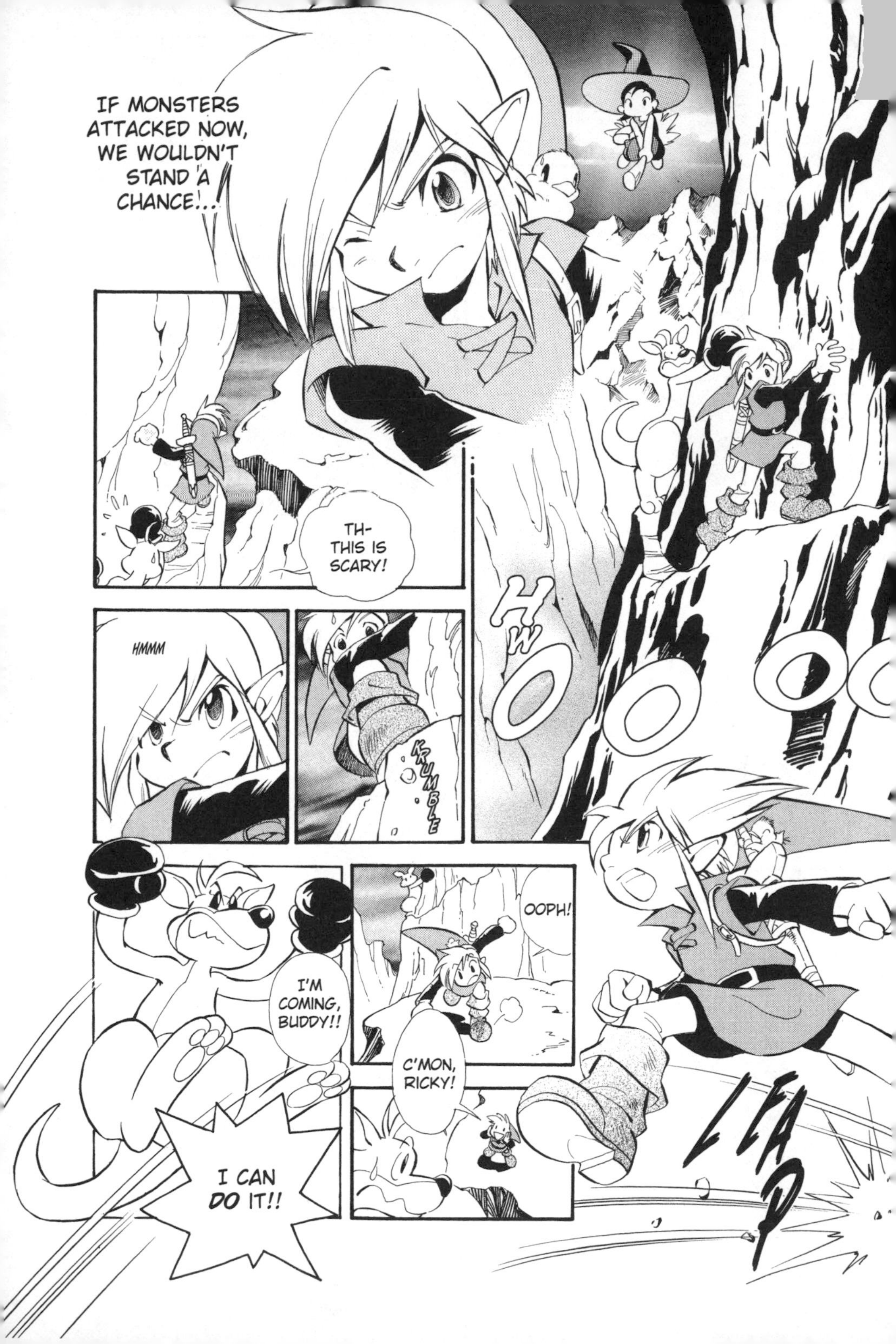
IF MONSTERS ATTACKED NOW, WE WOULDN'T STAND A CHANCE!...
HWOOOO
TH- THIS IS SCARY!
KRUMBLE
HMMM
LEAP
OOPH!
C'MON, RICKY!
I'M COMING, BUDDY!!
I CAN *DO* IT!!

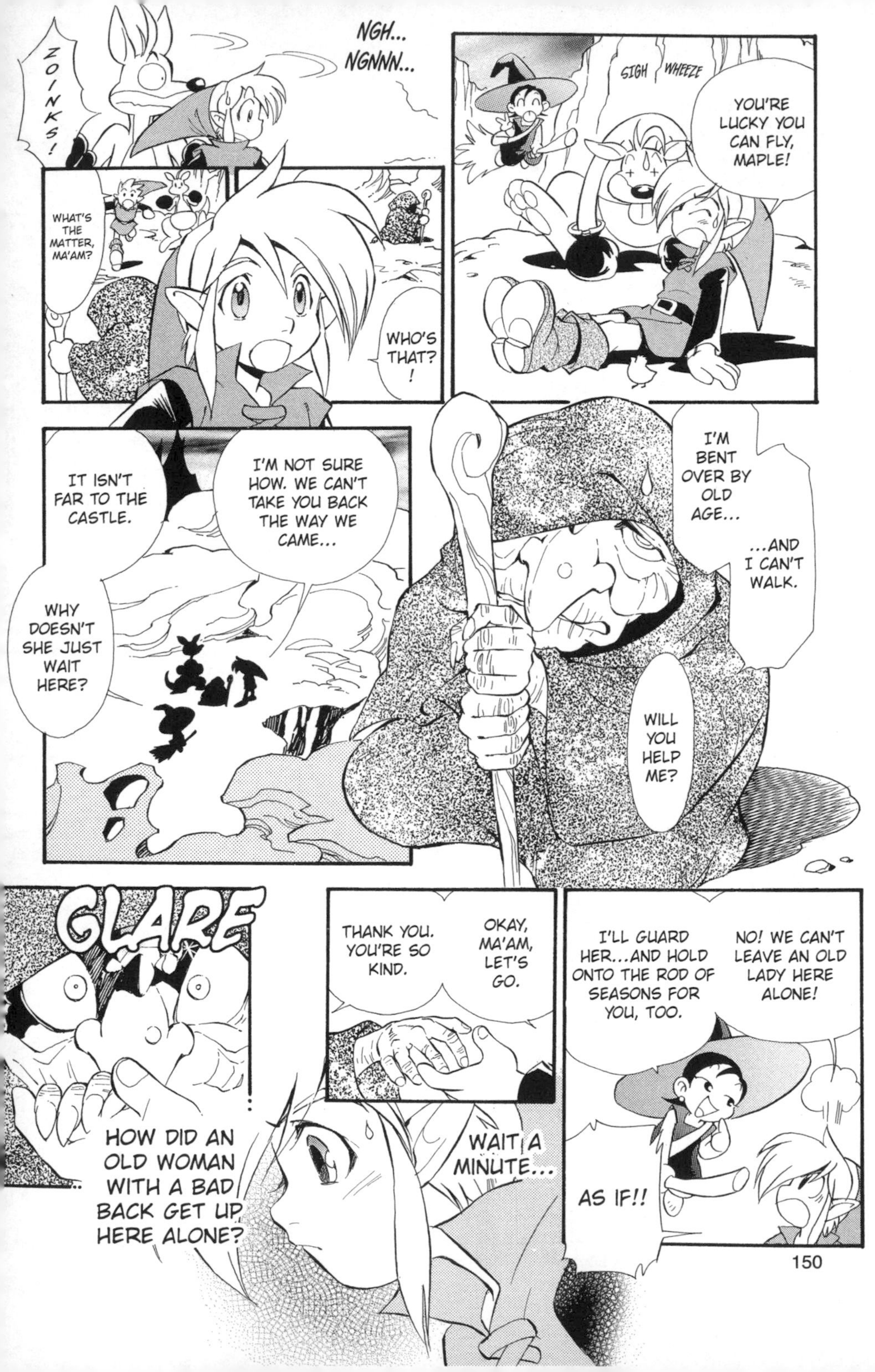
SIGH
WHEEZE
YOU'RE LUCKY YOU CAN FLY, MAPLE!
NGH... NGNNN...
ZOINKS!
WHO'S THAT?!
WHAT'S THE MATTER, MA'AM?
I'M BENT OVER BY OLD AGE...
...AND I CAN'T WALK.
WILL YOU HELP ME?
I'M NOT SURE HOW. WE CAN'T TAKE YOU BACK THE WAY WE CAME...
IT ISN'T FAR TO THE CASTLE.
WHY DOESN'T SHE JUST WAIT HERE?
?!
NO! WE CAN'T LEAVE AN OLD LADY HERE ALONE!
I'LL GUARD HER...AND HOLD ONTO THE ROD OF SEASONS FOR YOU, TOO.
AS IF!!
OKAY, MA'AM, LET'S GO.
THANK YOU. YOU'RE SO KIND.
WAIT A MINUTE...
GLARE
...
HOW DID AN OLD WOMAN WITH A BAD BACK GET UP HERE ALONE?

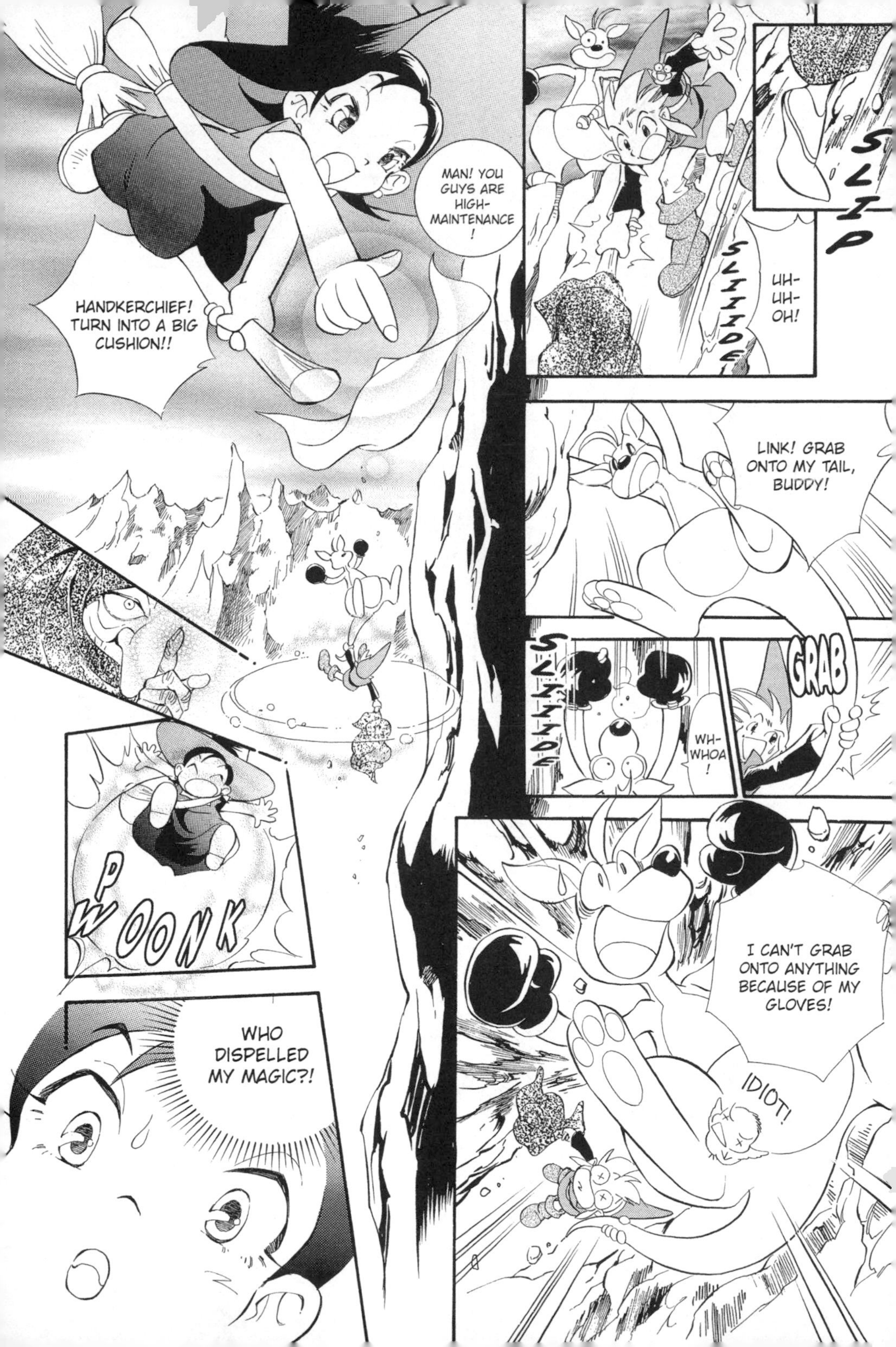
SLIP
SLIIIIDE
UH-UH-OH!
LINK! GRAB ONTO MY TAIL, BUDDY!
GRAB
SLIIIIDE
WH-WHOA!
I CAN'T GRAB ONTO ANYTHING BECAUSE OF MY GLOVES!
IDIOT!
MAN! YOU GUYS ARE HIGH-MAINTENANCE!
HANDKERCHIEF! TURN INTO A BIG CUSHION!!
PWOONK
WHO DISPELLED MY MAGIC?!

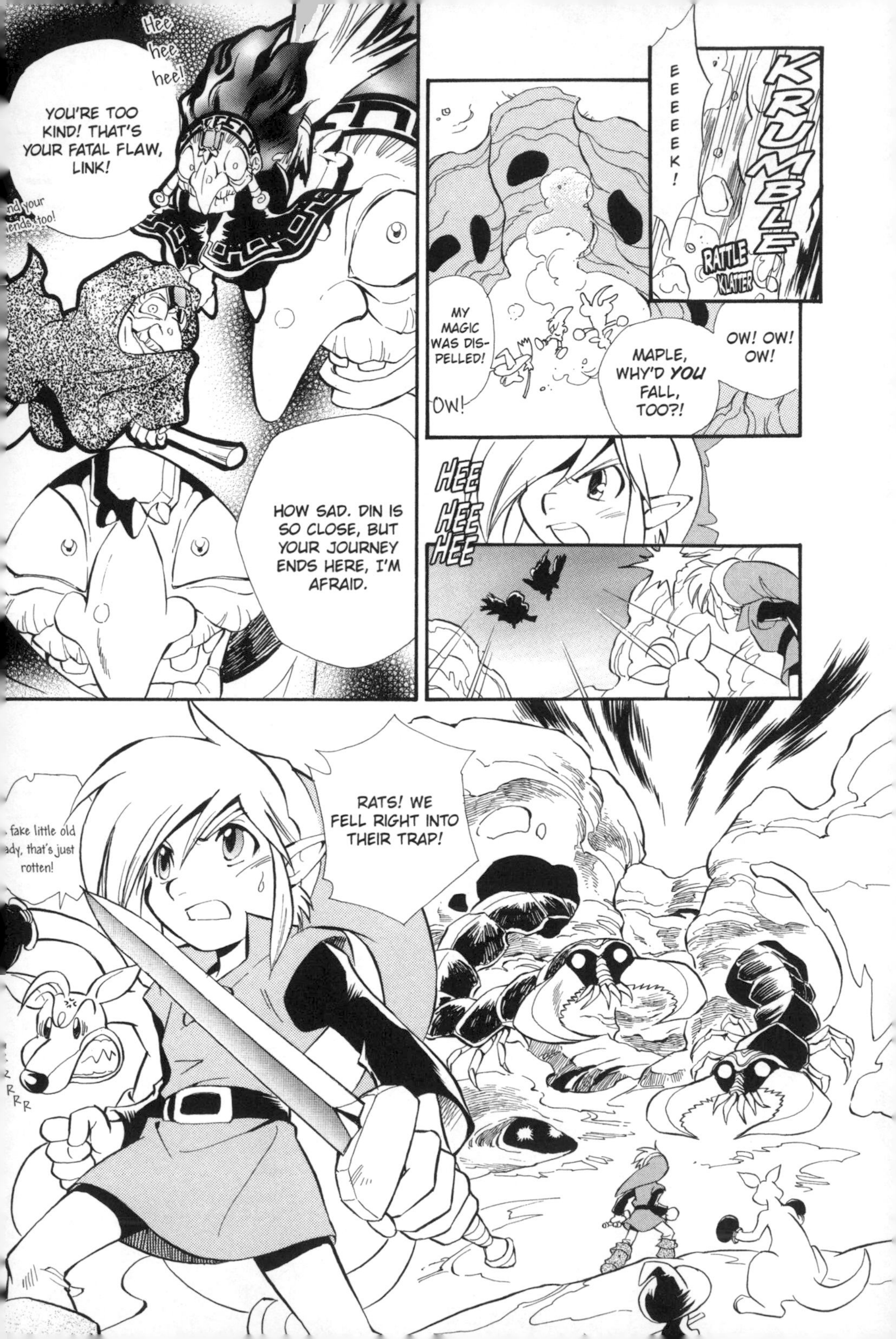

KRUMBLE
EEEEEEK!
RATTLE
KLATTER
OW! OW! OW!
MAPLE, WHY'D YOU FALL, TOO?!
MY MAGIC WAS DISPELLED!
OW!
HEE HEE HEE
Hee hee hee!
YOU'RE TOO KIND! THAT'S YOUR FATAL FLAW, LINK!
nd your iends, too!
HOW SAD. DIN IS SO CLOSE, BUT YOUR JOURNEY ENDS HERE, I'M AFRAID.
RATS! WE FELL RIGHT INTO THEIR TRAP!
fake little old ady, that's just rotten!
RRR

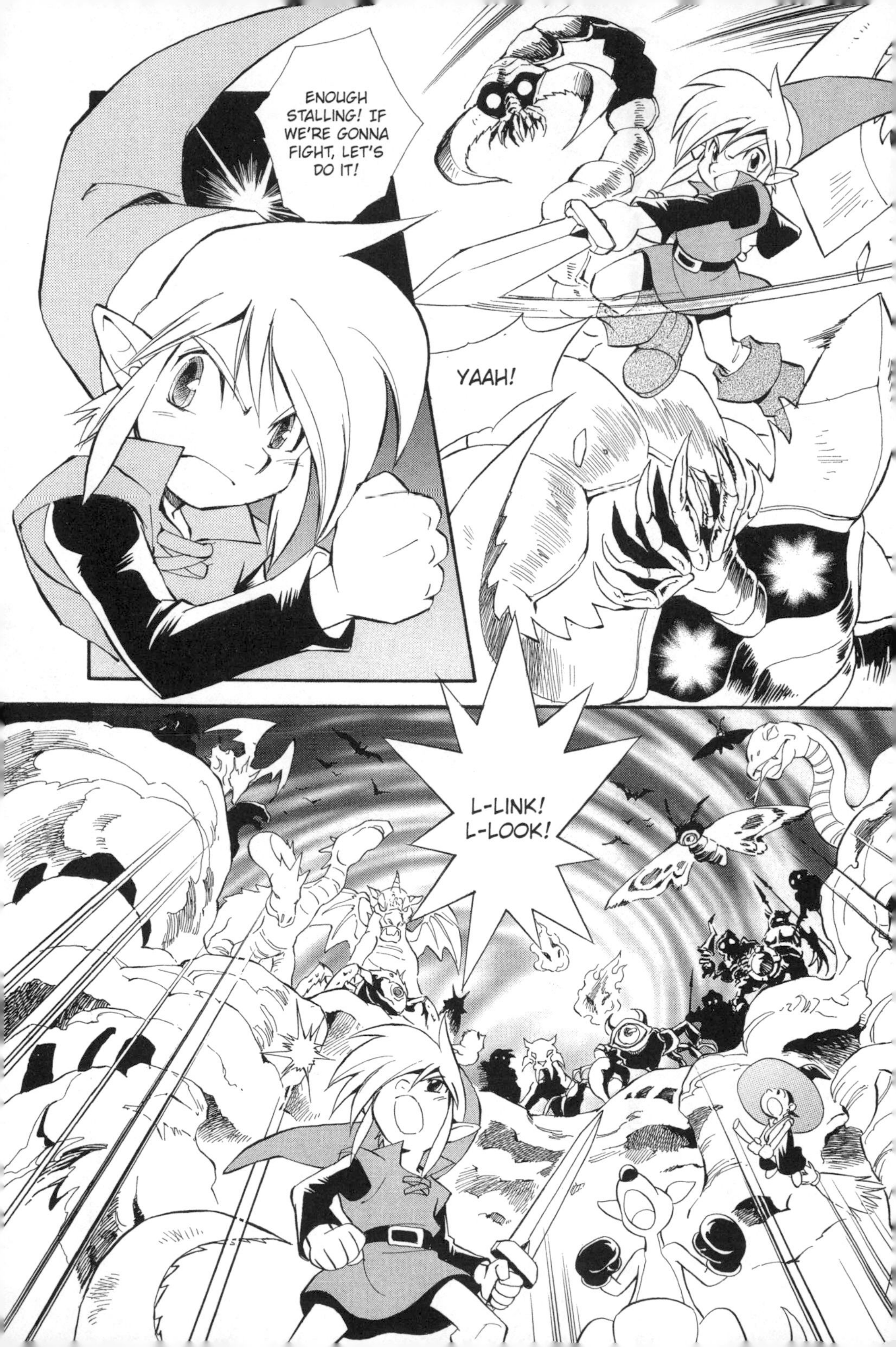
YAAH!
ENOUGH STALLING! IF WE'RE GONNA FIGHT, LET'S DO IT!
L-LINK! L-LOOK!

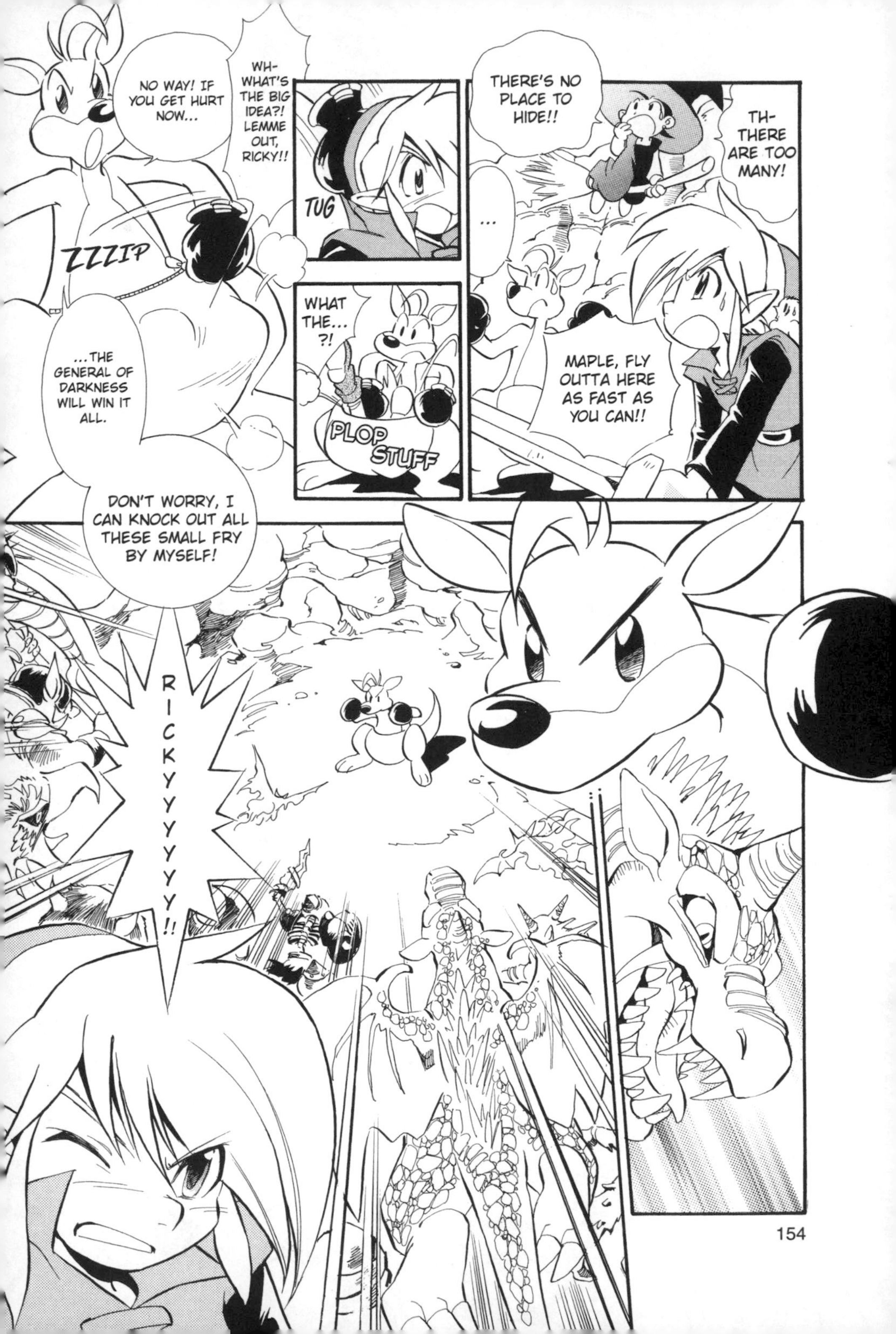
TH- THERE ARE TOO MANY!
THERE'S NO PLACE TO HIDE!!
...
MAPLE, FLY OUTTA HERE AS FAST AS YOU CAN!!
TUG
WH- WHAT'S THE BIG IDEA?! LEMME OUT, RICKY!!
WHAT THE... ?!
PLOP
STUFF
NO WAY! IF YOU GET HURT NOW...
ZZZIP
...THE GENERAL OF DARKNESS WILL WIN IT ALL.
DON'T WORRY, I CAN KNOCK OUT ALL THESE SMALL FRY BY MYSELF!
RICKYYYYYY!!

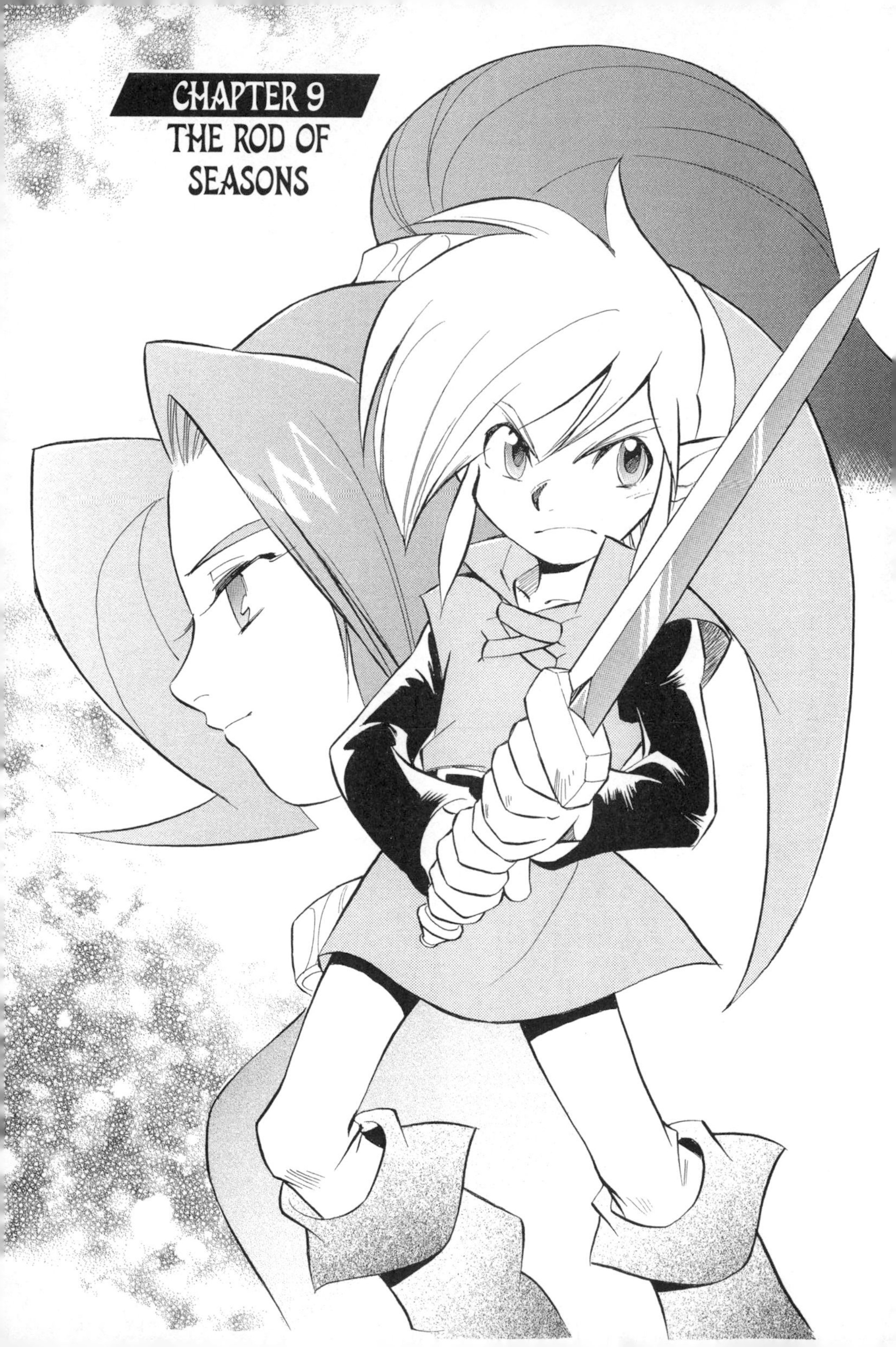
CHAPTER 9
THE ROD OF
SEASONS

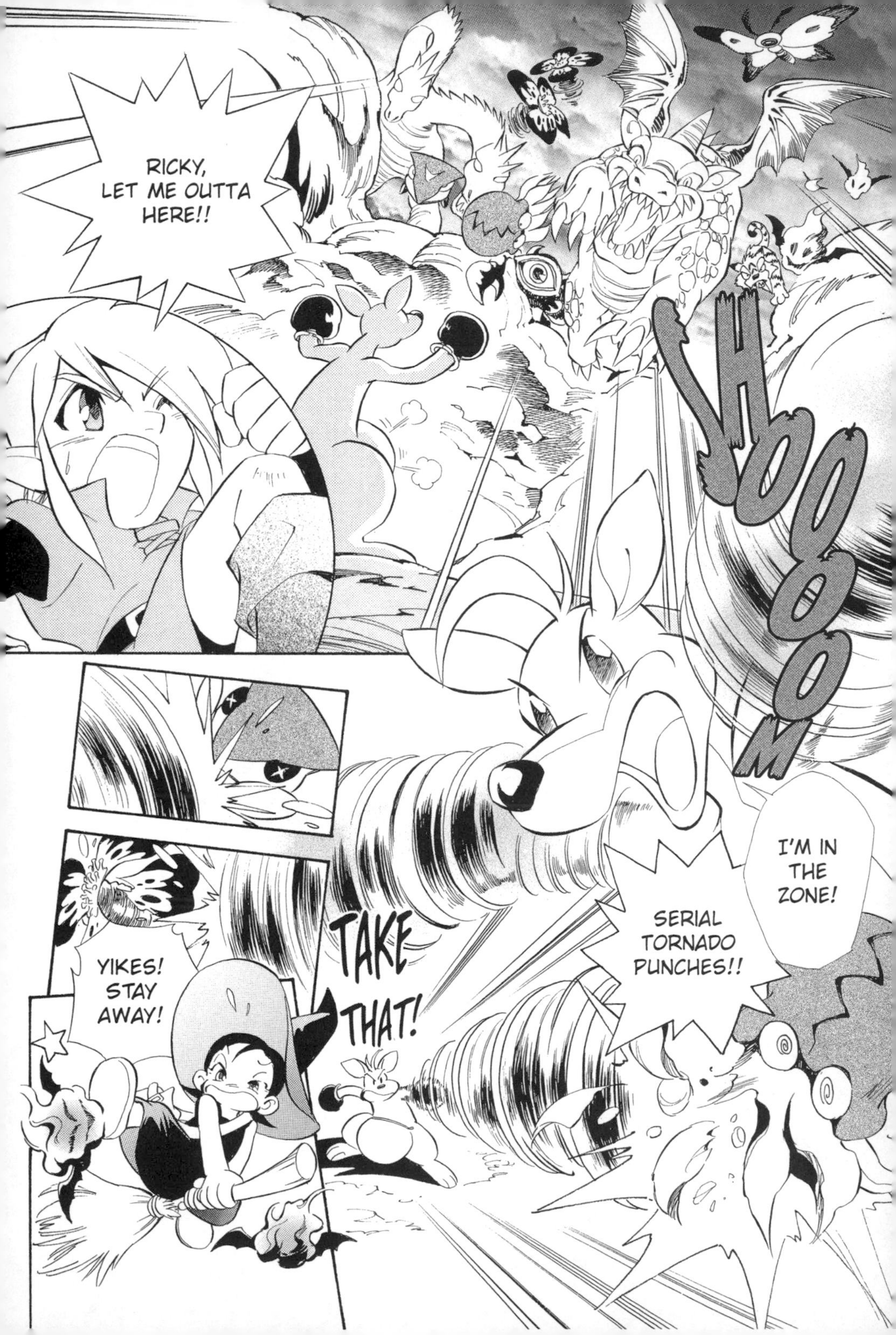
RICKY, LET ME OUTTA HERE!!
SHOOOOM
I'M IN THE ZONE!
SERIAL TORNADO PUNCHES!!
TAKE THAT!
YIKES! STAY AWAY!

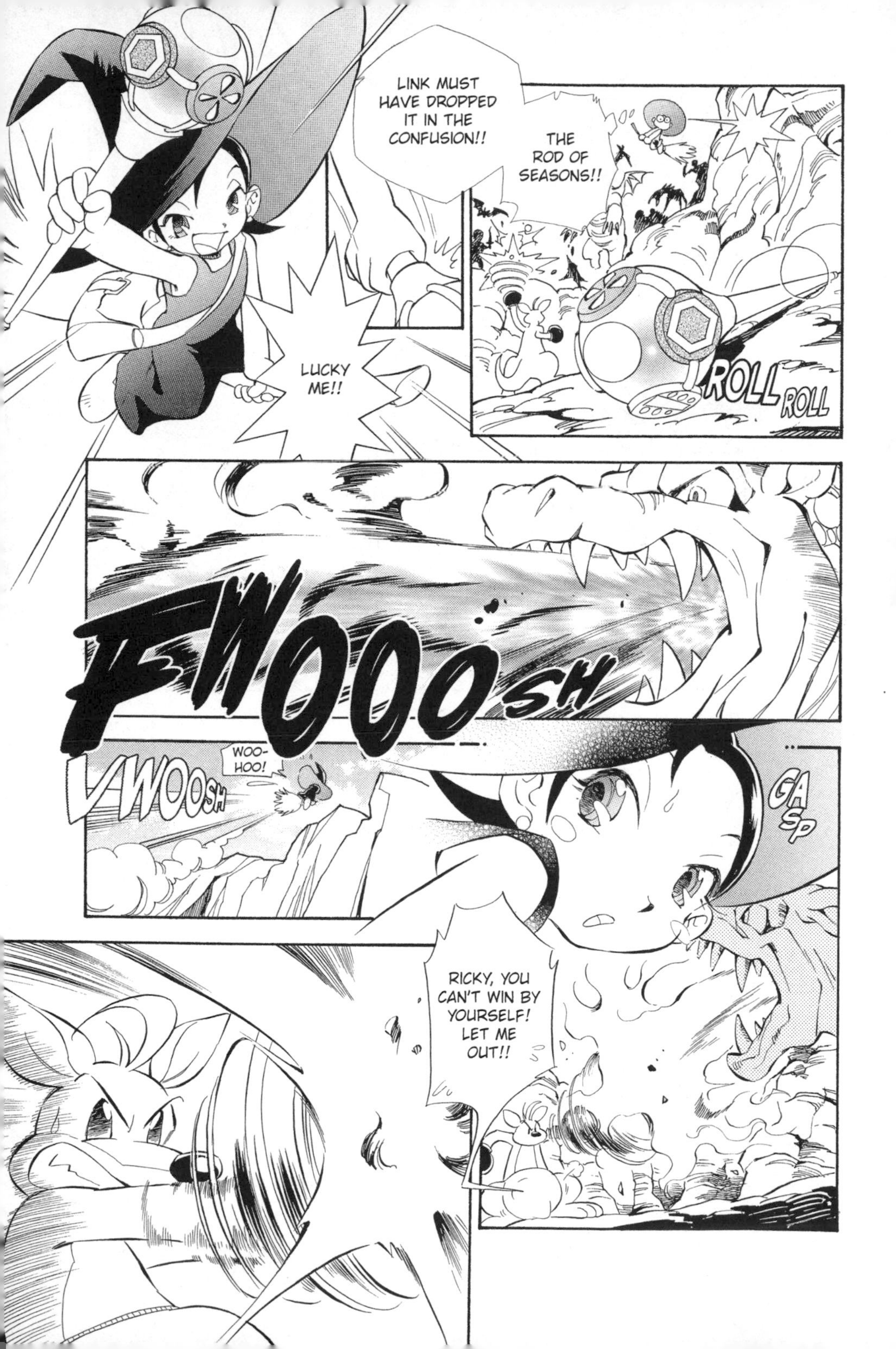
THE ROD OF SEASONS!!
ROLL ROLL
LINK MUST HAVE DROPPED IT IN THE CONFUSION!!
LUCKY ME!!
FWOOOSH
..
GASP
WOO-HOO!
VWOOSH
RICKY, YOU CAN'T WIN BY YOURSELF! LET ME OUT!!

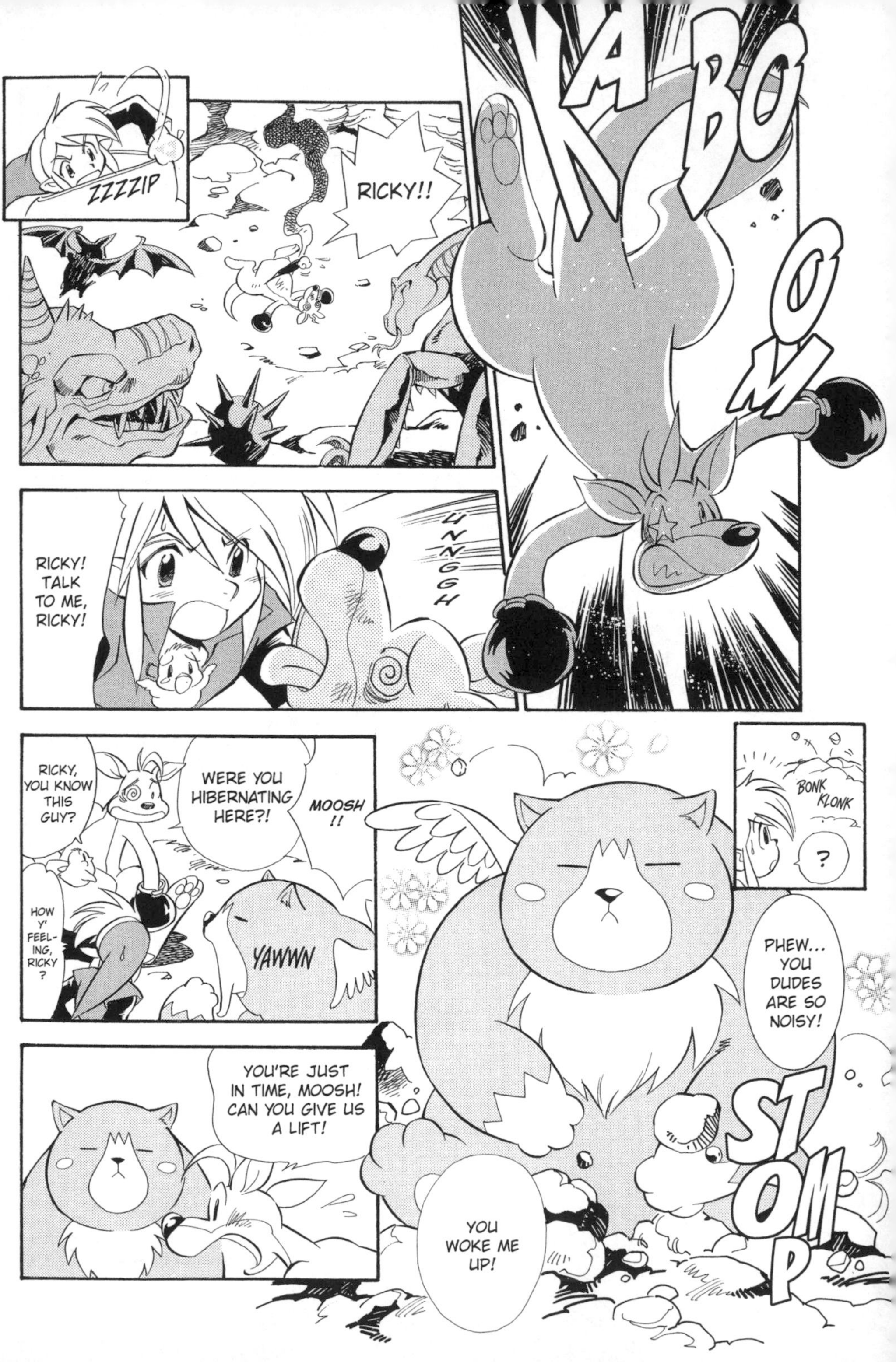
KABOOM
UNNGGH
RICKY!!
ZZZZIP
RICKY! TALK TO ME, RICKY!
BONK KLONK
?
PHEW... YOU DUDES ARE SO NOISY!
YOU WOKE ME UP!
STOMP
WERE YOU HIBERNATING HERE?!
MOOSH !!
RICKY, YOU KNOW THIS GUY?
YAWWN
HOW Y' FEEL-ING, RICKY ?
YOU'RE JUST IN TIME, MOOSH! CAN YOU GIVE US A LIFT!

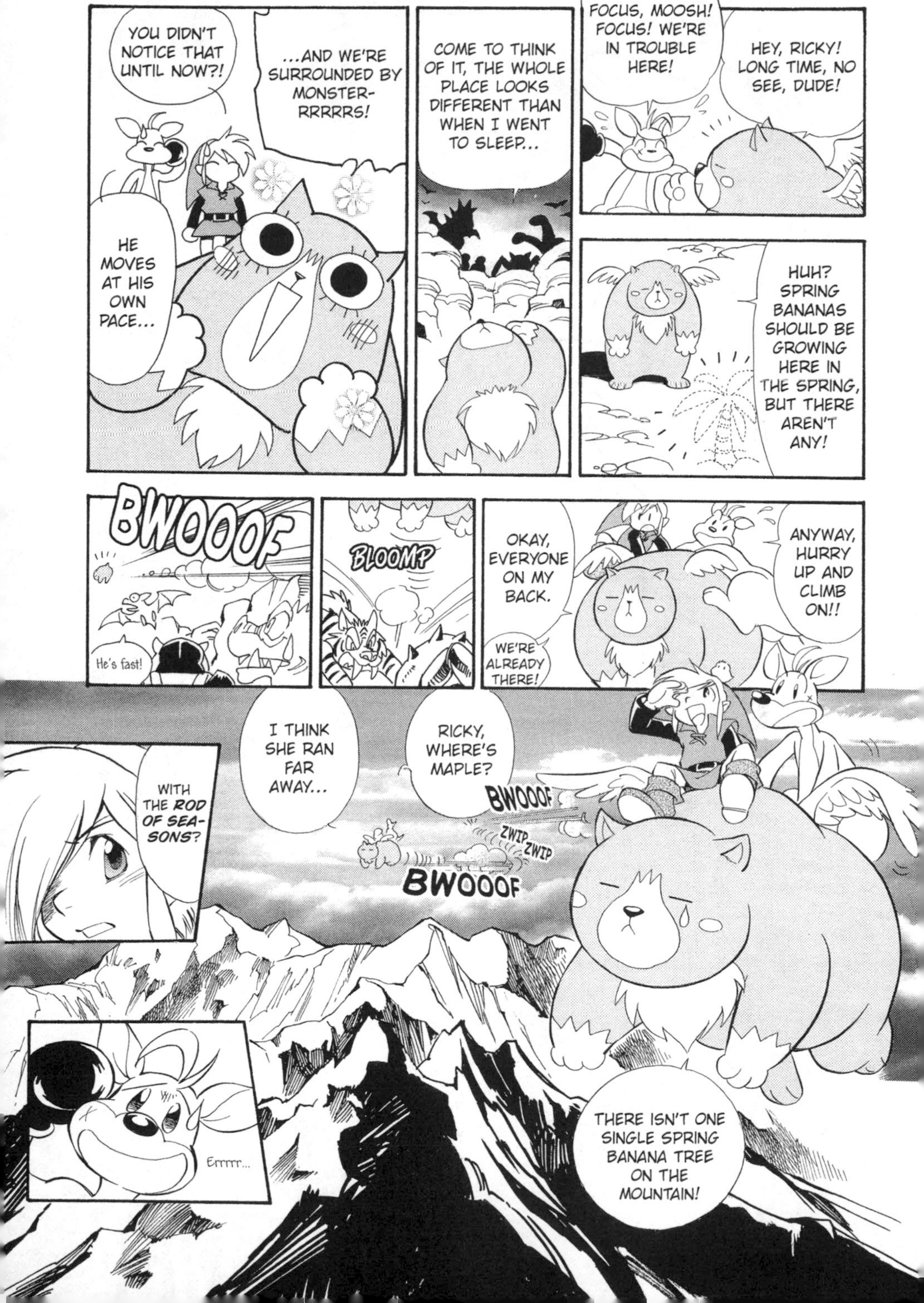
HEY, RICKY! LONG TIME, NO SEE, DUDE!
FOCUS, MOOSH! FOCUS! WE'RE IN TROUBLE HERE!
HUH? SPRING BANANAS SHOULD BE GROWING HERE IN THE SPRING, BUT THERE AREN'T ANY!
COME TO THINK OF IT, THE WHOLE PLACE LOOKS DIFFERENT THAN WHEN I WENT TO SLEEP...
...AND WE'RE SURROUNDED BY MONSTER-RRRRRS!
YOU DIDN'T NOTICE THAT UNTIL NOW?!
HE MOVES AT HIS OWN PACE...
ANYWAY, HURRY UP AND CLIMB ON!!
OKAY, EVERYONE ON MY BACK.
WE'RE ALREADY THERE!
BLOOMP
BWOOOF
He's fast!
RICKY, WHERE'S MAPLE?
BWOOOF
ZWIP ZWIP
I THINK SHE RAN FAR AWAY...
BWOOOF
WITH THE *ROD OF SEASONS*?
THERE ISN'T ONE SINGLE SPRING BANANA TREE ON THE MOUNTAIN!
Errrrr...

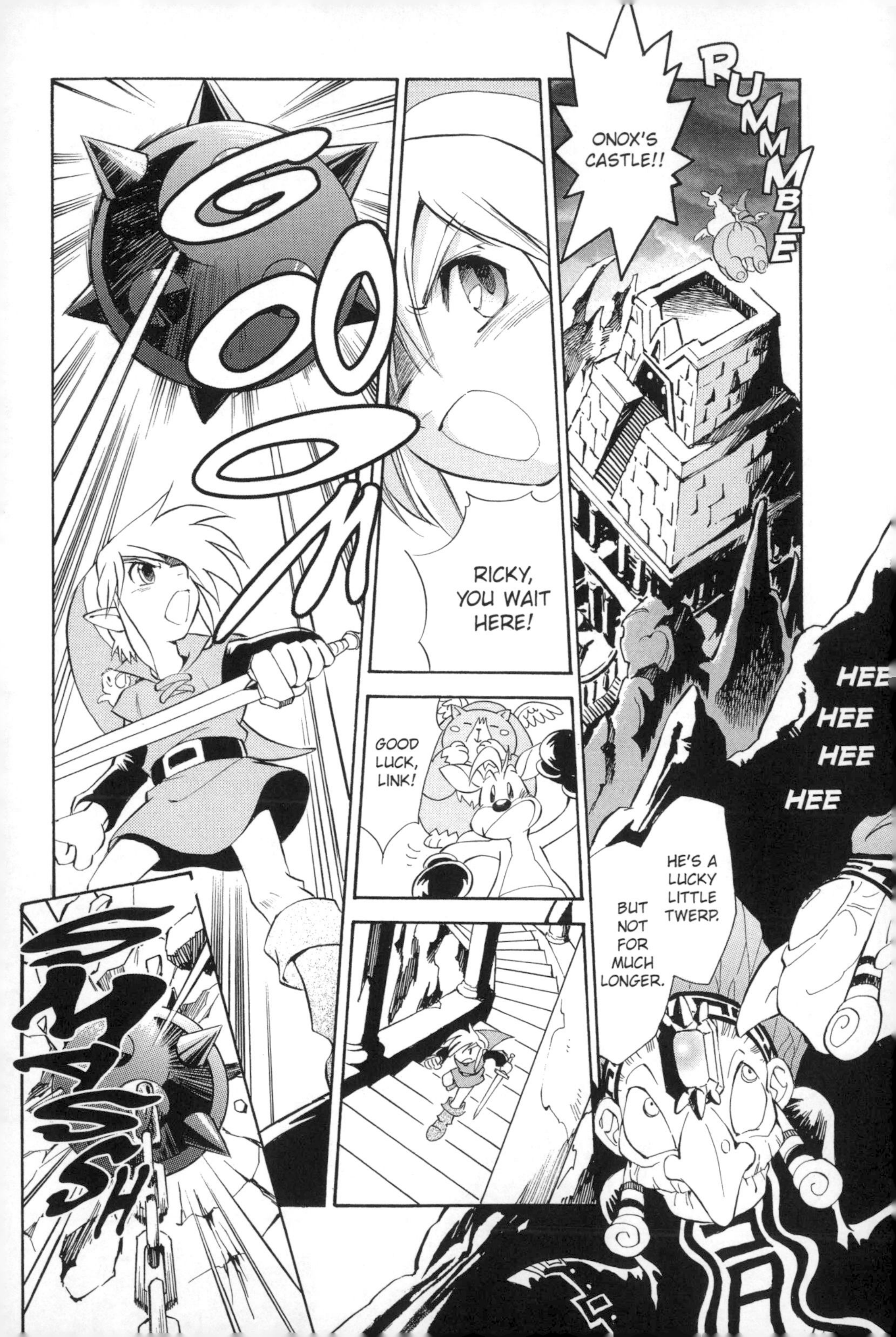
ONOX'S CASTLE!!
RUMMMBLE
HEE HEE HEE HEE
HE'S A LUCKY LITTLE TWERP.
BUT NOT FOR MUCH LONGER.
RICKY, YOU WAIT HERE!
GOOD LUCK, LINK!
GOOOOM
SMASH

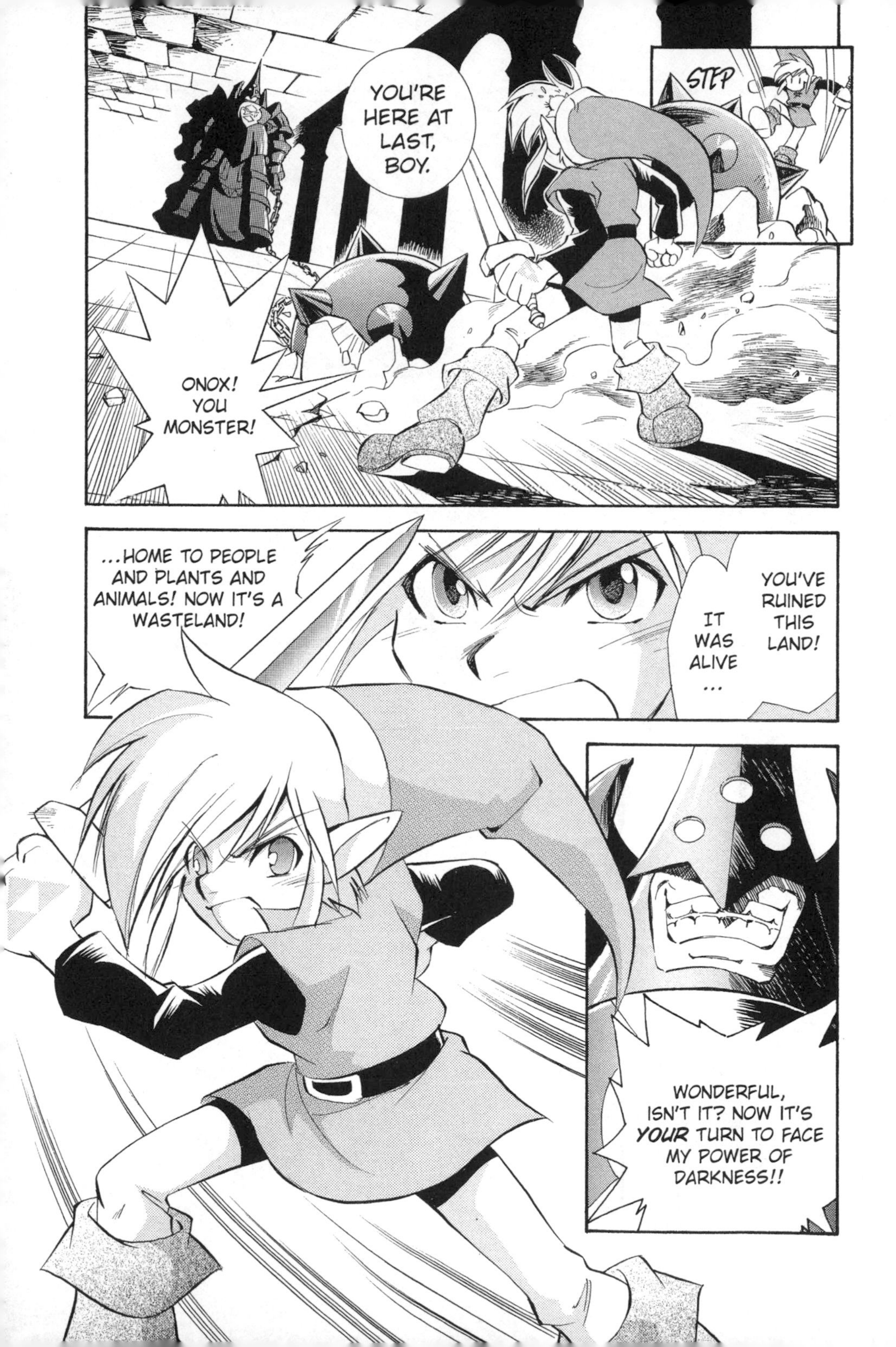
STEP
YOU'RE HERE AT LAST, BOY.
ONOX! YOU MONSTER!
YOU'VE RUINED THIS LAND!
IT WAS ALIVE ...
...HOME TO PEOPLE AND PLANTS AND ANIMALS! NOW IT'S A WASTELAND!
WONDERFUL, ISN'T IT? NOW IT'S **YOUR** TURN TO FACE MY POWER OF DARKNESS!!

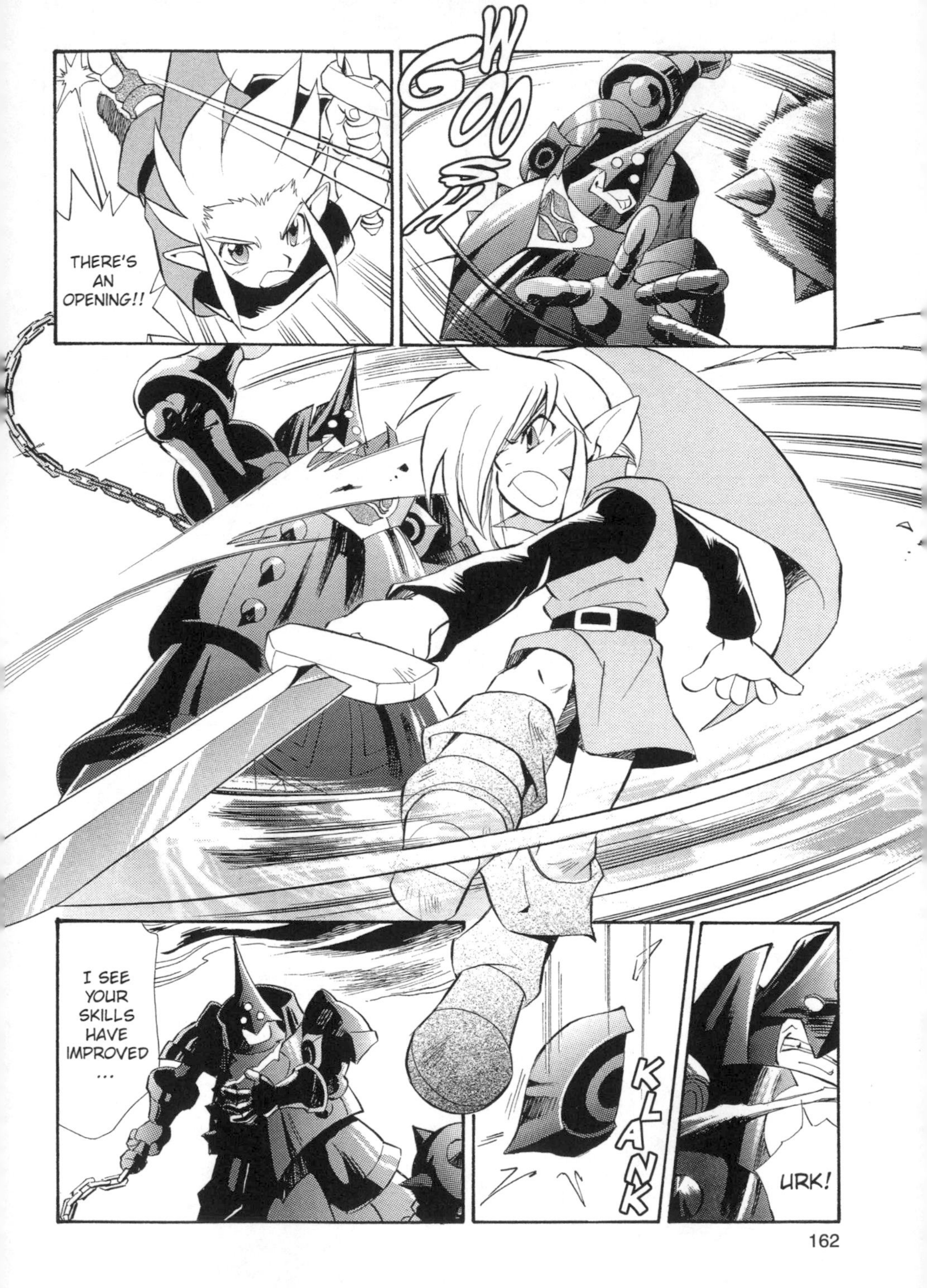
GWOOSH
THERE'S AN OPENING!!
URK!
KLANK
I SEE YOUR SKILLS HAVE IMPROVED ...

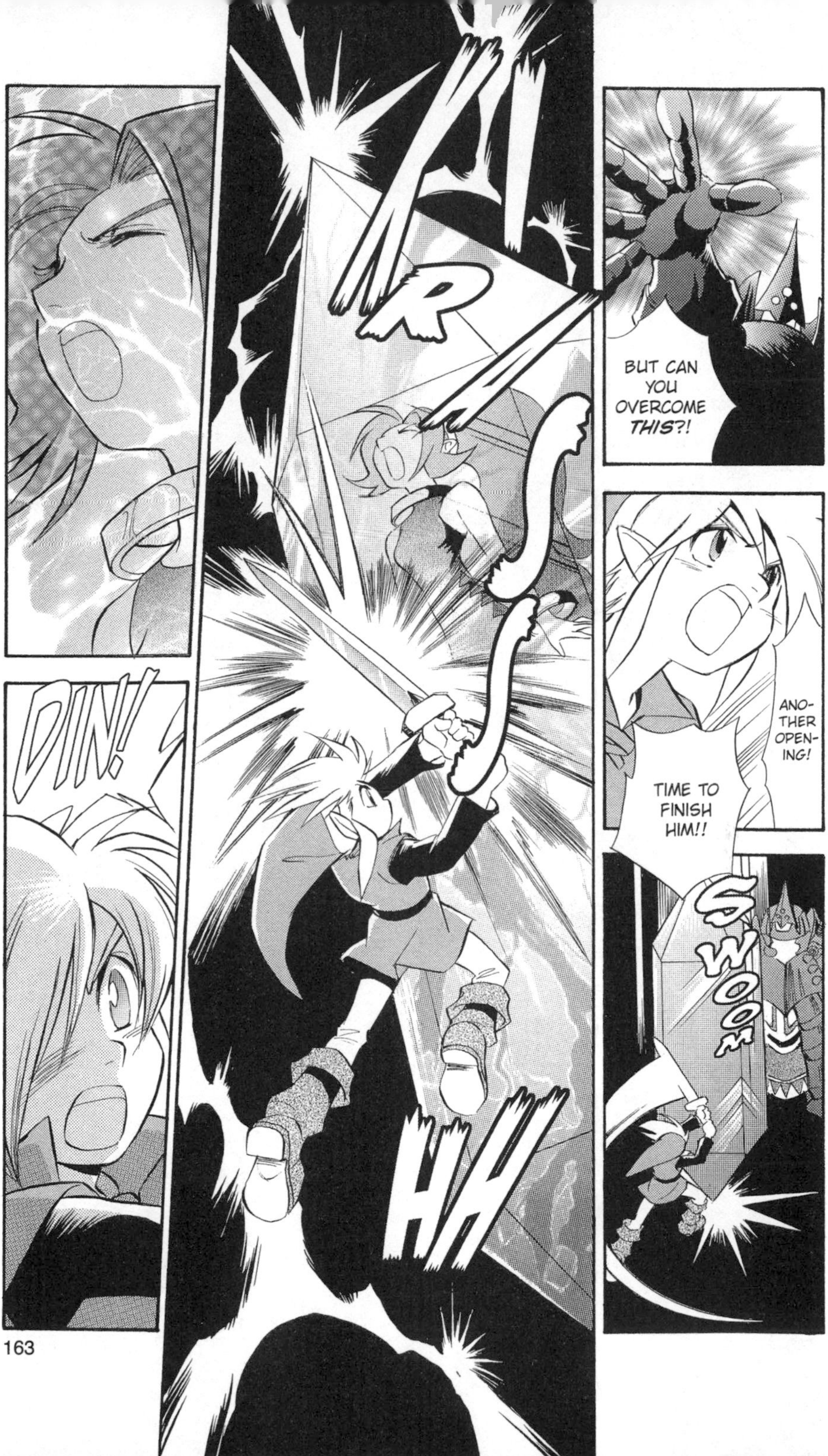
BUT CAN YOU OVERCOME *THIS*?!
ANO-THER OPEN-ING!
TIME TO FINISH HIM!!
SWOOM
R
HH
DIN!!

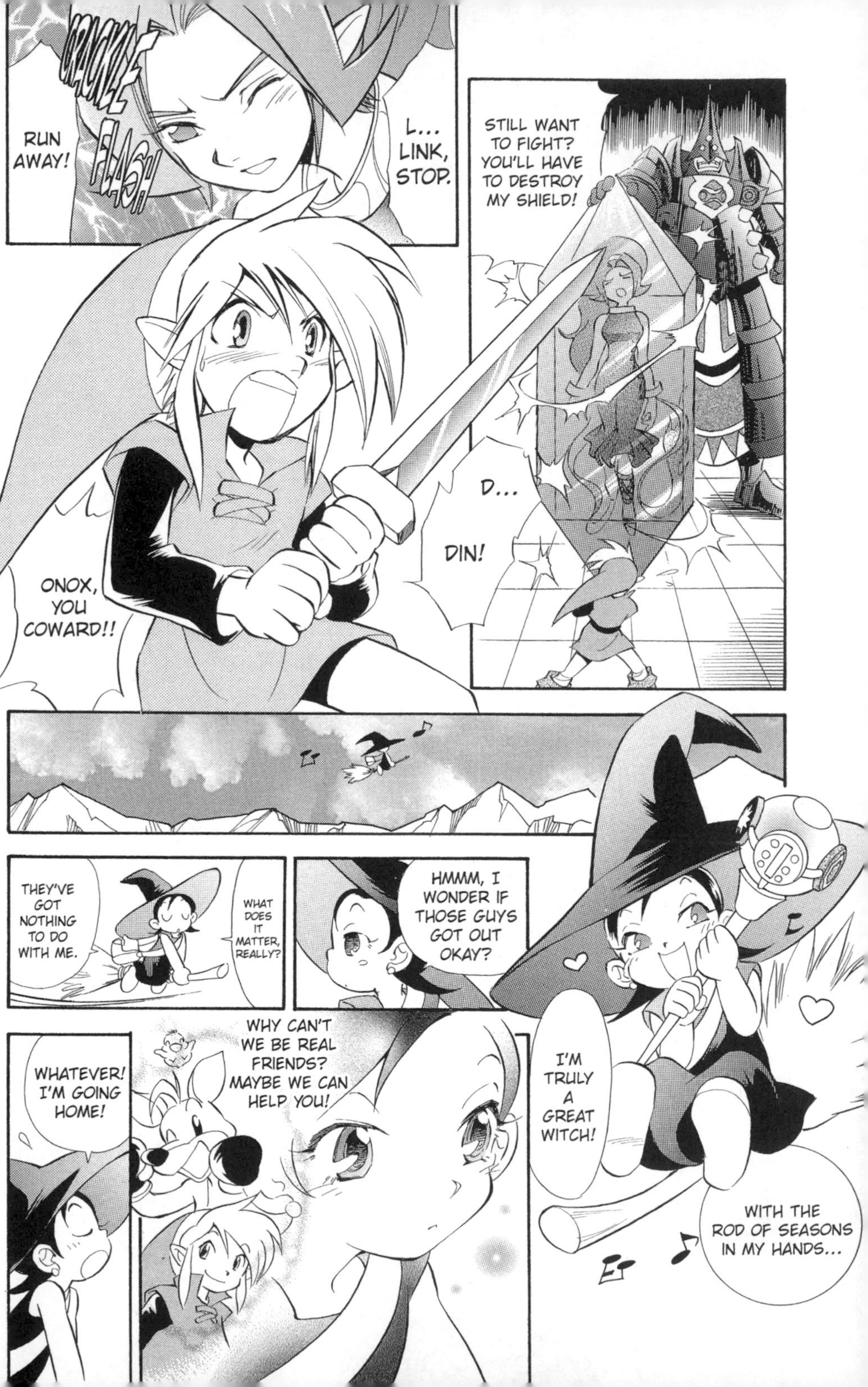
STILL WANT TO FIGHT? YOU'LL HAVE TO DESTROY MY SHIELD!
D...
DIN!
L... LINK, STOP.
CRACKLE FLASH
RUN AWAY!
ONOX, YOU COWARD!!
I'M TRULY A GREAT WITCH!
WITH THE ROD OF SEASONS IN MY HANDS...
HMMM, I WONDER IF THOSE GUYS GOT OUT OKAY?
WHAT DOES IT MATTER, REALLY?
THEY'VE GOT NOTHING TO DO WITH ME.
WHY CAN'T WE BE REAL FRIENDS? MAYBE WE CAN HELP YOU!
WHATEVER! I'M GOING HOME!

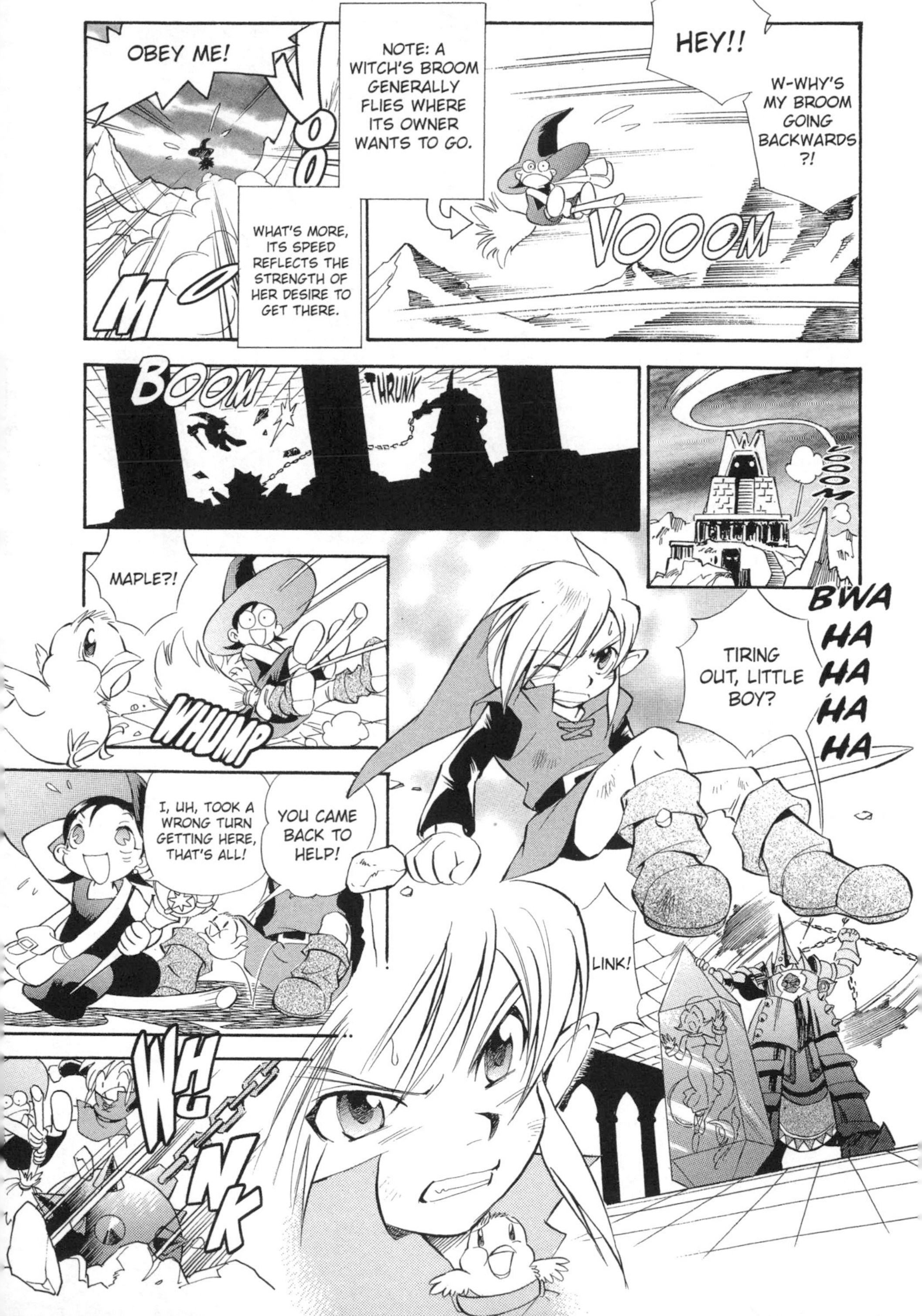
HEY!!
W-WHY'S MY BROOM GOING BACKWARDS ?!
VOOOM
NOTE: A WITCH'S BROOM GENERALLY FLIES WHERE ITS OWNER WANTS TO GO.
WHAT'S MORE, ITS SPEED REFLECTS THE STRENGTH OF HER DESIRE TO GET THERE.
OBEY ME!
VOOOM
VOOOM
THRUNK
BOOM
BWA HA HA HA HA HA
TIRING OUT, LITTLE BOY?
MAPLE?!
WHUMP
YOU CAME BACK TO HELP!
I, UH, TOOK A WRONG TURN GETTING HERE, THAT'S ALL!
LINK!
WHUNK

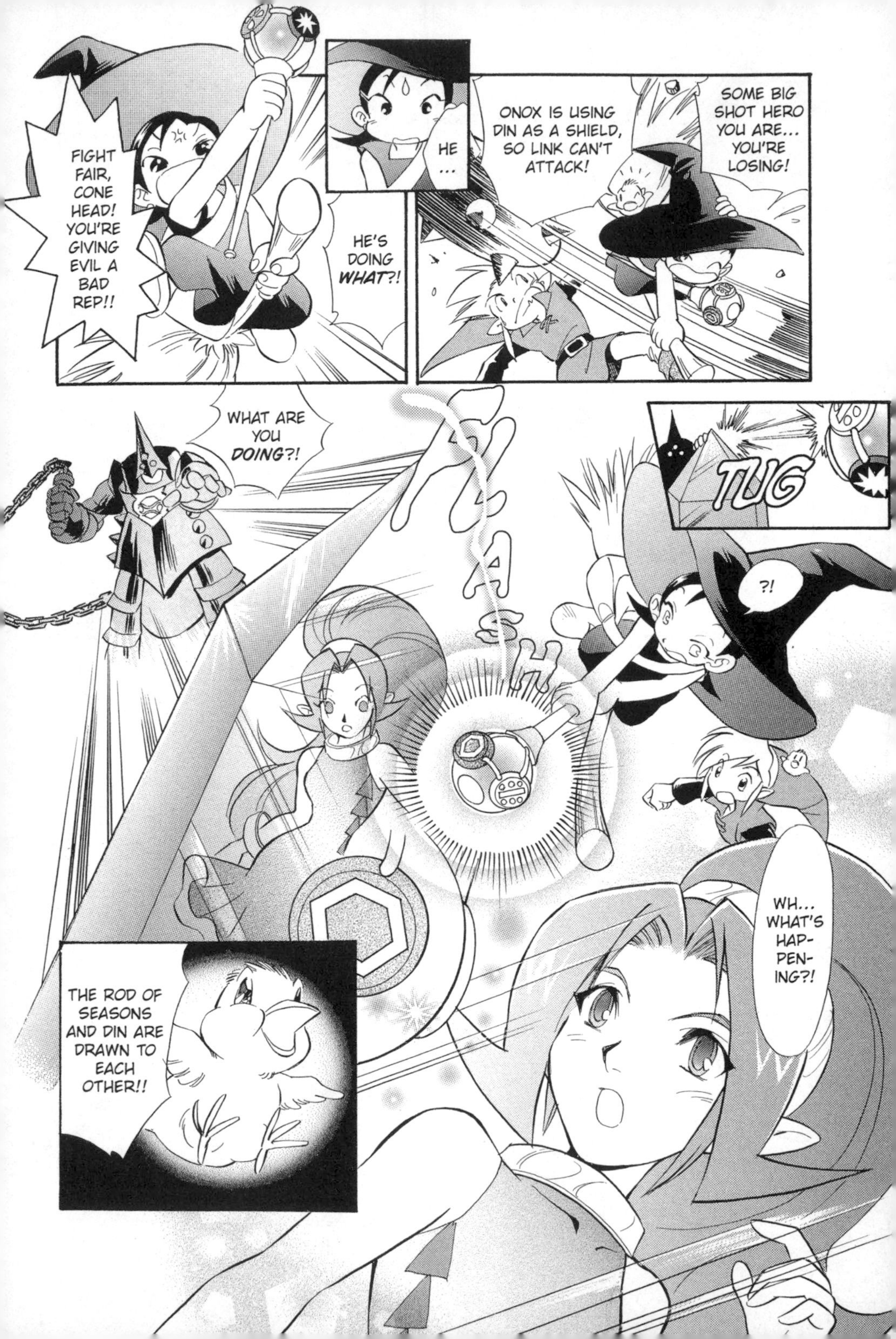
SOME BIG SHOT HERO YOU ARE... YOU'RE LOSING!
ONOX IS USING DIN AS A SHIELD, SO LINK CAN'T ATTACK!
HE ...
HE'S DOING *WHAT*?!
FIGHT FAIR, CONE HEAD! YOU'RE GIVING EVIL A BAD REP!!
TUG
?!
WHAT ARE YOU *DOING*?!
FLASH
WH... WHAT'S HAP-PEN-ING?!
THE ROD OF SEASONS AND DIN ARE DRAWN TO EACH OTHER!!

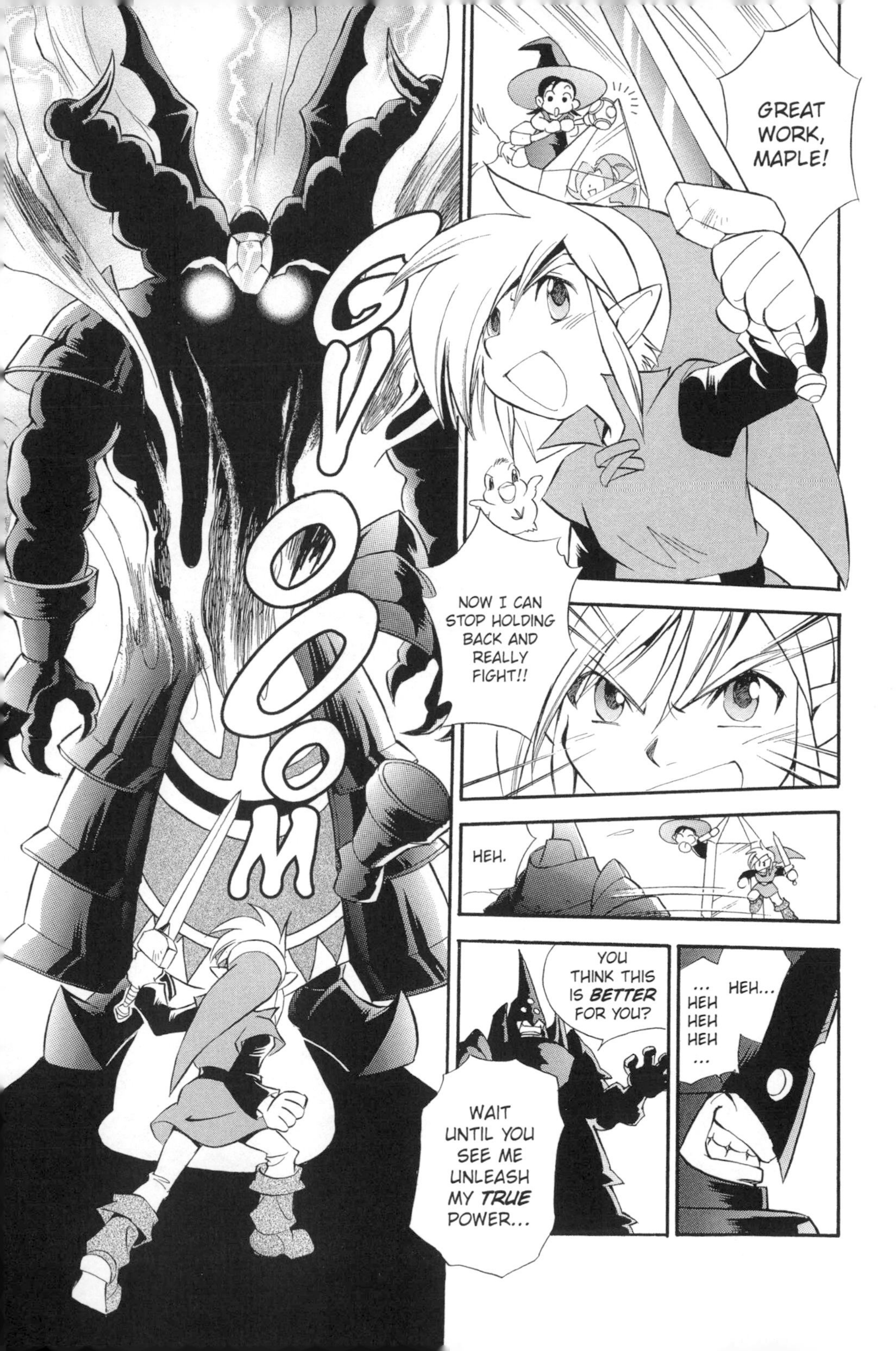
GREAT WORK, MAPLE!
NOW I CAN STOP HOLDING BACK AND REALLY FIGHT!!
HEH.
HEH... ... HEH HEH HEH ...
YOU THINK THIS IS **BETTER** FOR YOU?
WAIT UNTIL YOU SEE ME UNLEASH MY ***TRUE*** POWER...
VOOOOM

ROUGH CHARACTER ILLUSTRATION 4

Din is savvy and older than Link, so he looks up to her.

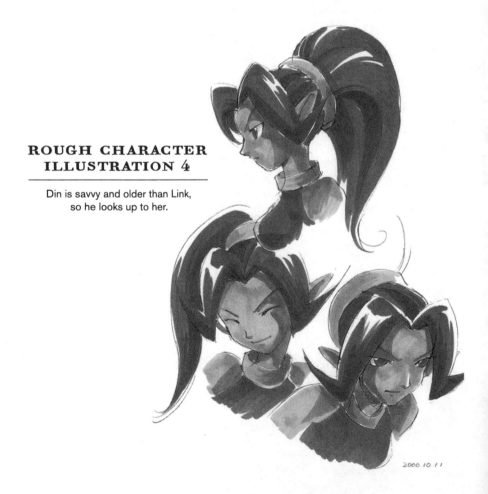

2000·10·11

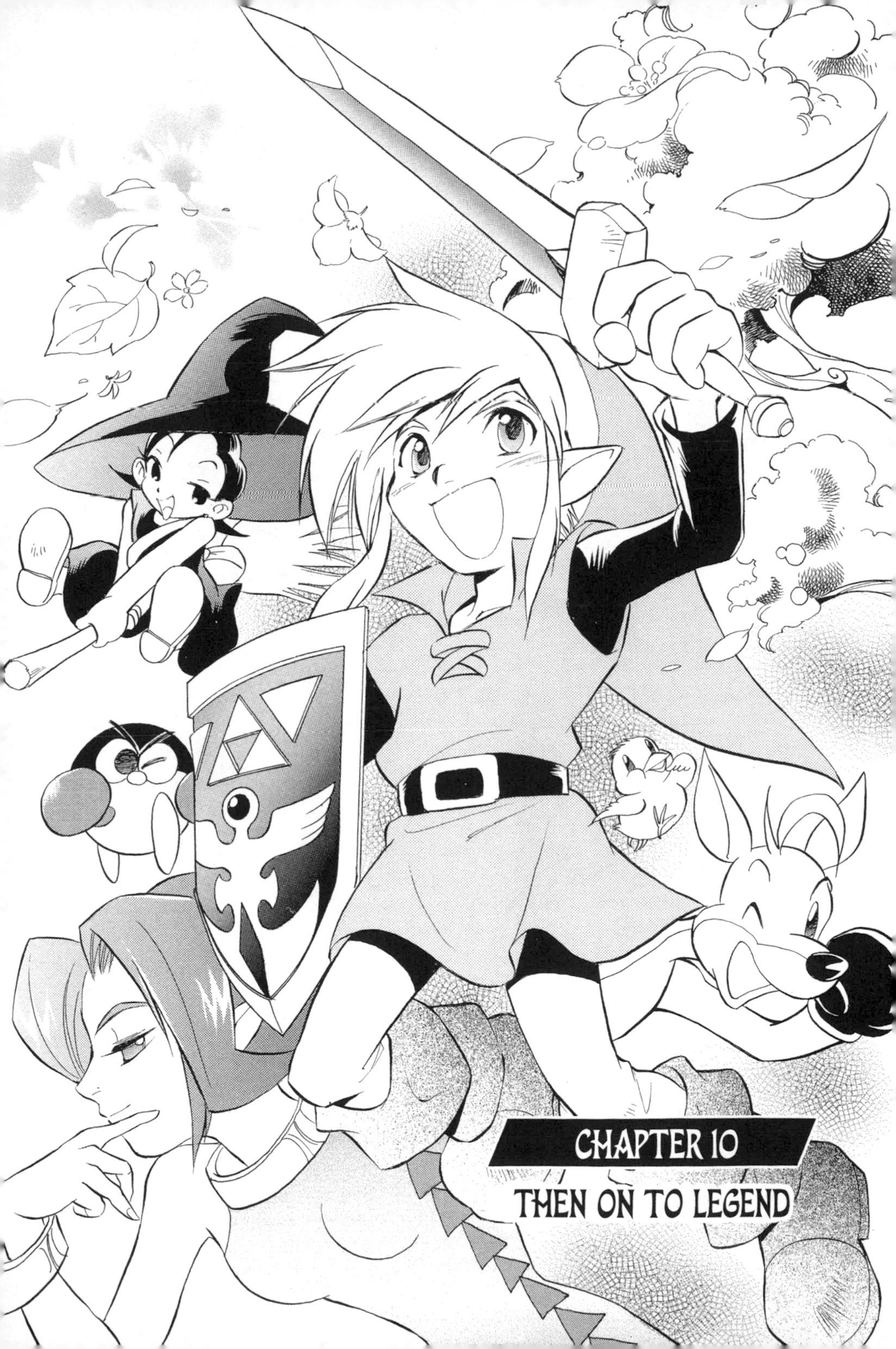
CHAPTER 10
THEN ON TO LEGEND

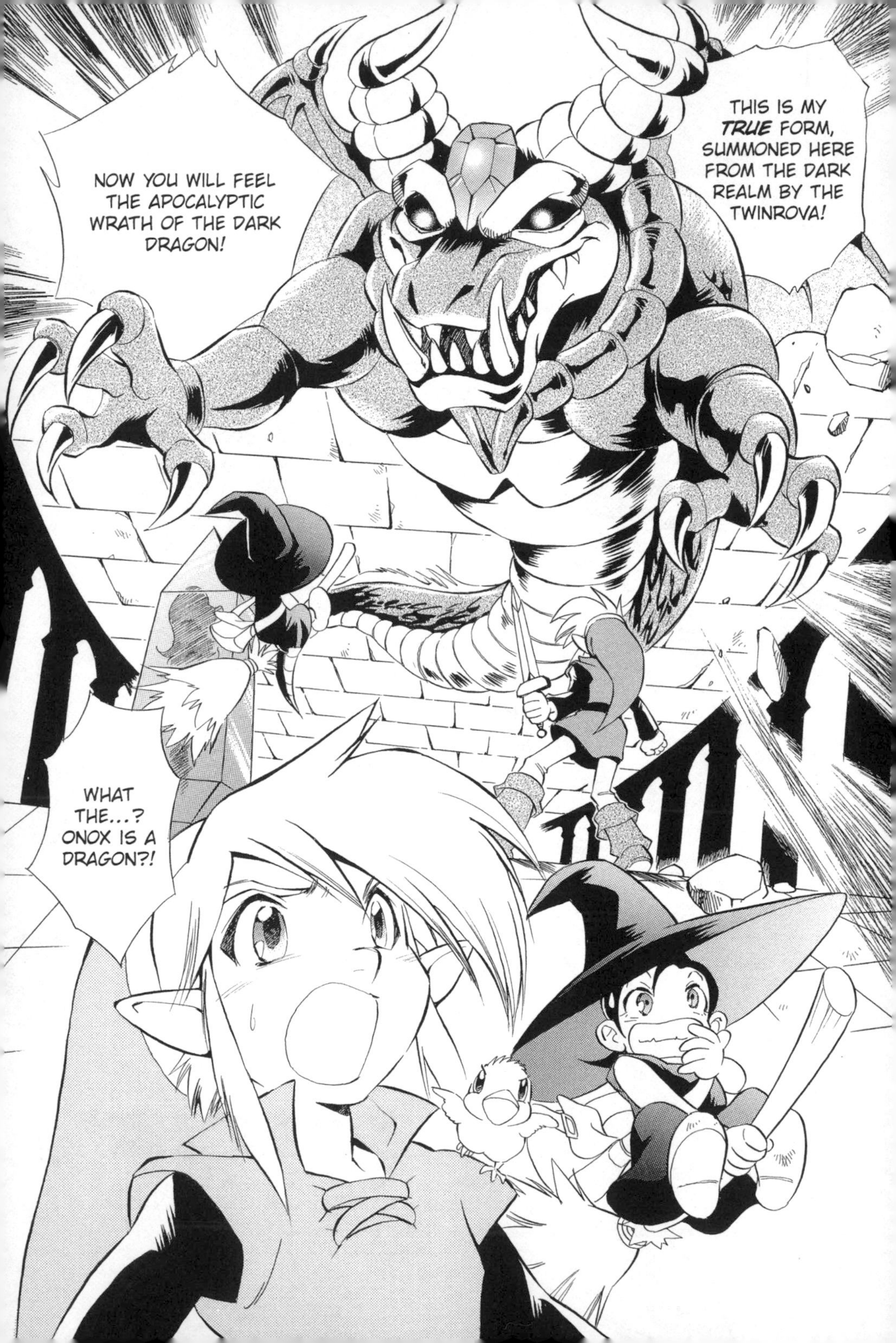
THIS IS MY **TRUE** FORM, SUMMONED HERE FROM THE DARK REALM BY THE TWINROVA!
NOW YOU WILL FEEL THE APOCALYPTIC WRATH OF THE DARK DRAGON!
WHAT THE...? ONOX IS A DRAGON?!

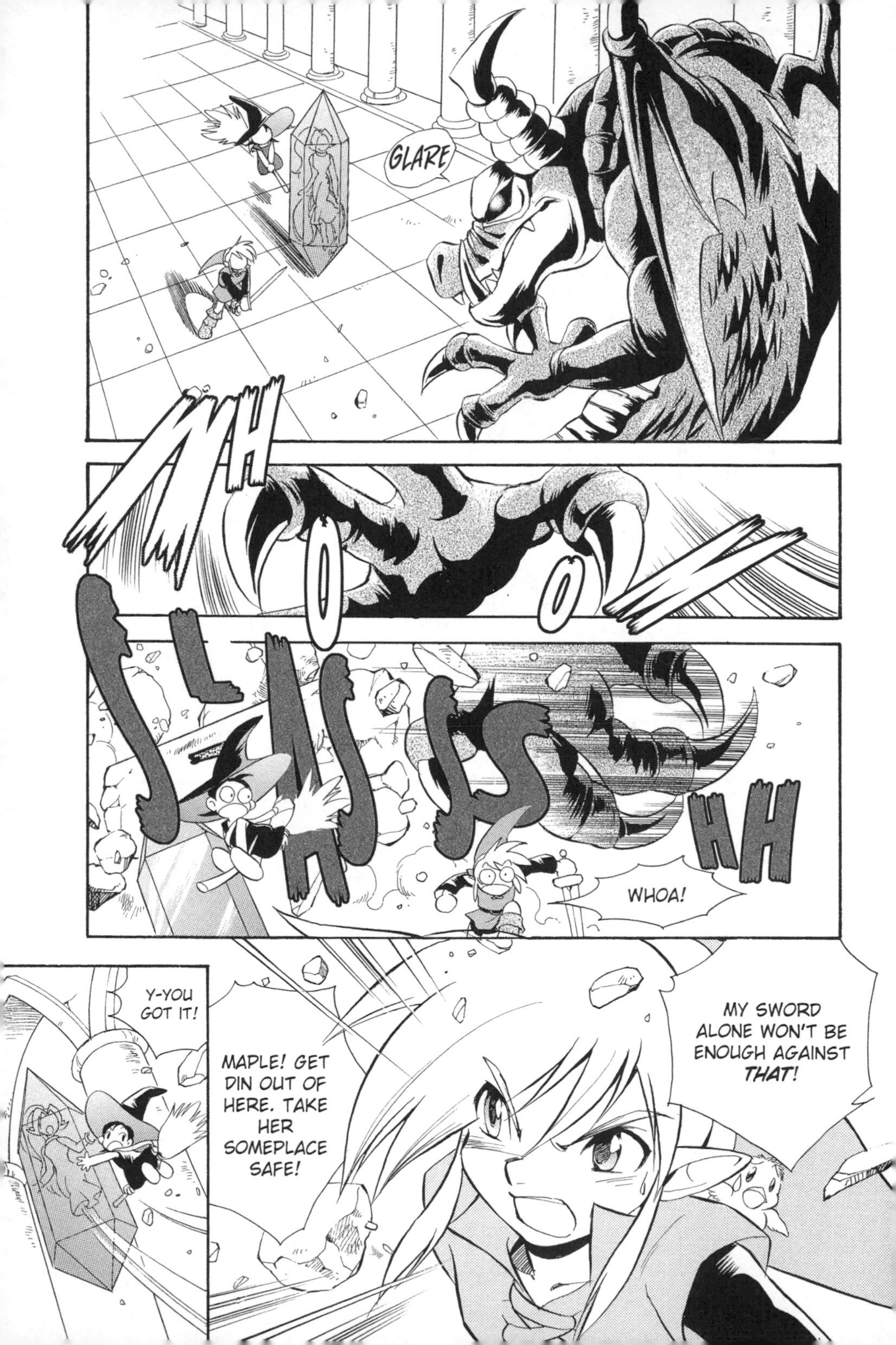
GLARE
WHOO
SLASHH
WHOA!
MY SWORD ALONE WON'T BE ENOUGH AGAINST *THAT*!
MAPLE! GET DIN OUT OF HERE. TAKE HER SOMEPLACE SAFE!
Y-YOU GOT IT!

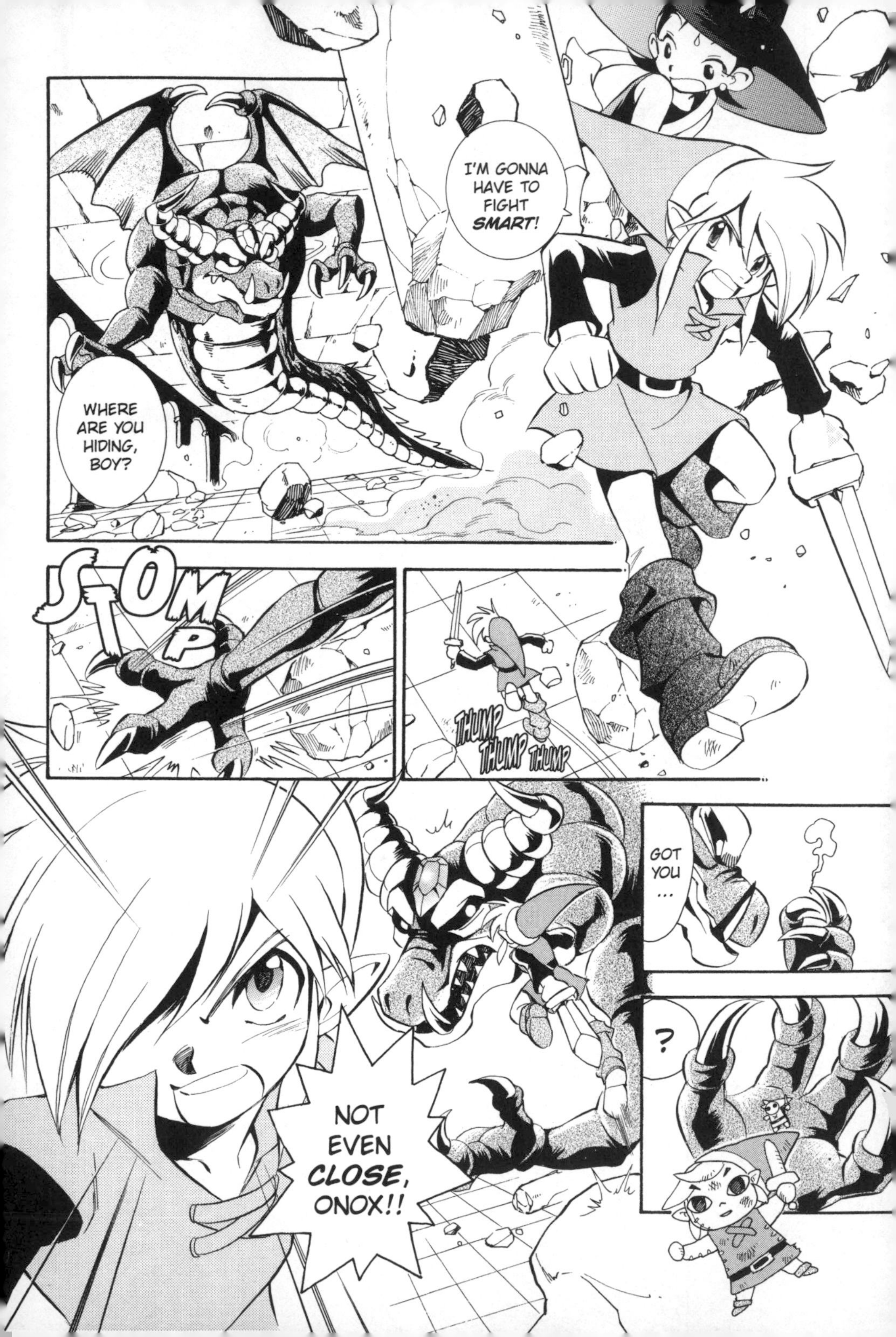

I'M GONNA HAVE TO FIGHT SMART!
WHERE ARE YOU HIDING, BOY?
THUMP THUMP THUMP
STOMP
GOT YOU ...
?
NOT EVEN CLOSE, ONOX!!

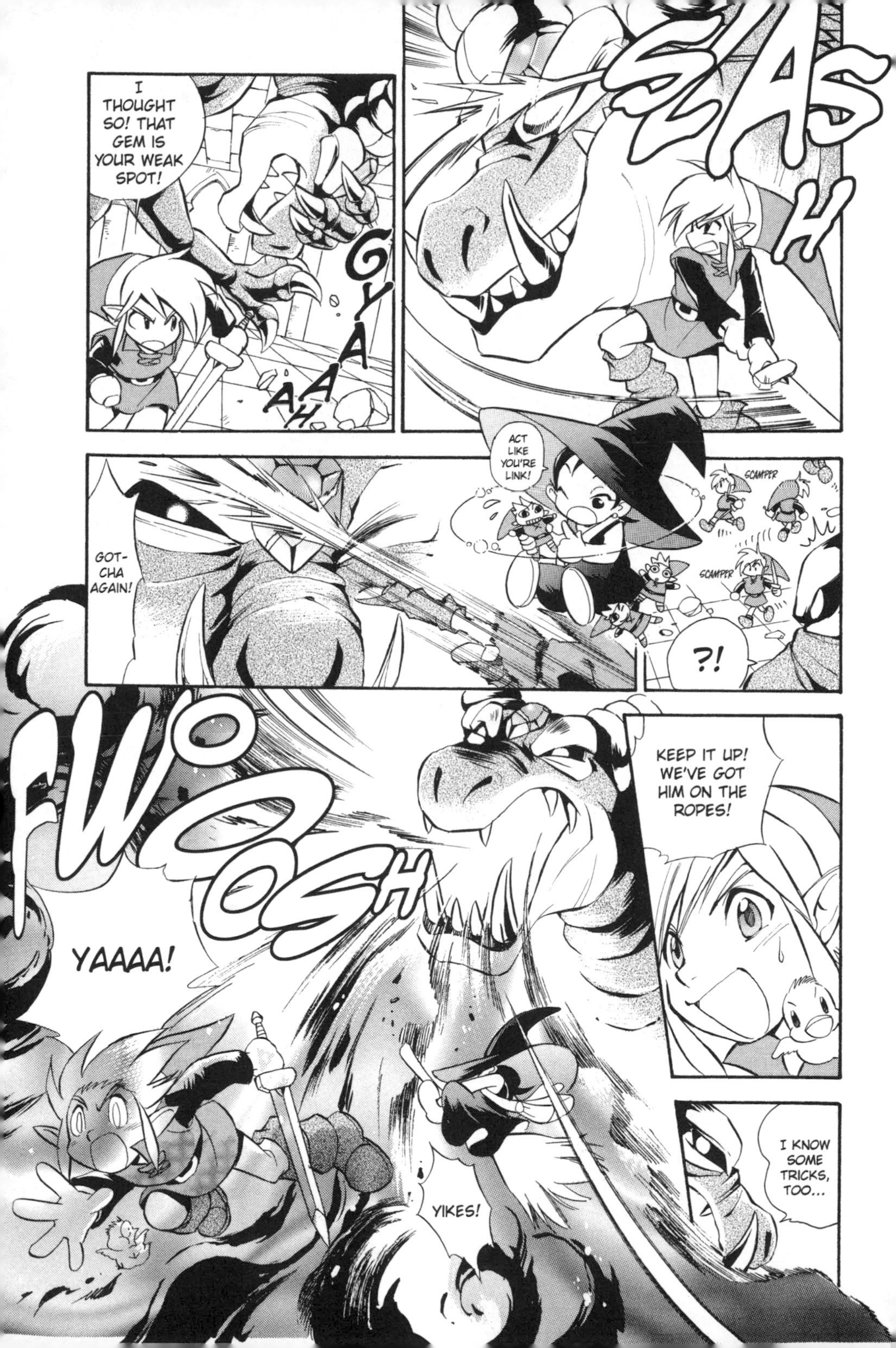
SLASH
I THOUGHT SO! THAT GEM IS YOUR WEAK SPOT!
GYAAAAAH
ACT LIKE YOU'RE LINK!
SCAMPER
SCAMPER
?!
GOT-CHA AGAIN!
KEEP IT UP! WE'VE GOT HIM ON THE ROPES!
I KNOW SOME TRICKS, TOO...
FWOOSH
YAAAA!
YIKES!

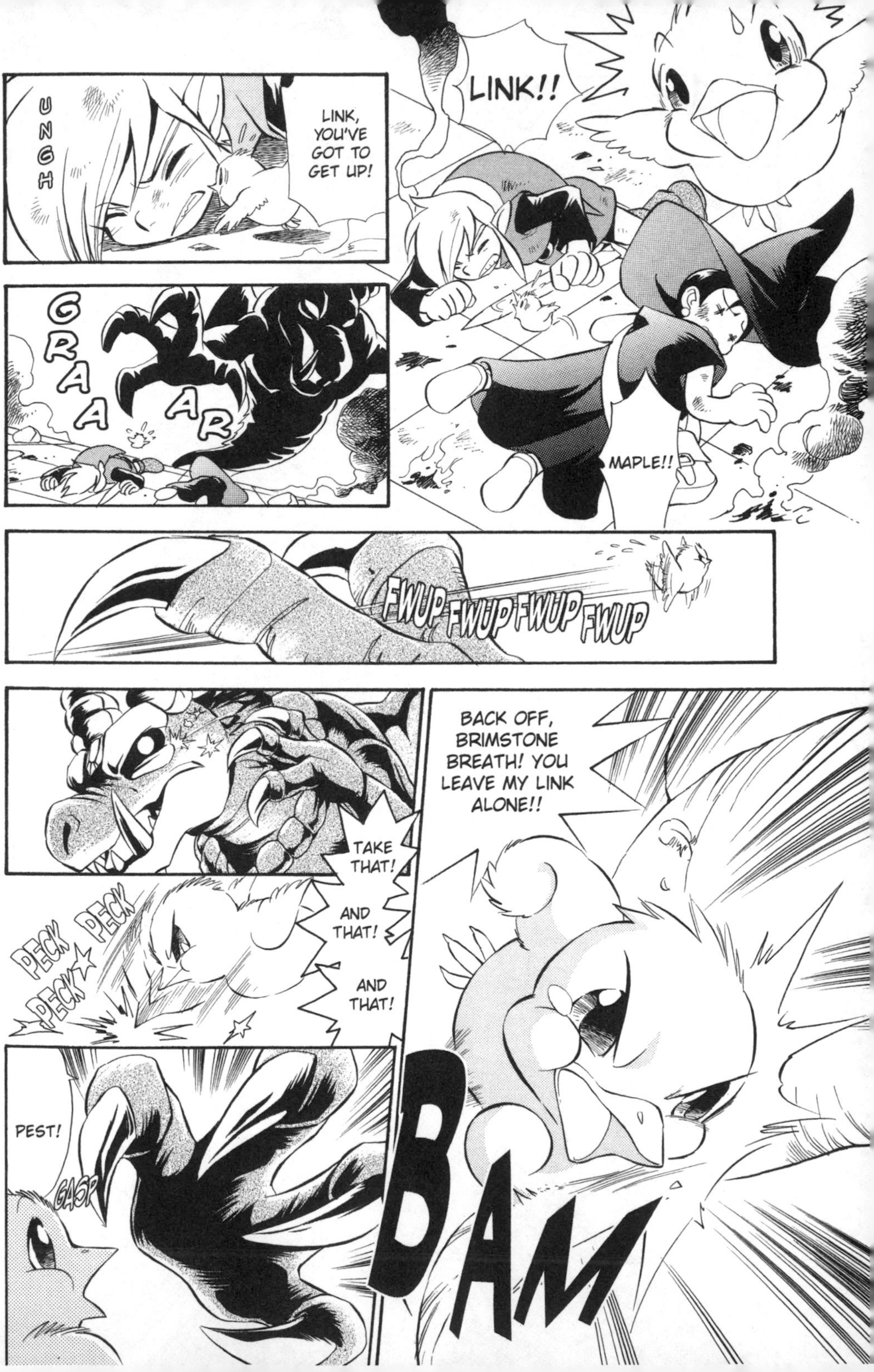
LINK!!
MAPLE!!
LINK, YOU'VE GOT TO GET UP!
UNGH
GRAAAAR
FWUP FWUP FWUP FWUP
BACK OFF, BRIMSTONE BREATH! YOU LEAVE MY LINK ALONE!!
BAM
TAKE THAT!
AND THAT!
AND THAT!
PECK PECK PECK
PEST!
GASP

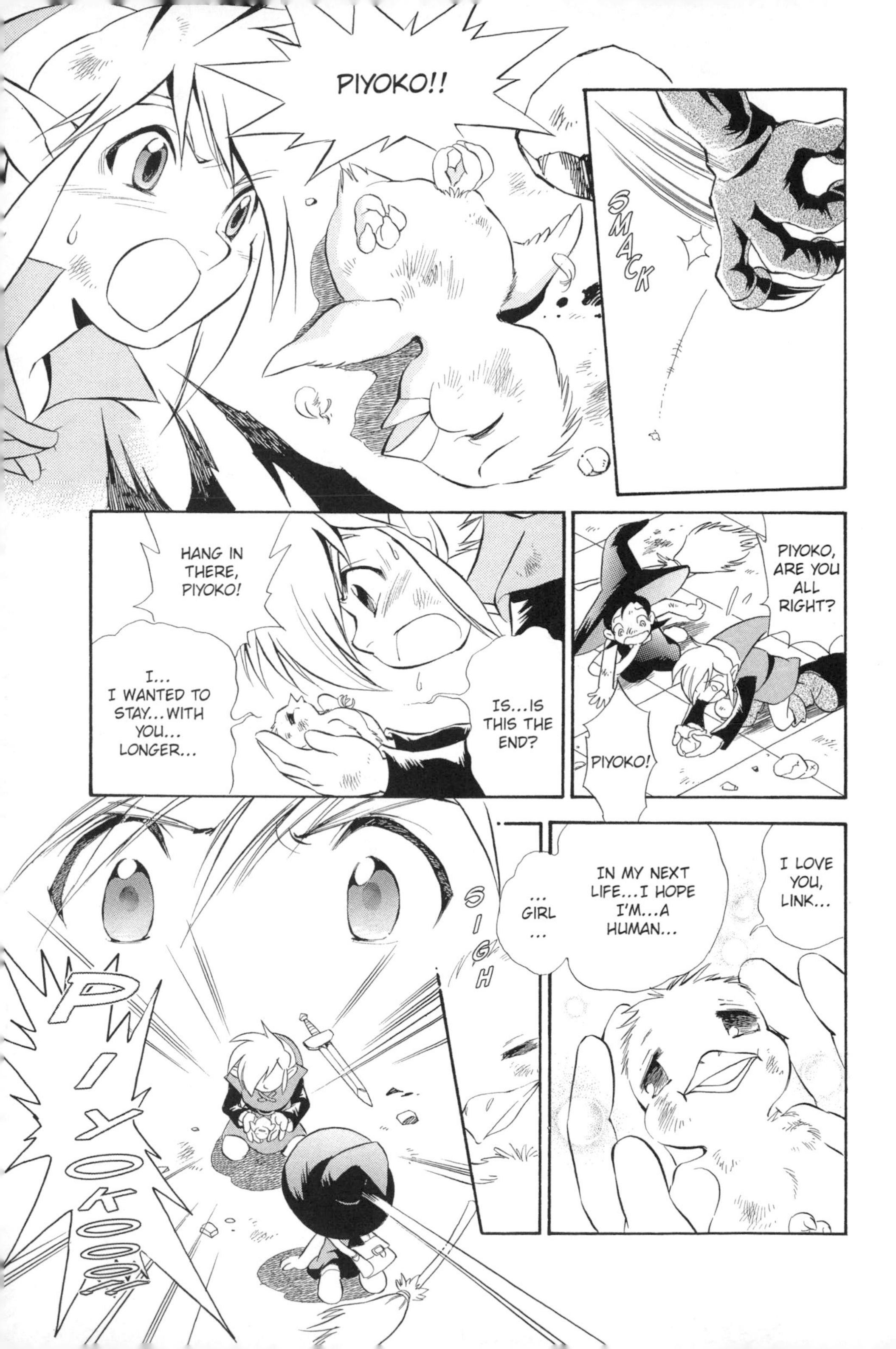
SMACK
PIYOKO!!
PIYOKO, ARE YOU ALL RIGHT?
PIYOKO!
HANG IN THERE, PIYOKO!
IS...IS THIS THE END?
I... I WANTED TO STAY...WITH YOU... LONGER...
I LOVE YOU, LINK...
IN MY NEXT LIFE...I HOPE I'M...A HUMAN...
...GIRL...
SIGH
PIYOKOOO!!

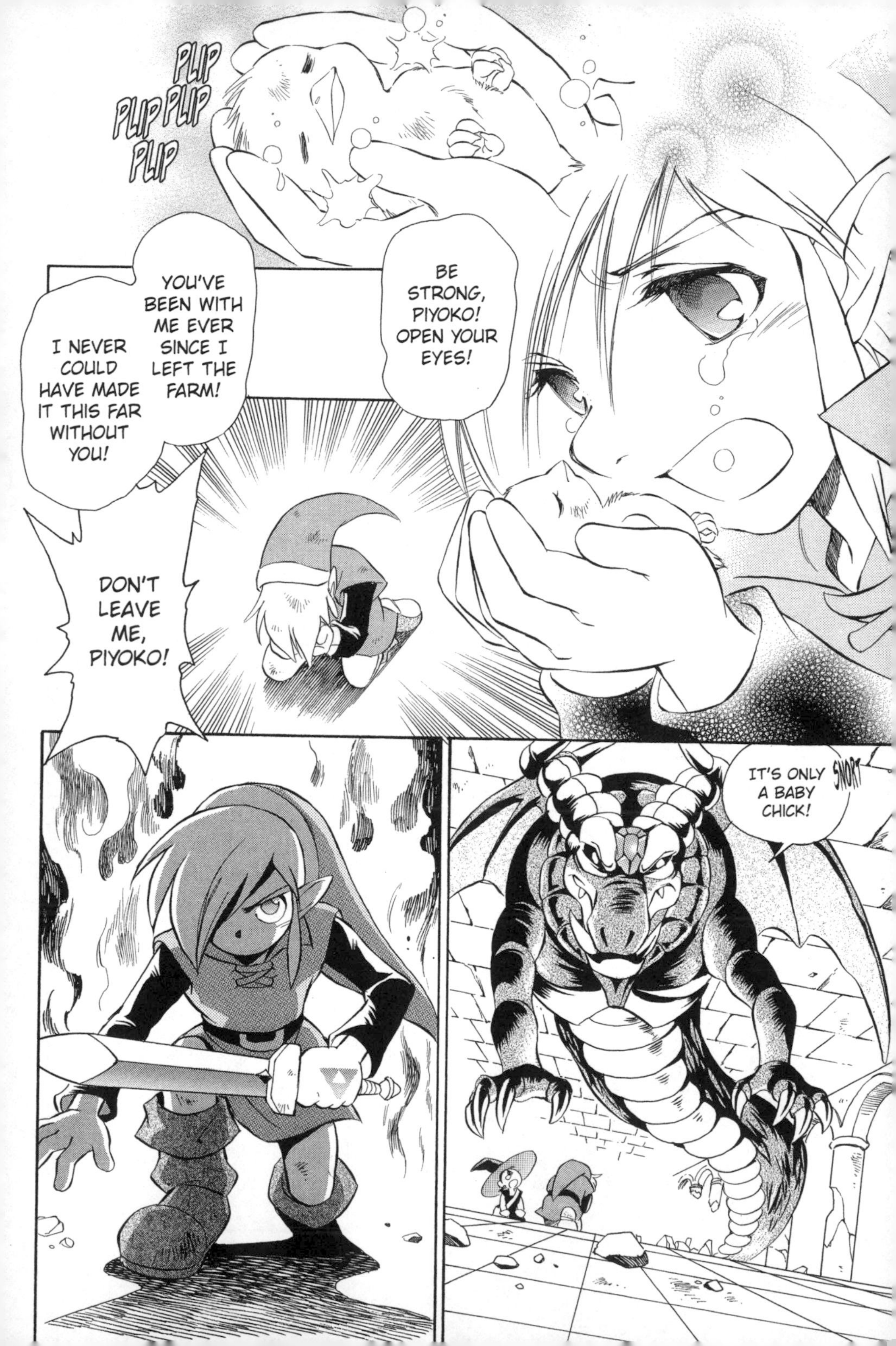
PLIP PLIP PLIP PLIP
BE STRONG, PIYOKO! OPEN YOUR EYES!
YOU'VE BEEN WITH ME EVER SINCE I LEFT THE FARM!
I NEVER COULD HAVE MADE IT THIS FAR WITHOUT YOU!
DON'T LEAVE ME, PIYOKO!
SNORT
IT'S ONLY A BABY CHICK!

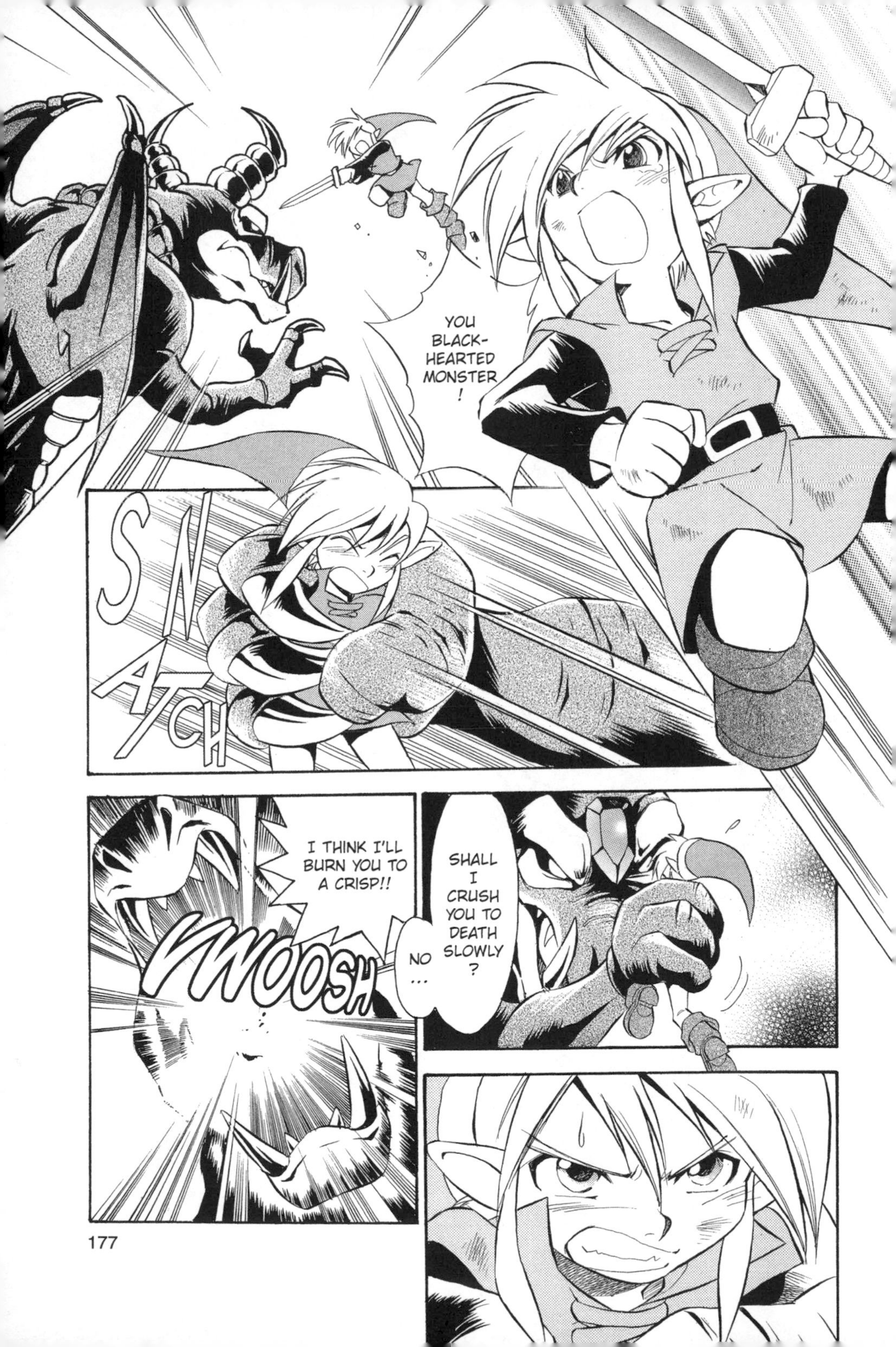
YOU BLACK-HEARTED MONSTER!
SNATCH
SHALL I CRUSH YOU TO DEATH SLOWLY?
NO...
I THINK I'LL BURN YOU TO A CRISP!!
VWOOSH

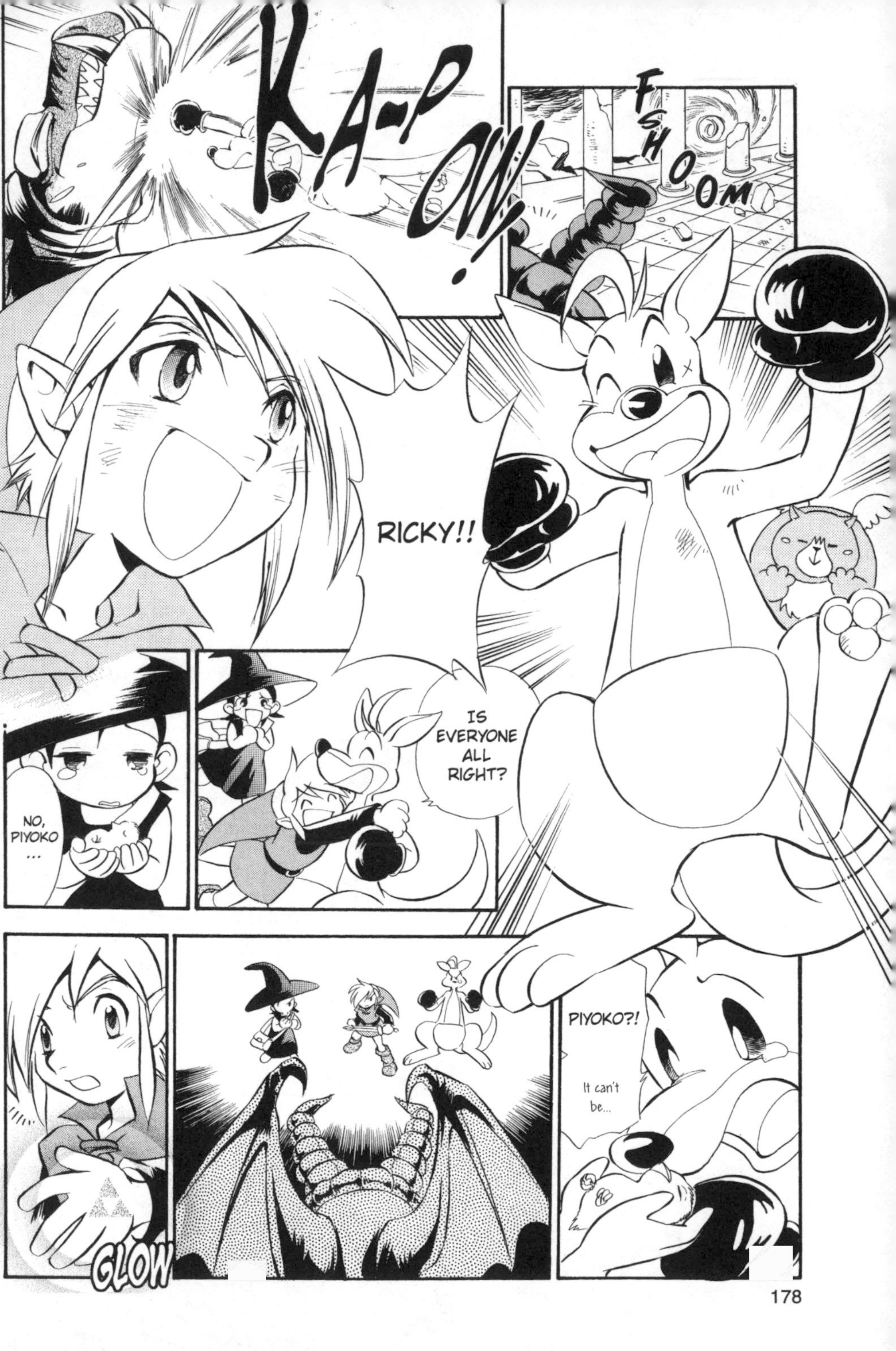
FSHOOOM
KA-POW!!
RICKY!!
IS EVERYONE ALL RIGHT?
NO, PIYOKO ...
PIYOKO?!
It can't be...
GLOW

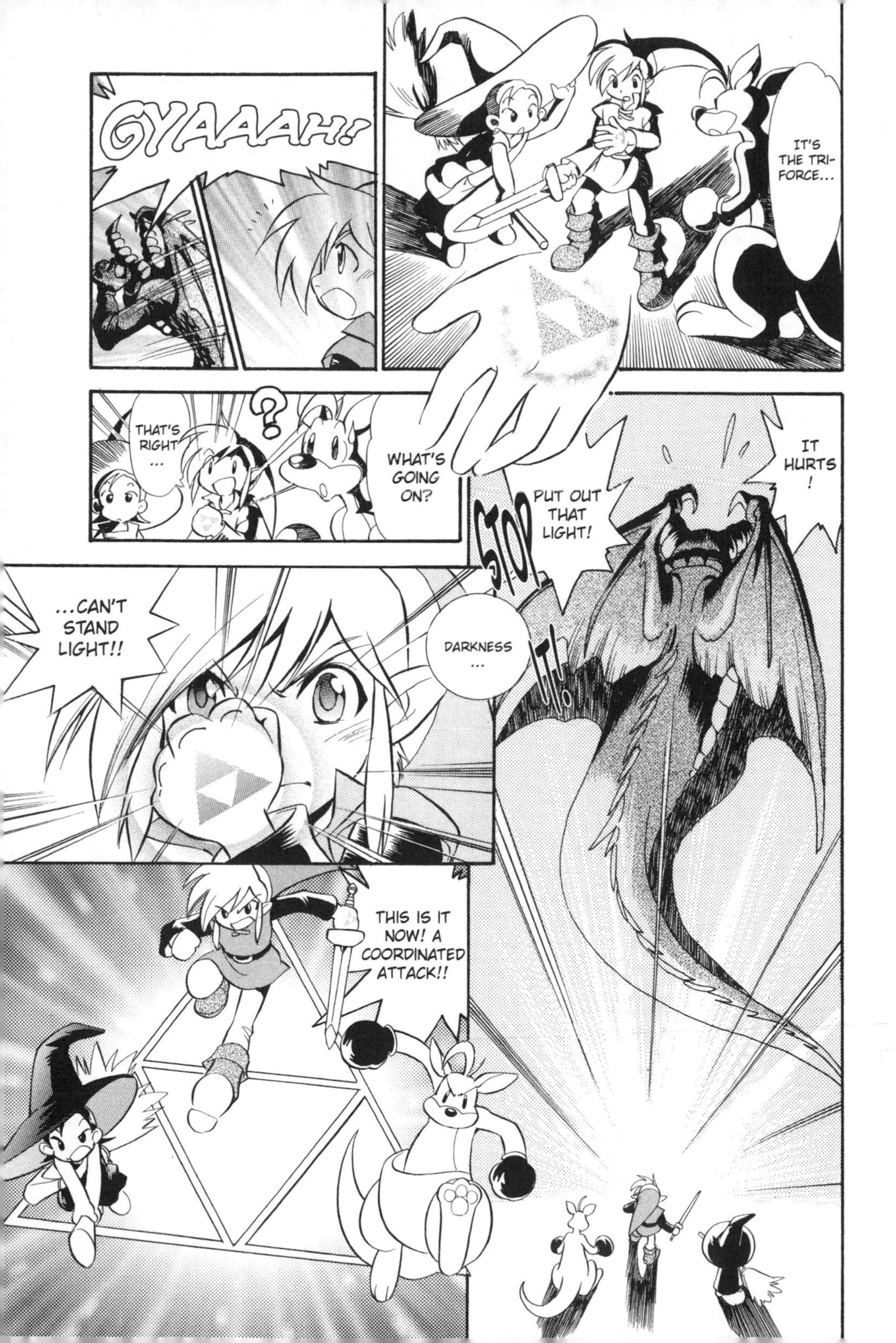
IT'S THE TRI-FORCE...
GYAAAH!
IT HURTS!
PUT OUT THAT LIGHT!
STOP IT!
?
WHAT'S GOING ON?
THAT'S RIGHT...
DARKNESS...
...CAN'T STAND LIGHT!!
THIS IS IT NOW! A COORDINATED ATTACK!!

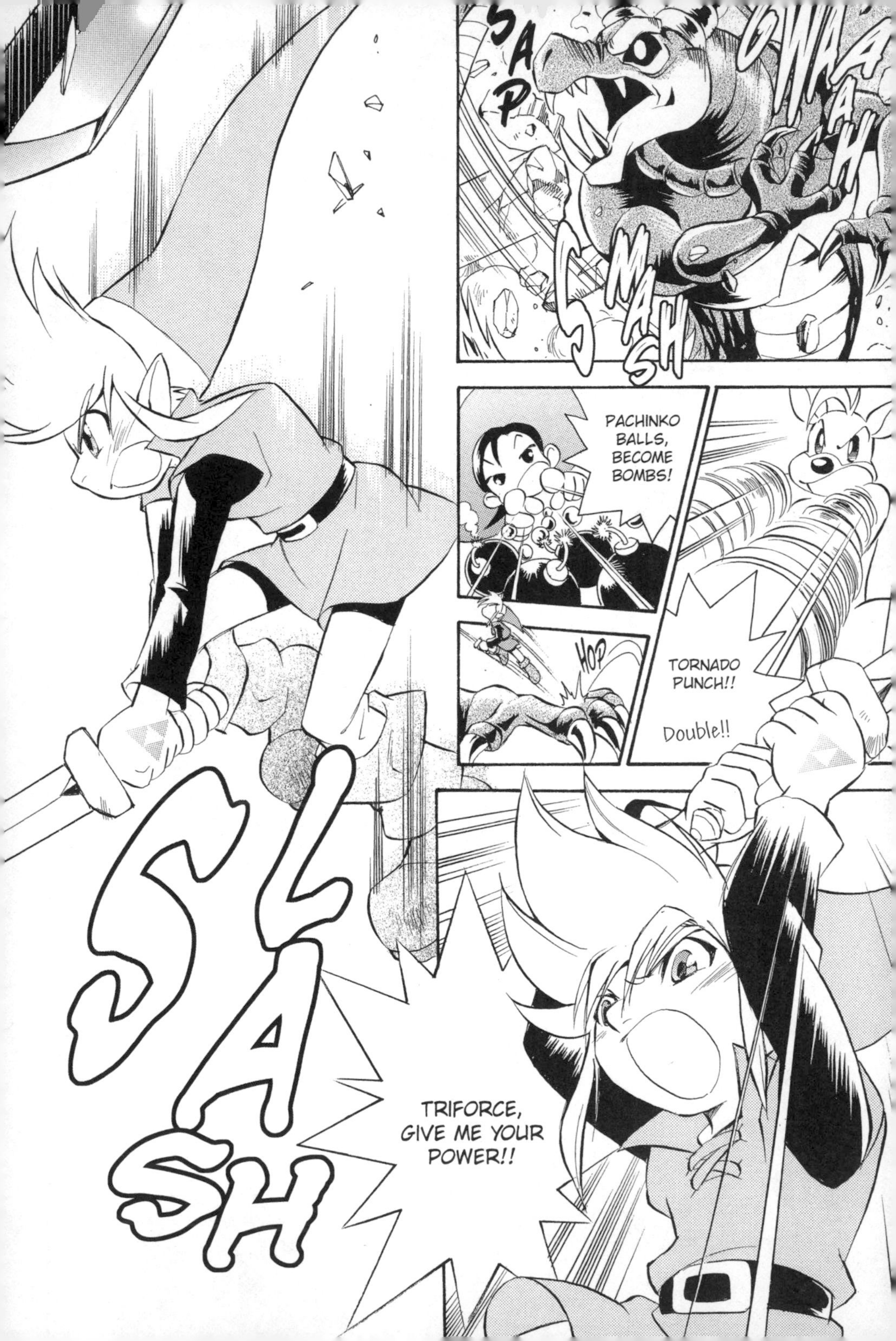
GWAAAH
SAP
SMASH
TORNADO PUNCH!!
Double!!
PACHINKO BALLS, BECOME BOMBS!
HOP
TRIFORCE, GIVE ME YOUR POWER!!
SLASH

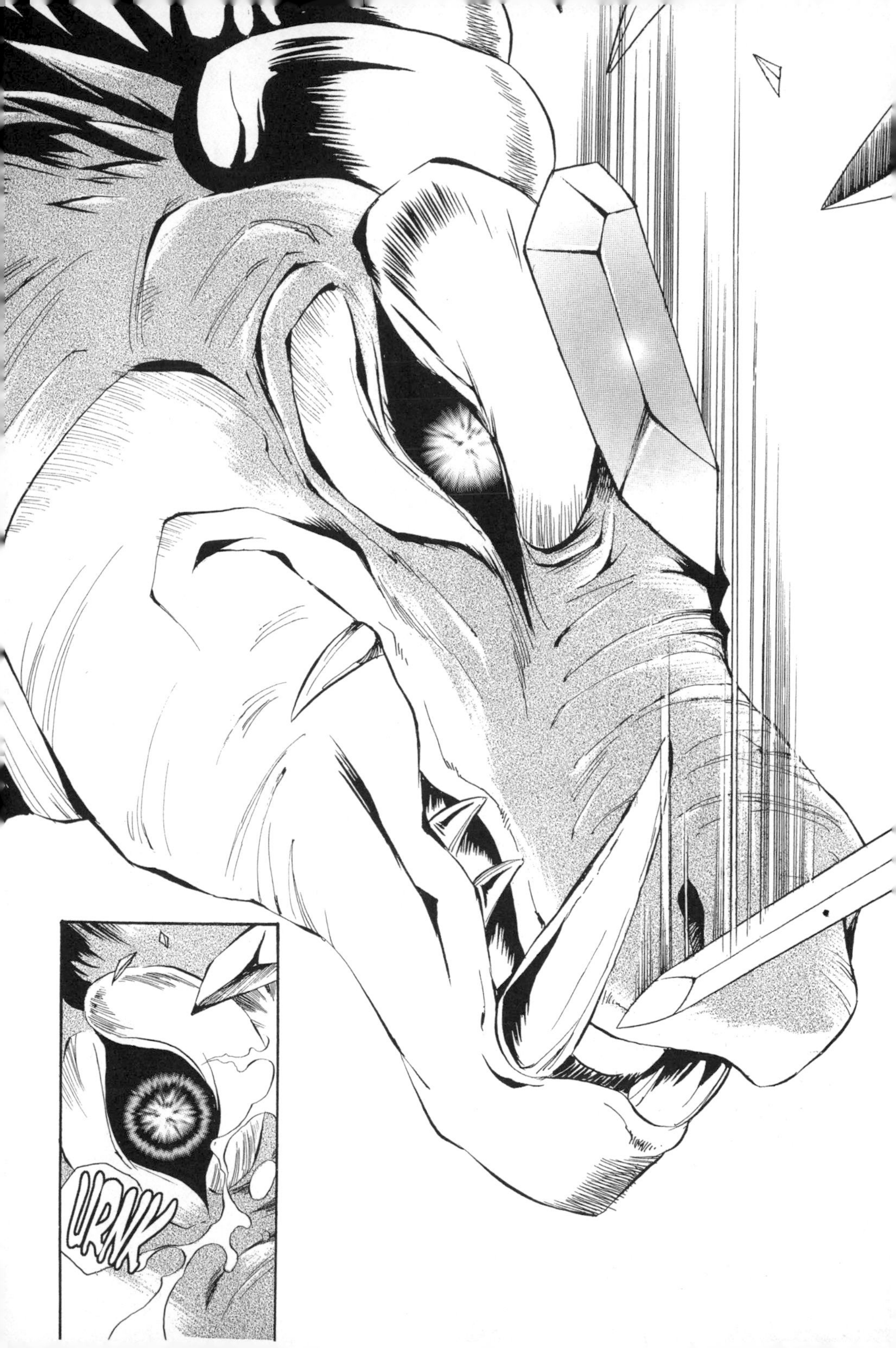
URNK

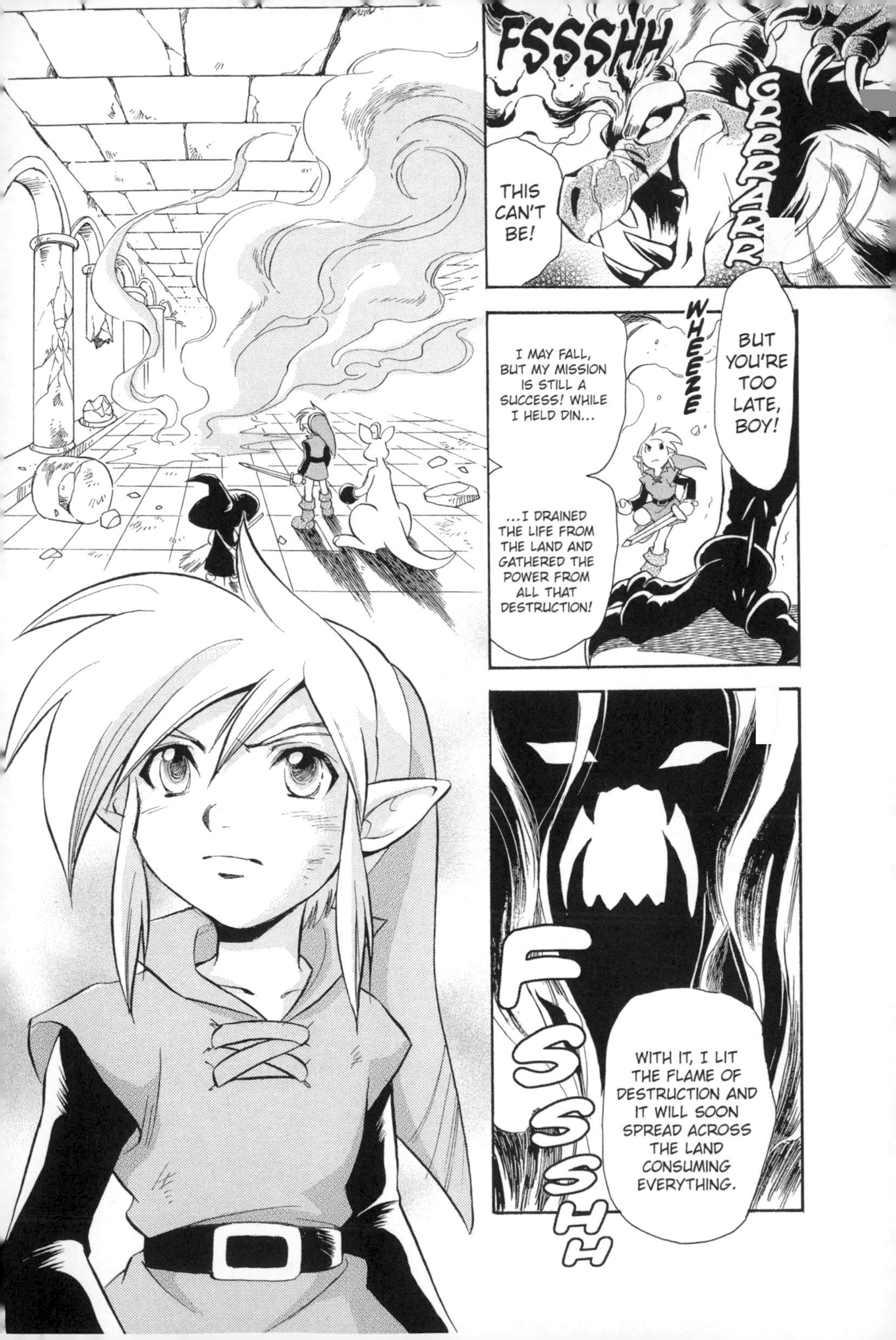
FSSSHH
GRRRARR
THIS CAN'T BE!
BUT YOU'RE TOO LATE, BOY!
WHEEZE
I MAY FALL, BUT MY MISSION IS STILL A SUCCESS! WHILE I HELD DIN...
...I DRAINED THE LIFE FROM THE LAND AND GATHERED THE POWER FROM ALL THAT DESTRUCTION!
WITH IT, I LIT THE FLAME OF DESTRUCTION AND IT WILL SOON SPREAD ACROSS THE LAND CONSUMING EVERYTHING.
FSSSHH

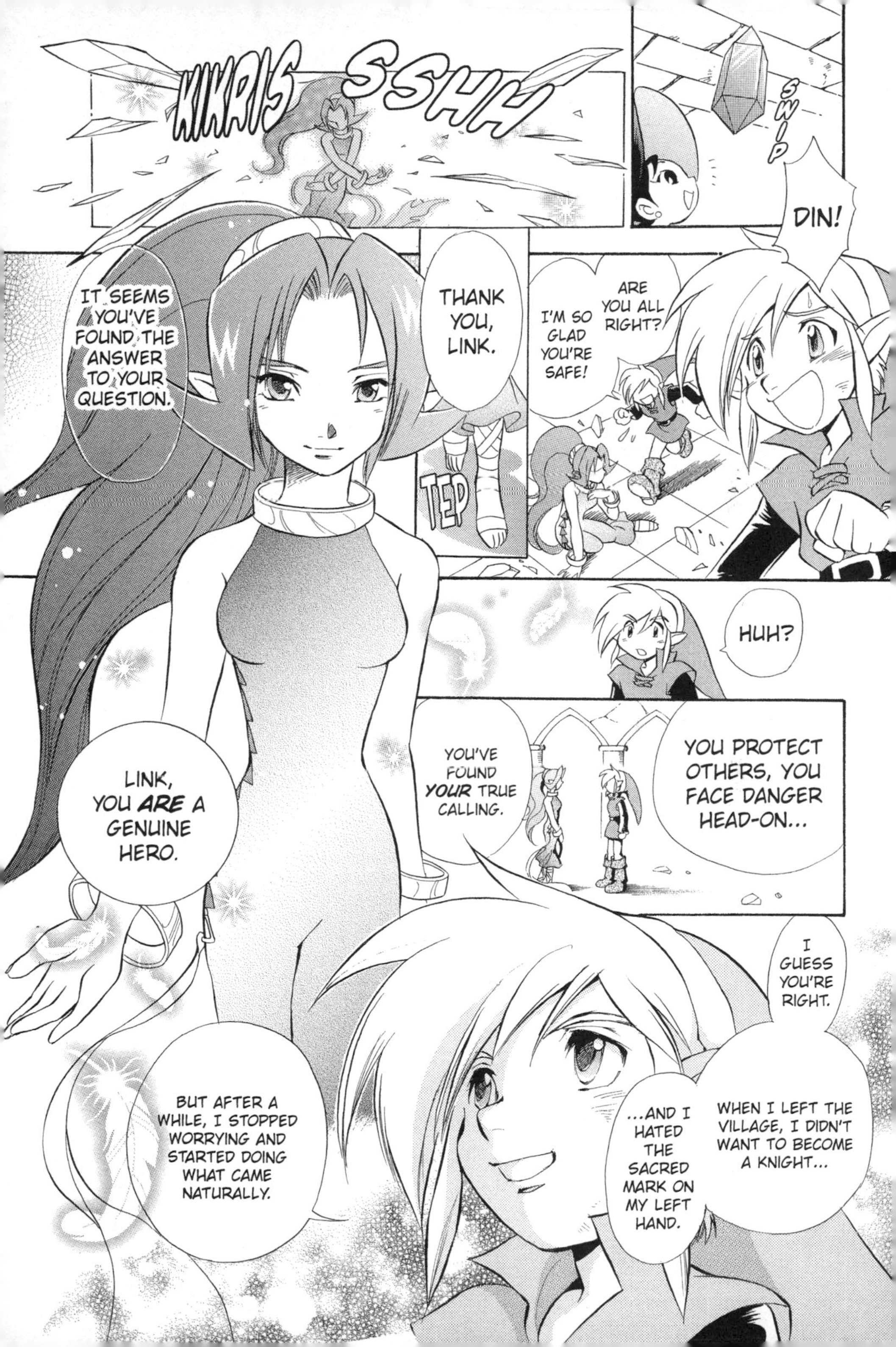
SWIP
DIN!
KIKRIS
SSHH
ARE YOU ALL RIGHT?
I'M SO GLAD YOU'RE SAFE!
THANK YOU, LINK.
TEP
IT SEEMS YOU'VE FOUND THE ANSWER TO YOUR QUESTION.
HUH?
YOU PROTECT OTHERS, YOU FACE DANGER HEAD-ON...
YOU'VE FOUND ***YOUR*** TRUE CALLING.
LINK, YOU ***ARE*** A GENUINE HERO.
I GUESS YOU'RE RIGHT.
WHEN I LEFT THE VILLAGE, I DIDN'T WANT TO BECOME A KNIGHT...
...AND I HATED THE SACRED MARK ON MY LEFT HAND.
BUT AFTER A WHILE, I STOPPED WORRYING AND STARTED DOING WHAT CAME NATURALLY.

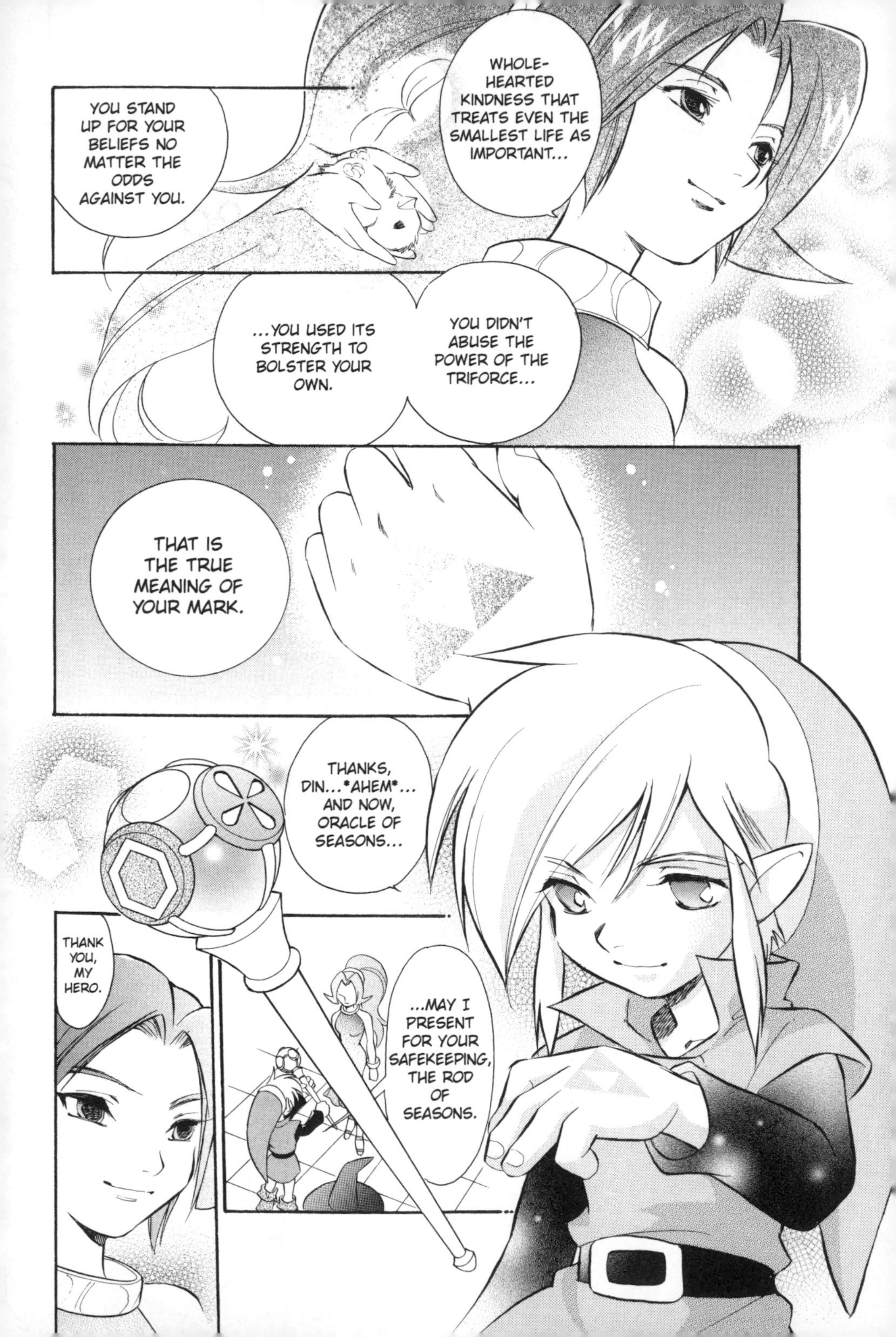
WHOLE-HEARTED KINDNESS THAT TREATS EVEN THE SMALLEST LIFE AS IMPORTANT...
YOU STAND UP FOR YOUR BELIEFS NO MATTER THE ODDS AGAINST YOU.
YOU DIDN'T ABUSE THE POWER OF THE TRIFORCE...
...YOU USED ITS STRENGTH TO BOLSTER YOUR OWN.
THAT IS THE TRUE MEANING OF YOUR MARK.
THANKS, DIN...*AHEM*... AND NOW, ORACLE OF SEASONS...
...MAY I PRESENT FOR YOUR SAFEKEEPING, THE ROD OF SEASONS.
THANK YOU, MY HERO.

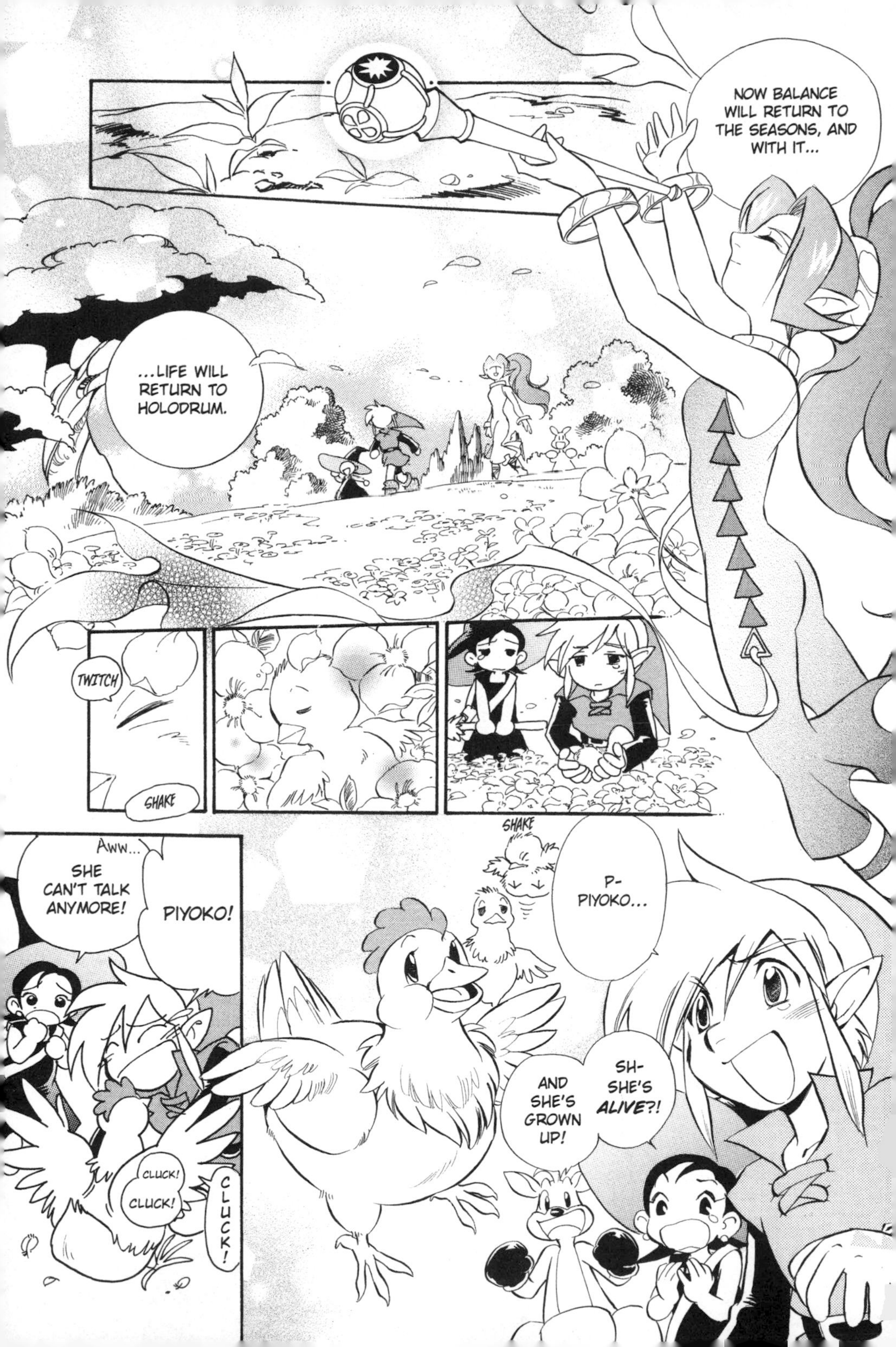

NOW BALANCE WILL RETURN TO THE SEASONS, AND WITH IT...
...LIFE WILL RETURN TO HOLODRUM.
TWITCH
SHAKE
SHAKE
P- PIYOKO...
SH- SHE'S *ALIVE*?!
AND SHE'S GROWN UP!
CLUCK!
PIYOKO!
Aww... SHE CAN'T TALK ANYMORE!
CLUCK!
CLUCK!

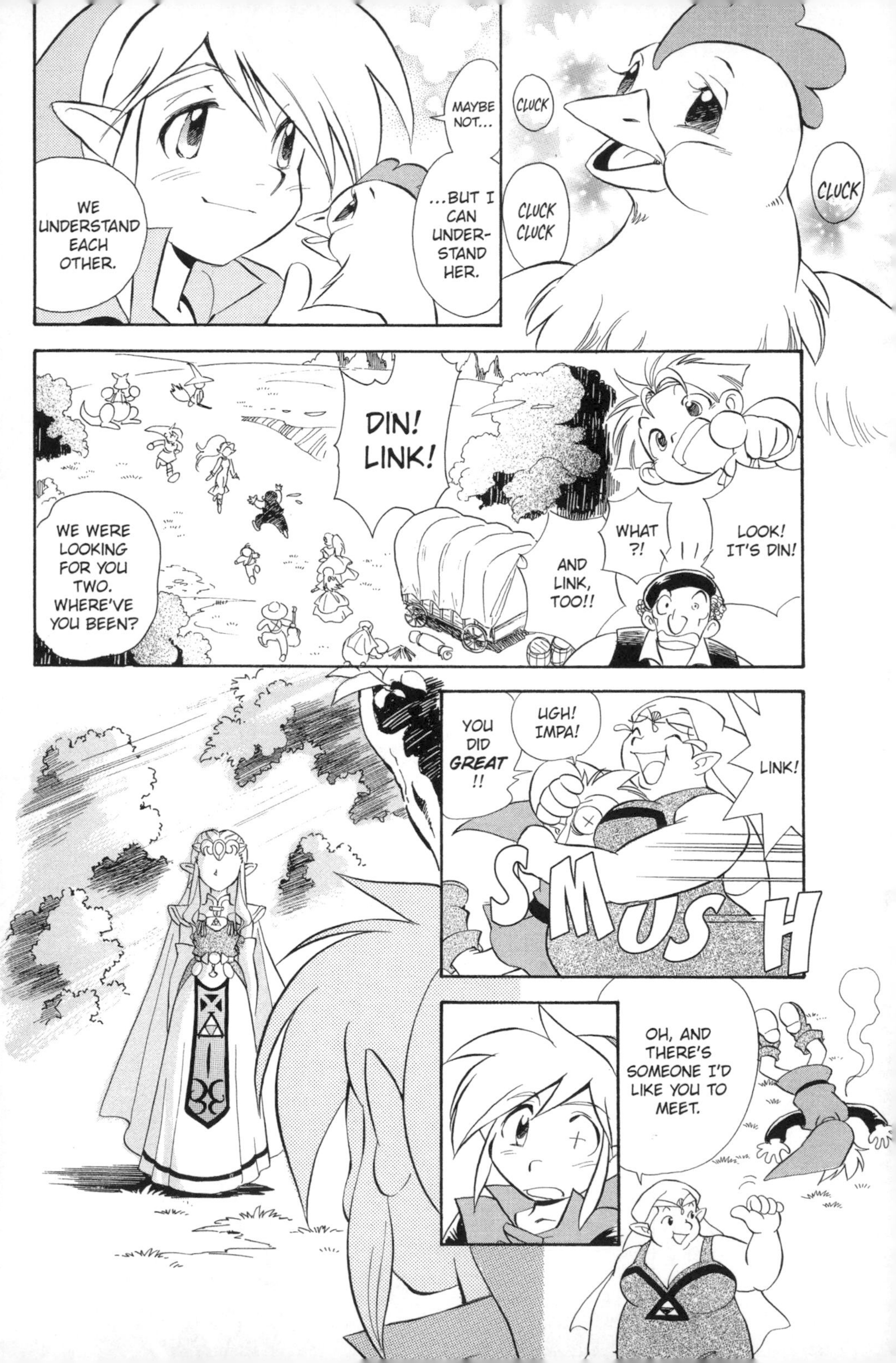
CLUCK
CLUCK
CLUCK CLUCK
MAYBE NOT...
...BUT I CAN UNDERSTAND HER.
WE UNDERSTAND EACH OTHER.
LOOK! IT'S DIN!
WHAT?!
AND LINK, TOO!!
DIN! LINK!
WE WERE LOOKING FOR YOU TWO. WHERE'VE YOU BEEN?
LINK!
UGH! IMPA!
YOU DID GREAT!!
SMUSH
OH, AND THERE'S SOMEONE I'D LIKE YOU TO MEET.

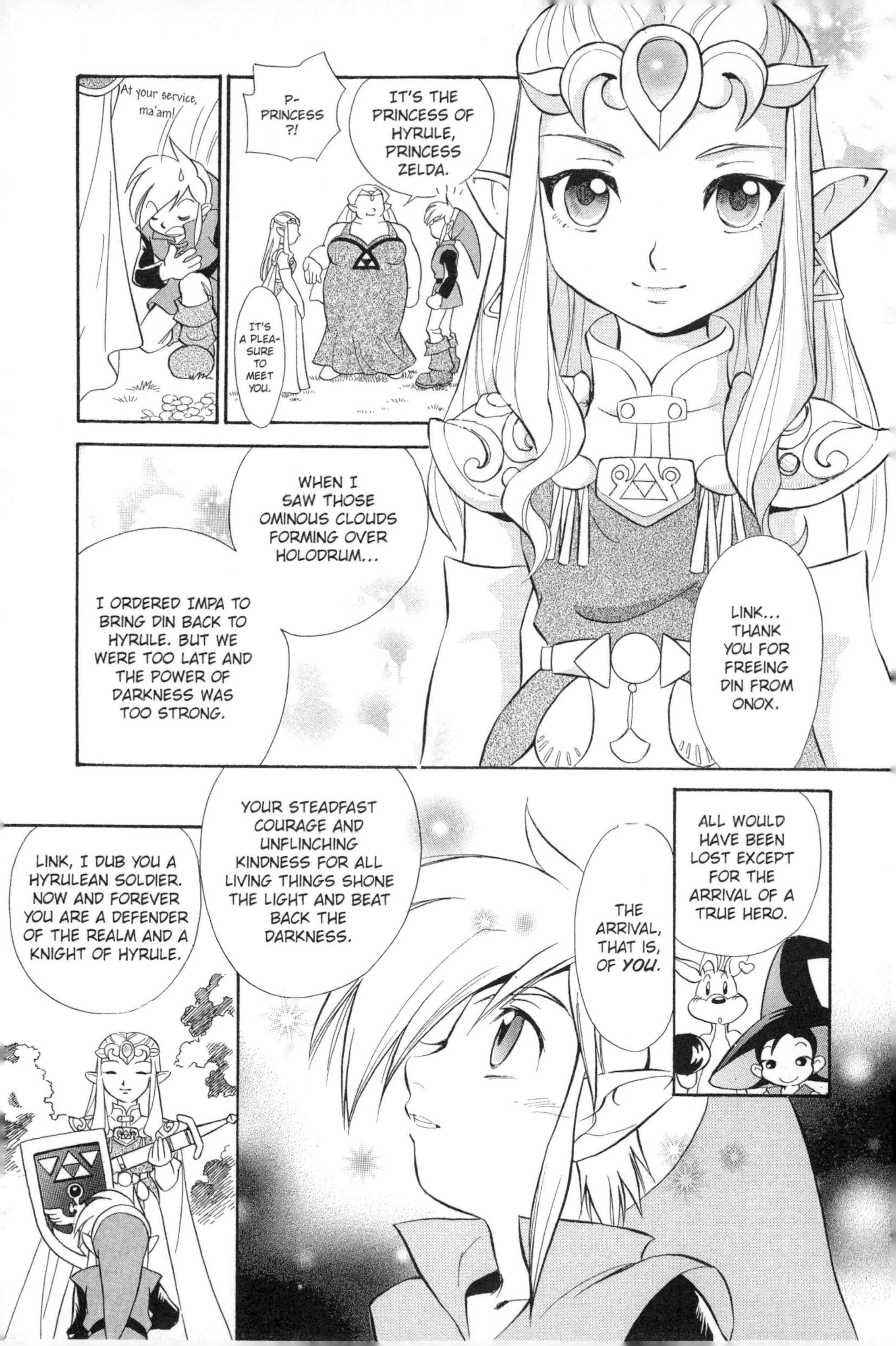
LINK... THANK YOU FOR FREEING DIN FROM ONOX.
IT'S THE PRINCESS OF HYRULE, PRINCESS ZELDA.
P-PRINCESS?!
IT'S A PLEASURE TO MEET YOU.
At your service, ma'am!
WHEN I SAW THOSE OMINOUS CLOUDS FORMING OVER HOLODRUM...
I ORDERED IMPA TO BRING DIN BACK TO HYRULE. BUT WE WERE TOO LATE AND THE POWER OF DARKNESS WAS TOO STRONG.
ALL WOULD HAVE BEEN LOST EXCEPT FOR THE ARRIVAL OF A TRUE HERO.
THE ARRIVAL, THAT IS, OF *YOU*.
YOUR STEADFAST COURAGE AND UNFLINCHING KINDNESS FOR ALL LIVING THINGS SHONE THE LIGHT AND BEAT BACK THE DARKNESS.
LINK, I DUB YOU A HYRULEAN SOLDIER. NOW AND FOREVER YOU ARE A DEFENDER OF THE REALM AND A KNIGHT OF HYRULE.

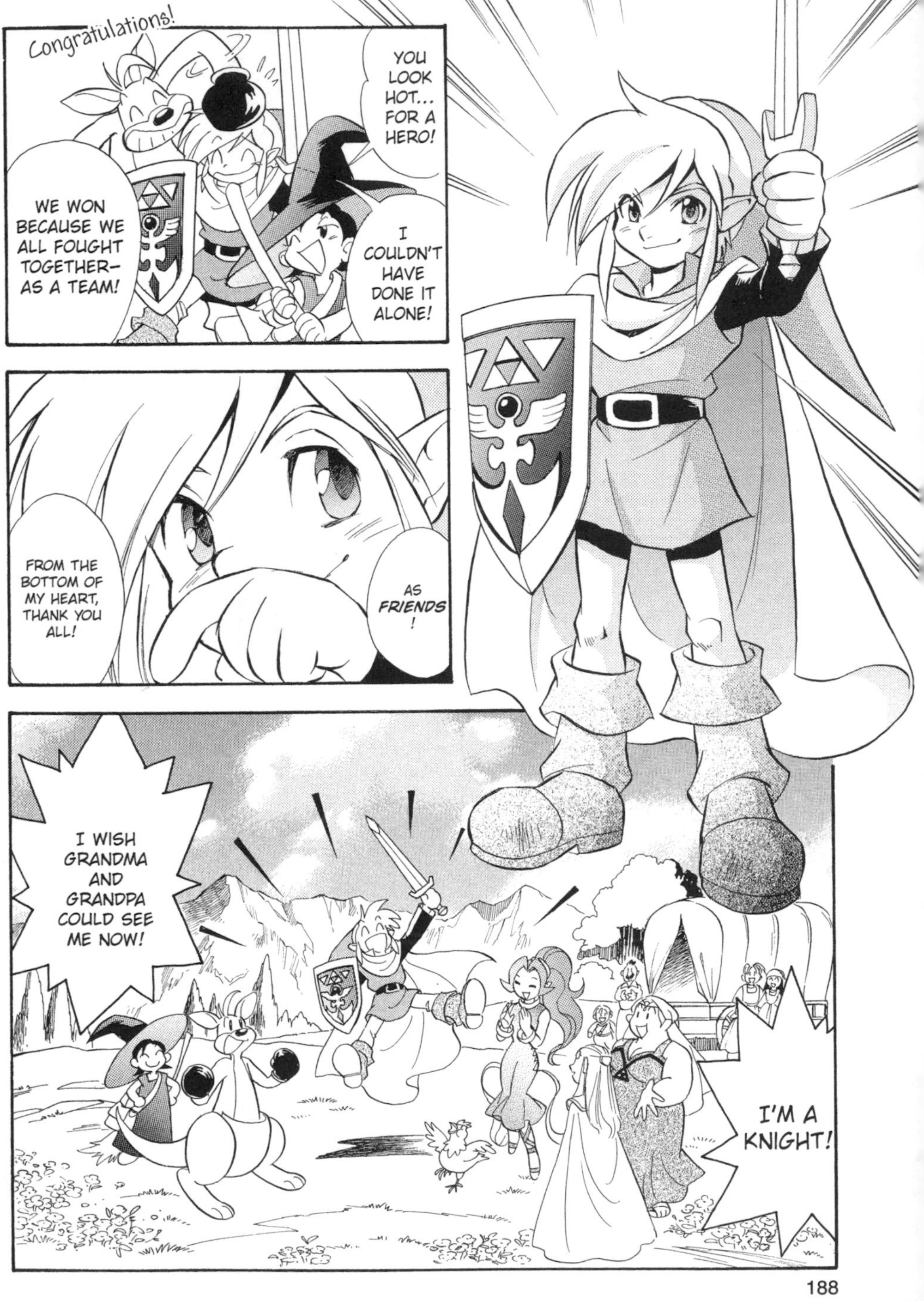
Congratulations!
YOU LOOK HOT... FOR A HERO!
I COULDN'T HAVE DONE IT ALONE!
WE WON BECAUSE WE ALL FOUGHT TOGETHER—AS A TEAM!
AS *FRIENDS*!
FROM THE BOTTOM OF MY HEART, THANK YOU ALL!
I'M A KNIGHT!
I WISH GRANDMA AND GRANDPA COULD SEE ME NOW!

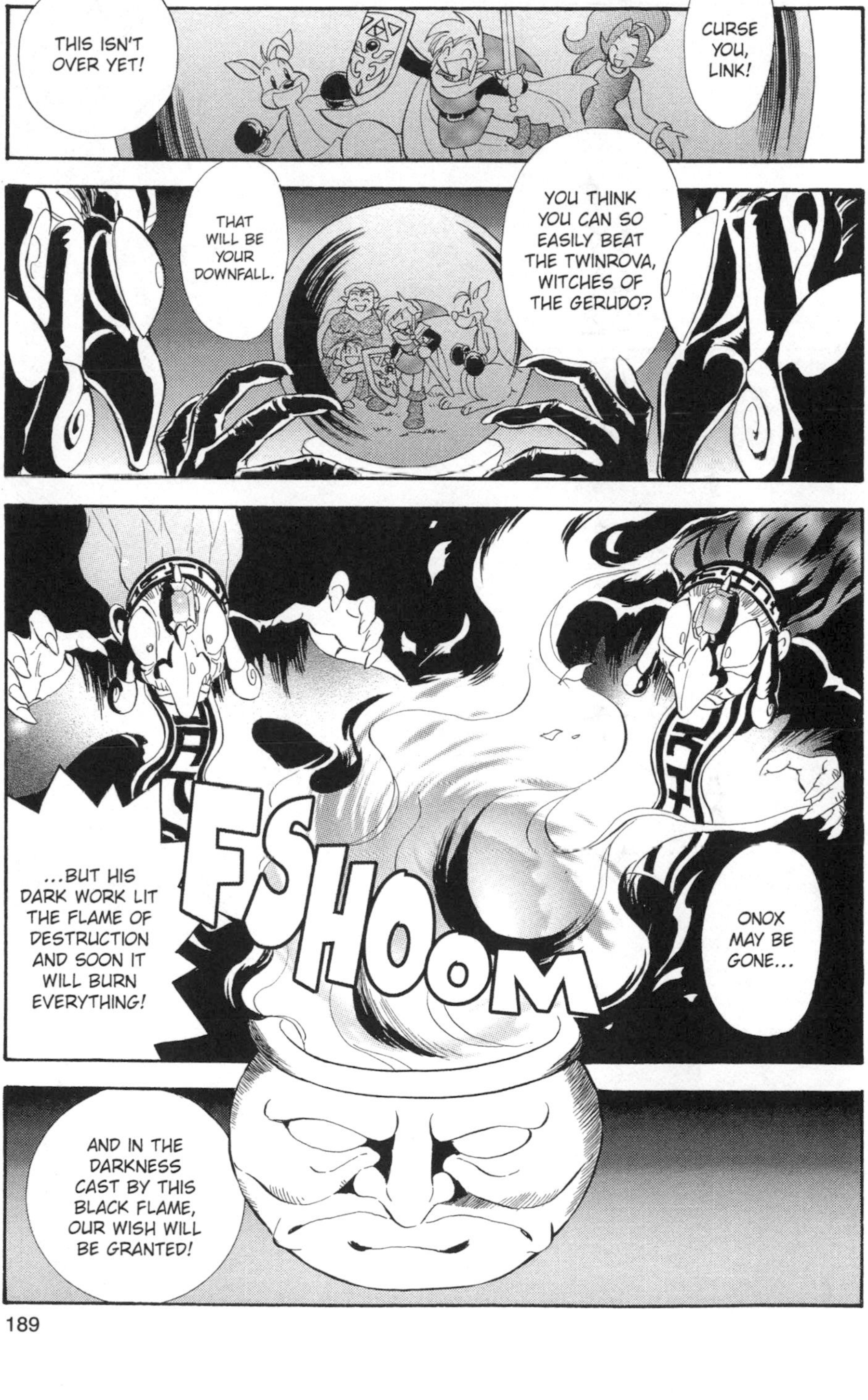
CURSE YOU, LINK!
THIS ISN'T OVER YET!
YOU THINK YOU CAN SO EASILY BEAT THE TWINROVA, WITCHES OF THE GERUDO?
THAT WILL BE YOUR DOWNFALL.
ONOX MAY BE GONE...
...BUT HIS DARK WORK LIT THE FLAME OF DESTRUCTION AND SOON IT WILL BURN EVERYTHING!
FSHOOM
AND IN THE DARKNESS CAST BY THIS BLACK FLAME, OUR WISH WILL BE GRANTED!

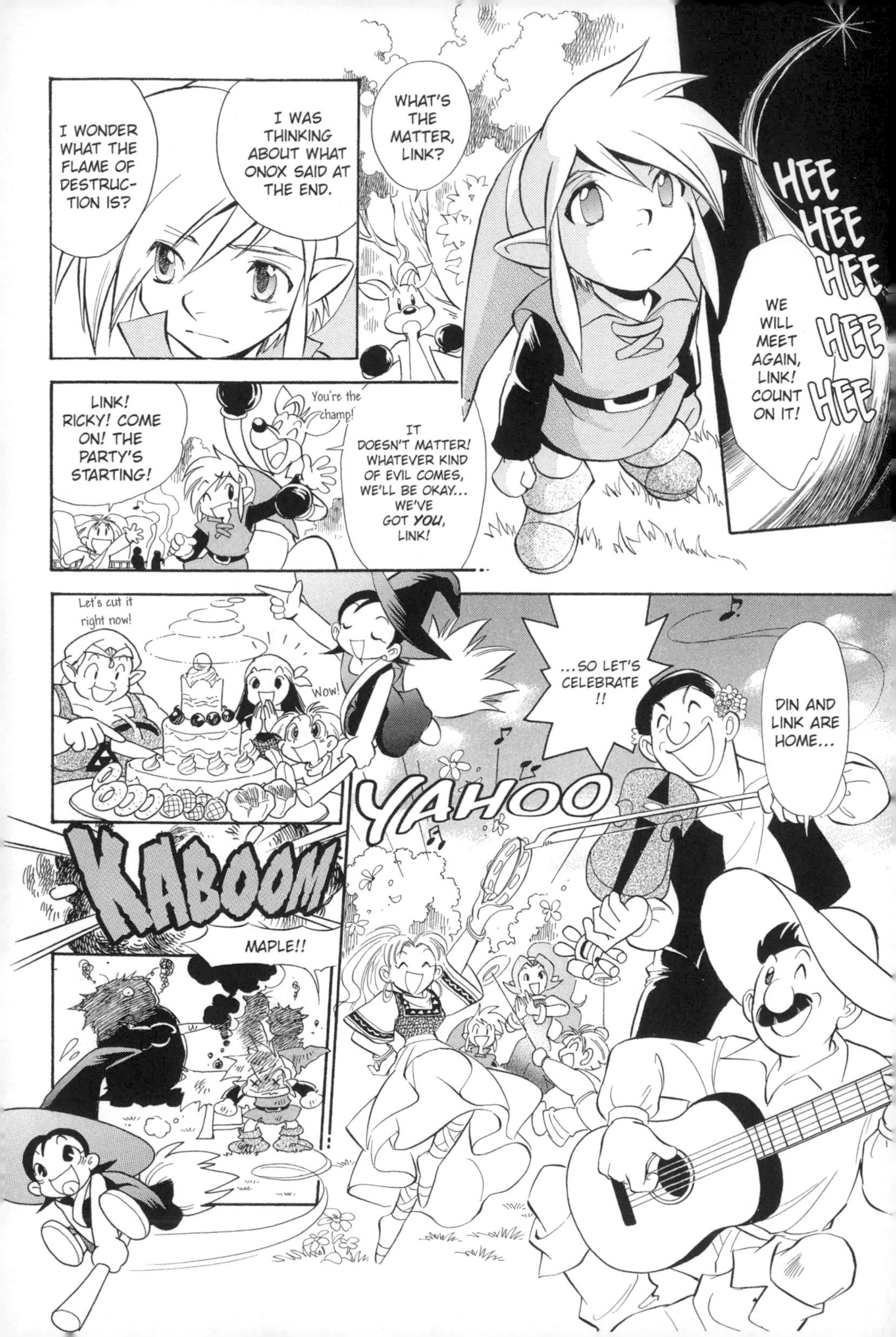
HEE HEE HEE HEE HEE
WE WILL MEET AGAIN, LINK! COUNT ON IT!
WHAT'S THE MATTER, LINK?
I WAS THINKING ABOUT WHAT ONOX SAID AT THE END.
I WONDER WHAT THE FLAME OF DESTRUCTION IS?
IT DOESN'T MATTER! WHATEVER KIND OF EVIL COMES, WE'LL BE OKAY... WE'VE GOT ***YOU***, LINK!
You're the champ!
LINK! RICKY! COME ON! THE PARTY'S STARTING!
DIN AND LINK ARE HOME...
...SO LET'S CELEBRATE !!
YAHOO
Let's cut it right now!
Wow!
KABOOM
MAPLE!!

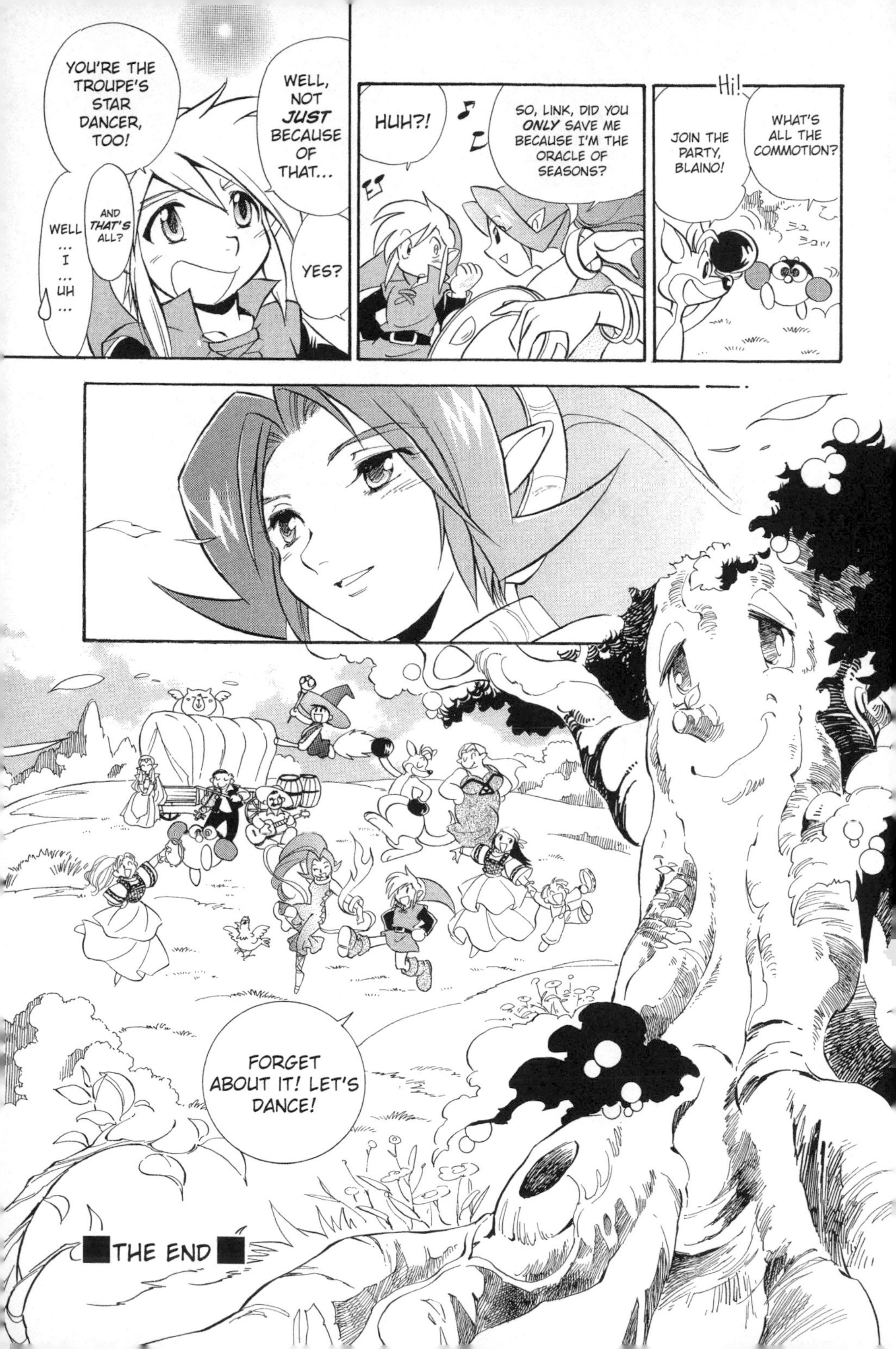

Hi!
WHAT'S ALL THE COMMOTION?
JOIN THE PARTY, BLAINO!
SO, LINK, DID YOU ONLY SAVE ME BECAUSE I'M THE ORACLE OF SEASONS?
HUH?!
WELL, NOT JUST BECAUSE OF THAT...
YOU'RE THE TROUPE'S STAR DANCER, TOO!
YES?
AND THAT'S ALL?
WELL... I... UH...
FORGET ABOUT IT! LET'S DANCE!
THE END

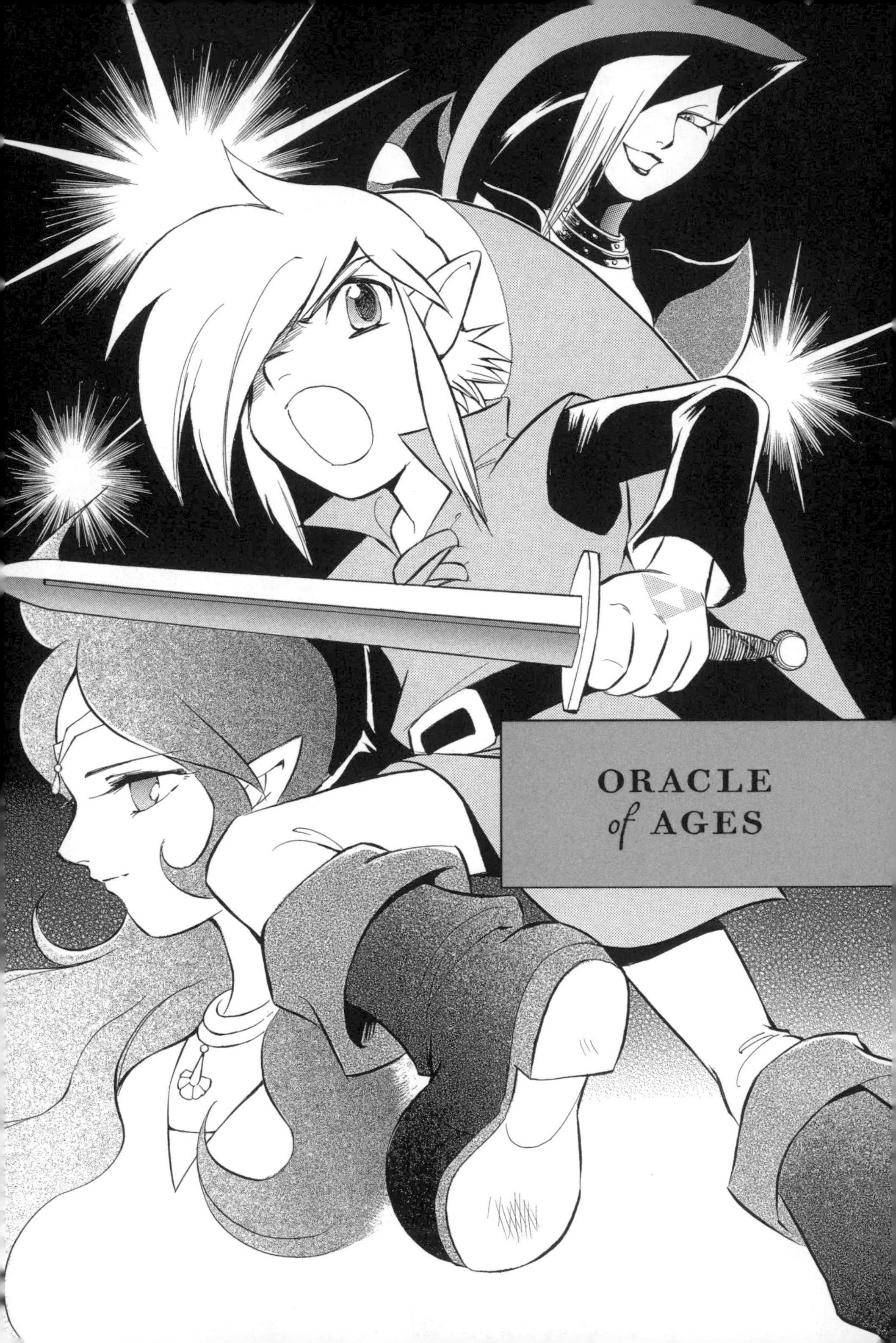
ORACLE
of AGES

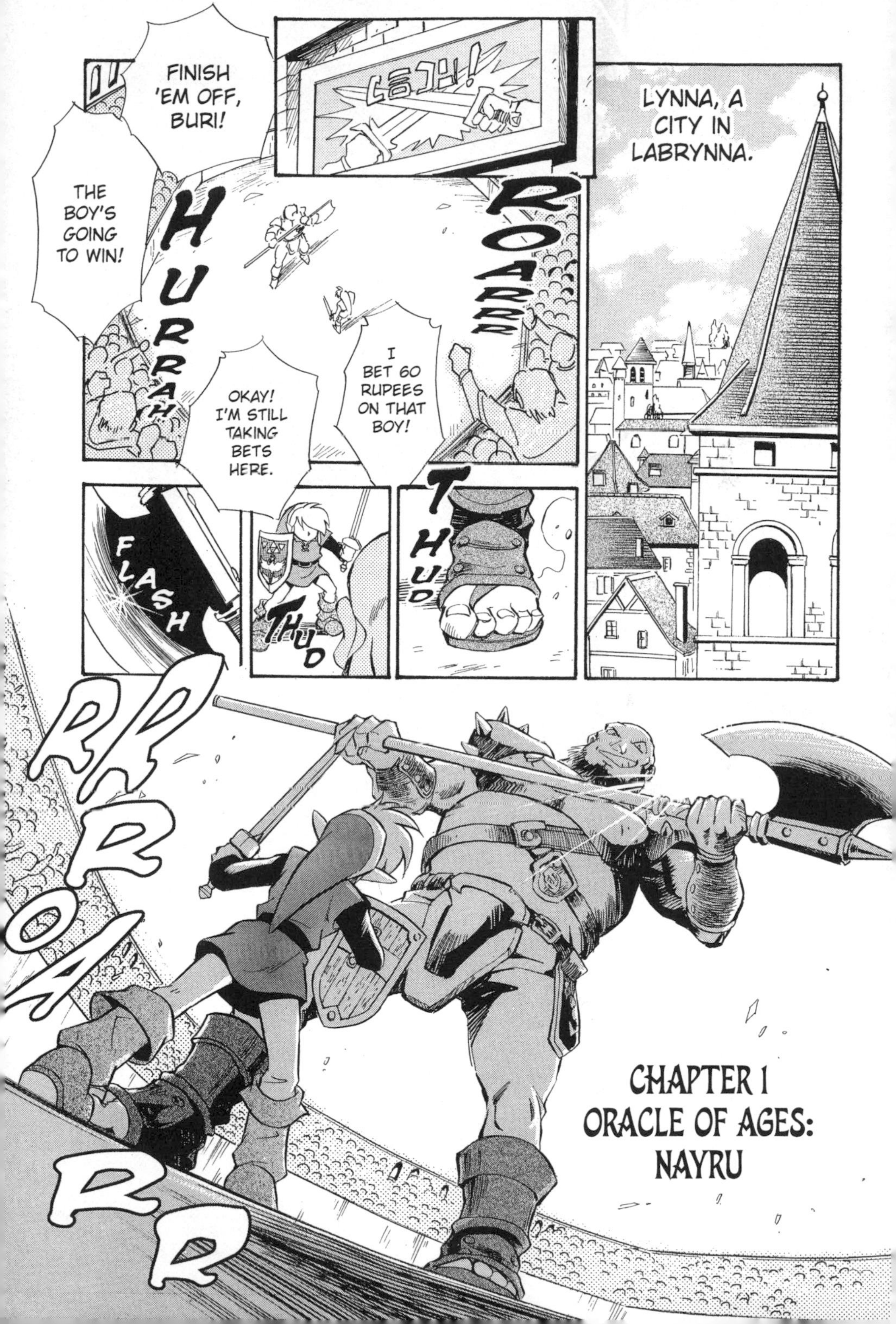
LYNNA, A CITY IN LABRYNNA.
FINISH 'EM OFF, BURI!
ROARRRR
THE BOY'S GOING TO WIN!
HURRAH
I BET 60 RUPEES ON THAT BOY!
OKAY! I'M STILL TAKING BETS HERE.
THUD
THUD
FLASH
RRROAARRR
CHAPTER 1
ORACLE OF AGES:
NAYRU

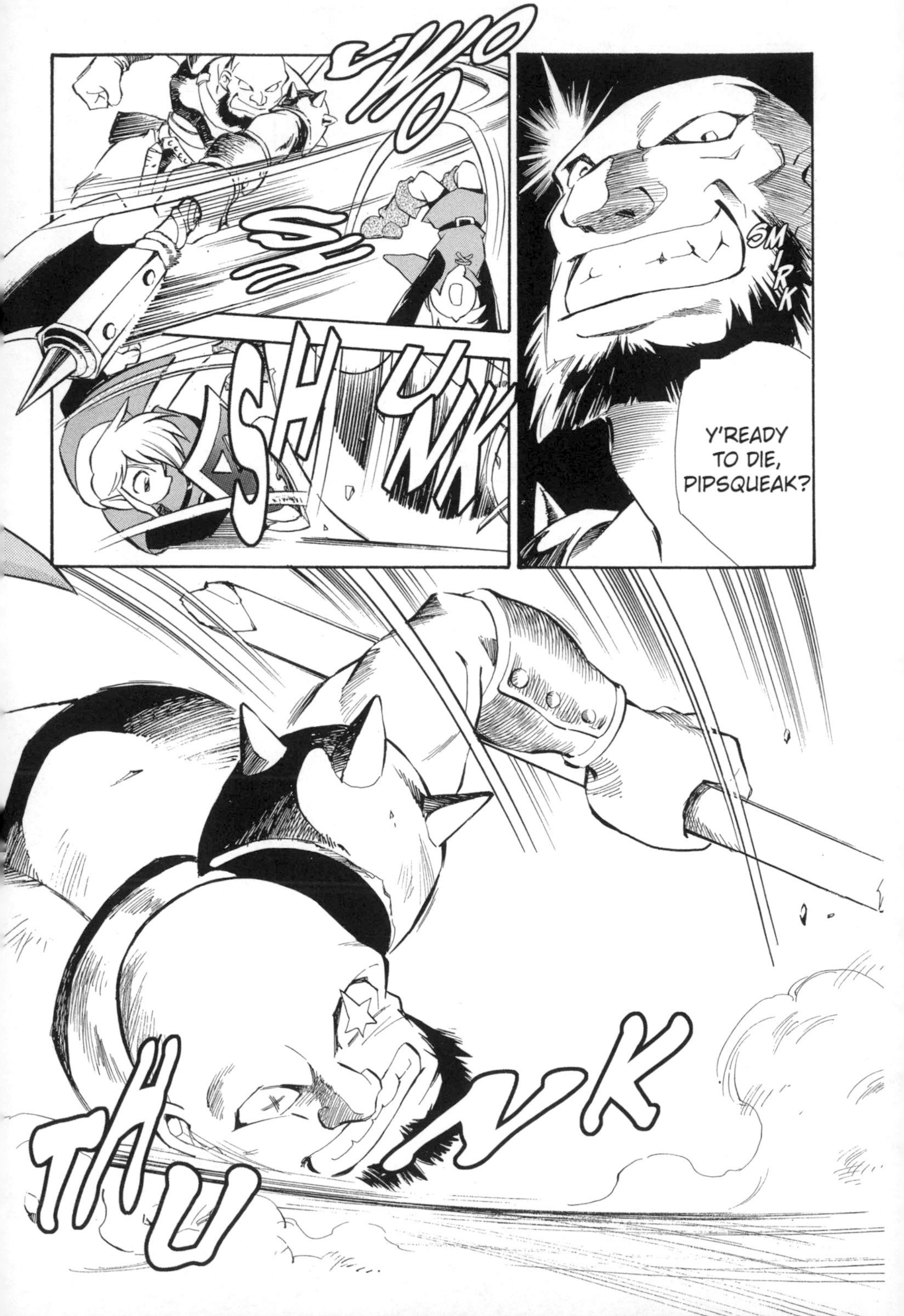
SMIRK
Y'READY TO DIE, PIPSQUEAK?
SHUNK
THUNK

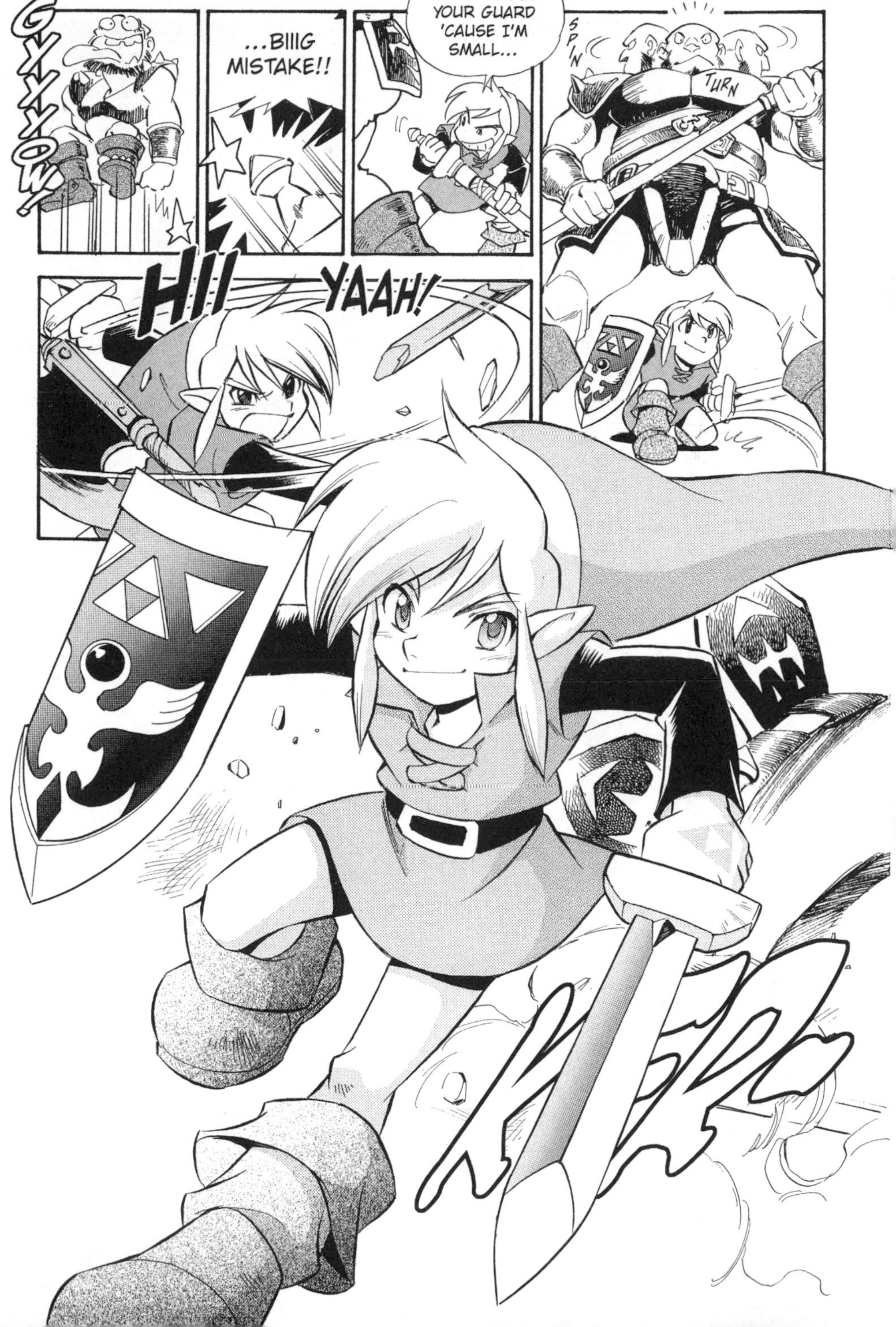
SPIN
TURN
YOU DROPPED YOUR GUARD 'CAUSE I'M SMALL...
...BIIIG MISTAKE!!
GYYYOW!
HII YAAH!

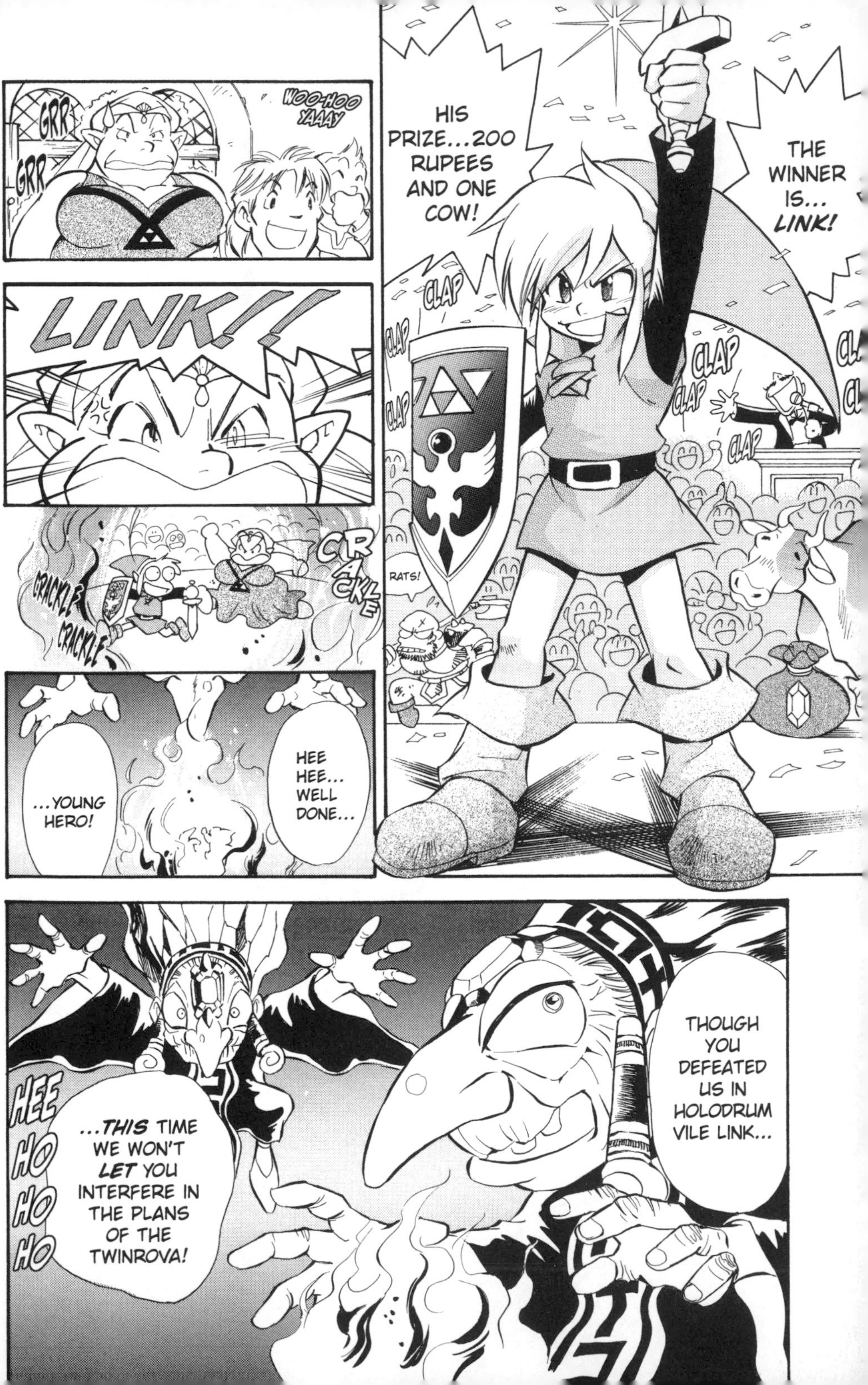
THE WINNER IS... LINK!
HIS PRIZE...200 RUPEES AND ONE COW!
CLAP
CLAP
CLAP
CLAP
CLAP
CLAP
CLAP
RATS!
WOO-HOO YAAAY
GRR
GRR
LINK!!
CRACKLE
CRACKLE
CRACKLE
HEE HEE... WELL DONE...
...YOUNG HERO!
THOUGH YOU DEFEATED US IN HOLODRUM VILE LINK...
...THIS TIME WE WON'T LET YOU INTERFERE IN THE PLANS OF THE TWINROVA!
HEE HO HO HO

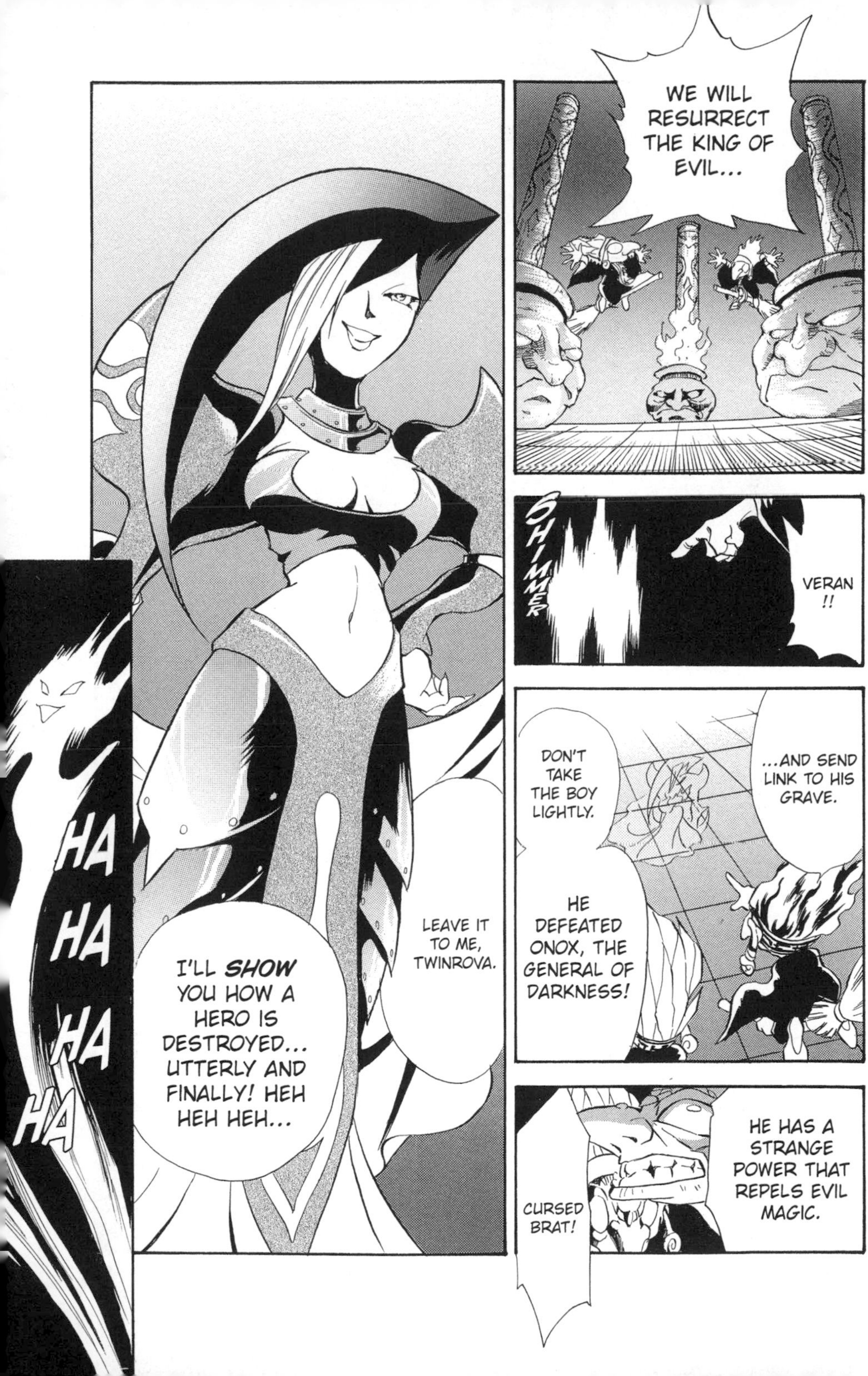

WE WILL RESURRECT THE KING OF EVIL...
SHIMMER
VERAN !!
...AND SEND LINK TO HIS GRAVE.
DON'T TAKE THE BOY LIGHTLY.
HE DEFEATED ONOX, THE GENERAL OF DARKNESS!
HE HAS A STRANGE POWER THAT REPELS EVIL MAGIC.
CURSED BRAT!
LEAVE IT TO ME, TWINROVA.
I'LL SHOW YOU HOW A HERO IS DESTROYED... UTTERLY AND FINALLY! HEH HEH HEH...
HA HA HA HA

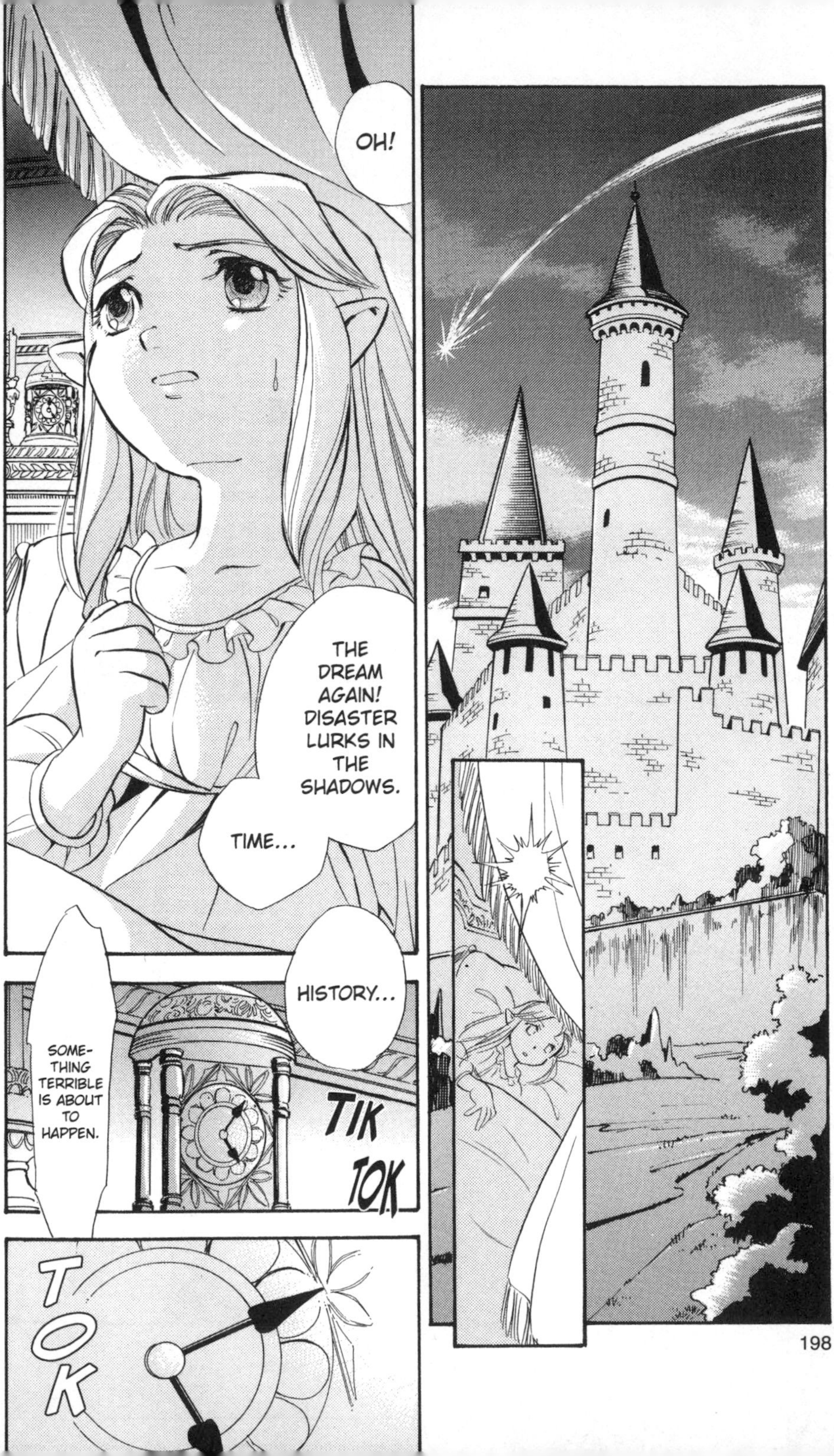
OH!
THE DREAM AGAIN! DISASTER LURKS IN THE SHADOWS.
TIME...
HISTORY...
SOME-THING TERRIBLE IS ABOUT TO HAPPEN.
TIK TOK
TOK

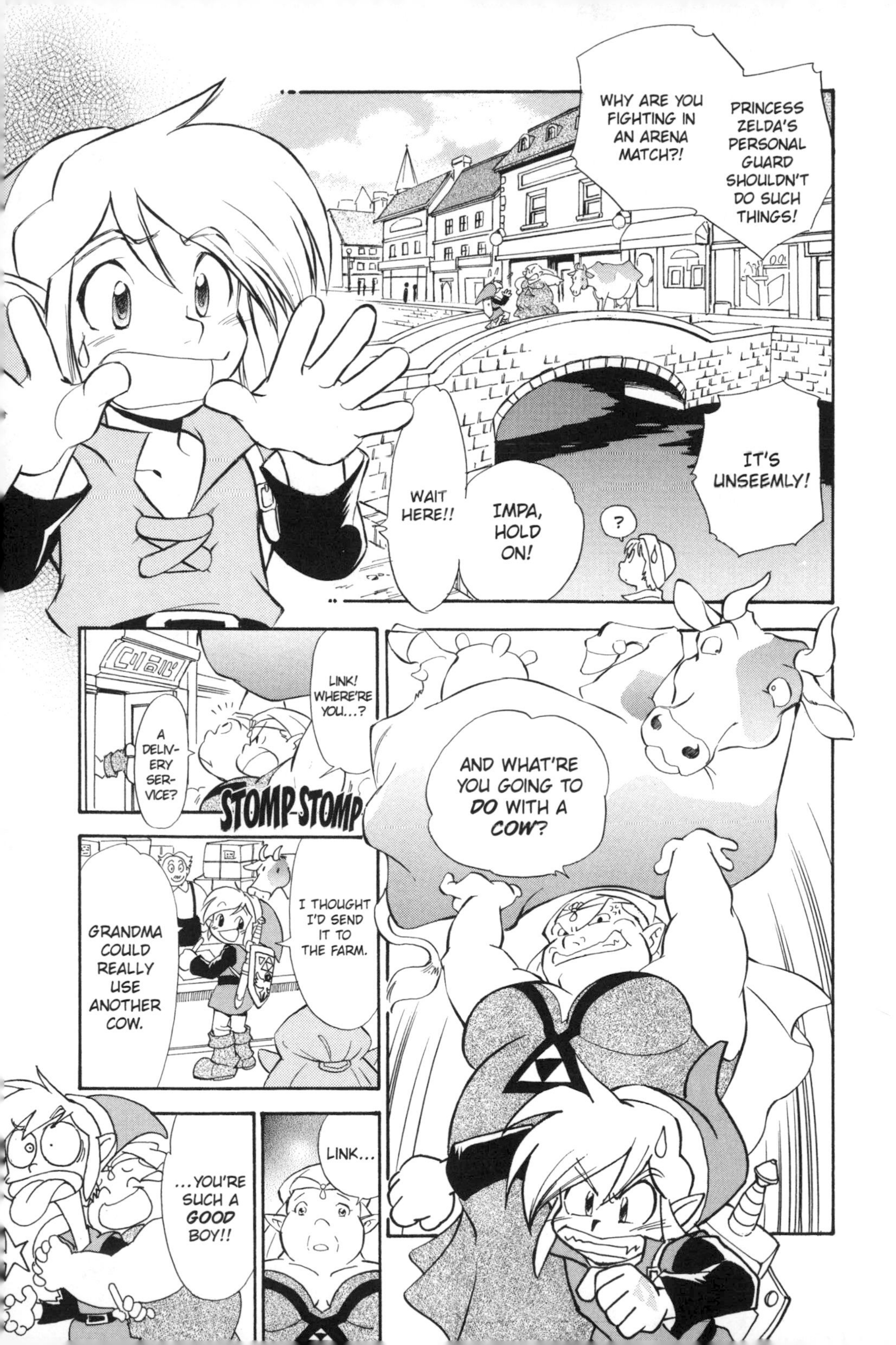
PRINCESS ZELDA'S PERSONAL GUARD SHOULDN'T DO SUCH THINGS!
WHY ARE YOU FIGHTING IN AN ARENA MATCH?!
IT'S UNSEEMLY!
?
IMPA, HOLD ON!
WAIT HERE!!
AND WHAT'RE YOU GOING TO *DO* WITH A *COW*?
LINK! WHERE'RE YOU...?
A DELIVERY SERVICE?
STOMP-STOMP
I THOUGHT I'D SEND IT TO THE FARM.
GRANDMA COULD REALLY USE ANOTHER COW.
LINK...
...YOU'RE SUCH A *GOOD* BOY!!

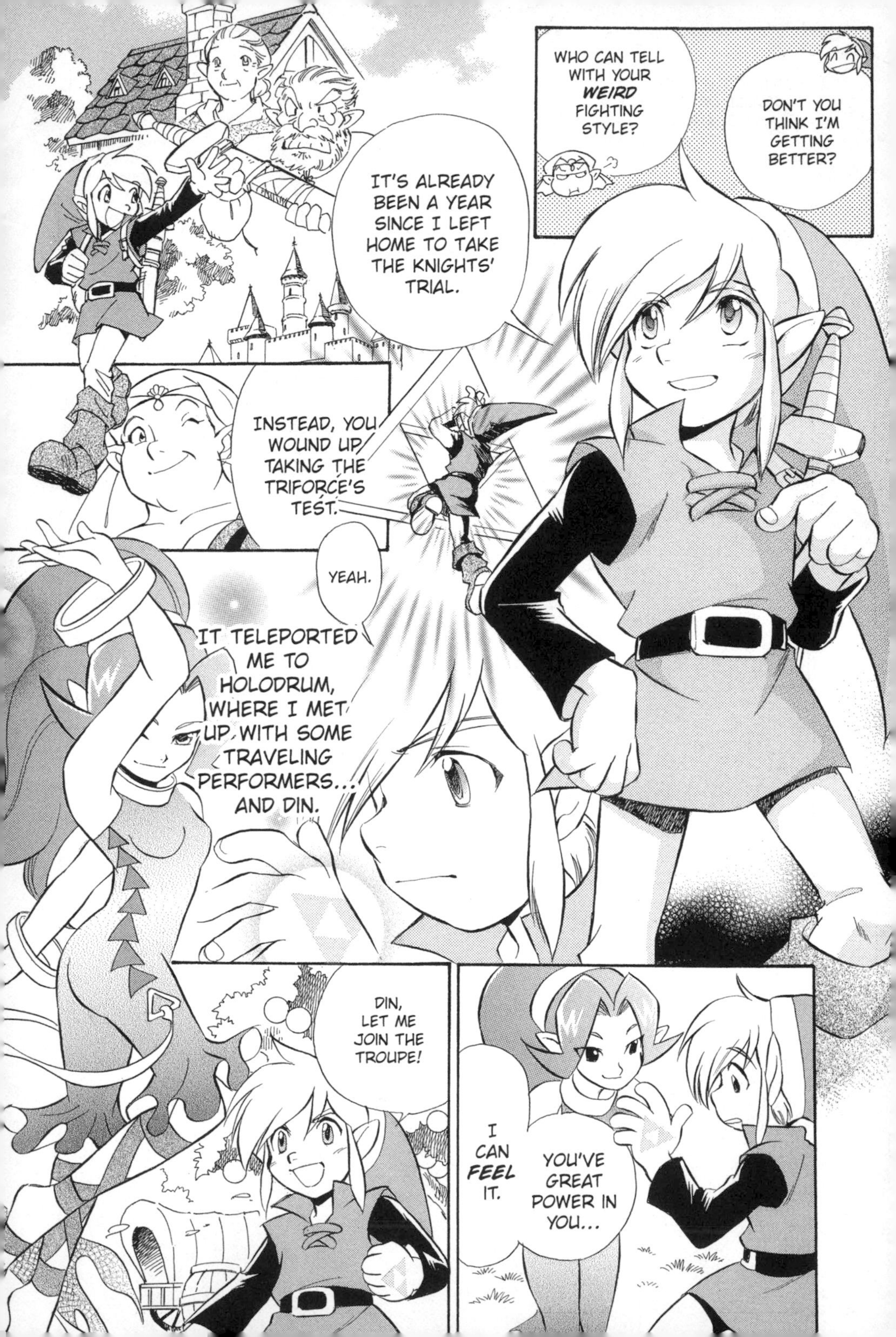
DON'T YOU THINK I'M GETTING BETTER?
WHO CAN TELL WITH YOUR **WEIRD** FIGHTING STYLE?
IT'S ALREADY BEEN A YEAR SINCE I LEFT HOME TO TAKE THE KNIGHTS' TRIAL.
INSTEAD, YOU WOUND UP TAKING THE TRIFORCE'S TEST.
YEAH.
IT TELEPORTED ME TO HOLODRUM, WHERE I MET UP WITH SOME TRAVELING PERFORMERS... AND DIN.
YOU'VE GREAT POWER IN YOU...
I CAN **FEEL** IT.
DIN, LET ME JOIN THE TROUPE!

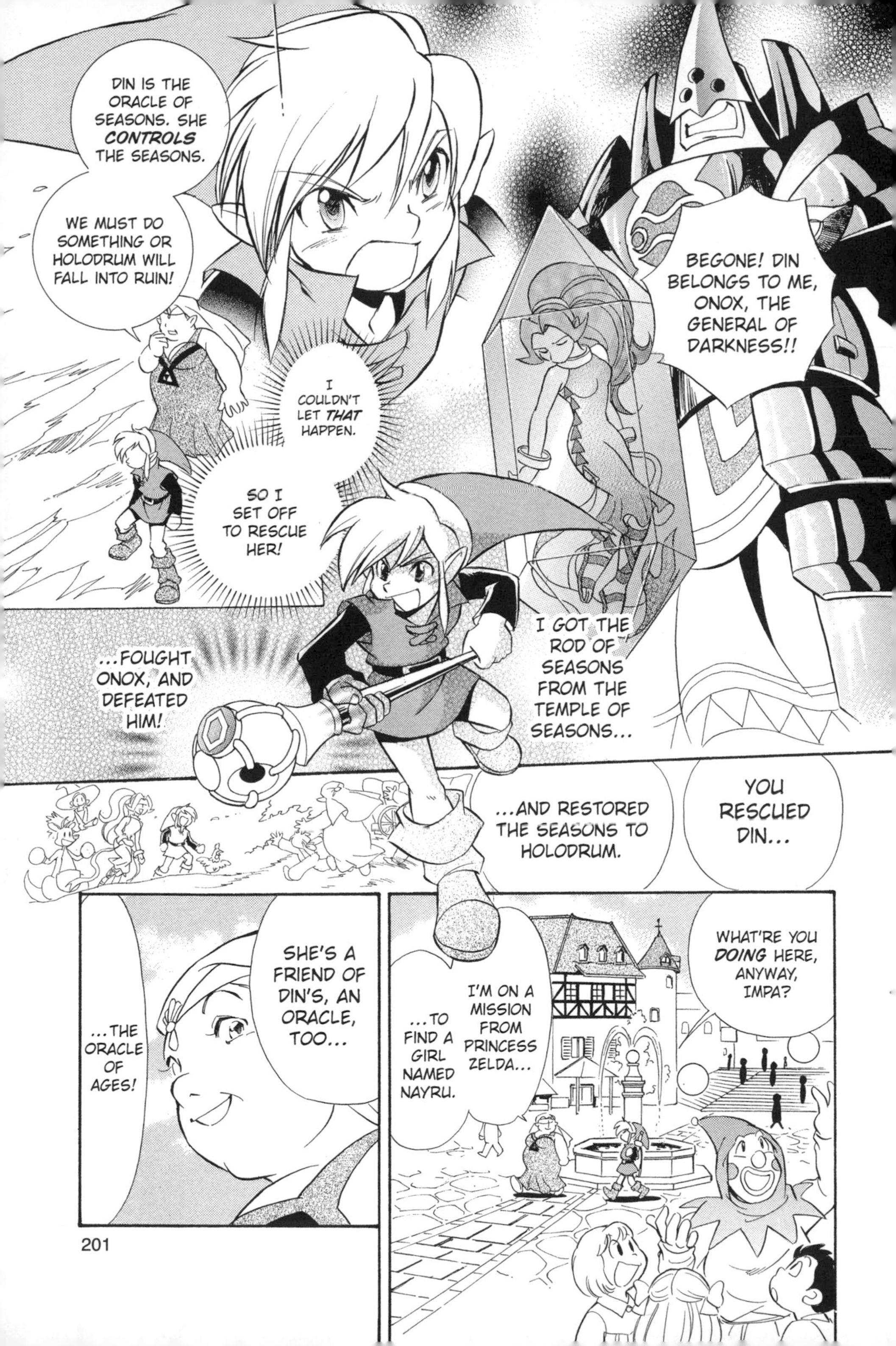

BEGONE! DIN BELONGS TO ME, ONOX, THE GENERAL OF DARKNESS!!
DIN IS THE ORACLE OF SEASONS. SHE *CONTROLS* THE SEASONS.
WE MUST DO SOMETHING OR HOLODRUM WILL FALL INTO RUIN!
I COULDN'T LET *THAT* HAPPEN.
SO I SET OFF TO RESCUE HER!
I GOT THE ROD OF SEASONS FROM THE TEMPLE OF SEASONS...
...FOUGHT ONOX, AND DEFEATED HIM!
...AND RESTORED THE SEASONS TO HOLODRUM.
YOU RESCUED DIN...
WHAT'RE YOU *DOING* HERE, ANYWAY, IMPA?
I'M ON A MISSION FROM PRINCESS ZELDA...
...TO FIND A GIRL NAMED NAYRU.
SHE'S A FRIEND OF DIN'S, AN ORACLE, TOO...
...THE ORACLE OF AGES!

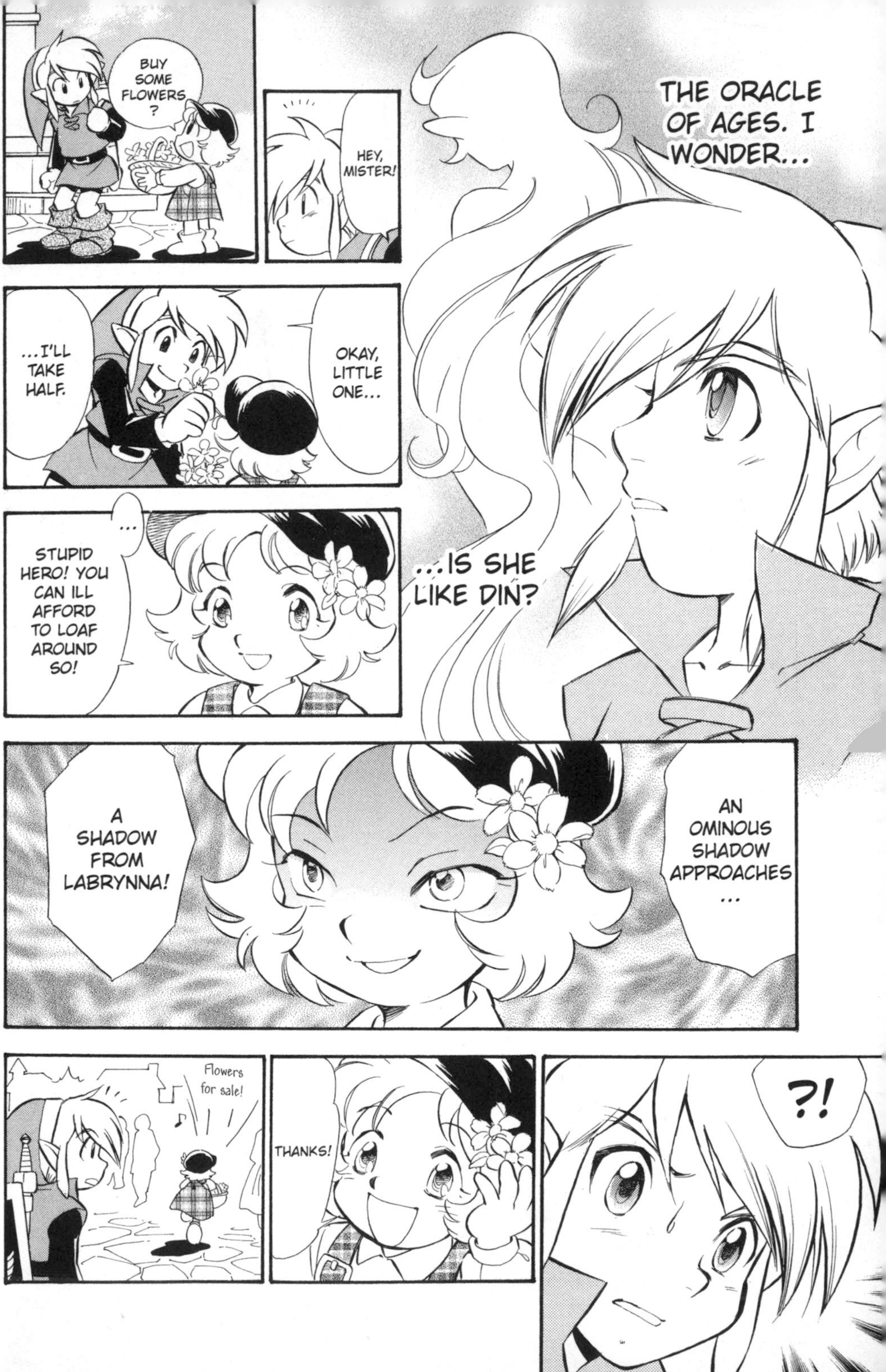

THE ORACLE OF AGES. I WONDER...
...IS SHE LIKE DIN?
HEY, MISTER!
BUY SOME FLOWERS ?
OKAY, LITTLE ONE...
...I'LL TAKE HALF.
...
STUPID HERO! YOU CAN ILL AFFORD TO LOAF AROUND SO!
AN OMINOUS SHADOW APPROACHES ...
A SHADOW FROM LABRYNNA!
?!
THANKS!
Flowers for sale!

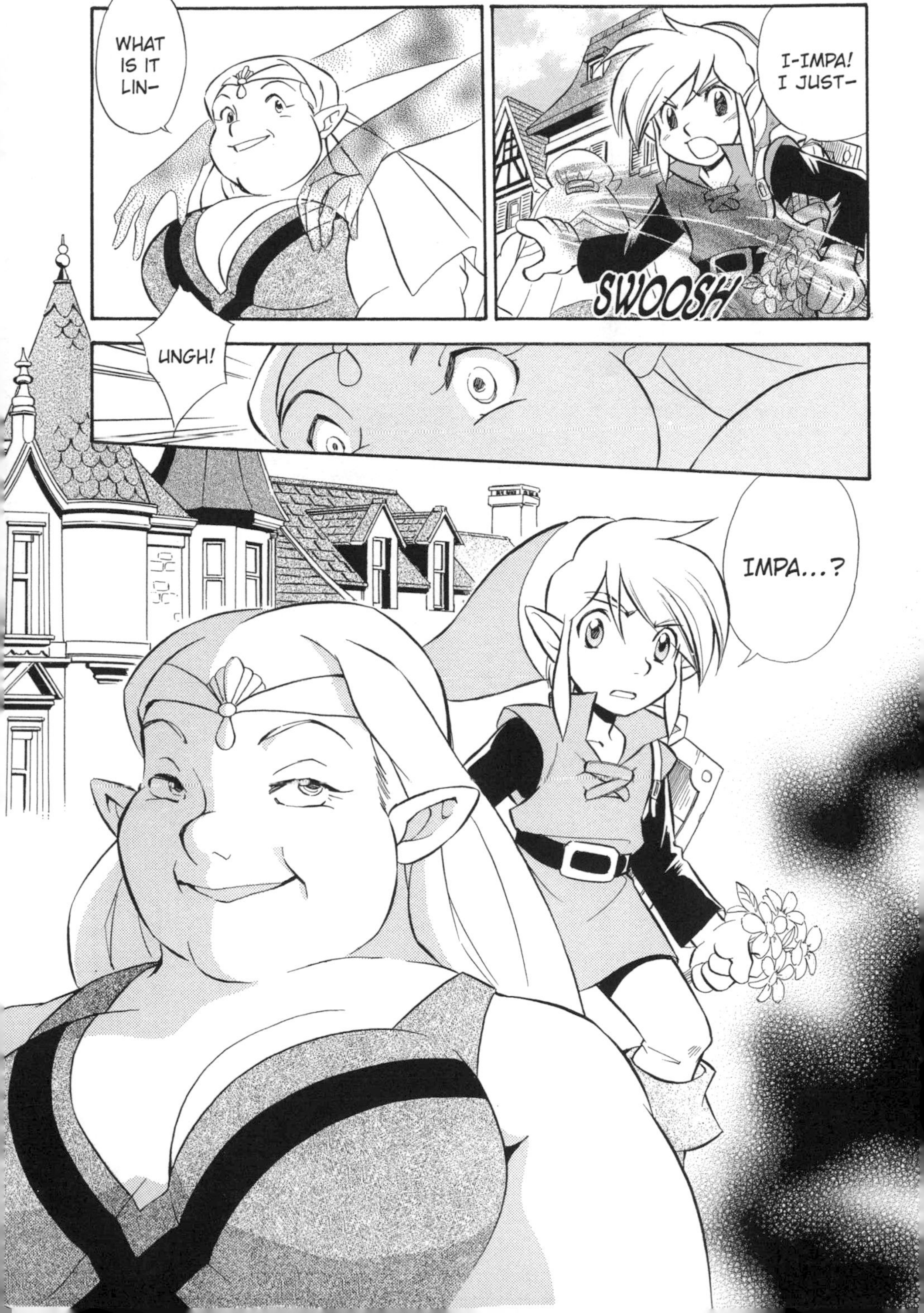
I-IMPA! I JUST-
SWOOSH
WHAT IS IT LIN-
UNGH!
IMPA...?

ROUGH CHARACTER
ILLUSTRATION 5

Maple. A capricious little witch.

Maple

2000 10·11

CHAPTER 2

SORCERESS OF SHADOWS: VERAN

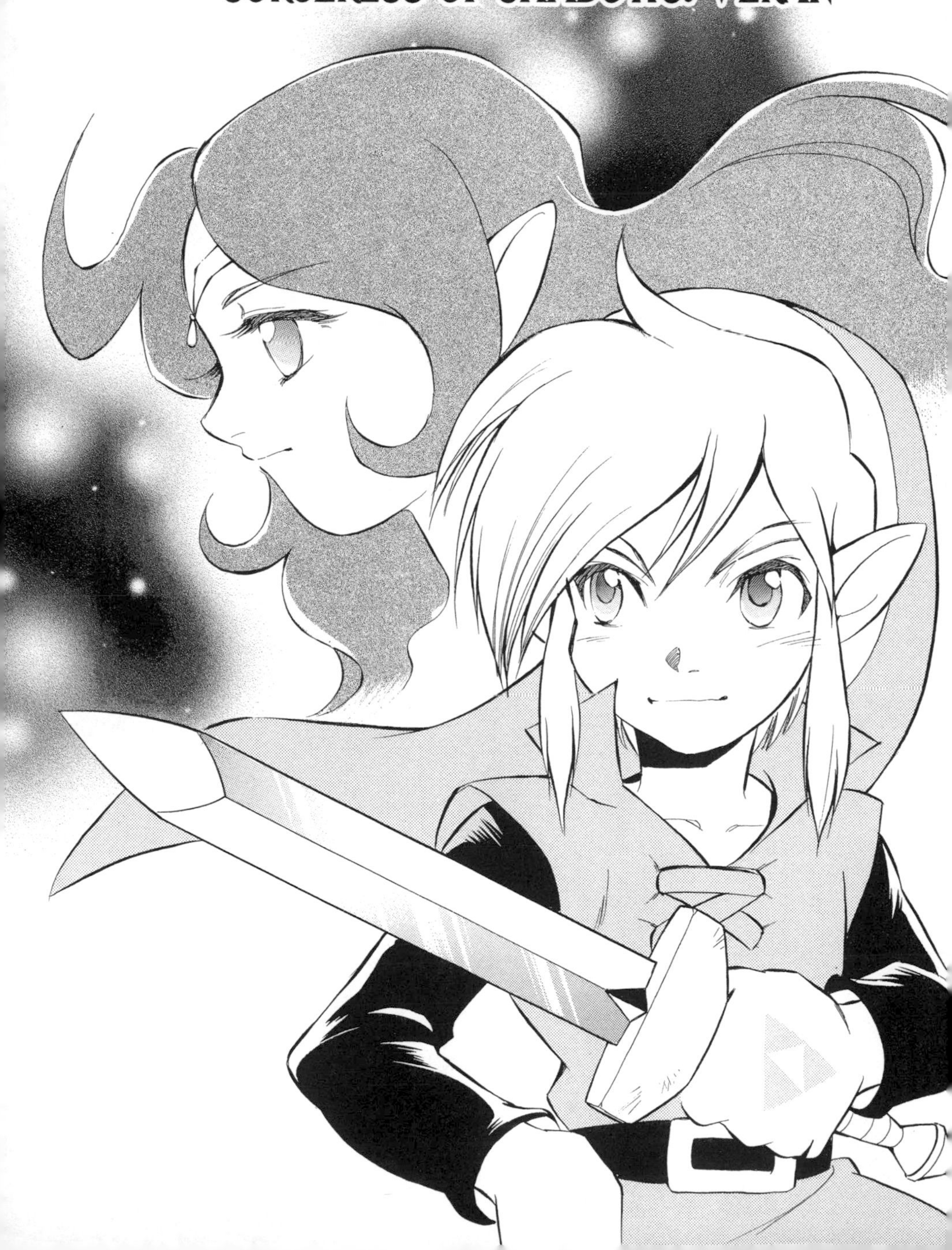

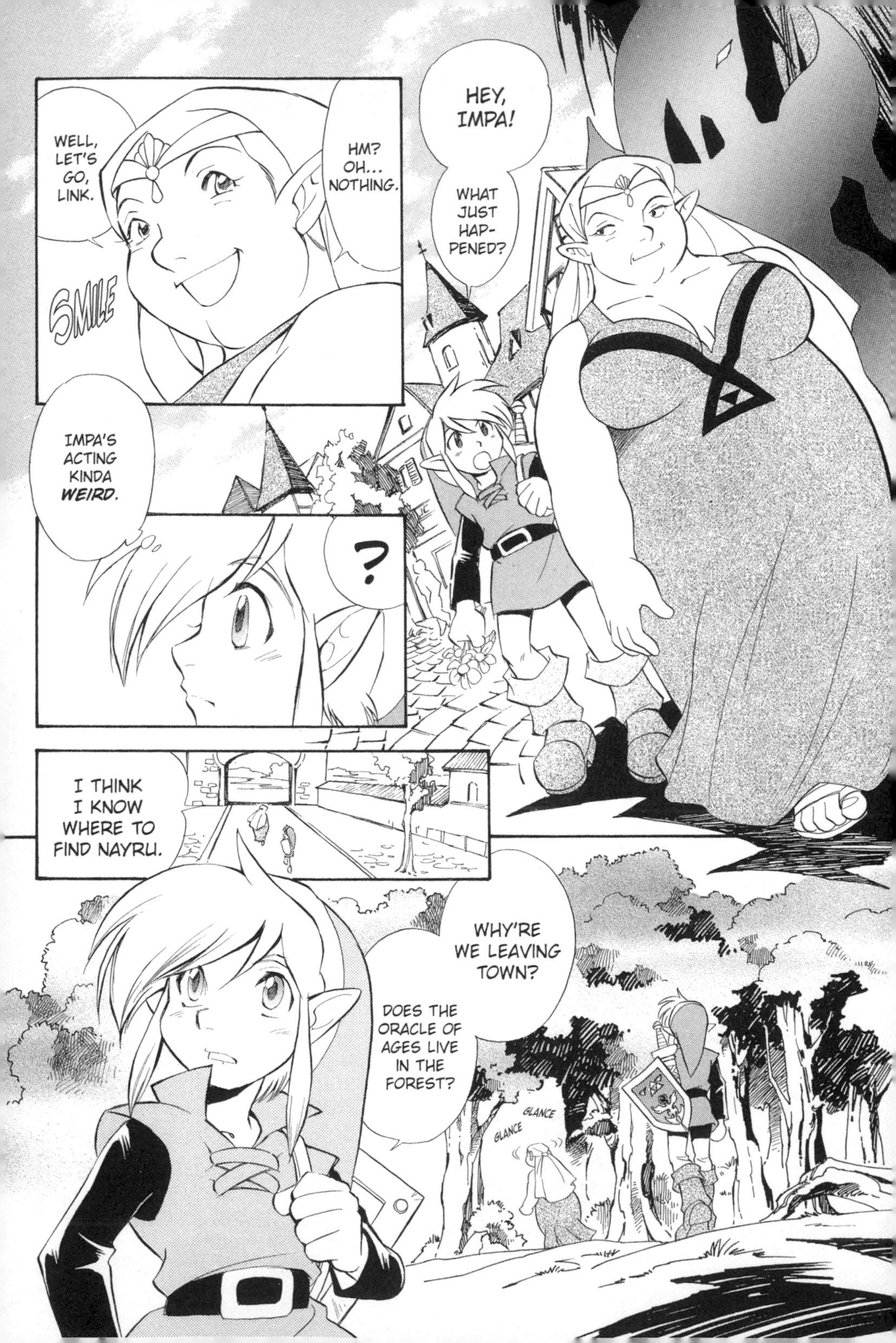
HEY, IMPA!
WHAT JUST HAP-PENED?
HM? OH... NOTHING.
WELL, LET'S GO, LINK.
SMILE
IMPA'S ACTING KINDA **WEIRD**.
?
I THINK I KNOW WHERE TO FIND NAYRU.
WHY'RE WE LEAVING TOWN?
DOES THE ORACLE OF AGES LIVE IN THE FOREST?
GLANCE
GLANCE

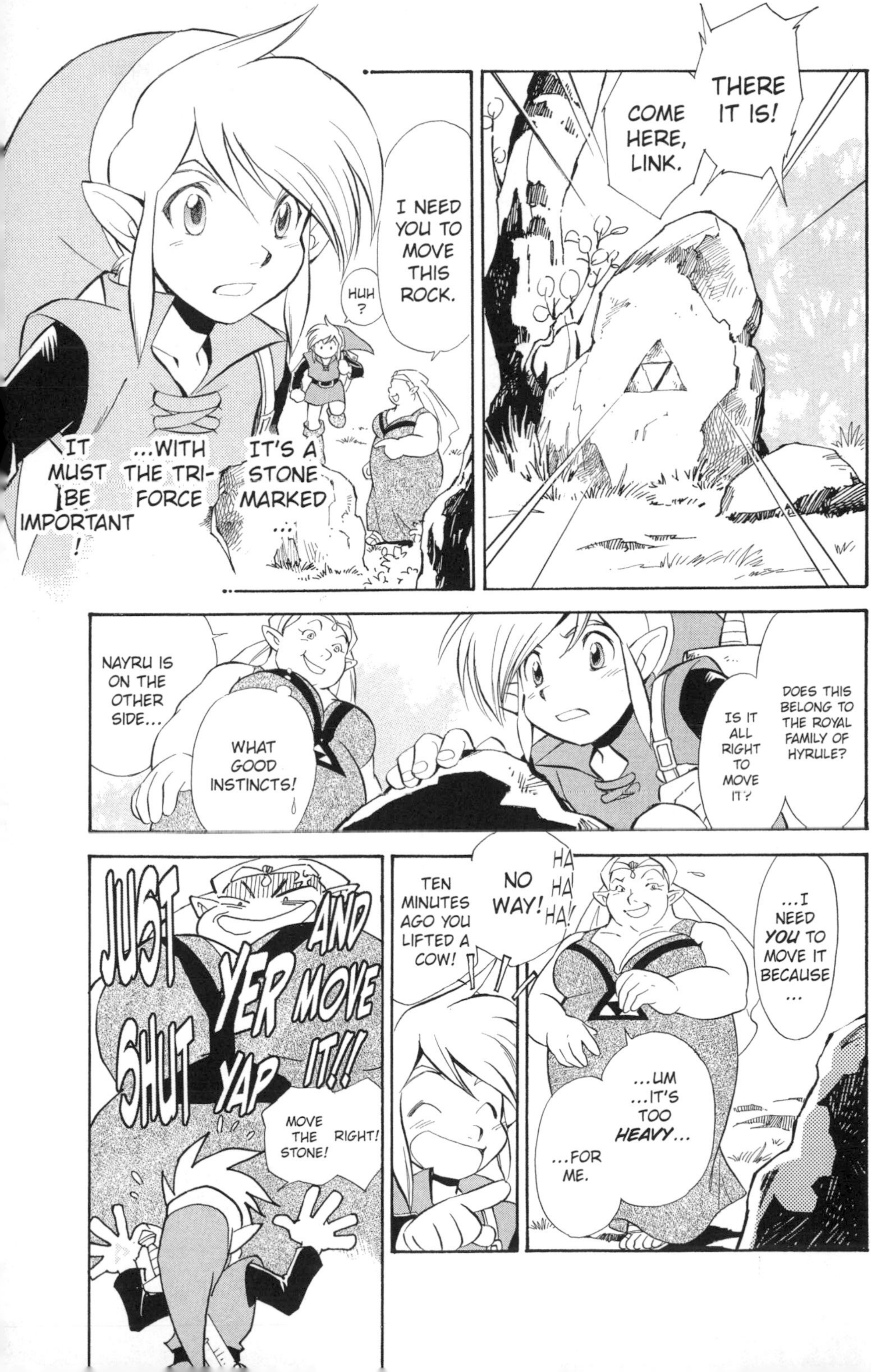
THERE IT IS!
COME HERE, LINK.
I NEED YOU TO MOVE THIS ROCK.
HUH?
IT'S A STONE MARKED
...WITH THE TRI-FORCE
IT MUST BE IMPORTANT!
DOES THIS BELONG TO THE ROYAL FAMILY OF HYRULE?
IS IT ALL RIGHT TO MOVE IT?
WHAT GOOD INSTINCTS!
NAYRU IS ON THE OTHER SIDE...
...I NEED YOU TO MOVE IT BECAUSE ...
...UM ...IT'S TOO HEAVY...
...FOR ME.
HA HA HA!
NO WAY!
TEN MINUTES AGO YOU LIFTED A COW!
JUST SHUT YER YAP AND MOVE IT!!
RIGHT!
MOVE THE STONE!

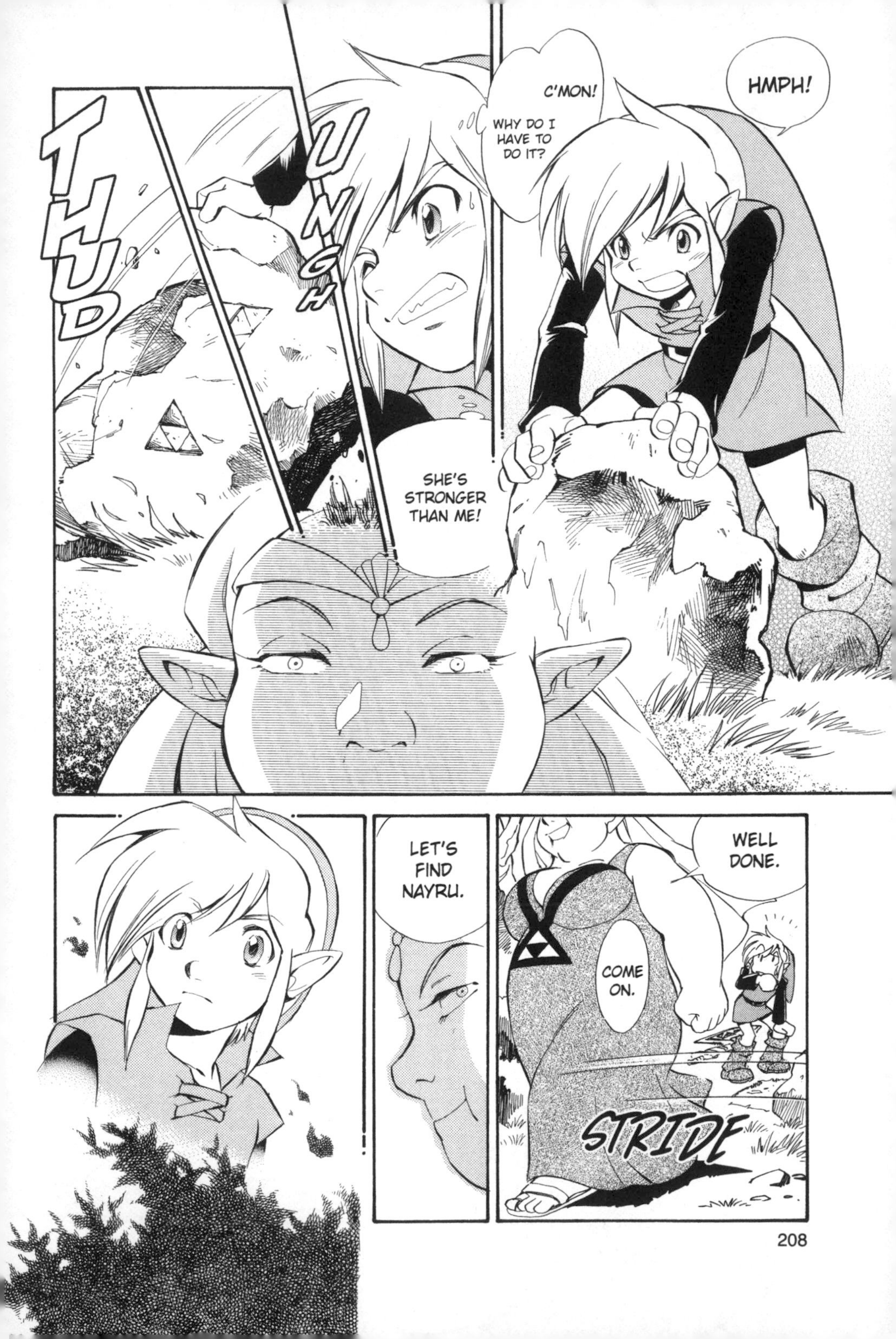
HMPH!
C'MON!
WHY DO I HAVE TO DO IT?
UUNGH
SHE'S STRONGER THAN ME!
THUD
WELL DONE.
COME ON.
STRIDE
LET'S FIND NAYRU.

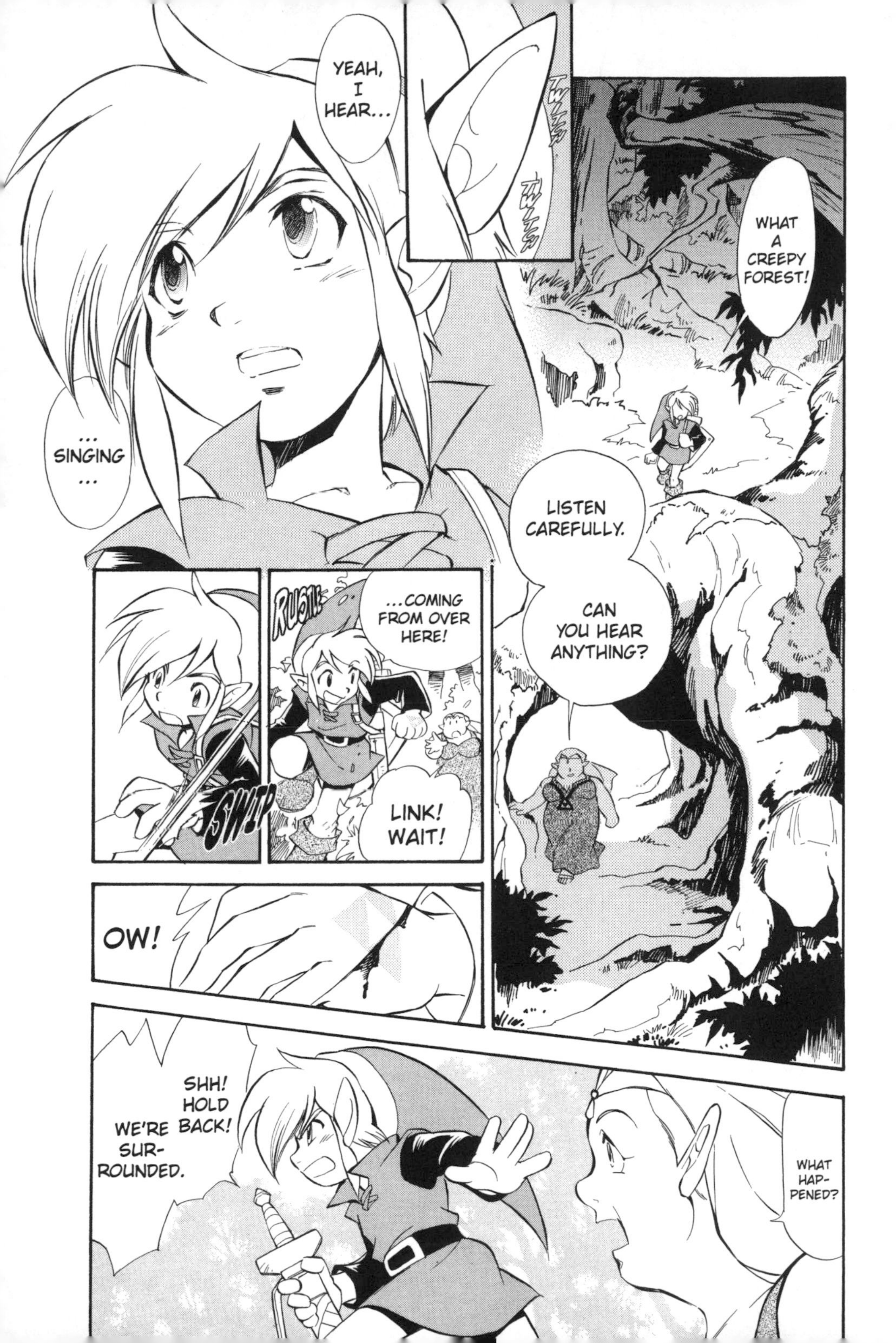
WHAT A CREEPY FOREST!
LISTEN CAREFULLY.
CAN YOU HEAR ANYTHING?
YEAH, I HEAR...
...SINGING...
...COMING FROM OVER HERE!
LINK! WAIT!
SWIP
OW!
WHAT HAPPENED?
SHH! HOLD BACK!
WE'RE SURROUNDED.

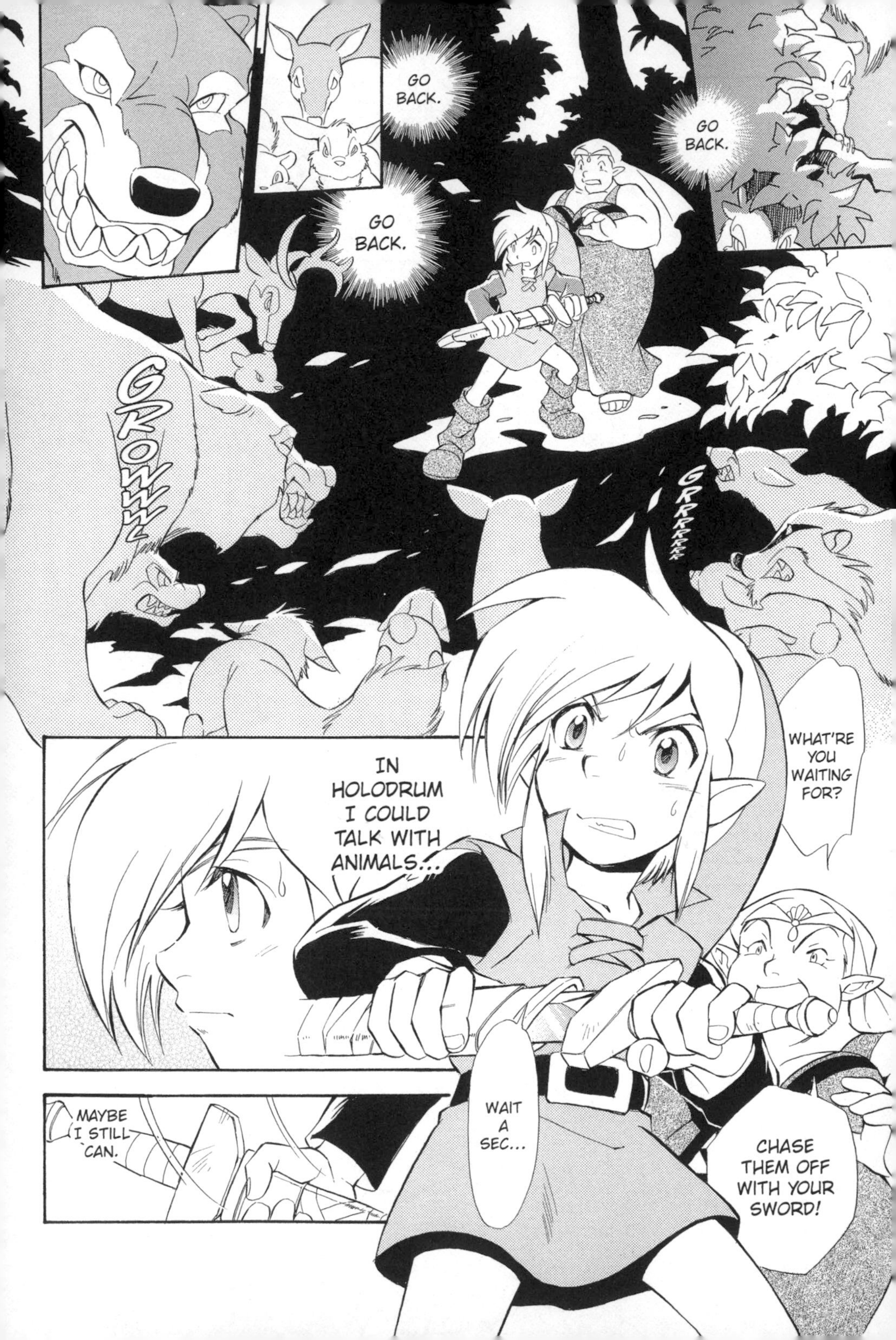
GO BACK.
GO BACK.
GO BACK.
GRRRRRR
GROWWW
WHAT'RE YOU WAITING FOR?
IN HOLODRUM I COULD TALK WITH ANIMALS...
CHASE THEM OFF WITH YOUR SWORD!
WAIT A SEC...
MAYBE I STILL CAN.

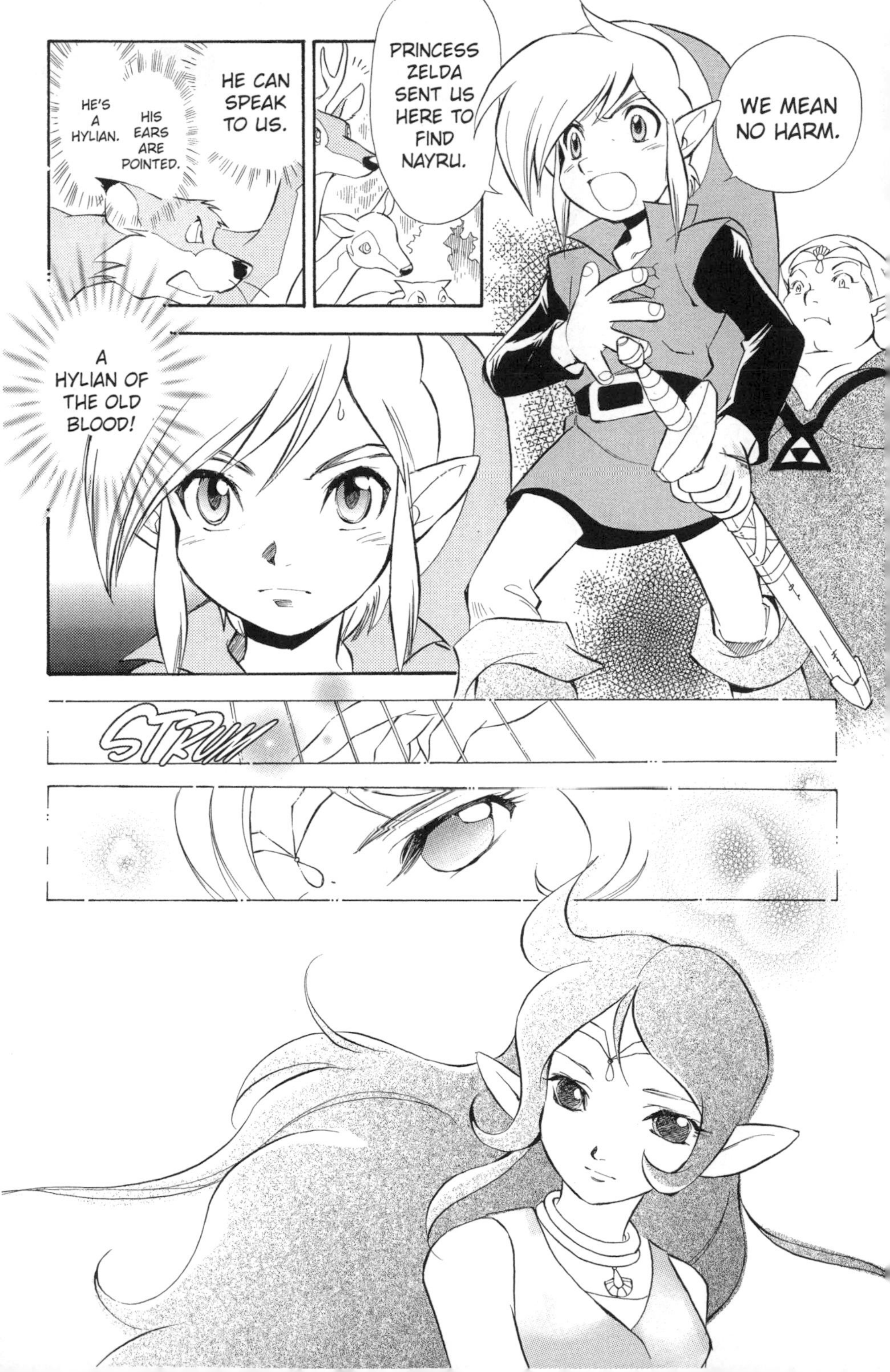

WE MEAN NO HARM.
PRINCESS ZELDA SENT US HERE TO FIND NAYRU.
HE CAN SPEAK TO US.
HIS EARS ARE POINTED.
HE'S A HYLIAN.
A HYLIAN OF THE OLD BLOOD!
STRUM

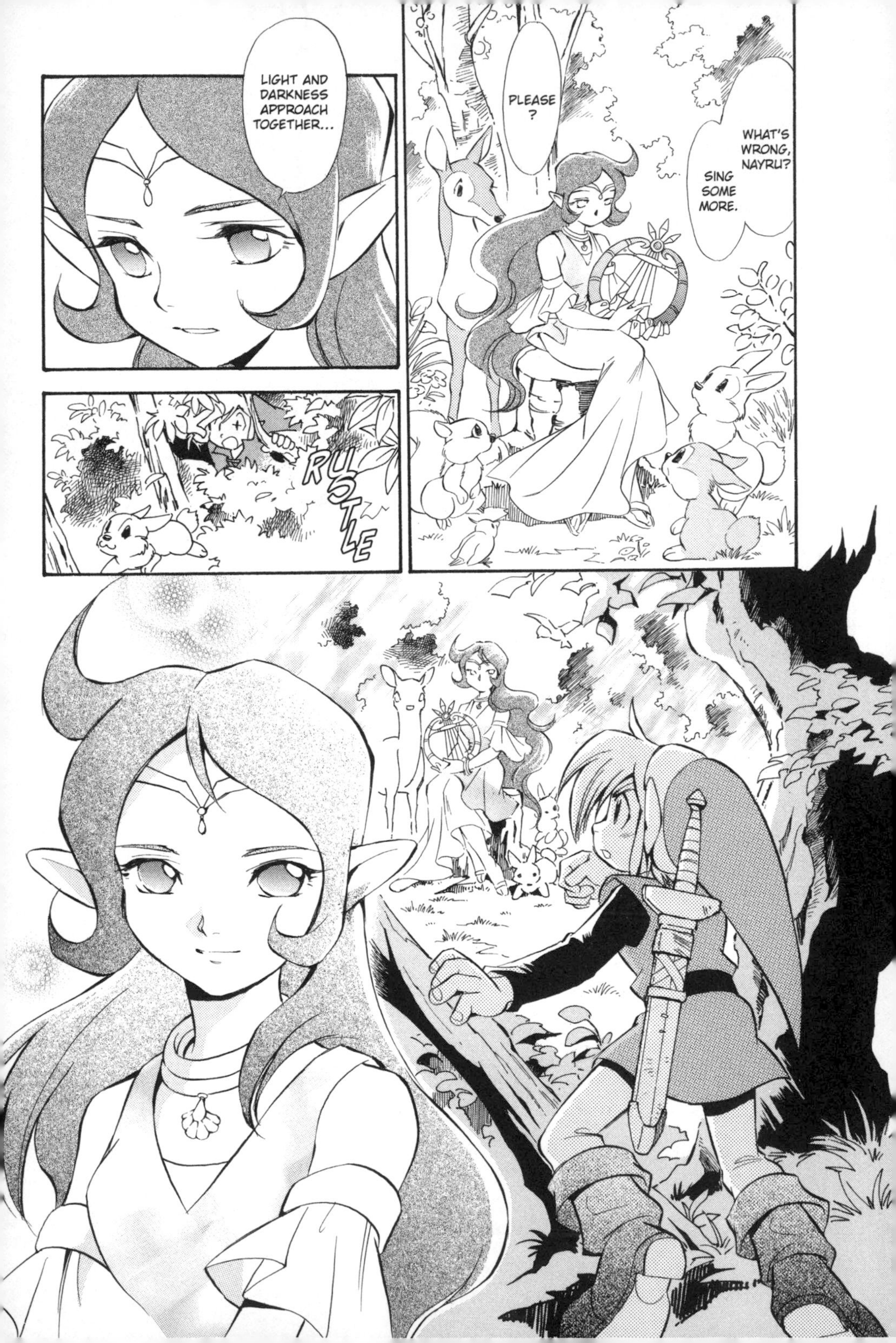
WHAT'S WRONG, NAYRU?
SING SOME MORE.
PLEASE?
LIGHT AND DARKNESS APPROACH TOGETHER...
RUSTLE

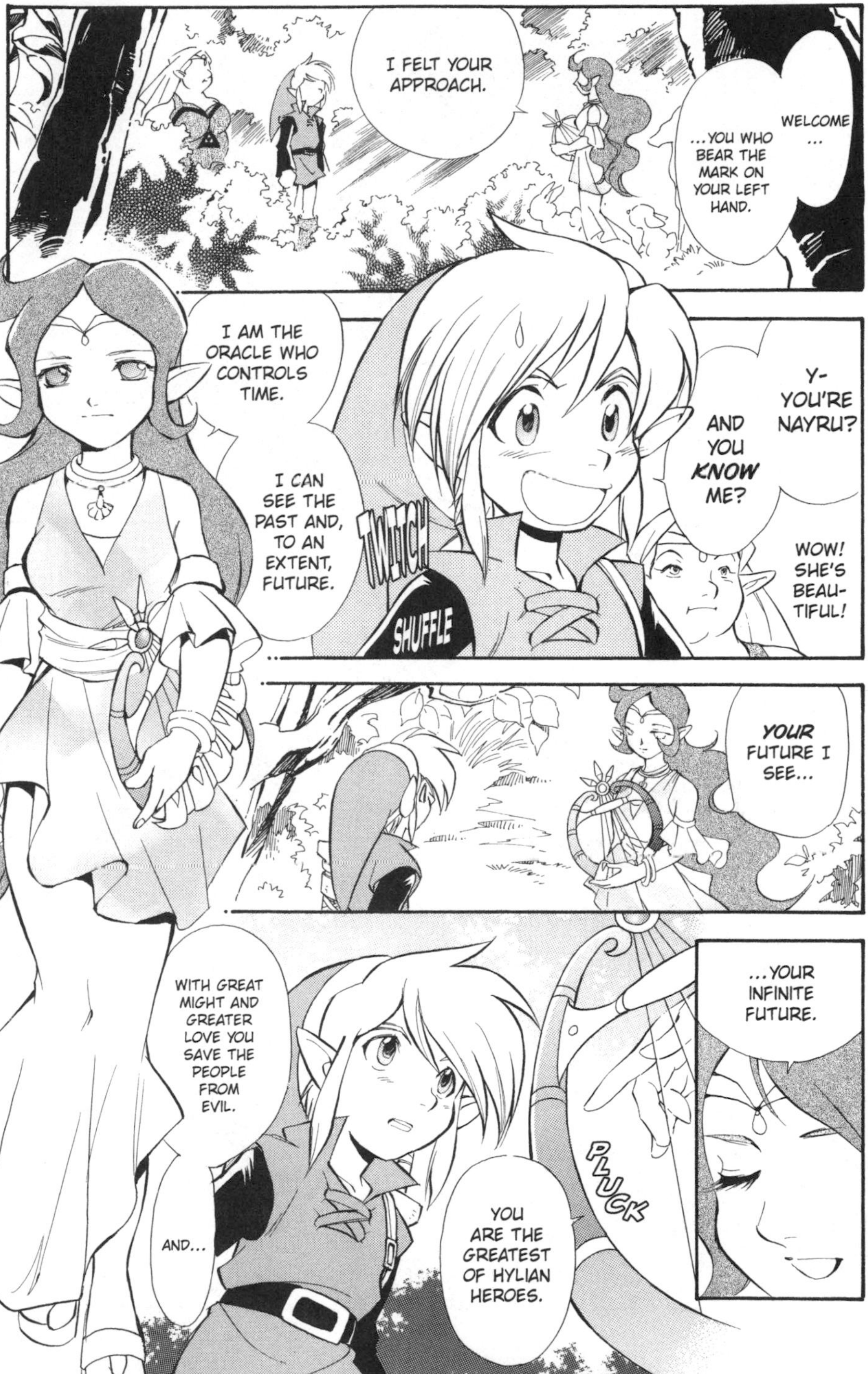
WELCOME...
...YOU WHO BEAR THE MARK ON YOUR LEFT HAND.
I FELT YOUR APPROACH.
Y-YOU'RE NAYRU?
AND YOU **KNOW** ME?
WOW! SHE'S BEAU-TIFUL!
TWITCH
SHUFFLE
I AM THE ORACLE WHO CONTROLS TIME.
I CAN SEE THE PAST AND, TO AN EXTENT, FUTURE.
YOUR FUTURE I SEE...
...YOUR INFINITE FUTURE.
PLUCK
WITH GREAT MIGHT AND GREATER LOVE YOU SAVE THE PEOPLE FROM EVIL.
AND...
YOU ARE THE GREATEST OF HYLIAN HEROES.

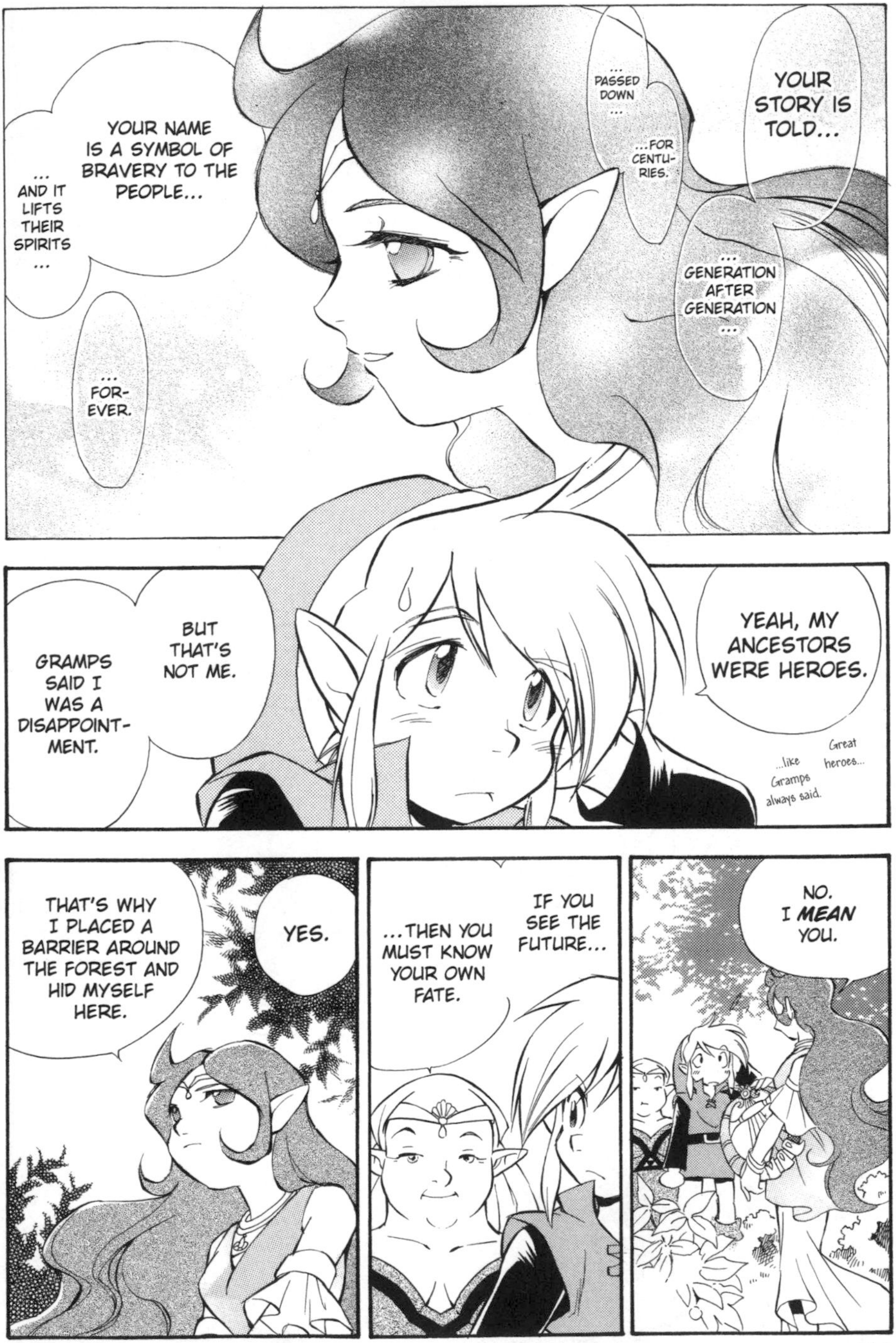
YOUR STORY IS TOLD...
...PASSED DOWN...
...FOR CENTURIES.
...GENERATION AFTER GENERATION...
YOUR NAME IS A SYMBOL OF BRAVERY TO THE PEOPLE...
...AND IT LIFTS THEIR SPIRITS...
...FOREVER.
YEAH, MY ANCESTORS WERE HEROES.
Great heroes...
...like Gramps always said.
BUT THAT'S NOT ME.
GRAMPS SAID I WAS A DISAPPOINTMENT.
NO. I *MEAN* YOU.
IF YOU SEE THE FUTURE...
...THEN YOU MUST KNOW YOUR OWN FATE.
YES.
THAT'S WHY I PLACED A BARRIER AROUND THE FOREST AND HID MYSELF HERE.

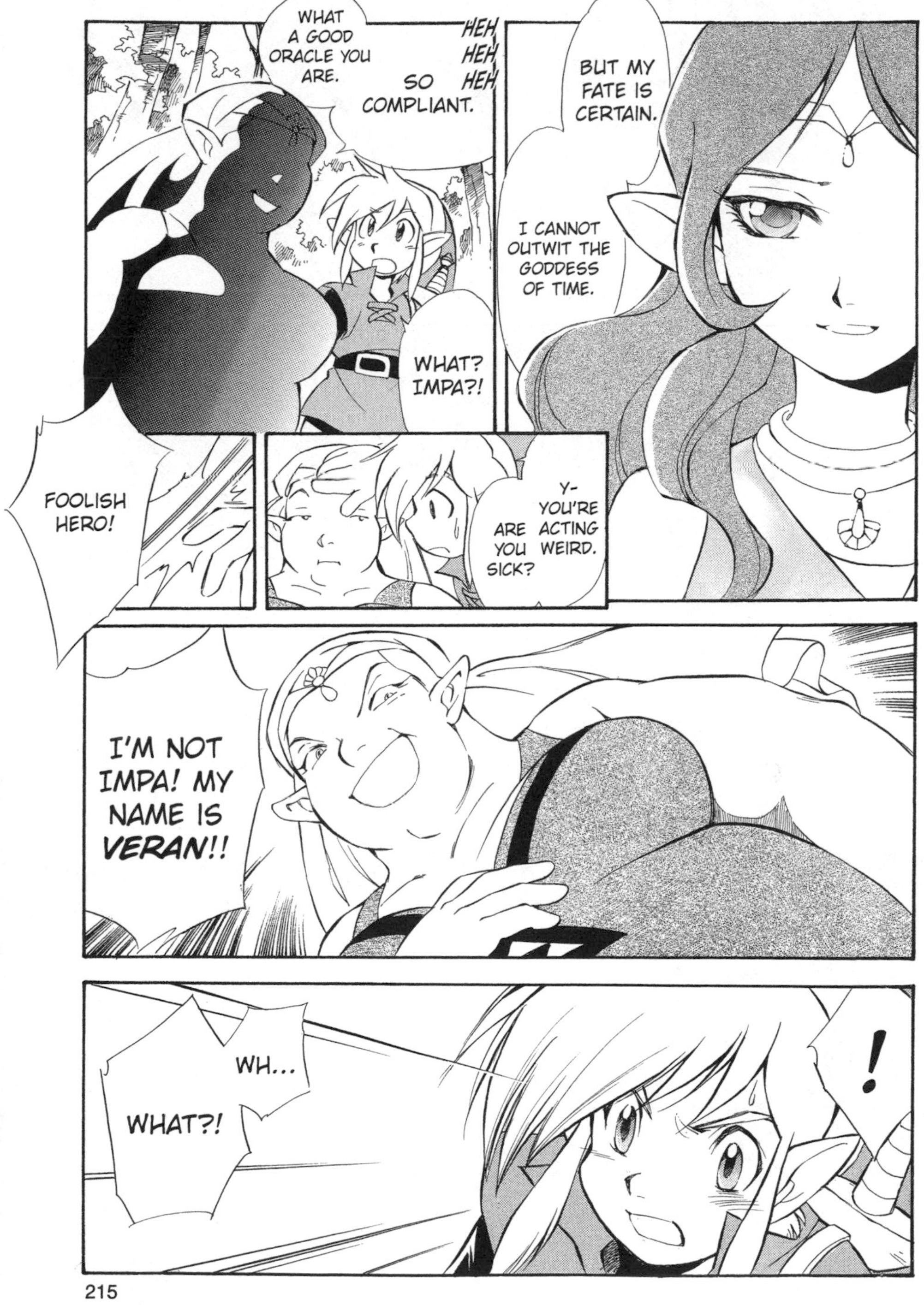
BUT MY FATE IS CERTAIN.
I CANNOT OUTWIT THE GODDESS OF TIME.
HEH HEH HEH
WHAT A GOOD ORACLE YOU ARE.
SO COMPLIANT.
WHAT? IMPA?!
Y- YOU'RE ACTING WEIRD.
ARE YOU SICK?
FOOLISH HERO!
I'M NOT IMPA! MY NAME IS *VERAN*!!
!
WH...
WHAT?!

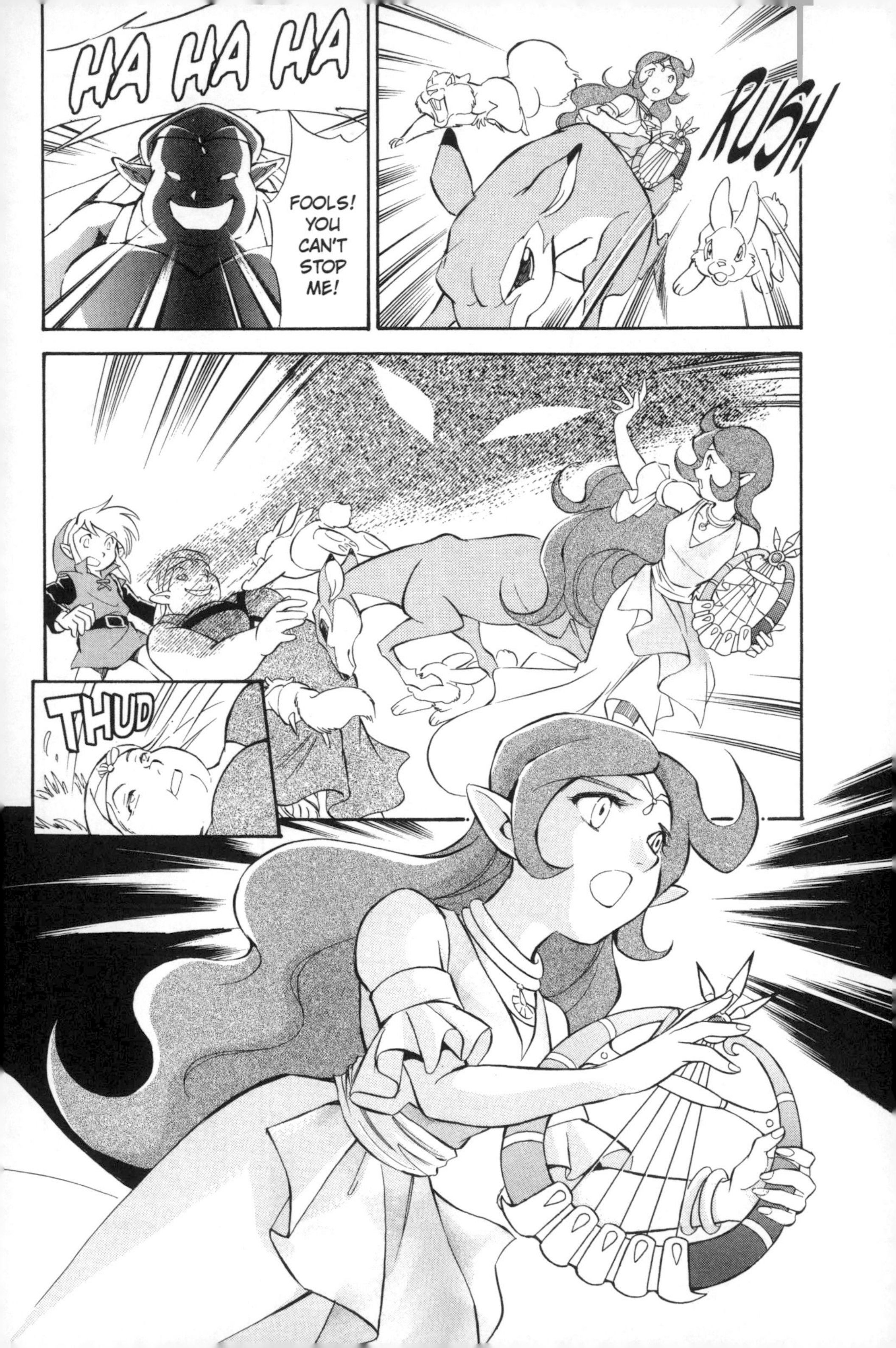
RUSH
HA HA HA
FOOLS! YOU CAN'T STOP ME!
THUD

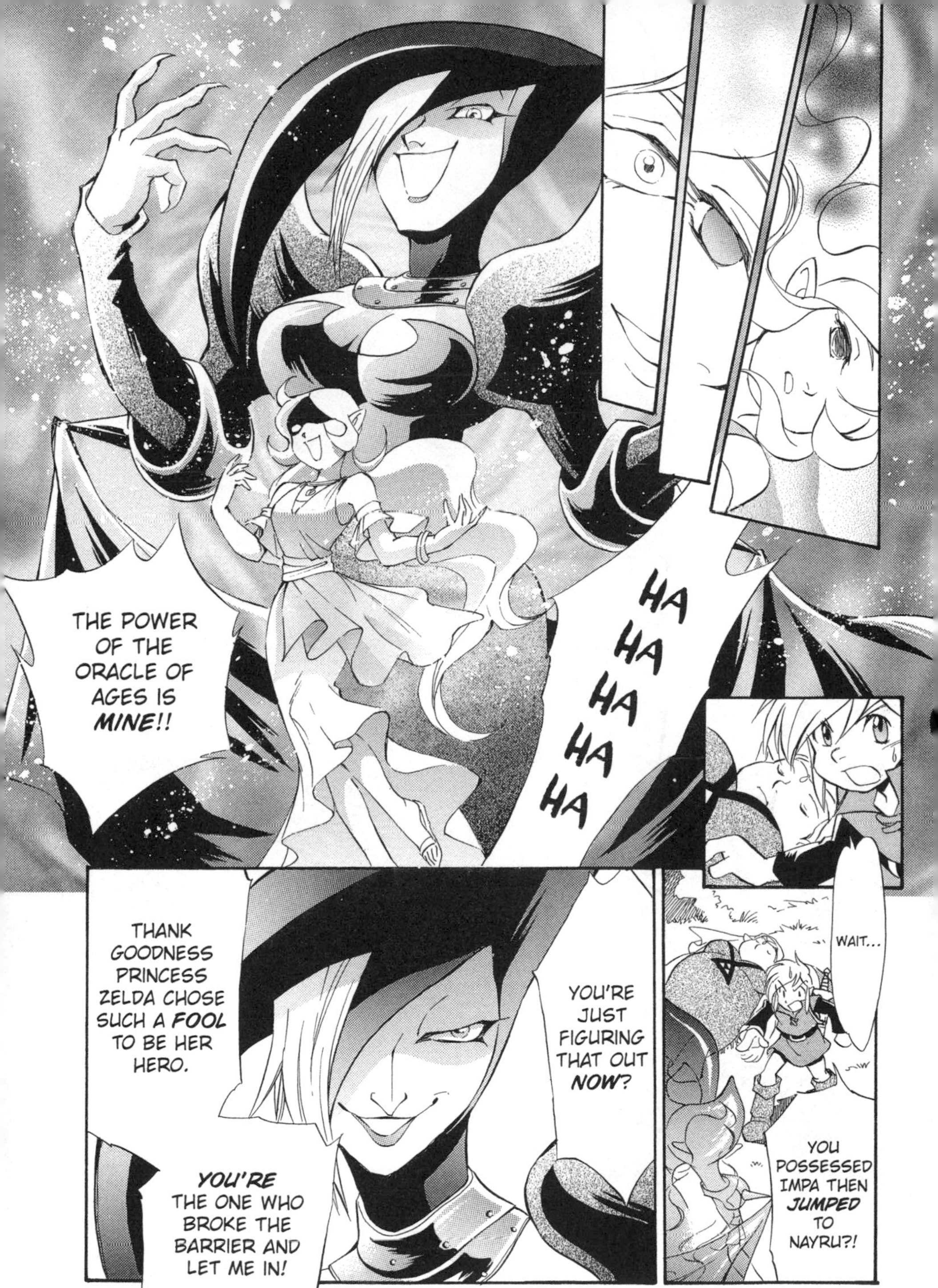

THE POWER OF THE ORACLE OF AGES IS MINE!!
HA HA HA HA HA HA
WAIT...
YOU POSSESSED IMPA THEN JUMPED TO NAYRU?!
YOU'RE JUST FIGURING THAT OUT NOW?
THANK GOODNESS PRINCESS ZELDA CHOSE SUCH A FOOL TO BE HER HERO.
YOU'RE THE ONE WHO BROKE THE BARRIER AND LET ME IN!

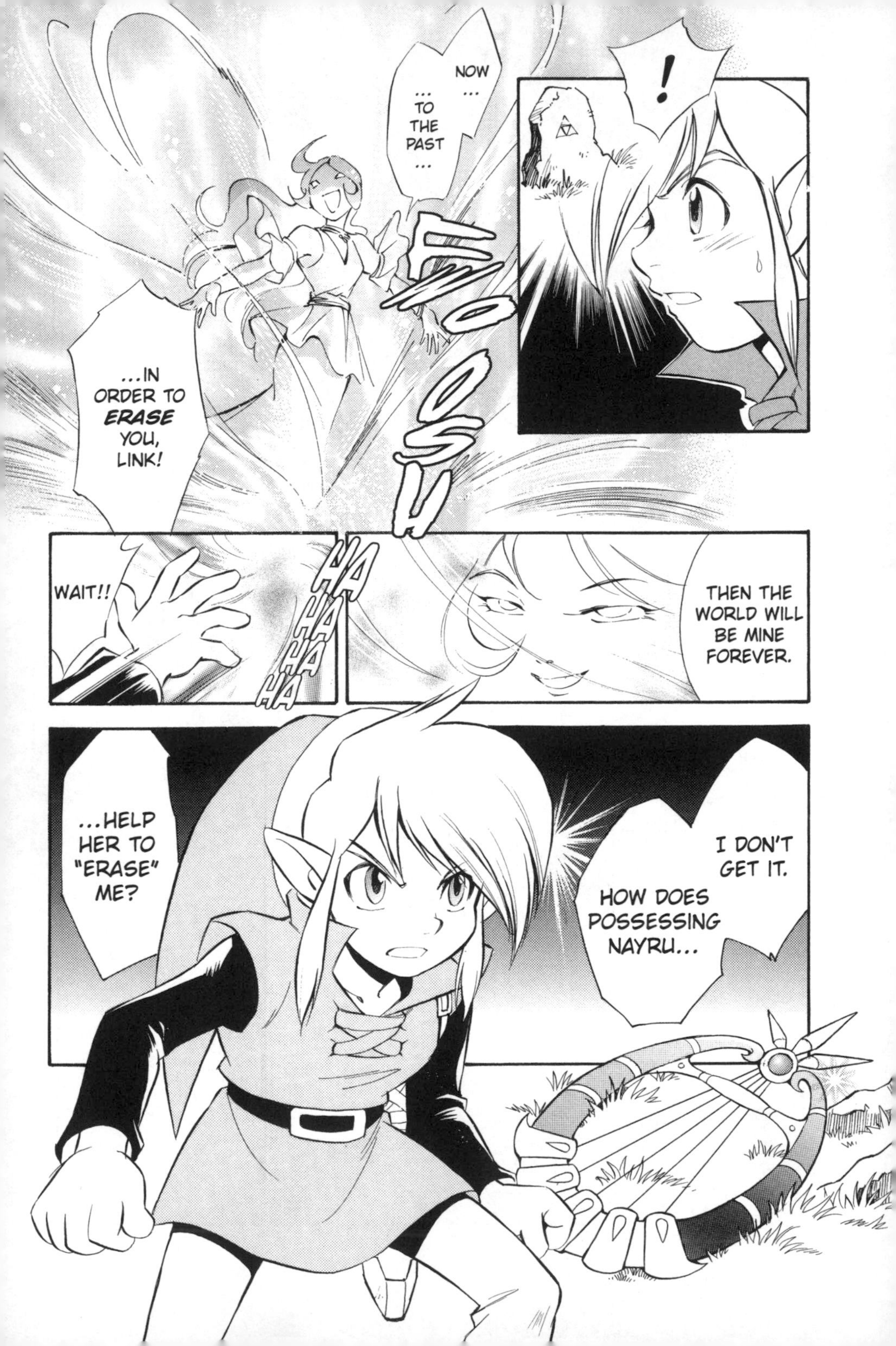
!
NOW... ...TO THE PAST...
...IN ORDER TO ERASE YOU, LINK!
FWOOOSH
THEN THE WORLD WILL BE MINE FOREVER.
HA HA HA HA HA
WAIT!!
I DON'T GET IT.
HOW DOES POSSESSING NAYRU...
...HELP HER TO "ERASE" ME?

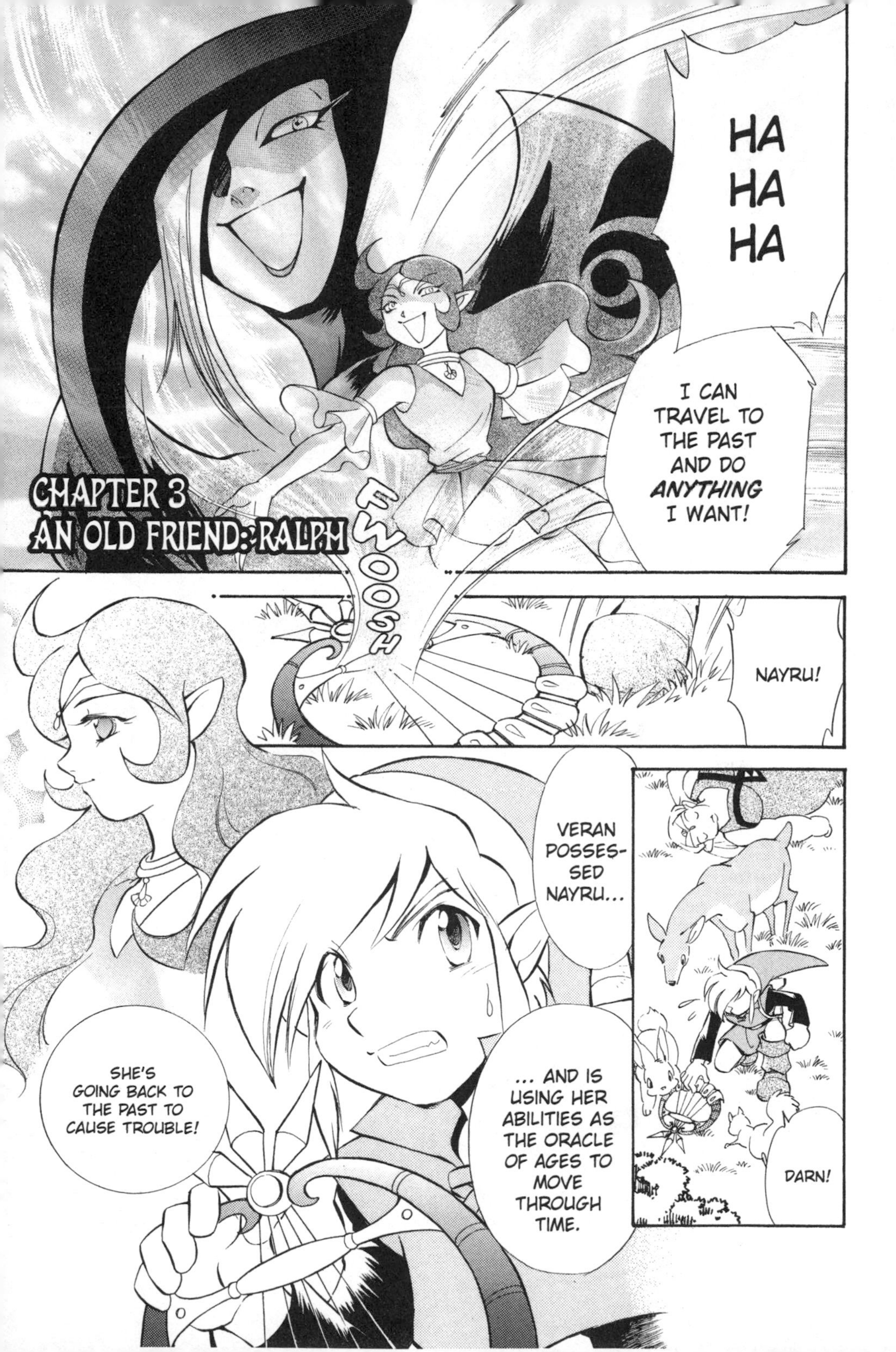
HA HA HA
I CAN TRAVEL TO THE PAST AND DO *ANYTHING* I WANT!
CHAPTER 3
AN OLD FRIEND: RALPH
FWOOOSH
NAYRU!
DARN!
VERAN POSSES-SED NAYRU...
... AND IS USING HER ABILITIES AS THE ORACLE OF AGES TO MOVE THROUGH TIME.
SHE'S GOING BACK TO THE PAST TO CAUSE TROUBLE!

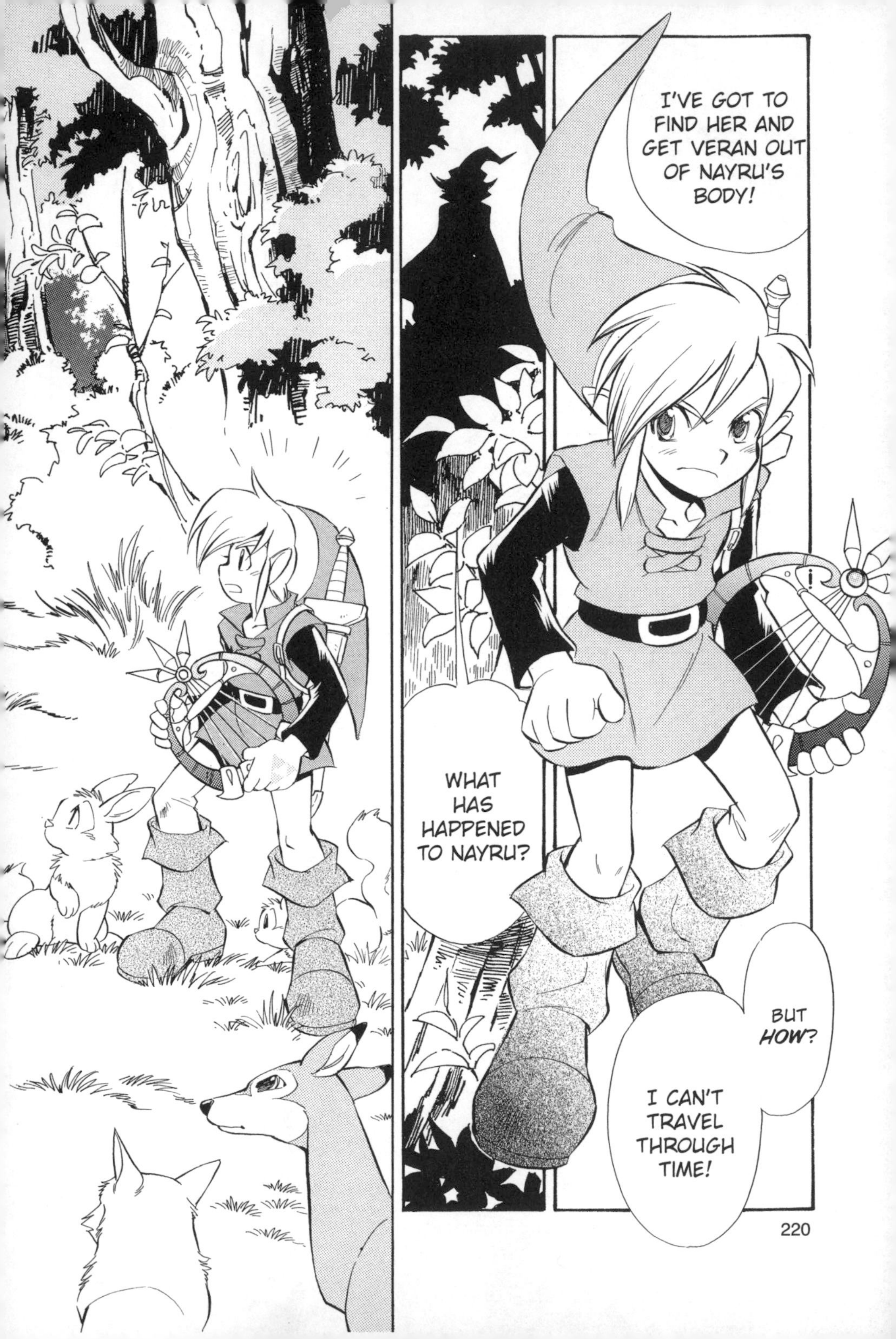
I'VE GOT TO FIND HER AND GET VERAN OUT OF NAYRU'S BODY!
WHAT HAS HAPPENED TO NAYRU?
BUT *HOW*?
I CAN'T TRAVEL THROUGH TIME!

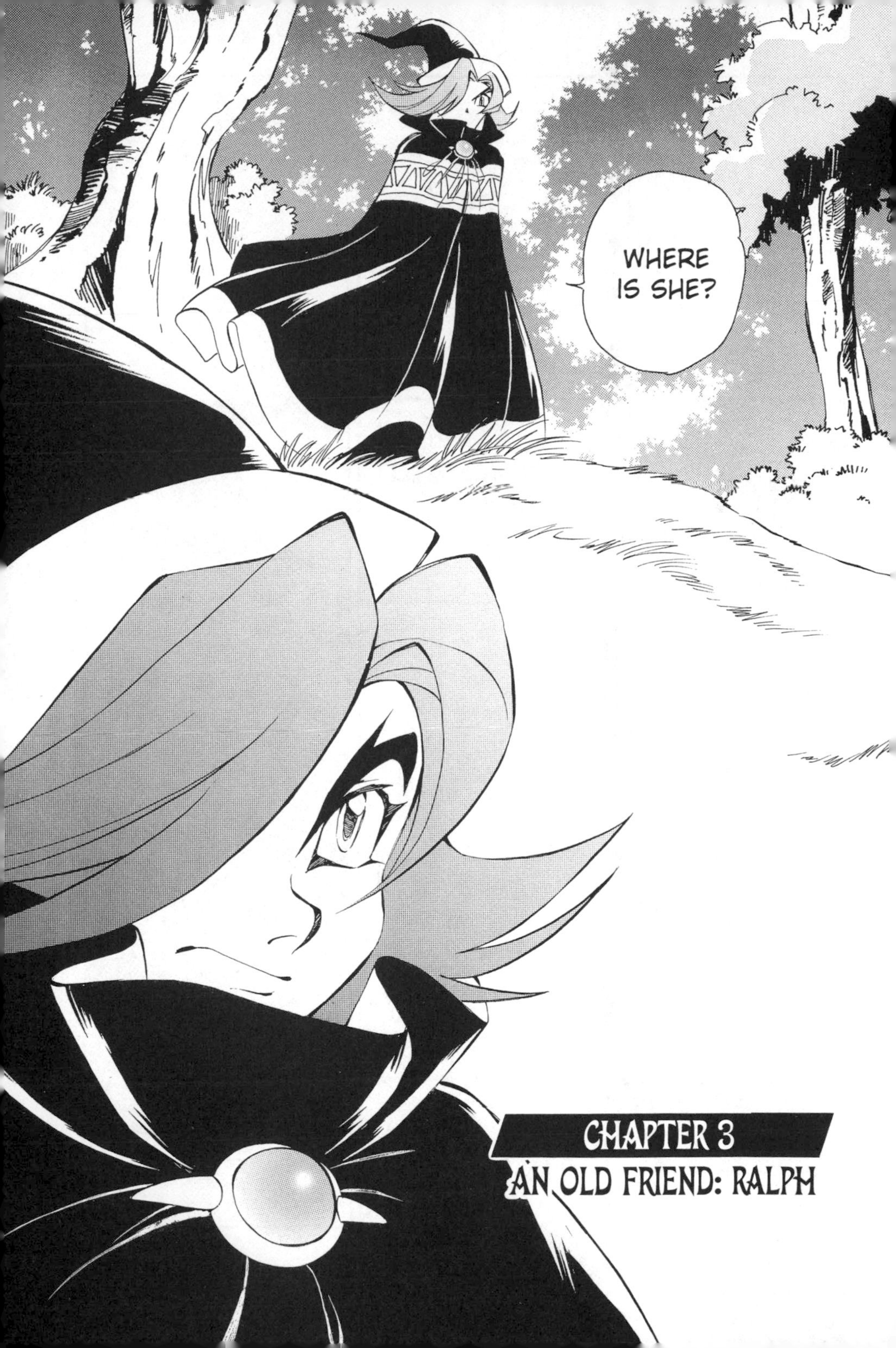
WHERE IS SHE?
CHAPTER 3
AN OLD FRIEND: RALPH

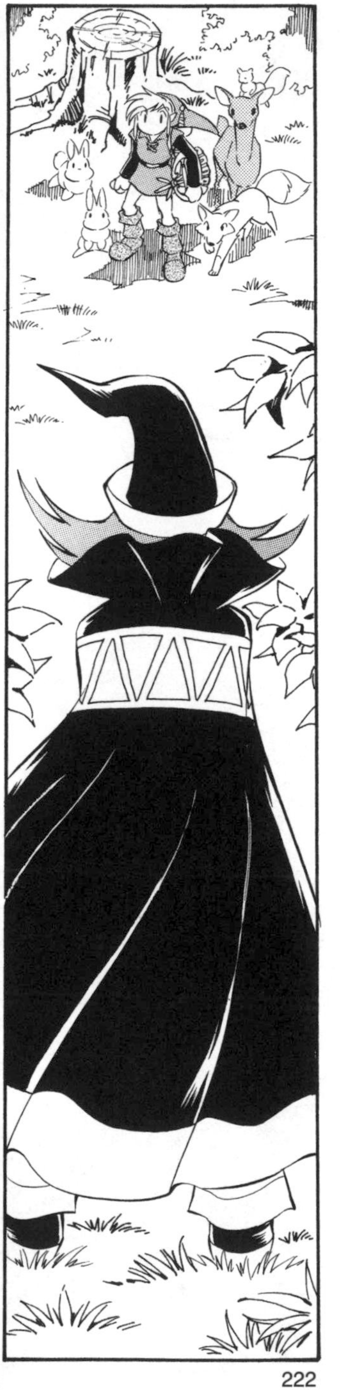
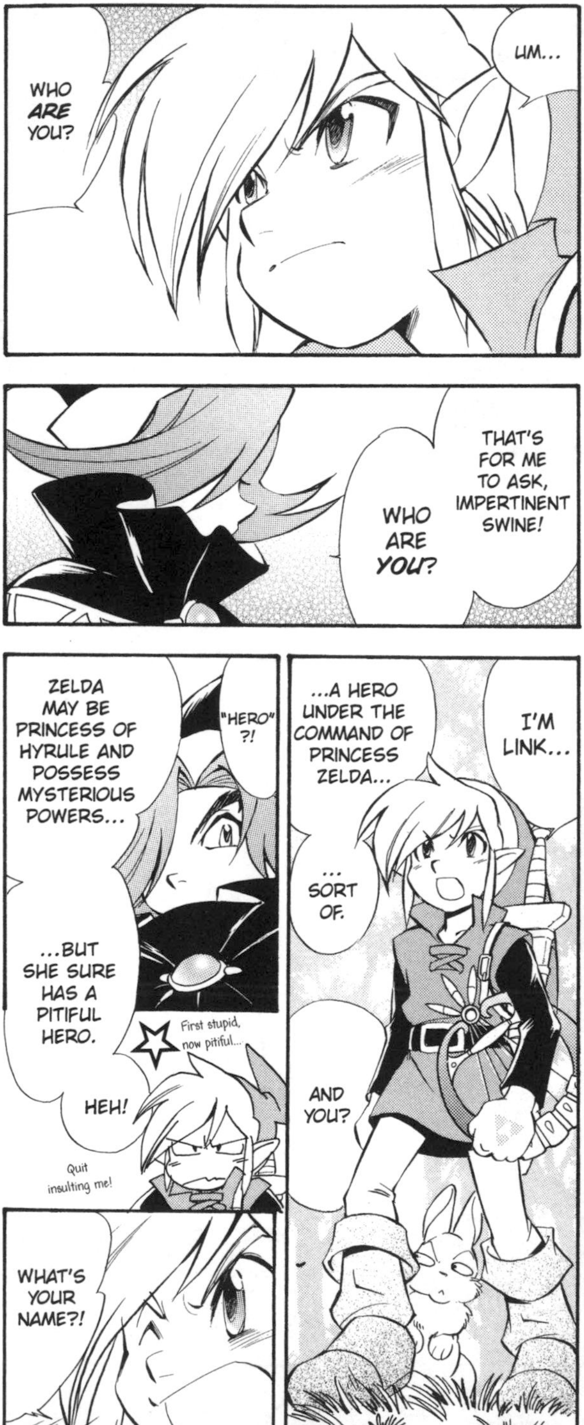
UM...
WHO ARE YOU?
THAT'S FOR ME TO ASK, IMPERTINENT SWINE!
WHO ARE YOU?
I'M LINK...
...A HERO UNDER THE COMMAND OF PRINCESS ZELDA...
... SORT OF.
AND YOU?
"HERO" ?!
ZELDA MAY BE PRINCESS OF HYRULE AND POSSESS MYSTERIOUS POWERS...
...BUT SHE SURE HAS A PITIFUL HERO.
HEH!
First stupid, now pitiful...
Quit insulting me!
WHAT'S YOUR NAME?!

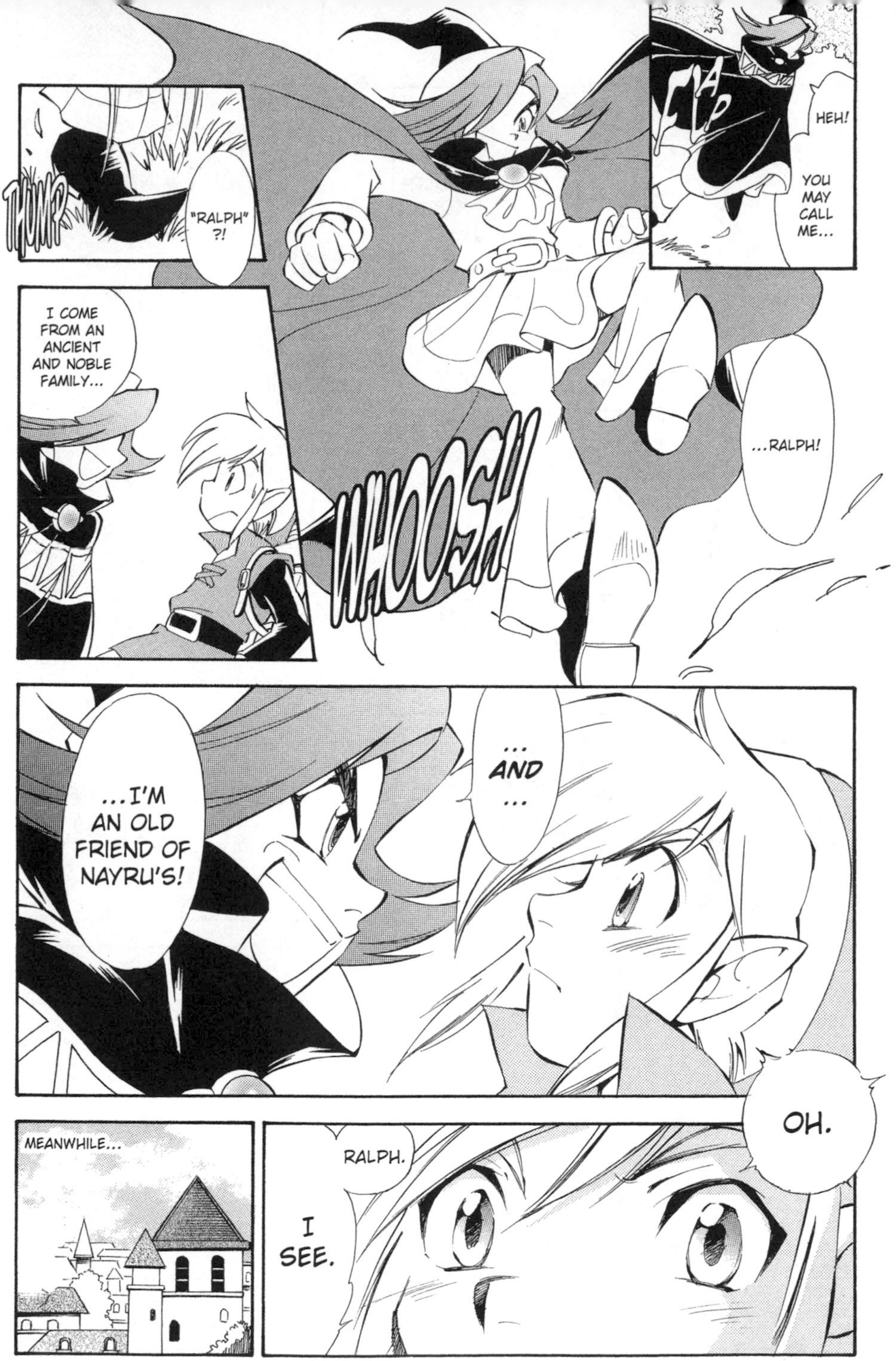
FLAP
HEH!
YOU MAY CALL ME...
...RALPH!
WHOOSH
THUMP
"RALPH" ?!
I COME FROM AN ANCIENT AND NOBLE FAMILY...
... AND ...
...I'M AN OLD FRIEND OF NAYRU'S!
OH.
RALPH.
I SEE.
MEANWHILE...

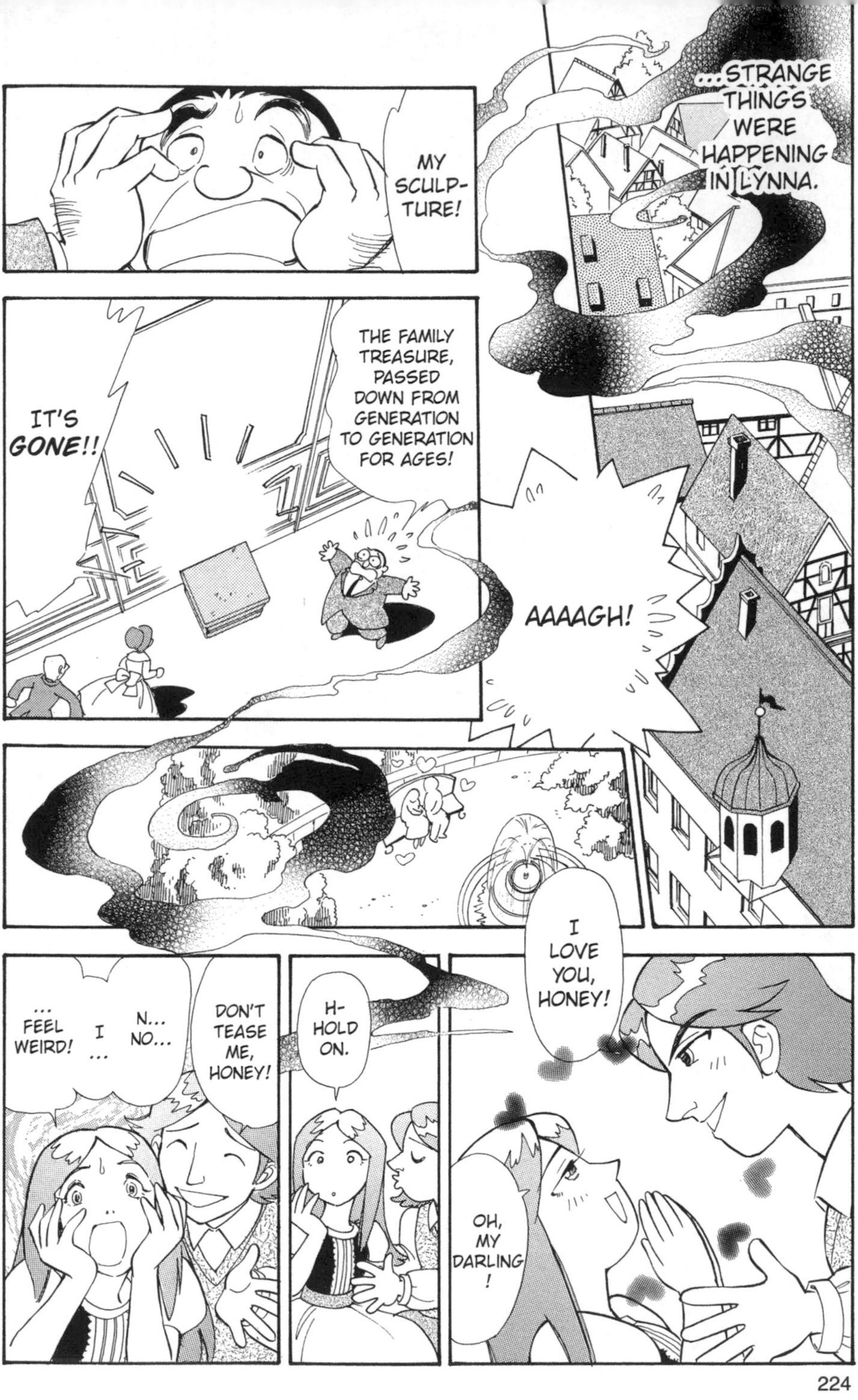
...STRANGE THINGS WERE HAPPENING IN LYNNA.
MY SCULP-TURE!
THE FAMILY TREASURE, PASSED DOWN FROM GENERATION TO GENERATION FOR AGES!
IT'S **GONE**!!
AAAAGH!
I LOVE YOU, HONEY!
OH, MY DARLING!
H-HOLD ON.
DON'T TEASE ME, HONEY!
N... NO... I ... FEEL WEIRD!

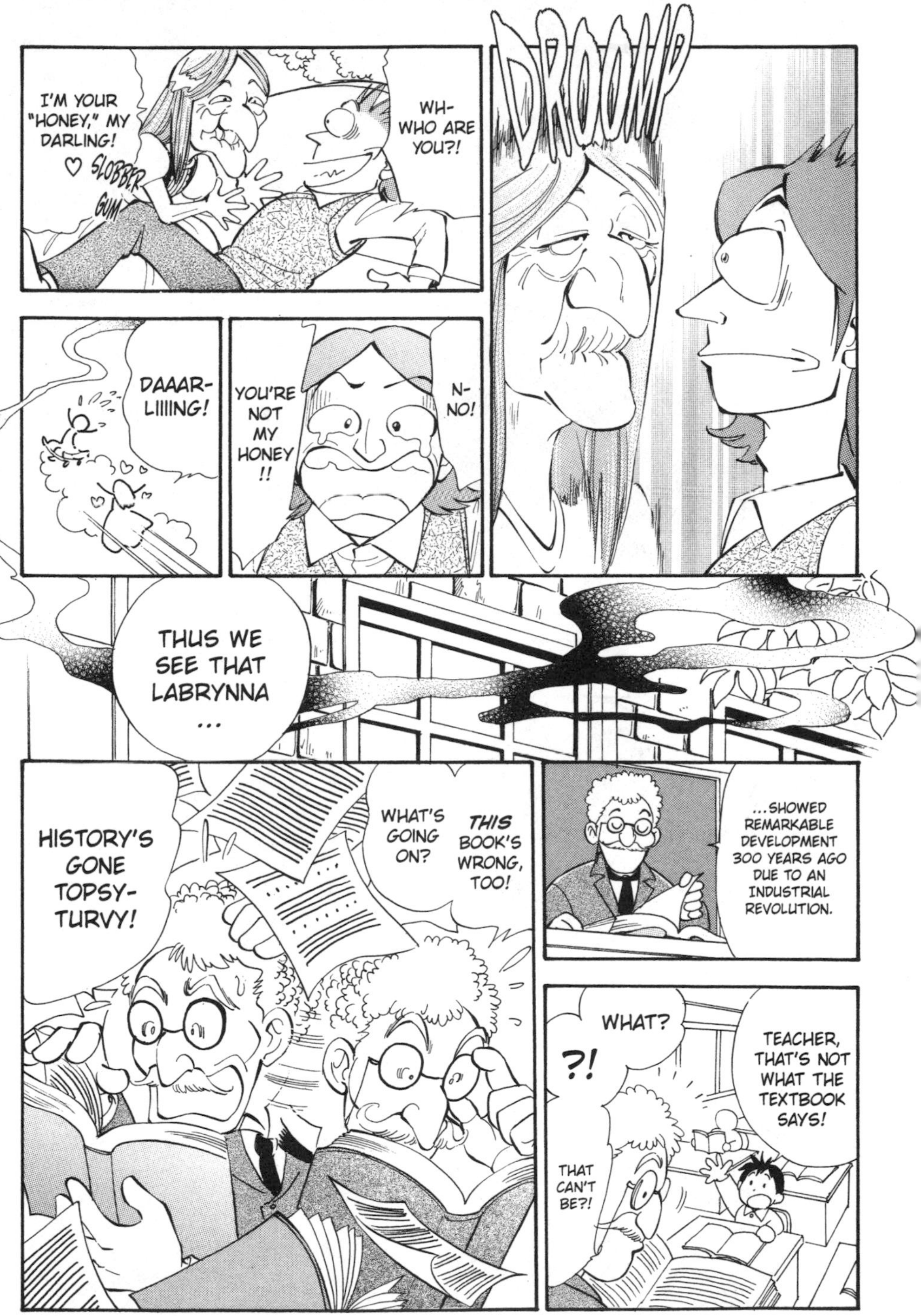
DROOMP
WH- WHO ARE YOU?!
I'M YOUR "HONEY," MY DARLING!
♡ SLOBBER GUM
N- NO!
YOU'RE NOT MY HONEY !!
DAAAR- LIIIING!
THUS WE SEE THAT LABRYNNA ...
...SHOWED REMARKABLE DEVELOPMENT 300 YEARS AGO DUE TO AN INDUSTRIAL REVOLUTION.
TEACHER, THAT'S NOT WHAT THE TEXTBOOK SAYS!
WHAT?
?!
THAT CAN'T BE?!
THIS BOOK'S WRONG, TOO!
WHAT'S GOING ON?
HISTORY'S GONE TOPSY-TURVY!

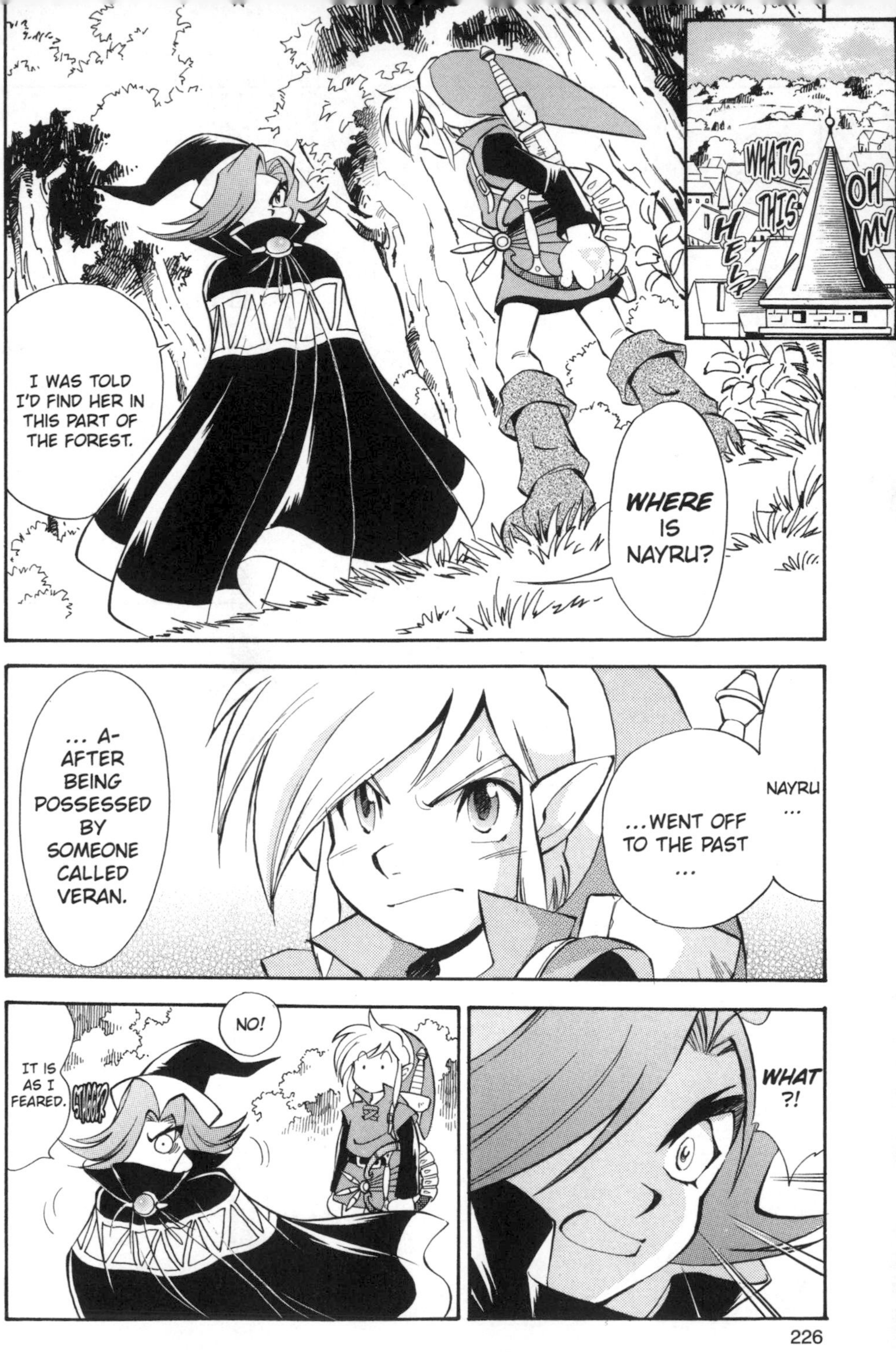
OH MY
WHAT'S THIS
HELP
WHERE IS NAYRU?
I WAS TOLD I'D FIND HER IN THIS PART OF THE FOREST.
NAYRU...
...WENT OFF TO THE PAST...
...A- AFTER BEING POSSESSED BY SOMEONE CALLED VERAN.
WHAT?!
NO!
IT IS AS I FEARED.

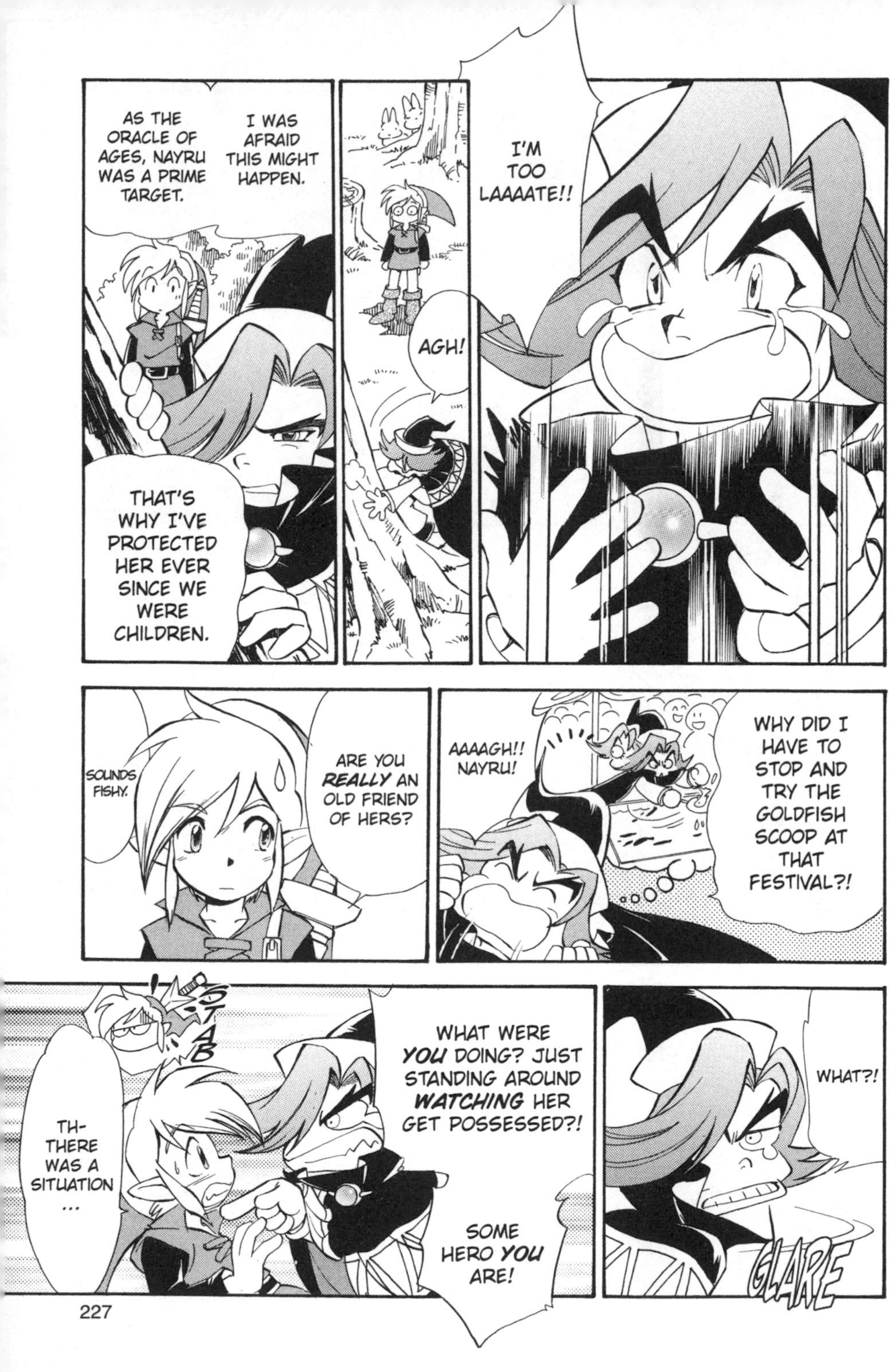
I'M TOO LAAAATE!!
AGH!
I WAS AFRAID THIS MIGHT HAPPEN.
AS THE ORACLE OF AGES, NAYRU WAS A PRIME TARGET.
THAT'S WHY I'VE PROTECTED HER EVER SINCE WE WERE CHILDREN.
WHY DID I HAVE TO STOP AND TRY THE GOLDFISH SCOOP AT THAT FESTIVAL?!
AAAAGH!! NAYRU!
ARE YOU *REALLY* AN OLD FRIEND OF HERS?
SOUNDS FISHY.
WHAT?!
GLARE
WHAT WERE *YOU* DOING? JUST STANDING AROUND *WATCHING* HER GET POSSESSED?!
STAB
TH-THERE WAS A SITUATION...
SOME HERO *YOU* ARE!

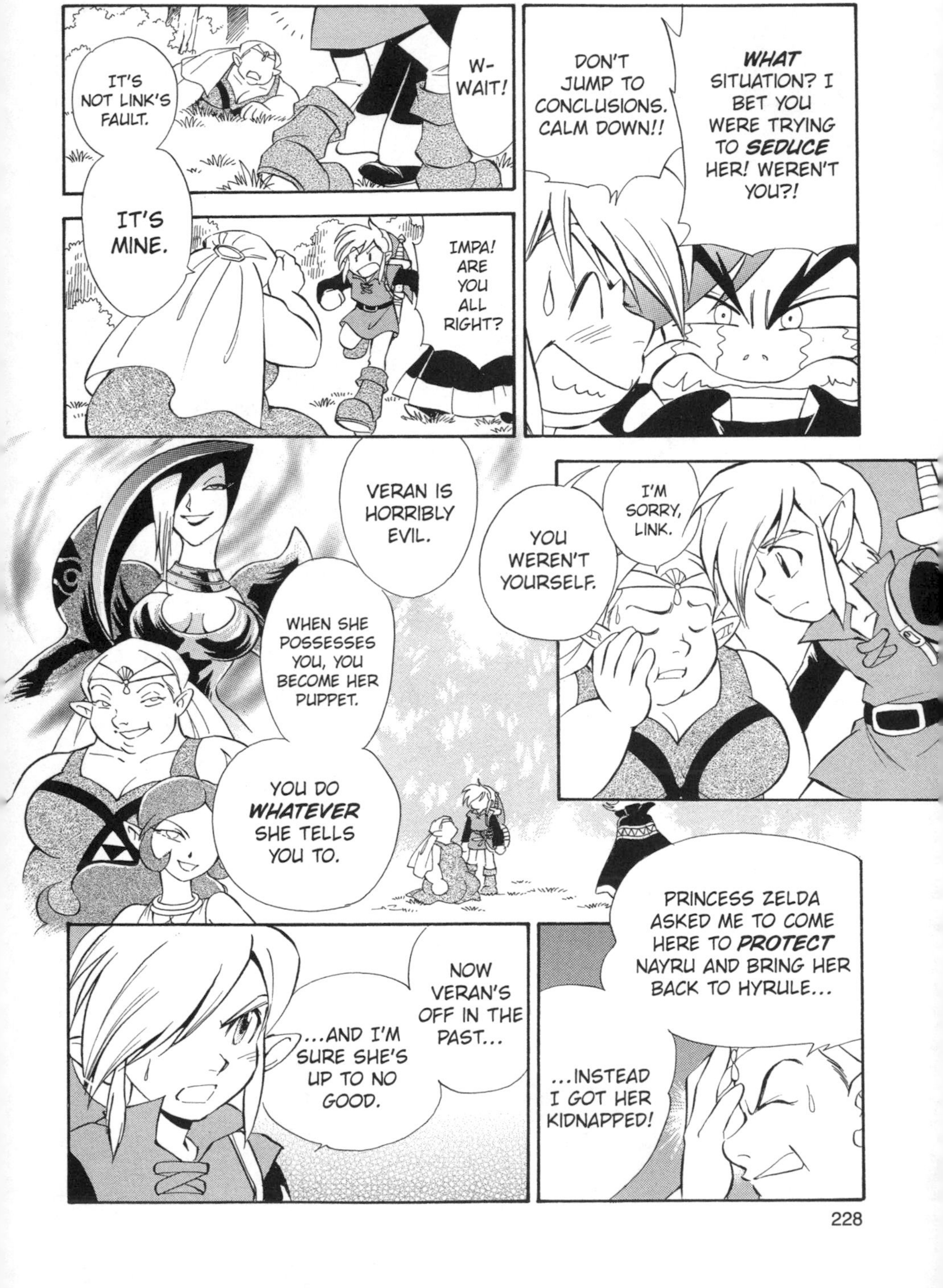
WHAT SITUATION? I BET YOU WERE TRYING TO SEDUCE HER! WEREN'T YOU?!
DON'T JUMP TO CONCLUSIONS. CALM DOWN!!
W-WAIT!
IT'S NOT LINK'S FAULT.
IMPA! ARE YOU ALL RIGHT?
IT'S MINE.
I'M SORRY, LINK.
YOU WEREN'T YOURSELF.
VERAN IS HORRIBLY EVIL.
WHEN SHE POSSESSES YOU, YOU BECOME HER PUPPET.
YOU DO WHATEVER SHE TELLS YOU TO.
PRINCESS ZELDA ASKED ME TO COME HERE TO PROTECT NAYRU AND BRING HER BACK TO HYRULE...
...INSTEAD I GOT HER KIDNAPPED!
NOW VERAN'S OFF IN THE PAST...
...AND I'M SURE SHE'S UP TO NO GOOD.

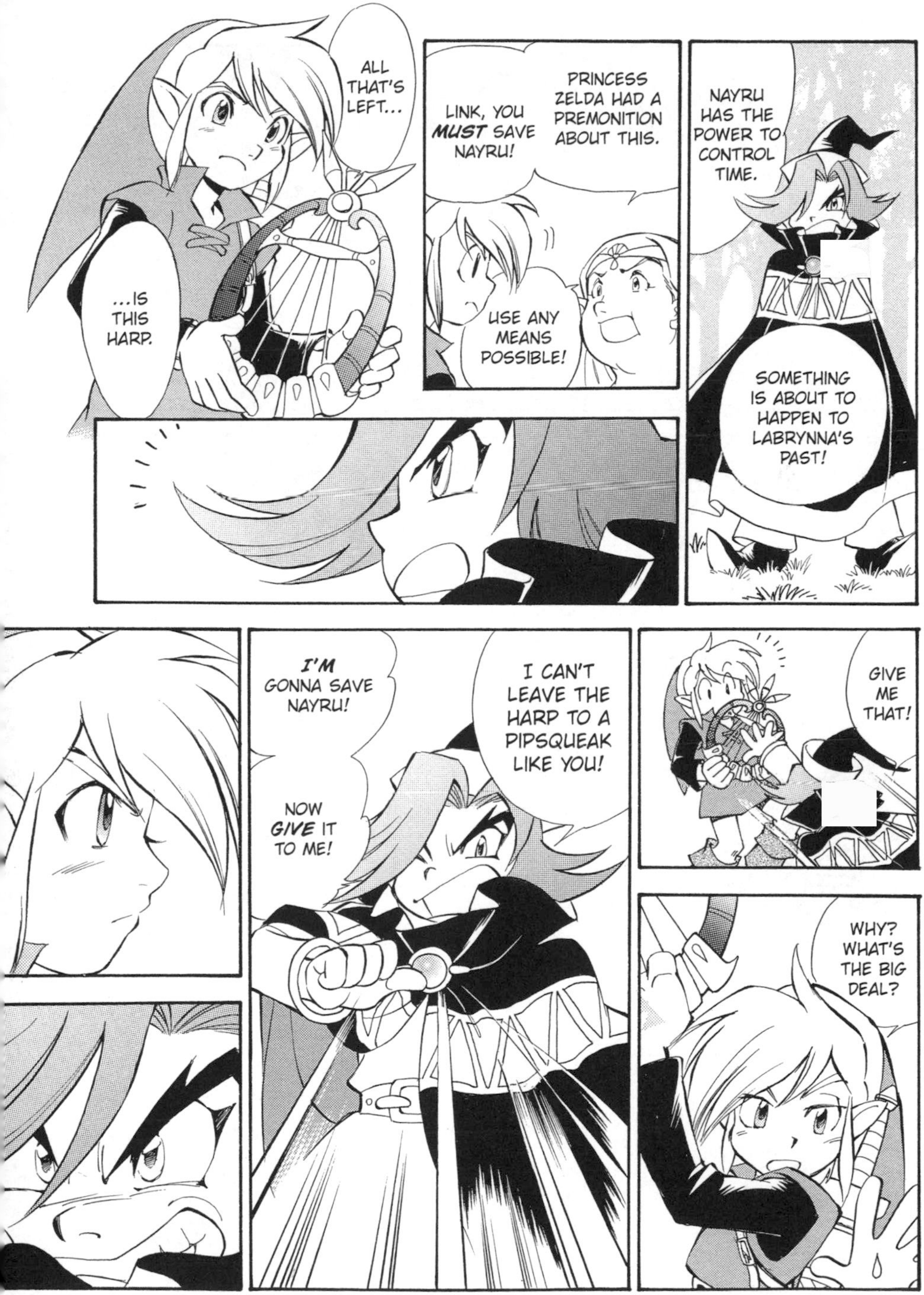
NAYRU HAS THE POWER TO CONTROL TIME.
SOMETHING IS ABOUT TO HAPPEN TO LABRYNNA'S PAST!
PRINCESS ZELDA HAD A PREMONITION ABOUT THIS.
LINK, YOU *MUST* SAVE NAYRU!
USE ANY MEANS POSSIBLE!
ALL THAT'S LEFT...
...IS THIS HARP.
GIVE ME THAT!
WHY? WHAT'S THE BIG DEAL?
I CAN'T LEAVE THE HARP TO A PIPSQUEAK LIKE YOU!
I'M GONNA SAVE NAYRU!
NOW *GIVE* IT TO ME!

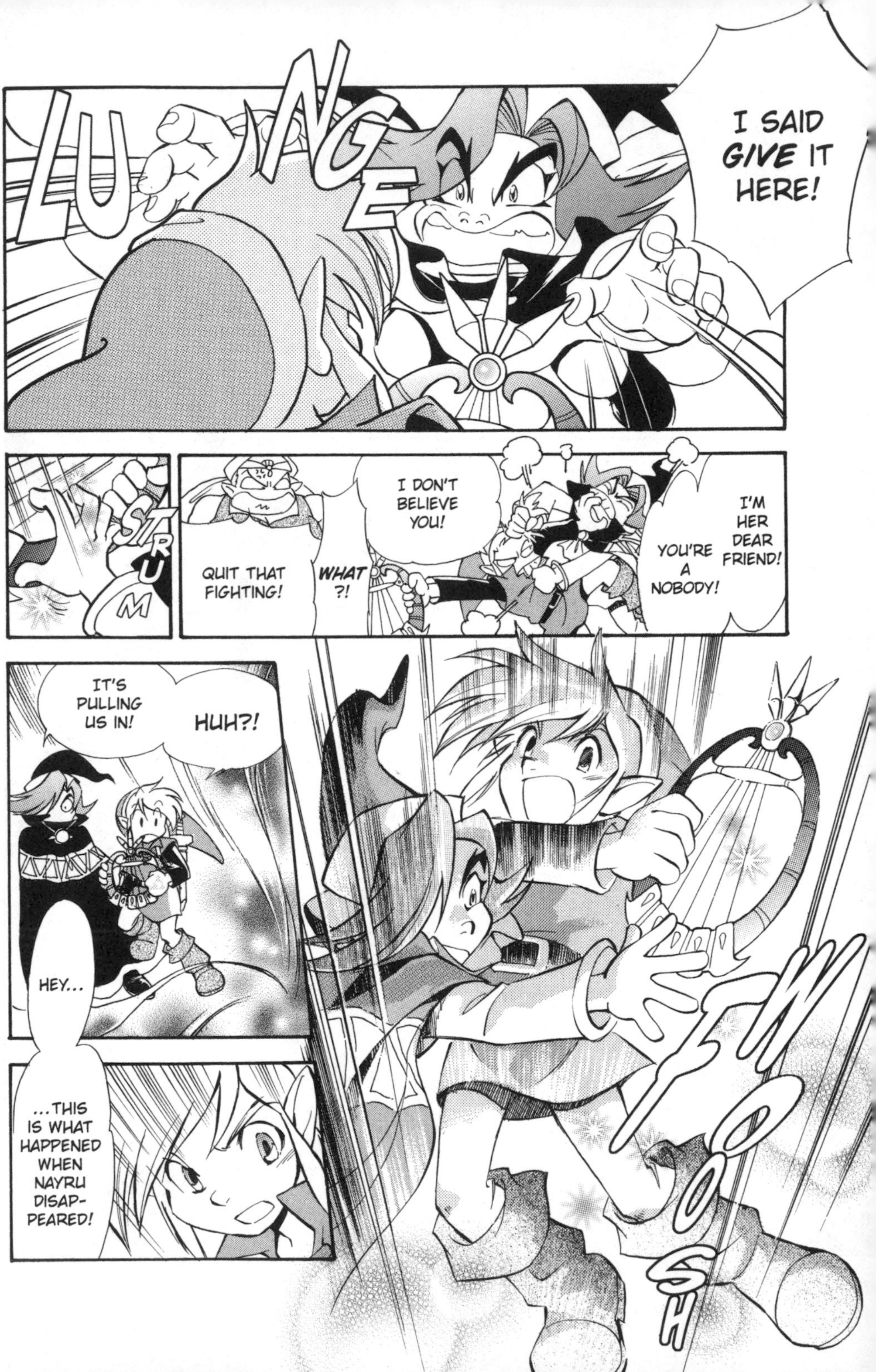
I SAID GIVE IT HERE!
LUNGE
I'M HER DEAR FRIEND!
YOU'RE A NOBODY!
I DON'T BELIEVE YOU!
WHAT?!
QUIT THAT FIGHTING!
STRUM
WHOOSH
HUH?!
IT'S PULLING US IN!
HEY...
...THIS IS WHAT HAPPENED WHEN NAYRU DISAP-PEARED!

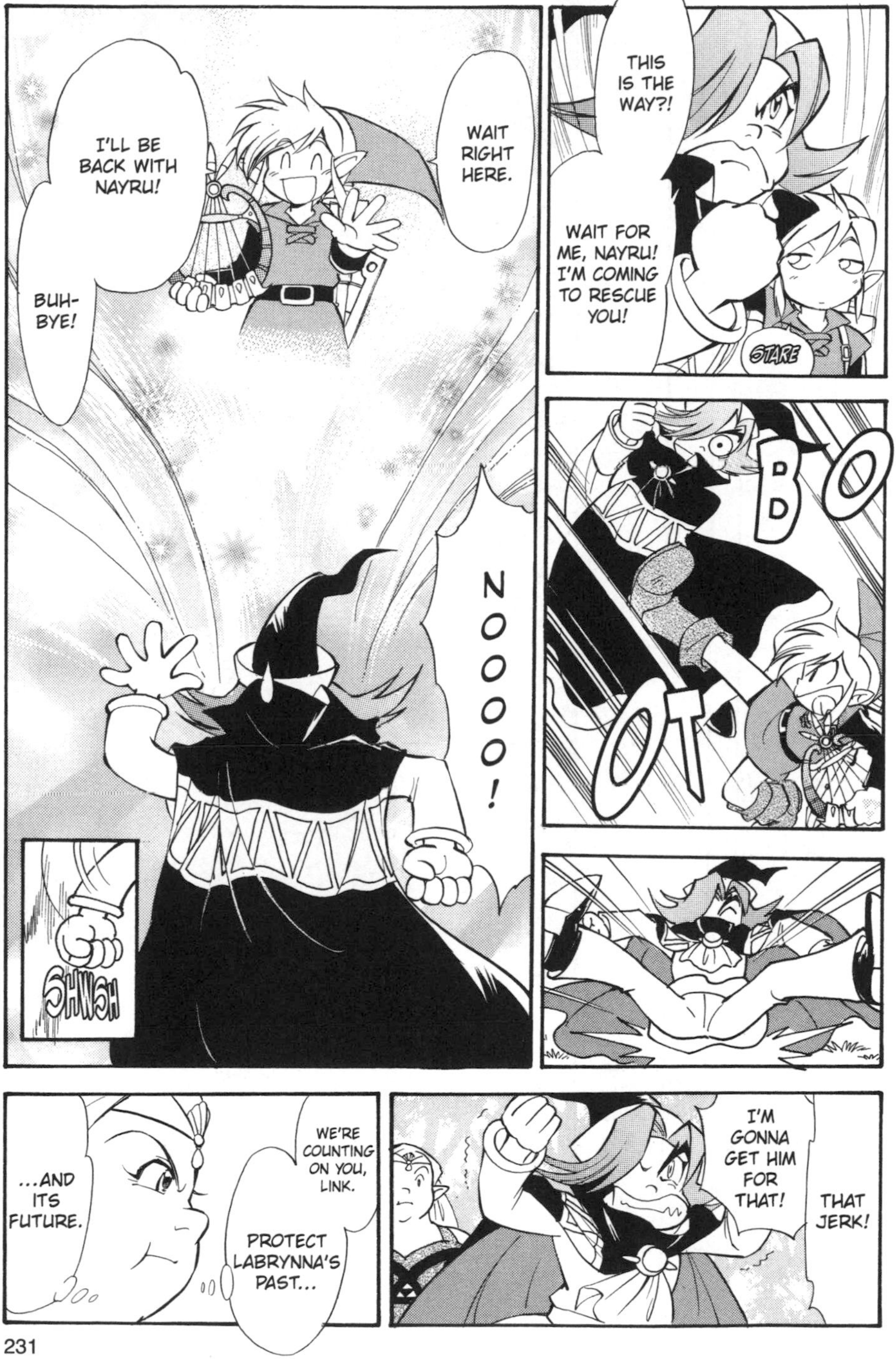
THIS IS THE WAY?!
WAIT FOR ME, NAYRU! I'M COMING TO RESCUE YOU!
STARE
BOOT
WAIT RIGHT HERE.
I'LL BE BACK WITH NAYRU!
BUH-BYE!
NOOOOO!
SHWSH
THAT JERK!
I'M GONNA GET HIM FOR THAT!
WE'RE COUNTING ON YOU, LINK.
PROTECT LABRYNNA'S PAST...
...AND ITS FUTURE.

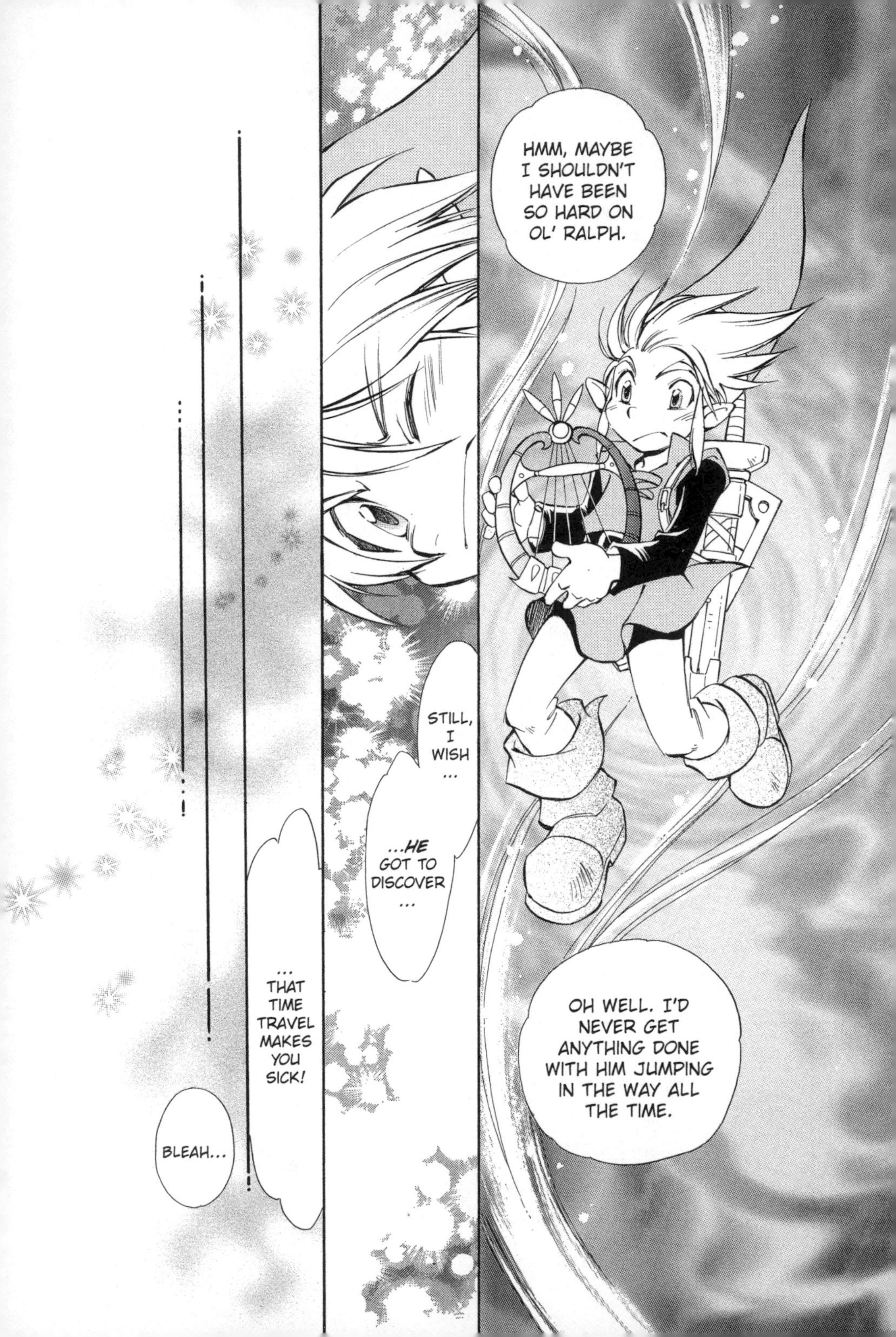
HMM, MAYBE I SHOULDN'T HAVE BEEN SO HARD ON OL' RALPH.
OH WELL. I'D NEVER GET ANYTHING DONE WITH HIM JUMPING IN THE WAY ALL THE TIME.
STILL, I WISH...
...HE GOT TO DISCOVER...
...THAT TIME TRAVEL MAKES YOU SICK!
BLEAH...

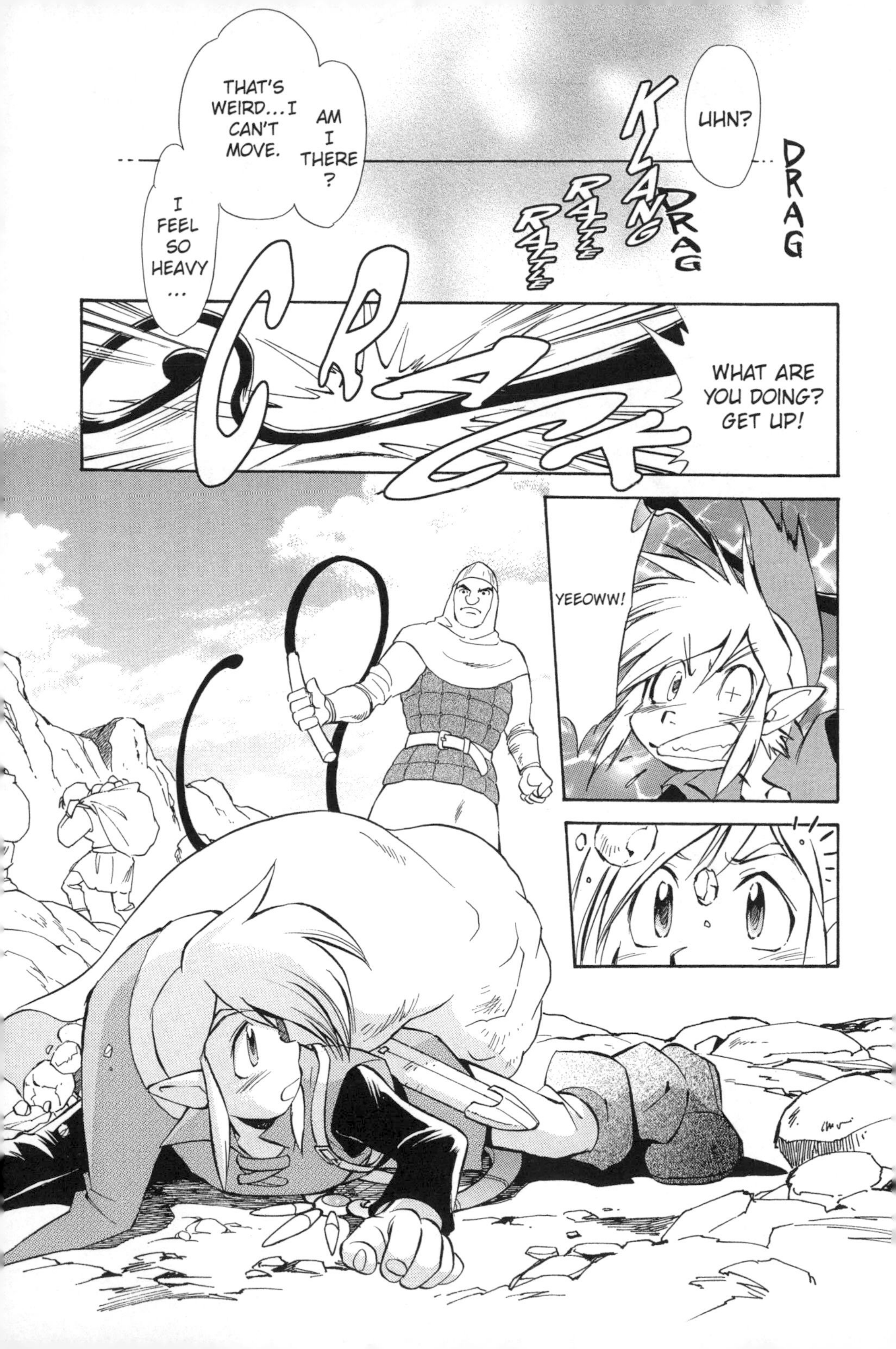

UHN?
DRAG
DRAG DRAG
KLANG
RATTLE
RATTLE
AM I THERE?
THAT'S WEIRD...I CAN'T MOVE.
I FEEL SO HEAVY...
WHAT ARE YOU DOING? GET UP!
CRACK
YEEOWW!

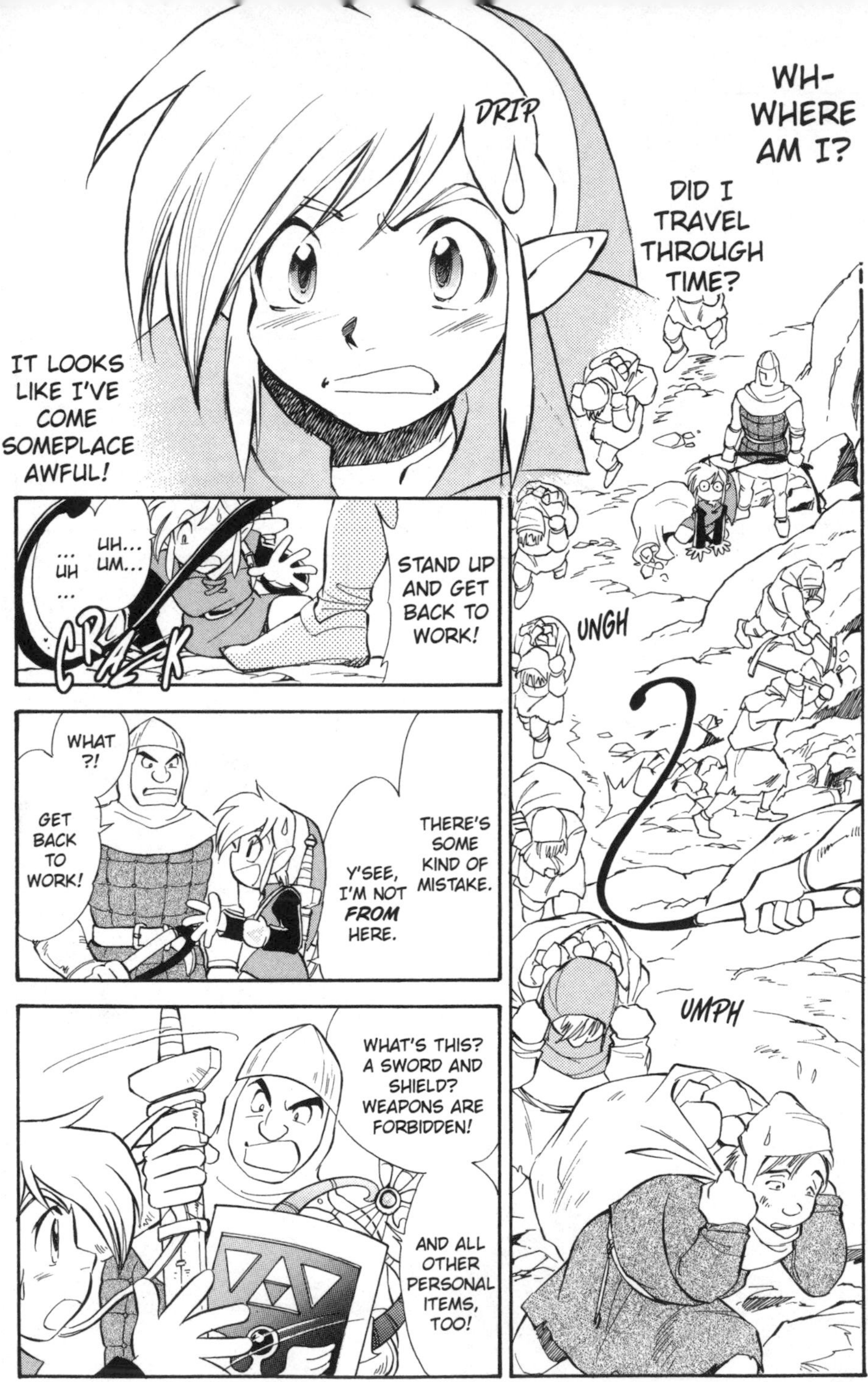
WH- WHERE AM I?
DID I TRAVEL THROUGH TIME?
DRIP
IT LOOKS LIKE I'VE COME SOMEPLACE AWFUL!
UNGH
UMPH
STAND UP AND GET BACK TO WORK!
UH... UM...
... UH ...
CRACK
THERE'S SOME KIND OF MISTAKE.
Y'SEE, I'M NOT *FROM* HERE.
WHAT ?!
GET BACK TO WORK!
WHAT'S THIS? A SWORD AND SHIELD? WEAPONS ARE FORBIDDEN!
AND ALL OTHER PERSONAL ITEMS, TOO!

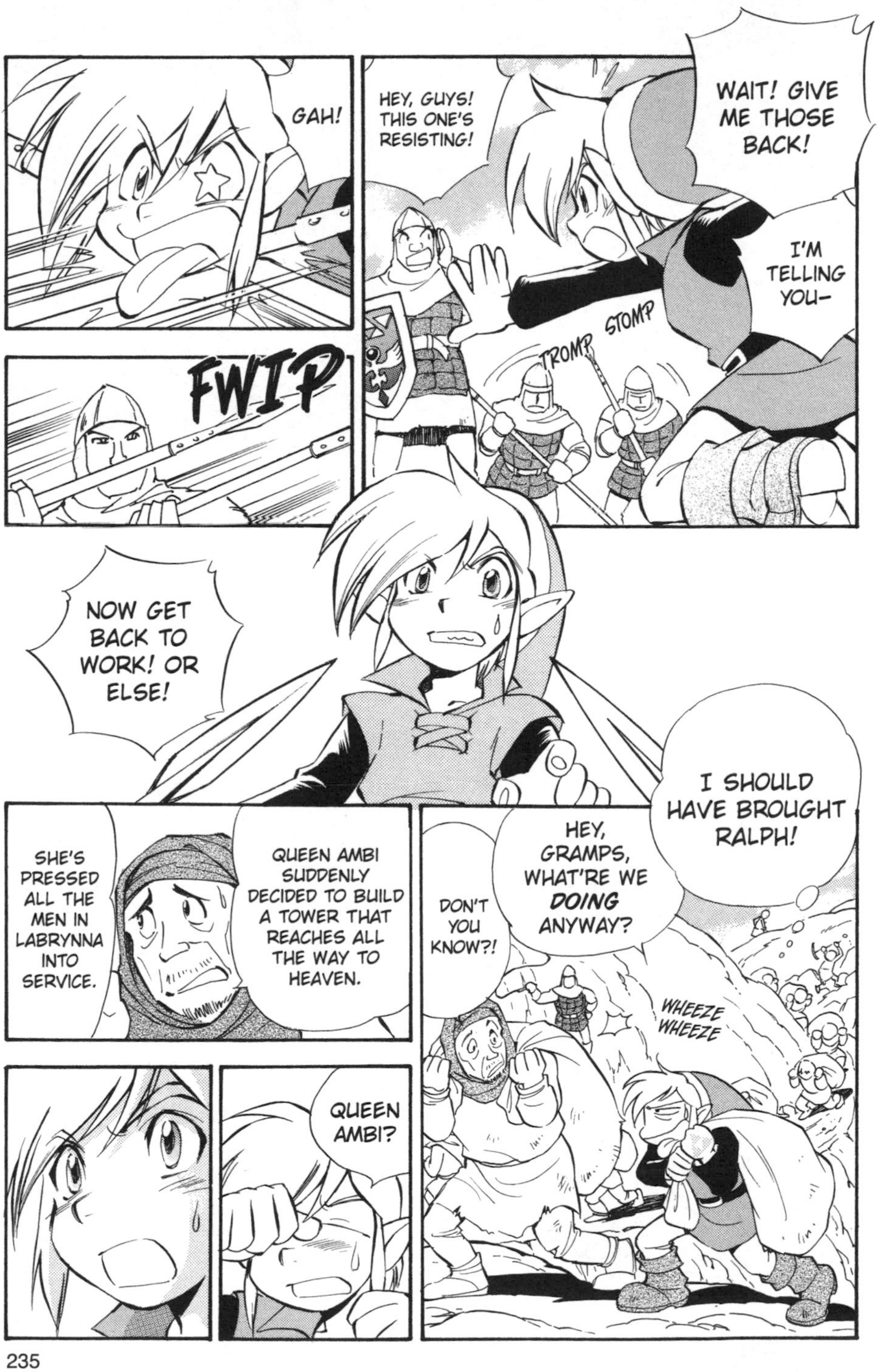
WAIT! GIVE ME THOSE BACK!
I'M TELLING YOU–
HEY, GUYS! THIS ONE'S RESISTING!
STOMP
TROMP
GAH!
FWIP
NOW GET BACK TO WORK! OR ELSE!
I SHOULD HAVE BROUGHT RALPH!
HEY, GRAMPS, WHAT'RE WE *DOING* ANYWAY?
DON'T YOU KNOW?!
WHEEZE WHEEZE
QUEEN AMBI SUDDENLY DECIDED TO BUILD A TOWER THAT REACHES ALL THE WAY TO HEAVEN.
SHE'S PRESSED ALL THE MEN IN LABRYNNA INTO SERVICE.
QUEEN AMBI?

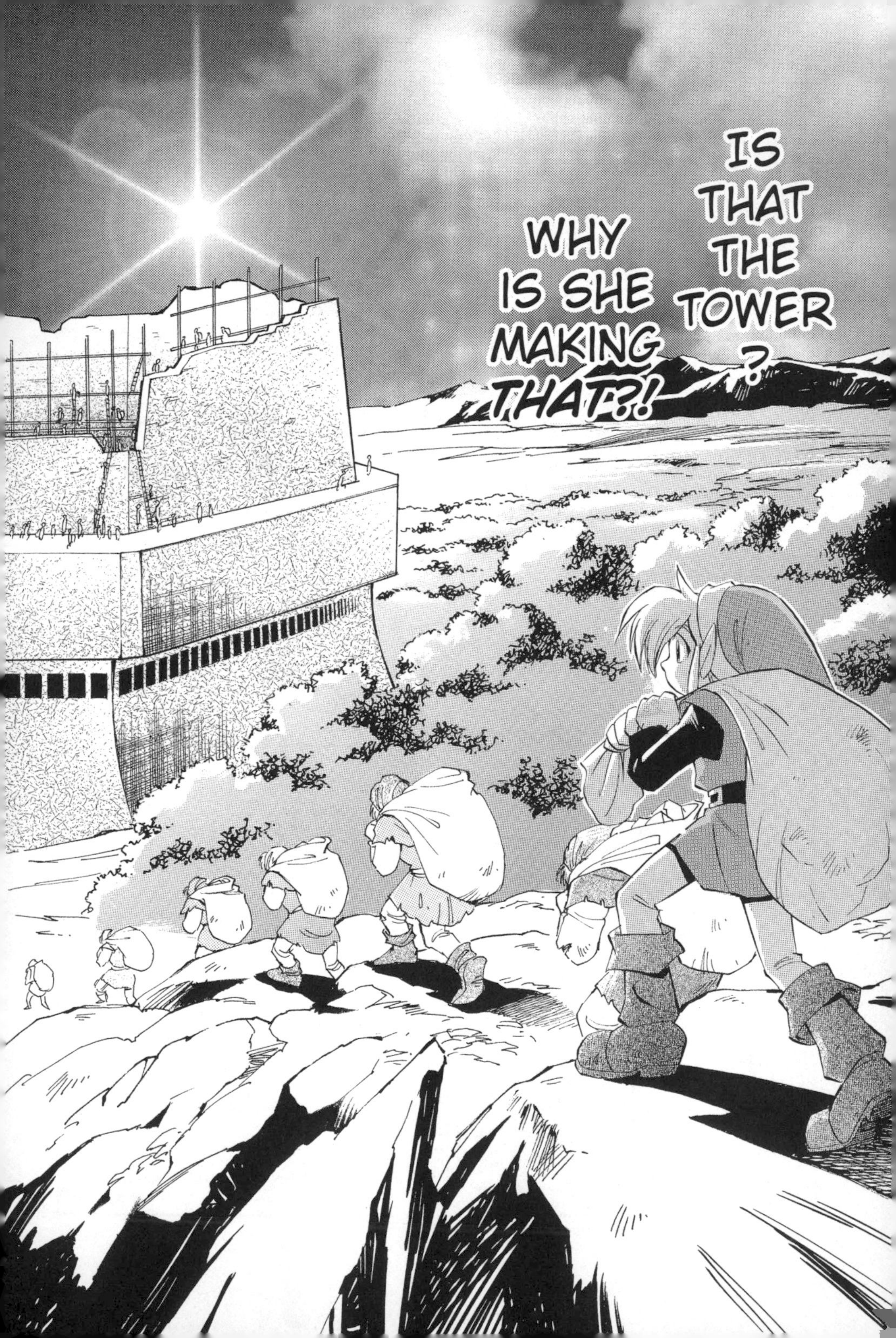
IS THAT THE TOWER?
WHY IS SHE MAKING THAT?!

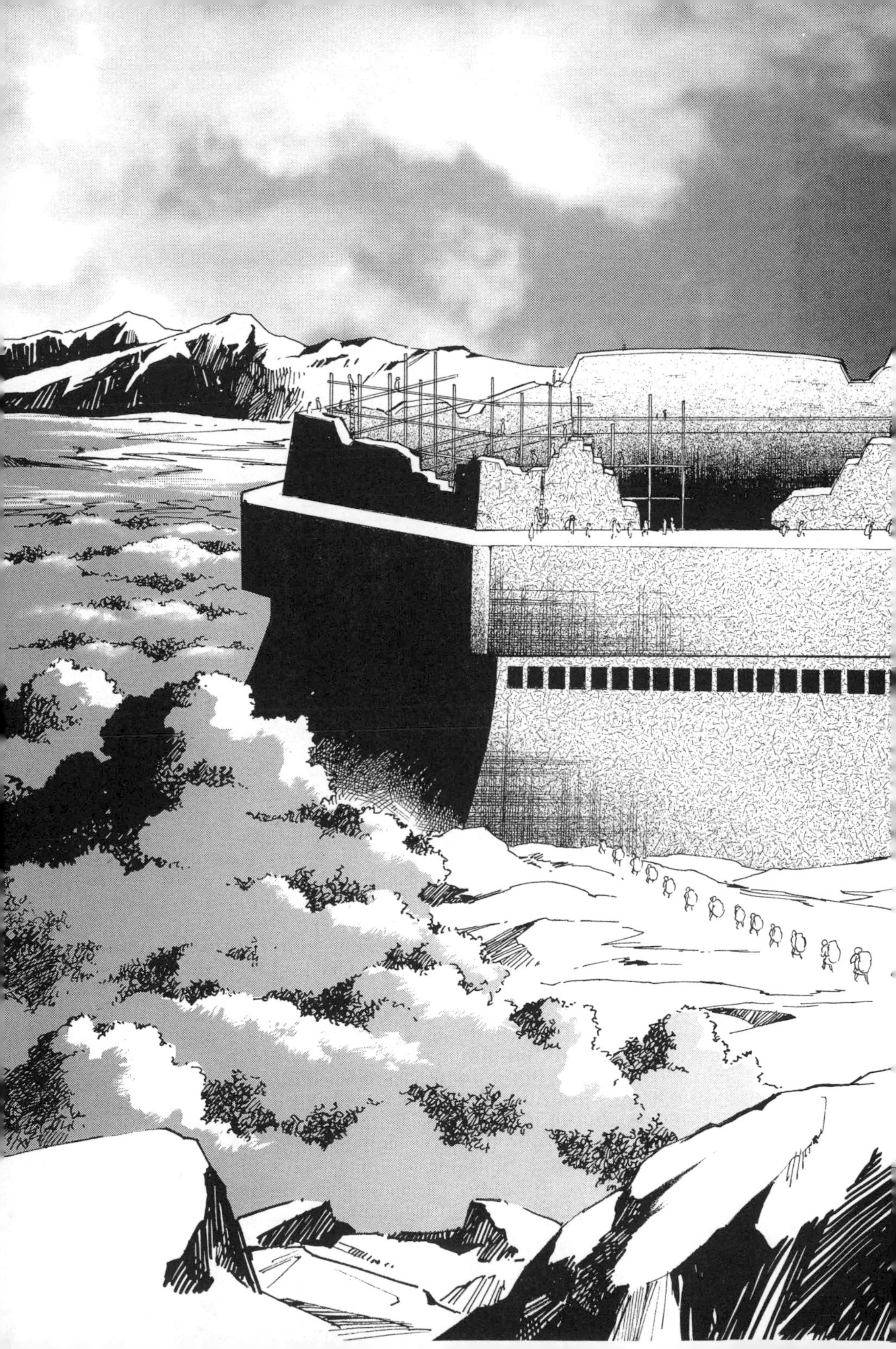

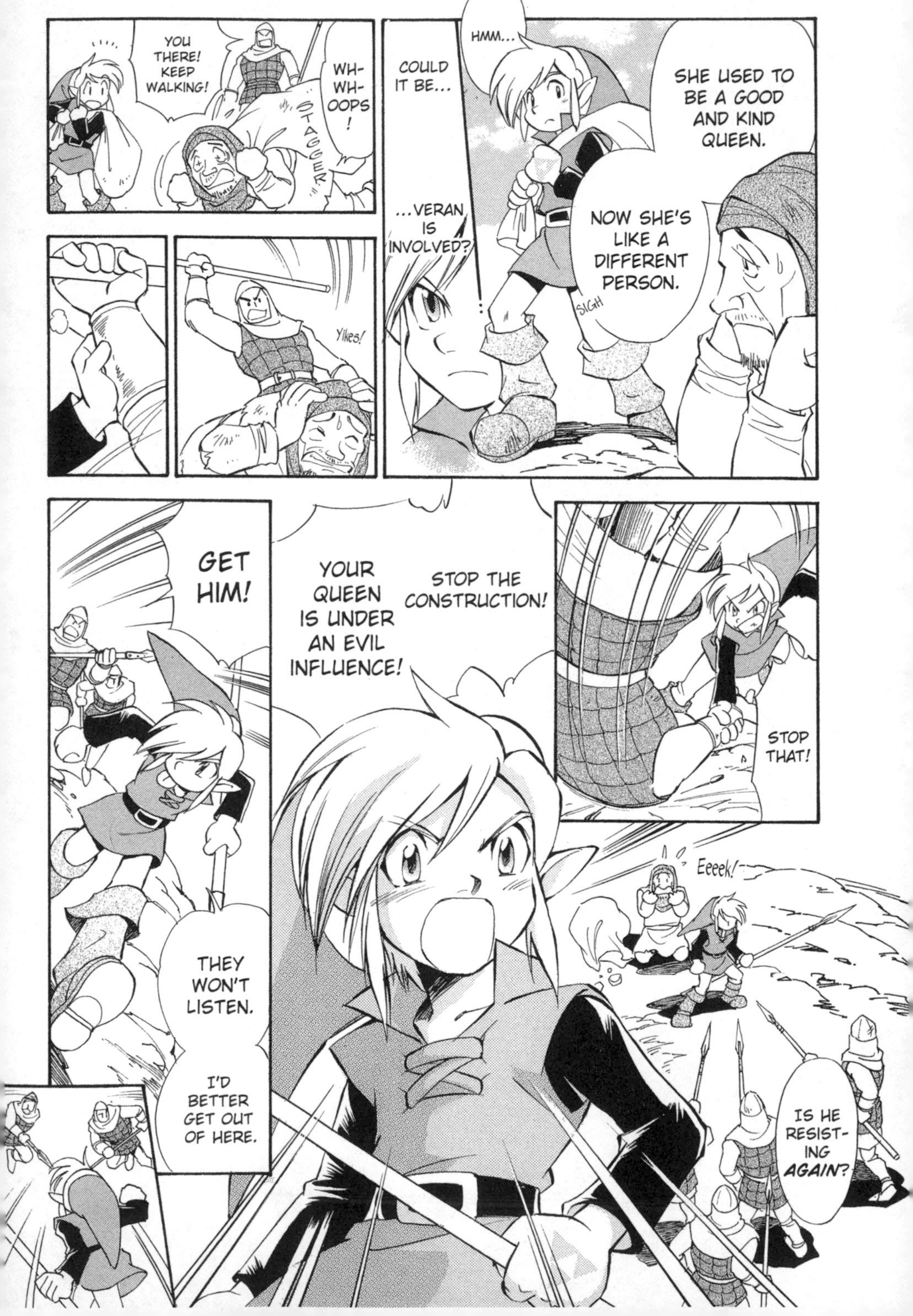
SHE USED TO BE A GOOD AND KIND QUEEN.
NOW SHE'S LIKE A DIFFERENT PERSON.
SIGH
HMM...
COULD IT BE...
...VERAN IS INVOLVED?
WH-WH-OOPS!
STAGGER
YOU THERE! KEEP WALKING!
Yikes!
STOP THAT!
STOP THE CONSTRUCTION!
YOUR QUEEN IS UNDER AN EVIL INFLUENCE!
Eeeek!
IS HE RESIST-ING AGAIN?
GET HIM!
THEY WON'T LISTEN.
I'D BETTER GET OUT OF HERE.

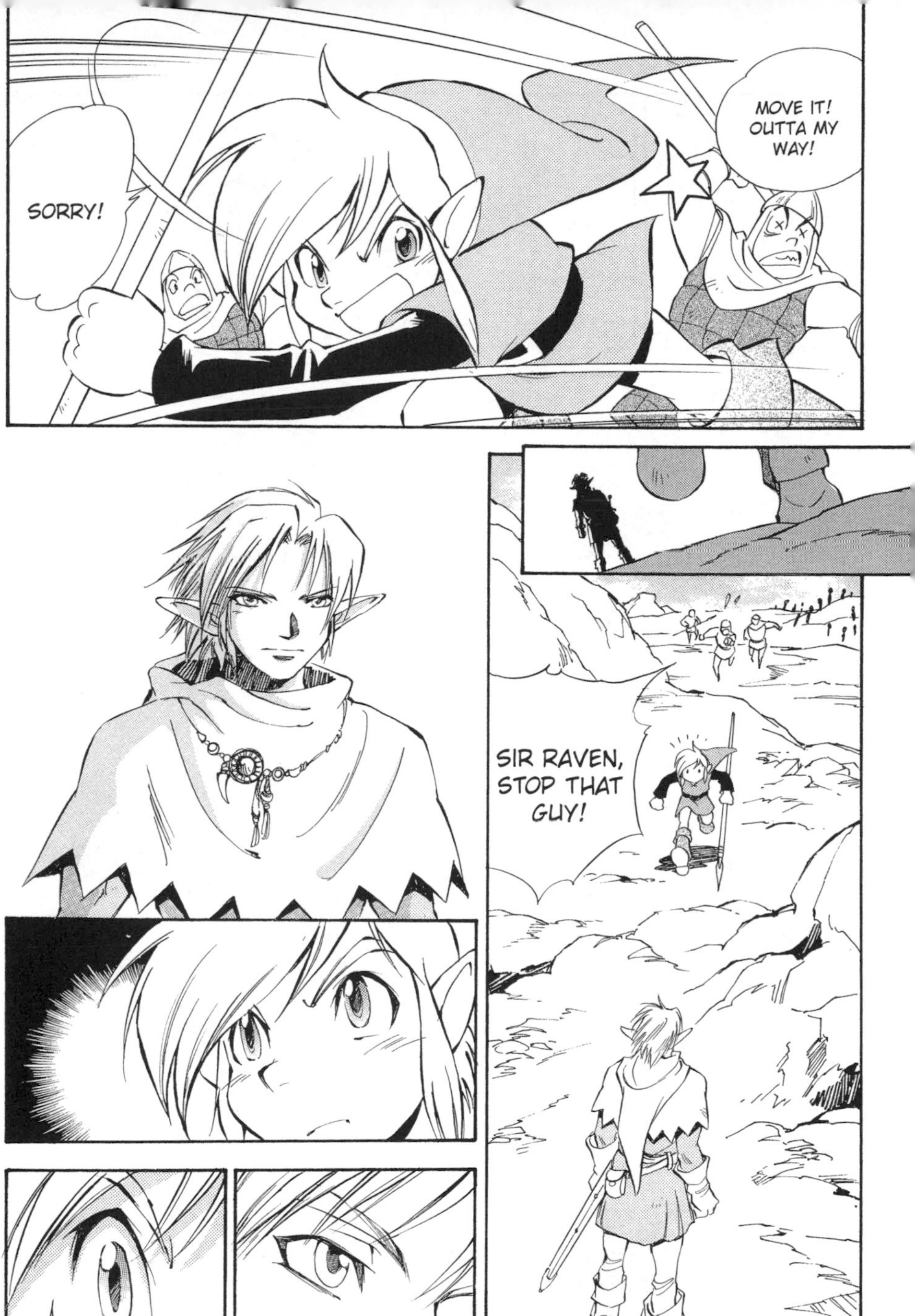
MOVE IT! OUTTA MY WAY!
SORRY!
SIR RAVEN, STOP THAT GUY!

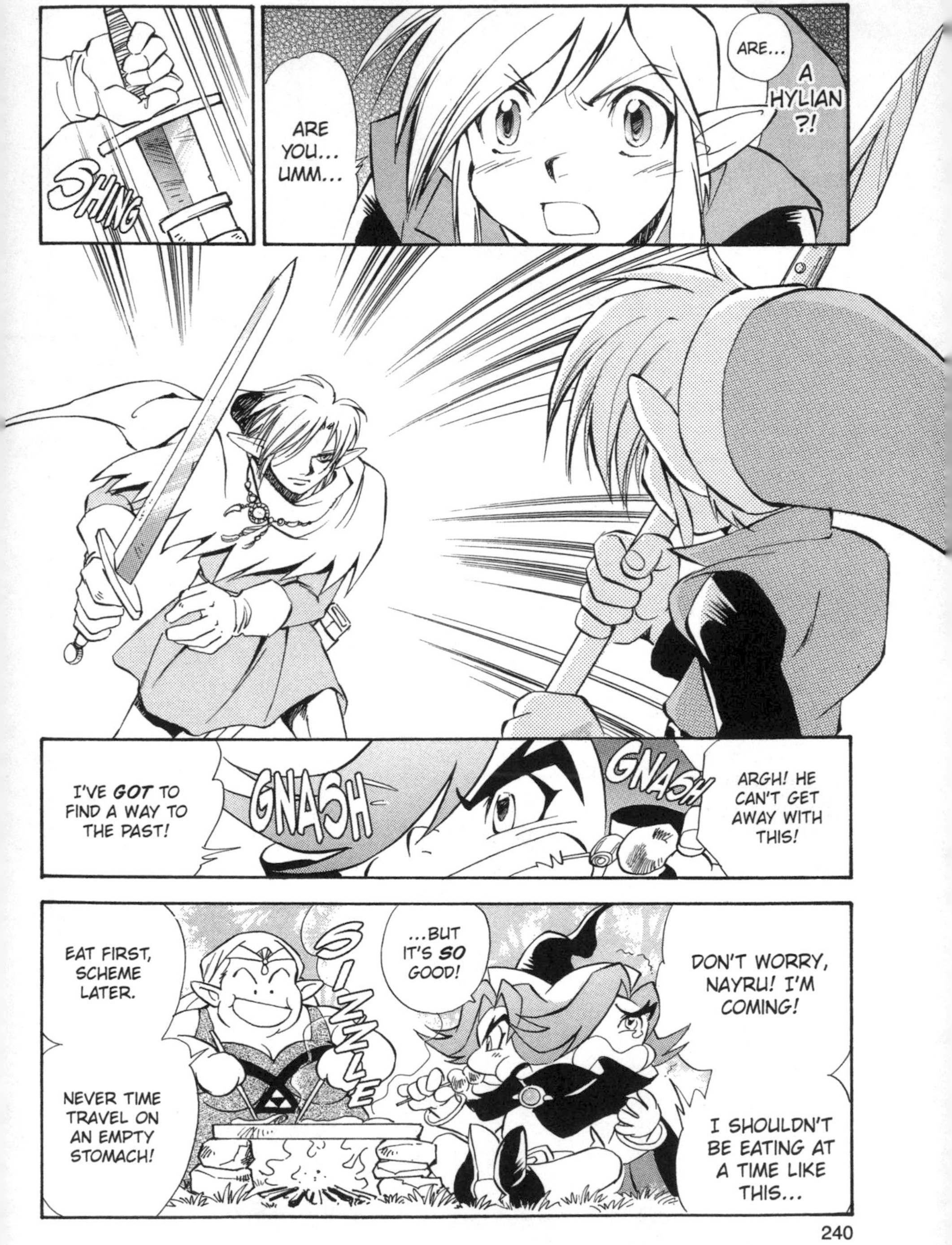
ARE...
A HYLIAN ?!
ARE YOU... UMM...
SHING
ARGH! HE CAN'T GET AWAY WITH THIS!
GNASH
GNASH
I'VE **GOT** TO FIND A WAY TO THE PAST!
DON'T WORRY, NAYRU! I'M COMING!
I SHOULDN'T BE EATING AT A TIME LIKE THIS...
...BUT IT'S **SO** GOOD!
SIZZLE
EAT FIRST, SCHEME LATER.
NEVER TIME TRAVEL ON AN EMPTY STOMACH!

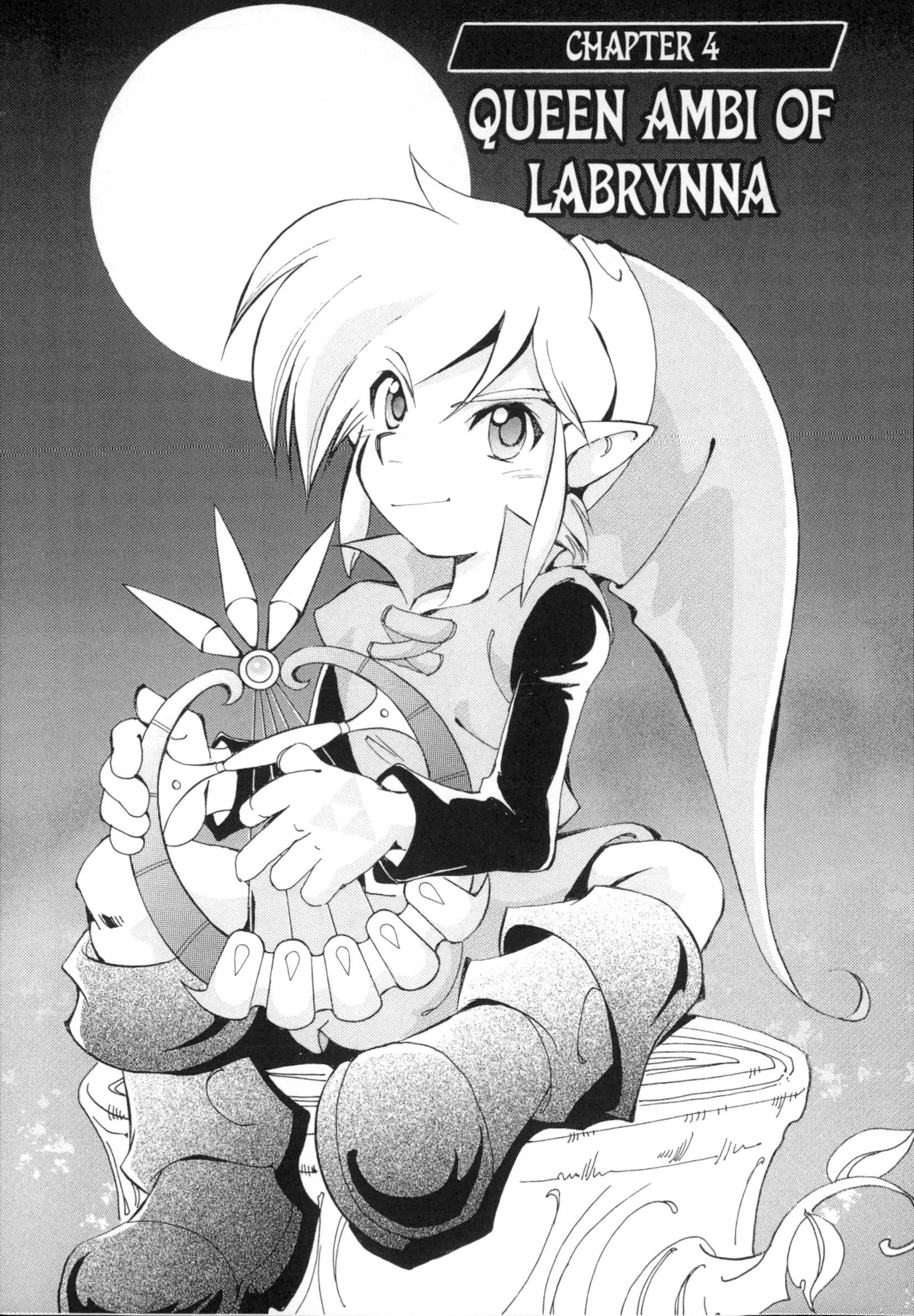
CHAPTER 4
QUEEN AMBI OF LABRYNNA

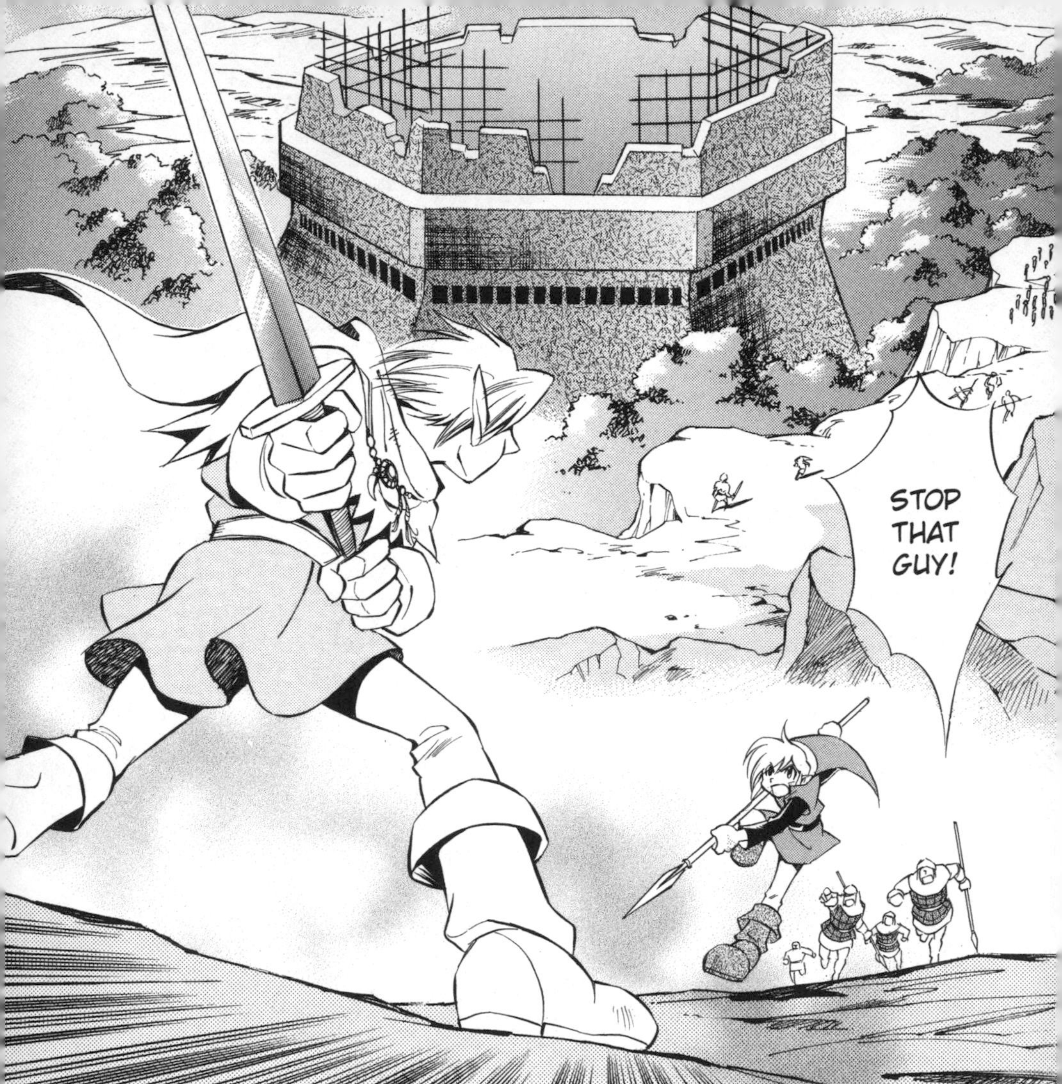
STOP THAT GUY!
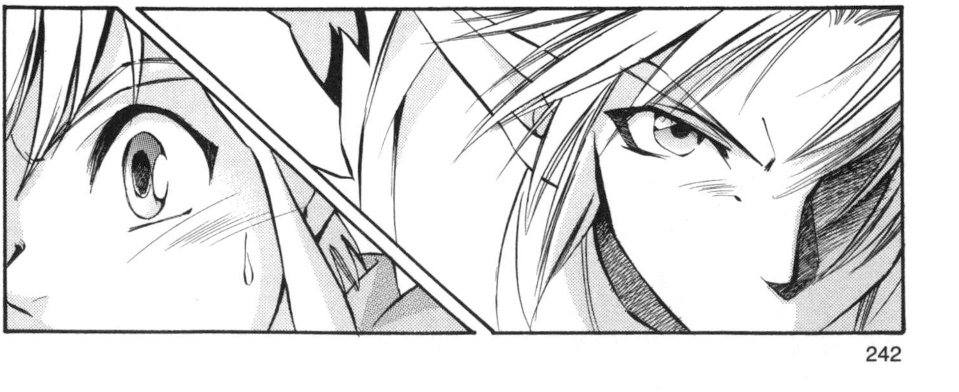

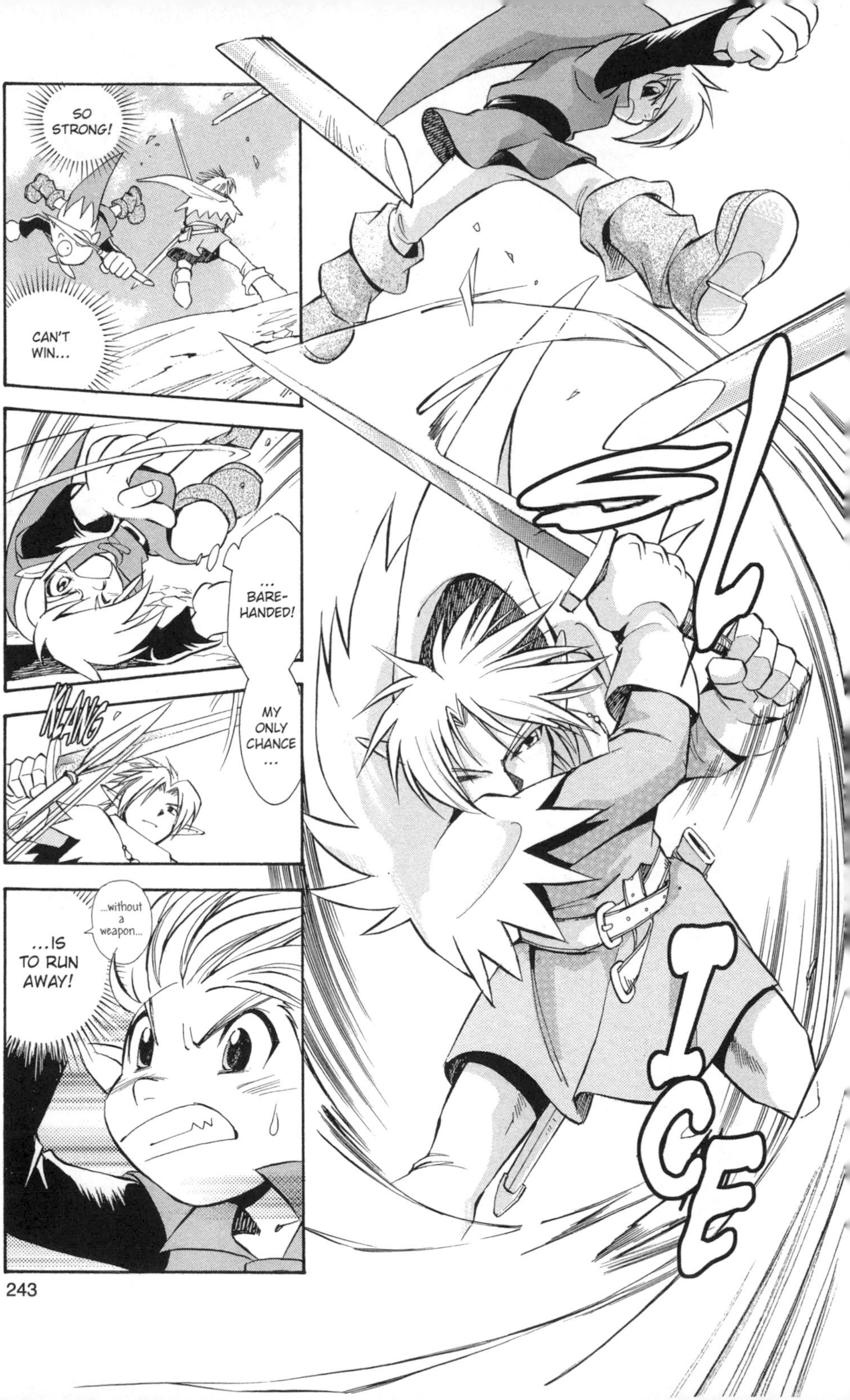
ICE
SO STRONG!
CAN'T WIN...
...BARE-HANDED!
KLANG
MY ONLY CHANCE ...
...without a weapon...
...IS TO RUN AWAY!

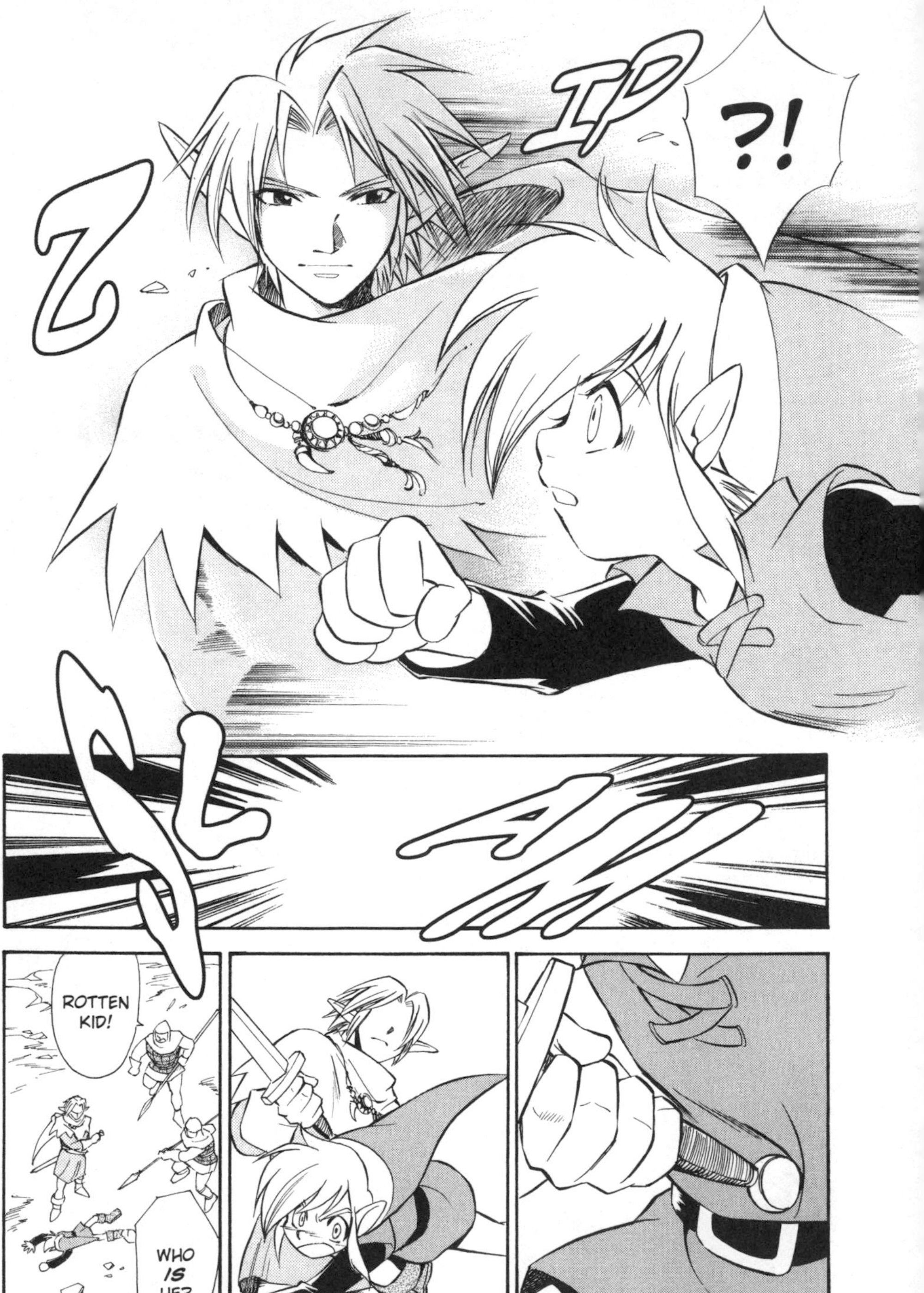
?!
ZIP
ROTTEN KID!
WHO *IS* HE?

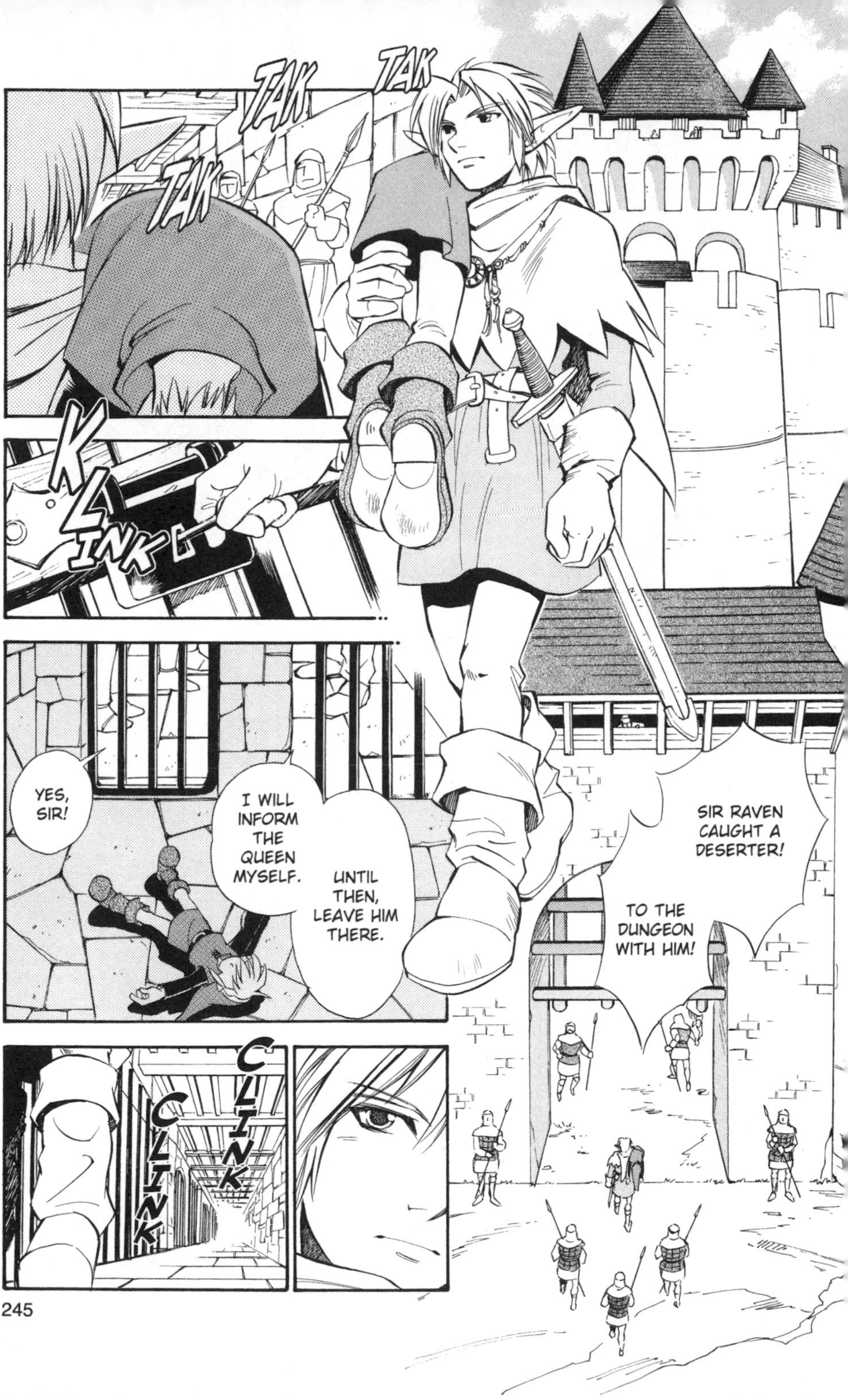
TAK
TAK
TAK
SIR RAVEN CAUGHT A DESERTER!
TO THE DUNGEON WITH HIM!
KLINK
I WILL INFORM THE QUEEN MYSELF.
UNTIL THEN, LEAVE HIM THERE.
YES, SIR!
CLINK
CLINK

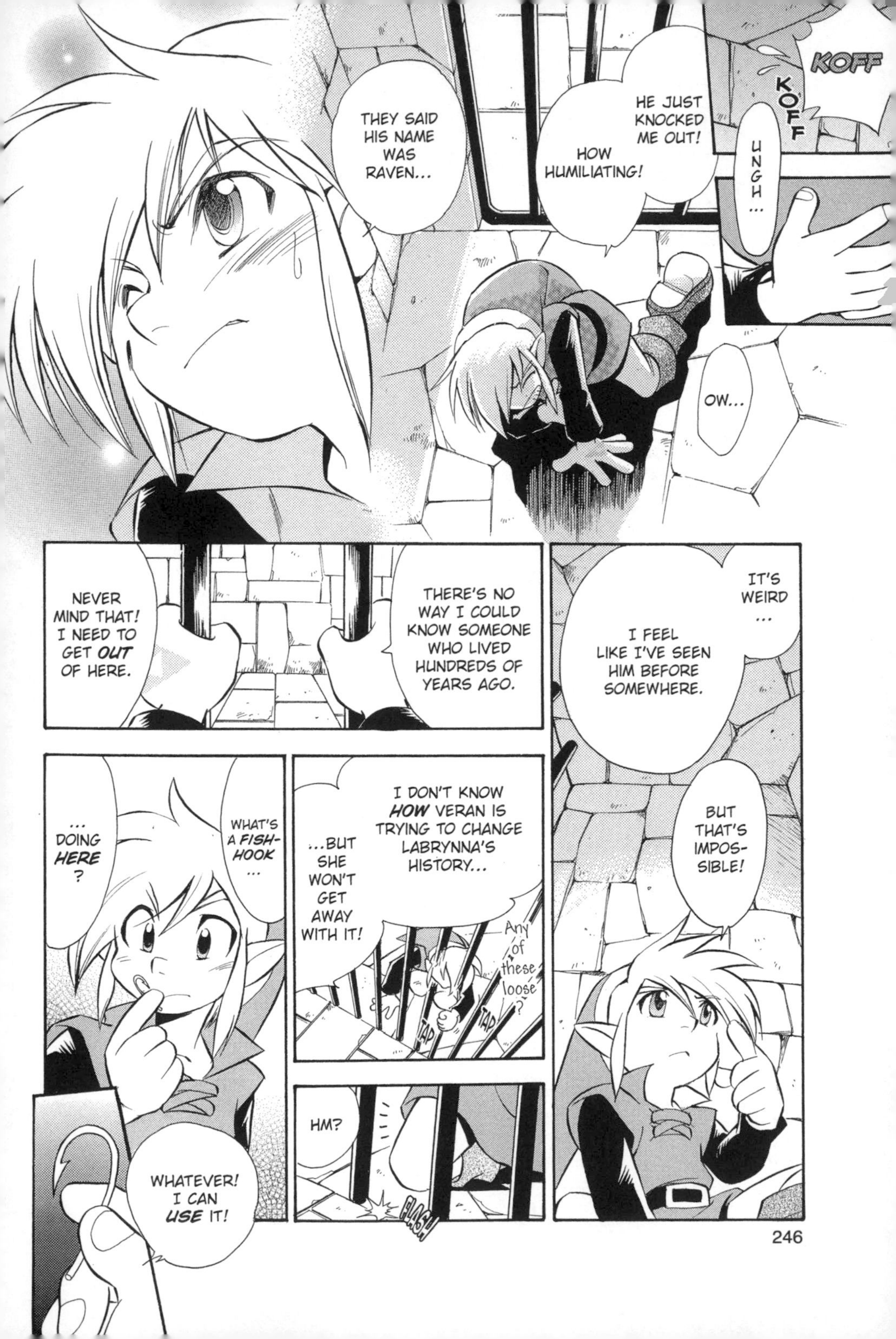
KOFF
KOFF
UNGH...
OW...
HE JUST KNOCKED ME OUT!
HOW HUMILIATING!
THEY SAID HIS NAME WAS RAVEN...
IT'S WEIRD...
I FEEL LIKE I'VE SEEN HIM BEFORE SOMEWHERE.
BUT THAT'S IMPOSSIBLE!
THERE'S NO WAY I COULD KNOW SOMEONE WHO LIVED HUNDREDS OF YEARS AGO.
NEVER MIND THAT! I NEED TO GET *OUT* OF HERE.
I DON'T KNOW ***HOW*** VERAN IS TRYING TO CHANGE LABRYNNA'S HISTORY...
...BUT SHE WON'T GET AWAY WITH IT!
Any of these loose?
TAP
TAP
HM?
FLASH
WHAT'S A ***FISH-HOOK***...
...DOING ***HERE***?
WHATEVER! I CAN ***USE*** IT!

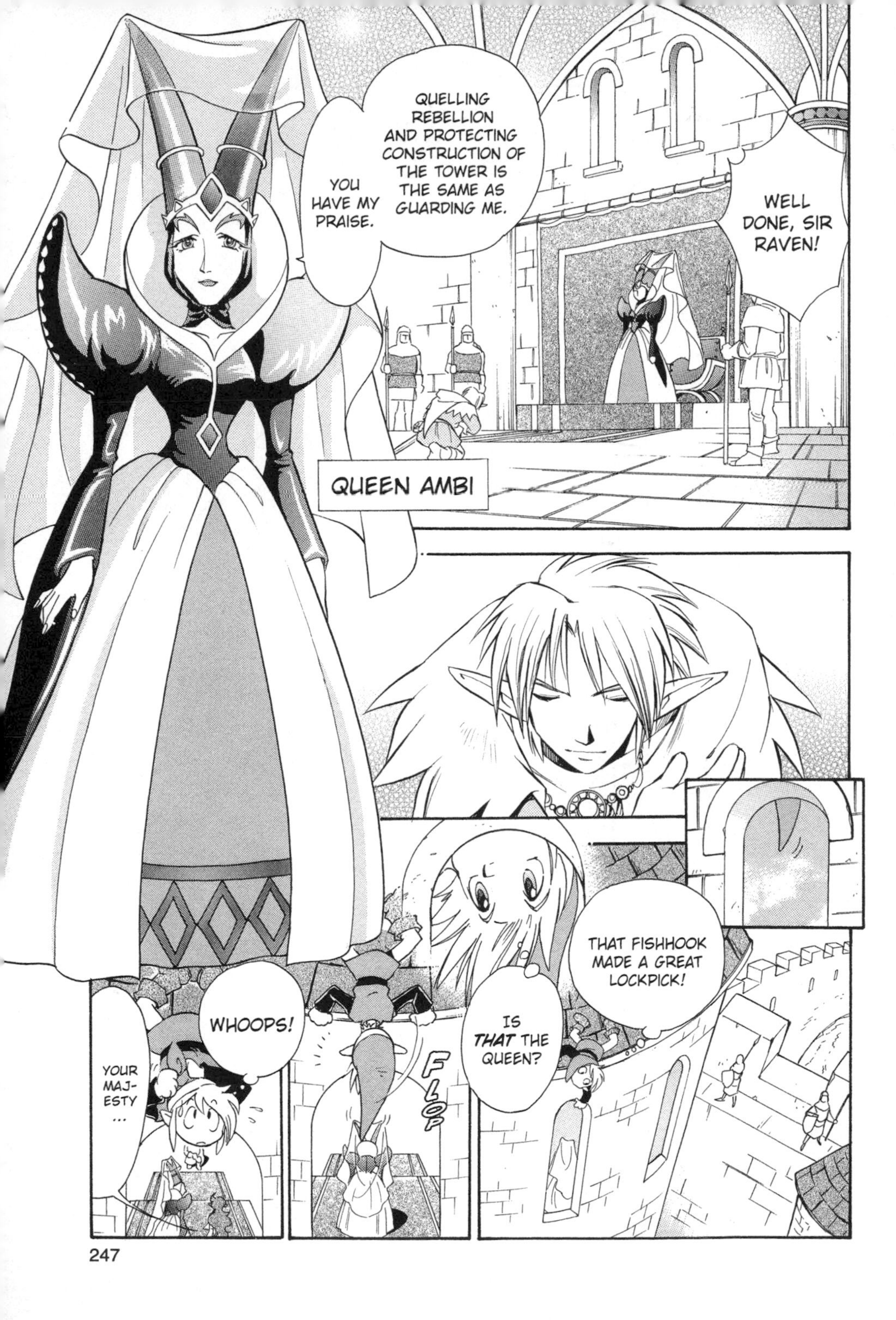
WELL DONE, SIR RAVEN!
QUELLING REBELLION AND PROTECTING CONSTRUCTION OF THE TOWER IS THE SAME AS GUARDING ME.
YOU HAVE MY PRAISE.
QUEEN AMBI
THAT FISHHOOK MADE A GREAT LOCKPICK!
IS *THAT* THE QUEEN?
FLOP
WHOOPS!
YOUR MAJ-ESTY ...

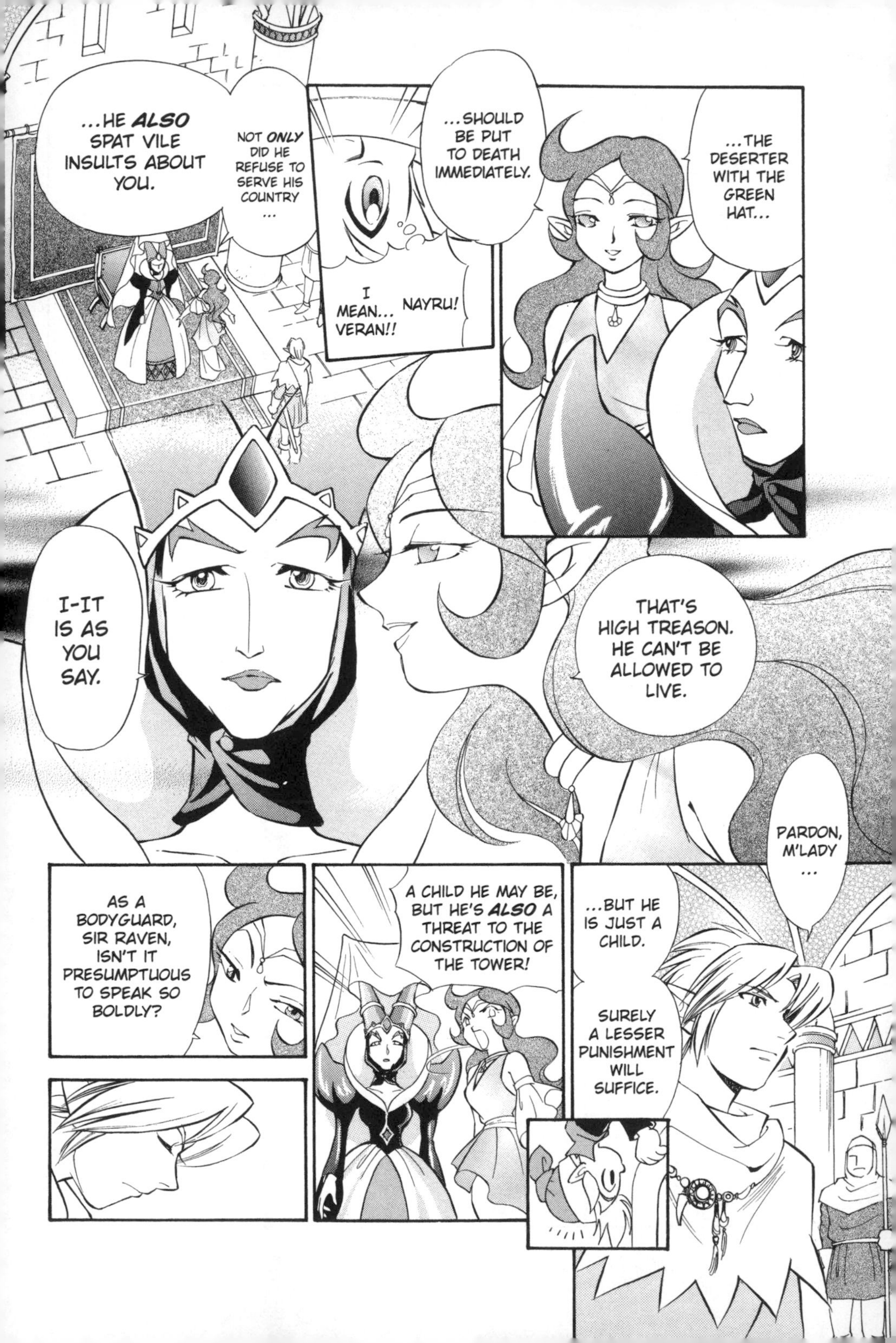
...THE DESERTER WITH THE GREEN HAT...
...SHOULD BE PUT TO DEATH IMMEDIATELY.
NAYRU!
I MEAN... VERAN!!
NOT ONLY DID HE REFUSE TO SERVE HIS COUNTRY ...
...HE ALSO SPAT VILE INSULTS ABOUT YOU.
THAT'S HIGH TREASON. HE CAN'T BE ALLOWED TO LIVE.
I-IT IS AS YOU SAY.
PARDON, M'LADY ...
...BUT HE IS JUST A CHILD.
SURELY A LESSER PUNISHMENT WILL SUFFICE.
A CHILD HE MAY BE, BUT HE'S ALSO A THREAT TO THE CONSTRUCTION OF THE TOWER!
AS A BODYGUARD, SIR RAVEN, ISN'T IT PRESUMPTUOUS TO SPEAK SO BOLDLY?

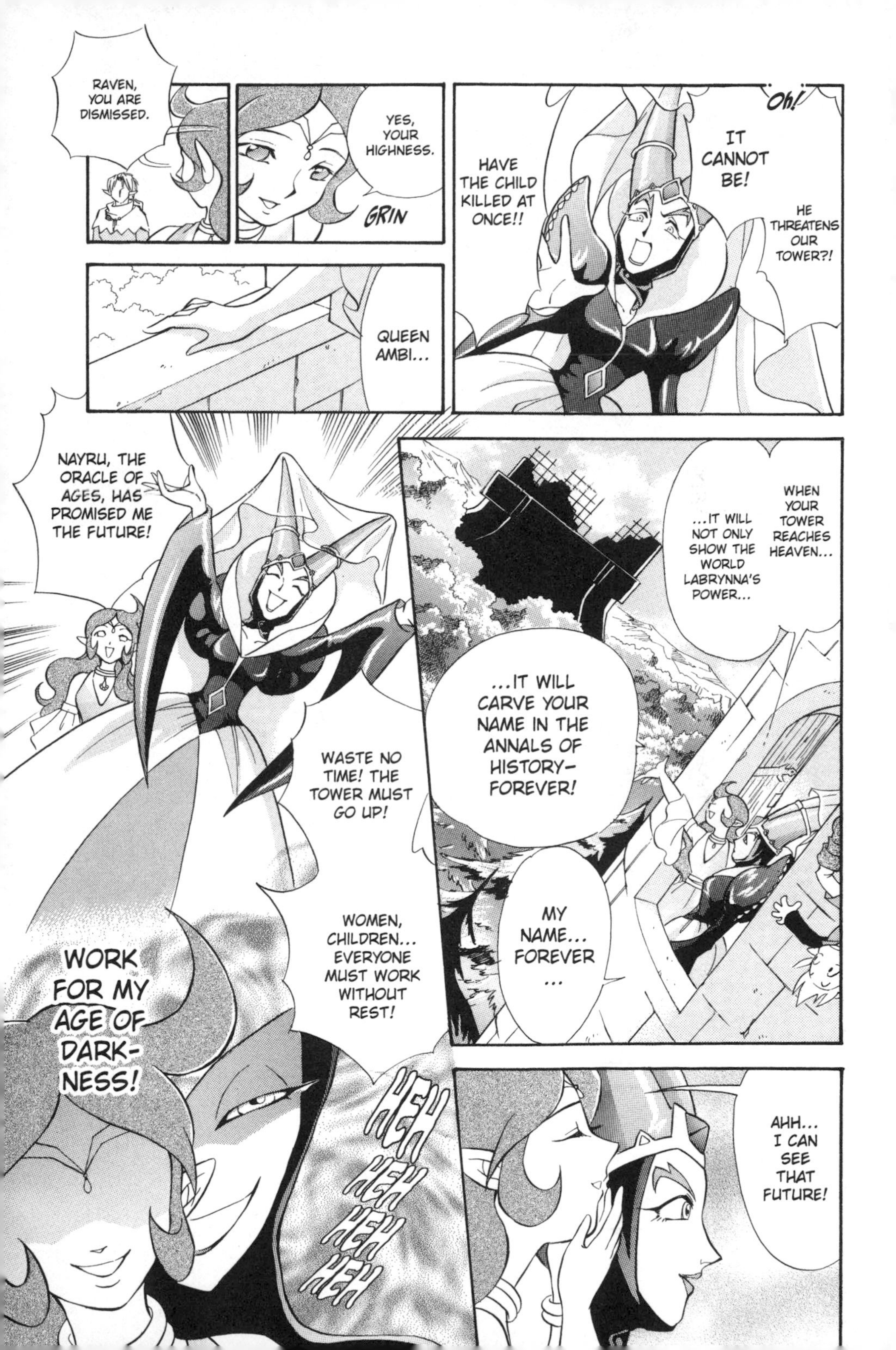
Oh!
IT CANNOT BE!
HE THREATENS OUR TOWER?!
HAVE THE CHILD KILLED AT ONCE!!
YES, YOUR HIGHNESS.
GRIN
RAVEN, YOU ARE DISMISSED.
QUEEN AMBI...
WHEN YOUR TOWER REACHES HEAVEN...
...IT WILL NOT ONLY SHOW THE WORLD LABRYNNA'S POWER...
...IT WILL CARVE YOUR NAME IN THE ANNALS OF HISTORY–FOREVER!
MY NAME... FOREVER...
NAYRU, THE ORACLE OF AGES, HAS PROMISED ME THE FUTURE!
WASTE NO TIME! THE TOWER MUST GO UP!
WOMEN, CHILDREN... EVERYONE MUST WORK WITHOUT REST!
AHH... I CAN SEE THAT FUTURE!
WORK FOR MY AGE OF DARK-NESS!
HEH HEH HEH HEH HEH

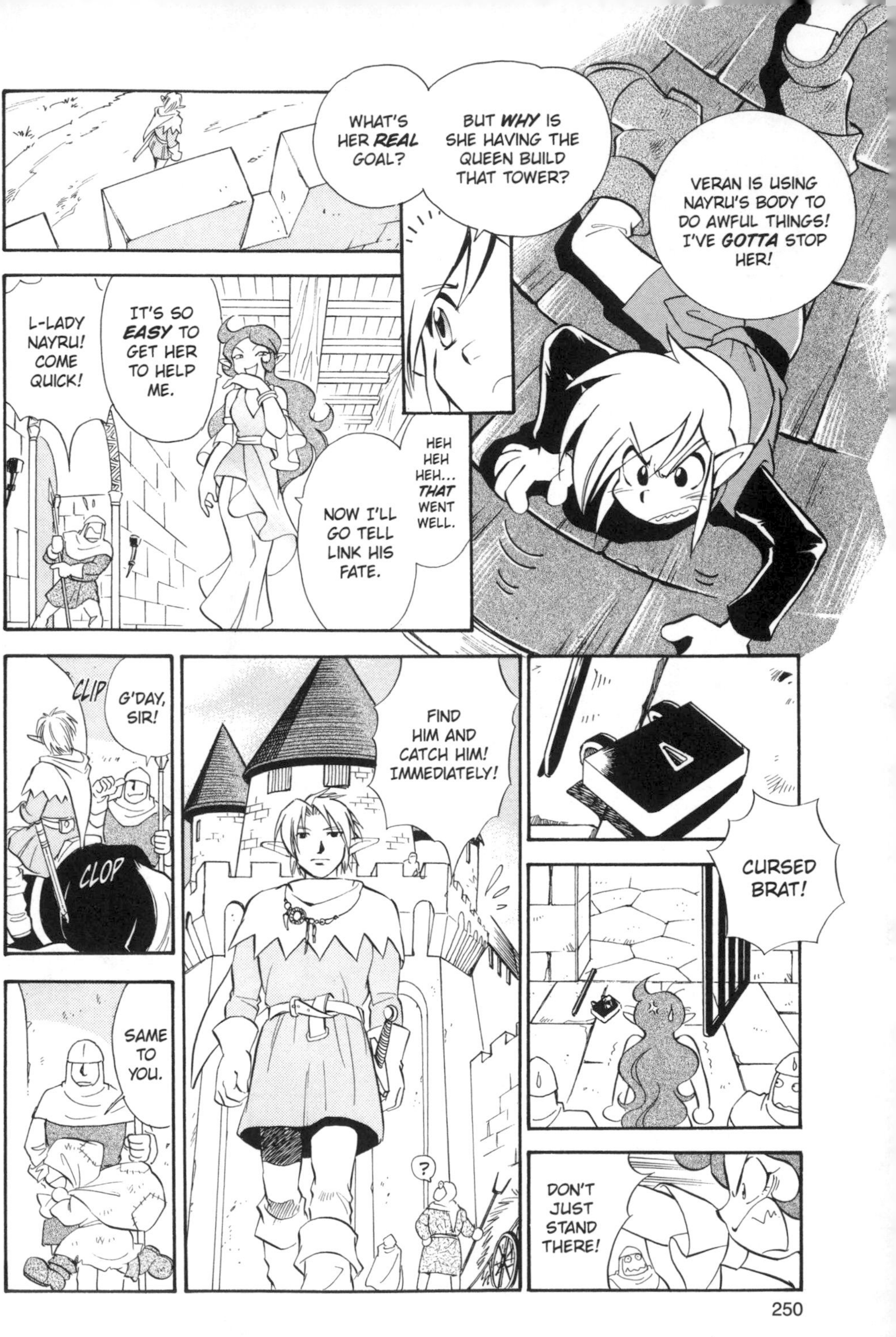
VERAN IS USING NAYRU'S BODY TO DO AWFUL THINGS! I'VE GOTTA STOP HER!
BUT WHY IS SHE HAVING THE QUEEN BUILD THAT TOWER?
WHAT'S HER REAL GOAL?
HEH HEH HEH... THAT WENT WELL.
IT'S SO EASY TO GET HER TO HELP ME.
NOW I'LL GO TELL LINK HIS FATE.
L-LADY NAYRU! COME QUICK!
CURSED BRAT!
DON'T JUST STAND THERE!
FIND HIM AND CATCH HIM! IMMEDIATELY!
CLIP
G'DAY, SIR!
CLOP
SAME TO YOU.

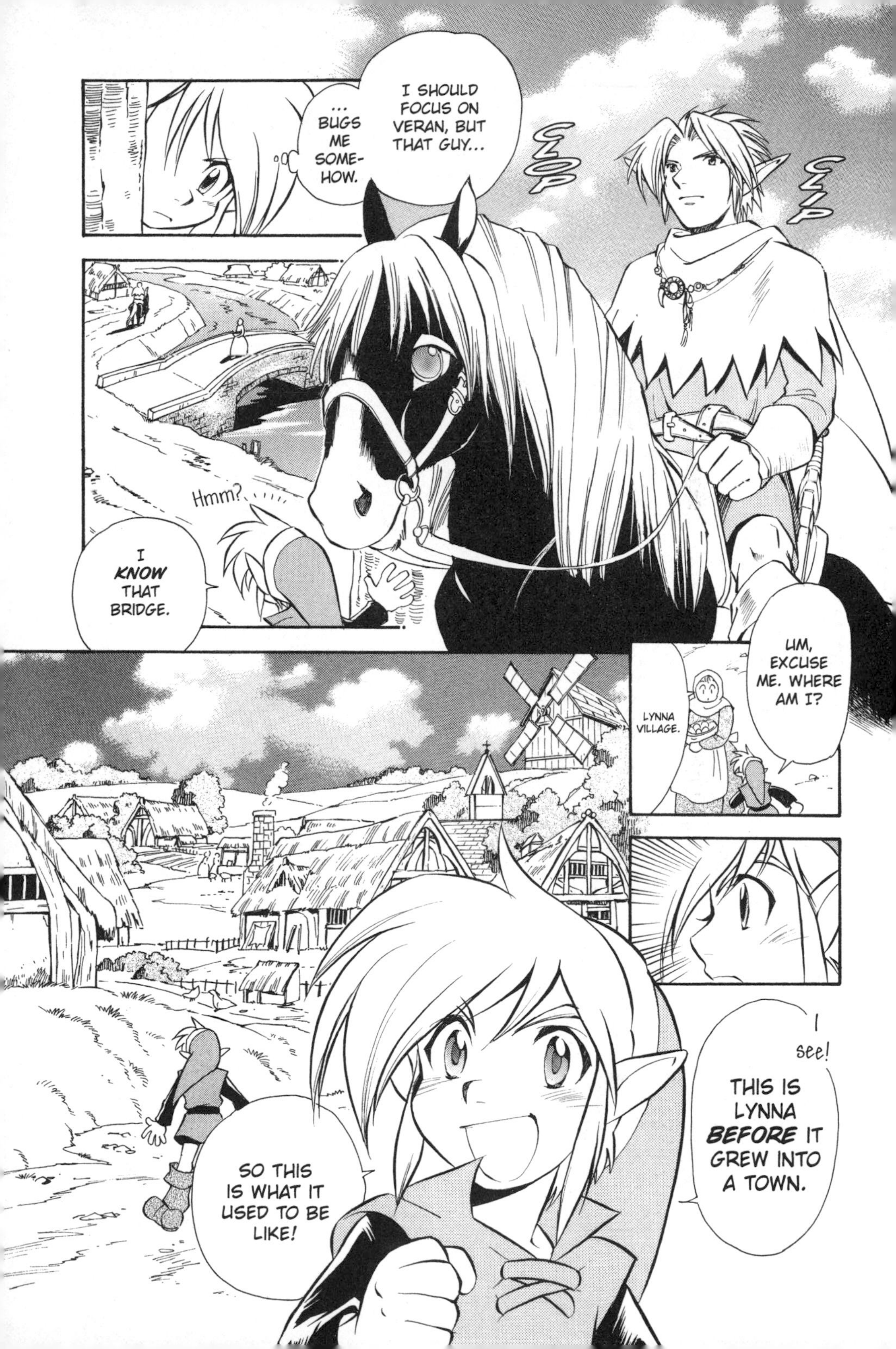
CLIP
CLOP
I SHOULD FOCUS ON VERAN, BUT THAT GUY...
... BUGS ME SOMEHOW.
Hmm?
I *KNOW* THAT BRIDGE.
UM, EXCUSE ME. WHERE AM I?
LYNNA VILLAGE.
I see!
THIS IS LYNNA *BEFORE* IT GREW INTO A TOWN.
SO THIS IS WHAT IT USED TO BE LIKE!

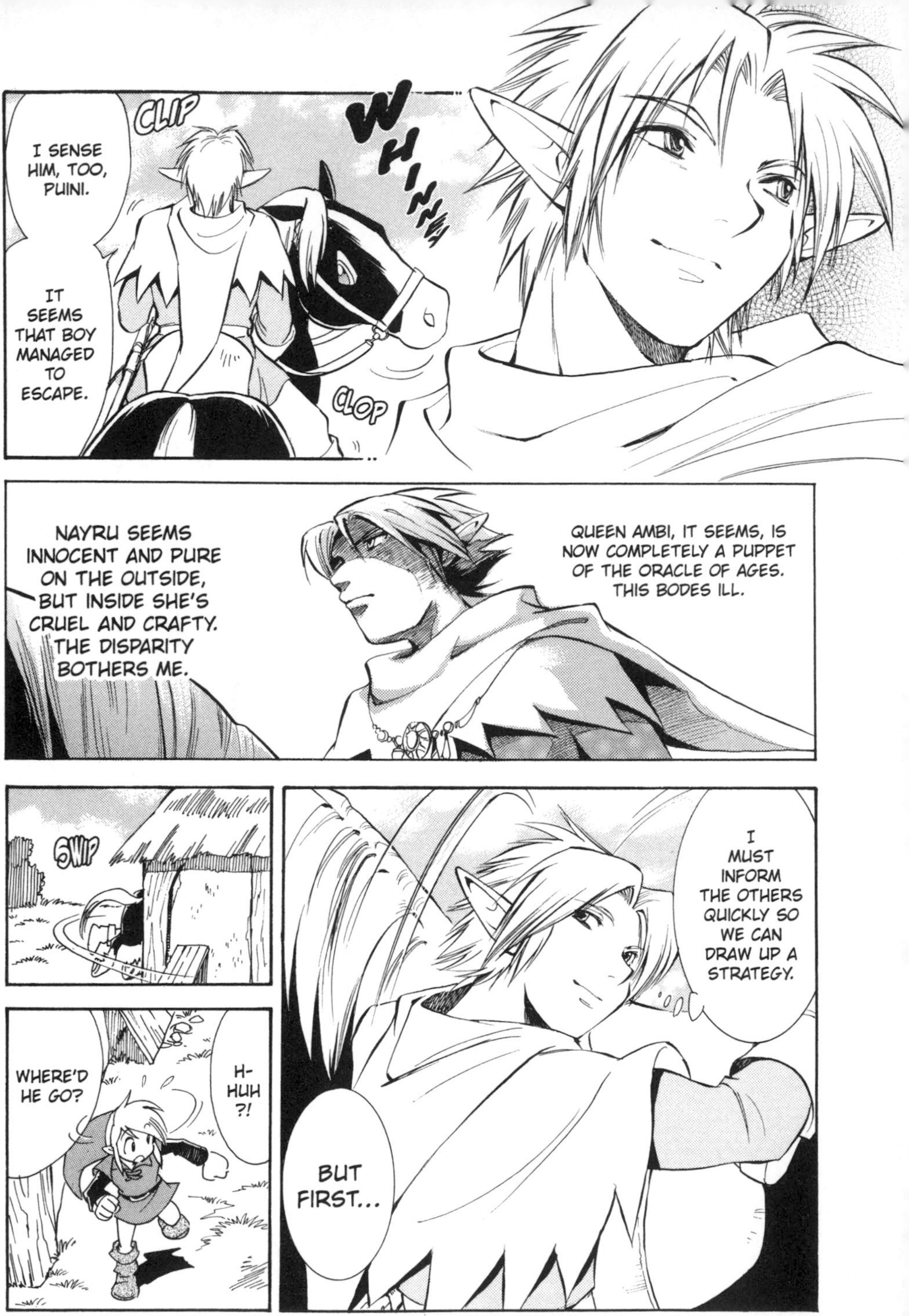
WHINNEY
CLIP
I SENSE HIM, TOO, PUINI.
CLOP
IT SEEMS THAT BOY MANAGED TO ESCAPE.
QUEEN AMBI, IT SEEMS, IS NOW COMPLETELY A PUPPET OF THE ORACLE OF AGES. THIS BODES ILL.
NAYRU SEEMS INNOCENT AND PURE ON THE OUTSIDE, BUT INSIDE SHE'S CRUEL AND CRAFTY. THE DISPARITY BOTHERS ME.
I MUST INFORM THE OTHERS QUICKLY SO WE CAN DRAW UP A STRATEGY.
BUT FIRST...
SWIP
H-HUH?!
WHERE'D HE GO?

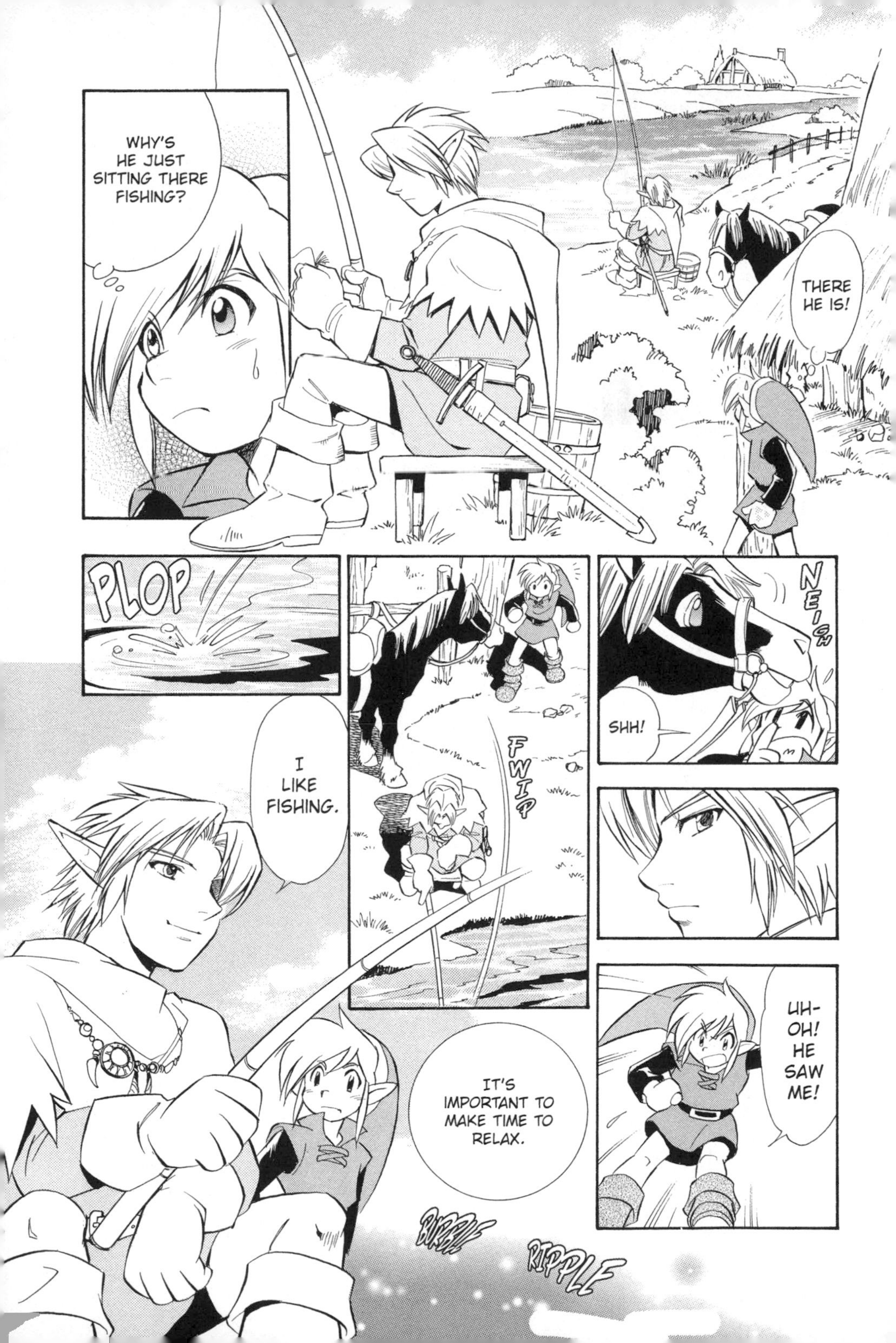
THERE HE IS!
WHY'S HE JUST SITTING THERE FISHING?
NEIGH
SHH!
UH-OH! HE SAW ME!
FWIP
PLOP
I LIKE FISHING.
IT'S IMPORTANT TO MAKE TIME TO RELAX.
BUBBLE
RIPPLE

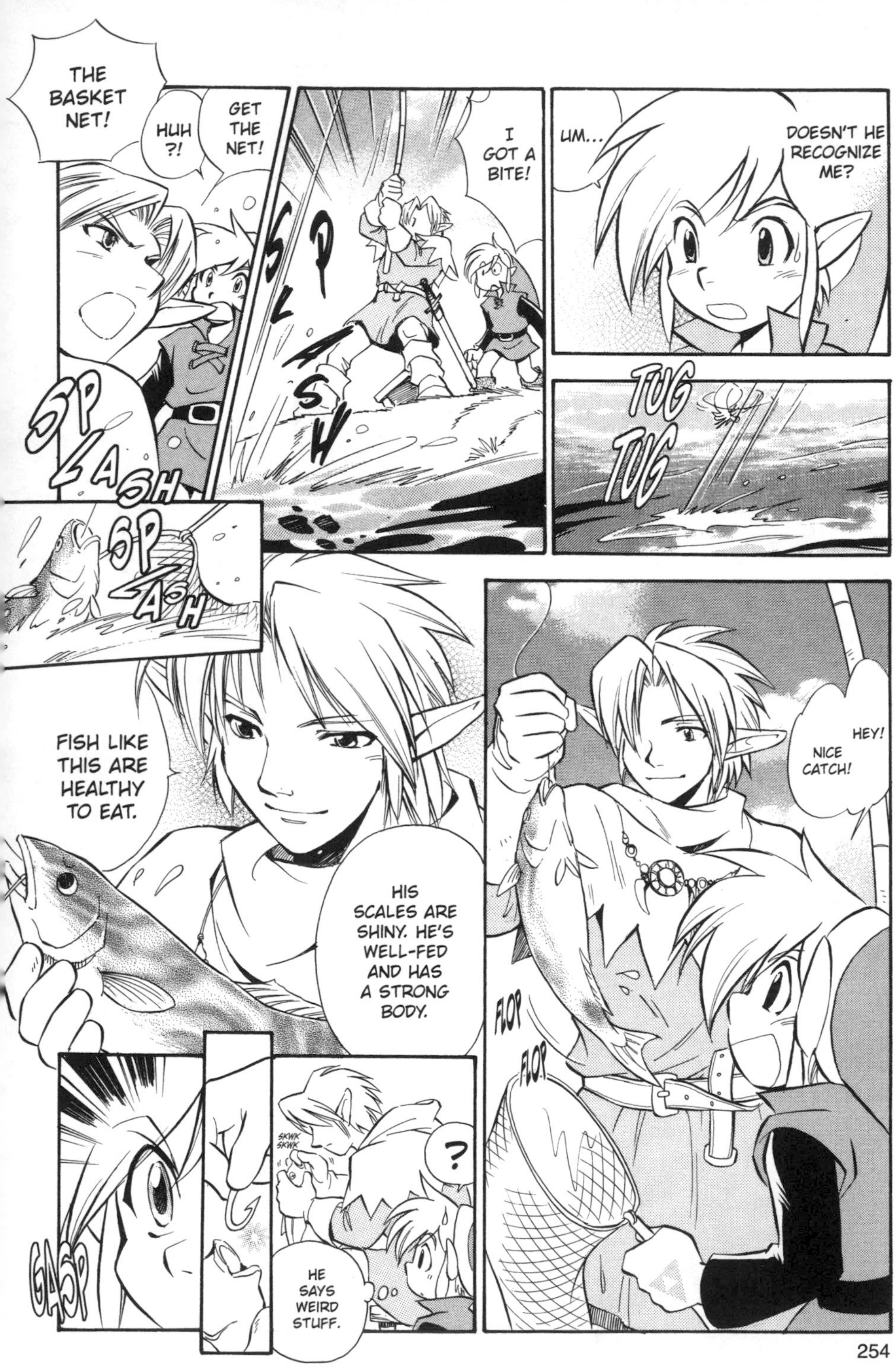
DOESN'T HE RECOGNIZE ME?
UM...
TUG TUG
I GOT A BITE!
SPLASH
GET THE NET!
HUH ?!
THE BASKET NET!
SPLASH
SPLASH
HEY! NICE CATCH!
FLOP FLOP
FISH LIKE THIS ARE HEALTHY TO EAT.
HIS SCALES ARE SHINY. HE'S WELL-FED AND HAS A STRONG BODY.
?
SKWK SKWK
HE SAYS WEIRD STUFF.
GASP

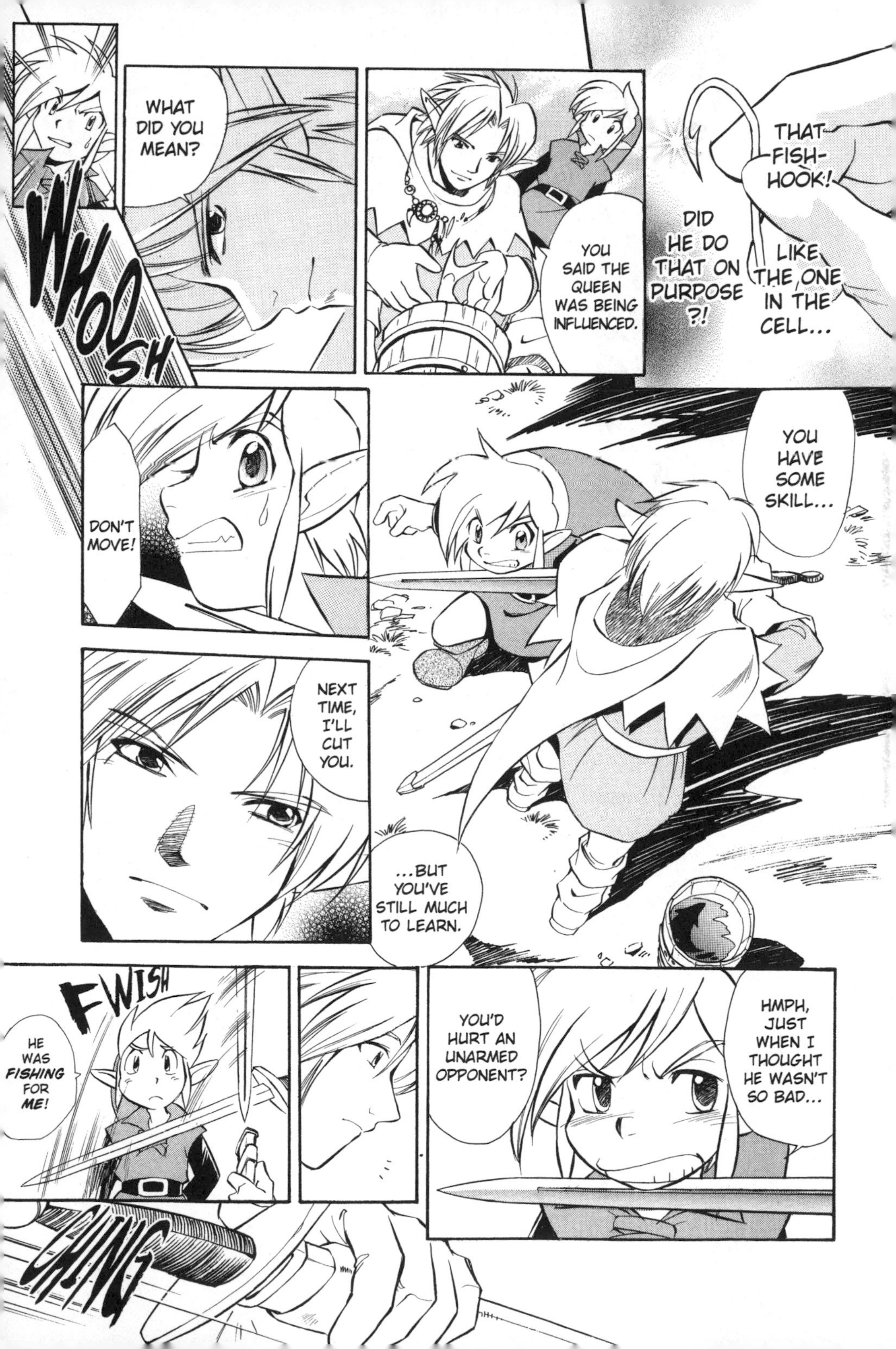
THAT FISH-HOOK!
LIKE THE ONE IN THE CELL...
DID HE DO THAT ON PURPOSE?!
YOU SAID THE QUEEN WAS BEING INFLUENCED.
WHAT DID YOU MEAN?
WHOOSH
YOU HAVE SOME SKILL...
...BUT YOU'VE STILL MUCH TO LEARN.
DON'T MOVE!
NEXT TIME, I'LL CUT YOU.
HMPH, JUST WHEN I THOUGHT HE WASN'T SO BAD...
YOU'D HURT AN UNARMED OPPONENT?
FWISH
HE WAS *FISHING* FOR *ME*!
CHING

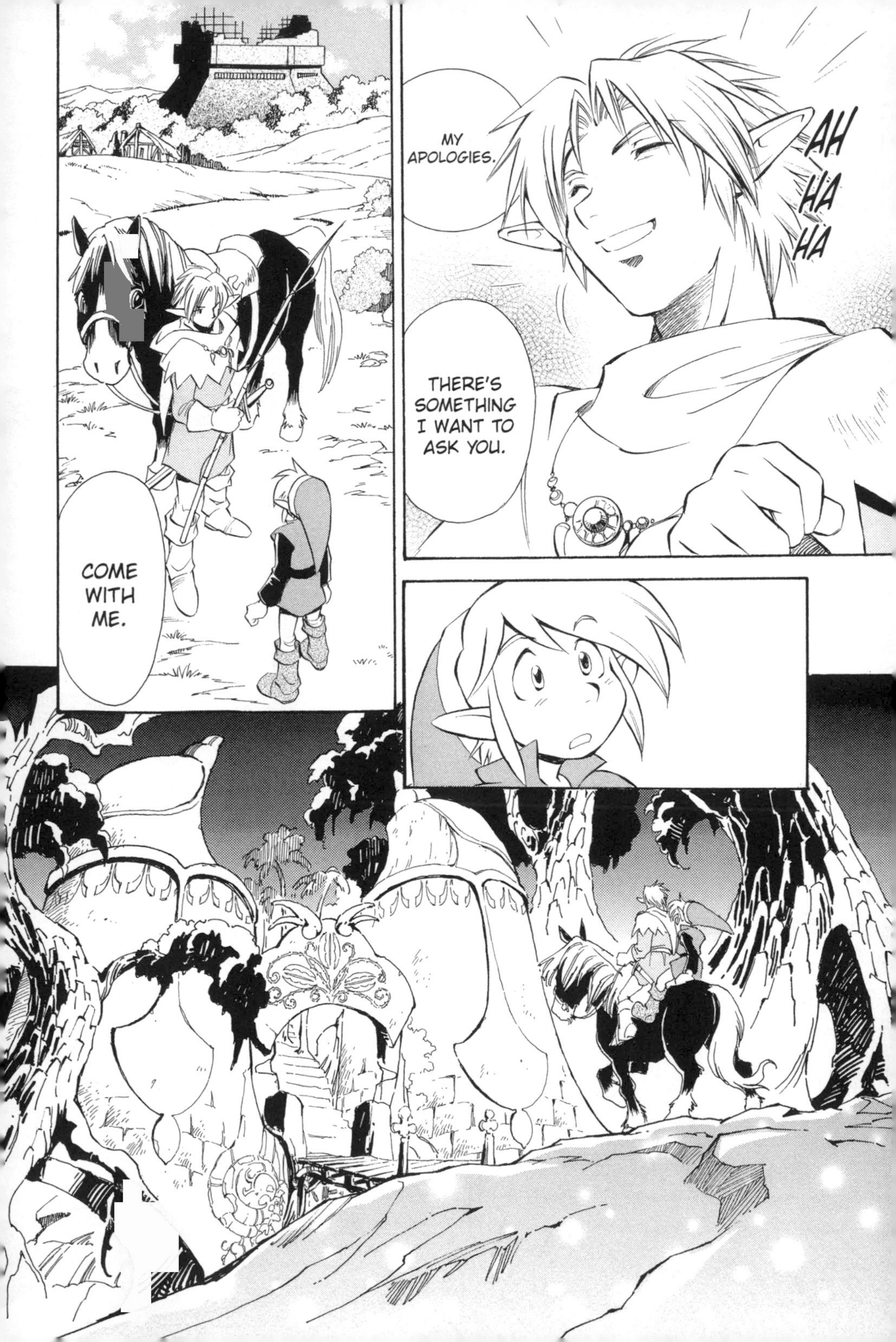
MY APOLOGIES.
AH HA HA HA
THERE'S SOMETHING I WANT TO ASK YOU.
COME WITH ME.

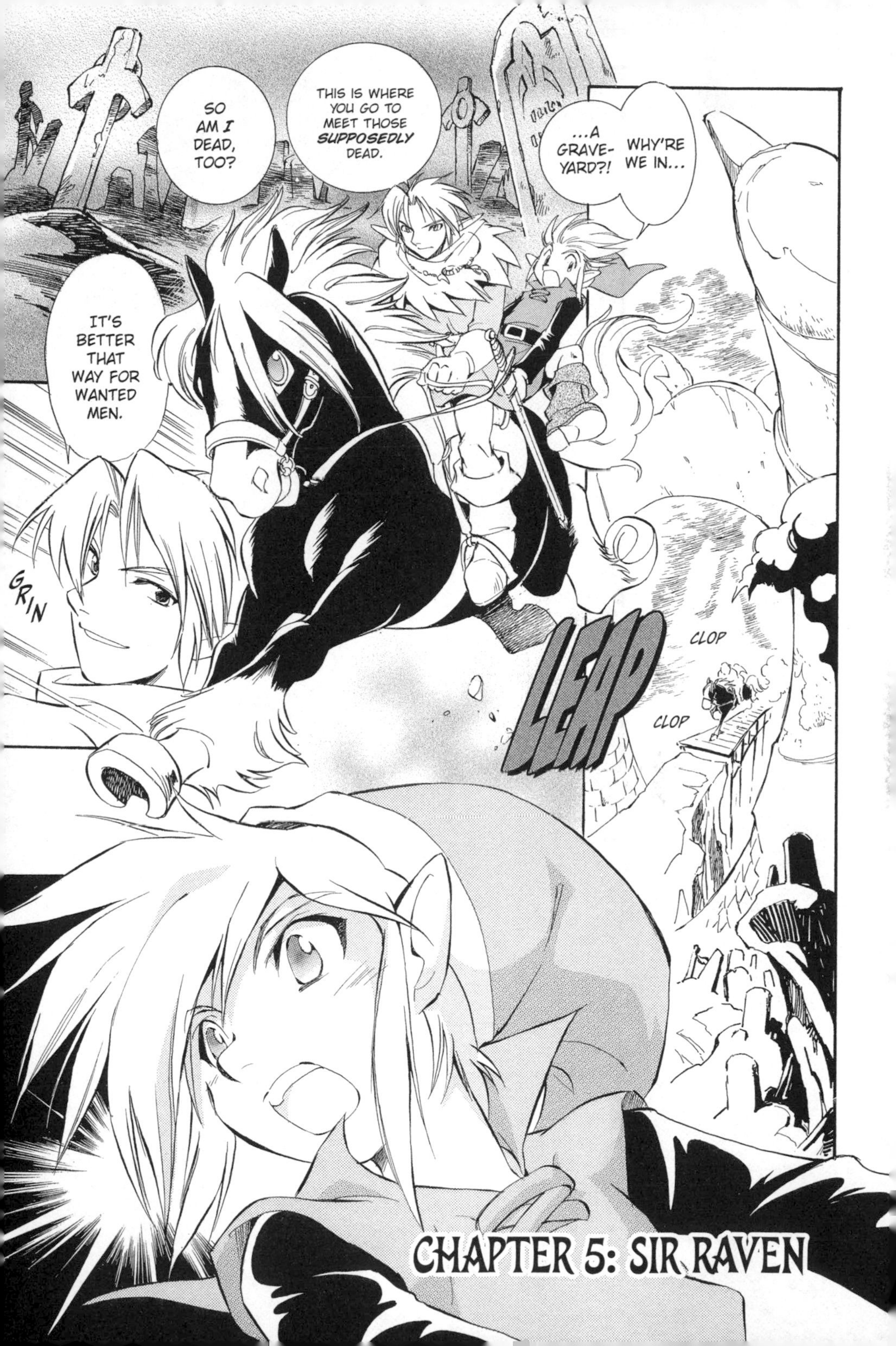
WHY'RE WE IN... ...A GRAVE-YARD?!
THIS IS WHERE YOU GO TO MEET THOSE SUPPOSEDLY DEAD.
SO AM I DEAD, TOO?
CLOP
CLOP
LEAP
IT'S BETTER THAT WAY FOR WANTED MEN.
GRIN

CHAPTER 5: SIR RAVEN

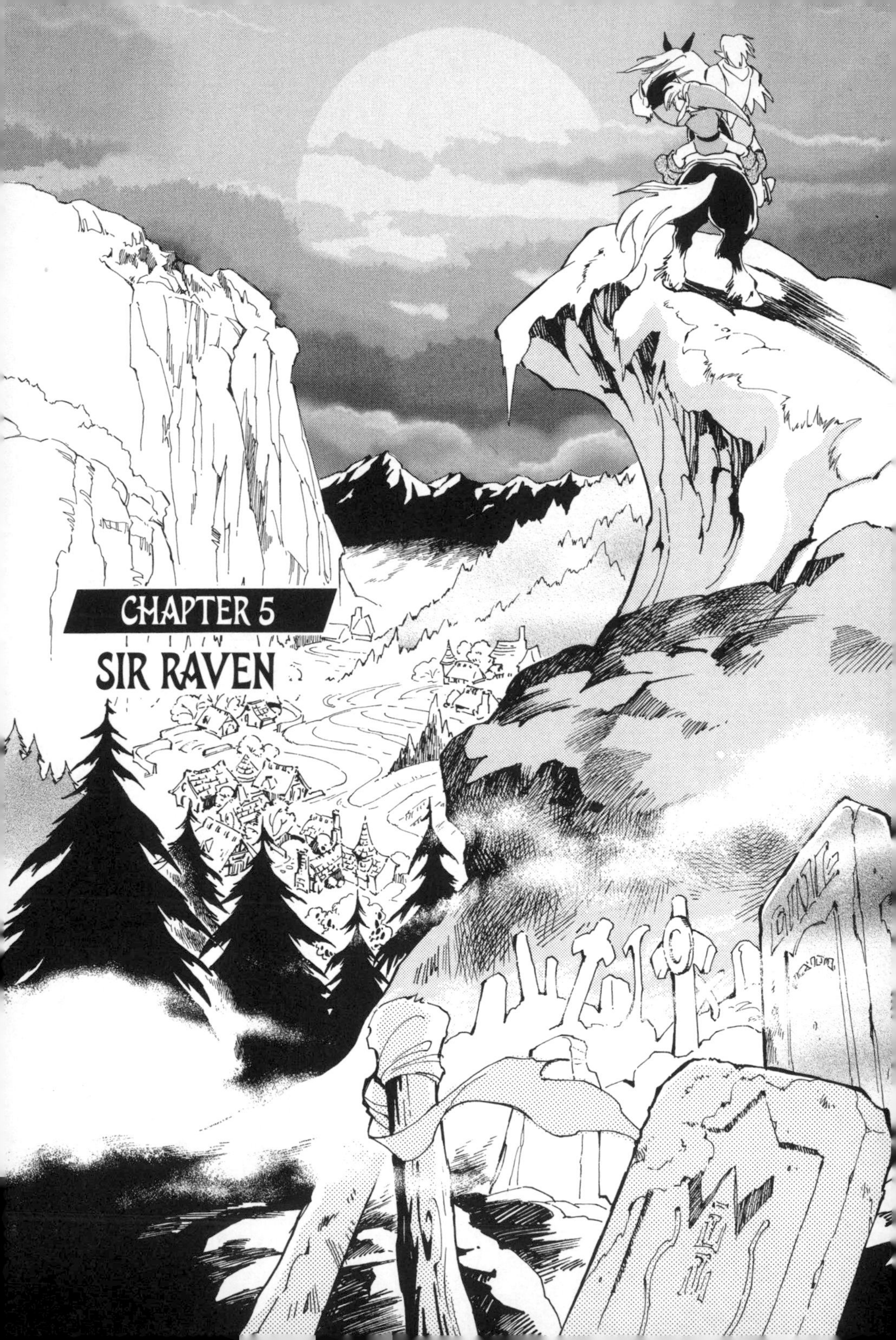
CHAPTER 5
SIR RAVEN

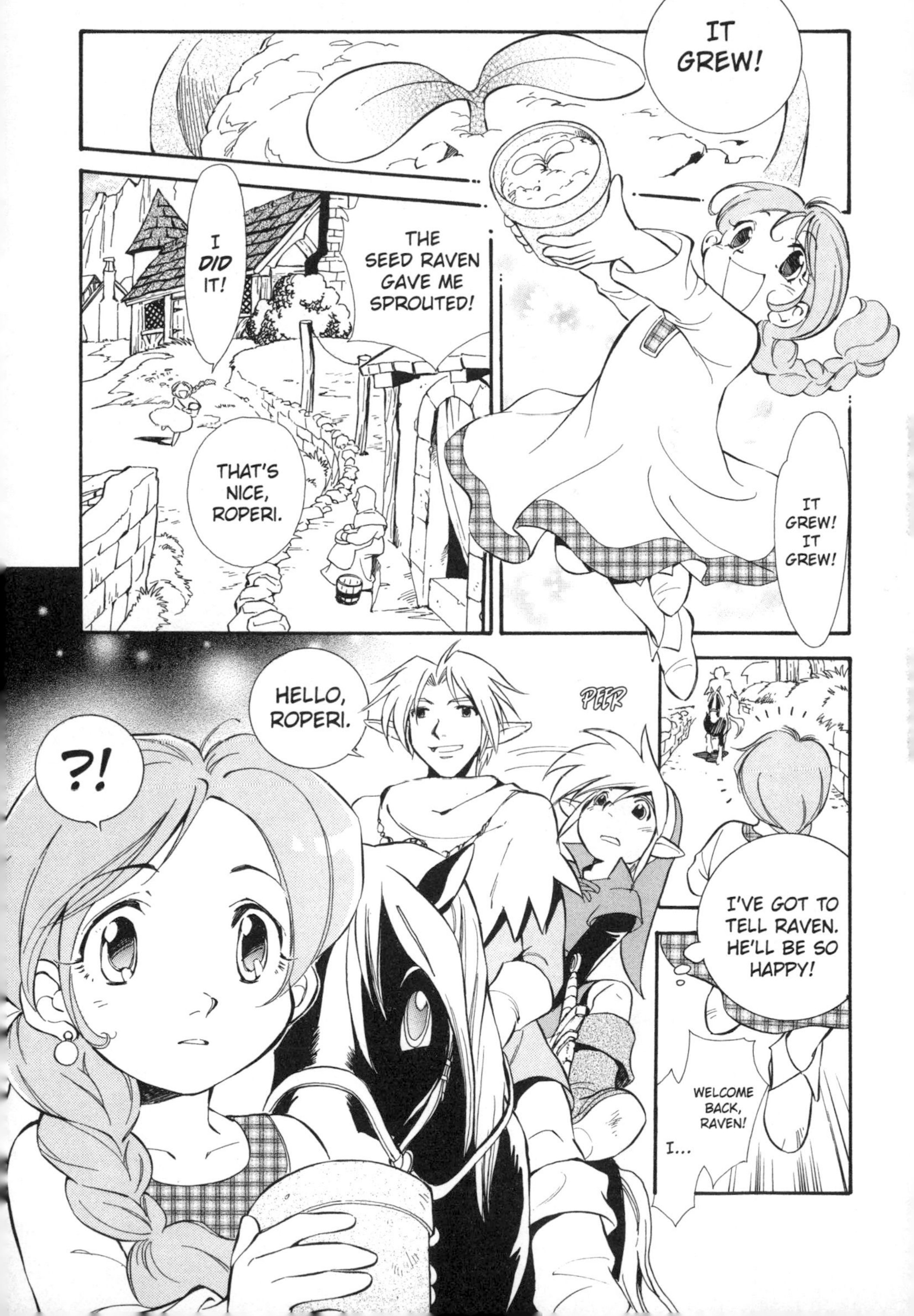

IT GREW!
IT GREW! IT GREW!
THE SEED RAVEN GAVE ME SPROUTED!
I *DID* IT!
THAT'S NICE, ROPERI.
PEER
I'VE GOT TO TELL RAVEN. HE'LL BE SO HAPPY!
WELCOME BACK, RAVEN!
I...
HELLO, ROPERI.
?!

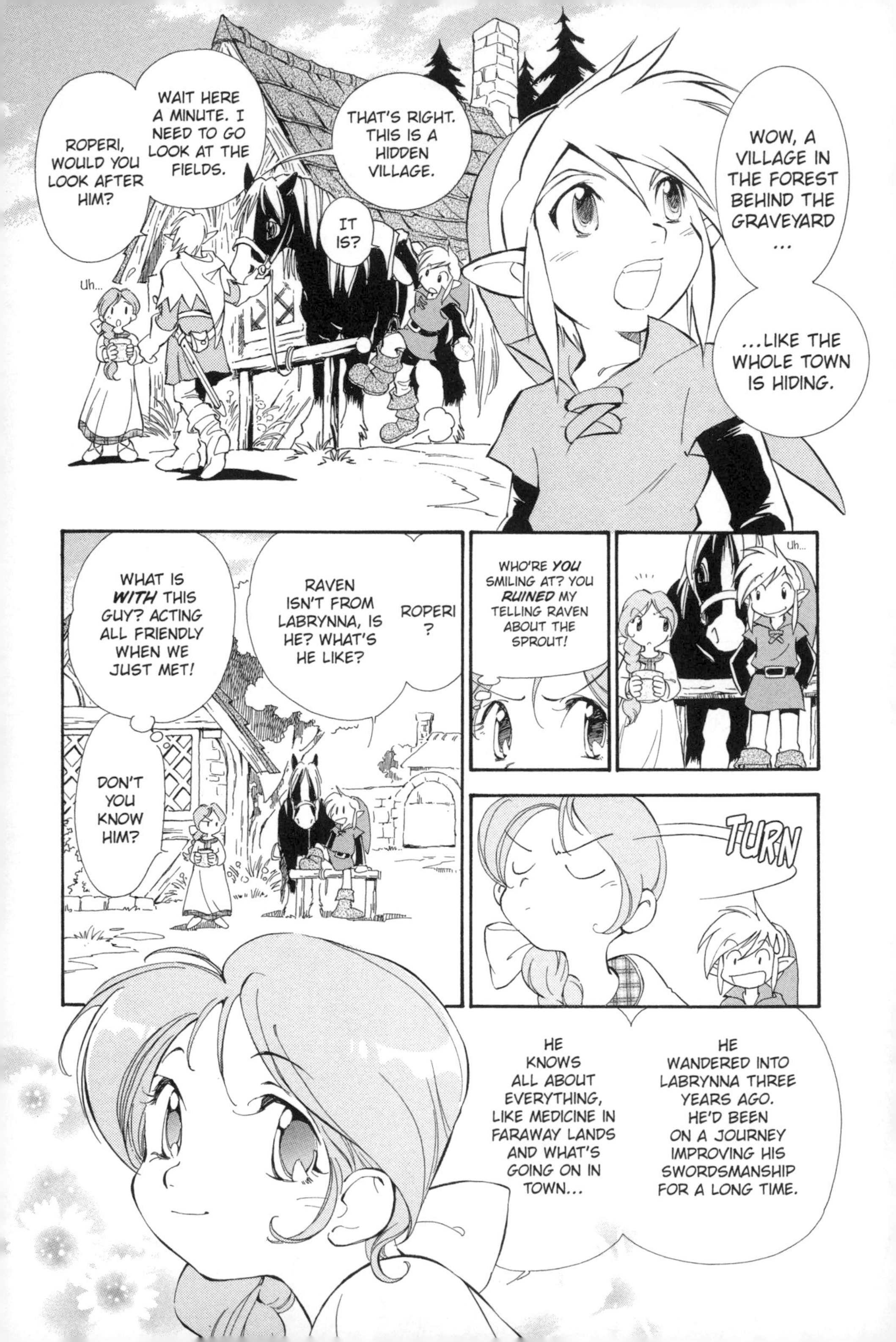

WOW, A VILLAGE IN THE FOREST BEHIND THE GRAVEYARD...
...LIKE THE WHOLE TOWN IS HIDING.
THAT'S RIGHT. THIS IS A HIDDEN VILLAGE.
IT IS?
WAIT HERE A MINUTE. I NEED TO GO LOOK AT THE FIELDS.
ROPERI, WOULD YOU LOOK AFTER HIM?
Uh...
Uh...
WHO'RE *YOU* SMILING AT? YOU *RUINED* MY TELLING RAVEN ABOUT THE SPROUT!
TURN
ROPERI?
RAVEN ISN'T FROM LABRYNNA, IS HE? WHAT'S HE LIKE?
WHAT IS *WITH* THIS GUY? ACTING ALL FRIENDLY WHEN WE JUST MET!
DON'T YOU KNOW HIM?
HE WANDERED INTO LABRYNNA THREE YEARS AGO. HE'D BEEN ON A JOURNEY IMPROVING HIS SWORDSMANSHIP FOR A LONG TIME.
HE KNOWS ALL ABOUT EVERYTHING, LIKE MEDICINE IN FARAWAY LANDS AND WHAT'S GOING ON IN TOWN...

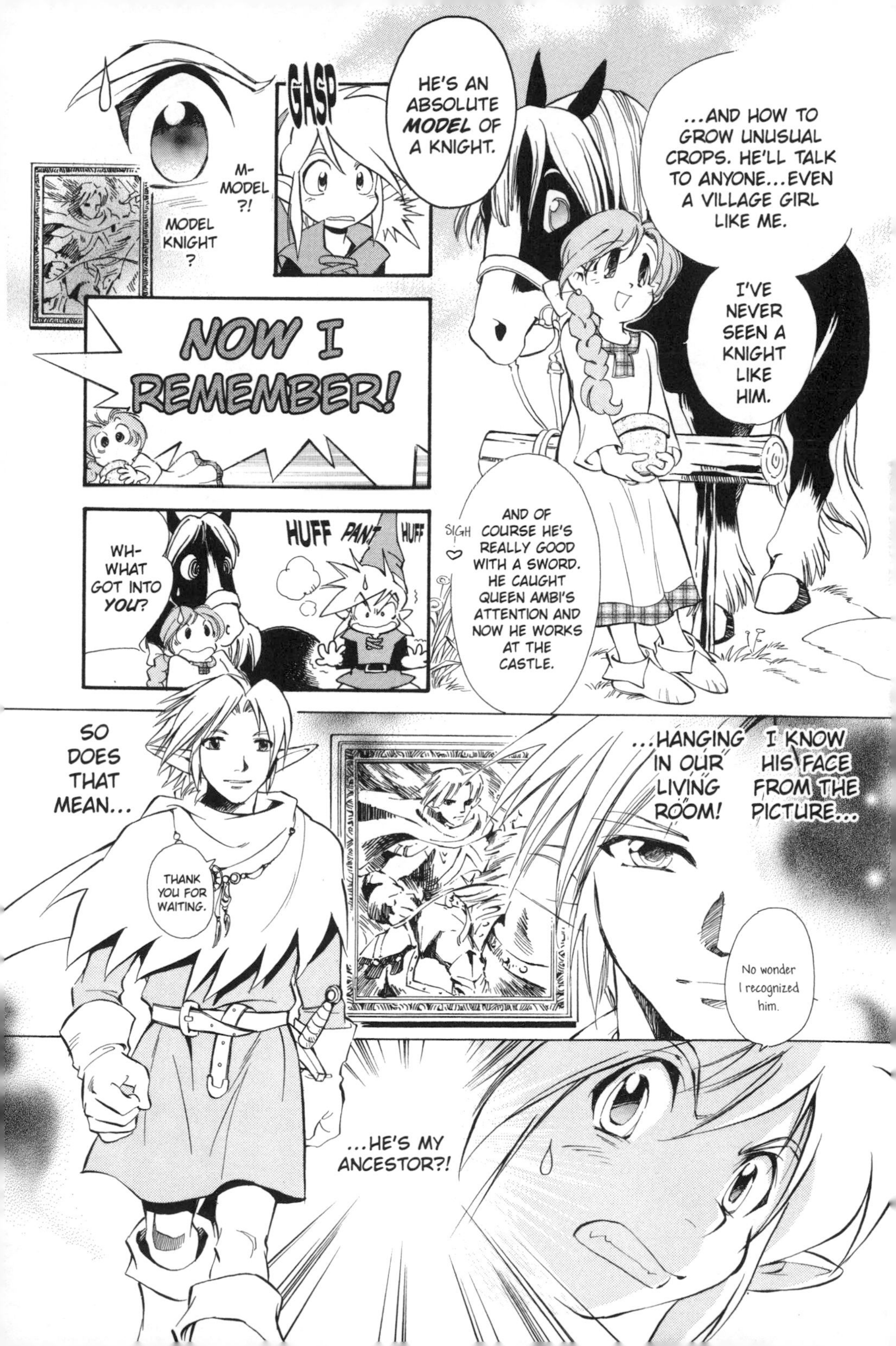
...AND HOW TO GROW UNUSUAL CROPS. HE'LL TALK TO ANYONE...EVEN A VILLAGE GIRL LIKE ME.
I'VE NEVER SEEN A KNIGHT LIKE HIM.
SIGH
AND OF COURSE HE'S REALLY GOOD WITH A SWORD. HE CAUGHT QUEEN AMBI'S ATTENTION AND NOW HE WORKS AT THE CASTLE.
HE'S AN ABSOLUTE MODEL OF A KNIGHT.
GASP
M-MODEL?!
MODEL KNIGHT?
NOW I REMEMBER!
HUFF PANT HUFF
WH-WHAT GOT INTO YOU?
I KNOW HIS FACE FROM THE PICTURE...
...HANGING IN OUR LIVING ROOM!
No wonder I recognized him.
SO DOES THAT MEAN...
THANK YOU FOR WAITING.
...HE'S MY ANCESTOR?!

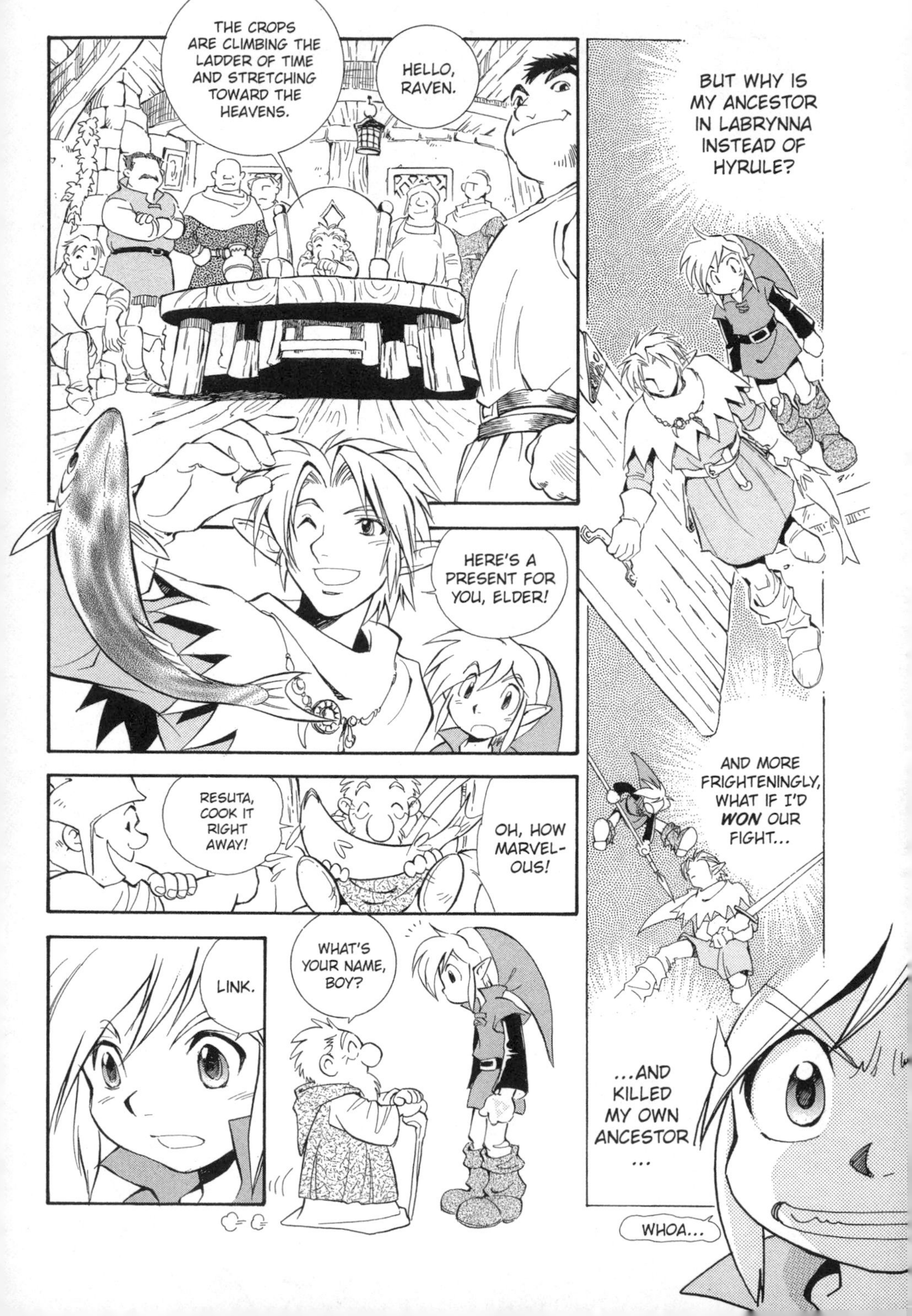
BUT WHY IS MY ANCESTOR IN LABRYNNA INSTEAD OF HYRULE?
AND MORE FRIGHTENINGLY, WHAT IF I'D **WON** OUR FIGHT...
...AND KILLED MY OWN ANCESTOR ...
WHOA...
HELLO, RAVEN.
THE CROPS ARE CLIMBING THE LADDER OF TIME AND STRETCHING TOWARD THE HEAVENS.
HERE'S A PRESENT FOR YOU, ELDER!
OH, HOW MARVEL-OUS!
RESUTA, COOK IT RIGHT AWAY!
WHAT'S YOUR NAME, BOY?
LINK.

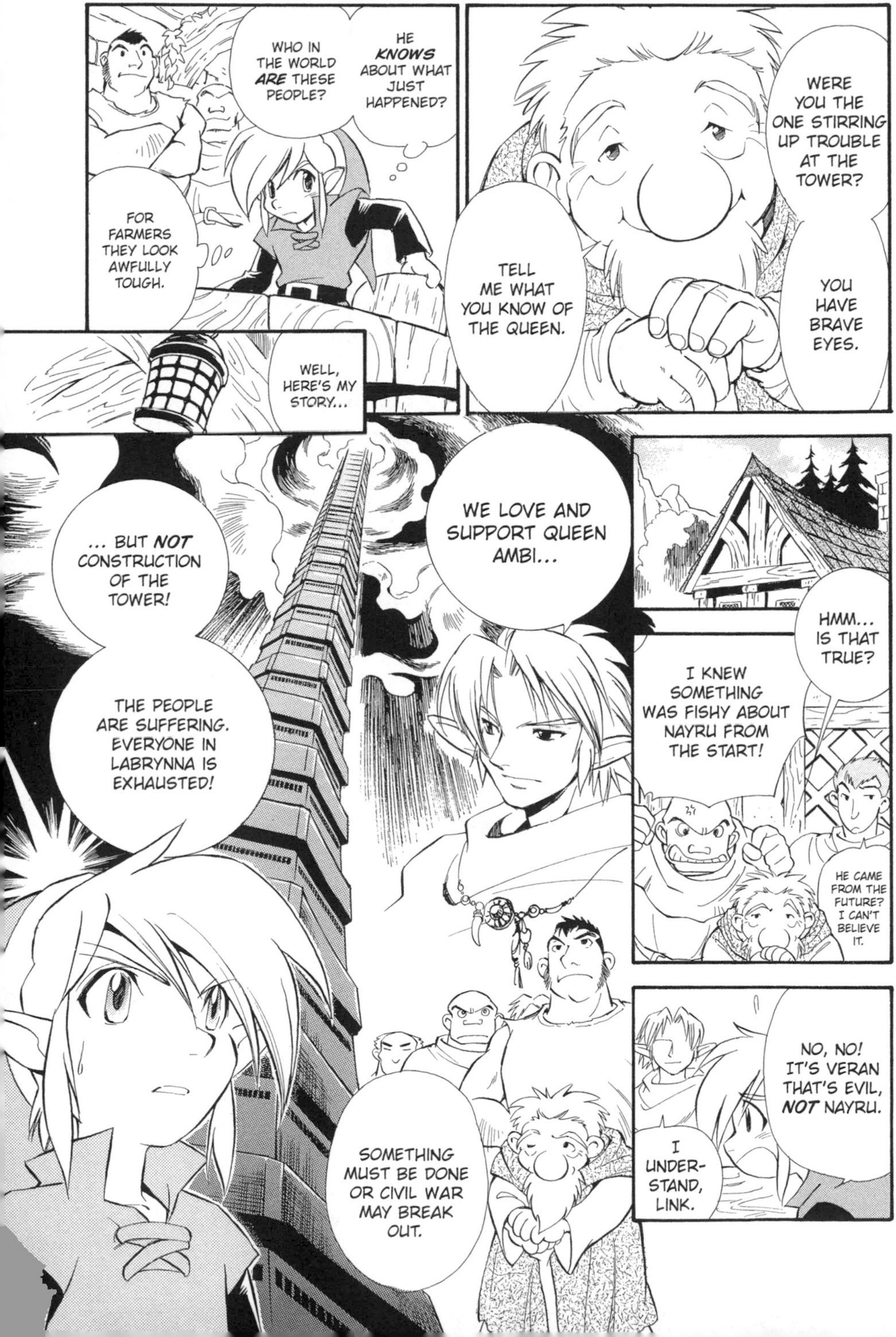
WERE YOU THE ONE STIRRING UP TROUBLE AT THE TOWER?
YOU HAVE BRAVE EYES.
TELL ME WHAT YOU KNOW OF THE QUEEN.
HE **KNOWS** ABOUT WHAT JUST HAPPENED?
WHO IN THE WORLD **ARE** THESE PEOPLE?
FOR FARMERS THEY LOOK AWFULLY TOUGH.
WELL, HERE'S MY STORY...
HMM... IS THAT TRUE?
I KNEW SOMETHING WAS FISHY ABOUT NAYRU FROM THE START!
HE CAME FROM THE FUTURE? I CAN'T BELIEVE IT.
NO, NO! IT'S VERAN THAT'S EVIL, **NOT** NAYRU.
I UNDER-STAND, LINK.
WE LOVE AND SUPPORT QUEEN AMBI...
... BUT **NOT** CONSTRUCTION OF THE TOWER!
THE PEOPLE ARE SUFFERING. EVERYONE IN LABRYNNA IS EXHAUSTED!
SOMETHING MUST BE DONE OR CIVIL WAR MAY BREAK OUT.

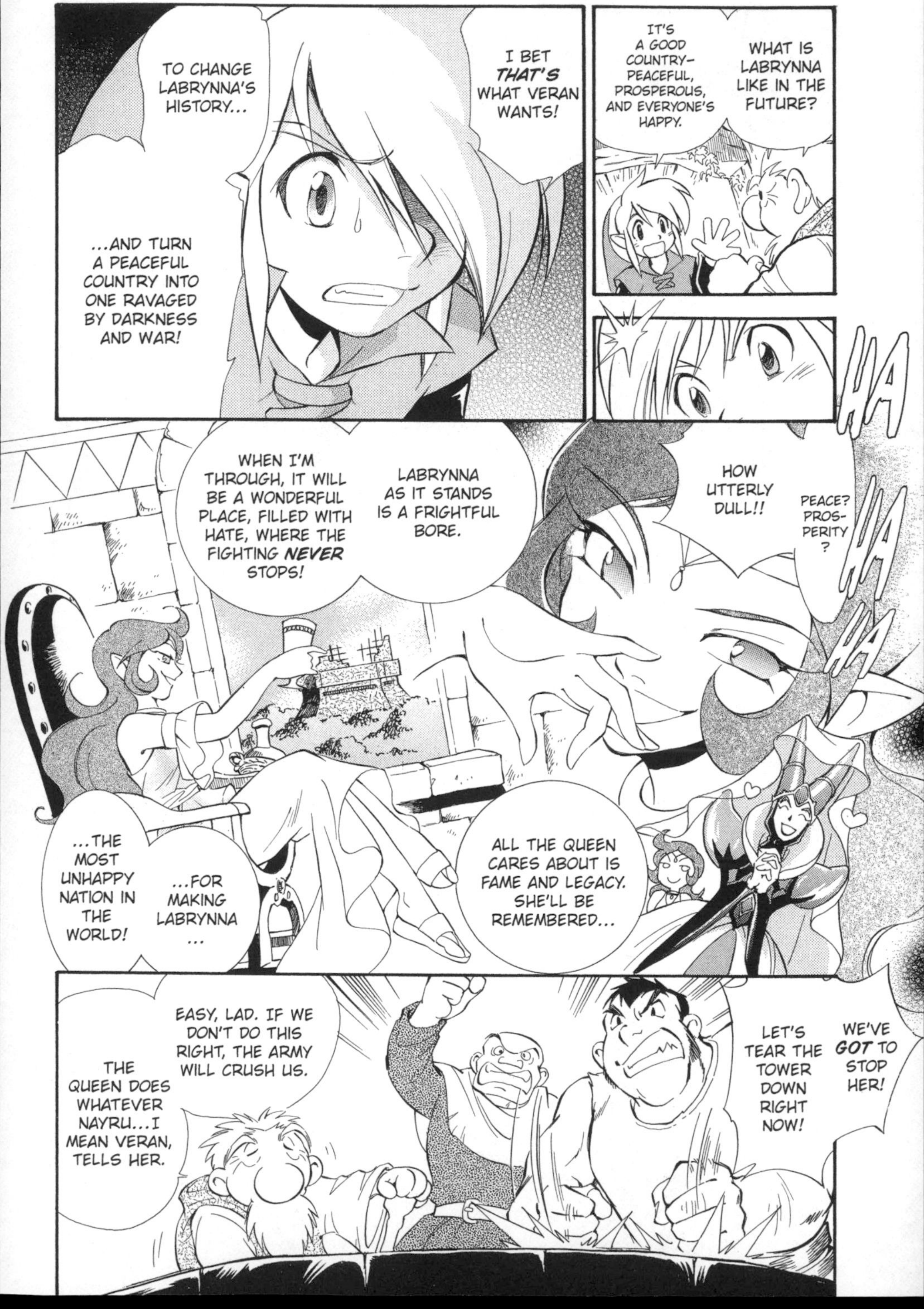
WHAT IS LABRYNNA LIKE IN THE FUTURE?
IT'S A GOOD COUNTRY—PEACEFUL, PROSPEROUS, AND EVERYONE'S HAPPY.
HA
I BET ***THAT'S*** WHAT VERAN WANTS!
TO CHANGE LABRYNNA'S HISTORY...
...AND TURN A PEACEFUL COUNTRY INTO ONE RAVAGED BY DARKNESS AND WAR!
HA HA HA HA
PEACE? PROS-PERITY?
HOW UTTERLY DULL!!
LABRYNNA AS IT STANDS IS A FRIGHTFUL BORE.
WHEN I'M THROUGH, IT WILL BE A WONDERFUL PLACE, FILLED WITH HATE, WHERE THE FIGHTING ***NEVER*** STOPS!
ALL THE QUEEN CARES ABOUT IS FAME AND LEGACY. SHE'LL BE REMEMBERED...
...FOR MAKING LABRYNNA...
...THE MOST UNHAPPY NATION IN THE WORLD!
WE'VE ***GOT*** TO STOP HER!
LET'S TEAR THE TOWER DOWN RIGHT NOW!
EASY, LAD. IF WE DON'T DO THIS RIGHT, THE ARMY WILL CRUSH US.
THE QUEEN DOES WHATEVER NAYRU...I MEAN VERAN, TELLS HER.

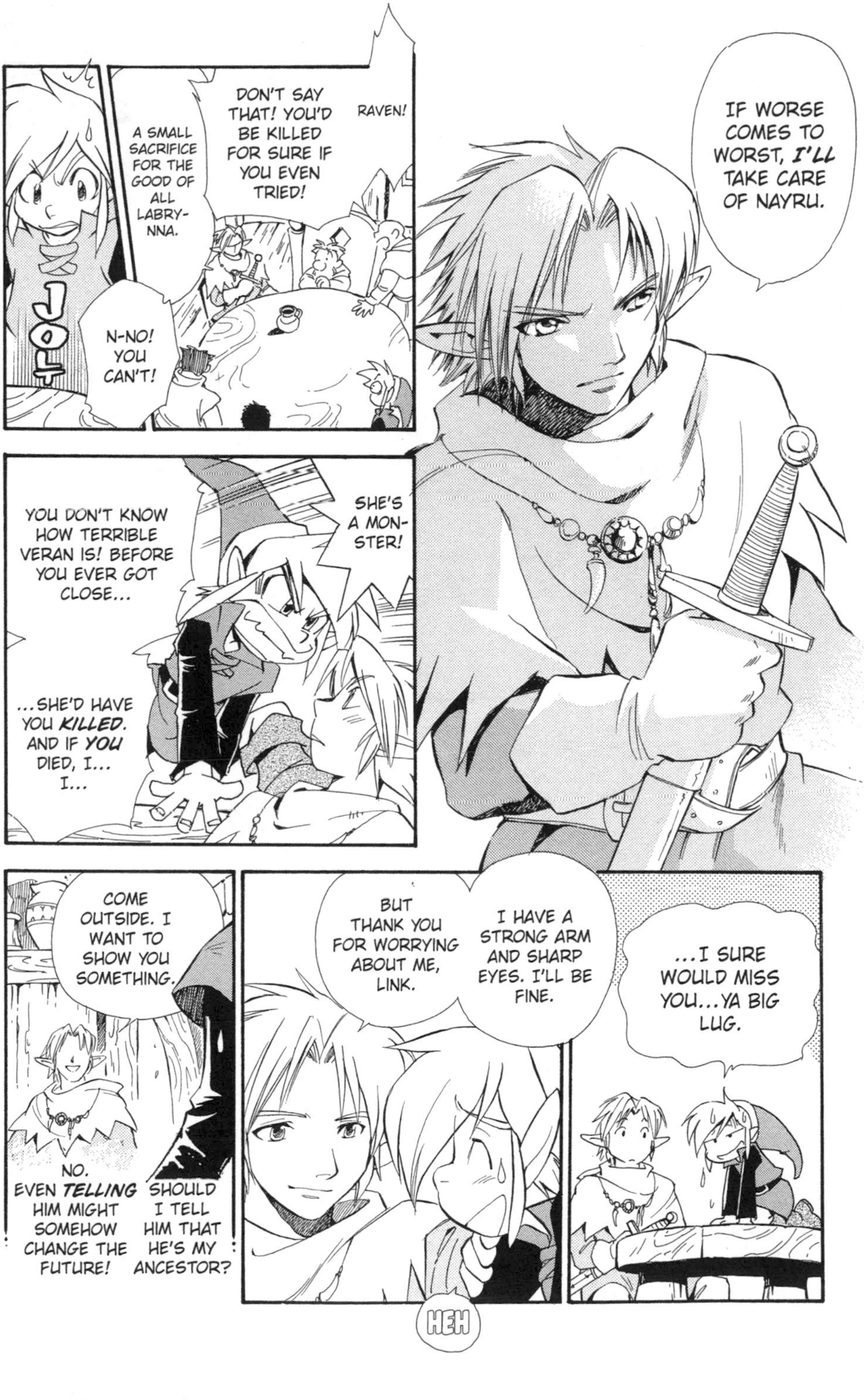

IF WORSE COMES TO WORST, I'LL TAKE CARE OF NAYRU.
RAVEN!
DON'T SAY THAT! YOU'D BE KILLED FOR SURE IF YOU EVEN TRIED!
A SMALL SACRIFICE FOR THE GOOD OF ALL LABRYNNA.
JOLT
N-NO! YOU CAN'T!
SHE'S A MONSTER!
YOU DON'T KNOW HOW TERRIBLE VERAN IS! BEFORE YOU EVER GOT CLOSE...
...SHE'D HAVE YOU KILLED. AND IF YOU DIED, I... I...
...I SURE WOULD MISS YOU...YA BIG LUG.
I HAVE A STRONG ARM AND SHARP EYES. I'LL BE FINE.
BUT THANK YOU FOR WORRYING ABOUT ME, LINK.
COME OUTSIDE. I WANT TO SHOW YOU SOMETHING.
SHOULD I TELL HIM THAT HE'S MY ANCESTOR?
NO. EVEN TELLING HIM MIGHT SOMEHOW CHANGE THE FUTURE!
HEH

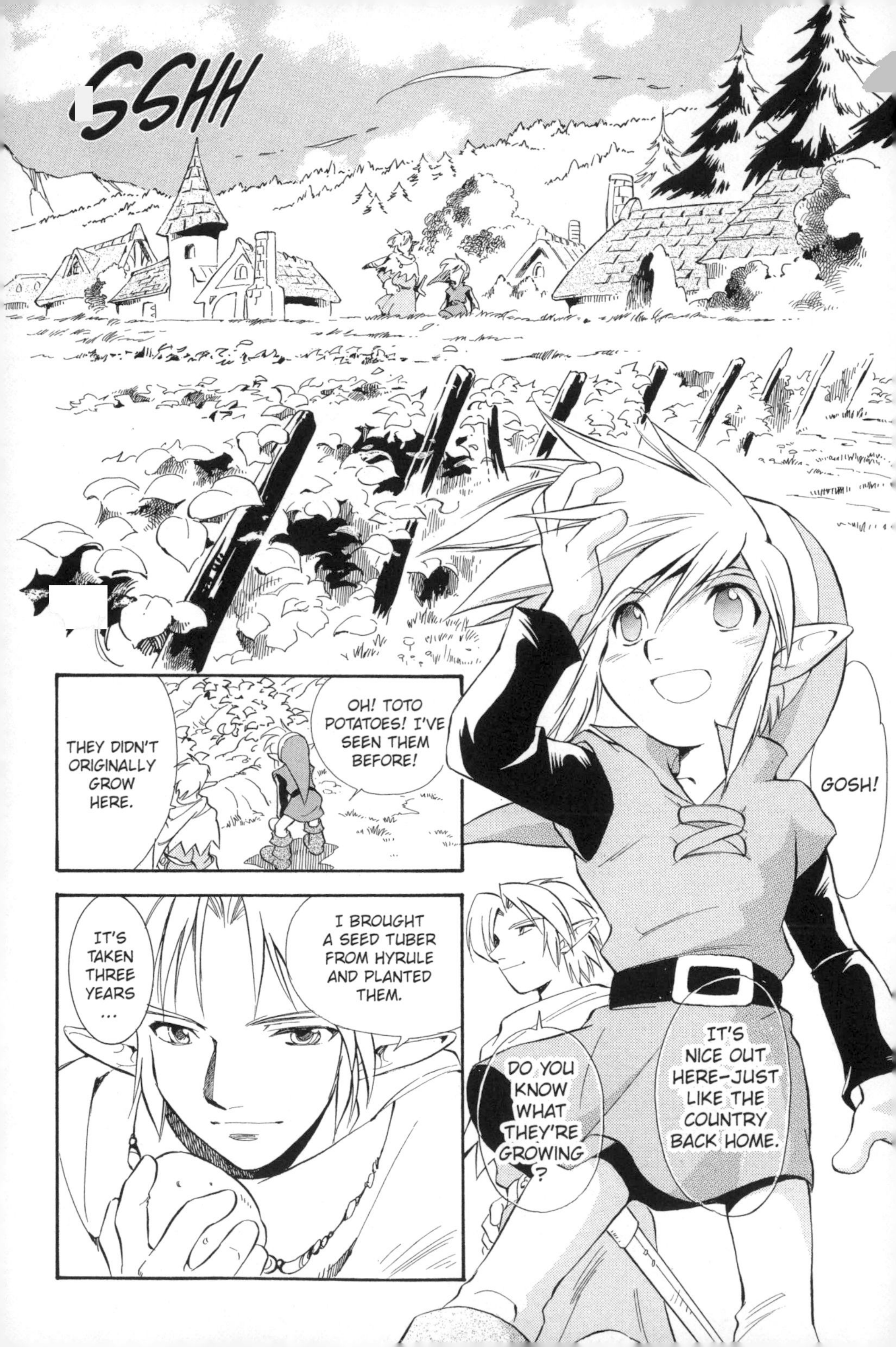
SSHH
GOSH!
IT'S NICE OUT HERE–JUST LIKE THE COUNTRY BACK HOME.
DO YOU KNOW WHAT THEY'RE GROWING?
OH! TOTO POTATOES! I'VE SEEN THEM BEFORE!
THEY DIDN'T ORIGINALLY GROW HERE.
I BROUGHT A SEED TUBER FROM HYRULE AND PLANTED THEM.
IT'S TAKEN THREE YEARS...

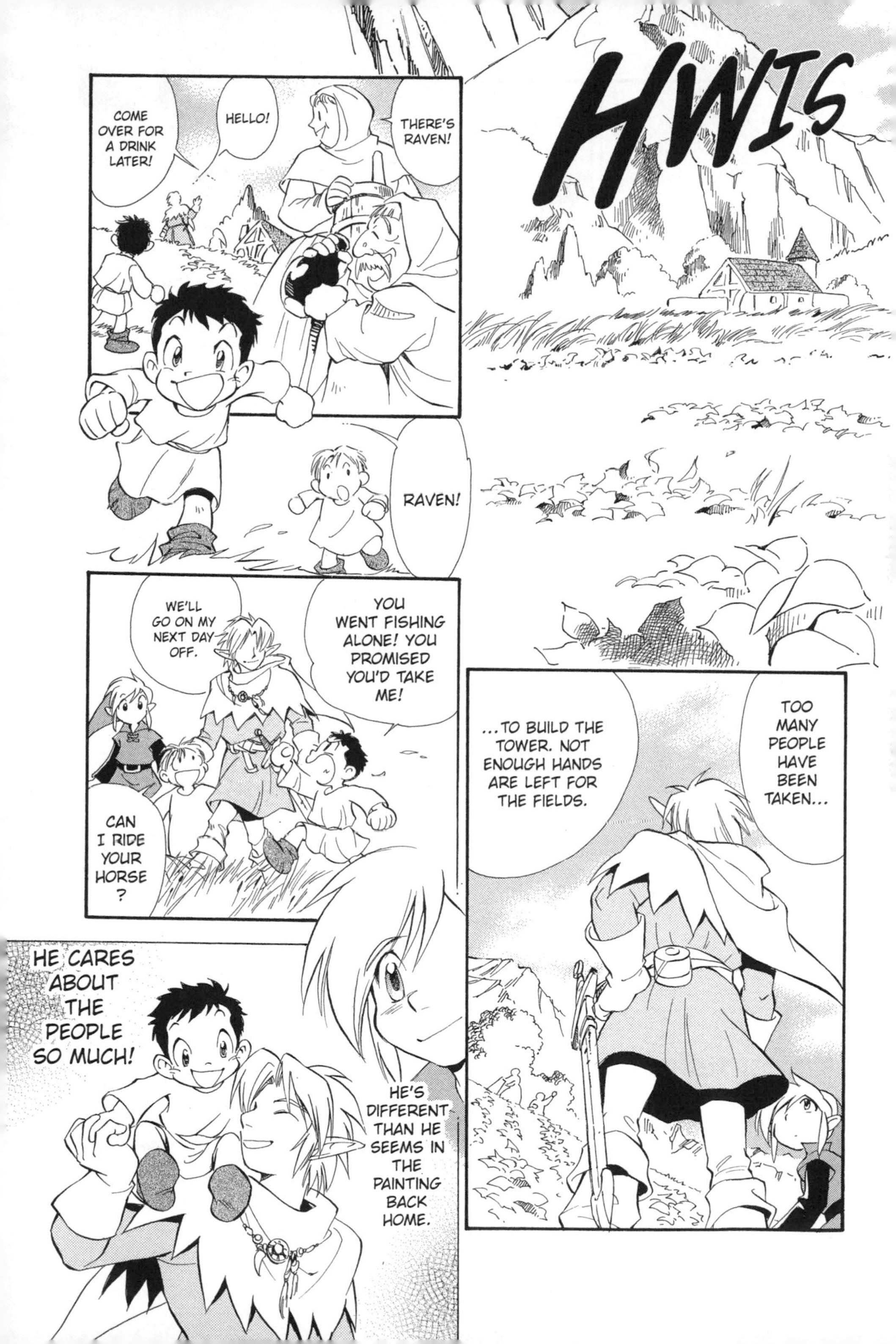
HWIS
THERE'S RAVEN!
HELLO!
COME OVER FOR A DRINK LATER!
RAVEN!
YOU WENT FISHING ALONE! YOU PROMISED YOU'D TAKE ME!
WE'LL GO ON MY NEXT DAY OFF.
CAN I RIDE YOUR HORSE?
TOO MANY PEOPLE HAVE BEEN TAKEN...
...TO BUILD THE TOWER. NOT ENOUGH HANDS ARE LEFT FOR THE FIELDS.
HE CARES ABOUT THE PEOPLE SO MUCH!
HE'S DIFFERENT THAN HE SEEMS IN THE PAINTING BACK HOME.

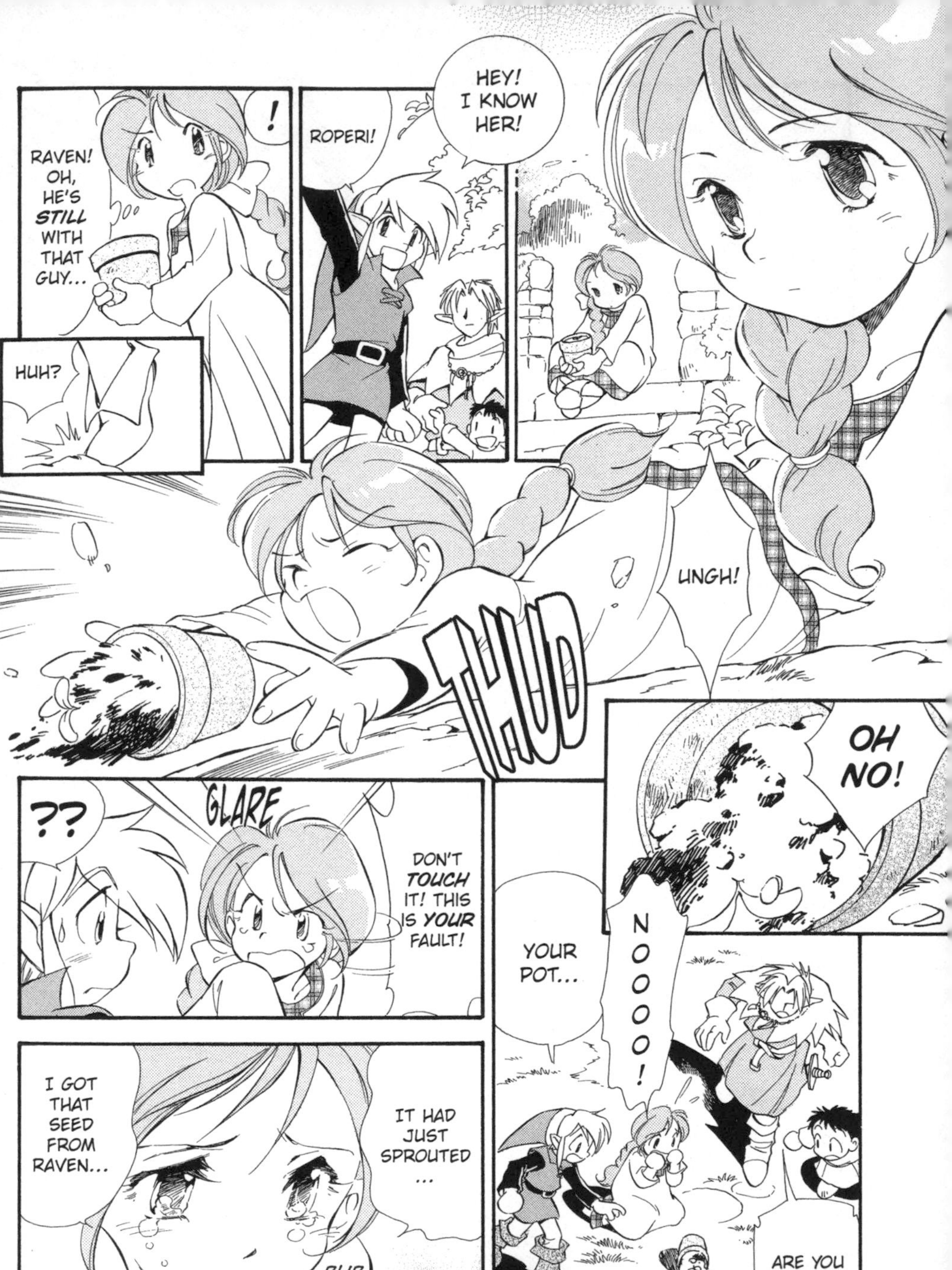
HEY! I KNOW HER!
ROPERI!
!
RAVEN! OH, HE'S ***STILL*** WITH THAT GUY...
HUH?
UNGH!
THUD
OH NO!
NOOOOO!
YOUR POT...
ARE YOU ALL RIGHT, ROPERI?
GLARE
??
DON'T ***TOUCH*** IT! THIS IS ***YOUR*** FAULT!
IT HAD JUST SPROUTED ...
I GOT THAT SEED FROM RAVEN...
PLIP
PLIP

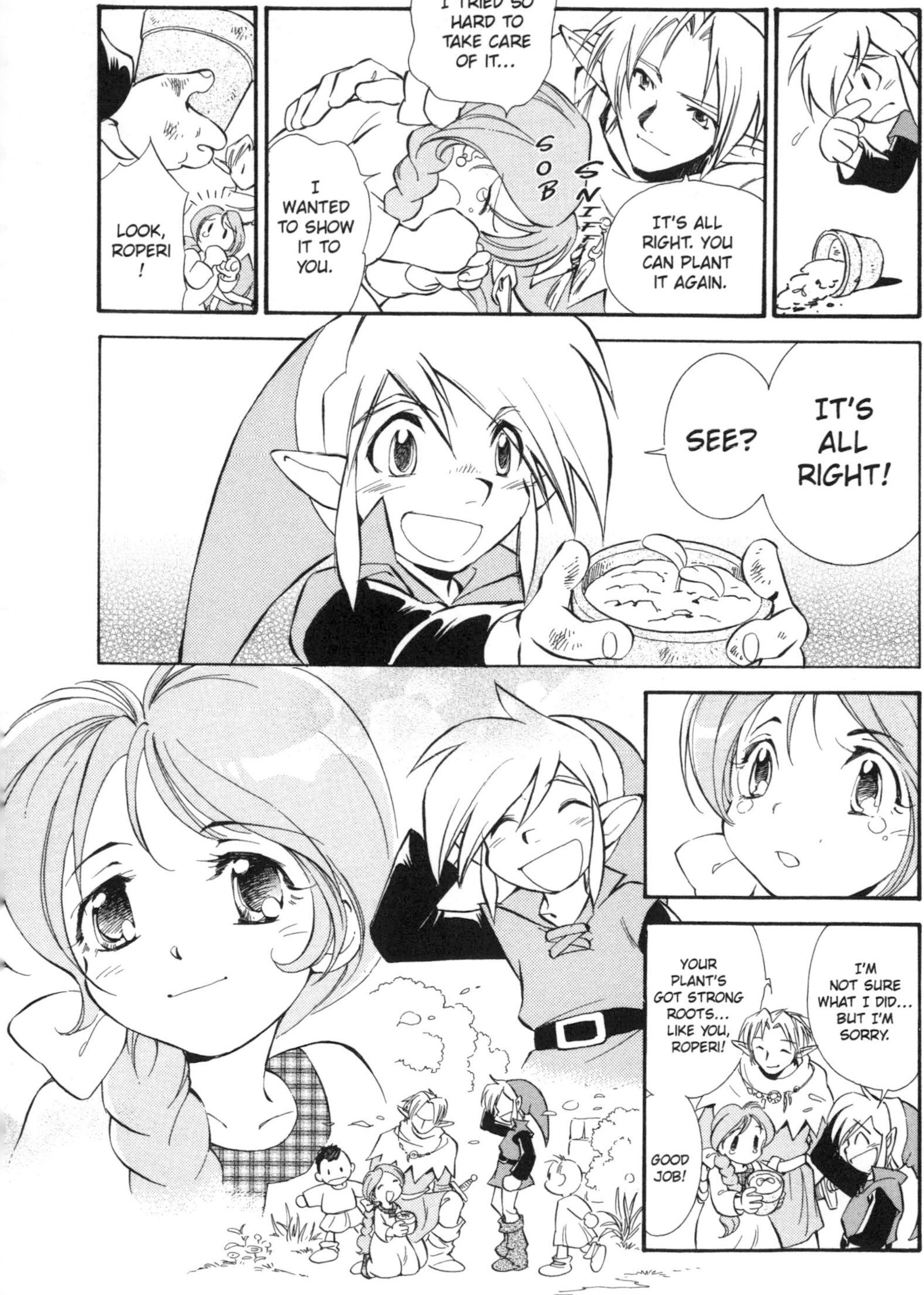
I TRIED SO HARD TO TAKE CARE OF IT...
SNIFF
SOB
I WANTED TO SHOW IT TO YOU.
IT'S ALL RIGHT. YOU CAN PLANT IT AGAIN.
LOOK, ROPERI!
SEE? IT'S ALL RIGHT!
I'M NOT SURE WHAT I DID... BUT I'M SORRY.
YOUR PLANT'S GOT STRONG ROOTS... LIKE YOU, ROPERI!
GOOD JOB!

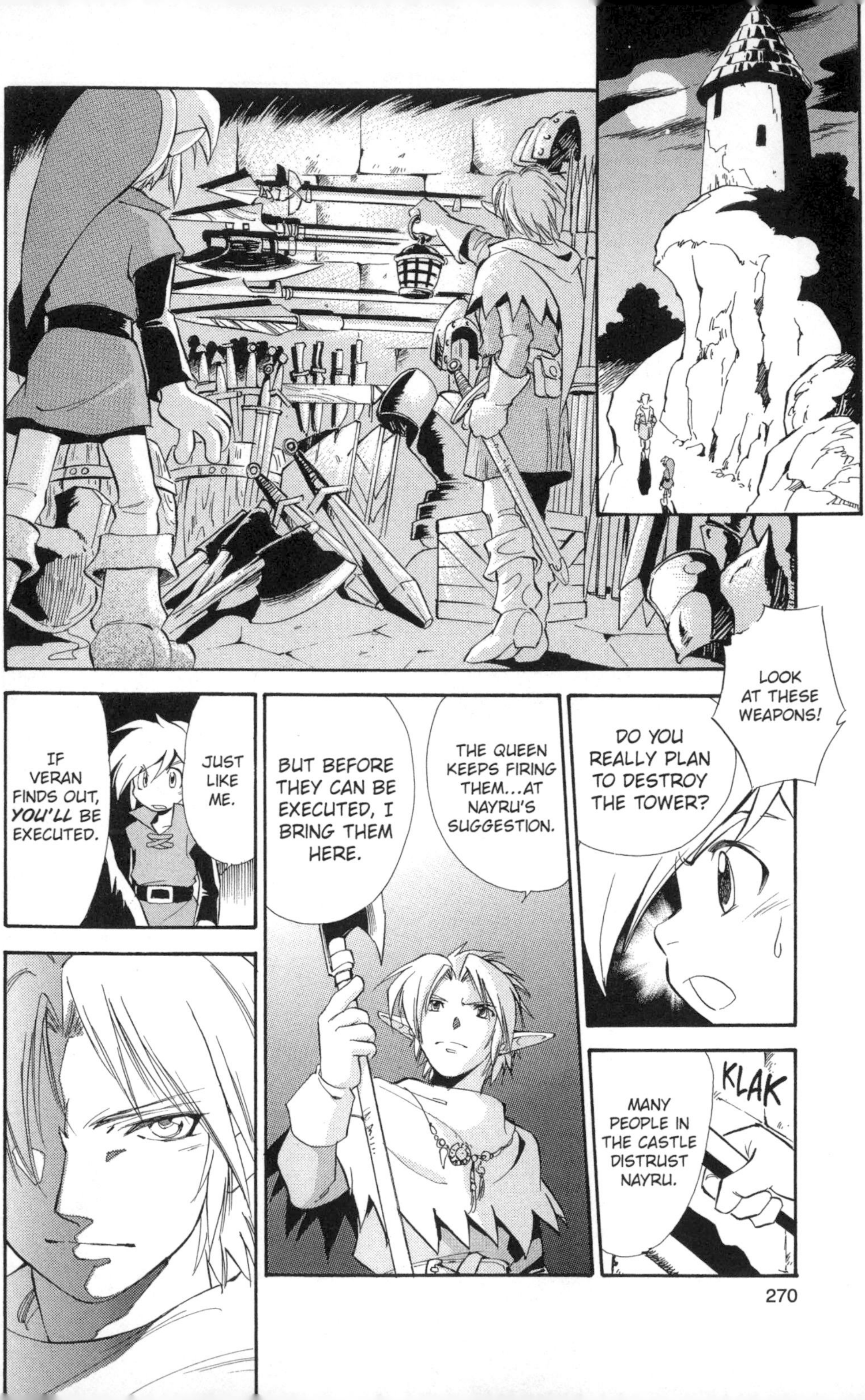
LOOK AT THESE WEAPONS!
DO YOU REALLY PLAN TO DESTROY THE TOWER?
KLAK
MANY PEOPLE IN THE CASTLE DISTRUST NAYRU.
THE QUEEN KEEPS FIRING THEM...AT NAYRU'S SUGGESTION.
BUT BEFORE THEY CAN BE EXECUTED, I BRING THEM HERE.
JUST LIKE ME.
IF VERAN FINDS OUT, *YOU'LL* BE EXECUTED.

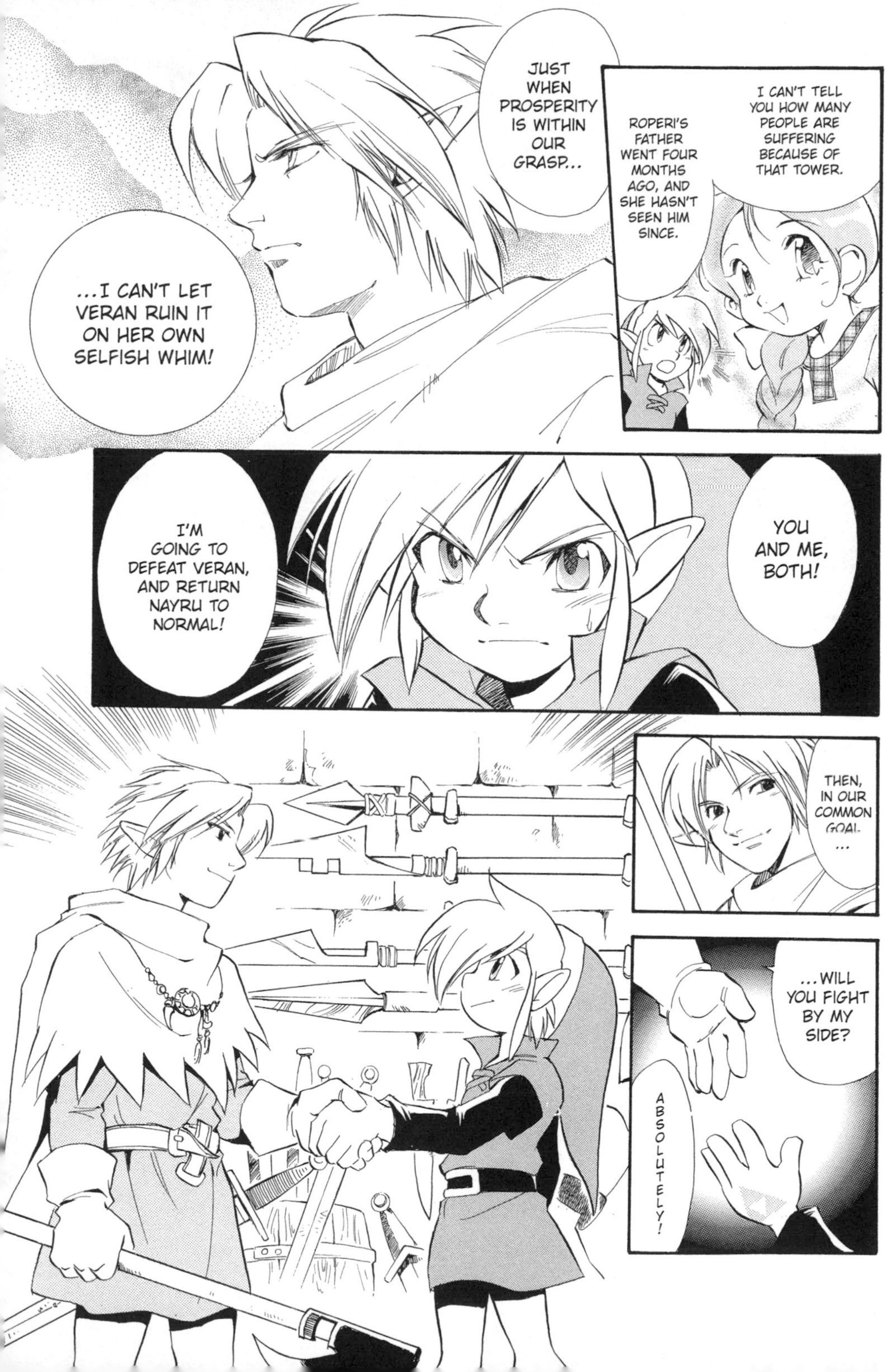
I CAN'T TELL YOU HOW MANY PEOPLE ARE SUFFERING BECAUSE OF THAT TOWER.
ROPERI'S FATHER WENT FOUR MONTHS AGO, AND SHE HASN'T SEEN HIM SINCE.
JUST WHEN PROSPERITY IS WITHIN OUR GRASP...
...I CAN'T LET VERAN RUIN IT ON HER OWN SELFISH WHIM!
YOU AND ME, BOTH!
I'M GOING TO DEFEAT VERAN, AND RETURN NAYRU TO NORMAL!
THEN, IN OUR COMMON GOAL...
...WILL YOU FIGHT BY MY SIDE?
ABSOLUTELY!

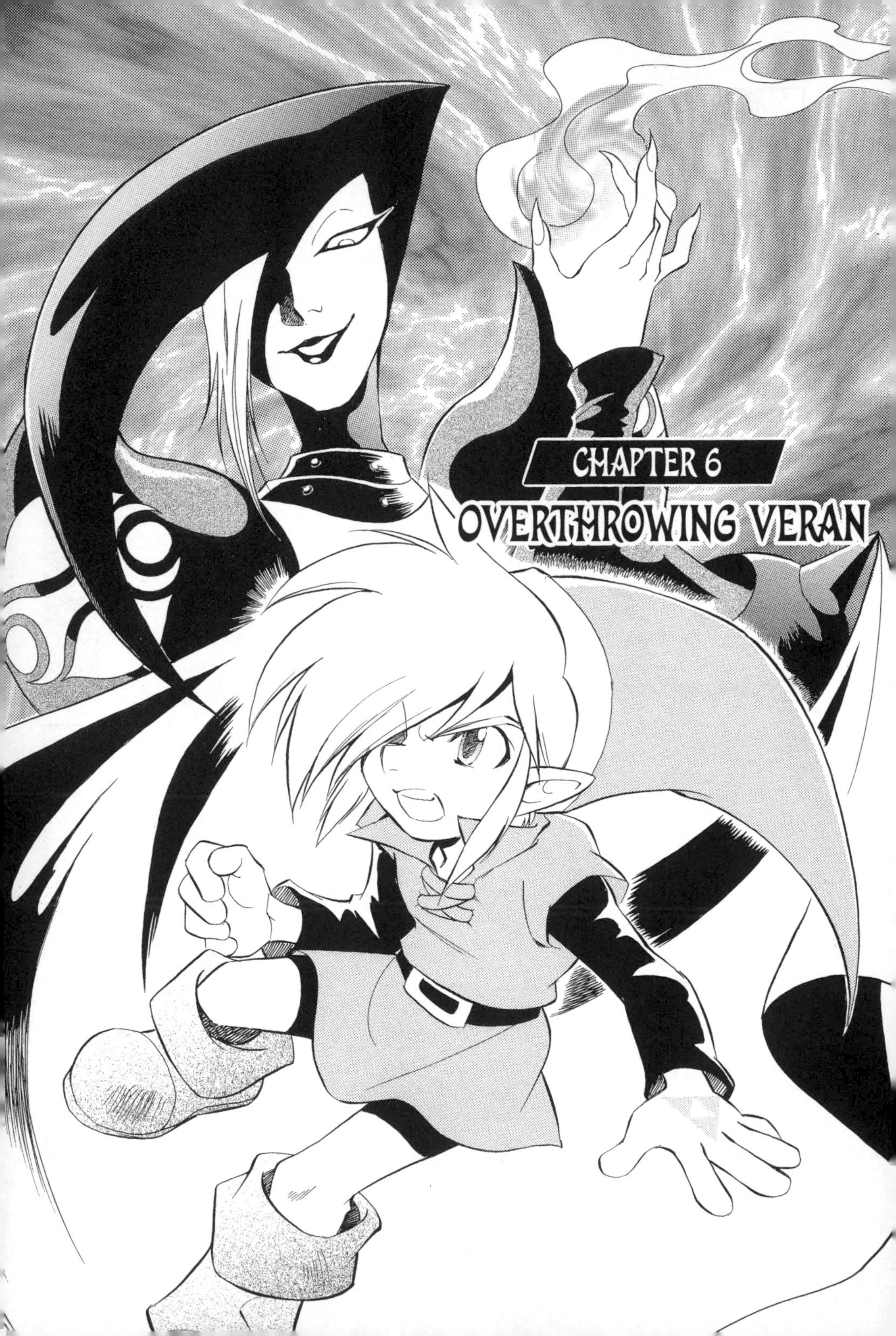
CHAPTER 6
OVERTHROWING VERAN

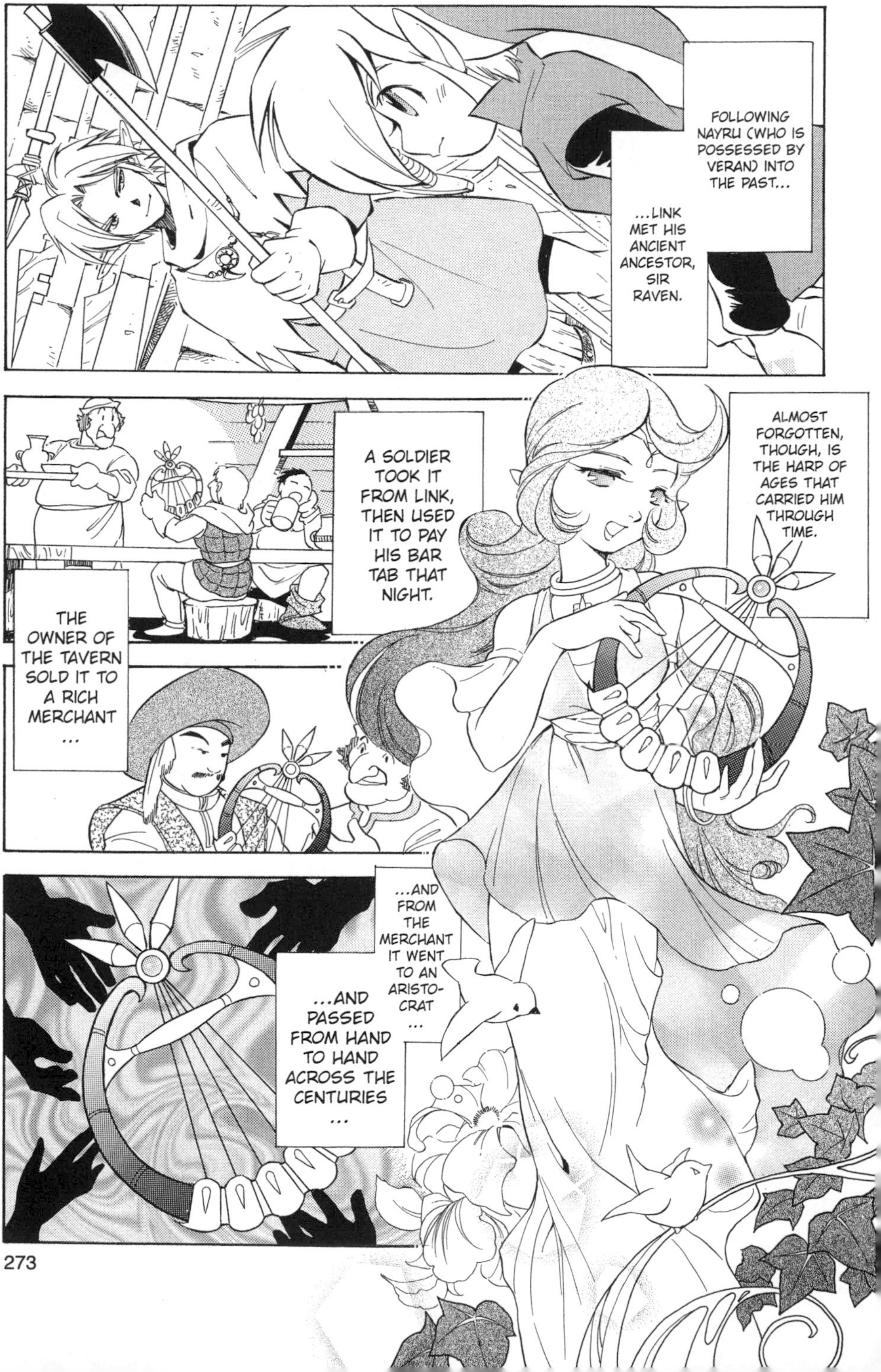
FOLLOWING NAYRU (WHO IS POSSESSED BY VERAN) INTO THE PAST...
...LINK MET HIS ANCIENT ANCESTOR, SIR RAVEN.
ALMOST FORGOTTEN, THOUGH, IS THE HARP OF AGES THAT CARRIED HIM THROUGH TIME.
A SOLDIER TOOK IT FROM LINK, THEN USED IT TO PAY HIS BAR TAB THAT NIGHT.
THE OWNER OF THE TAVERN SOLD IT TO A RICH MERCHANT...
...AND FROM THE MERCHANT IT WENT TO AN ARISTOCRAT...
...AND PASSED FROM HAND TO HAND ACROSS THE CENTURIES...

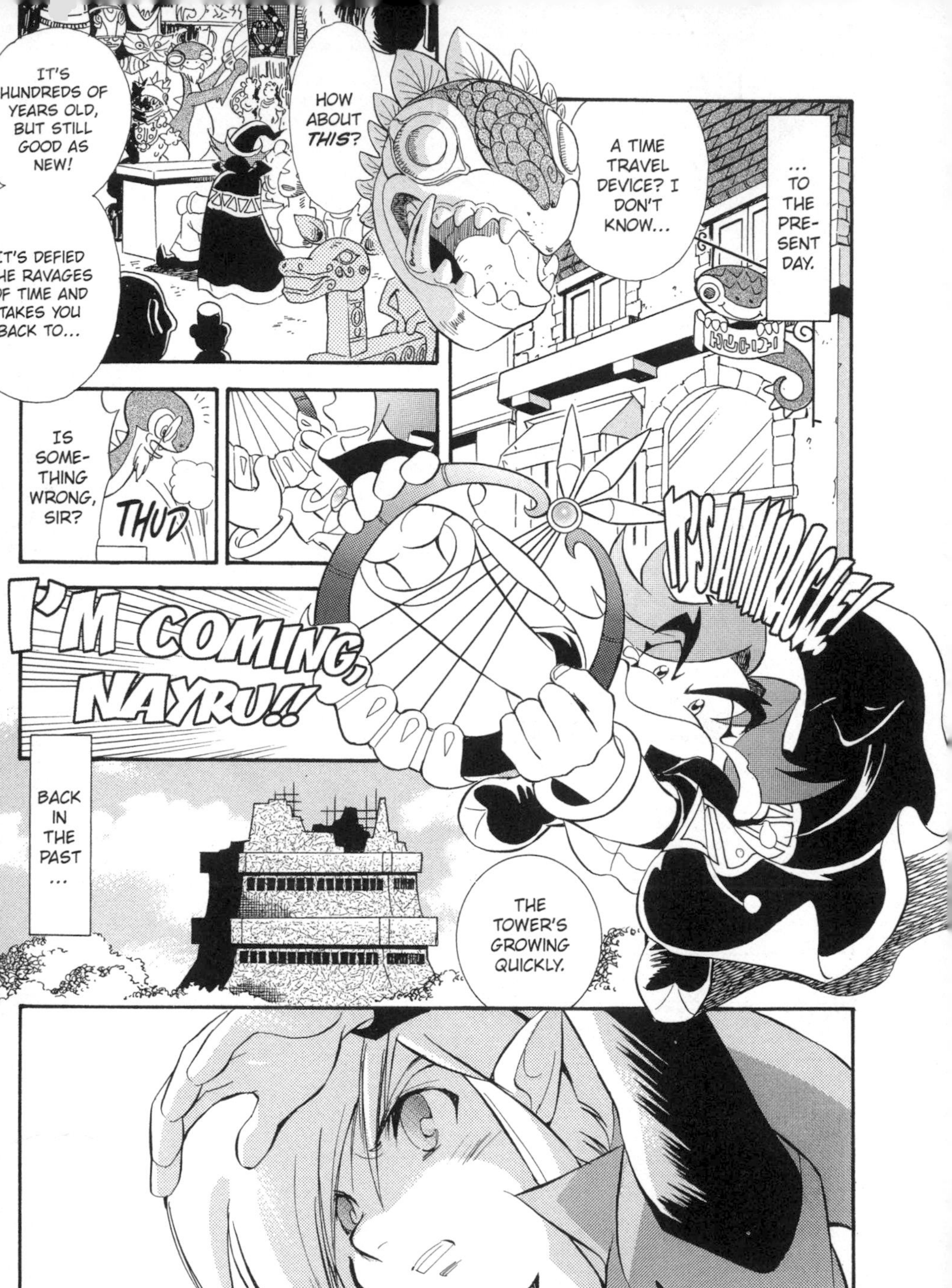

...TO THE PRESENT DAY.
A TIME TRAVEL DEVICE? I DON'T KNOW...
HOW ABOUT *THIS*?
IT'S HUNDREDS OF YEARS OLD, BUT STILL GOOD AS NEW!
IT'S DEFIED THE RAVAGES OF TIME AND TAKES YOU BACK TO...
IS SOMETHING WRONG, SIR?
THUD
IT'S A MIRACLE!
I'M COMING, NAYRU!!
BACK IN THE PAST...
THE TOWER'S GROWING QUICKLY.

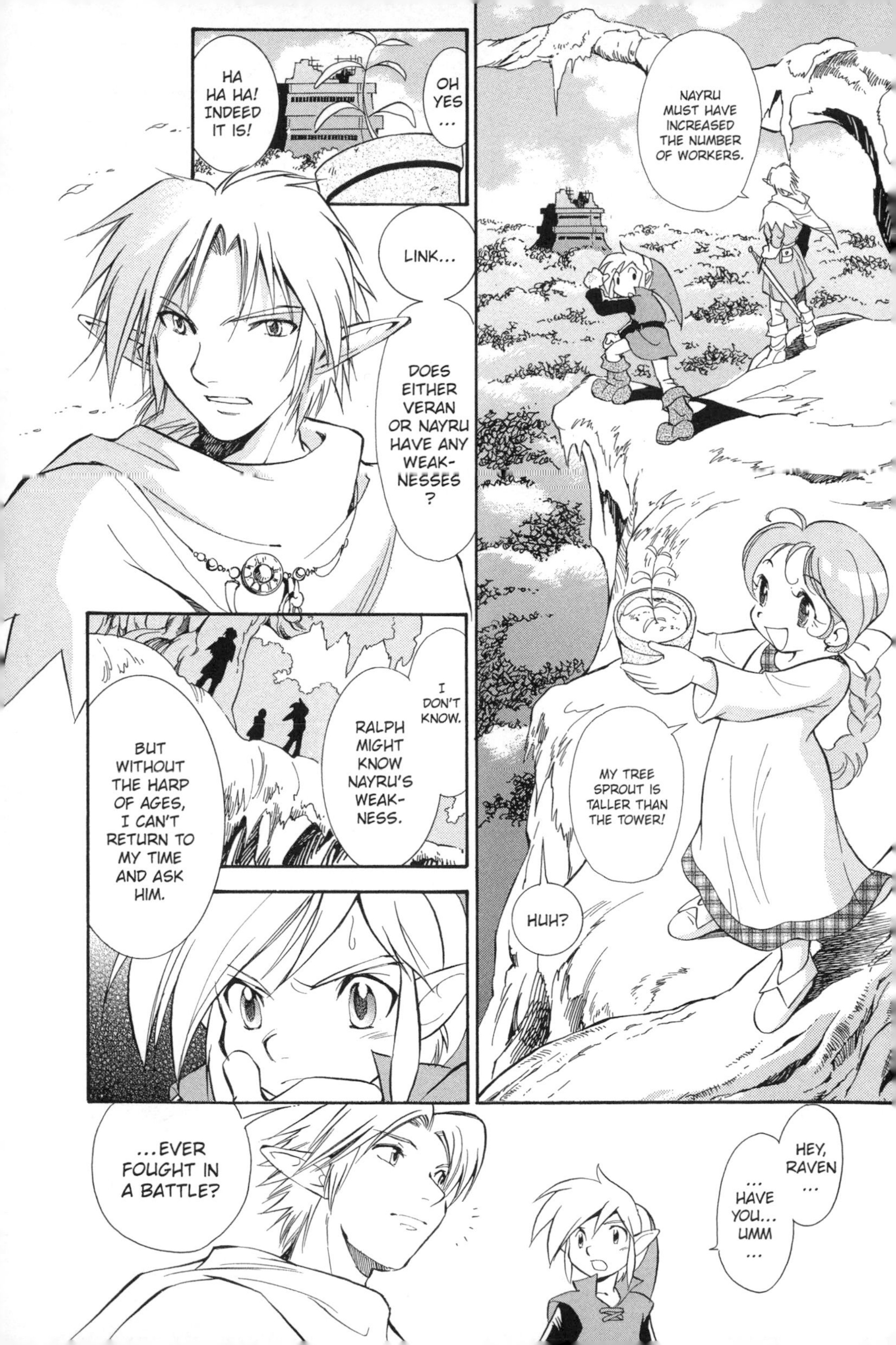
NAYRU MUST HAVE INCREASED THE NUMBER OF WORKERS.
MY TREE SPROUT IS TALLER THAN THE TOWER!
HUH?
OH YES ...
HA HA HA! INDEED IT IS!
LINK...
DOES EITHER VERAN OR NAYRU HAVE ANY WEAK-NESSES ?
I DON'T KNOW.
RALPH MIGHT KNOW NAYRU'S WEAK-NESS.
BUT WITHOUT THE HARP OF AGES, I CAN'T RETURN TO MY TIME AND ASK HIM.
HEY, RAVEN ...
... HAVE YOU... UMM ...
...EVER FOUGHT IN A BATTLE?

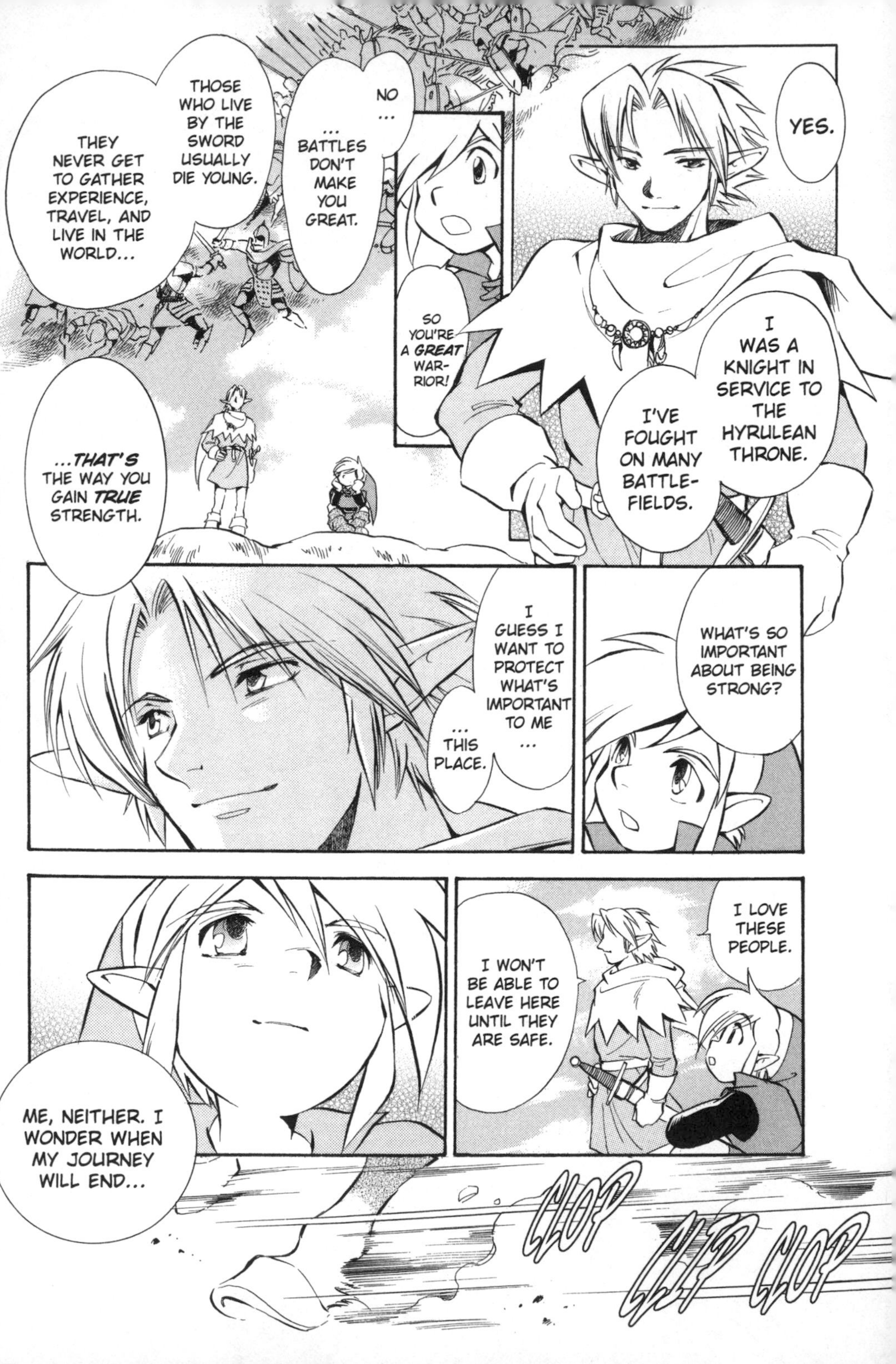
YES.
I WAS A KNIGHT IN SERVICE TO THE HYRULEAN THRONE.
I'VE FOUGHT ON MANY BATTLE-FIELDS.
SO YOU'RE A *GREAT* WAR-RIOR!
NO ...
... BATTLES DON'T MAKE YOU GREAT.
THOSE WHO LIVE BY THE SWORD USUALLY DIE YOUNG.
THEY NEVER GET TO GATHER EXPERIENCE, TRAVEL, AND LIVE IN THE WORLD...
...*THAT'S* THE WAY YOU GAIN *TRUE* STRENGTH.
WHAT'S SO IMPORTANT ABOUT BEING STRONG?
I GUESS I WANT TO PROTECT WHAT'S IMPORTANT TO ME ...
... THIS PLACE.
I LOVE THESE PEOPLE.
I WON'T BE ABLE TO LEAVE HERE UNTIL THEY ARE SAFE.
ME, NEITHER. I WONDER WHEN MY JOURNEY WILL END...
CLOP
CLOP CLOP

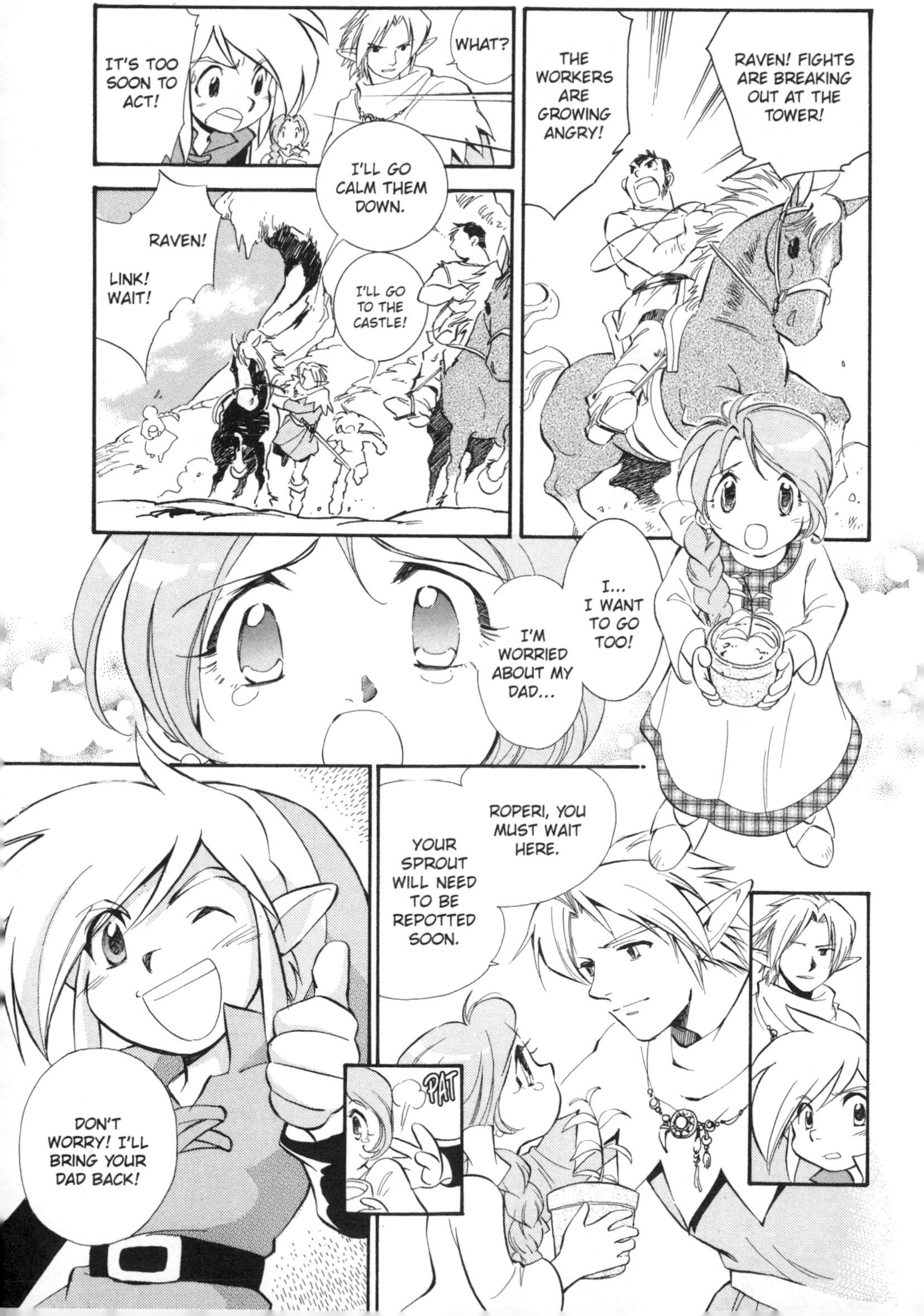
RAVEN! FIGHTS ARE BREAKING OUT AT THE TOWER!
THE WORKERS ARE GROWING ANGRY!
WHAT?
IT'S TOO SOON TO ACT!
I'LL GO CALM THEM DOWN.
I'LL GO TO THE CASTLE!
RAVEN!
LINK! WAIT!
I... I WANT TO GO TOO!
I'M WORRIED ABOUT MY DAD...
ROPERI, YOU MUST WAIT HERE.
YOUR SPROUT WILL NEED TO BE REPOTTED SOON.
PAT
DON'T WORRY! I'LL BRING YOUR DAD BACK!

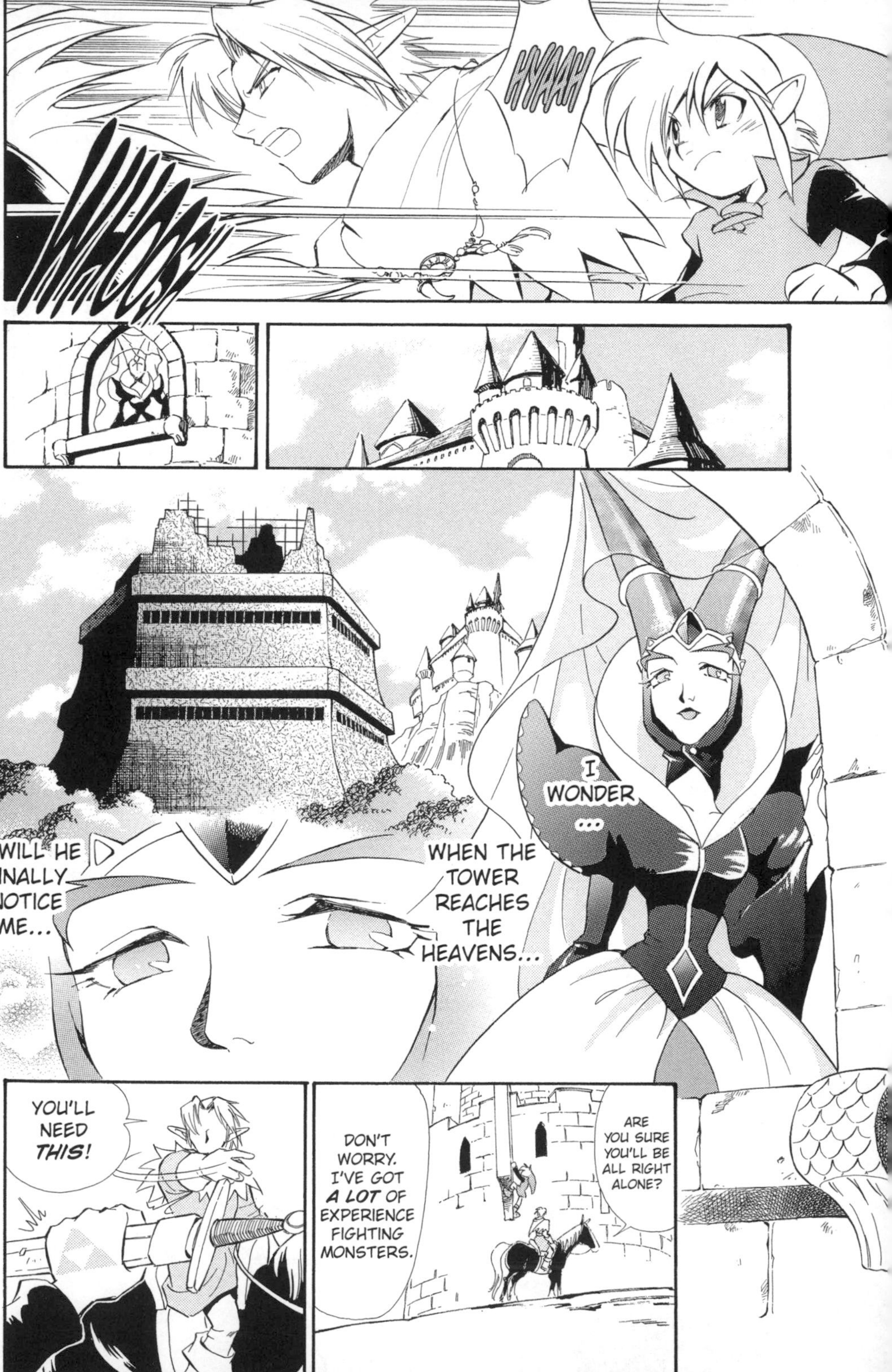
HYAAAH
WHOOSH!
I WONDER...
WHEN THE TOWER REACHES THE HEAVENS...
...WILL HE FINALLY NOTICE ME...
ARE YOU SURE YOU'LL BE ALL RIGHT ALONE?
DON'T WORRY. I'VE GOT ***A LOT*** OF EXPERIENCE FIGHTING MONSTERS.
YOU'LL NEED ***THIS***!

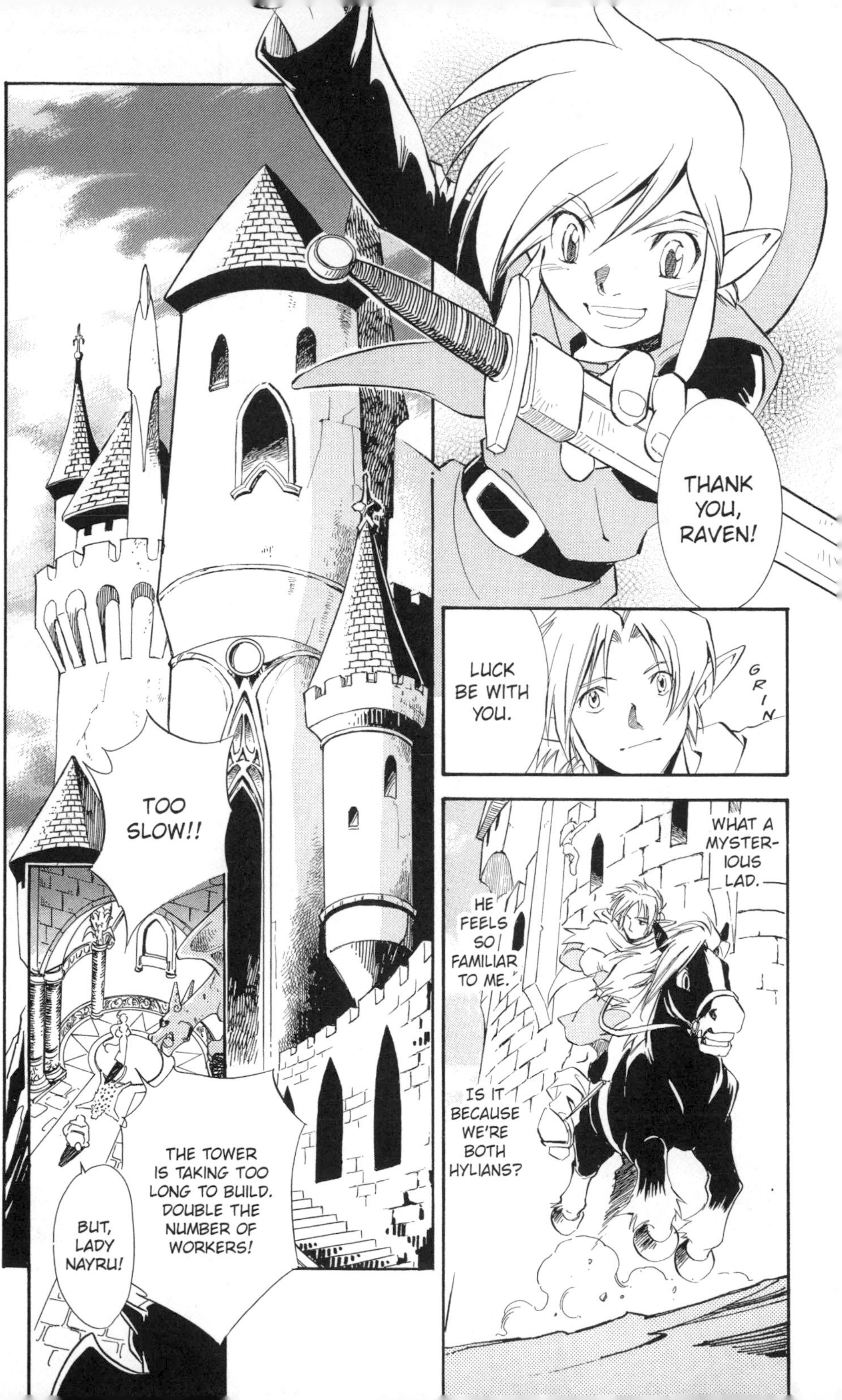
THANK YOU, RAVEN!
GRIN
LUCK BE WITH YOU.
WHAT A MYSTERIOUS LAD.
HE FEELS SO FAMILIAR TO ME.
IS IT BECAUSE WE'RE BOTH HYLIANS?
TOO SLOW!!
THE TOWER IS TAKING TOO LONG TO BUILD. DOUBLE THE NUMBER OF WORKERS!
BUT, LADY NAYRU!

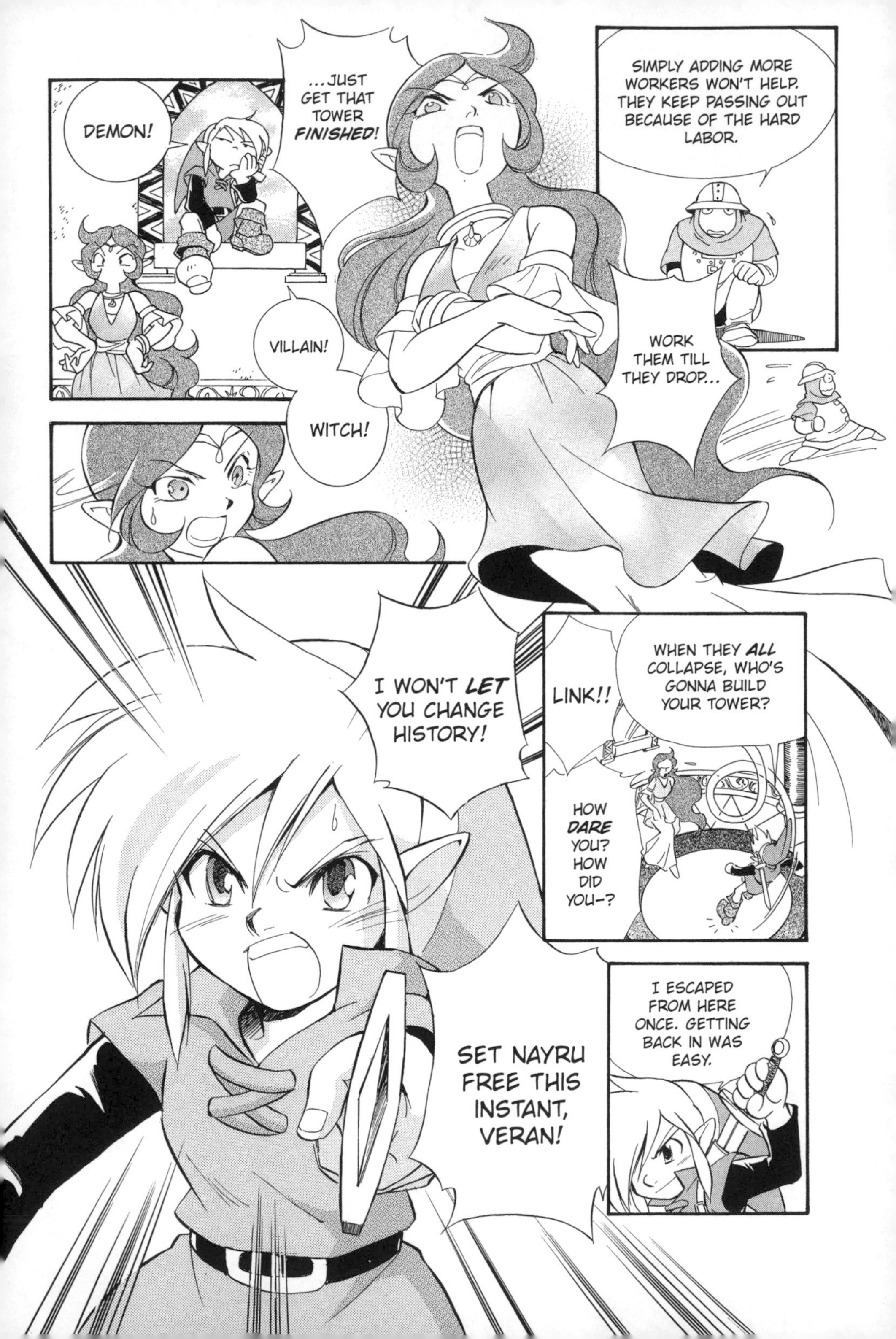
SIMPLY ADDING MORE WORKERS WON'T HELP. THEY KEEP PASSING OUT BECAUSE OF THE HARD LABOR.
WORK THEM TILL THEY DROP...
...JUST GET THAT TOWER *FINISHED*!
DEMON!
VILLAIN!
WITCH!
WHEN THEY *ALL* COLLAPSE, WHO'S GONNA BUILD YOUR TOWER?
LINK!!
HOW *DARE* YOU? HOW DID YOU-?
I ESCAPED FROM HERE ONCE. GETTING BACK IN WAS EASY.
I WON'T *LET* YOU CHANGE HISTORY!
SET NAYRU FREE THIS INSTANT, VERAN!

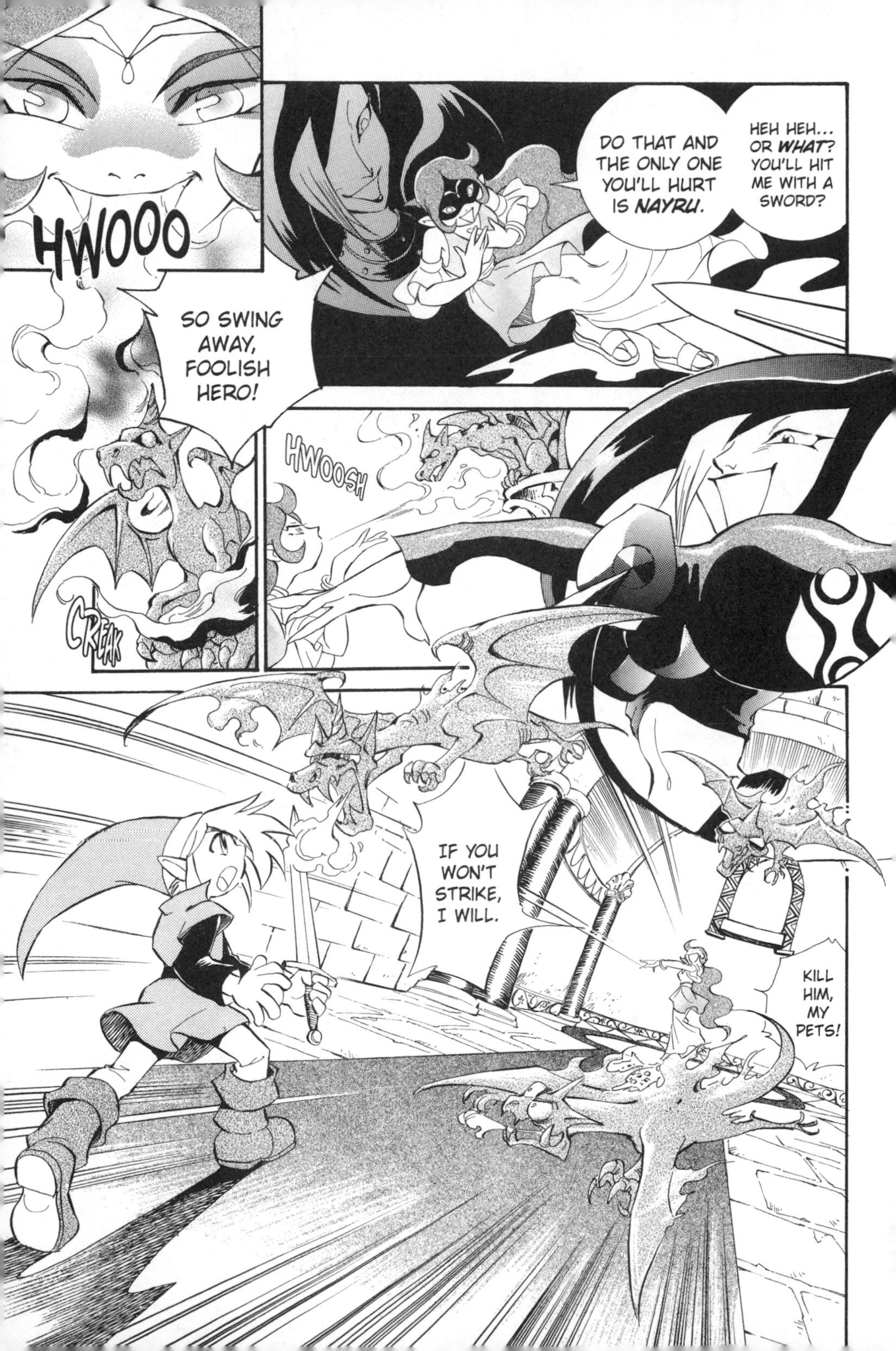
HEH HEH... OR *WHAT*? YOU'LL HIT ME WITH A SWORD?
DO THAT AND THE ONLY ONE YOU'LL HURT IS *NAYRU*.
SO SWING AWAY, FOOLISH HERO!
HWOOO
HWOOSH
CREAK
IF YOU WON'T STRIKE, I WILL.
KILL HIM, MY PETS!

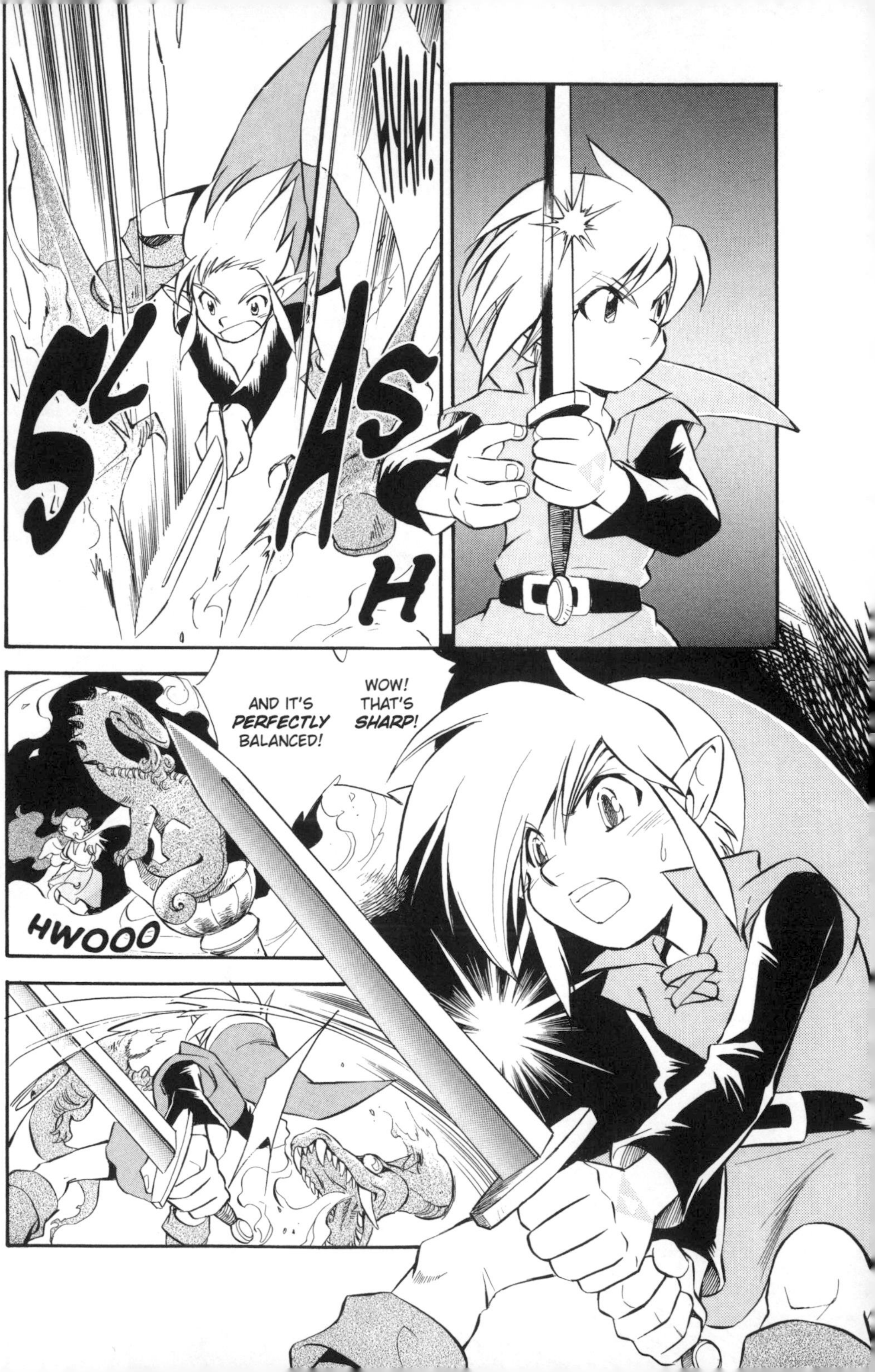
HYAH!
SLASH
WOW! THAT'S SHARP!
AND IT'S PERFECTLY BALANCED!
HWOOO

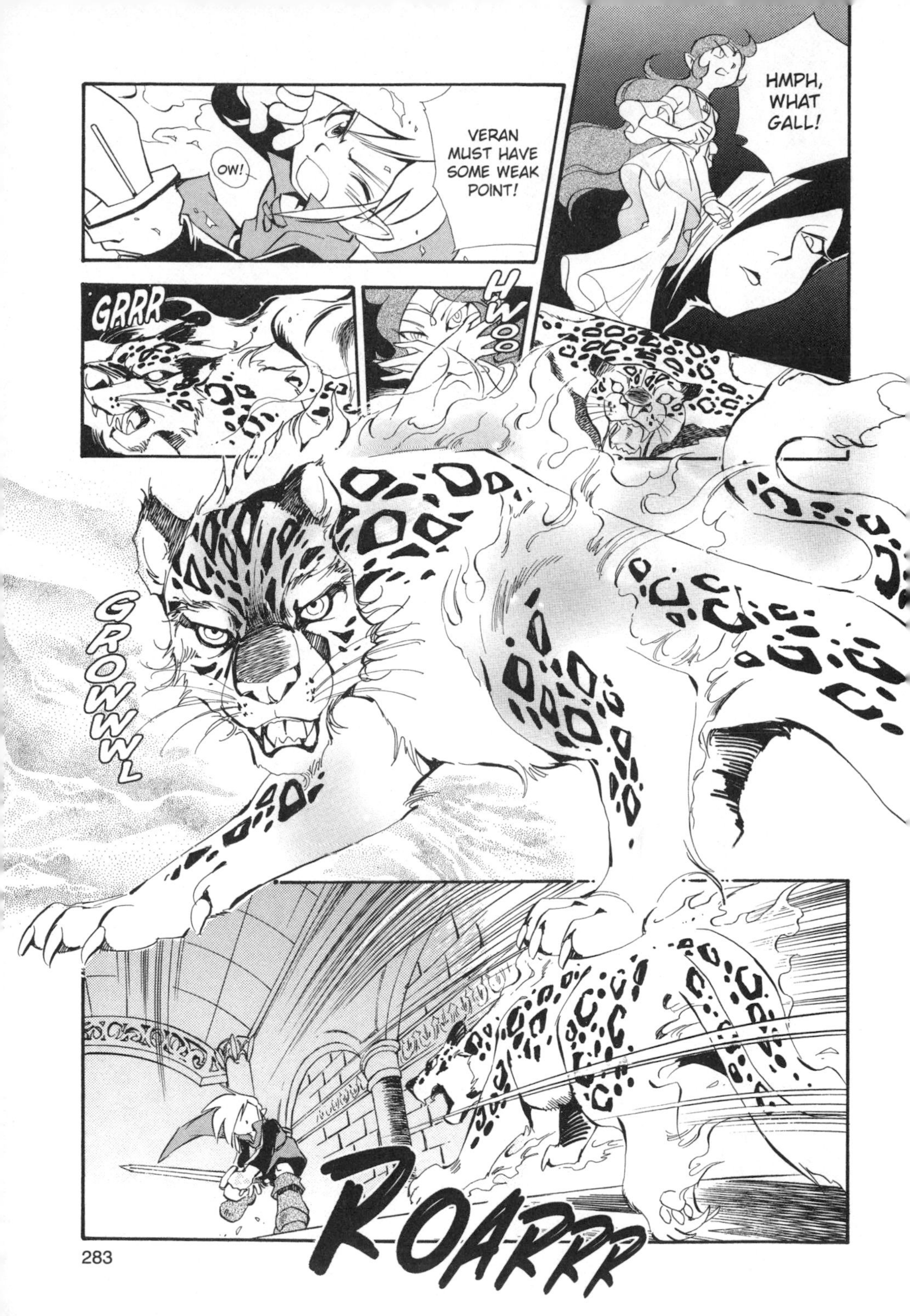
HMPH, WHAT GALL!
VERAN MUST HAVE SOME WEAK POINT!
OW!
HWOO
GRRR
GROWWWL
ROARRR

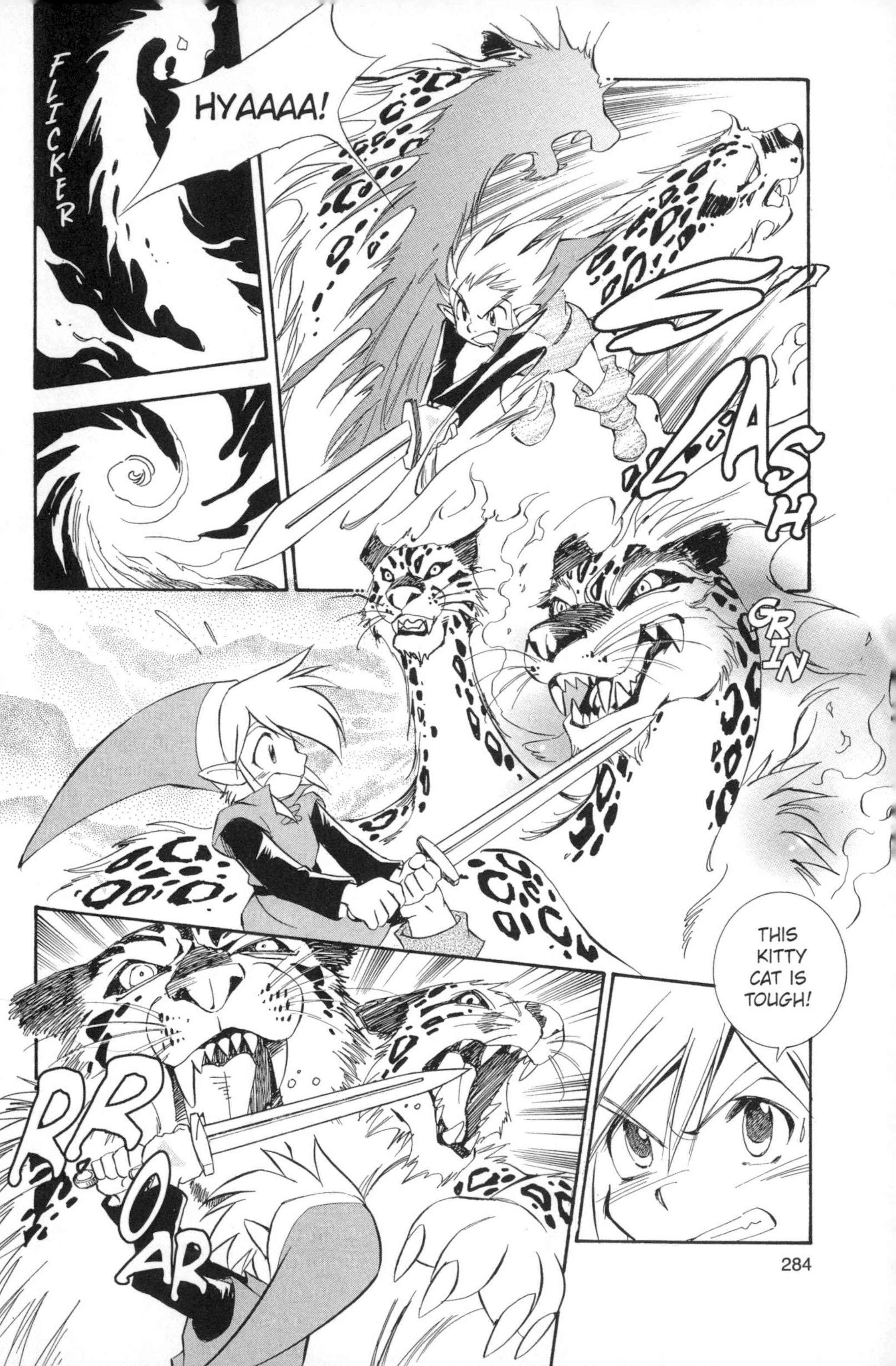
HYAAAA!
ZASH
FLICKER
GRIN
THIS KITTY CAT IS TOUGH!
RROOAR

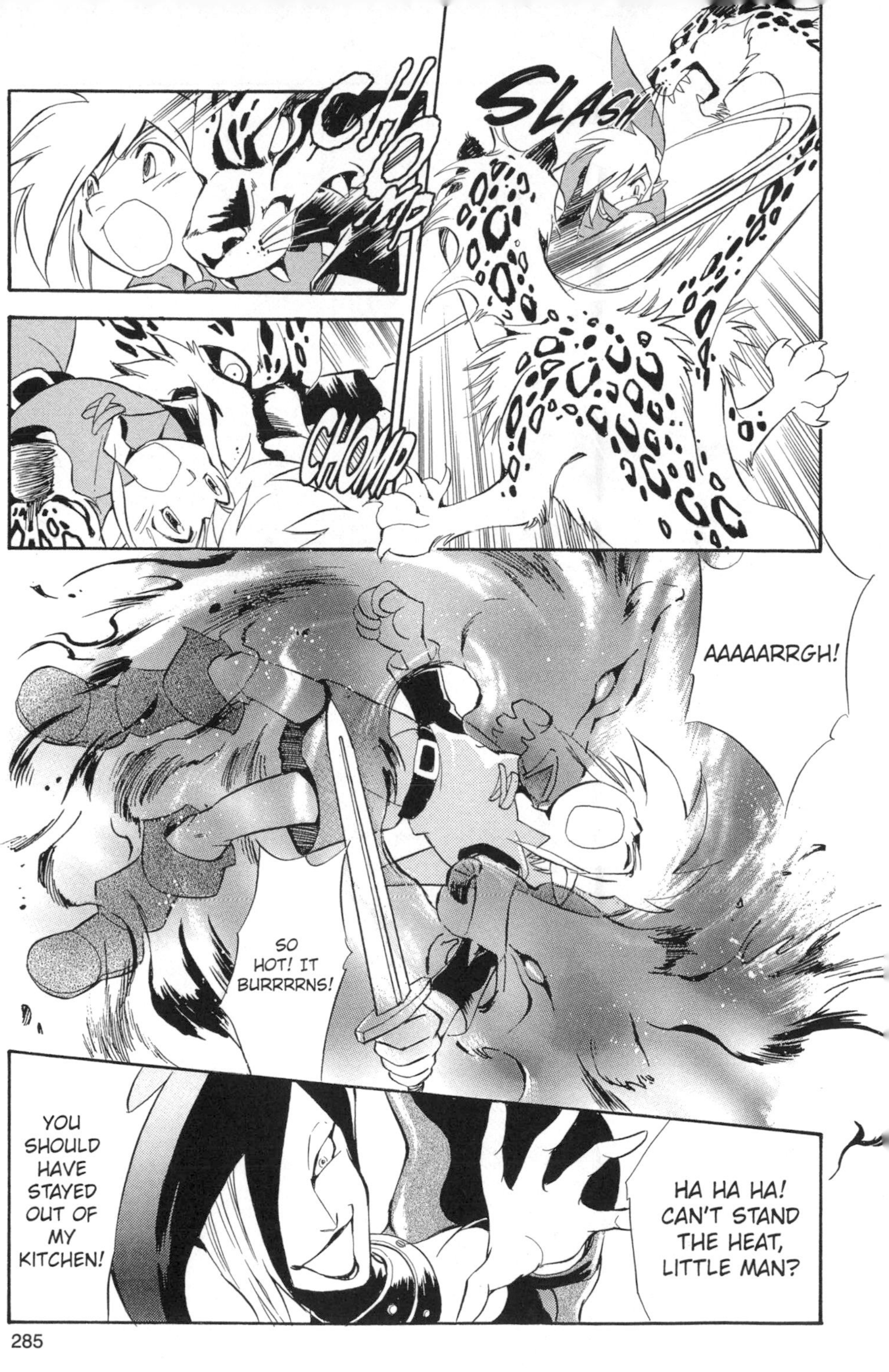
SLASH
CHOMP
AAAAARRGH!
SO HOT! IT BURRRRNS!
HA HA HA! CAN'T STAND THE HEAT, LITTLE MAN?
YOU SHOULD HAVE STAYED OUT OF MY KITCHEN!

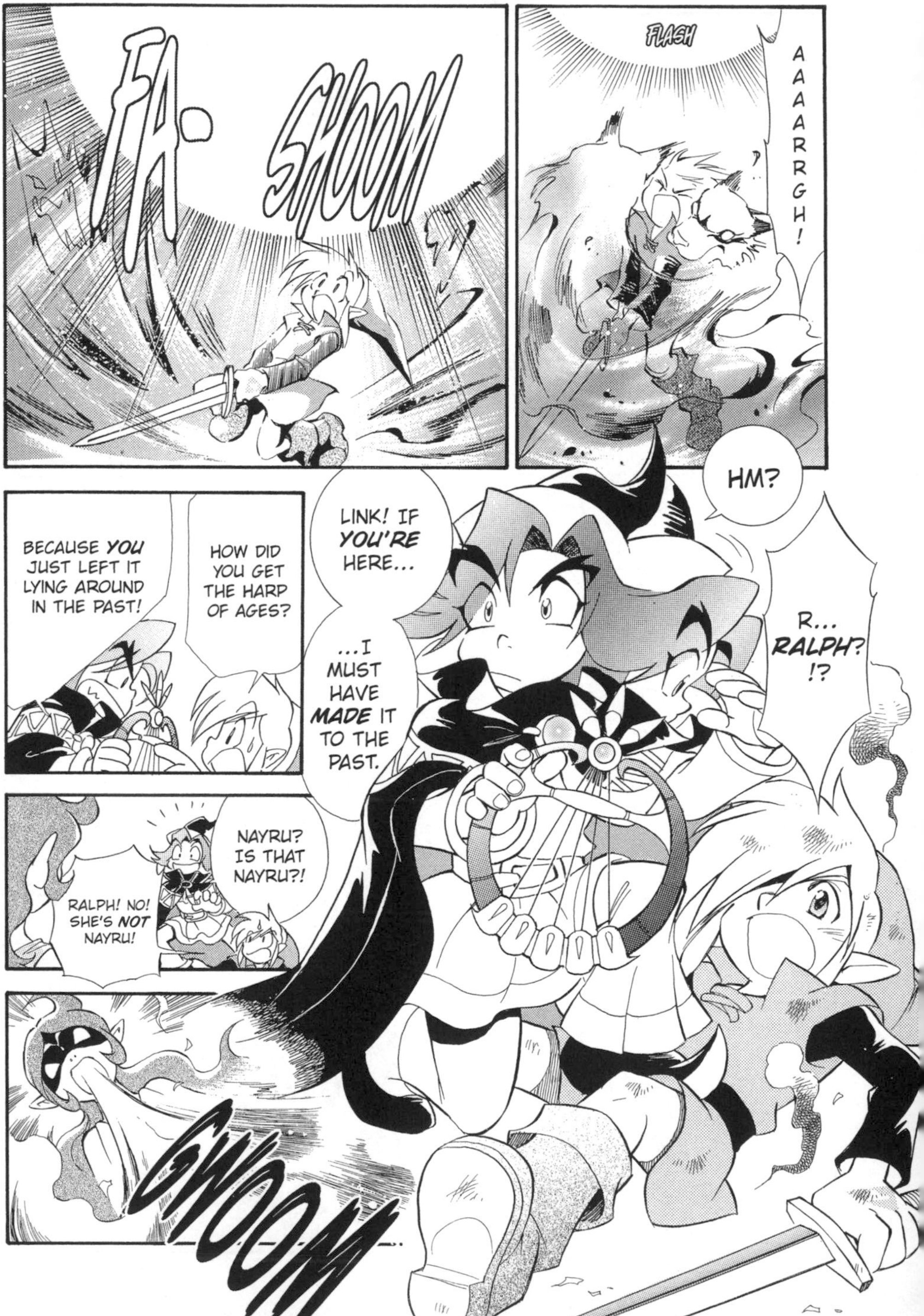
FLASH
AAAAARRGH!
FA-SHOOM
HM?
LINK! IF ***YOU'RE*** HERE...
R... ***RALPH***?!?
...I MUST HAVE ***MADE*** IT TO THE PAST.
HOW DID YOU GET THE HARP OF AGES?
BECAUSE ***YOU*** JUST LEFT IT LYING AROUND IN THE PAST!
NAYRU? IS THAT NAYRU?!
RALPH! NO! SHE'S ***NOT*** NAYRU!
GWOOM

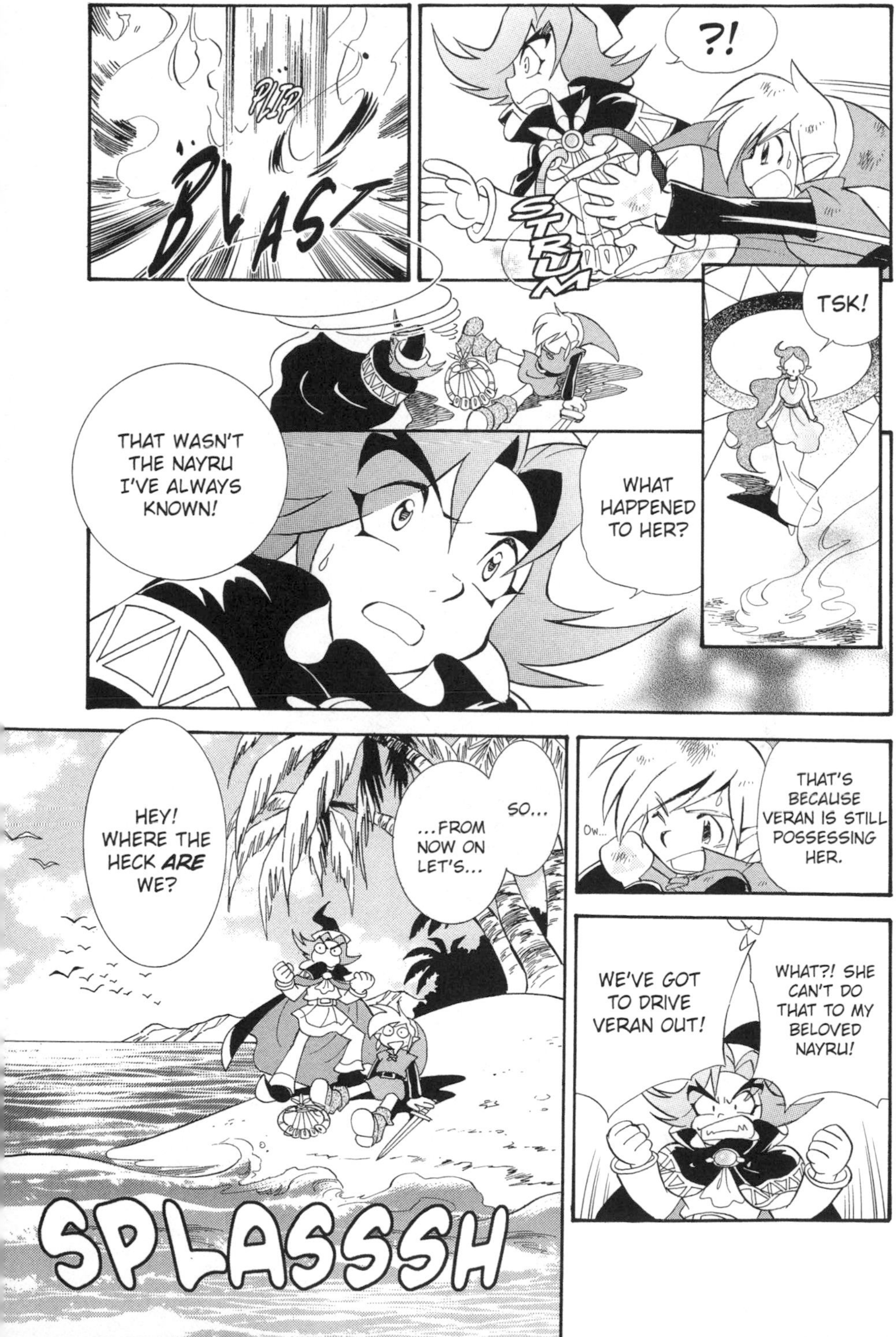

?!
STRUM
PLIP
BLAST
TSK!
WHAT HAPPENED TO HER?
THAT WASN'T THE NAYRU I'VE ALWAYS KNOWN!
THAT'S BECAUSE VERAN IS STILL POSSESSING HER.
OW...
WHAT?! SHE CAN'T DO THAT TO MY BELOVED NAYRU!
WE'VE GOT TO DRIVE VERAN OUT!
SO...
...FROM NOW ON LET'S...
HEY! WHERE THE HECK *ARE* WE?
SPLASSSH

ROUGH CHARACTER
ILLUSTRATION 6

Any way you look at her,
she's the bold mother type.

Impa

2000·10·11

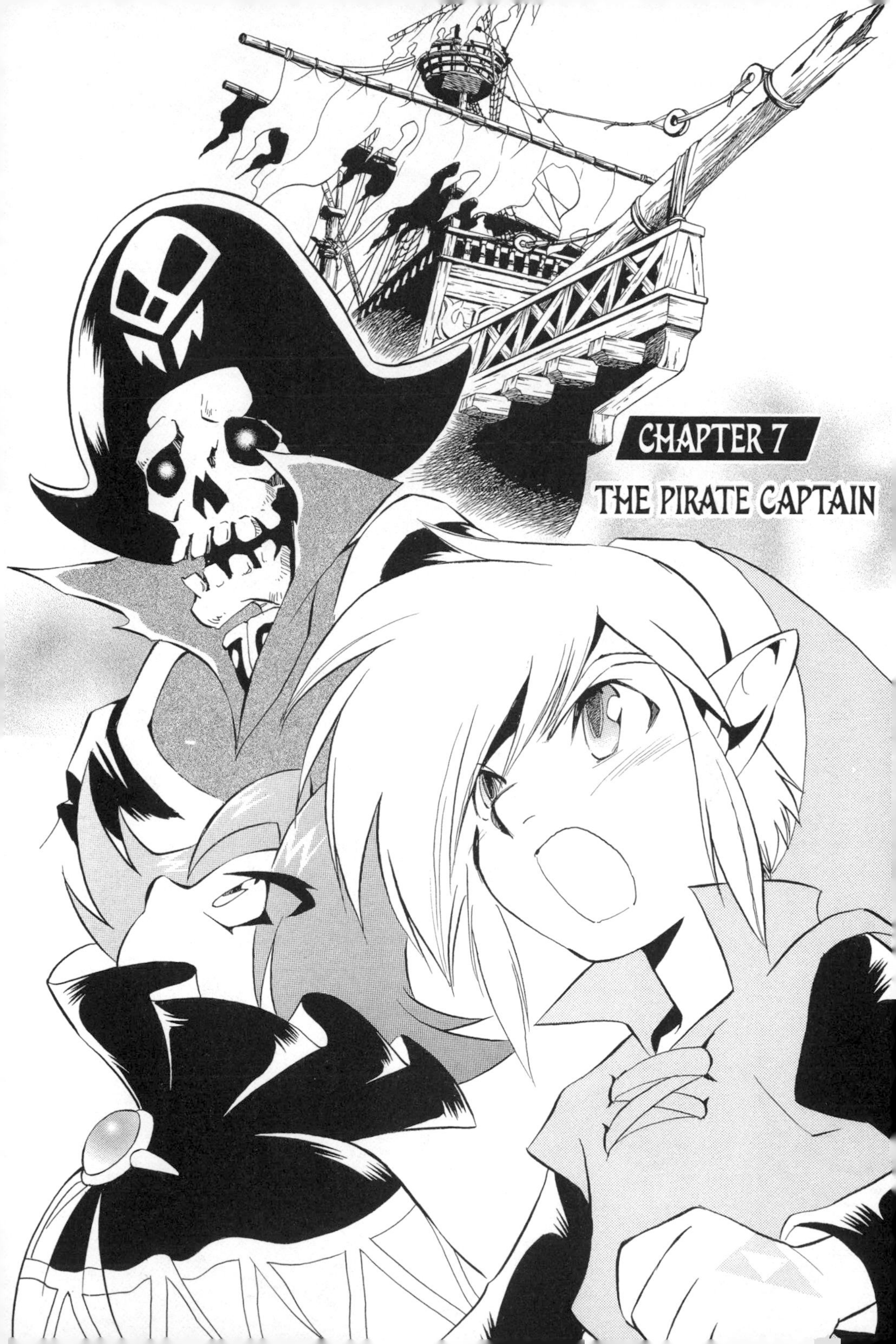
CHAPTER 7
THE PIRATE CAPTAIN

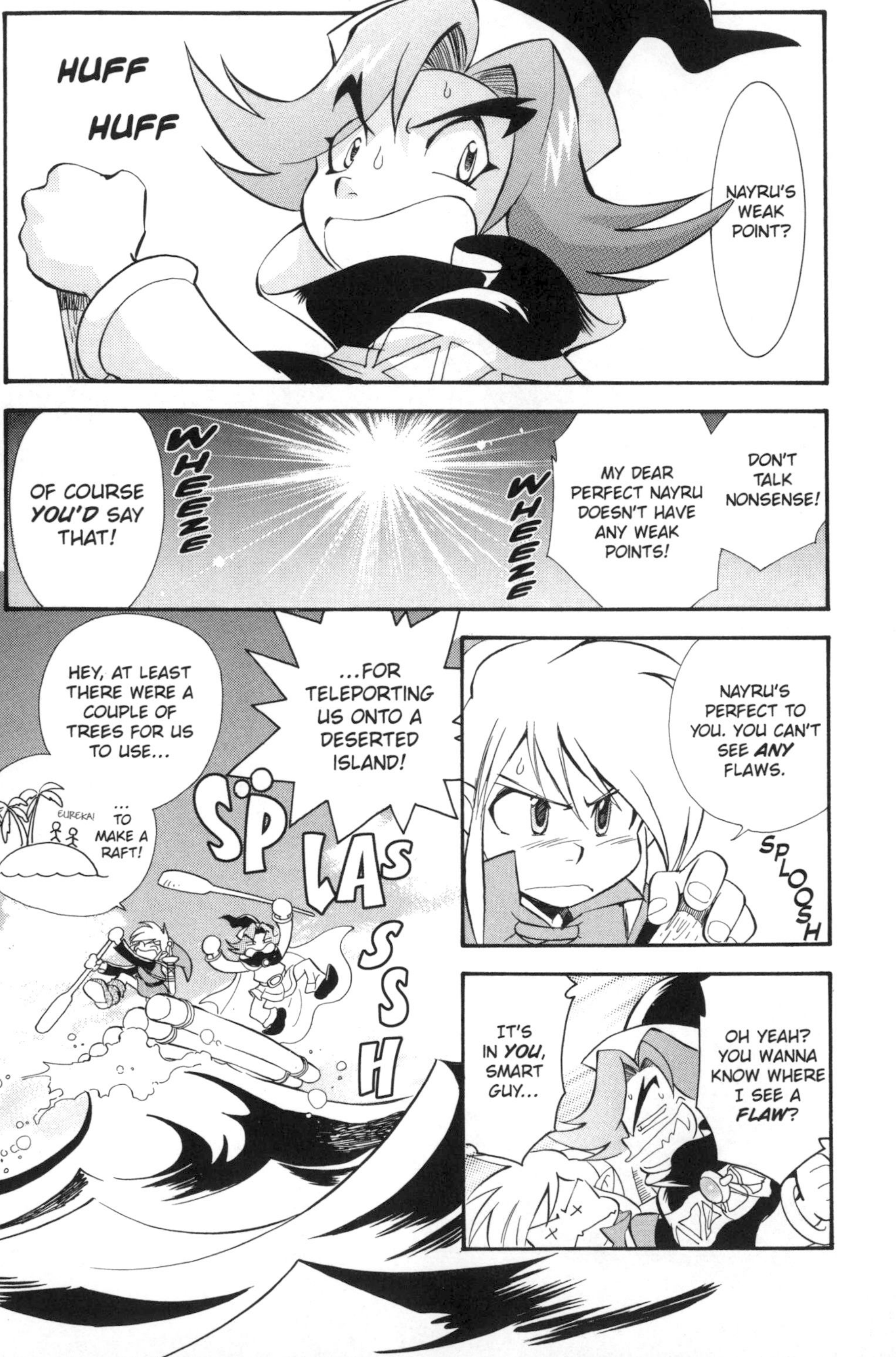
NAYRU'S WEAK POINT?
HUFF HUFF
DON'T TALK NONSENSE!
MY DEAR PERFECT NAYRU DOESN'T HAVE ANY WEAK POINTS!
WHEEZE
WHEEZE
OF COURSE *YOU'D* SAY THAT!
NAYRU'S PERFECT TO YOU. YOU CAN'T SEE *ANY* FLAWS.
SPLOOSH
OH YEAH? YOU WANNA KNOW WHERE I SEE A *FLAW*?
IT'S IN *YOU*, SMART GUY...
...FOR TELEPORTING US ONTO A DESERTED ISLAND!
HEY, AT LEAST THERE WERE A COUPLE OF TREES FOR US TO USE...
EUREKA!
...TO MAKE A RAFT!
SPLASSSH

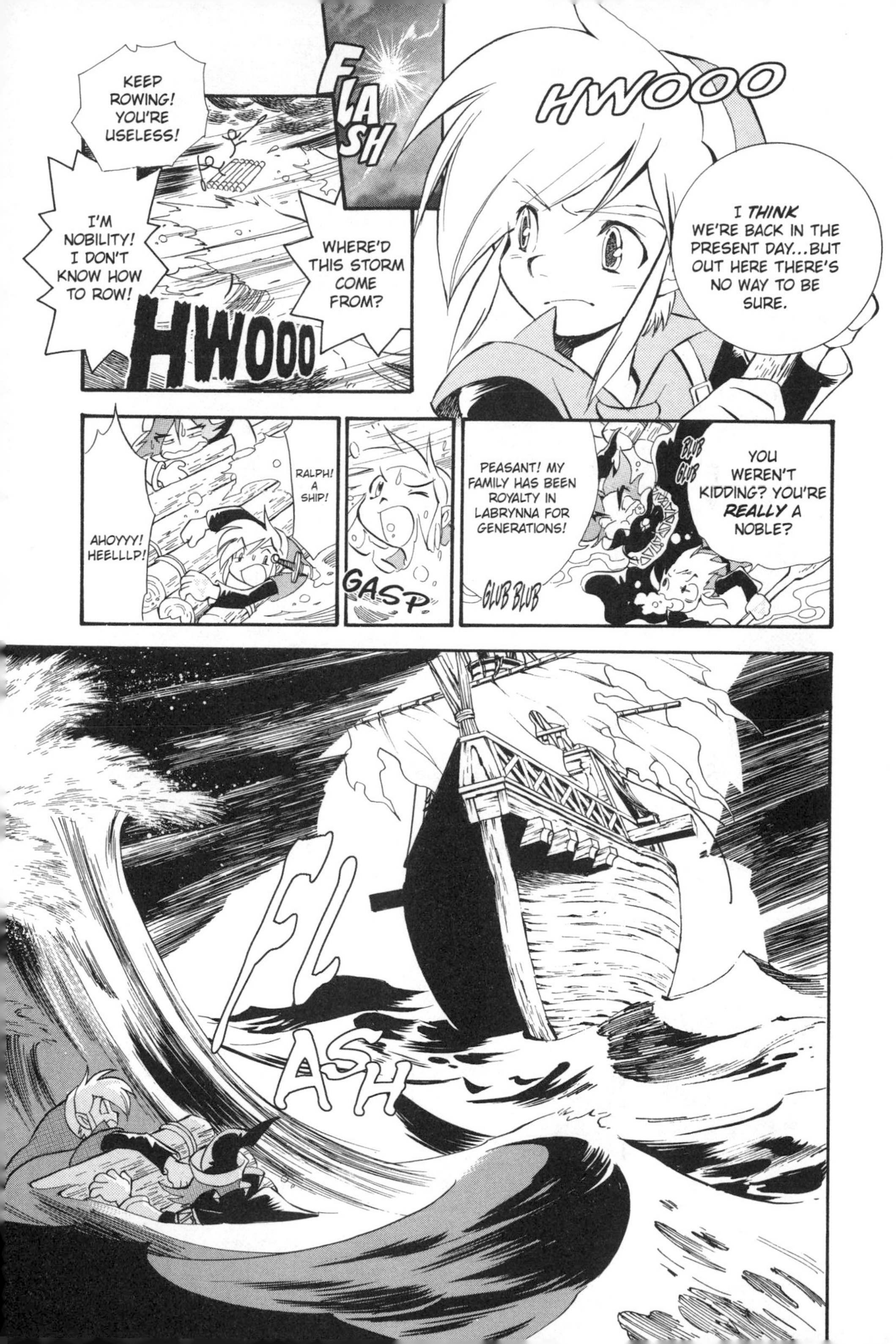
HWOOOO
I THINK WE'RE BACK IN THE PRESENT DAY...BUT OUT HERE THERE'S NO WAY TO BE SURE.
FLASH
KEEP ROWING! YOU'RE USELESS!
WHERE'D THIS STORM COME FROM?
I'M NOBILITY! I DON'T KNOW HOW TO ROW!
HWOOO
YOU WEREN'T KIDDING? YOU'RE REALLY A NOBLE?
BLUB BLUB
PEASANT! MY FAMILY HAS BEEN ROYALTY IN LABRYNNA FOR GENERATIONS!
GLUB BLUB
GASP
RALPH! A SHIP!
AHOYYY! HEELLLP!
FL
ASH

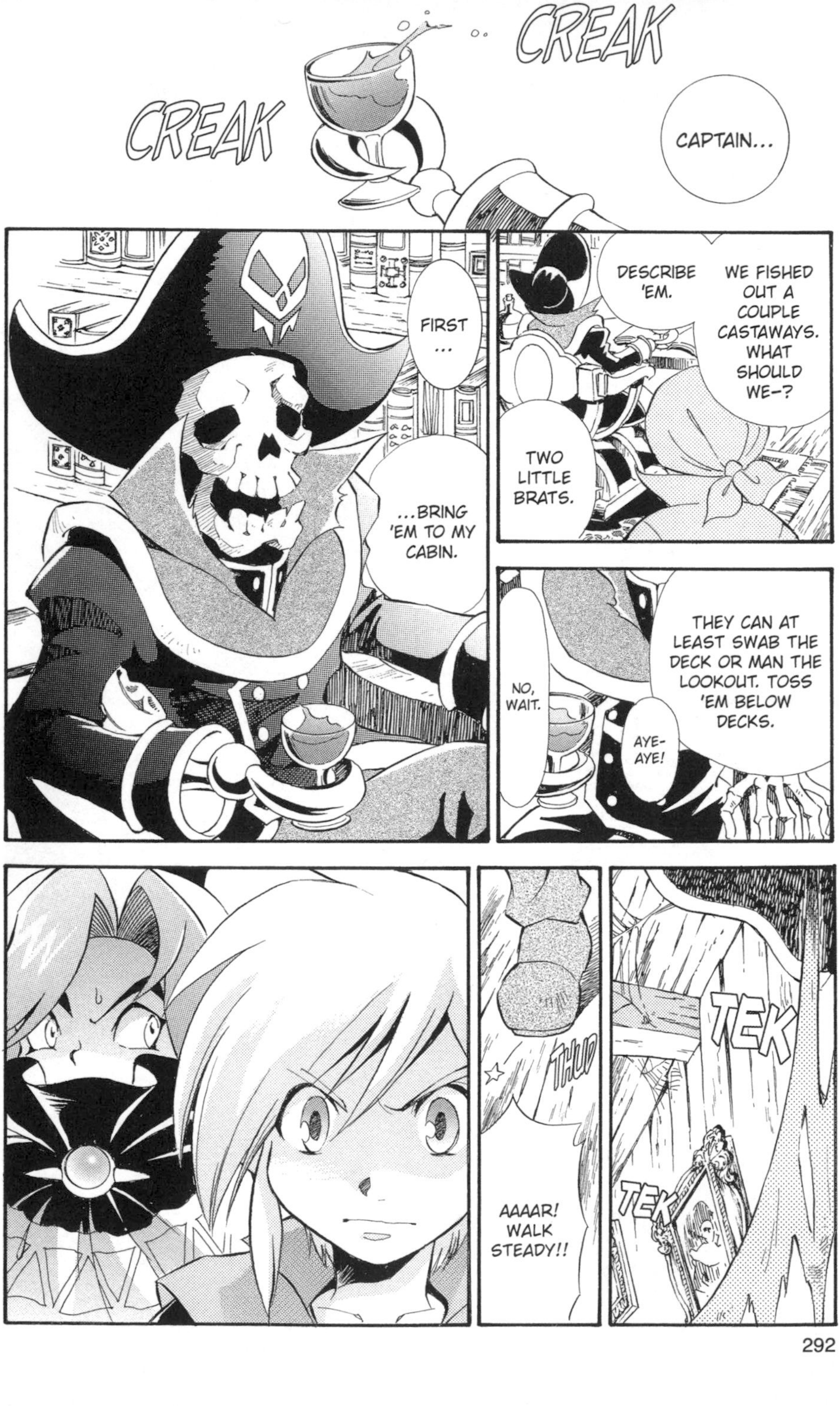
CREAK
CREAK
CAPTAIN...
WE FISHED OUT A COUPLE CASTAWAYS. WHAT SHOULD WE–?
DESCRIBE 'EM.
TWO LITTLE BRATS.
THEY CAN AT LEAST SWAB THE DECK OR MAN THE LOOKOUT. TOSS 'EM BELOW DECKS.
AYE-AYE!
NO, WAIT.
FIRST ...
...BRING 'EM TO MY CABIN.
TEK
TEK
THUD
AAAAR! WALK STEADY!!

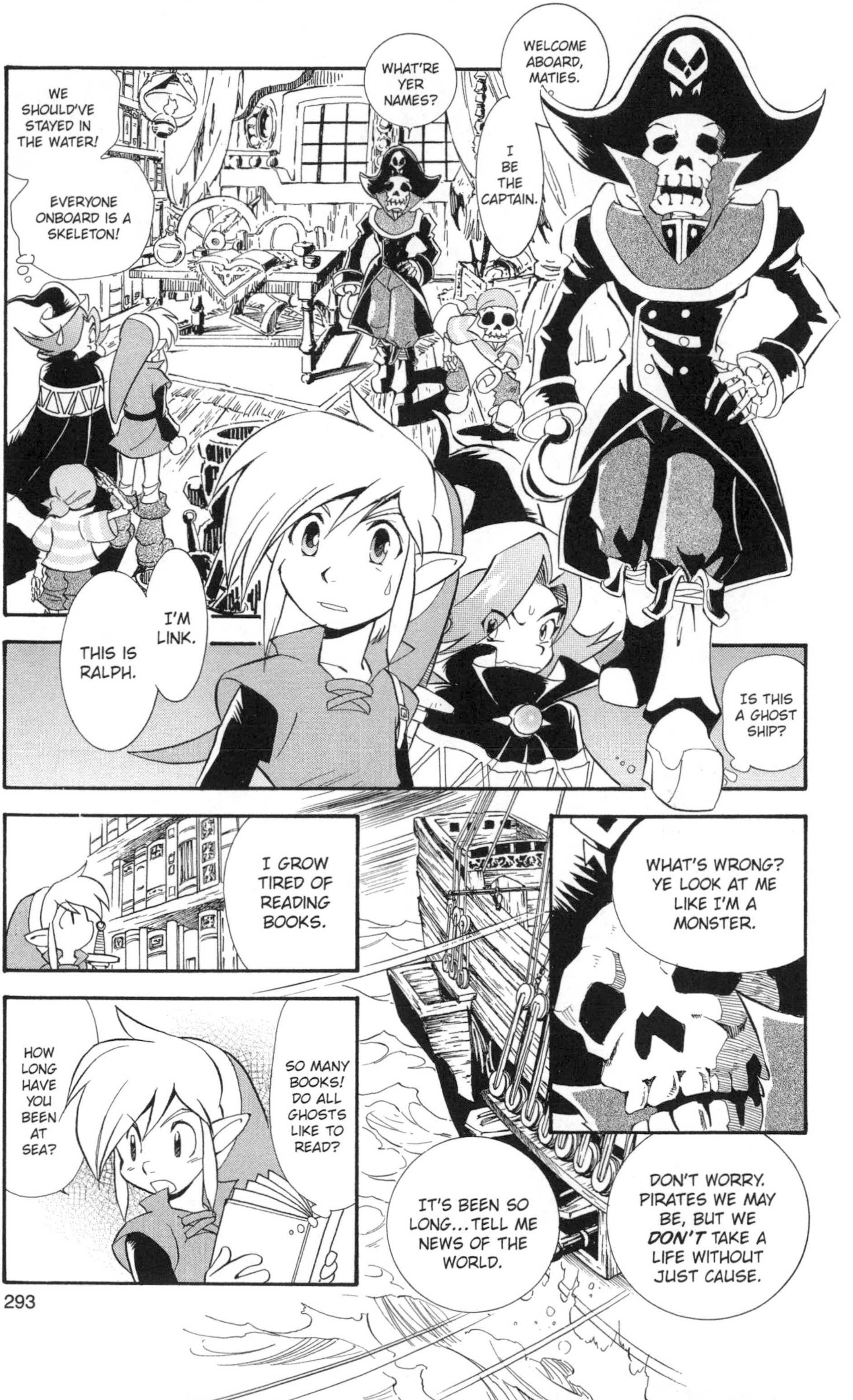
WELCOME ABOARD, MATIES.
I BE THE CAPTAIN.
WHAT'RE YER NAMES?
WE SHOULD'VE STAYED IN THE WATER!
EVERYONE ONBOARD IS A SKELETON!
IS THIS A GHOST SHIP?
I'M LINK.
THIS IS RALPH.
WHAT'S WRONG? YE LOOK AT ME LIKE I'M A MONSTER.
DON'T WORRY. PIRATES WE MAY BE, BUT WE ***DON'T*** TAKE A LIFE WITHOUT JUST CAUSE.
IT'S BEEN SO LONG...TELL ME NEWS OF THE WORLD.
I GROW TIRED OF READING BOOKS.
SO MANY BOOKS! DO ALL GHOSTS LIKE TO READ?
HOW LONG HAVE YOU BEEN AT SEA?

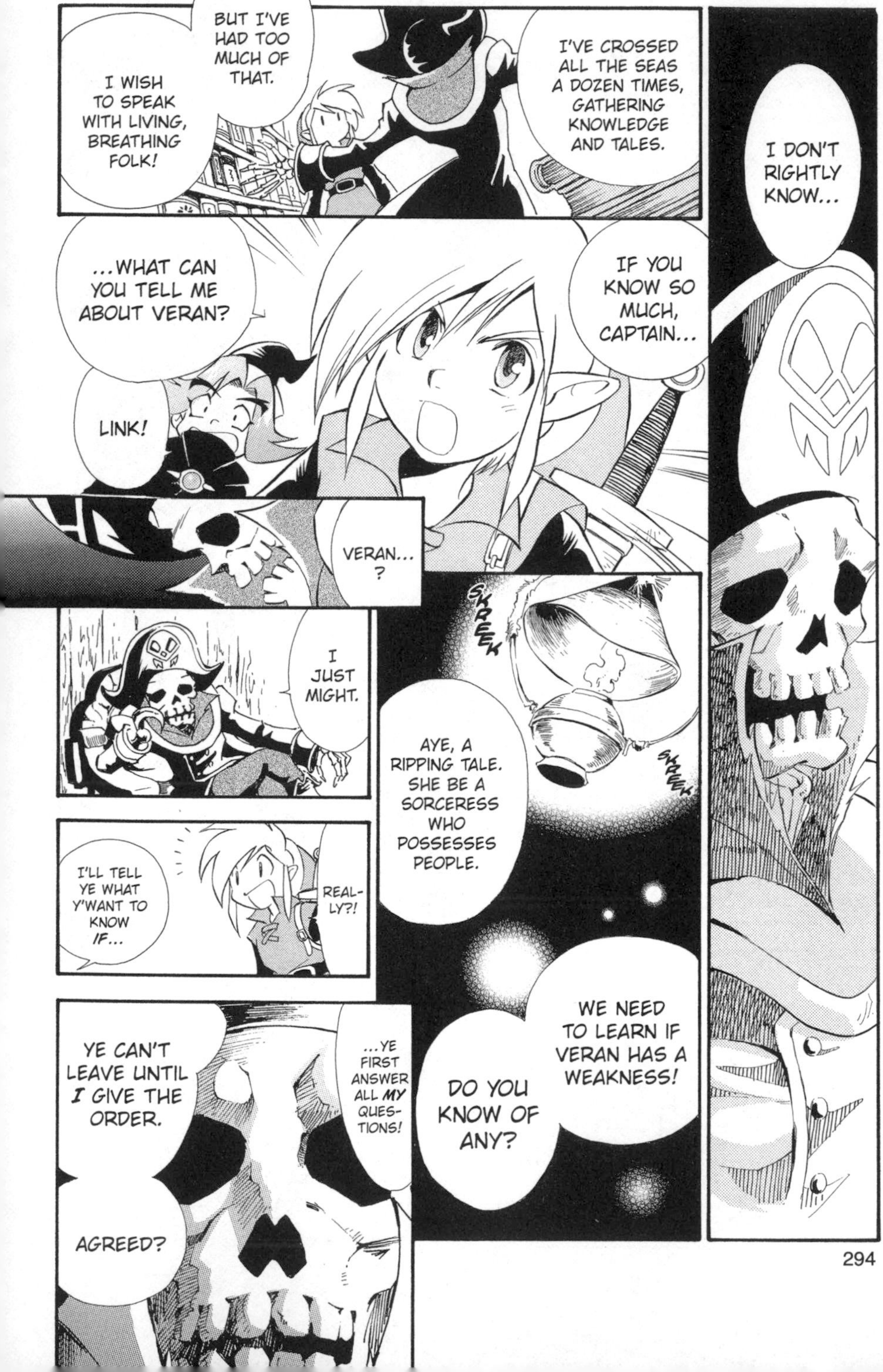

I DON'T RIGHTLY KNOW...
I'VE CROSSED ALL THE SEAS A DOZEN TIMES, GATHERING KNOWLEDGE AND TALES.
BUT I'VE HAD TOO MUCH OF THAT.
I WISH TO SPEAK WITH LIVING, BREATHING FOLK!
IF YOU KNOW SO MUCH, CAPTAIN...
...WHAT CAN YOU TELL ME ABOUT VERAN?
LINK!
VERAN... ?
SKREEK
SKREEK
AYE, A RIPPING TALE. SHE BE A SORCERESS WHO POSSESSES PEOPLE.
WE NEED TO LEARN IF VERAN HAS A WEAKNESS!
DO YOU KNOW OF ANY?
I JUST MIGHT.
REAL-LY?!
I'LL TELL YE WHAT Y'WANT TO KNOW IF...
...YE FIRST ANSWER ALL MY QUES-TIONS!
YE CAN'T LEAVE UNTIL I GIVE THE ORDER.
AGREED?

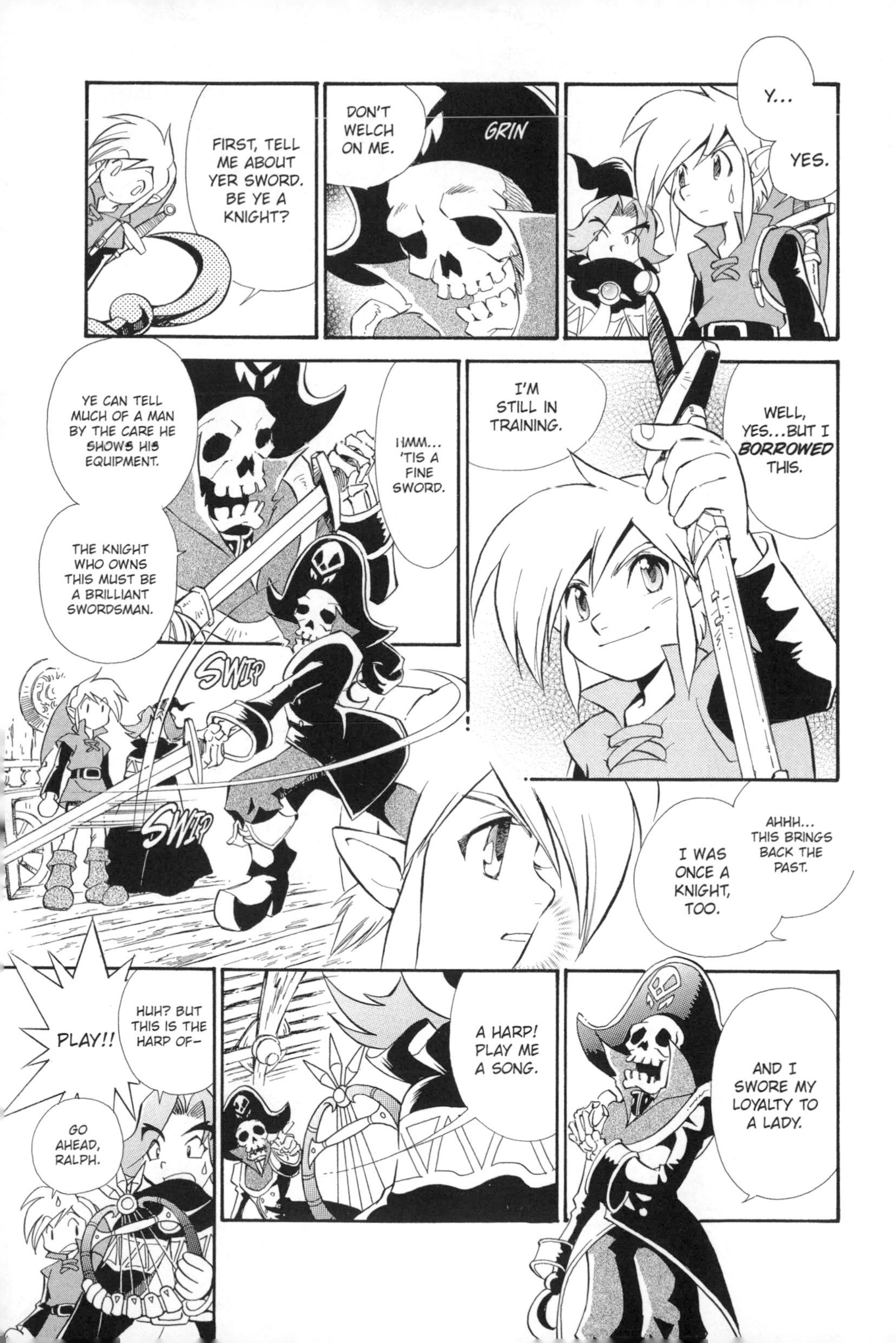
Y...
YES.
GRIN
DON'T WELCH ON ME.
FIRST, TELL ME ABOUT YER SWORD. BE YE A KNIGHT?
WELL, YES...BUT I **BORROWED** THIS.
I'M STILL IN TRAINING.
HMM... 'TIS A FINE SWORD.
YE CAN TELL MUCH OF A MAN BY THE CARE HE SHOWS HIS EQUIPMENT.
THE KNIGHT WHO OWNS THIS MUST BE A BRILLIANT SWORDSMAN.
SWIP
SWIP
AHHH... THIS BRINGS BACK THE PAST.
I WAS ONCE A KNIGHT, TOO.
AND I SWORE MY LOYALTY TO A LADY.
A HARP! PLAY ME A SONG.
HUH? BUT THIS IS THE HARP OF-
PLAY!!
GO AHEAD, RALPH.

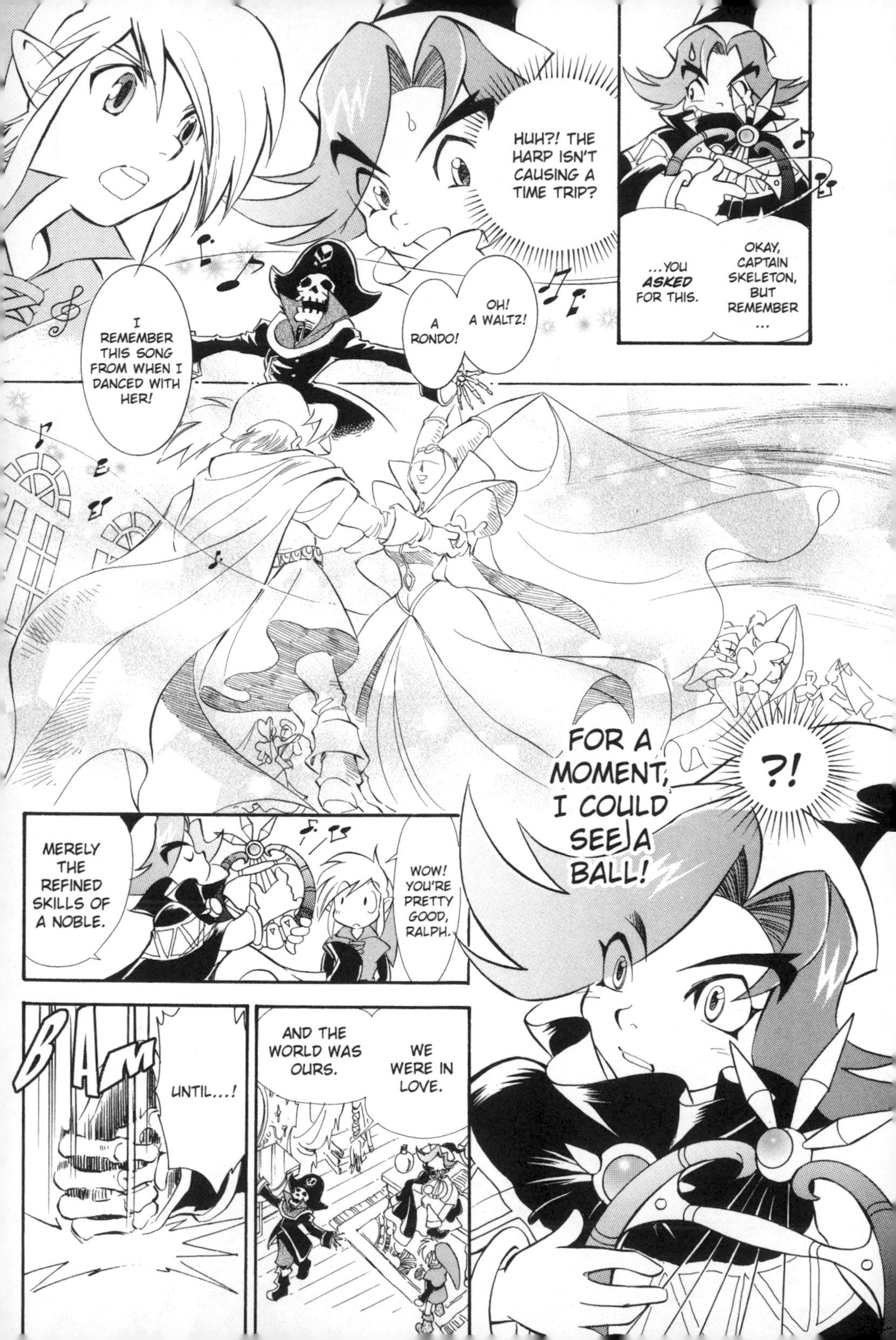
OKAY, CAPTAIN SKELETON, BUT REMEMBER ...
...YOU **ASKED** FOR THIS.
HUH?! THE HARP ISN'T CAUSING A TIME TRIP?
OH! A WALTZ!
A RONDO!
I REMEMBER THIS SONG FROM WHEN I DANCED WITH HER!
?!
FOR A MOMENT, I COULD SEE A BALL!
WOW! YOU'RE PRETTY GOOD, RALPH.
MERELY THE REFINED SKILLS OF A NOBLE.
WE WERE IN LOVE.
AND THE WORLD WAS OURS.
UNTIL...!
BAM

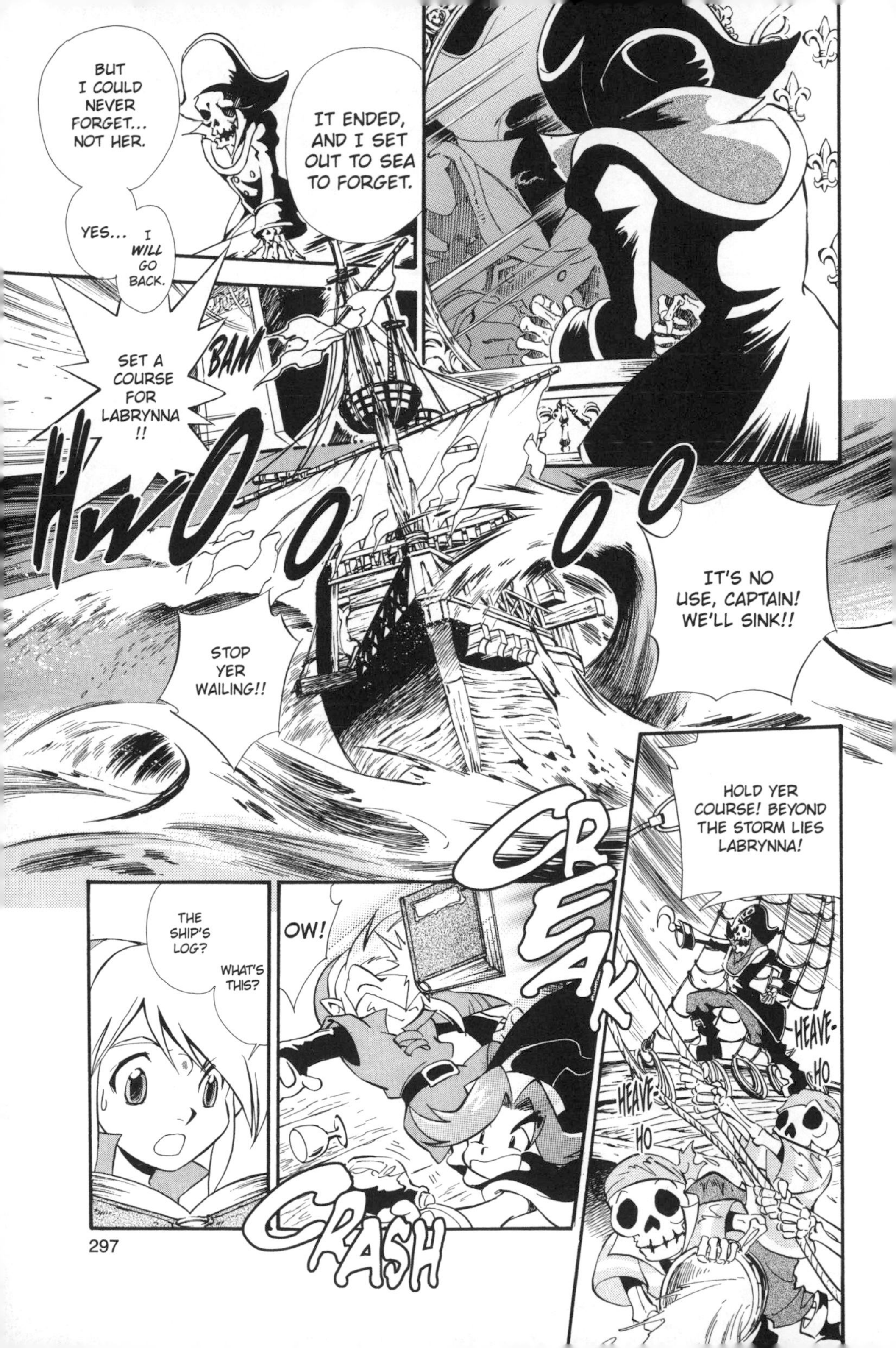
IT ENDED, AND I SET OUT TO SEA TO FORGET.
BUT I COULD NEVER FORGET... NOT HER.
YES... I WILL GO BACK.
SET A COURSE FOR LABRYNNA!!
BAM
HWOOOOO
IT'S NO USE, CAPTAIN! WE'LL SINK!!
STOP YER WAILING!!
HOLD YER COURSE! BEYOND THE STORM LIES LABRYNNA!
HEAVE-HO
HEAVE-HO
CREAK
OW!
CRASH
THE SHIP'S LOG?
WHAT'S THIS?

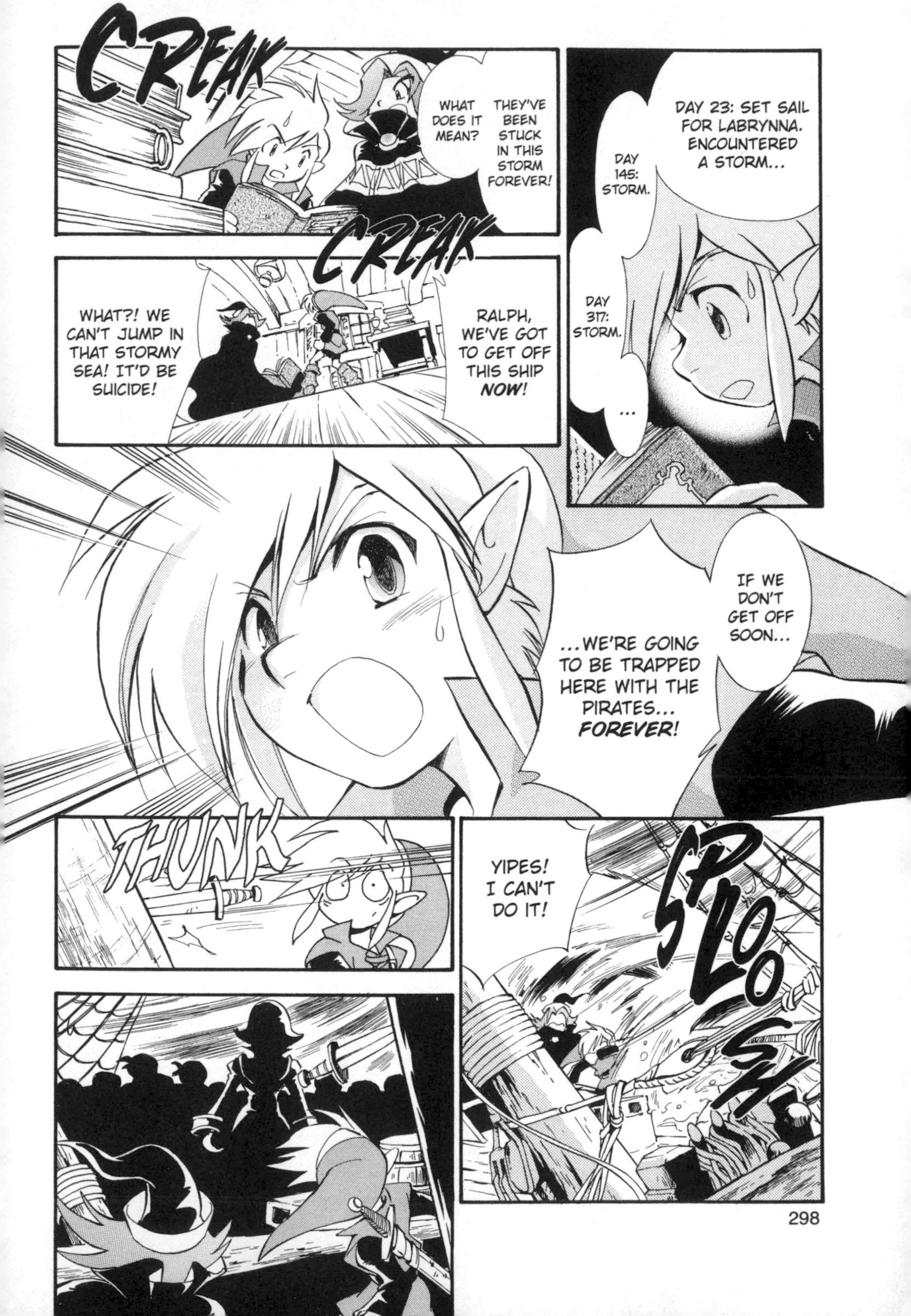

DAY 23: SET SAIL FOR LABRYNNA. ENCOUNTERED A STORM...
DAY 145: STORM.
DAY 317: STORM.
...
CREAK
THEY'VE BEEN STUCK IN THIS STORM FOREVER!
WHAT DOES IT MEAN?
CREAK
RALPH, WE'VE GOT TO GET OFF THIS SHIP *NOW*!
WHAT?! WE CAN'T JUMP IN THAT STORMY SEA! IT'D BE SUICIDE!
IF WE DON'T GET OFF SOON...
...WE'RE GOING TO BE TRAPPED HERE WITH THE PIRATES... ***FOREVER***!
SPLOOSH
YIPES! I CAN'T DO IT!
THUNK

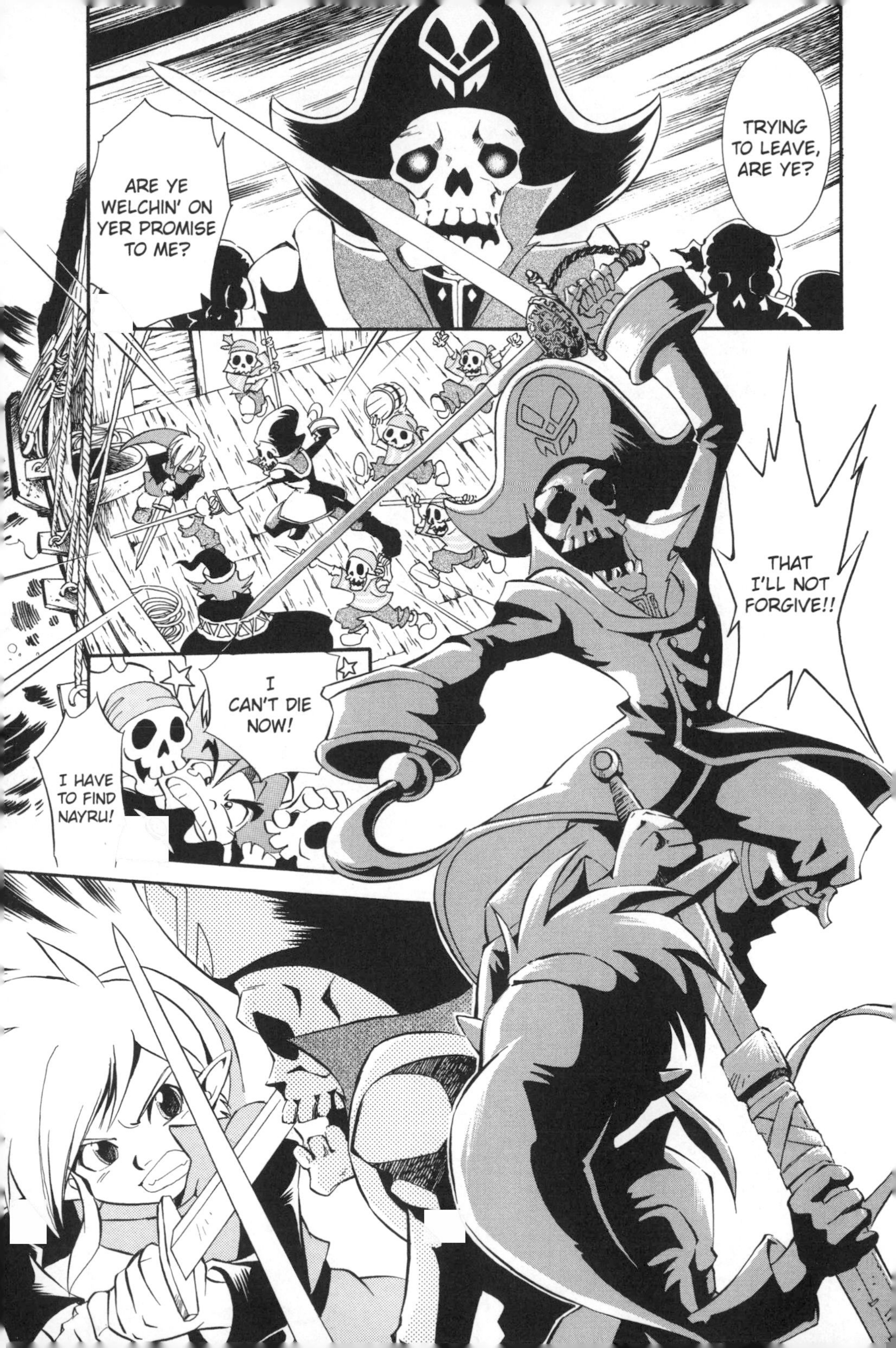
TRYING TO LEAVE, ARE YE?
ARE YE WELCHIN' ON YER PROMISE TO ME?
THAT I'LL NOT FORGIVE!!
I CAN'T DIE NOW!
I HAVE TO FIND NAYRU!

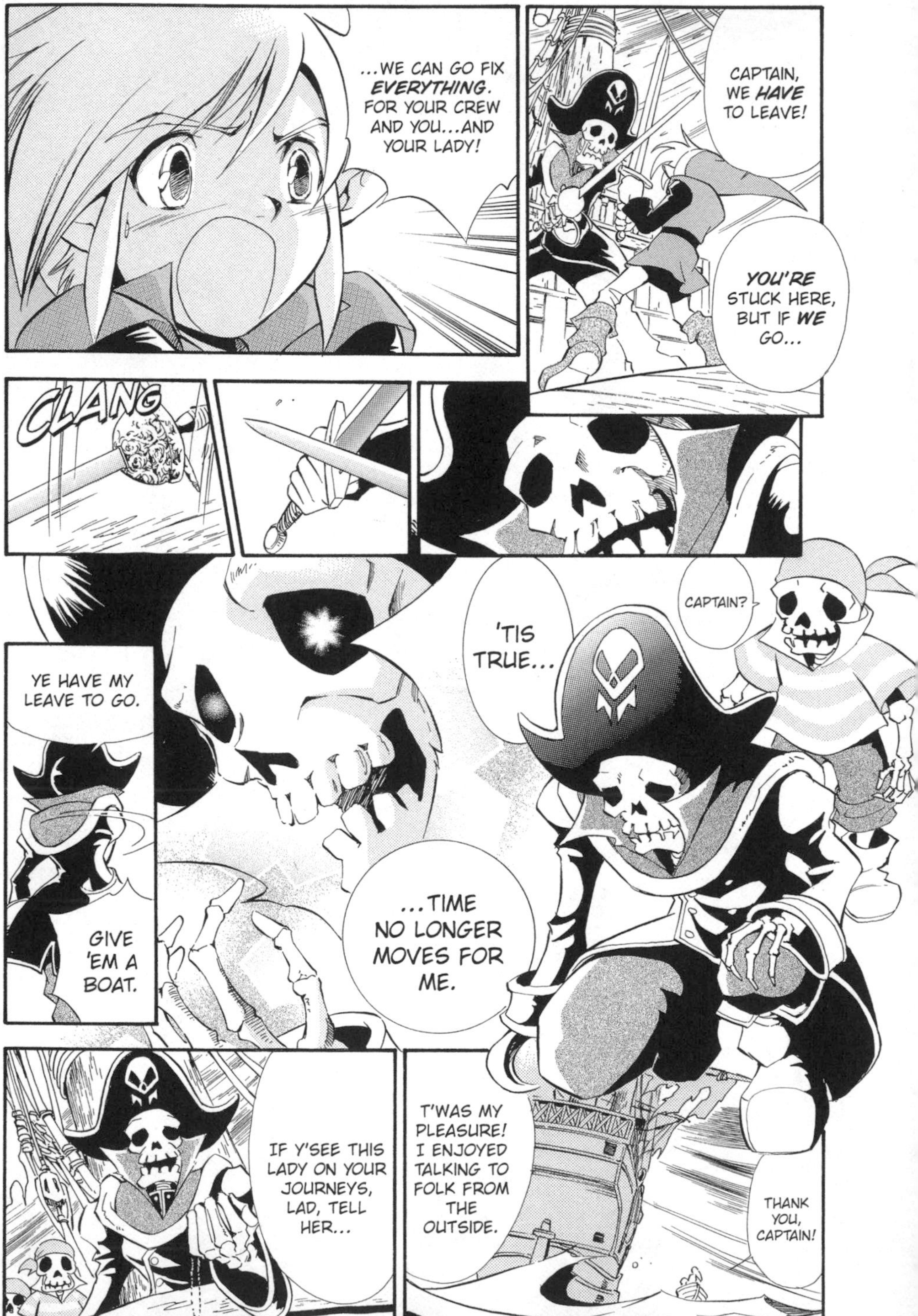
CAPTAIN, WE HAVE TO LEAVE!
YOU'RE STUCK HERE, BUT IF WE GO...
...WE CAN GO FIX EVERYTHING. FOR YOUR CREW AND YOU...AND YOUR LADY!
CLANG
CAPTAIN?
'TIS TRUE...
...TIME NO LONGER MOVES FOR ME.
YE HAVE MY LEAVE TO GO.
GIVE 'EM A BOAT.
THANK YOU, CAPTAIN!
T'WAS MY PLEASURE! I ENJOYED TALKING TO FOLK FROM THE OUTSIDE.
IF Y'SEE THIS LADY ON YOUR JOURNEYS, LAD, TELL HER...

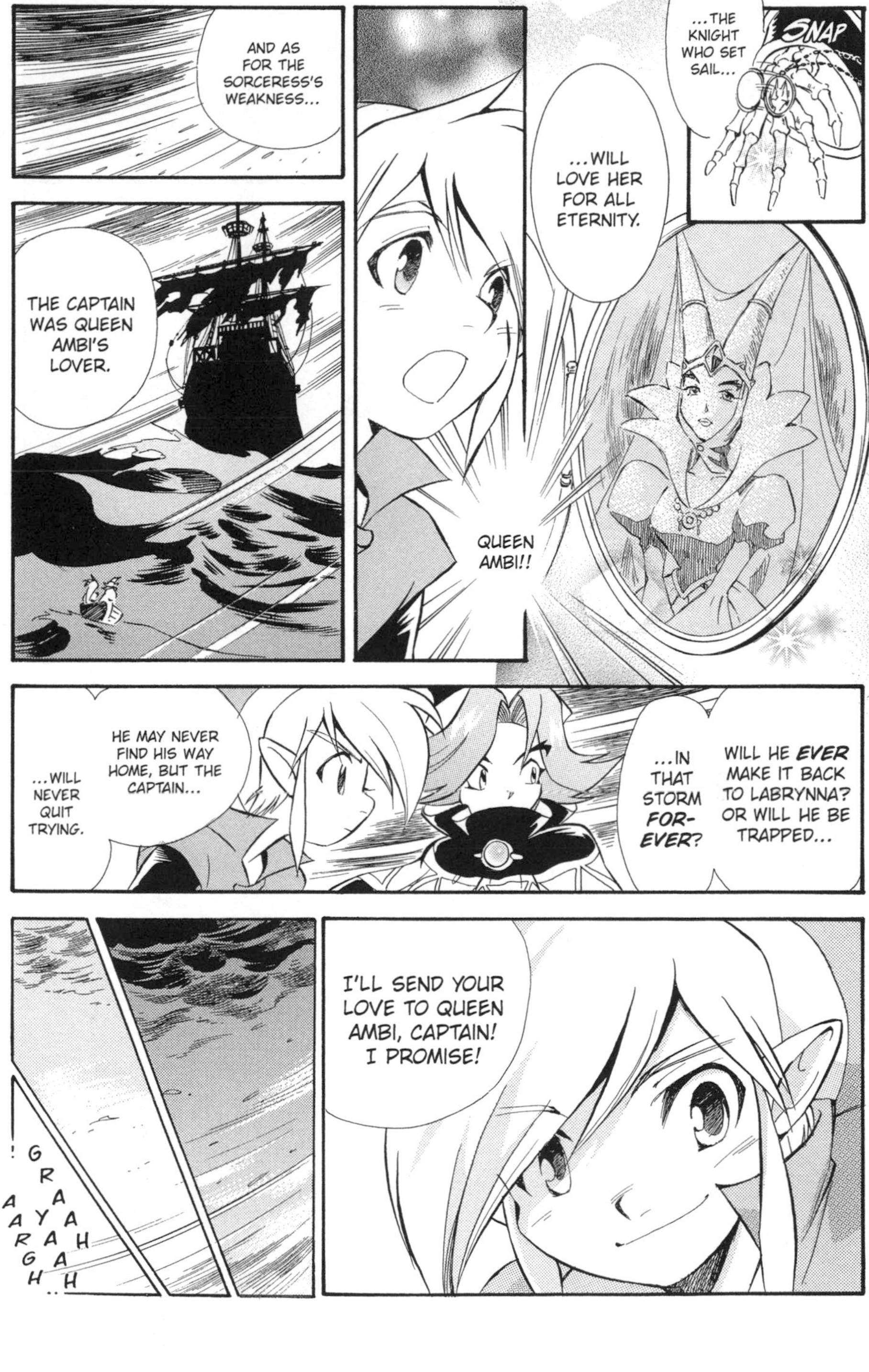
...THE KNIGHT WHO SET SAIL...
SNAP
...WILL LOVE HER FOR ALL ETERNITY.
QUEEN AMBI!!
AND AS FOR THE SORCERESS'S WEAKNESS...
THE CAPTAIN WAS QUEEN AMBI'S LOVER.
WILL HE *EVER* MAKE IT BACK TO LABRYNNA? OR WILL HE BE TRAPPED...
...IN THAT STORM *FOREVER*?
HE MAY NEVER FIND HIS WAY HOME, BUT THE CAPTAIN...
...WILL NEVER QUIT TRYING.
I'LL SEND YOUR LOVE TO QUEEN AMBI, CAPTAIN! I PROMISE!
GRAAH!
YAAH
AARGH..

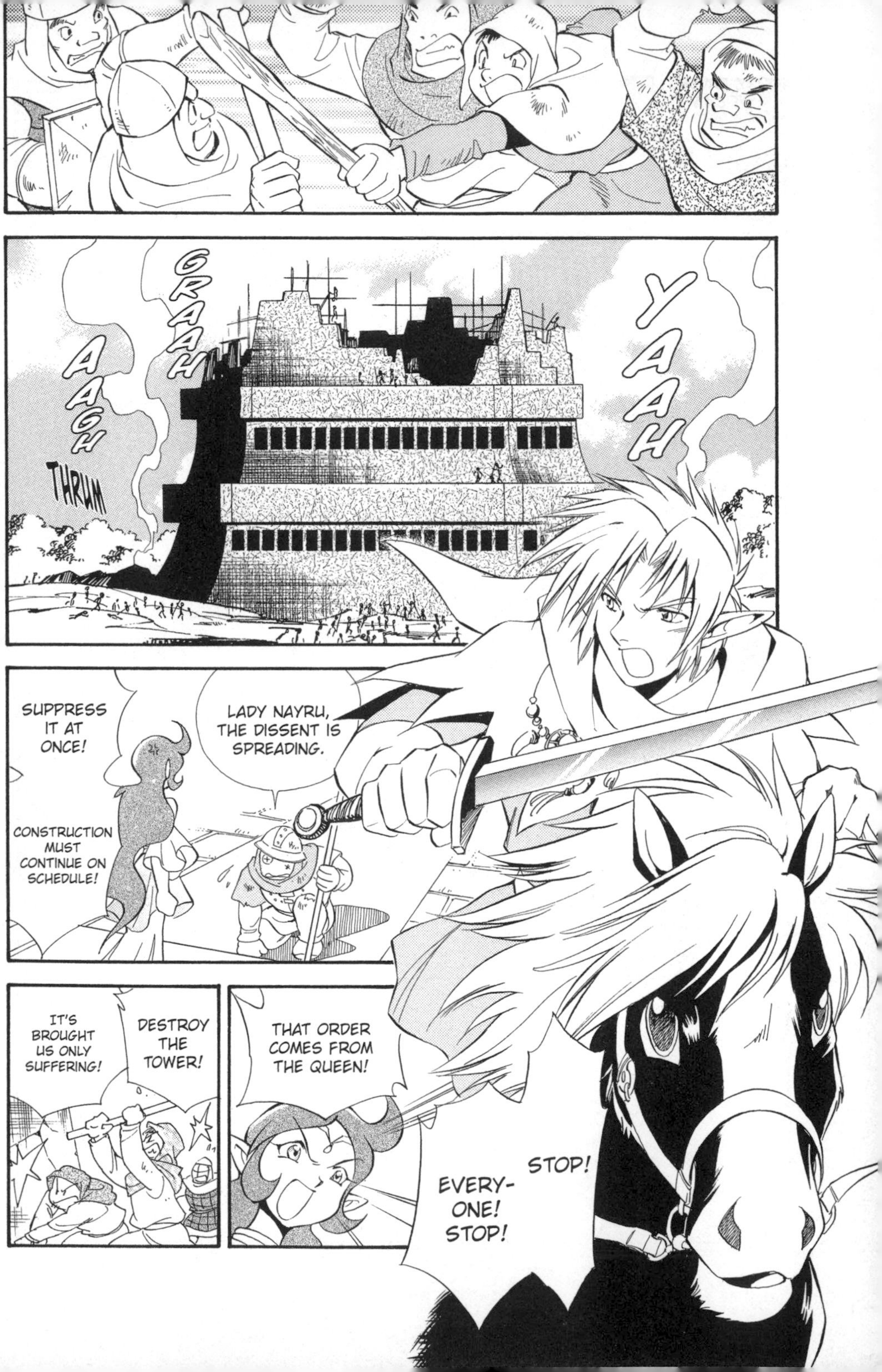
YAAAH
GRAAAH
AAAGH
THRUM
LADY NAYRU, THE DISSENT IS SPREADING.
SUPPRESS IT AT ONCE!
CONSTRUCTION MUST CONTINUE ON SCHEDULE!
THAT ORDER COMES FROM THE QUEEN!
DESTROY THE TOWER!
IT'S BROUGHT US ONLY SUFFERING!
STOP!
EVERY-ONE! STOP!

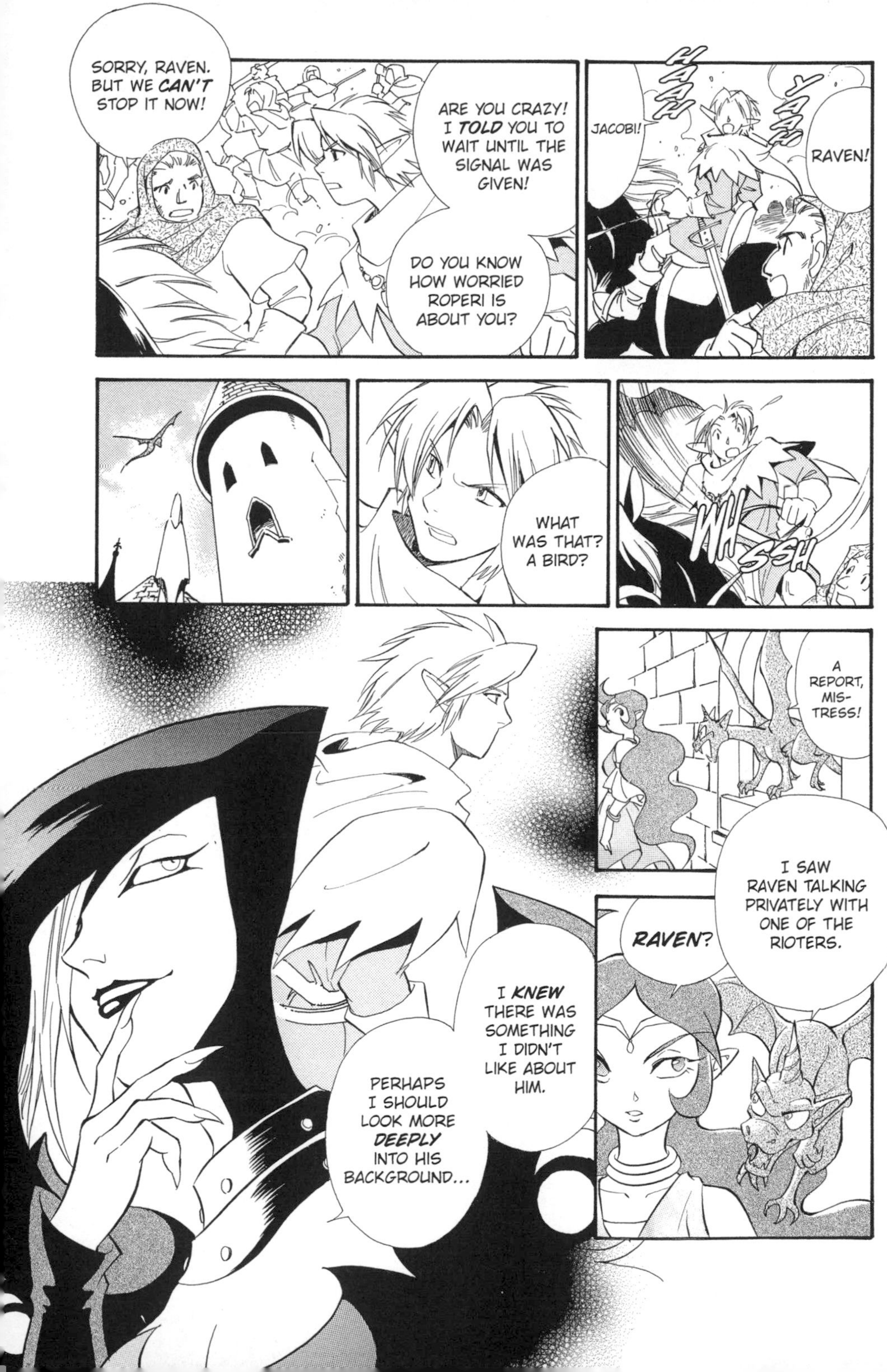
YAAAH
RAVEN!
HAAAH
JACOBI!
ARE YOU CRAZY! I TOLD YOU TO WAIT UNTIL THE SIGNAL WAS GIVEN!
DO YOU KNOW HOW WORRIED ROPERI IS ABOUT YOU?
SORRY, RAVEN. BUT WE CAN'T STOP IT NOW!
WHSSH
WHAT WAS THAT? A BIRD?
A REPORT, MISTRESS!
I SAW RAVEN TALKING PRIVATELY WITH ONE OF THE RIOTERS.
RAVEN?
I KNEW THERE WAS SOMETHING I DIDN'T LIKE ABOUT HIM.
PERHAPS I SHOULD LOOK MORE DEEPLY INTO HIS BACKGROUND...

CHAPTER 8
RAMROCK

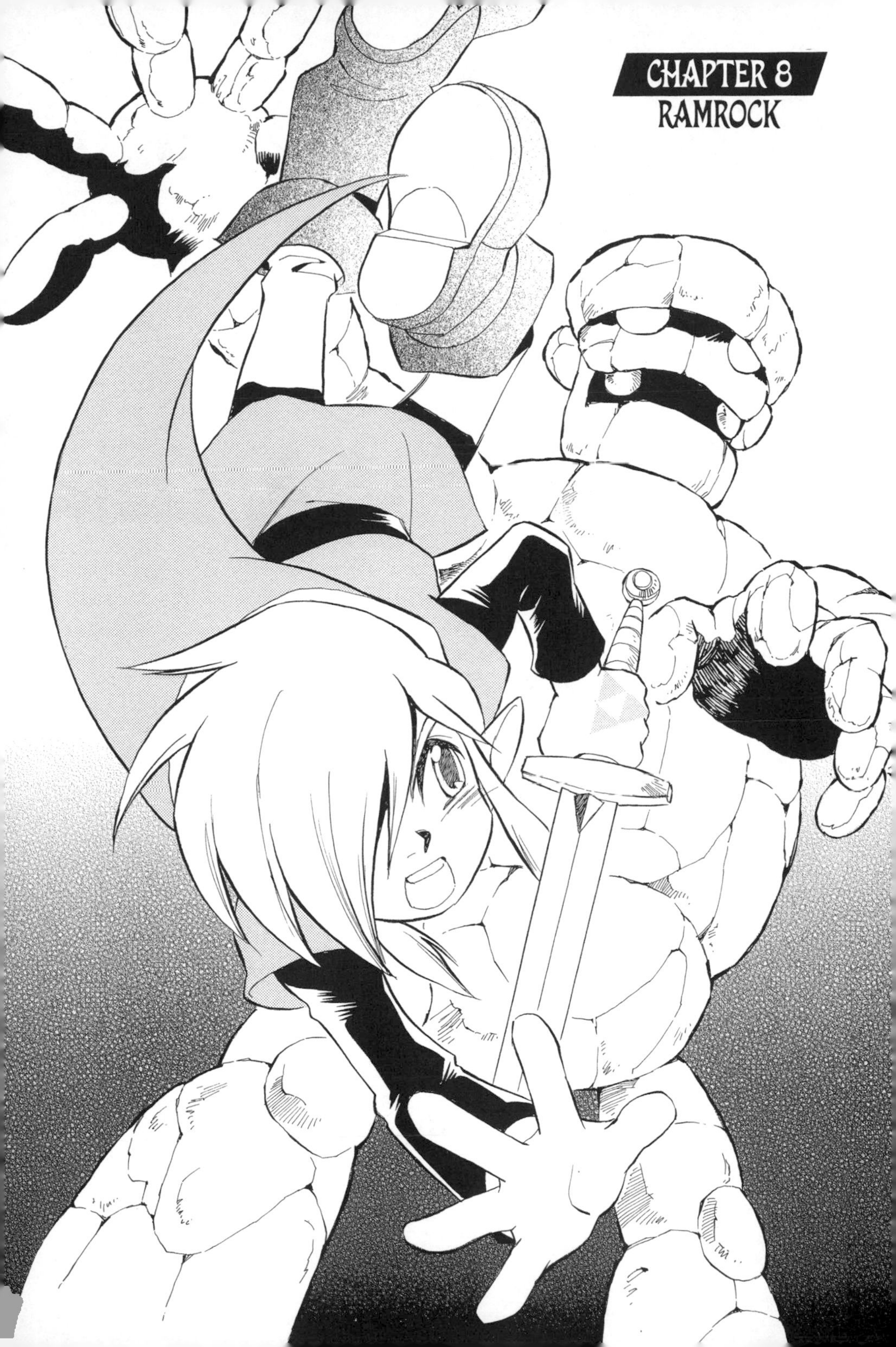

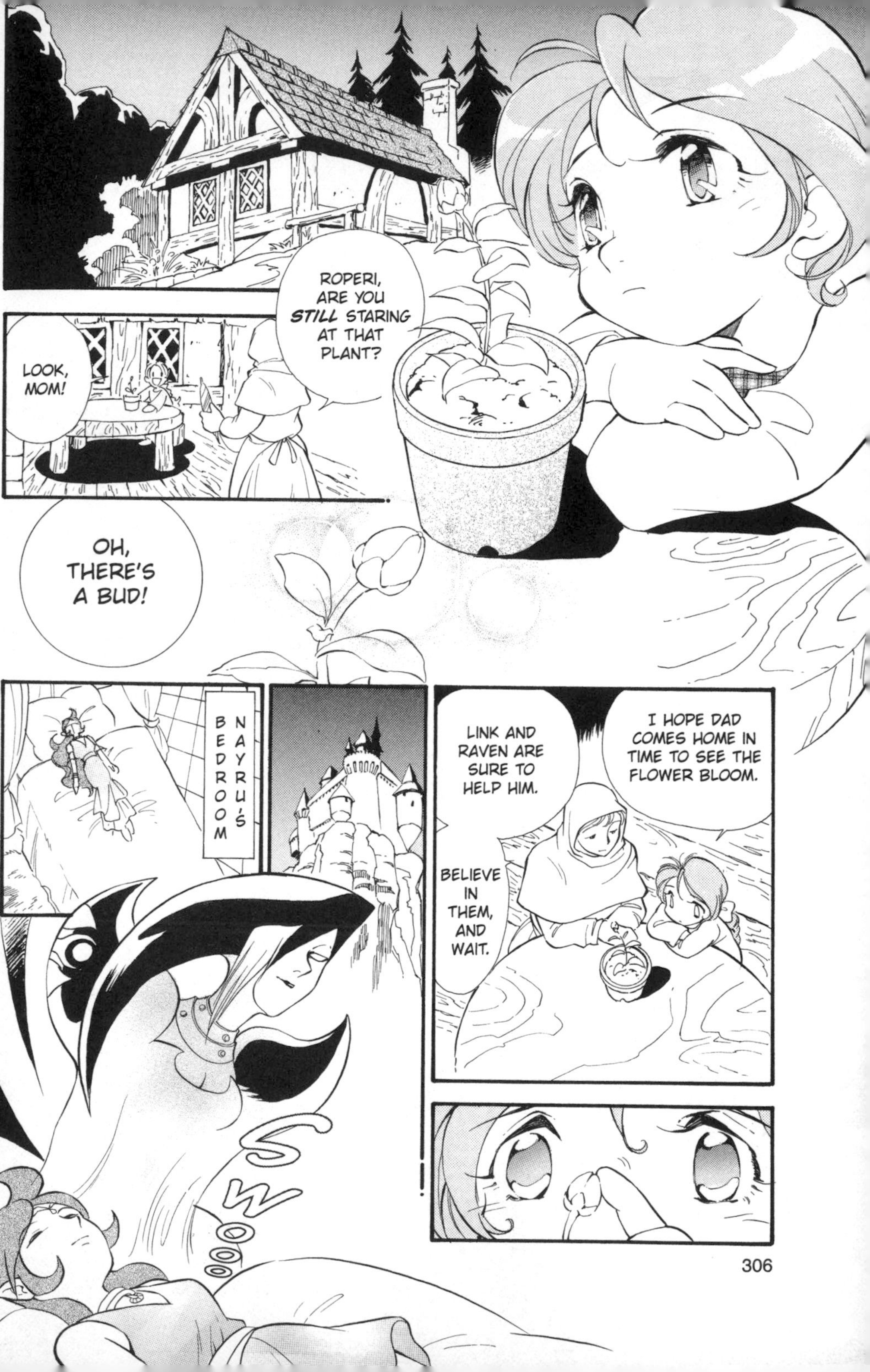
ROPERI, ARE YOU STILL STARING AT THAT PLANT?
LOOK, MOM!
OH, THERE'S A BUD!
I HOPE DAD COMES HOME IN TIME TO SEE THE FLOWER BLOOM.
LINK AND RAVEN ARE SURE TO HELP HIM.
BELIEVE IN THEM, AND WAIT.
NAYRU'S BEDROOM
SWOOO

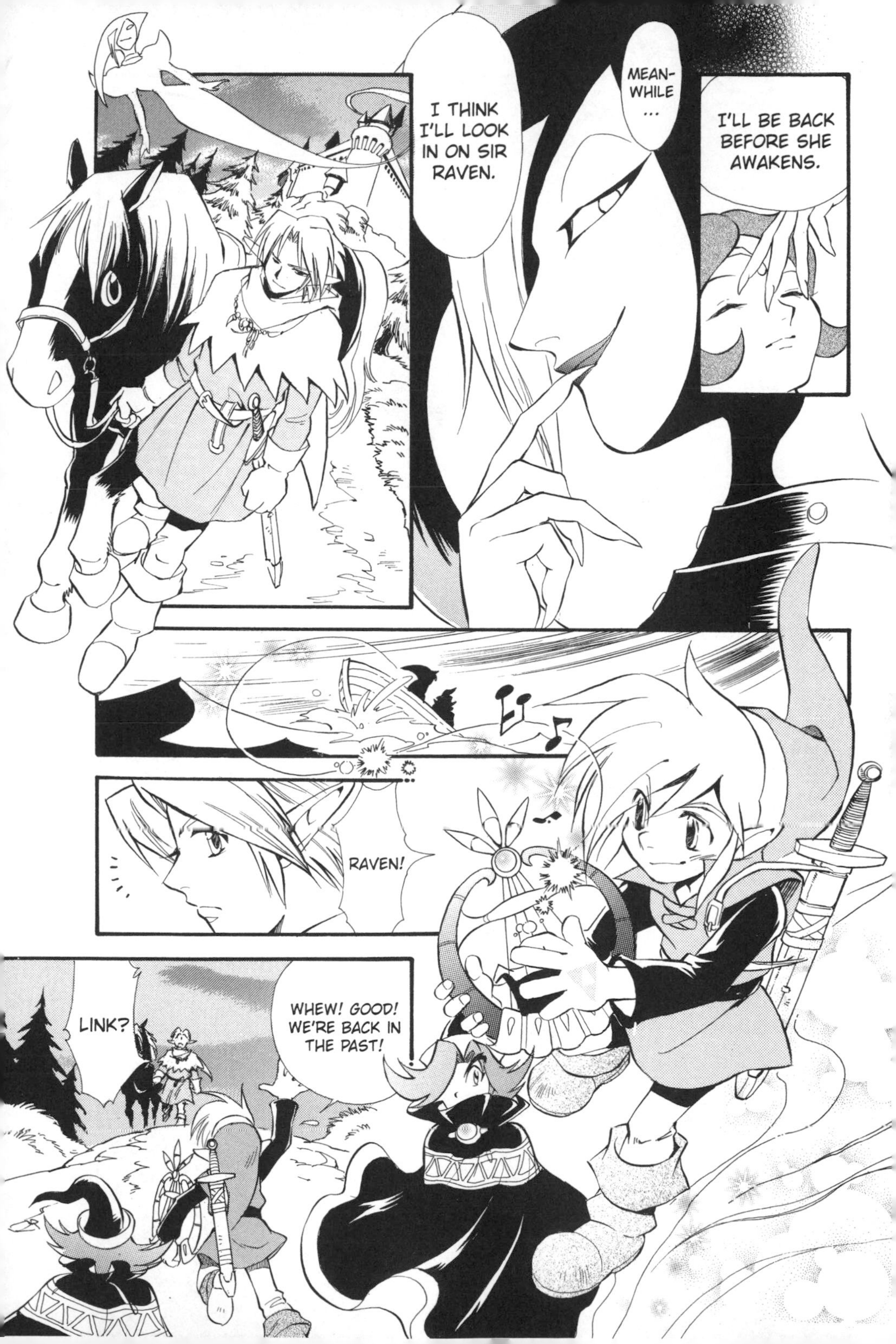
I'LL BE BACK BEFORE SHE AWAKENS.
MEAN-WHILE ...
I THINK I'LL LOOK IN ON SIR RAVEN.
RAVEN!
WHEW! GOOD! WE'RE BACK IN THE PAST!
LINK?

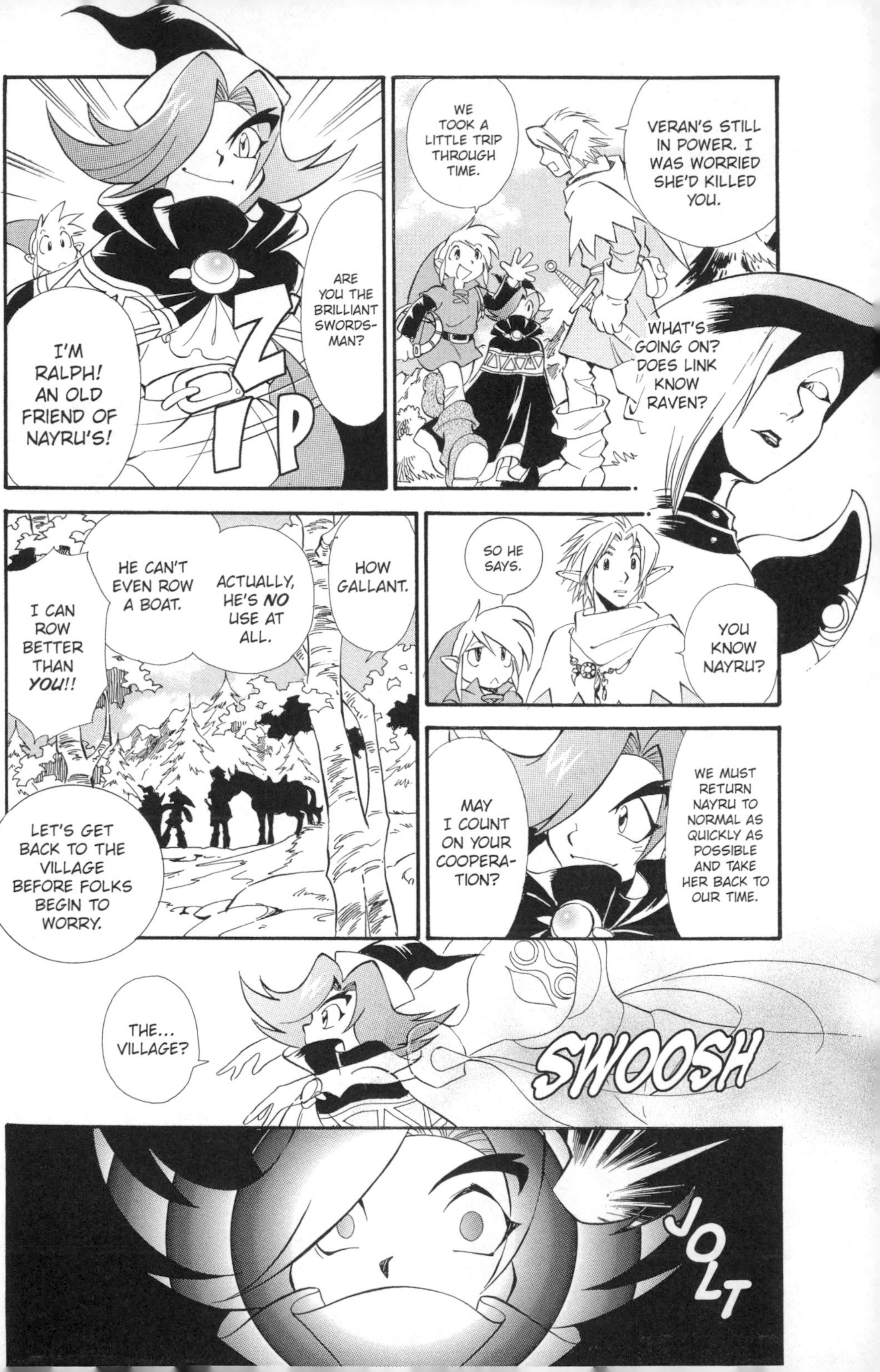
VERAN'S STILL IN POWER. I WAS WORRIED SHE'D KILLED YOU.
WE TOOK A LITTLE TRIP THROUGH TIME.
WHAT'S GOING ON? DOES LINK KNOW RAVEN?
ARE YOU THE BRILLIANT SWORDS-MAN?
ZIP
I'M RALPH! AN OLD FRIEND OF NAYRU'S!
YOU KNOW NAYRU?
SO HE SAYS.
WE MUST RETURN NAYRU TO NORMAL AS QUICKLY AS POSSIBLE AND TAKE HER BACK TO OUR TIME.
MAY I COUNT ON YOUR COOPERA-TION?
HOW GALLANT.
ACTUALLY, HE'S *NO* USE AT ALL.
HE CAN'T EVEN ROW A BOAT.
I CAN ROW BETTER THAN *YOU*!!
LET'S GET BACK TO THE VILLAGE BEFORE FOLKS BEGIN TO WORRY.
SWOOSH
THE... VILLAGE?
JOLT

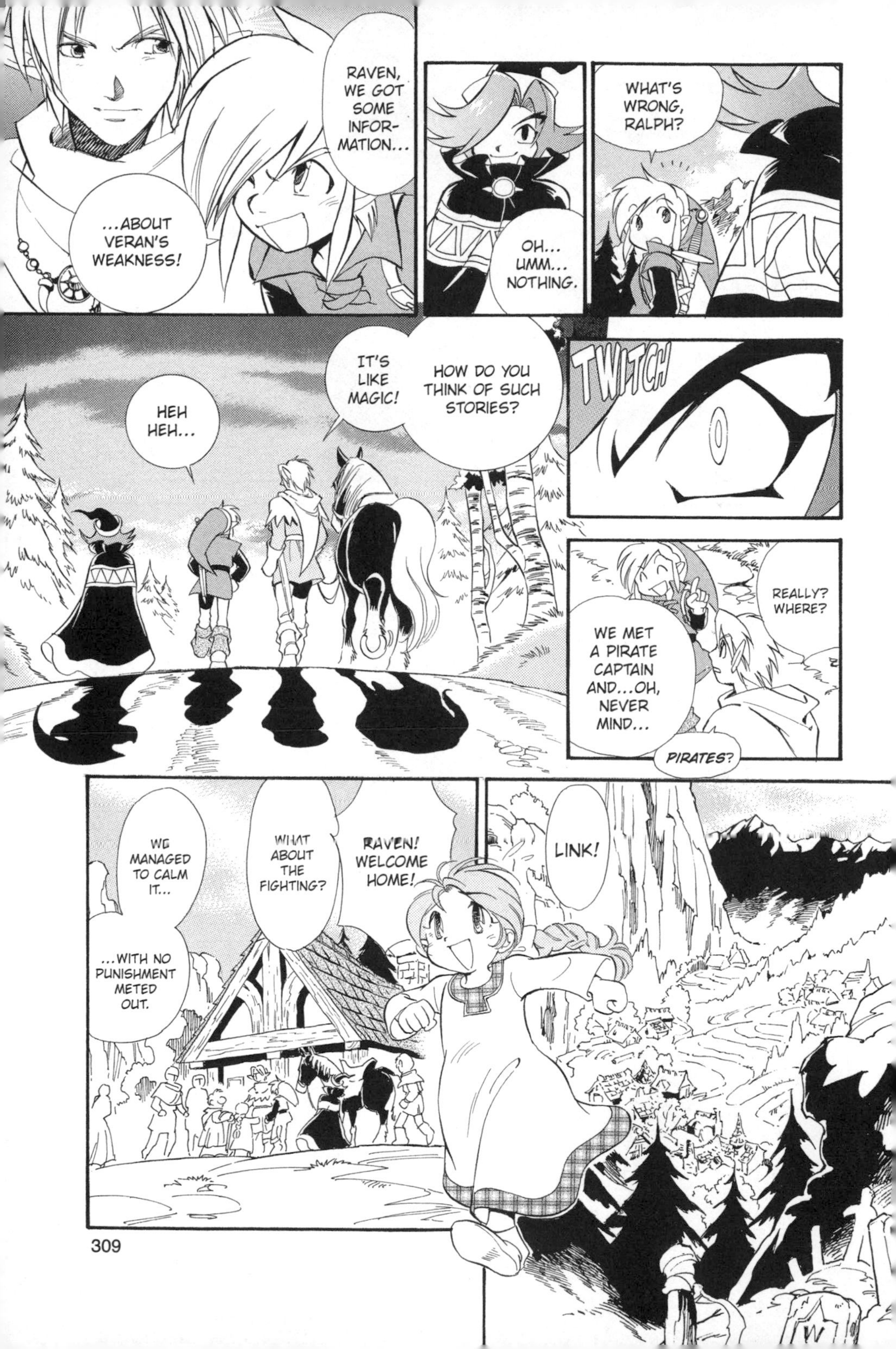
WHAT'S WRONG, RALPH?
OH... UMM... NOTHING.
RAVEN, WE GOT SOME INFORMATION...
...ABOUT VERAN'S WEAKNESS!
TWITCH
REALLY? WHERE?
WE MET A PIRATE CAPTAIN AND...OH, NEVER MIND...
PIRATES?
HOW DO YOU THINK OF SUCH STORIES?
IT'S LIKE MAGIC!
HEH HEH...
LINK!
RAVEN! WELCOME HOME!
WHAT ABOUT THE FIGHTING?
WE MANAGED TO CALM IT...
...WITH NO PUNISHMENT METED OUT.

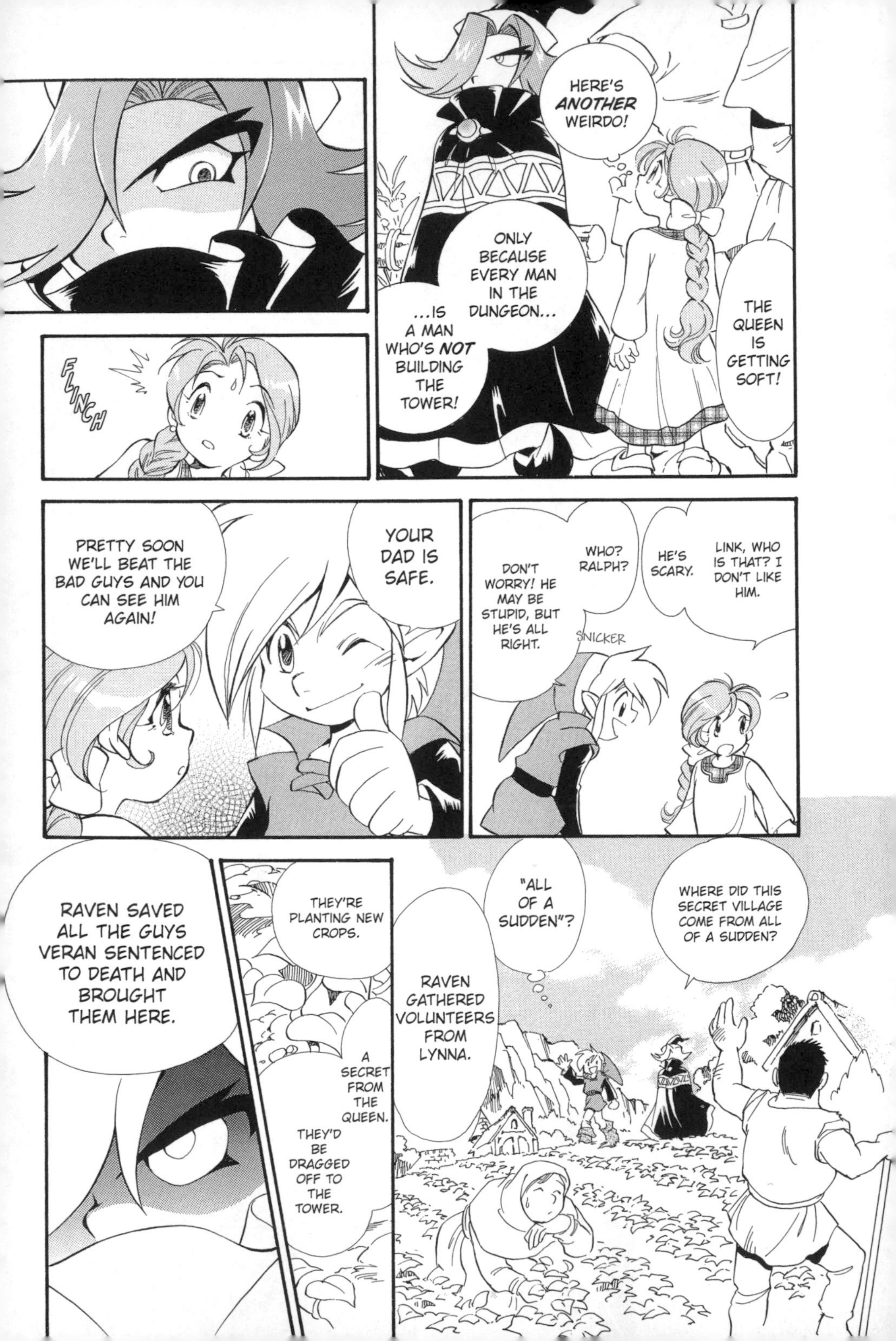
HERE'S ANOTHER WEIRDO!
THE QUEEN IS GETTING SOFT!
ONLY BECAUSE EVERY MAN IN THE DUNGEON...
...IS A MAN WHO'S NOT BUILDING THE TOWER!
FLINCH
LINK, WHO IS THAT? I DON'T LIKE HIM.
HE'S SCARY.
WHO? RALPH?
DON'T WORRY! HE MAY BE STUPID, BUT HE'S ALL RIGHT.
SNICKER
YOUR DAD IS SAFE.
PRETTY SOON WE'LL BEAT THE BAD GUYS AND YOU CAN SEE HIM AGAIN!
WHERE DID THIS SECRET VILLAGE COME FROM ALL OF A SUDDEN?
"ALL OF A SUDDEN"?
THEY'RE PLANTING NEW CROPS.
RAVEN GATHERED VOLUNTEERS FROM LYNNA.
A SECRET FROM THE QUEEN.
THEY'D BE DRAGGED OFF TO THE TOWER.
RAVEN SAVED ALL THE GUYS VERAN SENTENCED TO DEATH AND BROUGHT THEM HERE.

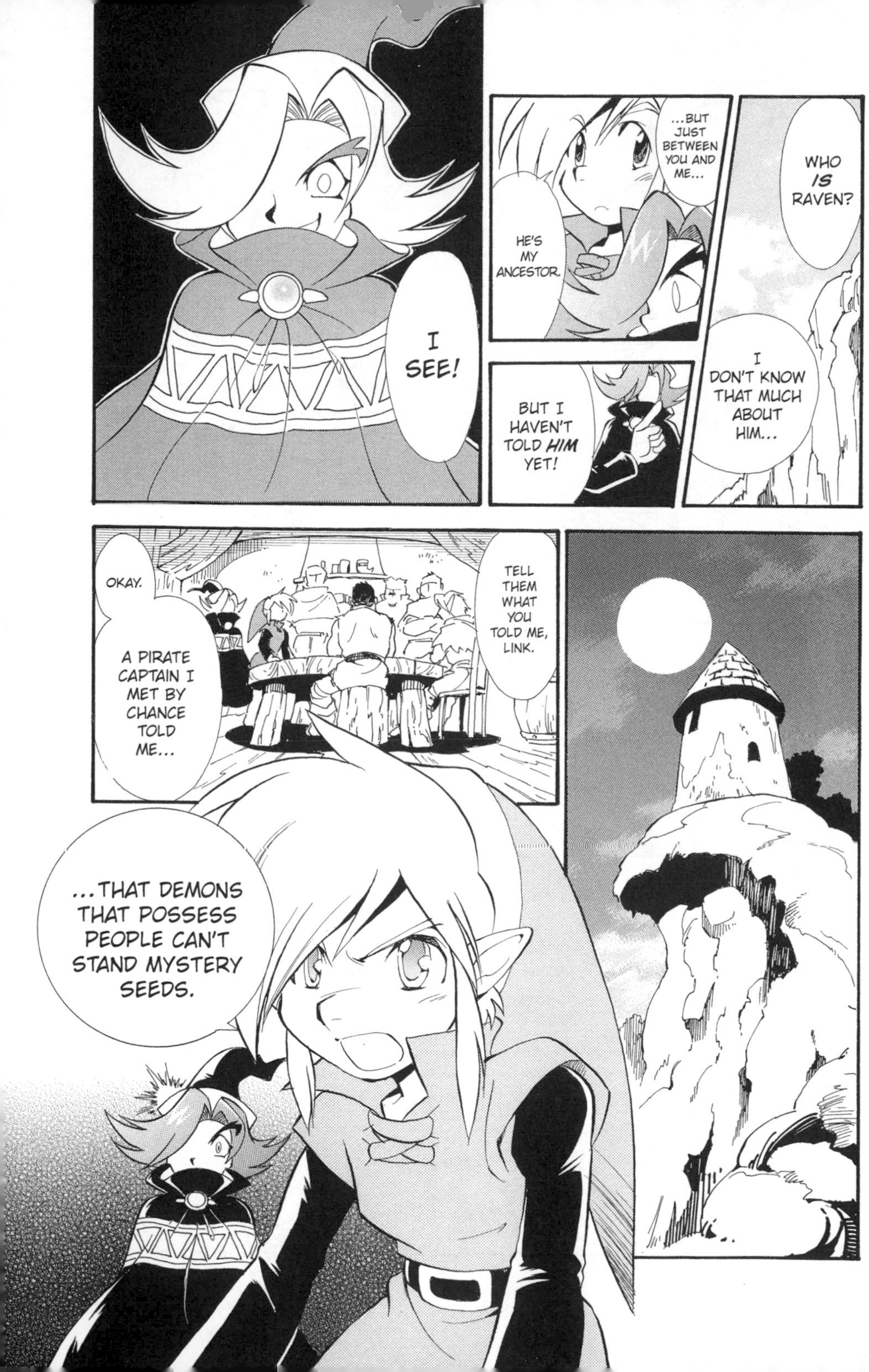
WHO *IS* RAVEN?
I DON'T KNOW THAT MUCH ABOUT HIM...
...BUT JUST BETWEEN YOU AND ME...
HE'S MY ANCESTOR.
BUT I HAVEN'T TOLD *HIM* YET!
I SEE!
TELL THEM WHAT YOU TOLD ME, LINK.
OKAY.
A PIRATE CAPTAIN I MET BY CHANCE TOLD ME...
...THAT DEMONS THAT POSSESS PEOPLE CAN'T STAND MYSTERY SEEDS.

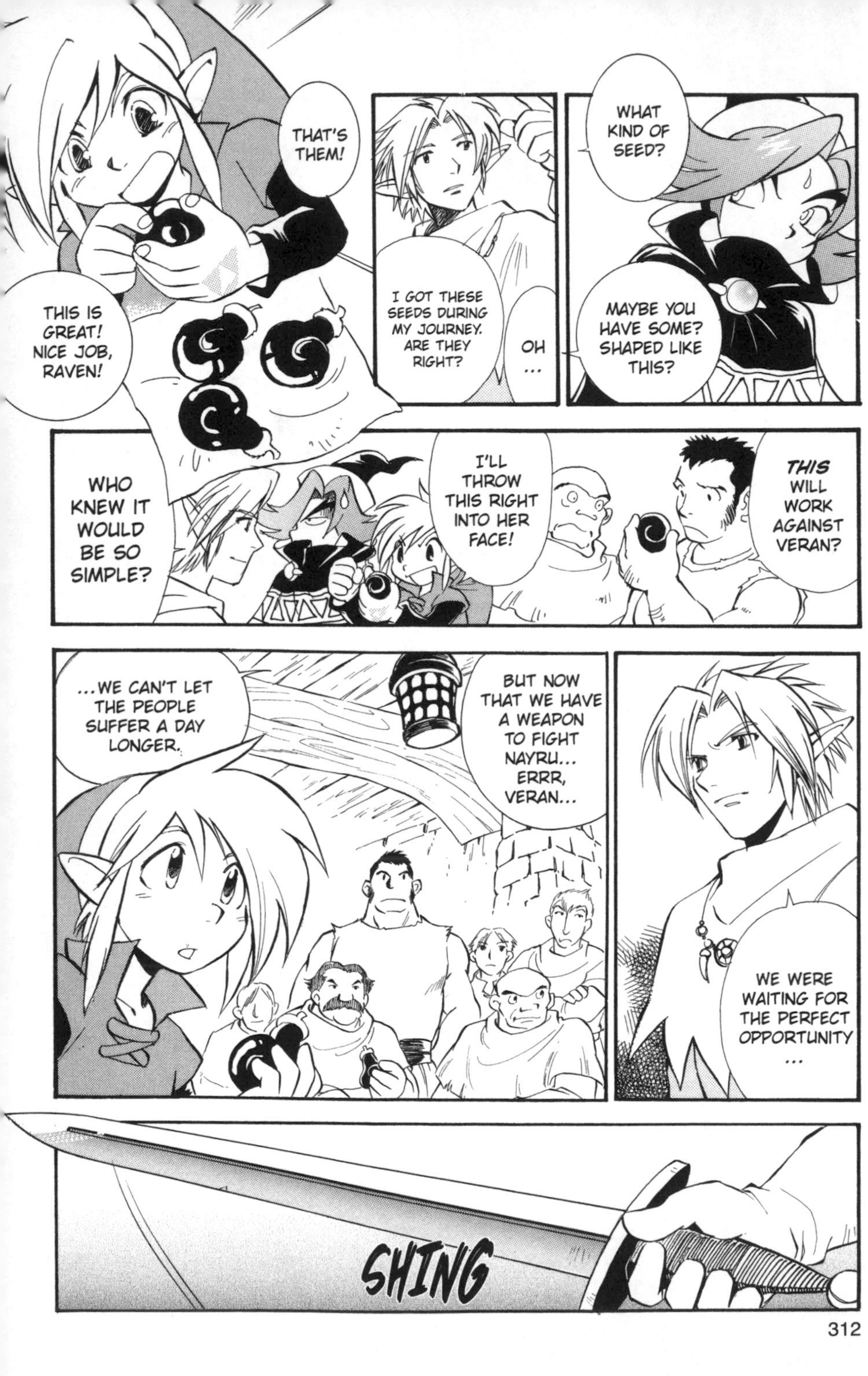
WHAT KIND OF SEED?
MAYBE YOU HAVE SOME? SHAPED LIKE THIS?
I GOT THESE SEEDS DURING MY JOURNEY. ARE THEY RIGHT?
OH ...
THAT'S THEM!
THIS IS GREAT! NICE JOB, RAVEN!
THIS WILL WORK AGAINST VERAN?
I'LL THROW THIS RIGHT INTO HER FACE!
WHO KNEW IT WOULD BE SO SIMPLE?
WE WERE WAITING FOR THE PERFECT OPPORTUNITY ...
BUT NOW THAT WE HAVE A WEAPON TO FIGHT NAYRU... ERRR, VERAN...
...WE CAN'T LET THE PEOPLE SUFFER A DAY LONGER.
SHING

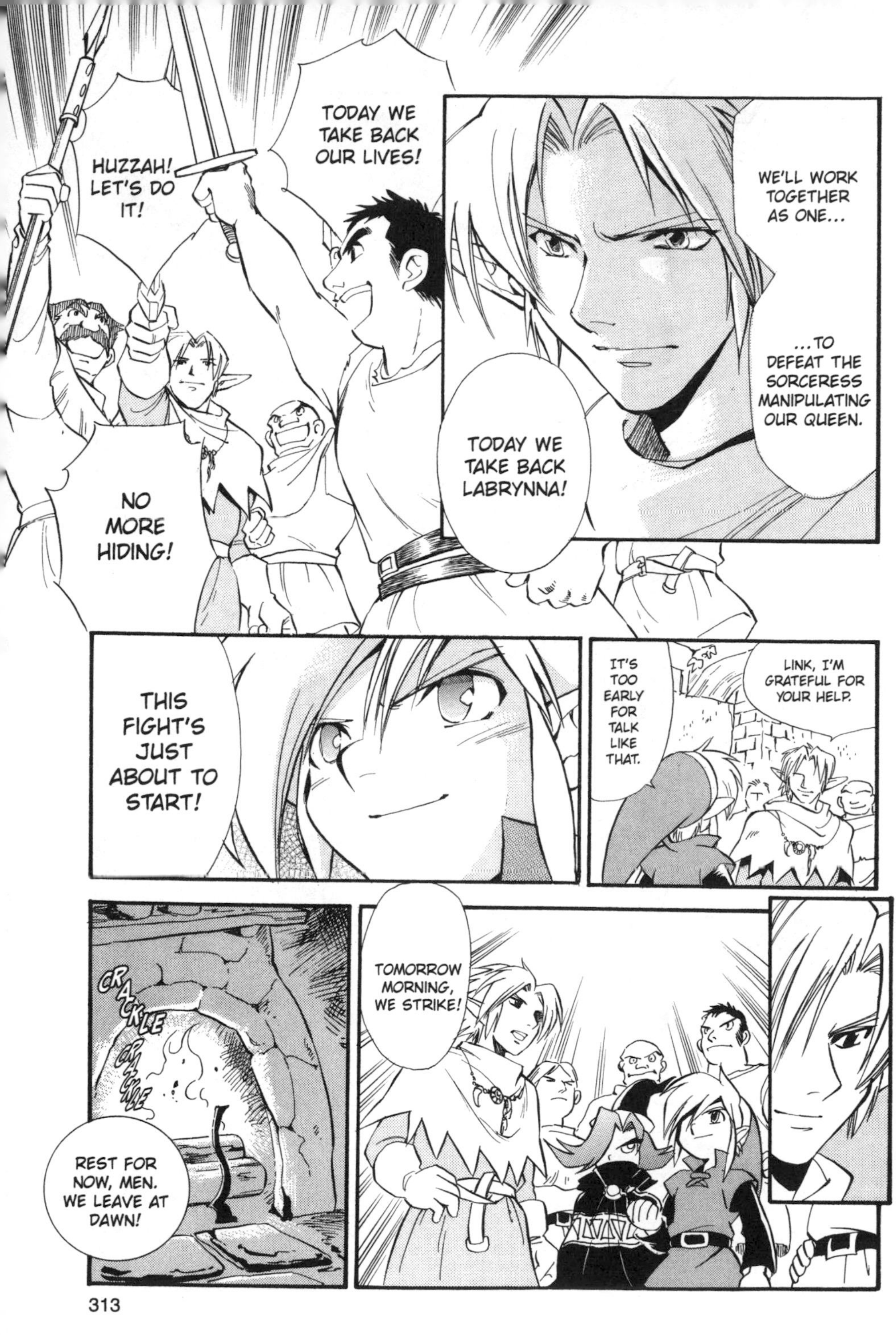
WE'LL WORK TOGETHER AS ONE...
...TO DEFEAT THE SORCERESS MANIPULATING OUR QUEEN.
TODAY WE TAKE BACK LABRYNNA!
TODAY WE TAKE BACK OUR LIVES!
HUZZAH! LET'S DO IT!
NO MORE HIDING!
LINK, I'M GRATEFUL FOR YOUR HELP.
IT'S TOO EARLY FOR TALK LIKE THAT.
THIS FIGHT'S JUST ABOUT TO START!
TOMORROW MORNING, WE STRIKE!
CRACKLE
CRACKLE
REST FOR NOW, MEN. WE LEAVE AT DAWN!

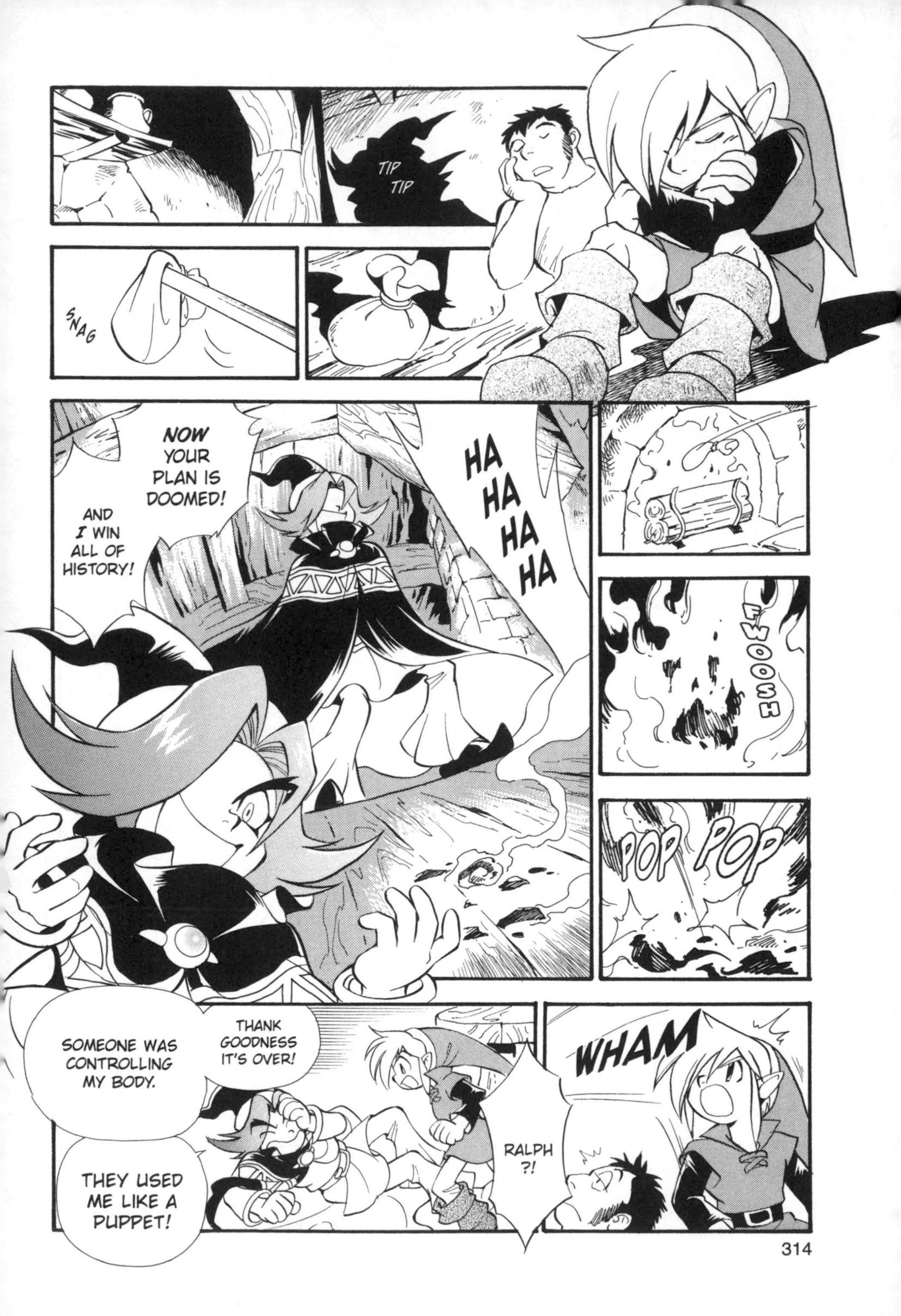
TIP TIP
SNAG
FWOOSH
POP POP
HA HA HA HA
NOW YOUR PLAN IS DOOMED!
AND I WIN ALL OF HISTORY!
WHAM
RALPH ?!
THANK GOODNESS IT'S OVER!
SOMEONE WAS CONTROLLING MY BODY.
THEY USED ME LIKE A PUPPET!

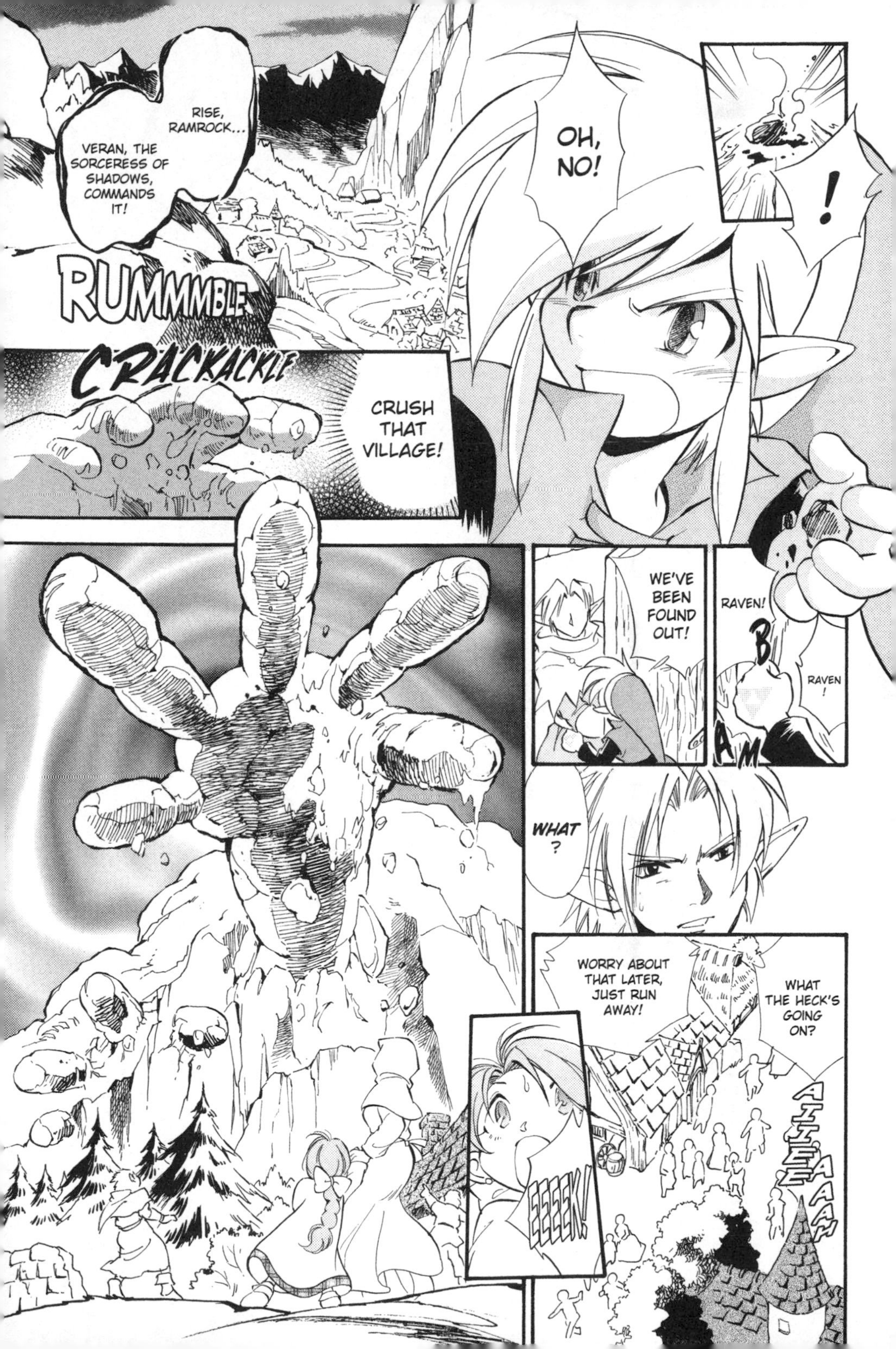
!
OH, NO!
RISE, RAMROCK...
VERAN, THE SORCERESS OF SHADOWS, COMMANDS IT!
RUMMMBLE
CRACKACKLE
CRUSH THAT VILLAGE!
RAVEN!
BAM
RAVEN!
WE'VE BEEN FOUND OUT!
WHAT?
WHAT THE HECK'S GOING ON?
WORRY ABOUT THAT LATER, JUST RUN AWAY!
AIIEEAAAH
EEEEK!

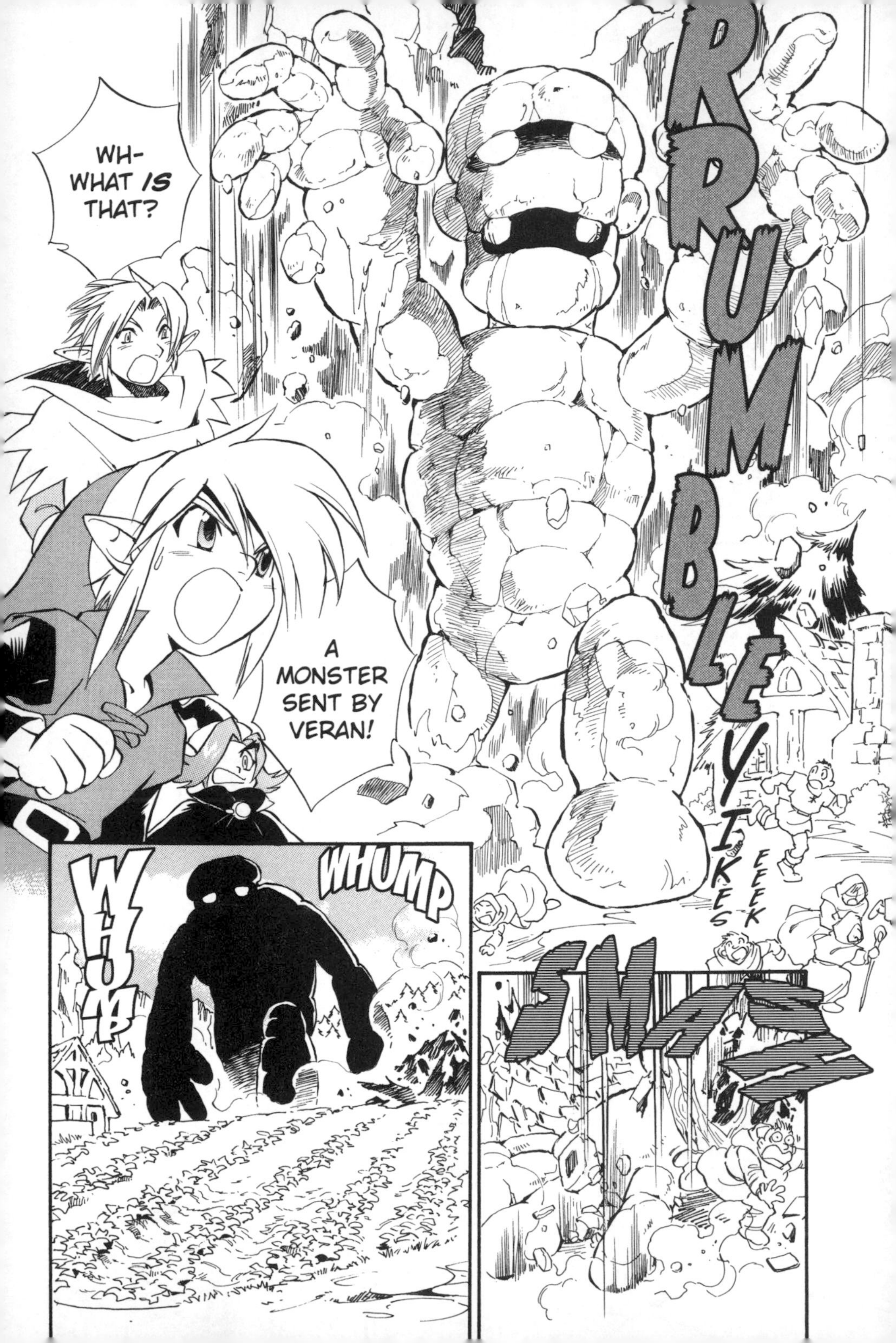
RRUMBLE
WH- WHAT *IS* THAT?
A MONSTER SENT BY VERAN!
YIKES
EEEK
SMASH
WHUMP
WHUMP

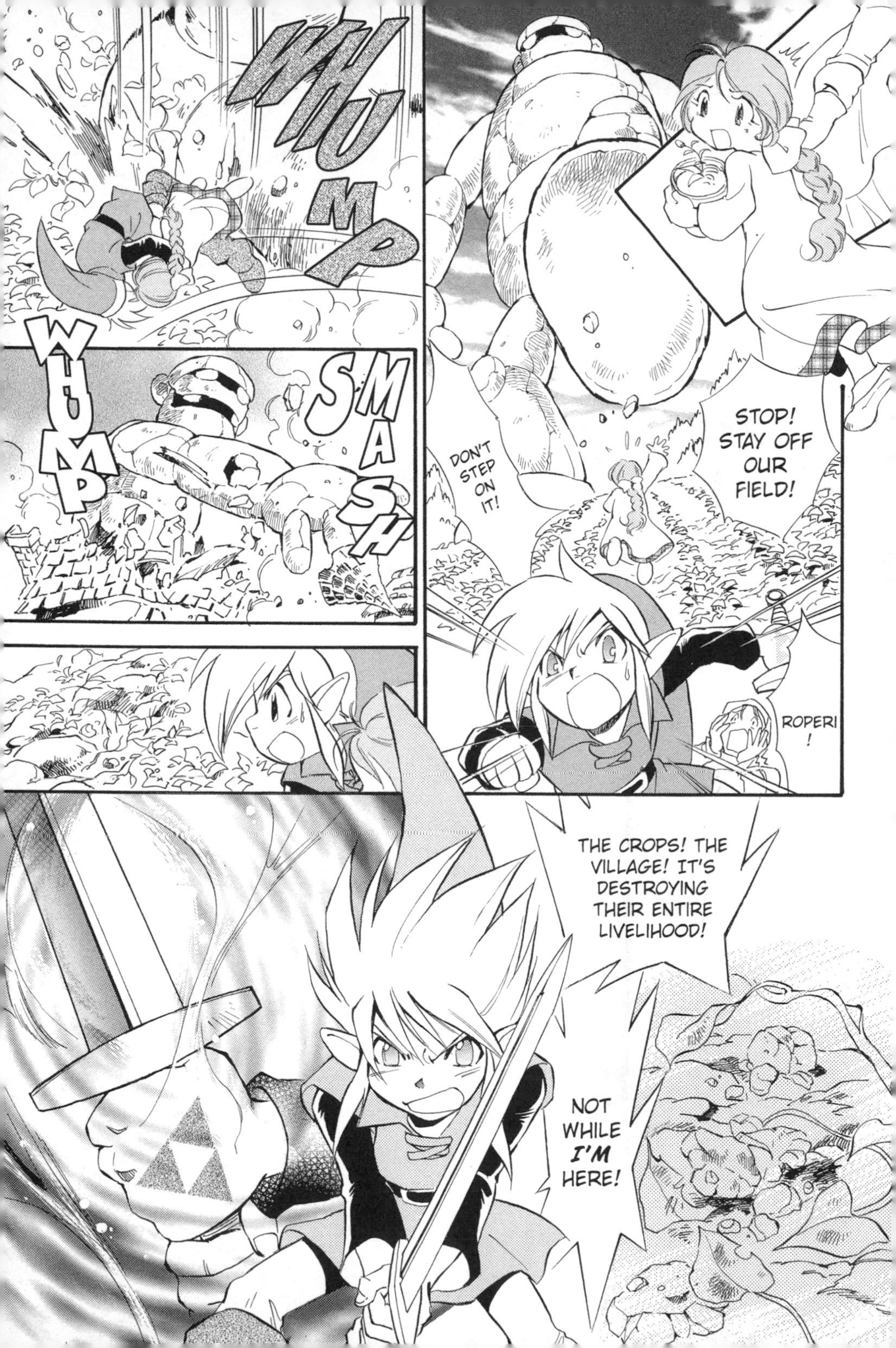
STOP! STAY OFF OUR FIELD!
DON'T STEP ON IT!
ROPERI!
WHUMP
SMASH
WHUMP
THE CROPS! THE VILLAGE! IT'S DESTROYING THEIR ENTIRE LIVELIHOOD!
NOT WHILE *I'M* HERE!

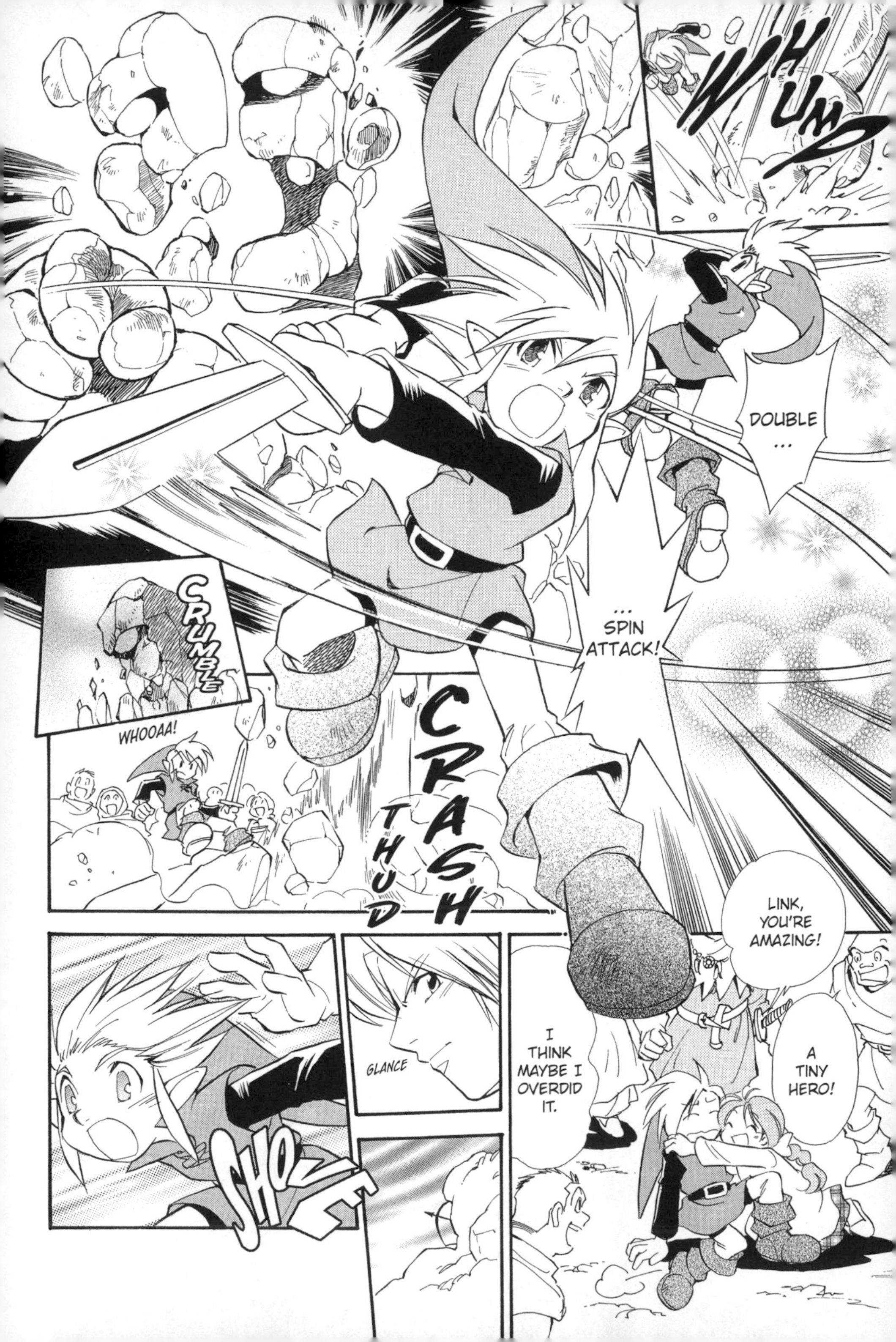
WHUMP
DOUBLE ...
... SPIN ATTACK!
CRASH
THUD
CRUMBLE
WHOOAA!
LINK, YOU'RE AMAZING!
A TINY HERO!
I THINK MAYBE I OVERDID IT.
GLANCE

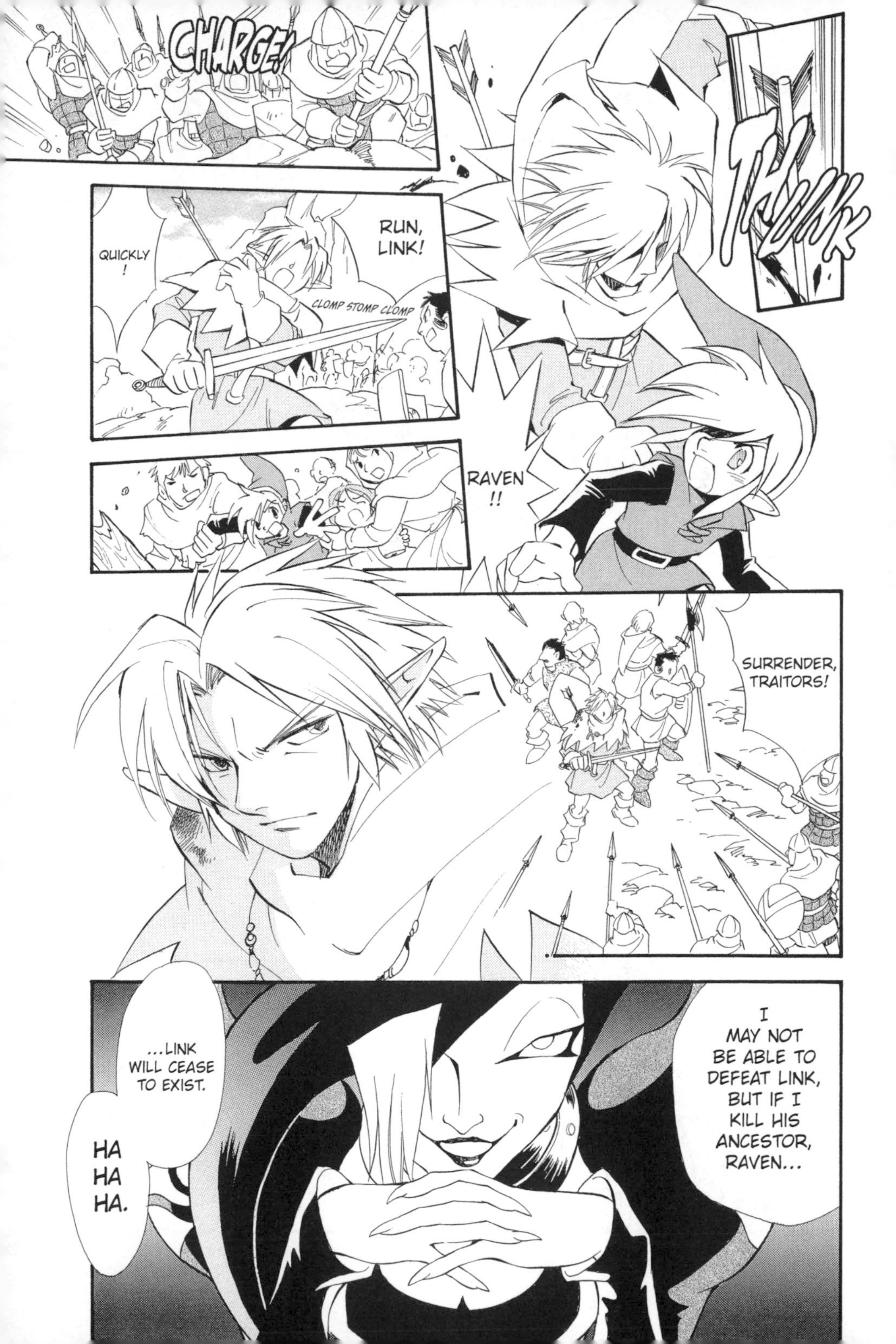

THUNK
CHARGE!
RUN, LINK!
QUICKLY!
CLOMP STOMP CLOMP
RAVEN!!
SURRENDER, TRAITORS!
I MAY NOT BE ABLE TO DEFEAT LINK, BUT IF I KILL HIS ANCESTOR, RAVEN...
...LINK WILL CEASE TO EXIST.
HA HA HA.

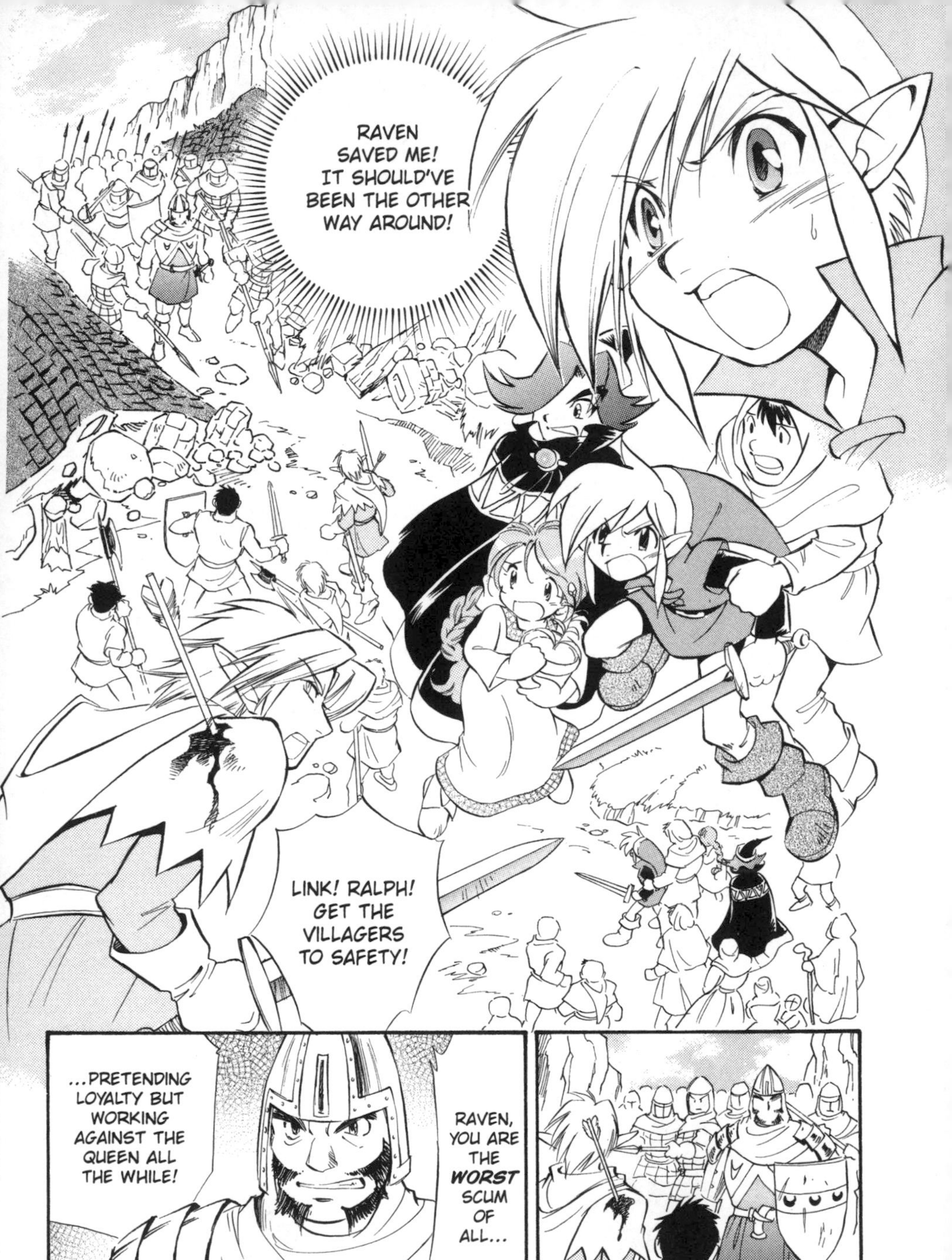
RAVEN SAVED ME! IT SHOULD'VE BEEN THE OTHER WAY AROUND!
LINK! RALPH! GET THE VILLAGERS TO SAFETY!
RAVEN, YOU ARE THE ***WORST*** SCUM OF ALL...
...PRETENDING LOYALTY BUT WORKING AGAINST THE QUEEN ALL THE WHILE!

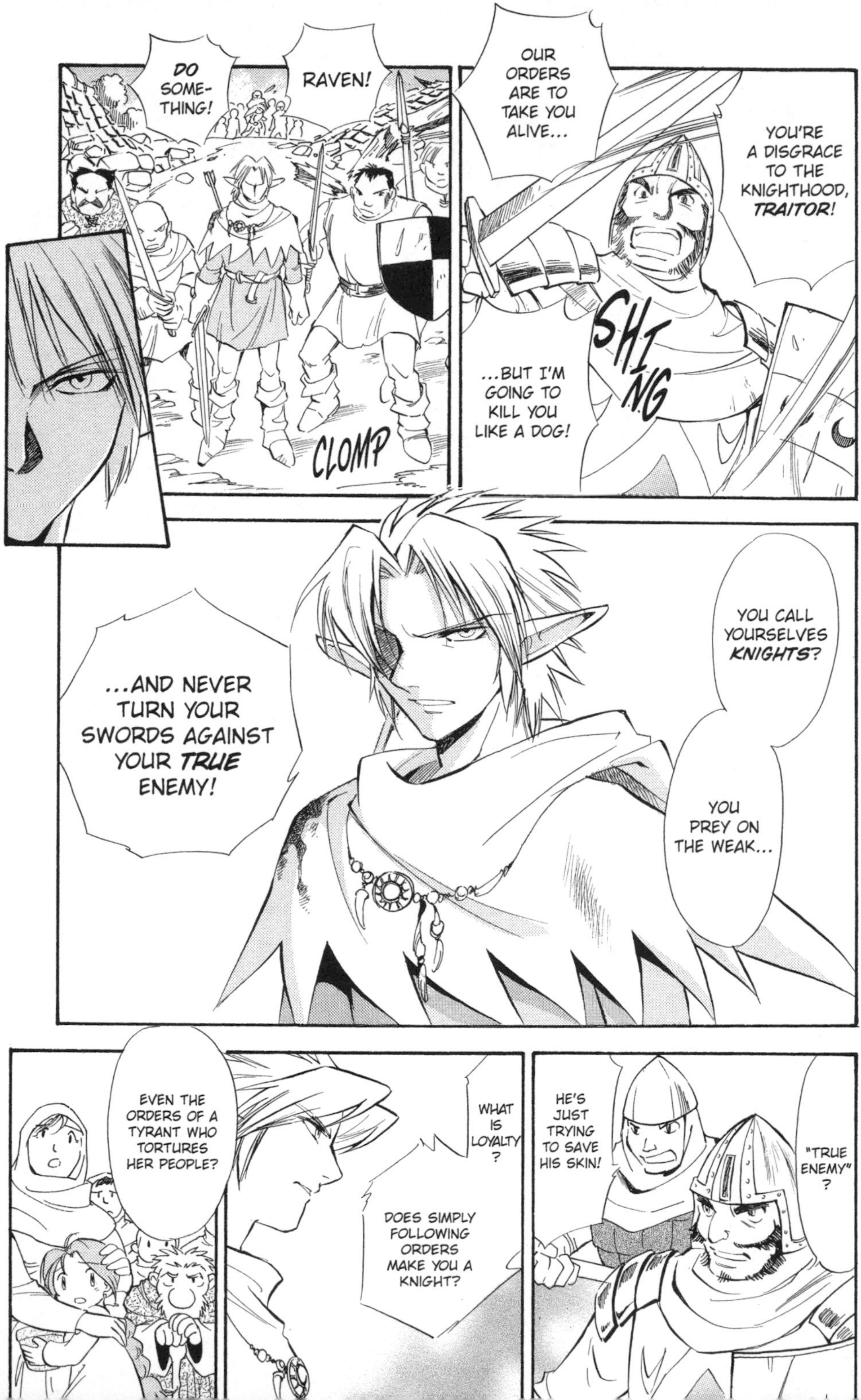
OUR ORDERS ARE TO TAKE YOU ALIVE...
YOU'RE A DISGRACE TO THE KNIGHTHOOD, *TRAITOR!*
SHING
...BUT I'M GOING TO KILL YOU LIKE A DOG!
RAVEN!
DO SOME-THING!
CLOMP
YOU CALL YOURSELVES *KNIGHTS*?
YOU PREY ON THE WEAK...
...AND NEVER TURN YOUR SWORDS AGAINST YOUR *TRUE* ENEMY!
"TRUE ENEMY"?
HE'S JUST TRYING TO SAVE HIS SKIN!
WHAT IS LOYALTY?
DOES SIMPLY FOLLOWING ORDERS MAKE YOU A KNIGHT?
EVEN THE ORDERS OF A TYRANT WHO TORTURES HER PEOPLE?

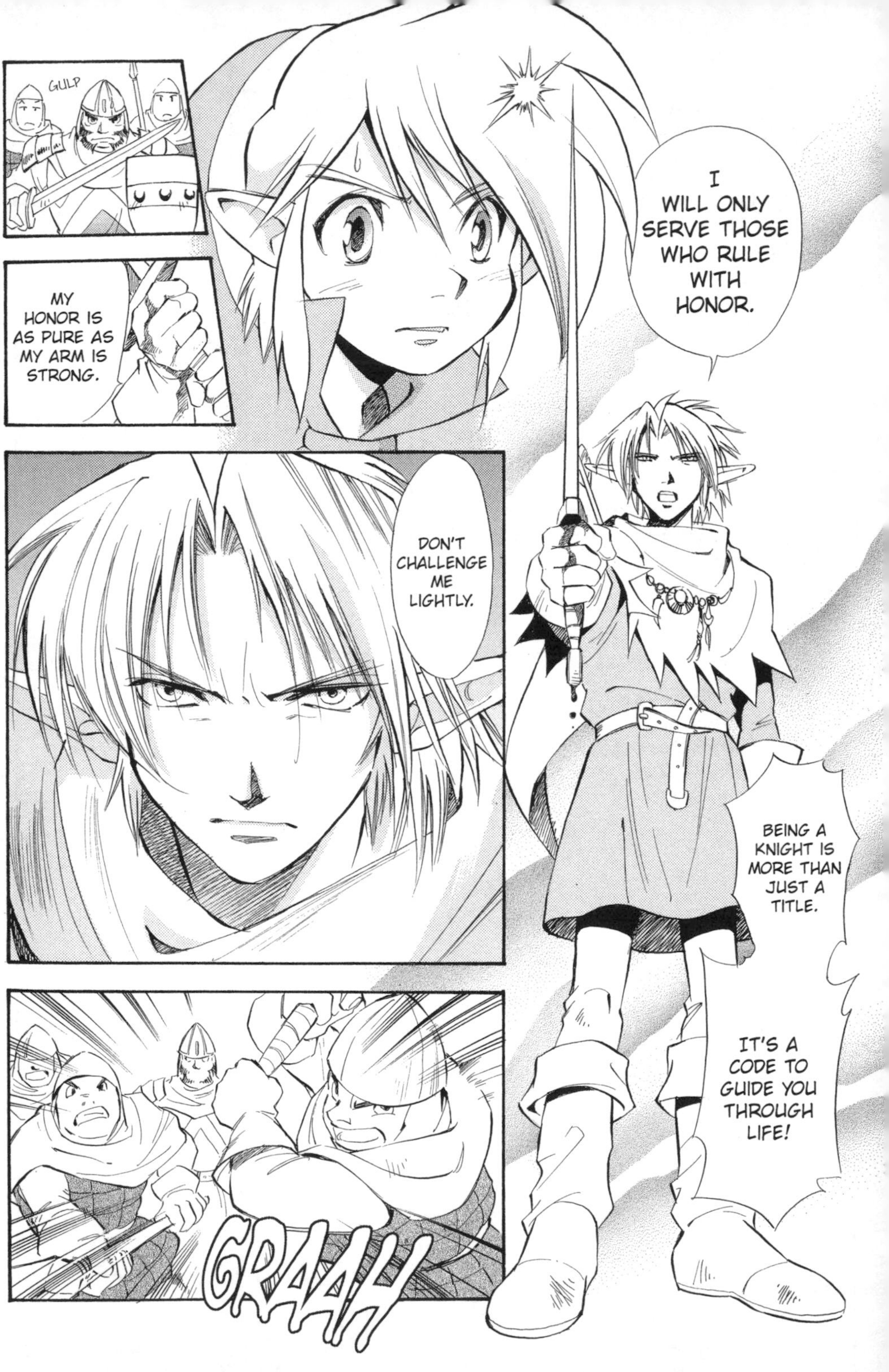
I WILL ONLY SERVE THOSE WHO RULE WITH HONOR.
BEING A KNIGHT IS MORE THAN JUST A TITLE.
IT'S A CODE TO GUIDE YOU THROUGH LIFE!
GULP
MY HONOR IS AS PURE AS MY ARM IS STRONG.
DON'T CHALLENGE ME LIGHTLY.
GRAAH

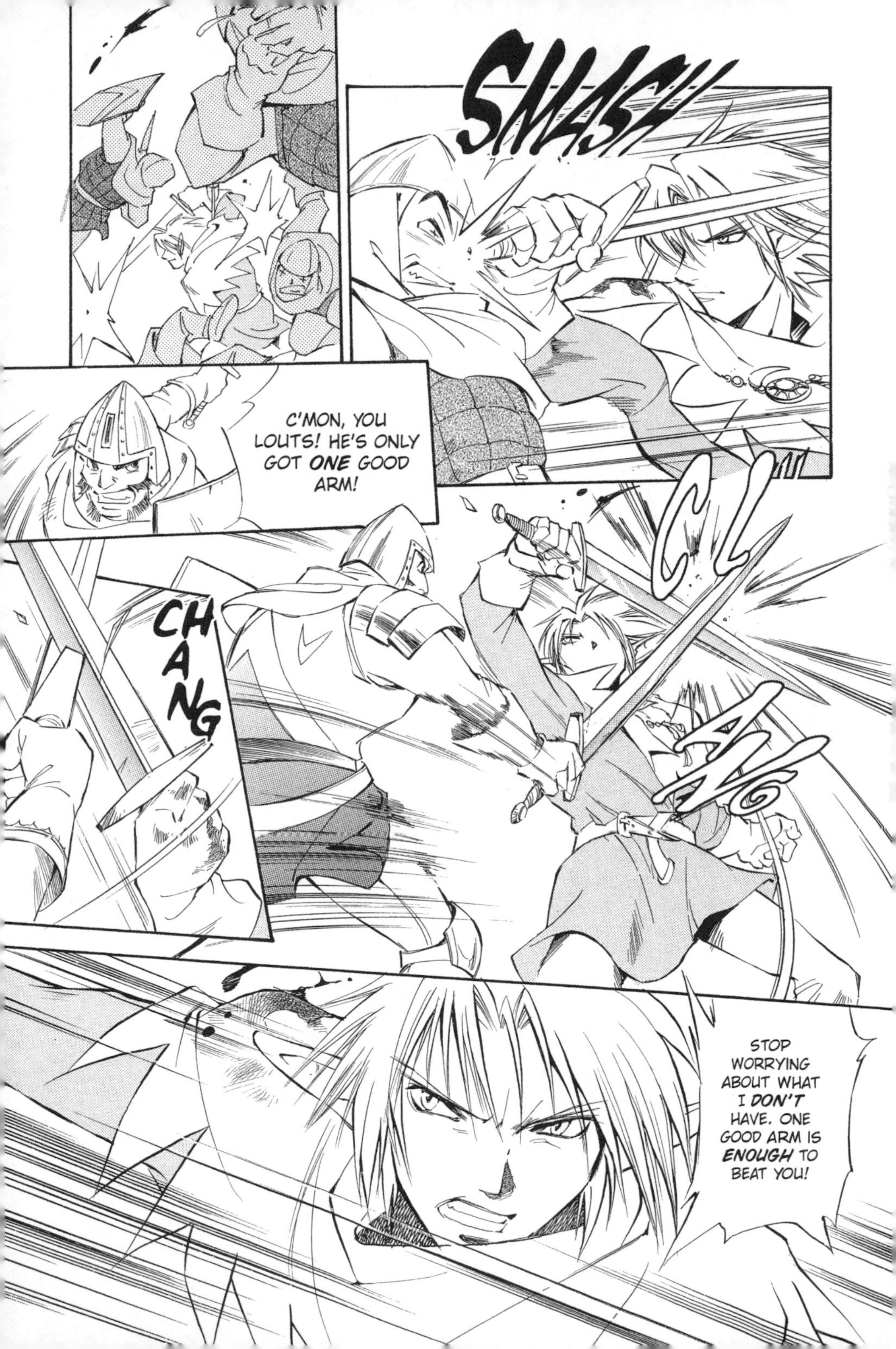
SMASH
C'MON, YOU LOUTS! HE'S ONLY GOT ONE GOOD ARM!
CLANG
CHANG
STOP WORRYING ABOUT WHAT I DON'T HAVE. ONE GOOD ARM IS ENOUGH TO BEAT YOU!

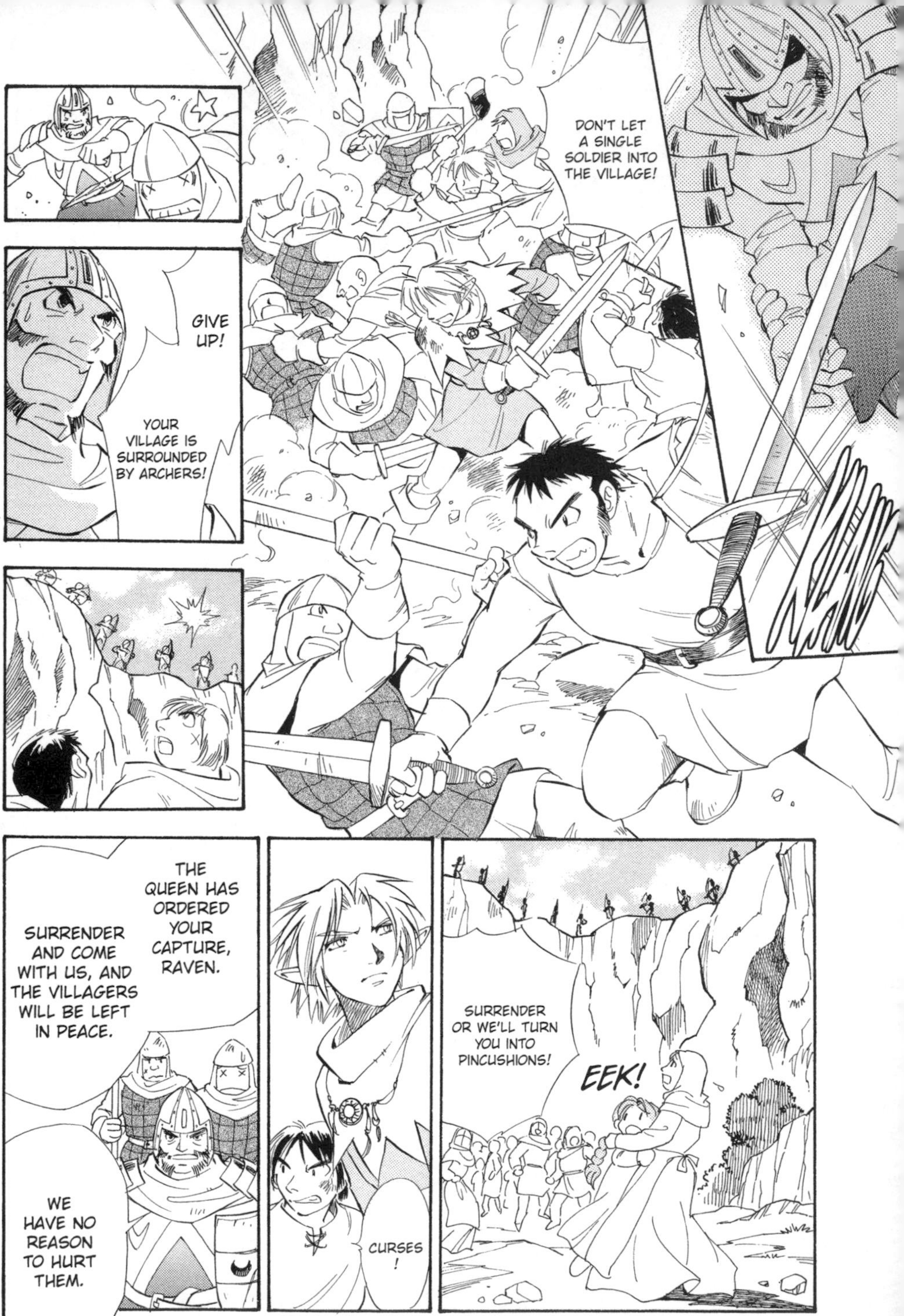
DON'T LET A SINGLE SOLDIER INTO THE VILLAGE!
GIVE UP!
YOUR VILLAGE IS SURROUNDED BY ARCHERS!
SURRENDER OR WE'LL TURN YOU INTO PINCUSHIONS!
EEK!
CURSES!
THE QUEEN HAS ORDERED YOUR CAPTURE, RAVEN.
SURRENDER AND COME WITH US, AND THE VILLAGERS WILL BE LEFT IN PEACE.
WE HAVE NO REASON TO HURT THEM.

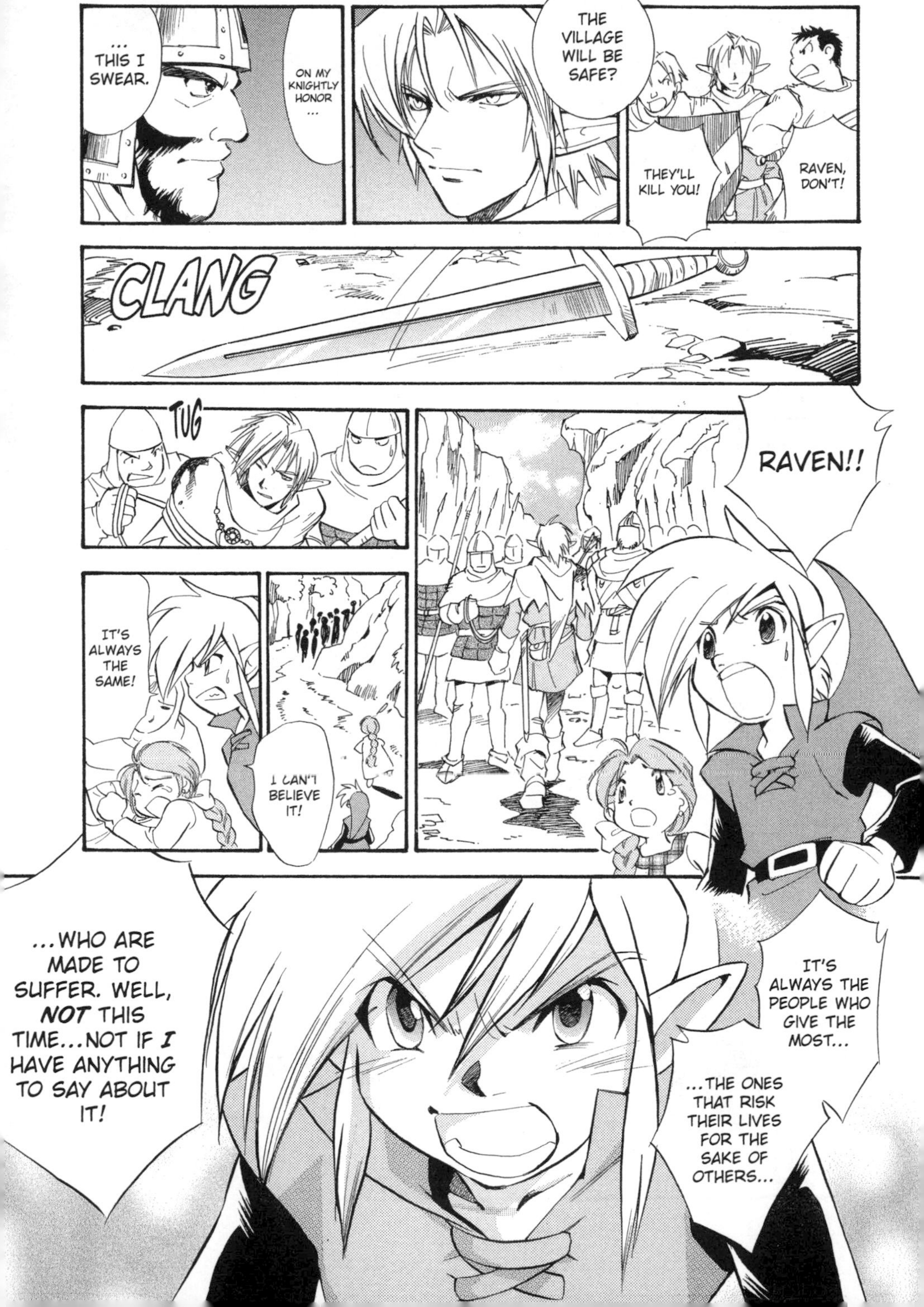
RAVEN, DON'T!
THEY'LL KILL YOU!
THE VILLAGE WILL BE SAFE?
ON MY KNIGHTLY HONOR ...
... THIS I SWEAR.
CLANG
RAVEN!!
TUG
I CAN'T BELIEVE IT!
IT'S ALWAYS THE SAME!
IT'S ALWAYS THE PEOPLE WHO GIVE THE MOST...
...THE ONES THAT RISK THEIR LIVES FOR THE SAKE OF OTHERS...
...WHO ARE MADE TO SUFFER. WELL, **NOT** THIS TIME...NOT IF *I* HAVE ANYTHING TO SAY ABOUT IT!

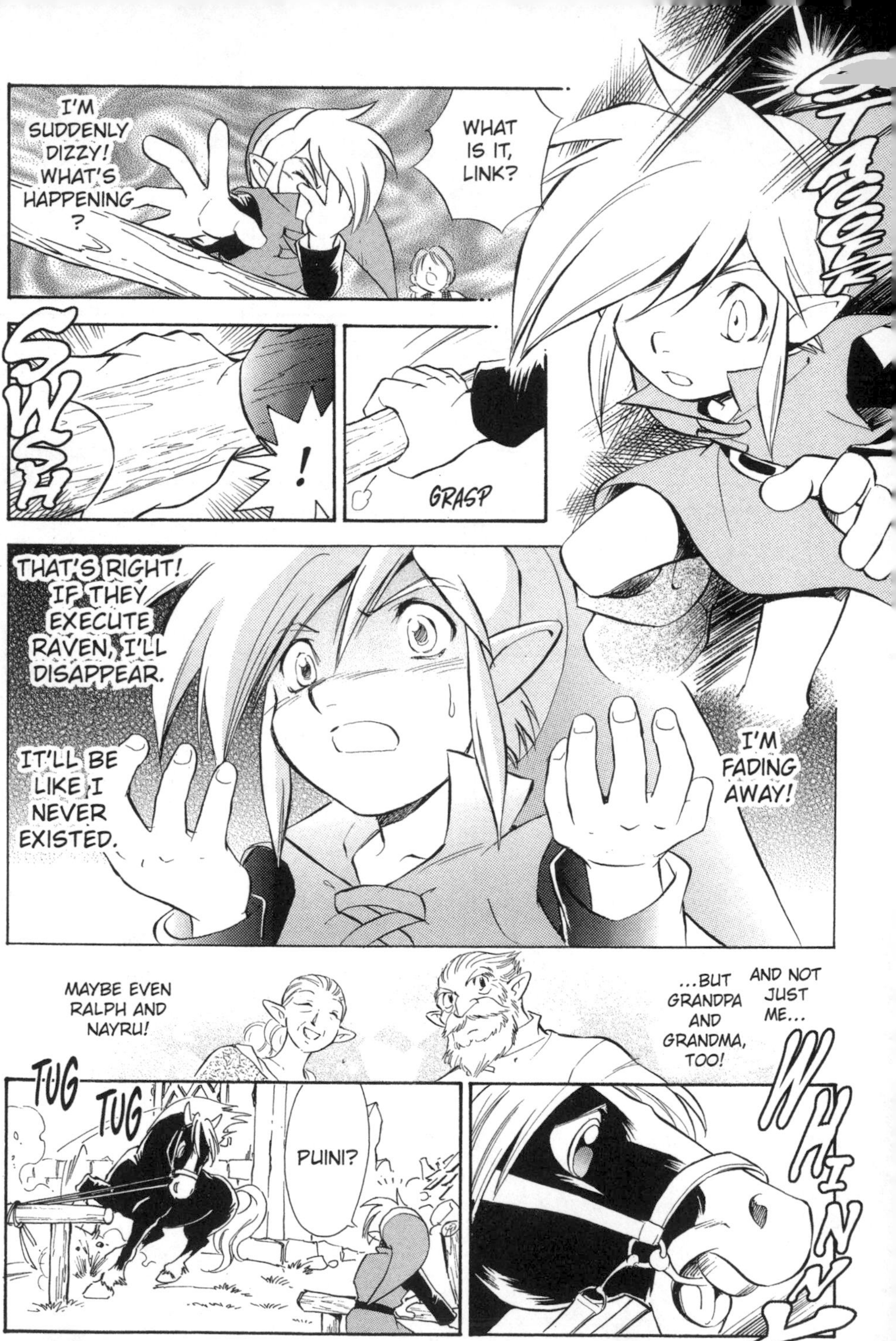
STAGGER
WHAT IS IT, LINK?
I'M SUDDENLY DIZZY! WHAT'S HAPPENING?
GRASP
!
SWISH
I'M FADING AWAY!
THAT'S RIGHT! IF THEY EXECUTE RAVEN, I'LL DISAPPEAR.
IT'LL BE LIKE I NEVER EXISTED.
AND NOT JUST ME...
...BUT GRANDPA AND GRANDMA, TOO!
MAYBE EVEN RALPH AND NAYRU!
WHINNY
TUG
TUG
PUINI?

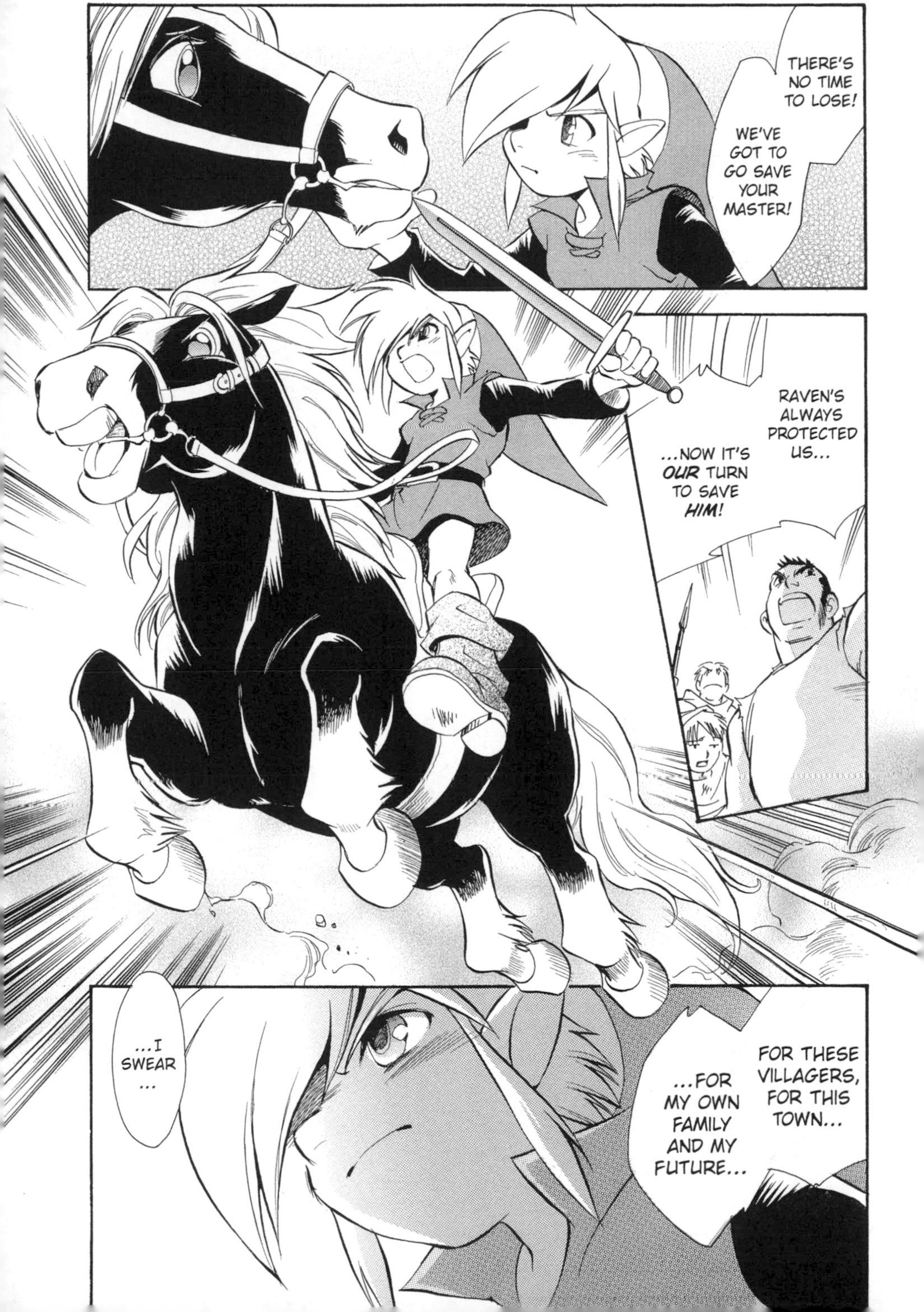
THERE'S NO TIME TO LOSE!
WE'VE GOT TO GO SAVE YOUR MASTER!
RAVEN'S ALWAYS PROTECTED US...
...NOW IT'S *OUR* TURN TO SAVE *HIM*!
FOR THESE VILLAGERS, FOR THIS TOWN...
...FOR MY OWN FAMILY AND MY FUTURE...
...I SWEAR...

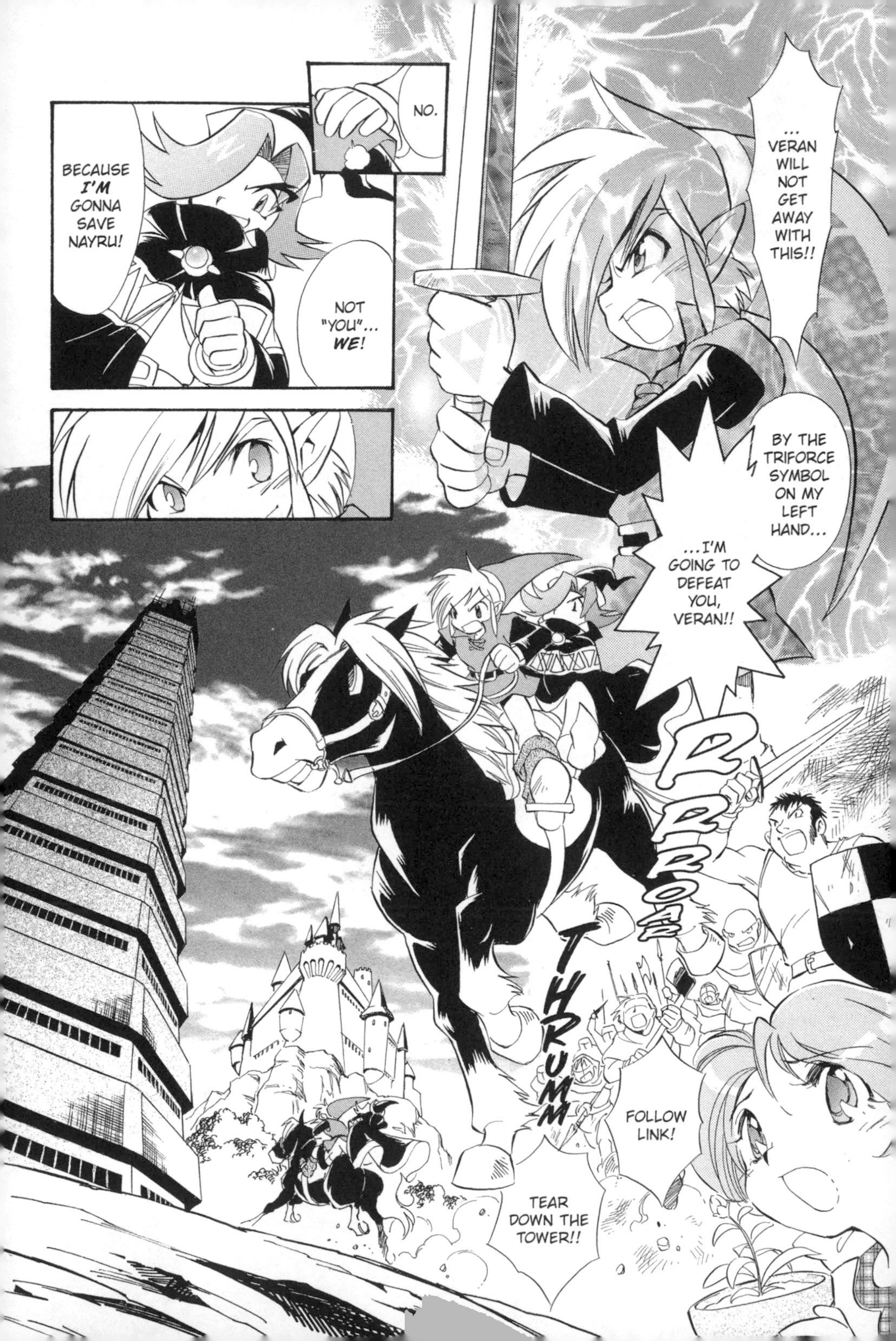

...VERAN WILL NOT GET AWAY WITH THIS!!
BECAUSE *I'M* GONNA SAVE NAYRU!
NO.
NOT "YOU"... ***WE!***
BY THE TRIFORCE SYMBOL ON MY LEFT HAND...
...I'M GOING TO DEFEAT YOU, VERAN!!
BRROOM
THHRUMM
FOLLOW LINK!
TEAR DOWN THE TOWER!!

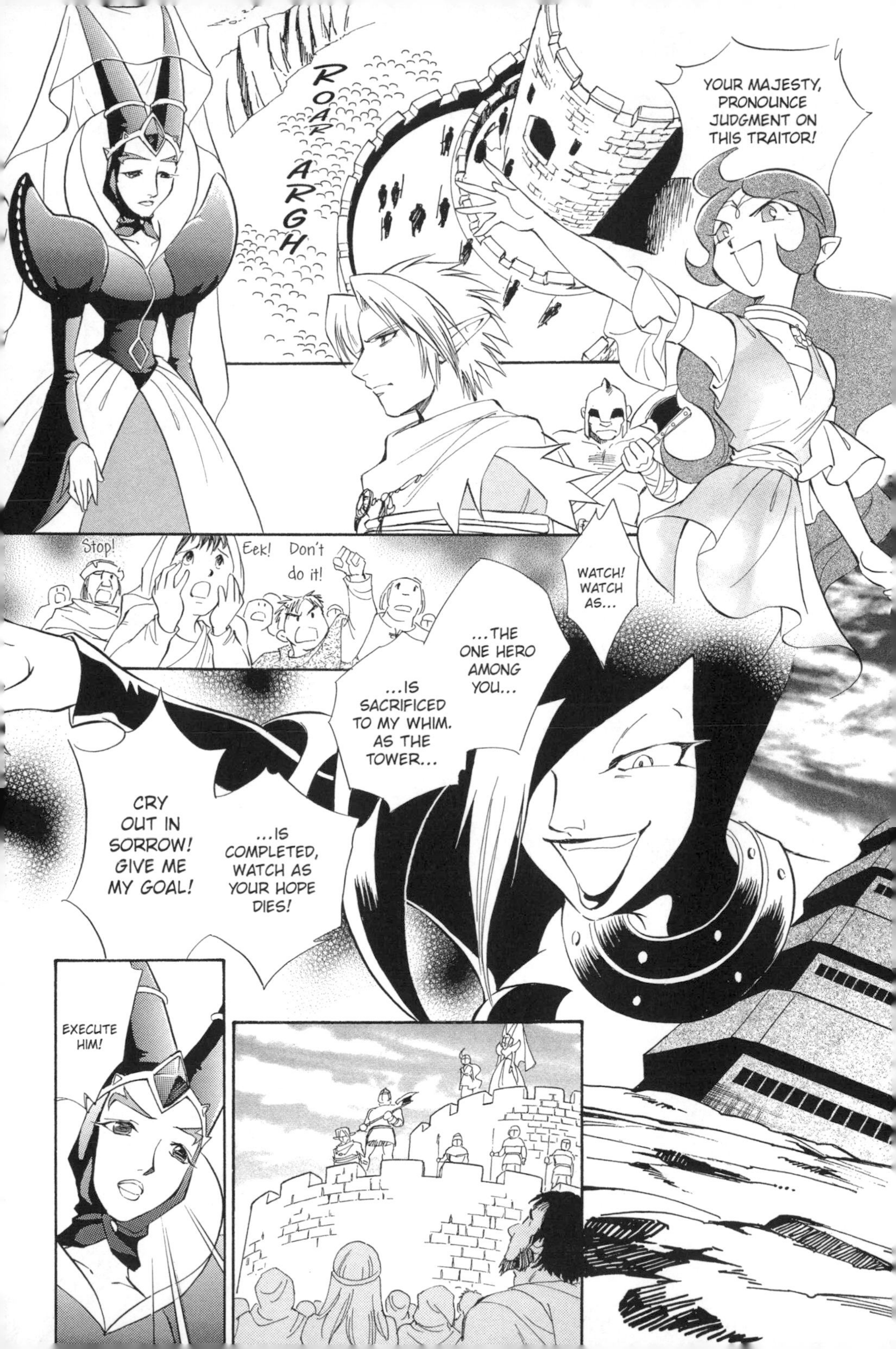
YOUR MAJESTY, PRONOUNCE JUDGMENT ON THIS TRAITOR!
ROAR
ARGH
WATCH! WATCH AS...
...THE ONE HERO AMONG YOU...
...IS SACRIFICED TO MY WHIM. AS THE TOWER...
...IS COMPLETED, WATCH AS YOUR HOPE DIES!
CRY OUT IN SORROW! GIVE ME MY GOAL!
Don't do it!
Eek!
Stop!
EXECUTE HIM!

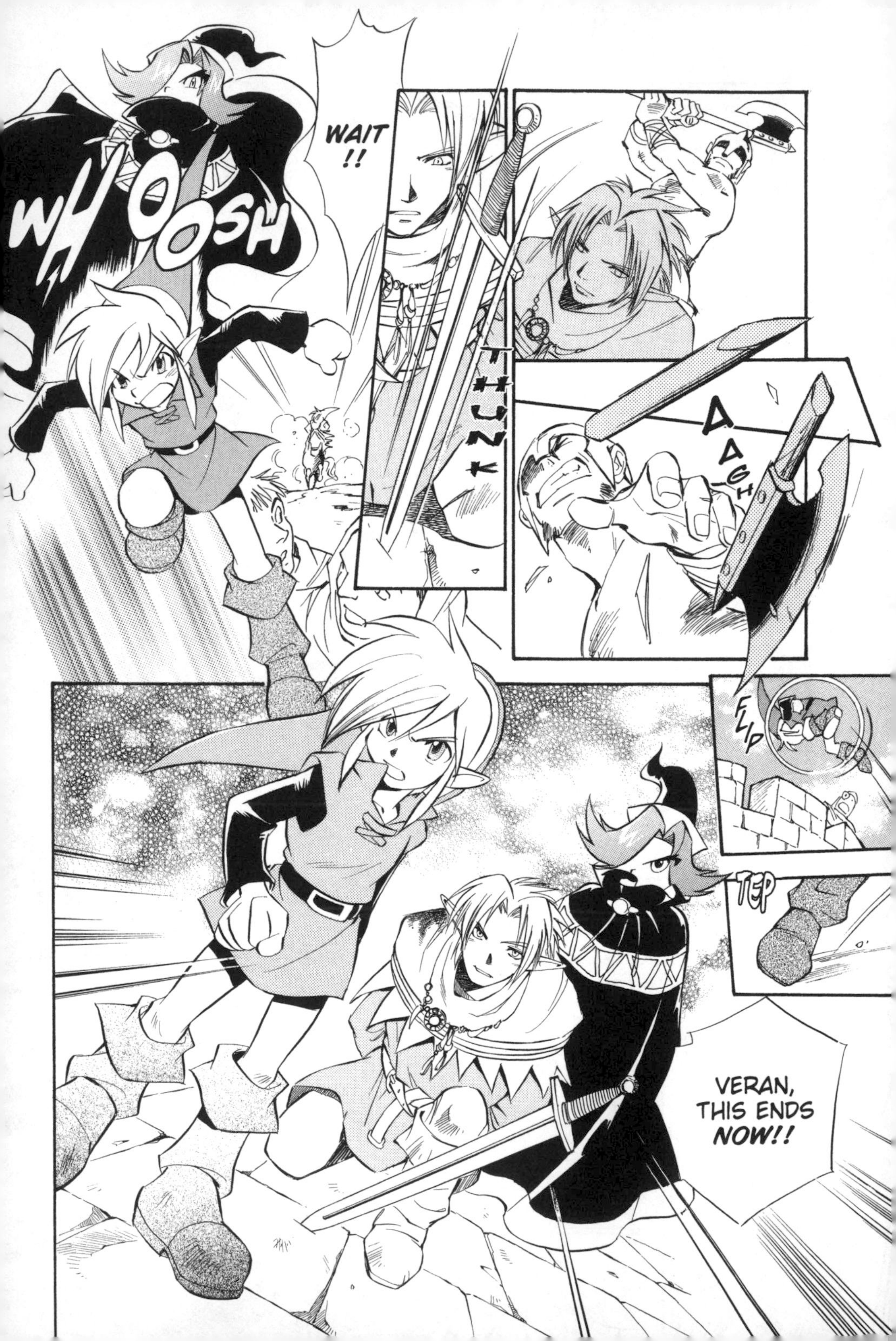
AAGH
THUNK
WAIT!!
WHOOSH
FLIP
TEP
VERAN, THIS ENDS NOW!!

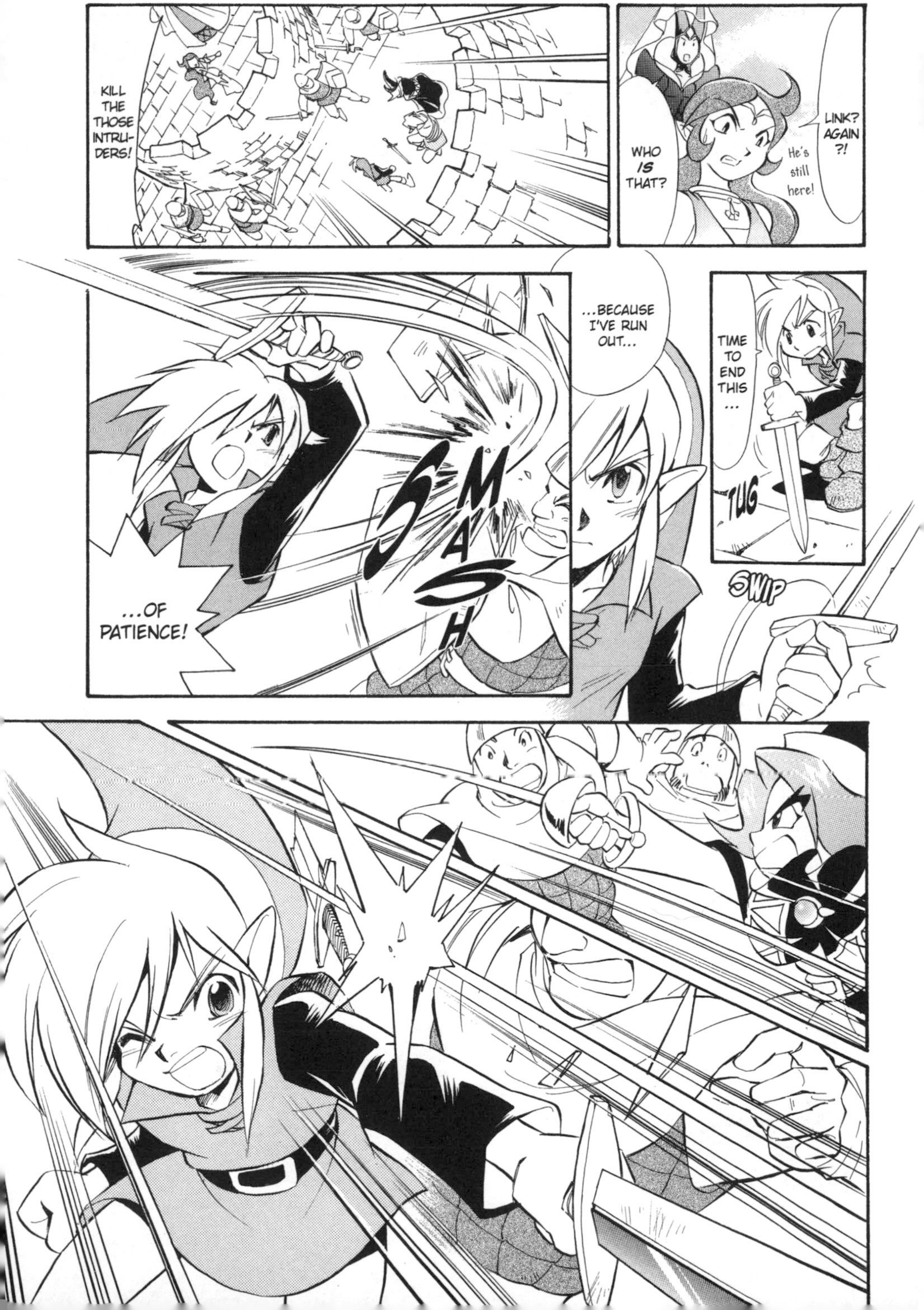
LINK? AGAIN ?!
He's still here!
WHO IS THAT?
KILL THE THOSE INTRUDERS!
TIME TO END THIS ...
TUG
SWIP
...BECAUSE I'VE RUN OUT...
SMASH
...OF PATIENCE!

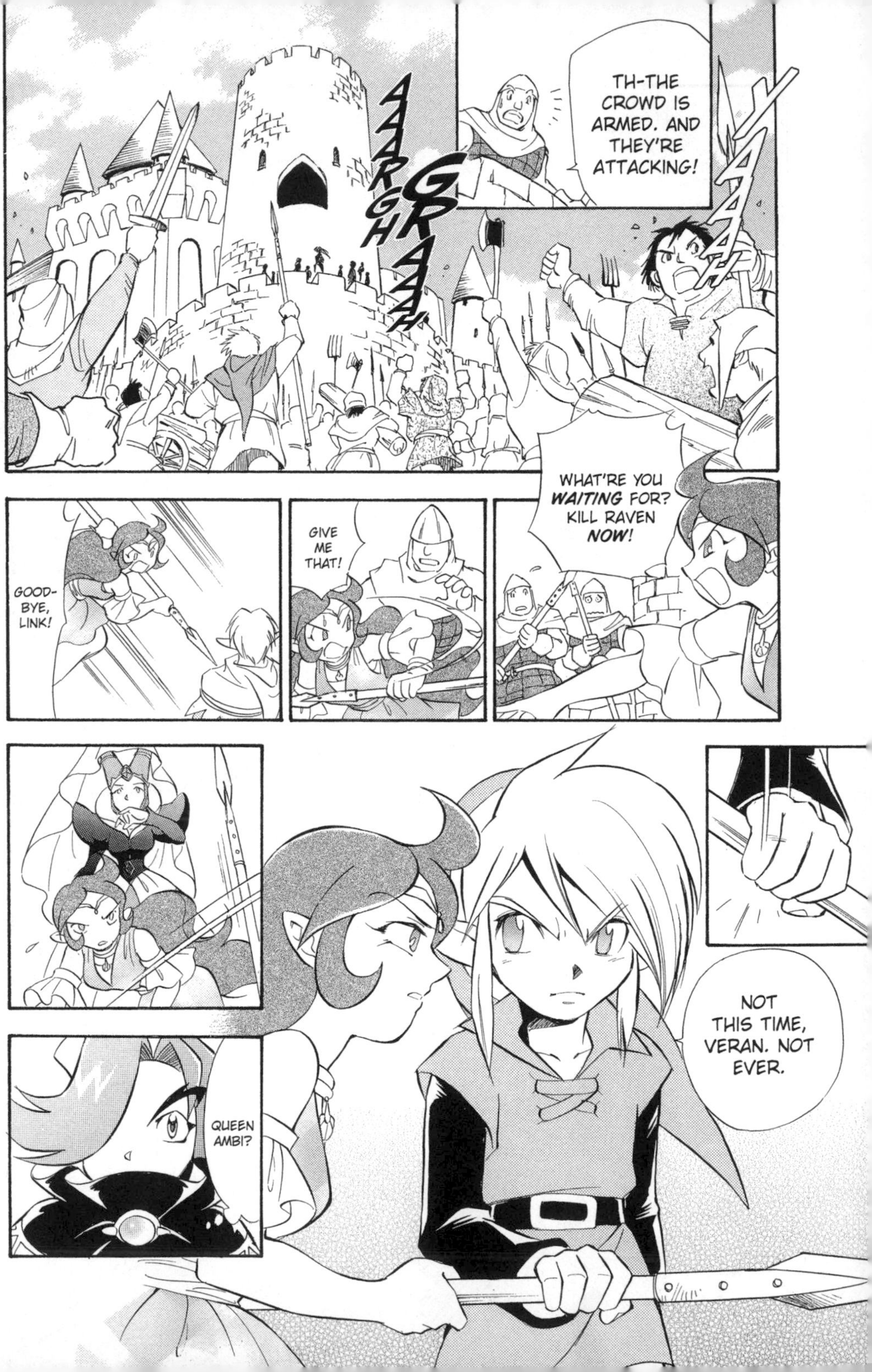
TH-THE CROWD IS ARMED. AND THEY'RE ATTACKING!
YAAAAH
GRAAAH
AAAARGH
WHAT'RE YOU *WAITING* FOR? KILL RAVEN *NOW!*
GIVE ME THAT!
GOOD-BYE, LINK!
NOT THIS TIME, VERAN. NOT EVER.
QUEEN AMBI?

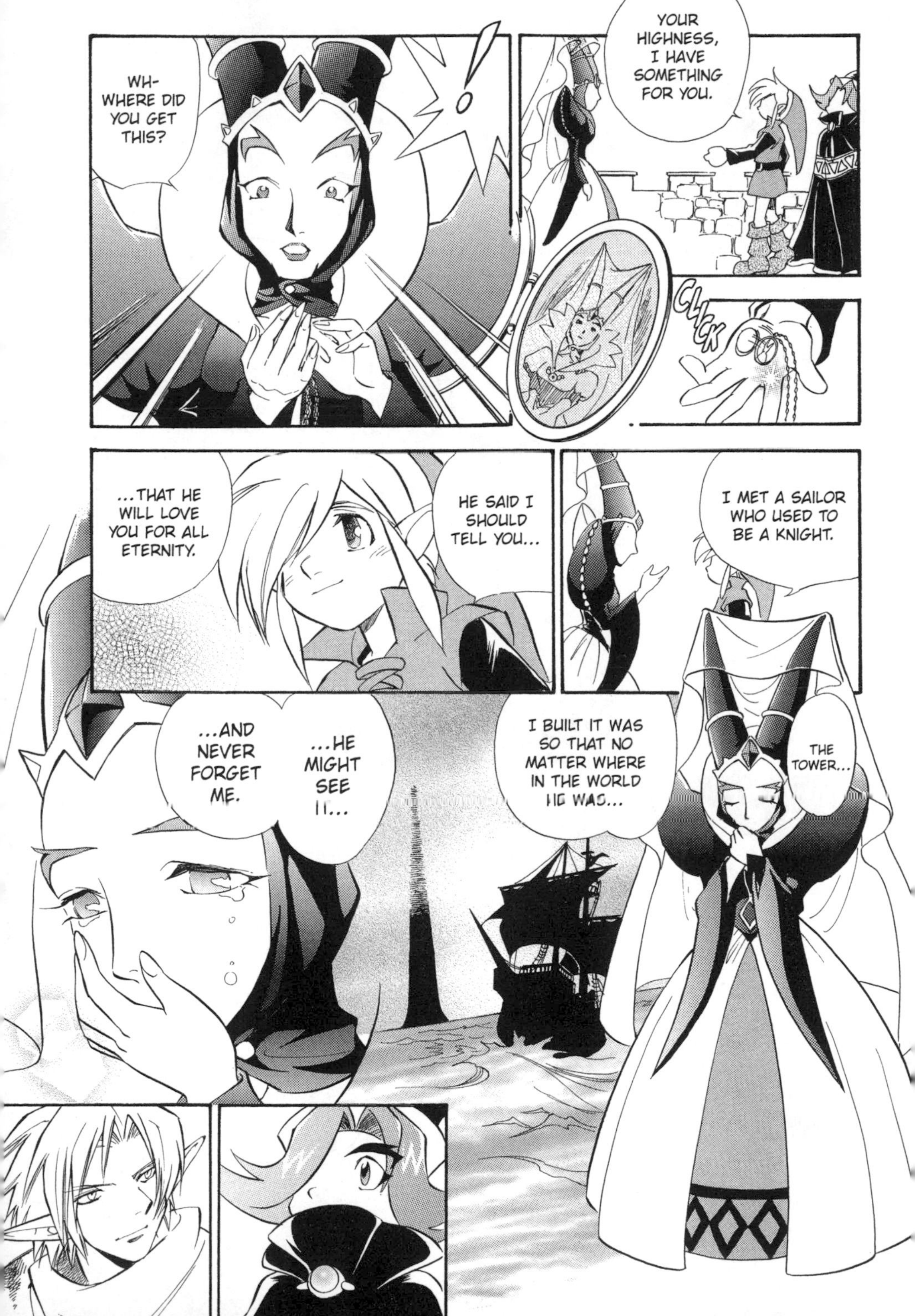
YOUR HIGHNESS, I HAVE SOMETHING FOR YOU.
CLICK
!
WH- WHERE DID YOU GET THIS?
I MET A SAILOR WHO USED TO BE A KNIGHT.
HE SAID I SHOULD TELL YOU...
...THAT HE WILL LOVE YOU FOR ALL ETERNITY.
THE TOWER...
I BUILT IT WAS SO THAT NO MATTER WHERE IN THE WORLD HE WAS...
...HE MIGHT SEE IT...
...AND NEVER FORGET ME.

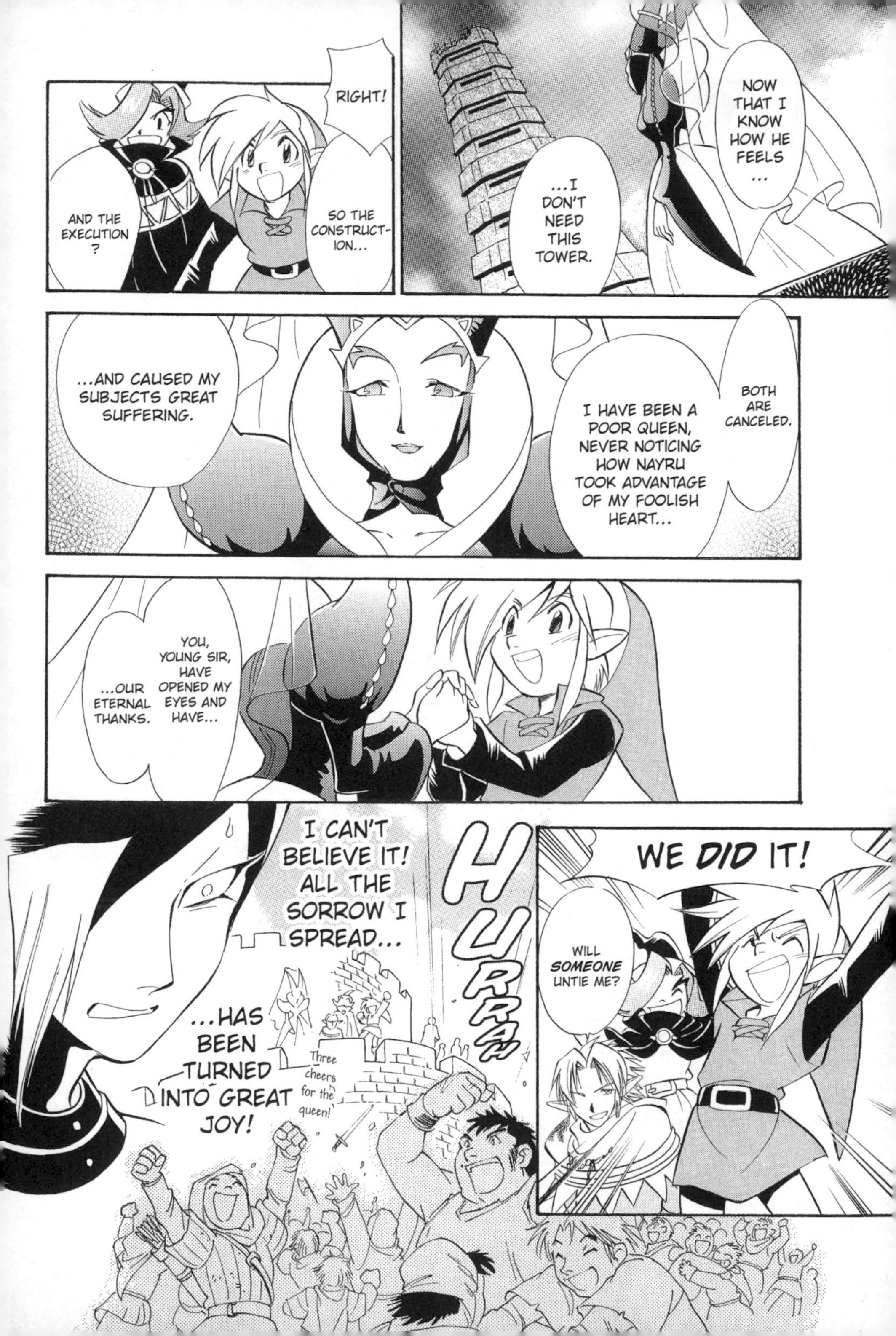
NOW THAT I KNOW HOW HE FEELS...
...I DON'T NEED THIS TOWER.
RIGHT!
SO THE CONSTRUCT-ION...
AND THE EXECUTION?
BOTH ARE CANCELED.
I HAVE BEEN A POOR QUEEN, NEVER NOTICING HOW NAYRU TOOK ADVANTAGE OF MY FOOLISH HEART...
...AND CAUSED MY SUBJECTS GREAT SUFFERING.
YOU, YOUNG SIR, HAVE OPENED MY EYES AND HAVE...
...OUR ETERNAL THANKS.
WE *DID* IT!
WILL *SOMEONE* UNTIE ME?
HURRAH
I CAN'T BELIEVE IT! ALL THE SORROW I SPREAD...
...HAS BEEN TURNED INTO GREAT JOY!
Three cheers for the queen!

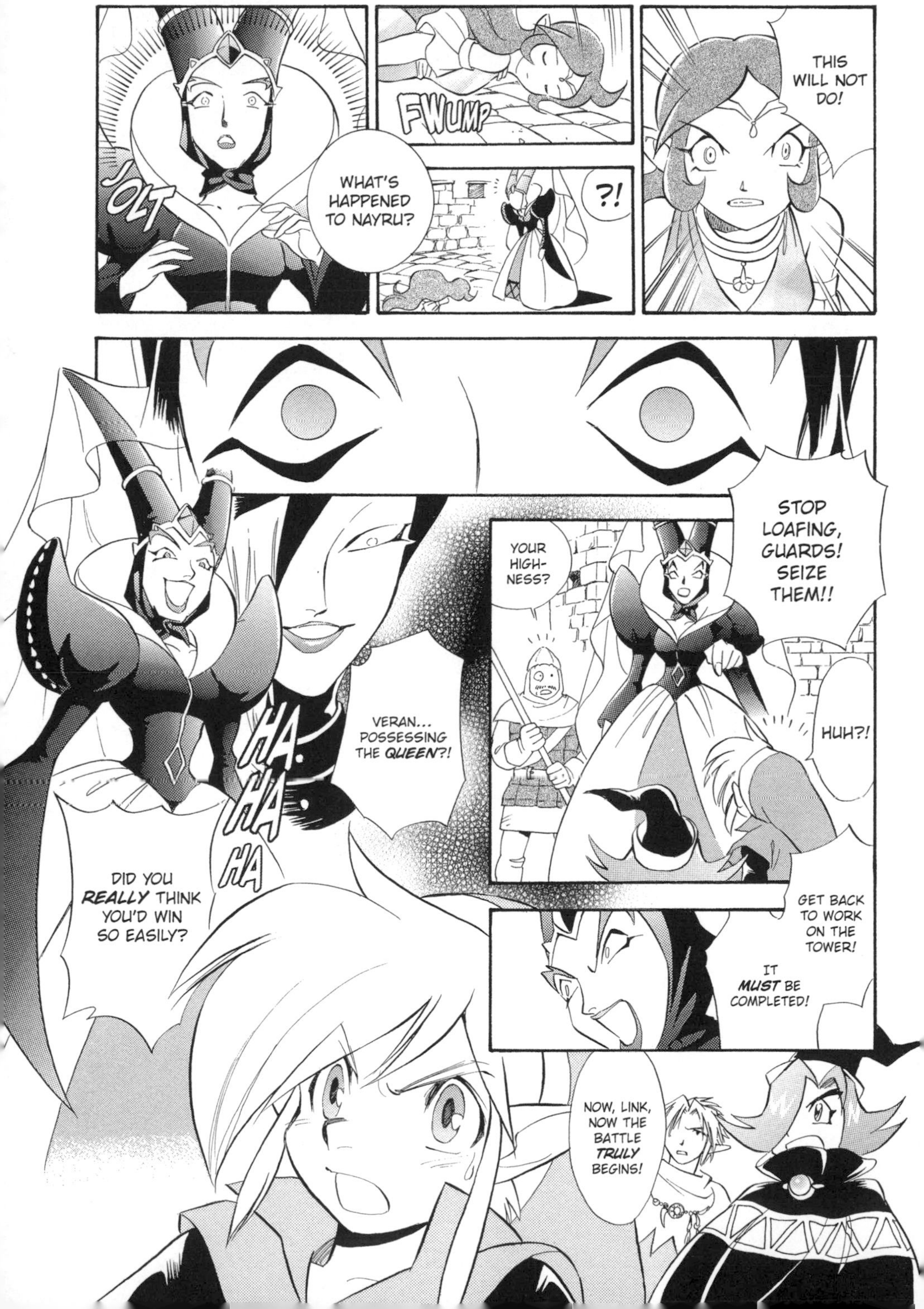
THIS WILL NOT DO!
FWUMP
?!
WHAT'S HAPPENED TO NAYRU?
JOLT
STOP LOAFING, GUARDS! SEIZE THEM!!
YOUR HIGH-NESS?
HUH?!
GET BACK TO WORK ON THE TOWER!
IT *MUST* BE COMPLETED!
VERAN... POSSESSING THE *QUEEN*?!
HA HA HA HA
DID YOU *REALLY* THINK YOU'D WIN SO EASILY?
NOW, LINK, NOW THE BATTLE *TRULY* BEGINS!

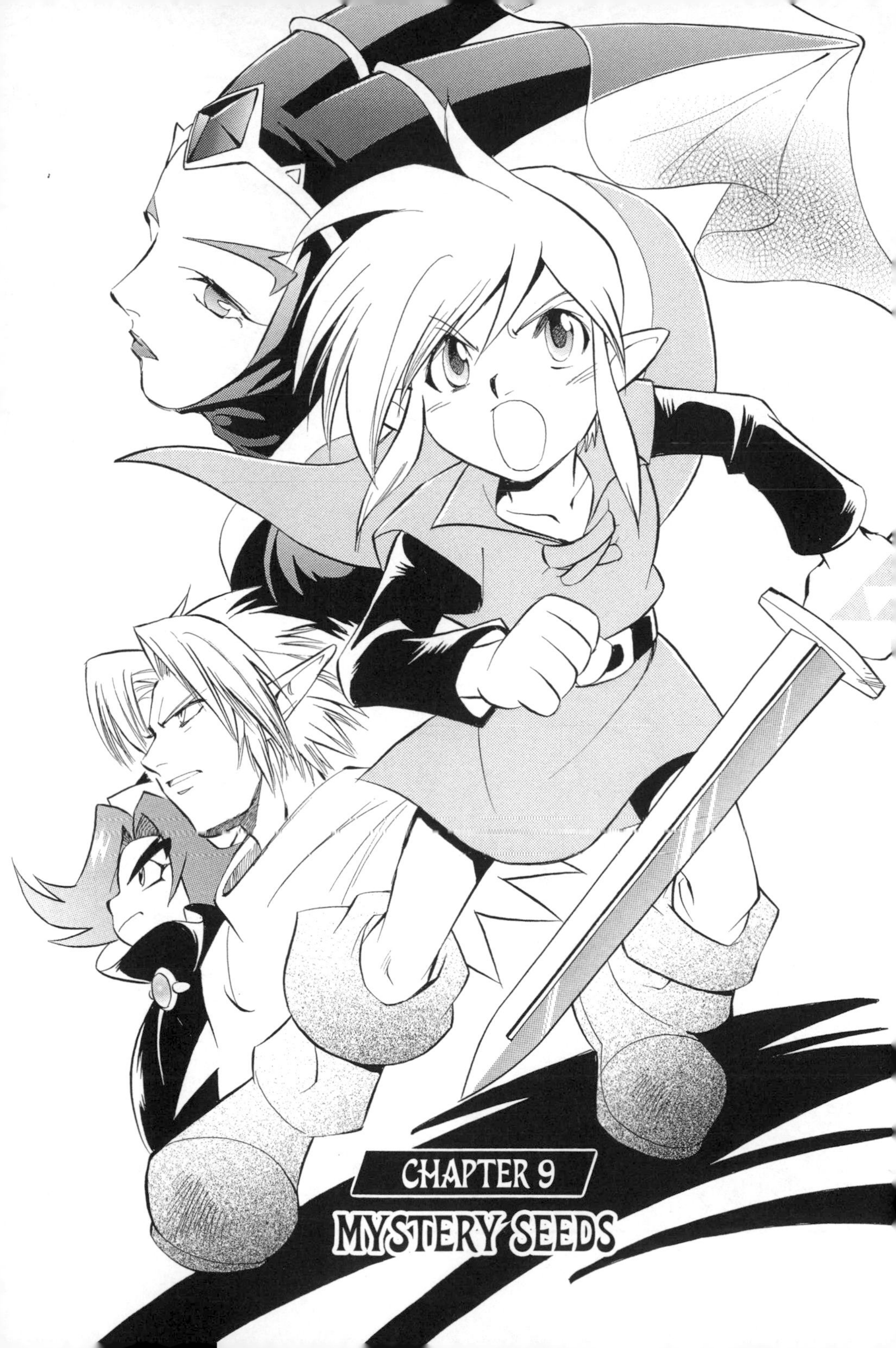
CHAPTER 9
MYSTERY SEEDS

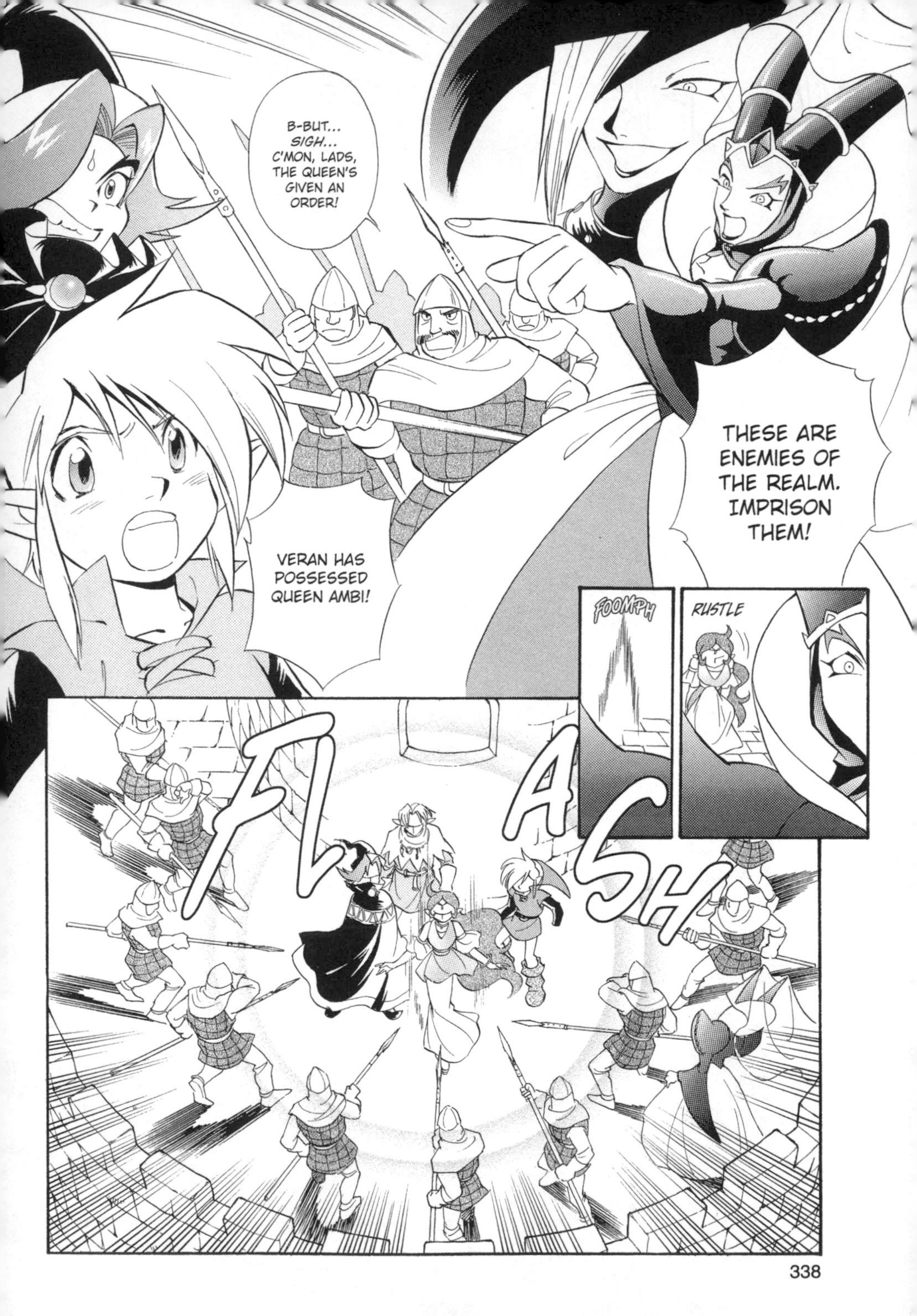
THESE ARE ENEMIES OF THE REALM. IMPRISON THEM!
B-BUT... SIGH... C'MON, LADS, THE QUEEN'S GIVEN AN ORDER!
VERAN HAS POSSESSED QUEEN AMBI!
RUSTLE
FOOMPH
FLASH

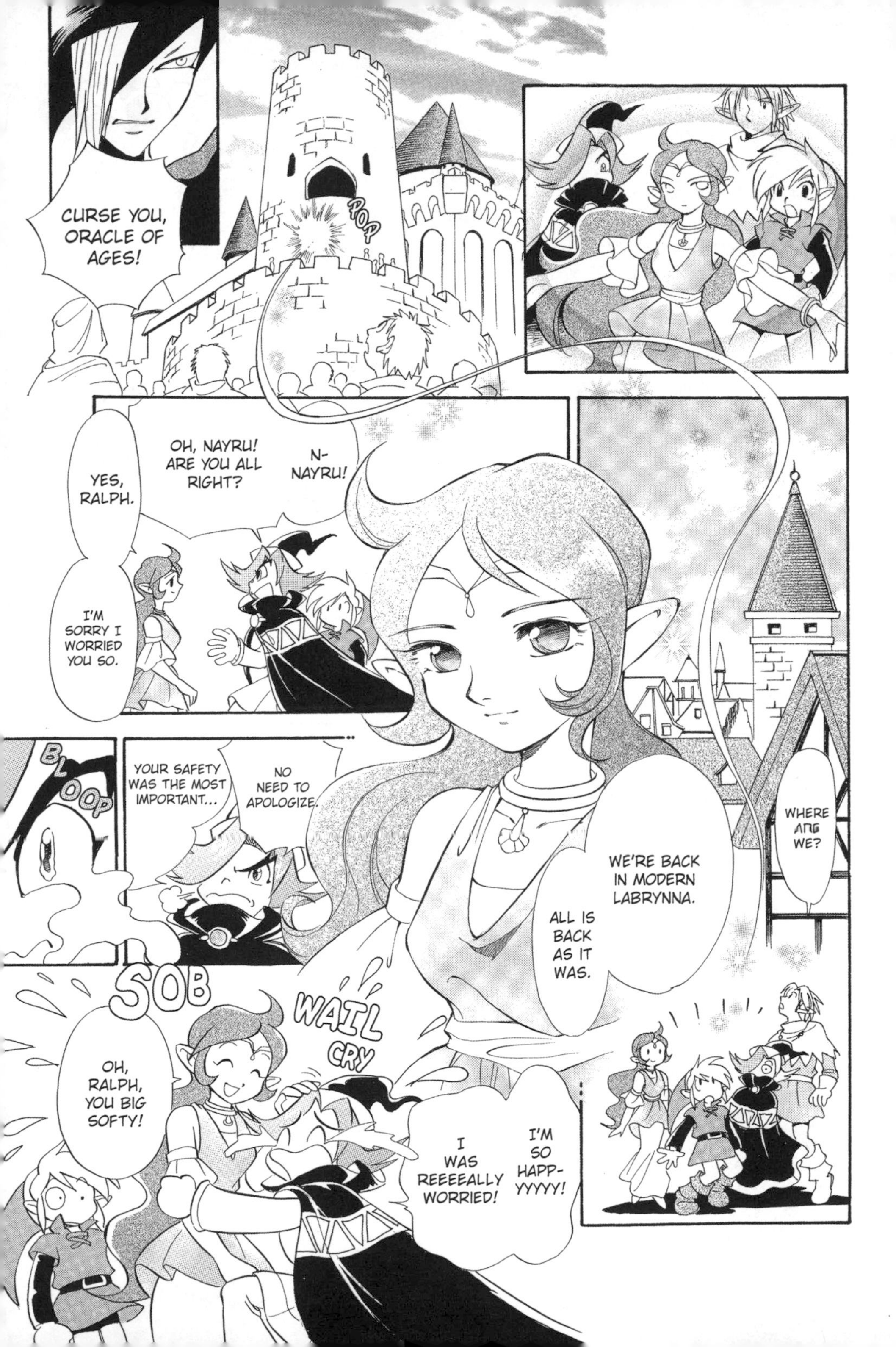
POP
CURSE YOU, ORACLE OF AGES!
WHERE ARE WE?
WE'RE BACK IN MODERN LABRYNNA.
ALL IS BACK AS IT WAS.
N-NAYRU!
OH, NAYRU! ARE YOU ALL RIGHT?
YES, RALPH.
I'M SORRY I WORRIED YOU SO.
NO NEED TO APOLOGIZE.
YOUR SAFETY WAS THE MOST IMPORTANT...
BLOOP
I'M SO HAPPY-YYYYY!
I WAS REEEEALLY WORRIED!
WAIL
CRY
SOB
OH, RALPH, YOU BIG SOFTY!

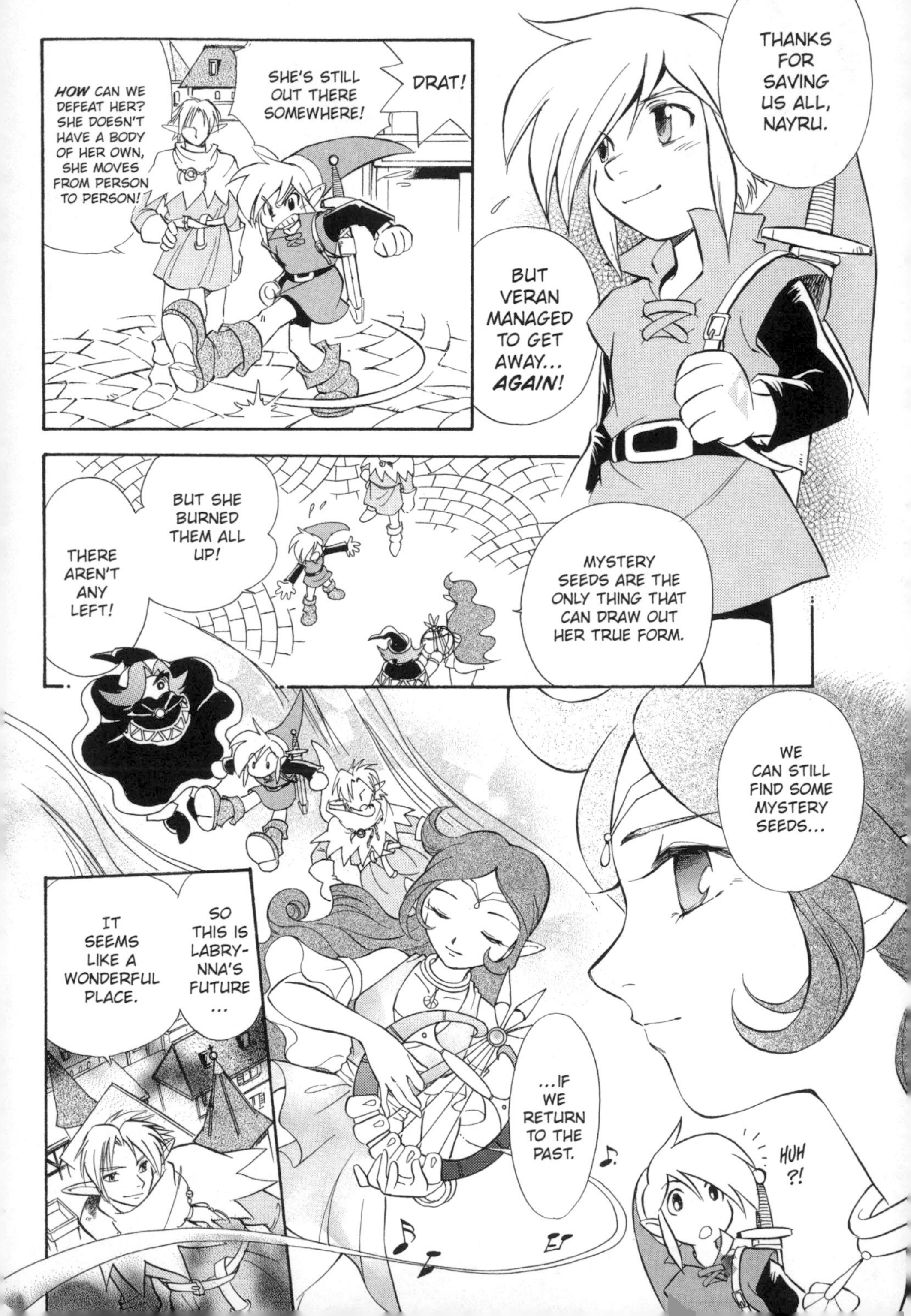
THANKS FOR SAVING US ALL, NAYRU.
BUT VERAN MANAGED TO GET AWAY... AGAIN!
DRAT!
SHE'S STILL OUT THERE SOMEWHERE!
HOW CAN WE DEFEAT HER? SHE DOESN'T HAVE A BODY OF HER OWN, SHE MOVES FROM PERSON TO PERSON!
MYSTERY SEEDS ARE THE ONLY THING THAT CAN DRAW OUT HER TRUE FORM.
BUT SHE BURNED THEM ALL UP!
THERE AREN'T ANY LEFT!
WE CAN STILL FIND SOME MYSTERY SEEDS...
...IF WE RETURN TO THE PAST.
SO THIS IS LABRYNNA'S FUTURE ...
IT SEEMS LIKE A WONDERFUL PLACE.
HUH ?!

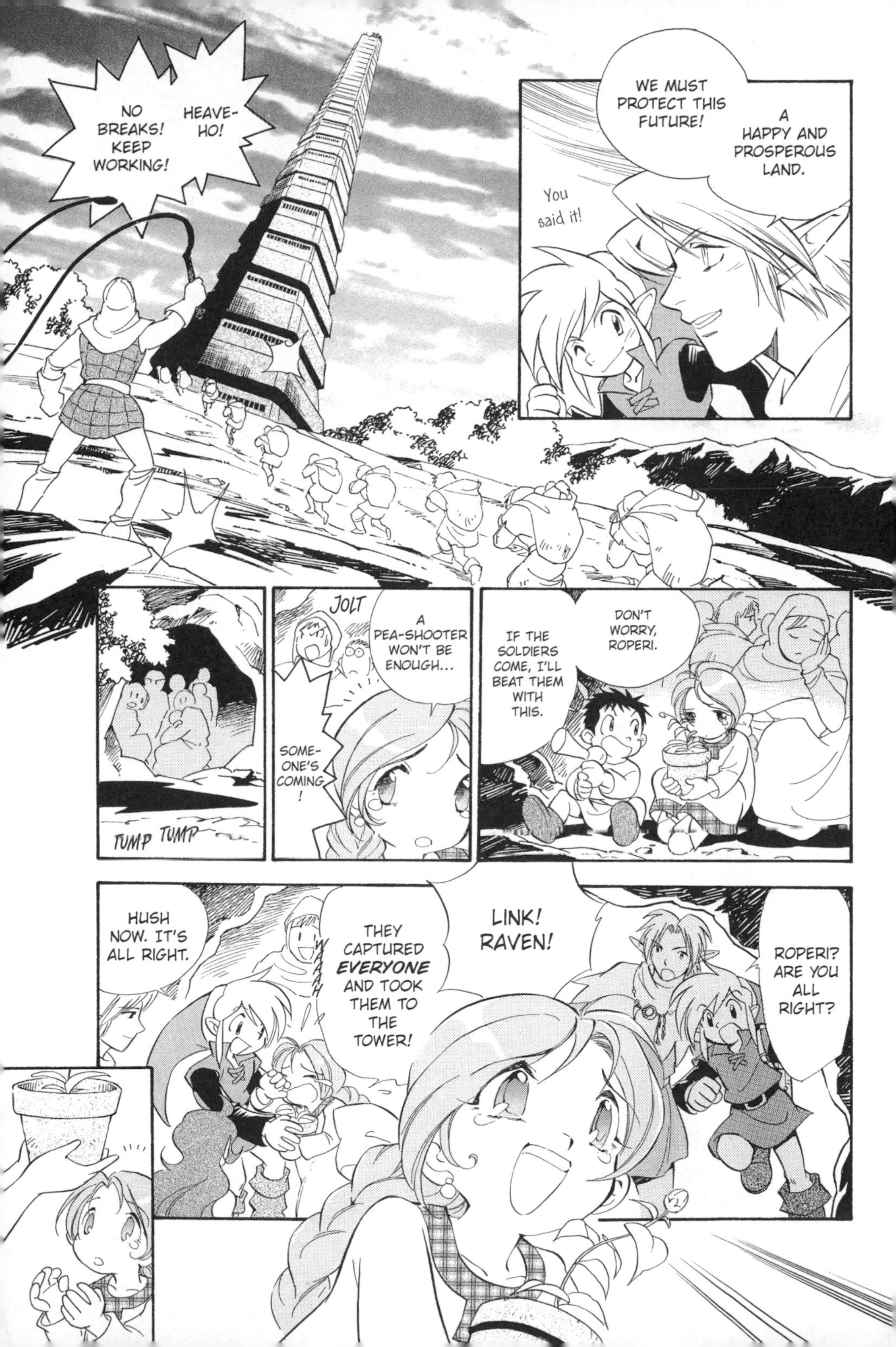
WE MUST PROTECT THIS FUTURE!
A HAPPY AND PROSPEROUS LAND.
You said it!
HEAVE-HO!
NO BREAKS! KEEP WORKING!
DON'T WORRY, ROPERI.
IF THE SOLDIERS COME, I'LL BEAT THEM WITH THIS.
A PEA-SHOOTER WON'T BE ENOUGH...
JOLT
SOME-ONE'S COMING!
TUMP TUMP
ROPERI? ARE YOU ALL RIGHT?
LINK! RAVEN!
THEY CAPTURED ***EVERYONE*** AND TOOK THEM TO THE TOWER!
WAAAH
HUSH NOW. IT'S ALL RIGHT.

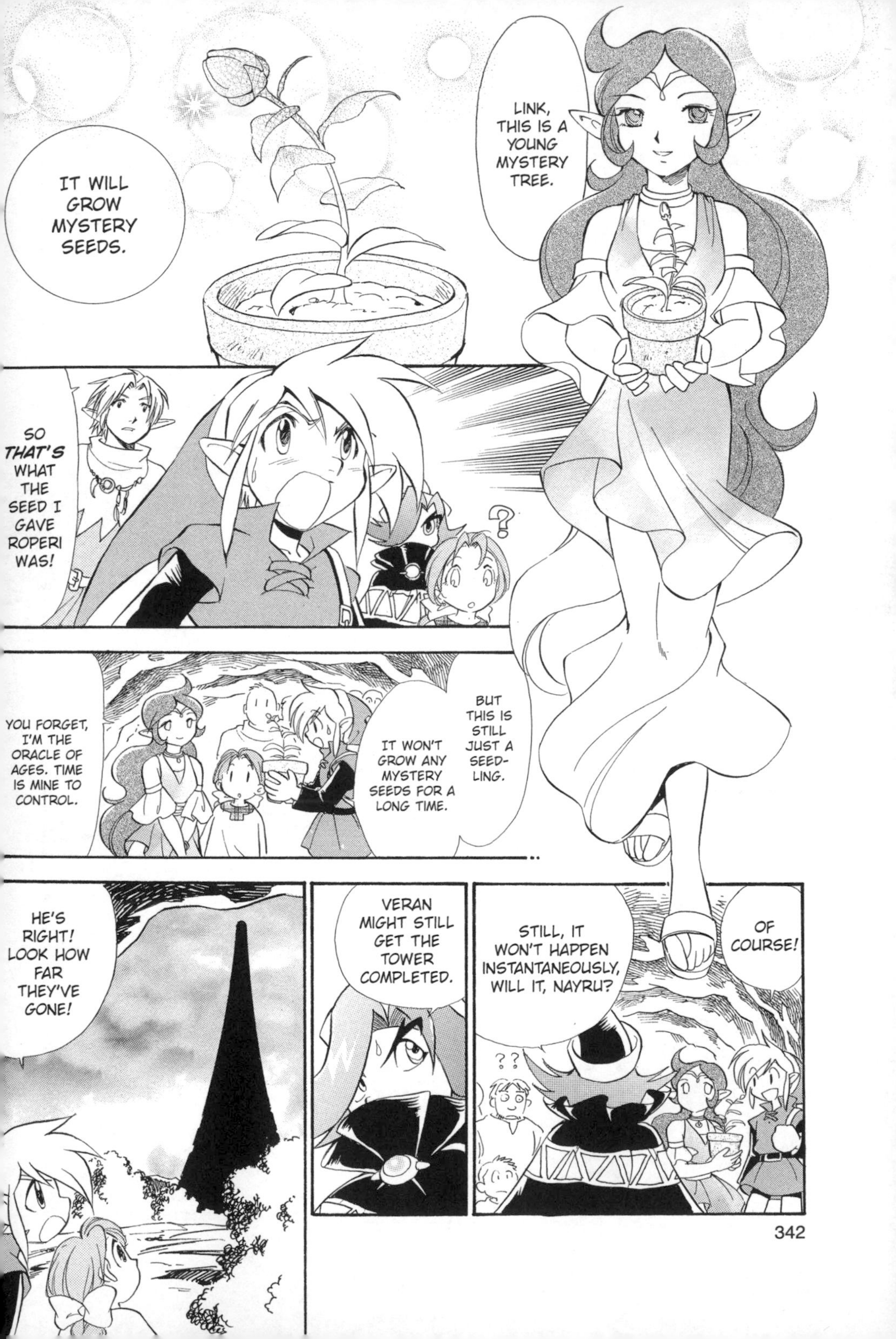
LINK, THIS IS A YOUNG MYSTERY TREE.
IT WILL GROW MYSTERY SEEDS.
SO *THAT'S* WHAT THE SEED I GAVE ROPERI WAS!
?
BUT THIS IS STILL JUST A SEED-LING.
IT WON'T GROW ANY MYSTERY SEEDS FOR A LONG TIME.
YOU FORGET, I'M THE ORACLE OF AGES. TIME IS MINE TO CONTROL.
STILL, IT WON'T HAPPEN INSTANTANEOUSLY, WILL IT, NAYRU?
OF COURSE!
??
VERAN MIGHT STILL GET THE TOWER COMPLETED.
HE'S RIGHT! LOOK HOW FAR THEY'VE GONE!

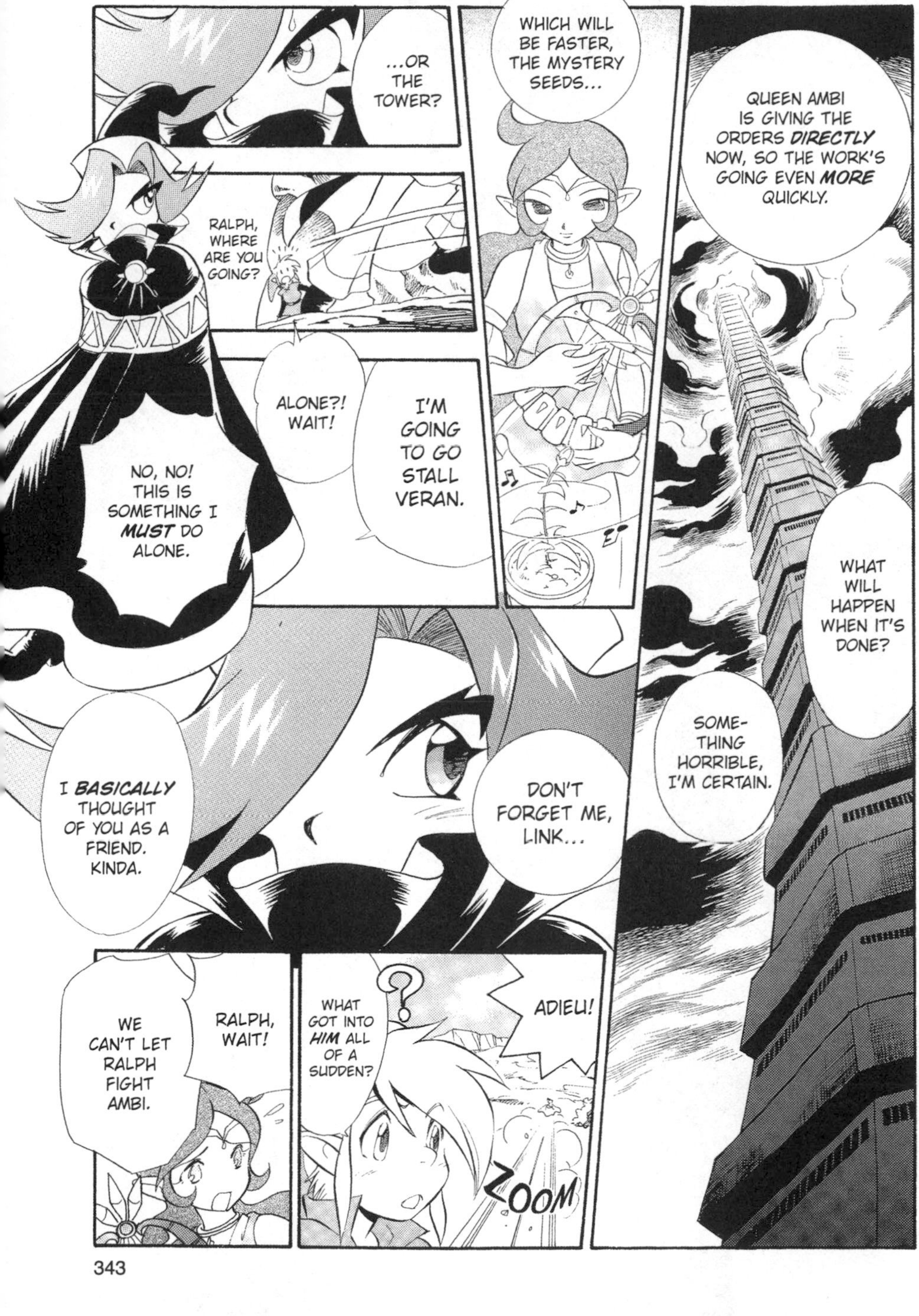
QUEEN AMBI IS GIVING THE ORDERS *DIRECTLY* NOW, SO THE WORK'S GOING EVEN *MORE* QUICKLY.
WHAT WILL HAPPEN WHEN IT'S DONE?
SOME-THING HORRIBLE, I'M CERTAIN.
WHICH WILL BE FASTER, THE MYSTERY SEEDS...
...OR THE TOWER?
RALPH, WHERE ARE YOU GOING?
I'M GOING TO GO STALL VERAN.
ALONE?! WAIT!
NO, NO! THIS IS SOMETHING I *MUST* DO ALONE.
DON'T FORGET ME, LINK...
I *BASICALLY* THOUGHT OF YOU AS A FRIEND. KINDA.
ADIEU!
WHAT GOT INTO *HIM* ALL OF A SUDDEN?
ZOOM
RALPH, WAIT!
WE CAN'T LET RALPH FIGHT AMBI.

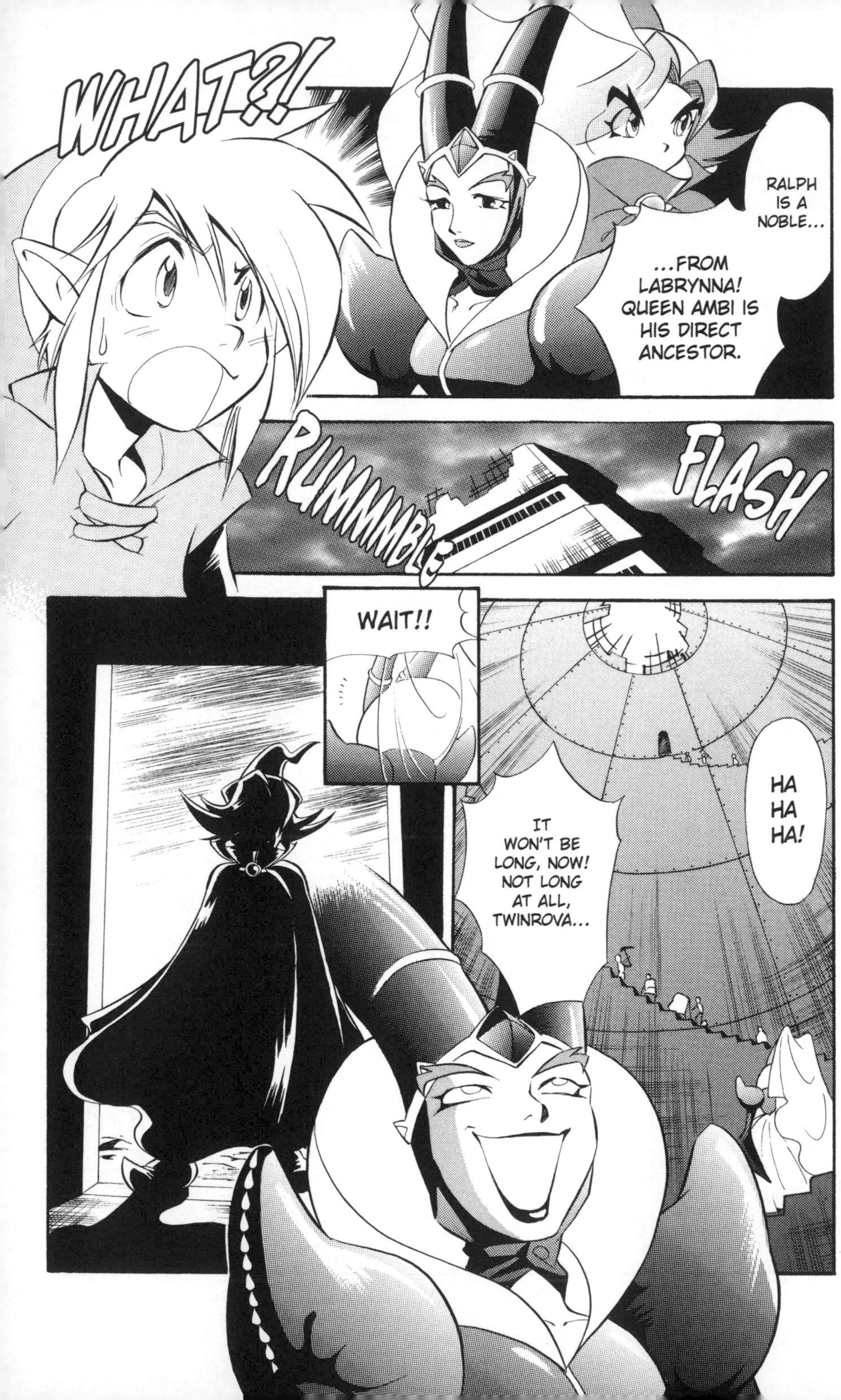
RALPH IS A NOBLE...
...FROM LABRYNNA! QUEEN AMBI IS HIS DIRECT ANCESTOR.
WHAT?!
FLASH
RUMMMBLE
HA HA HA!
IT WON'T BE LONG, NOW! NOT LONG AT ALL, TWINROVA...
WAIT!!

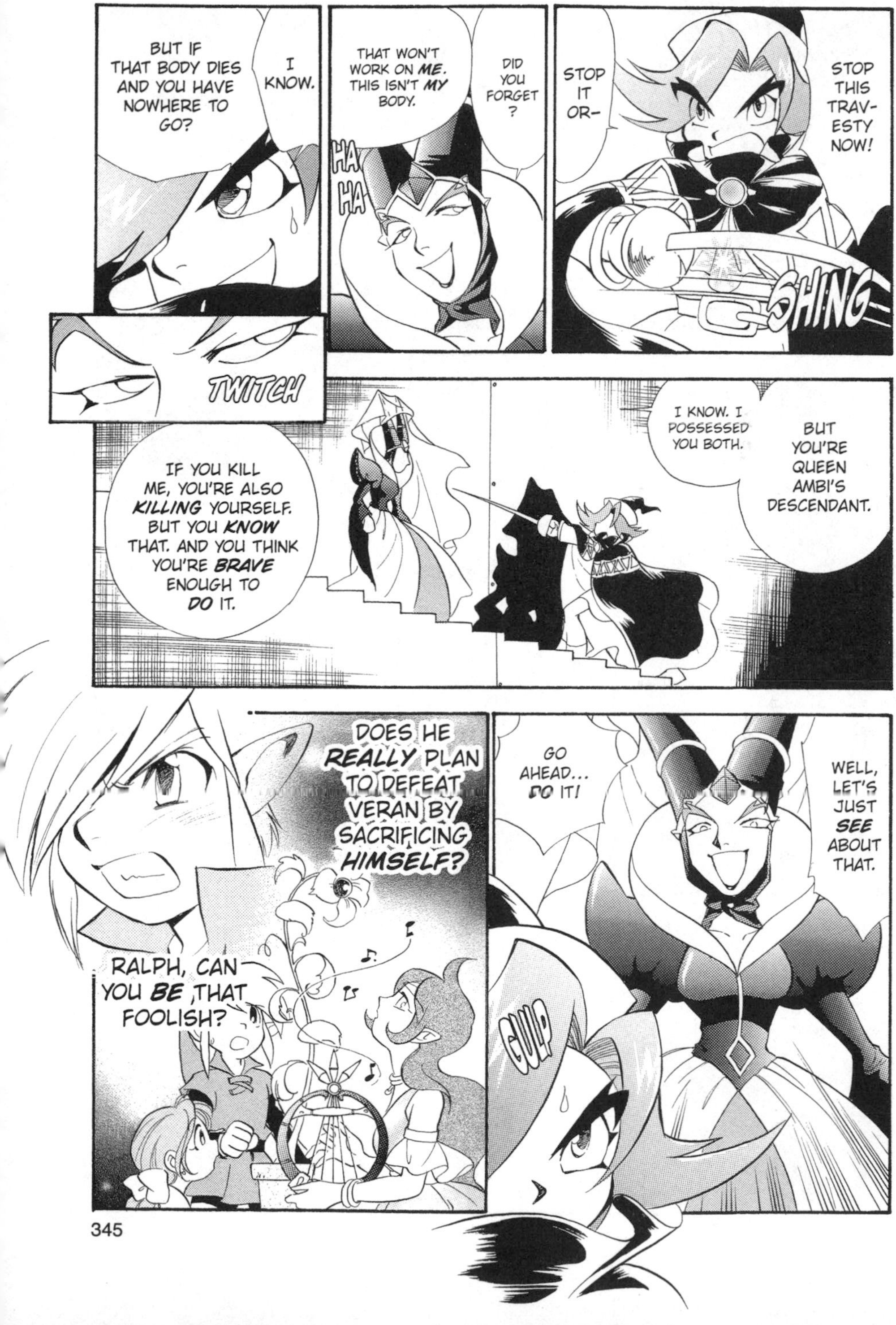
STOP THIS TRAV-ESTY NOW!
STOP IT OR–
SHING
DID YOU FORGET?
THAT WON'T WORK ON **ME.** THIS ISN'T **MY** BODY.
HA HA
I KNOW.
BUT IF THAT BODY DIES AND YOU HAVE NOWHERE TO GO?
TWITCH
BUT YOU'RE QUEEN AMBI'S DESCENDANT.
I KNOW. I POSSESSED YOU BOTH.
IF YOU KILL ME, YOU'RE ALSO **KILLING** YOURSELF. BUT YOU **KNOW** THAT. AND YOU THINK YOU'RE **BRAVE** ENOUGH TO **DO** IT.
WELL, LET'S JUST **SEE** ABOUT THAT.
GO AHEAD... **DO** IT!
GULP
DOES HE **REALLY** PLAN TO DEFEAT VERAN BY SACRIFICING **HIMSELF?**
RALPH, CAN YOU **BE** THAT FOOLISH?

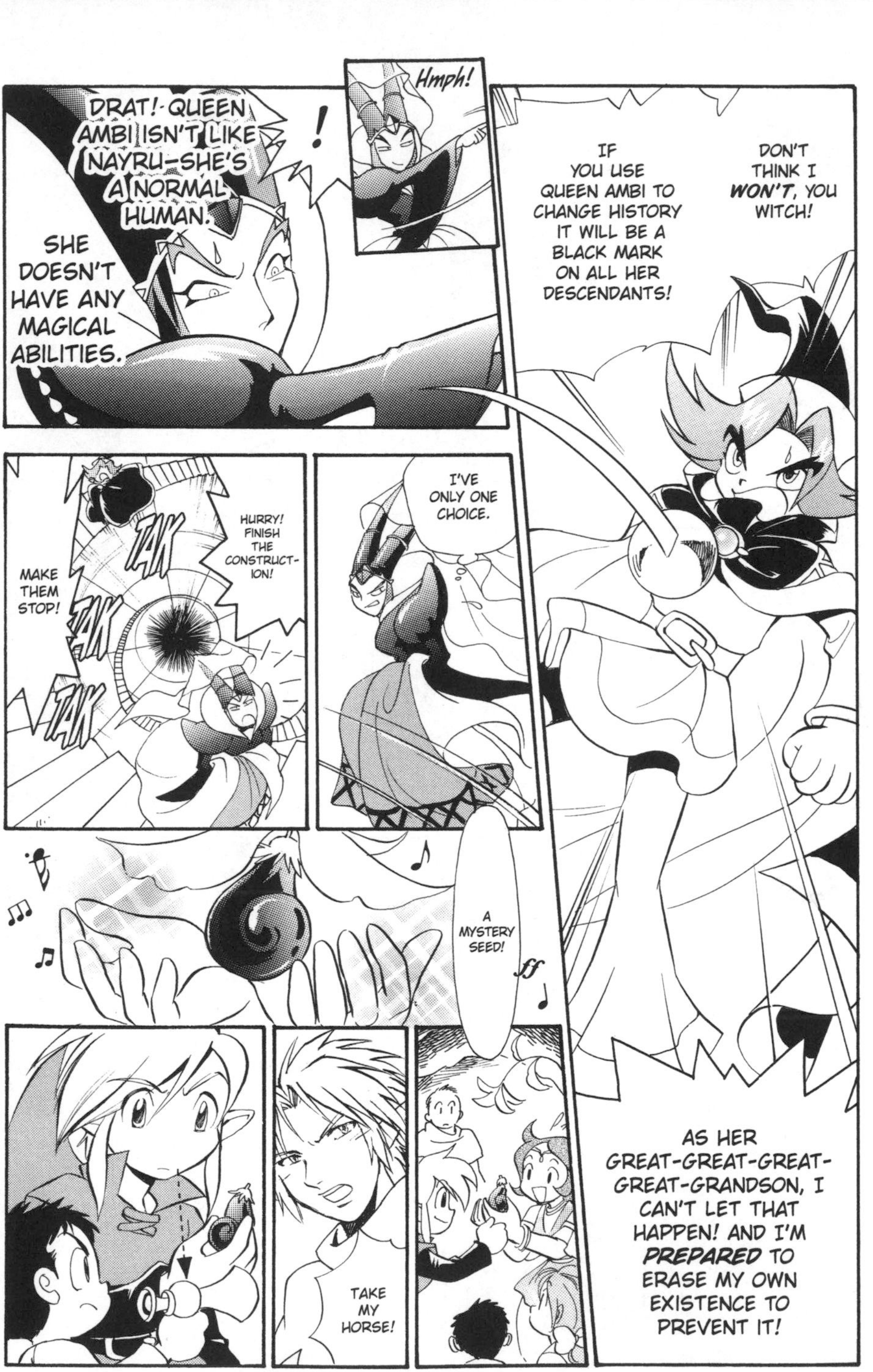
DON'T THINK I *WON'T*, YOU WITCH!
IF YOU USE QUEEN AMBI TO CHANGE HISTORY IT WILL BE A BLACK MARK ON ALL HER DESCENDANTS!
AS HER GREAT-GREAT-GREAT-GREAT-GRANDSON, I CAN'T LET THAT HAPPEN! AND I'M ***PREPARED*** TO ERASE MY OWN EXISTENCE TO PREVENT IT!
Hmph!
!
DRAT! QUEEN AMBI ISN'T LIKE NAYRU-SHE'S A NORMAL HUMAN.
SHE DOESN'T HAVE ANY MAGICAL ABILITIES.
I'VE ONLY ONE CHOICE.
HURRY! FINISH THE CONSTRUCTION!
TAK
TAK
TAK
MAKE THEM STOP!
A MYSTERY SEED!
TAKE MY HORSE!

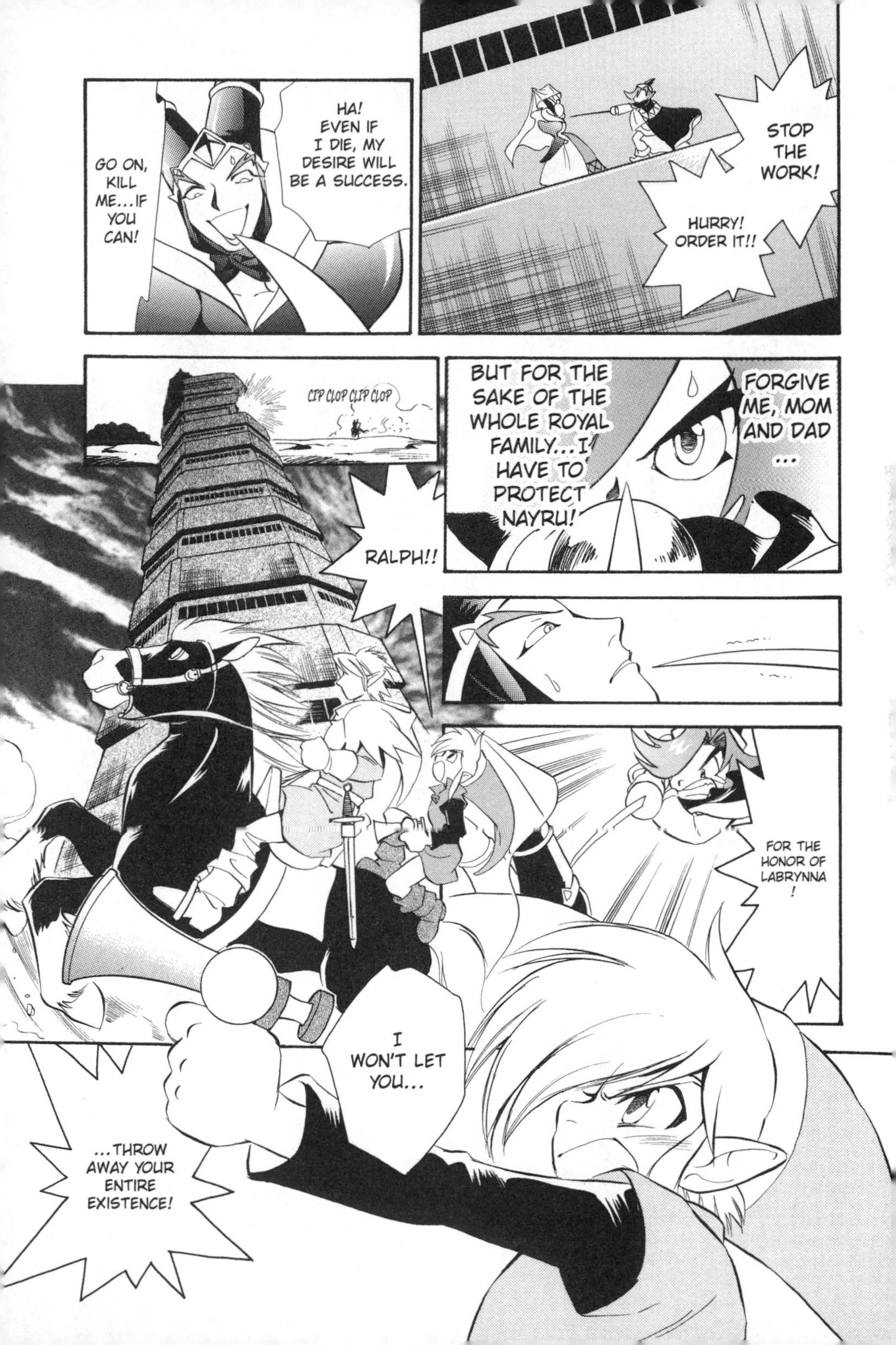
STOP THE WORK!
HURRY! ORDER IT!!
HA! EVEN IF I DIE, MY DESIRE WILL BE A SUCCESS.
GO ON, KILL ME...IF YOU CAN!
FORGIVE ME, MOM AND DAD ...
BUT FOR THE SAKE OF THE WHOLE ROYAL FAMILY...I HAVE TO PROTECT NAYRU!
FOR THE HONOR OF LABRYNNA!
CLIP CLOP CLIP CLOP
RALPH!!
I WON'T LET YOU...
...THROW AWAY YOUR ENTIRE EXISTENCE!

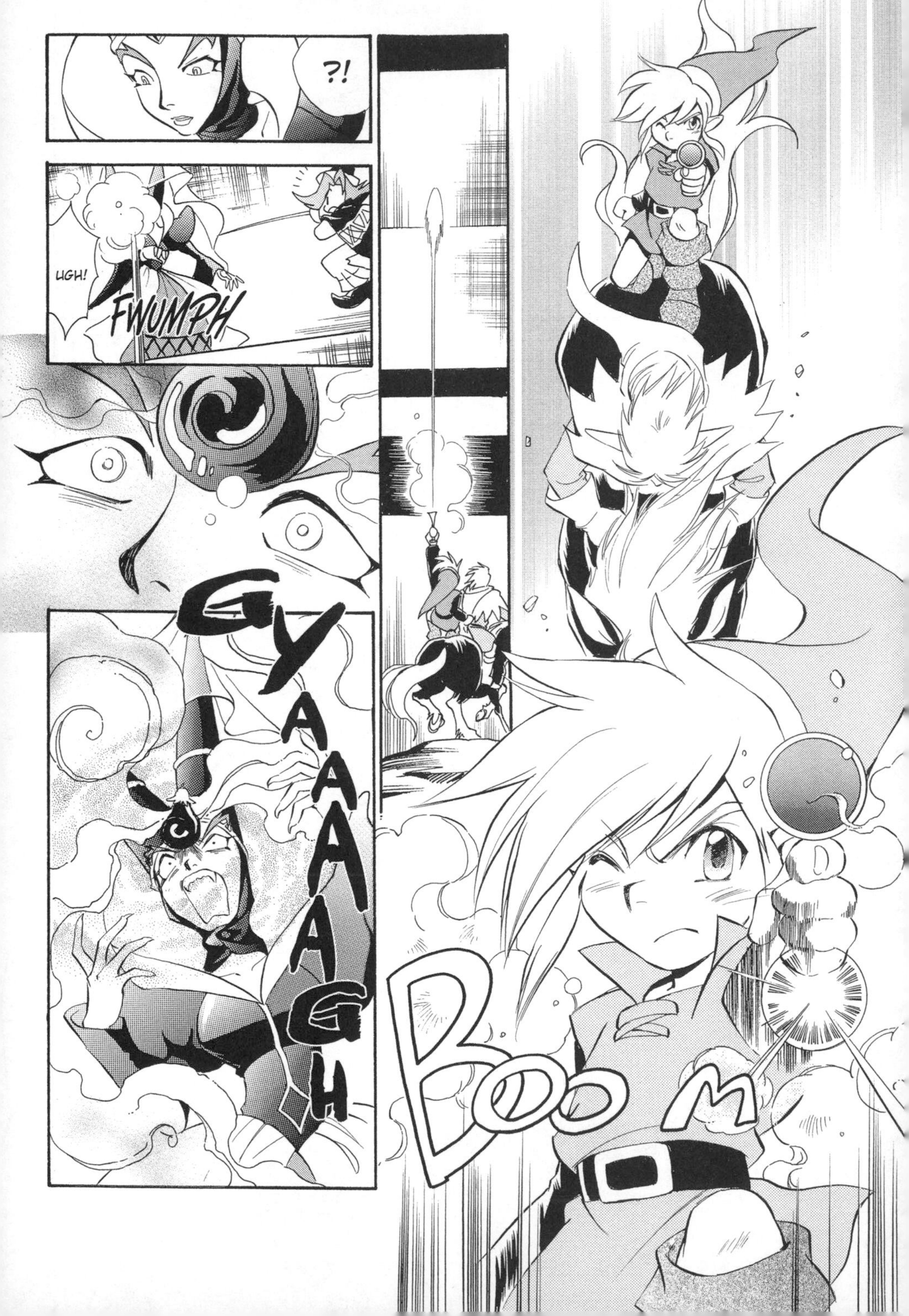
BOOM
?!
UGH!
FWUMPH
GYAAAAGH

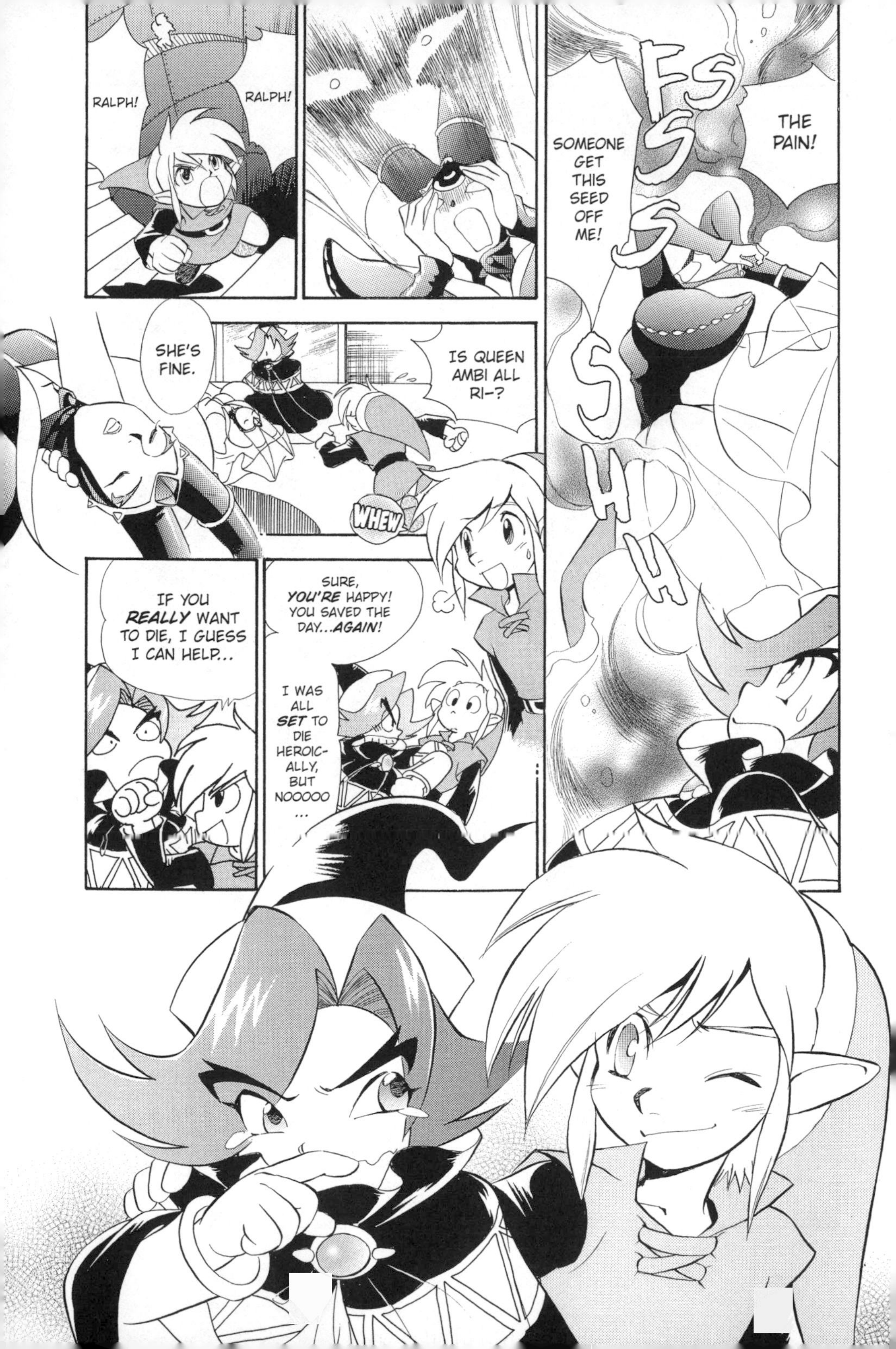
FSSSHH
THE PAIN!
SOMEONE GET THIS SEED OFF ME!
RALPH!
RALPH!
IS QUEEN AMBI ALL RI–?
SHE'S FINE.
WHEW
SURE, *YOU'RE* HAPPY! YOU SAVED THE DAY...*AGAIN!*
I WAS ALL *SET* TO DIE HEROIC-ALLY, BUT NOOOOO...
IF YOU *REALLY* WANT TO DIE, I GUESS I CAN HELP...

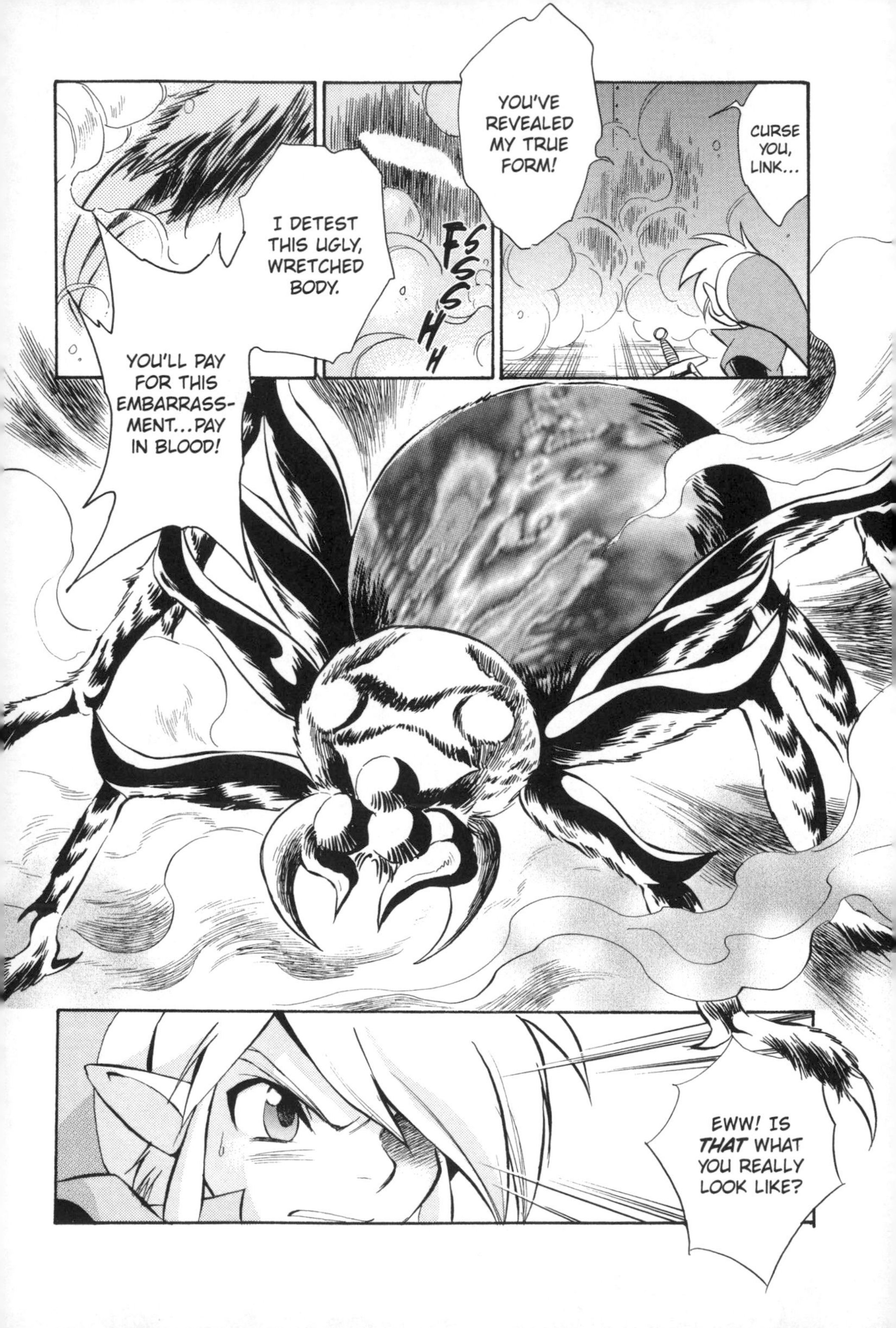
CURSE YOU, LINK...
YOU'VE REVEALED MY TRUE FORM!
FSSHH
I DETEST THIS UGLY, WRETCHED BODY.
YOU'LL PAY FOR THIS EMBARRASS-MENT...PAY IN BLOOD!
EWW! IS **THAT** WHAT YOU REALLY LOOK LIKE?

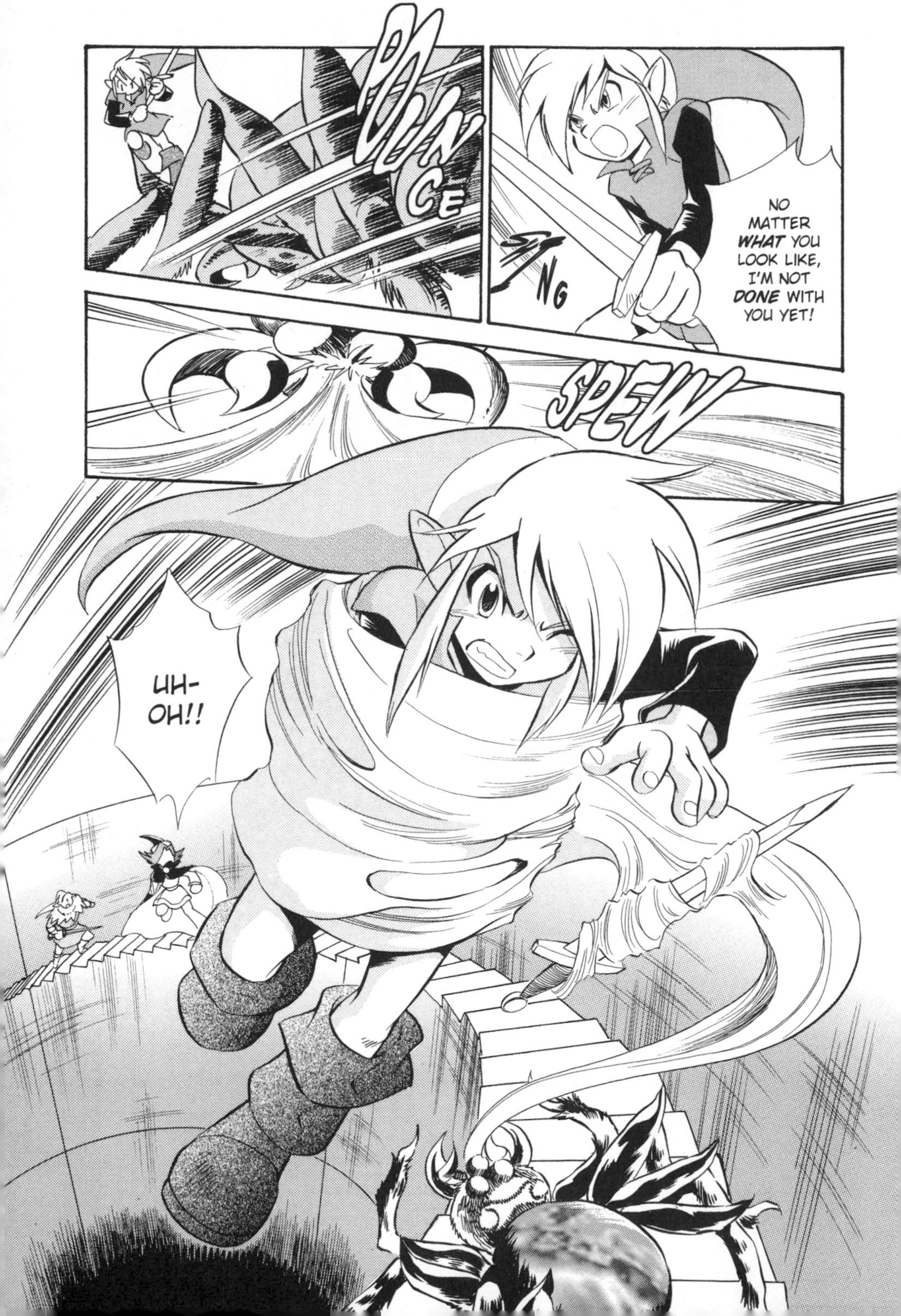
NO MATTER WHAT YOU LOOK LIKE, I'M NOT DONE WITH YOU YET!
SHING
POUNCE
SPEW
UH-OH!!

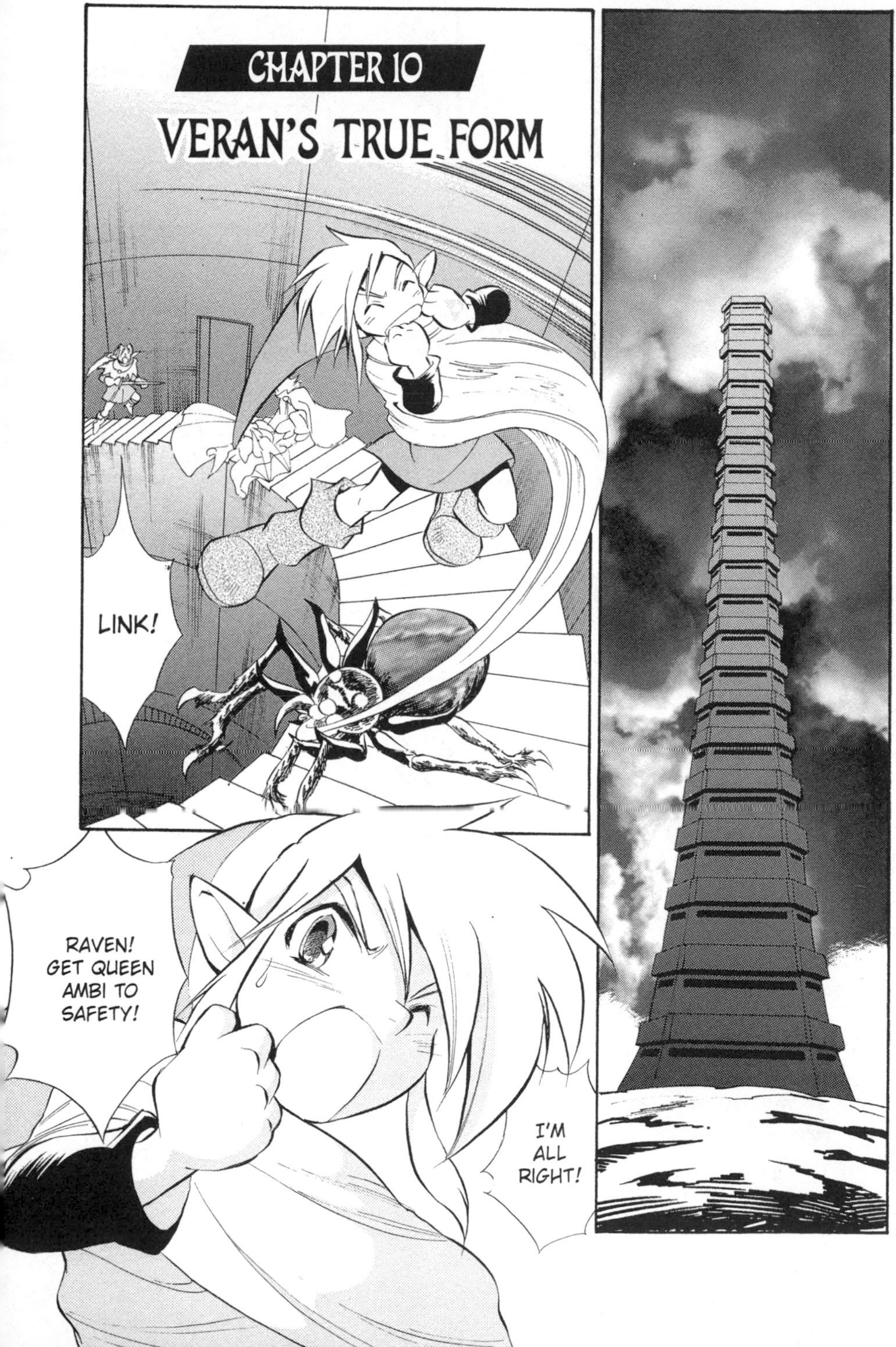
CHAPTER 10
VERAN'S TRUE FORM
LINK!
RAVEN! GET QUEEN AMBI TO SAFETY!
I'M ALL RIGHT!

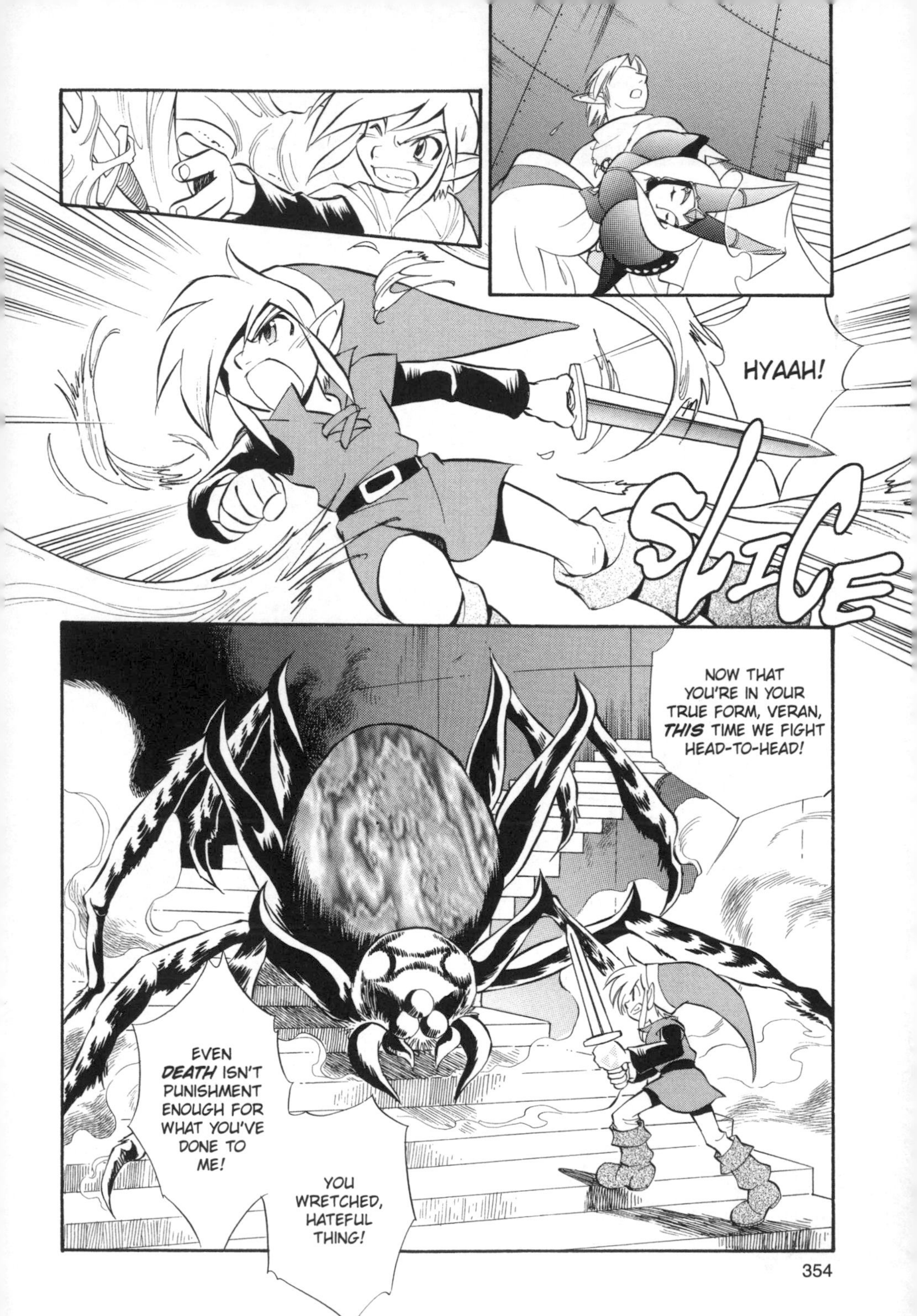
HYAAH!
SLICE
NOW THAT YOU'RE IN YOUR TRUE FORM, VERAN, THIS TIME WE FIGHT HEAD-TO-HEAD!
EVEN DEATH ISN'T PUNISHMENT ENOUGH FOR WHAT YOU'VE DONE TO ME!
YOU WRETCHED, HATEFUL THING!

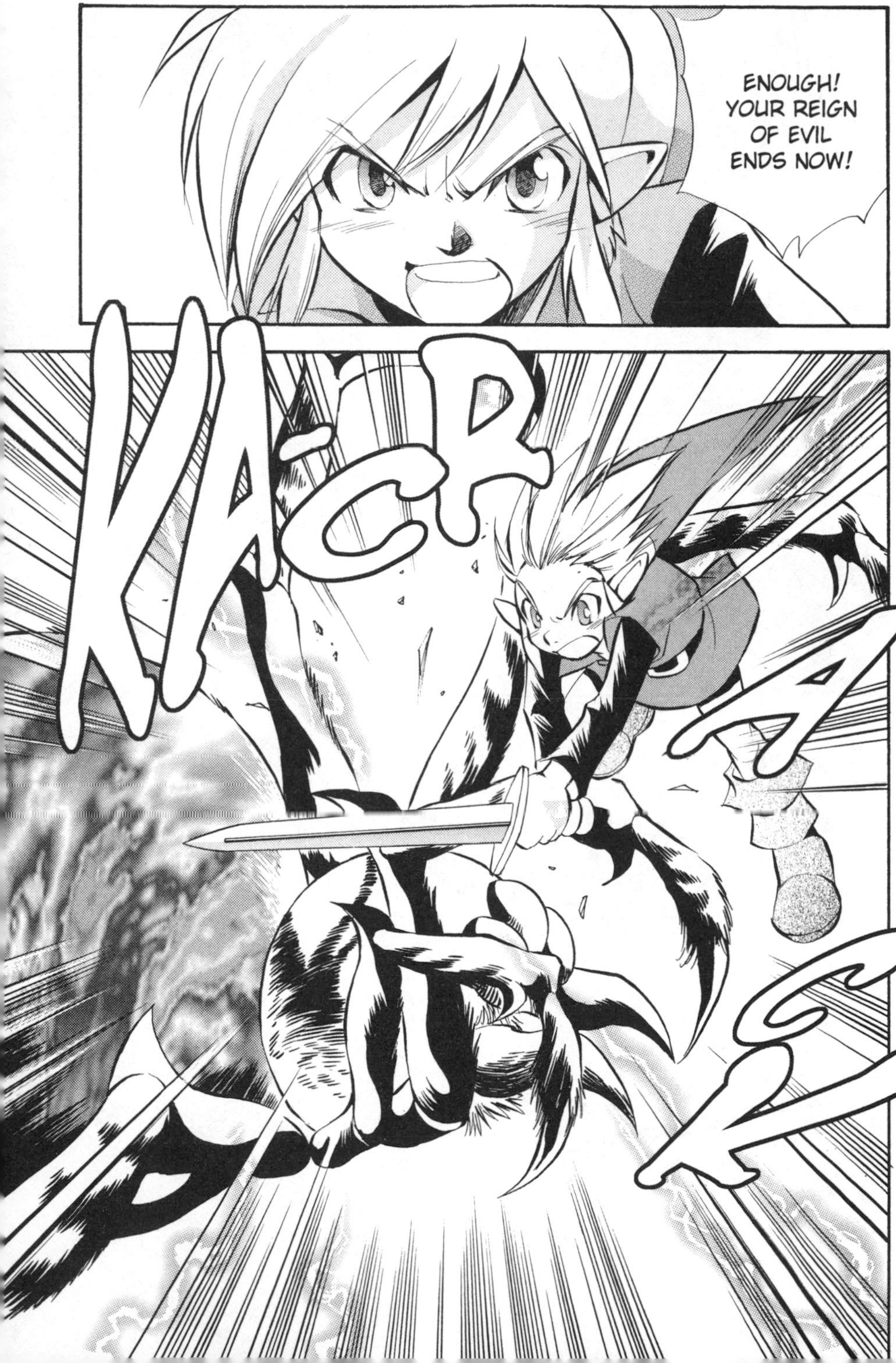
ENOUGH! YOUR REIGN OF EVIL ENDS NOW!
KA-CRACK

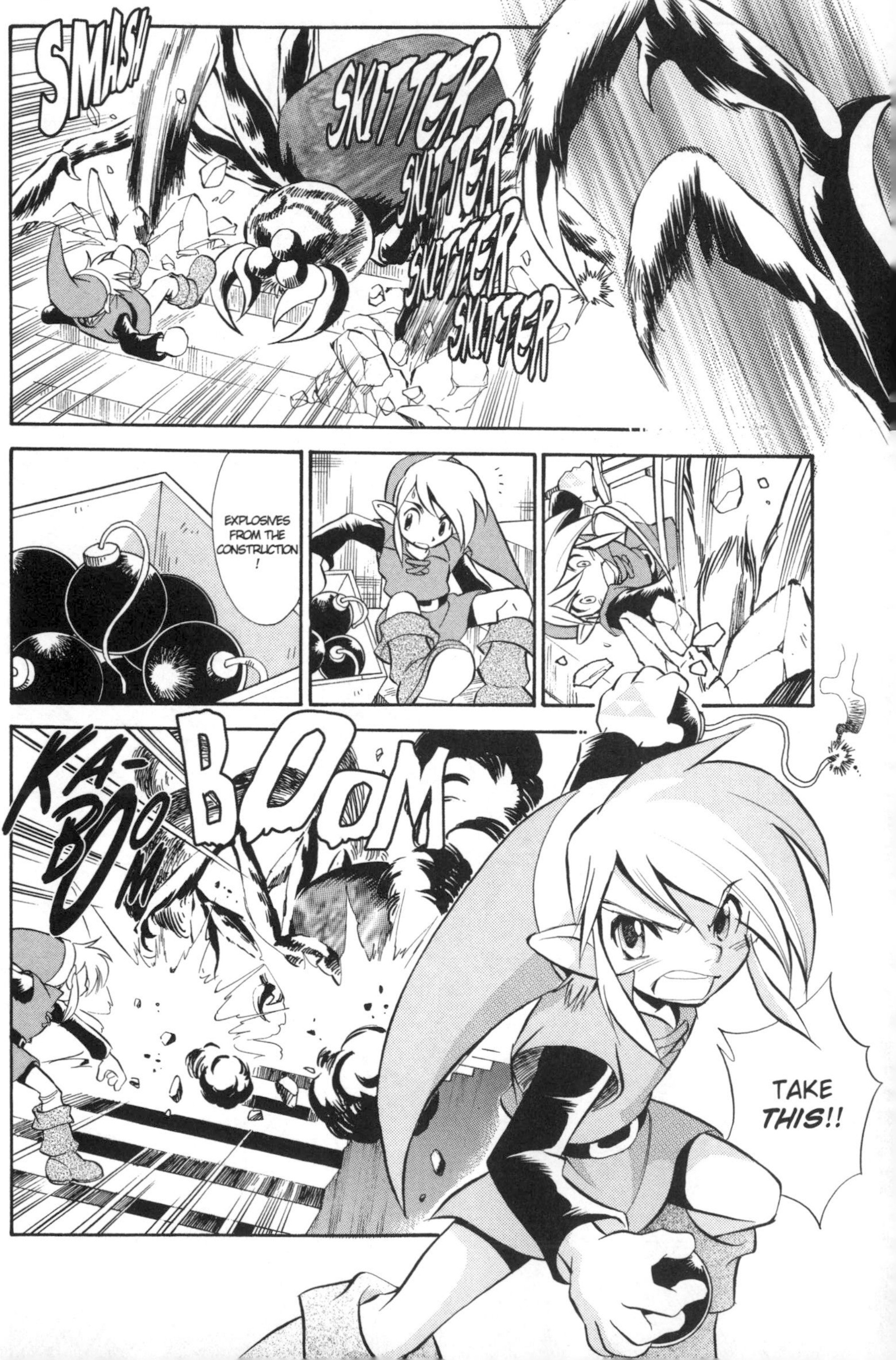
SKITTER
SKITTER
SKITTER
SKITTER
SKITTER
SMASH
EXPLOSIVES FROM THE CONSTRUCTION!
TAKE THIS!!
BOOM
KA-BOOM

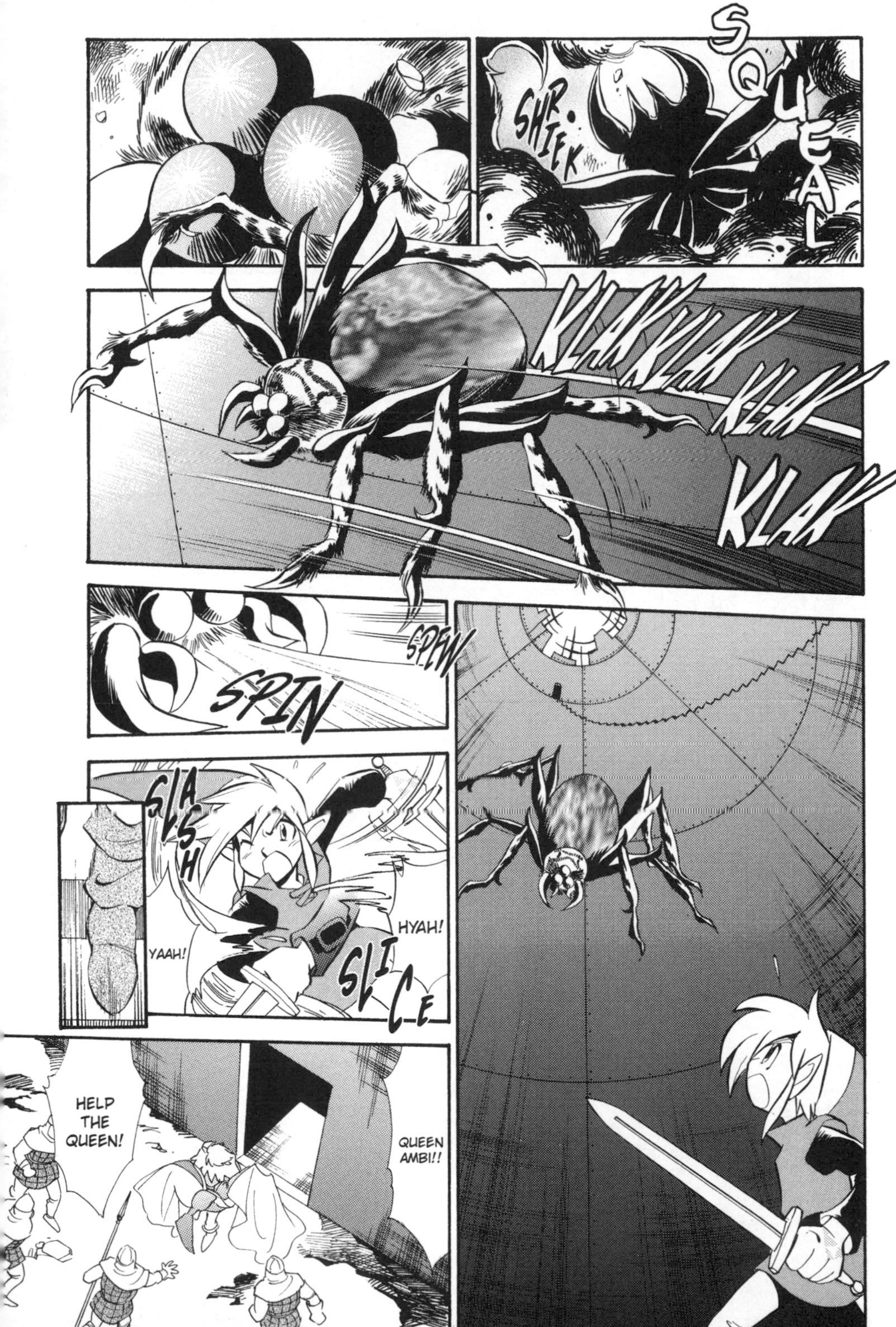
SQUEAL
SHRIEK
KLAK KLAK KLAK
KLAK
SPEW
SPIN
SLASH
HYAH!
YAAH!
SLICE
QUEEN AMBI!!
HELP THE QUEEN!

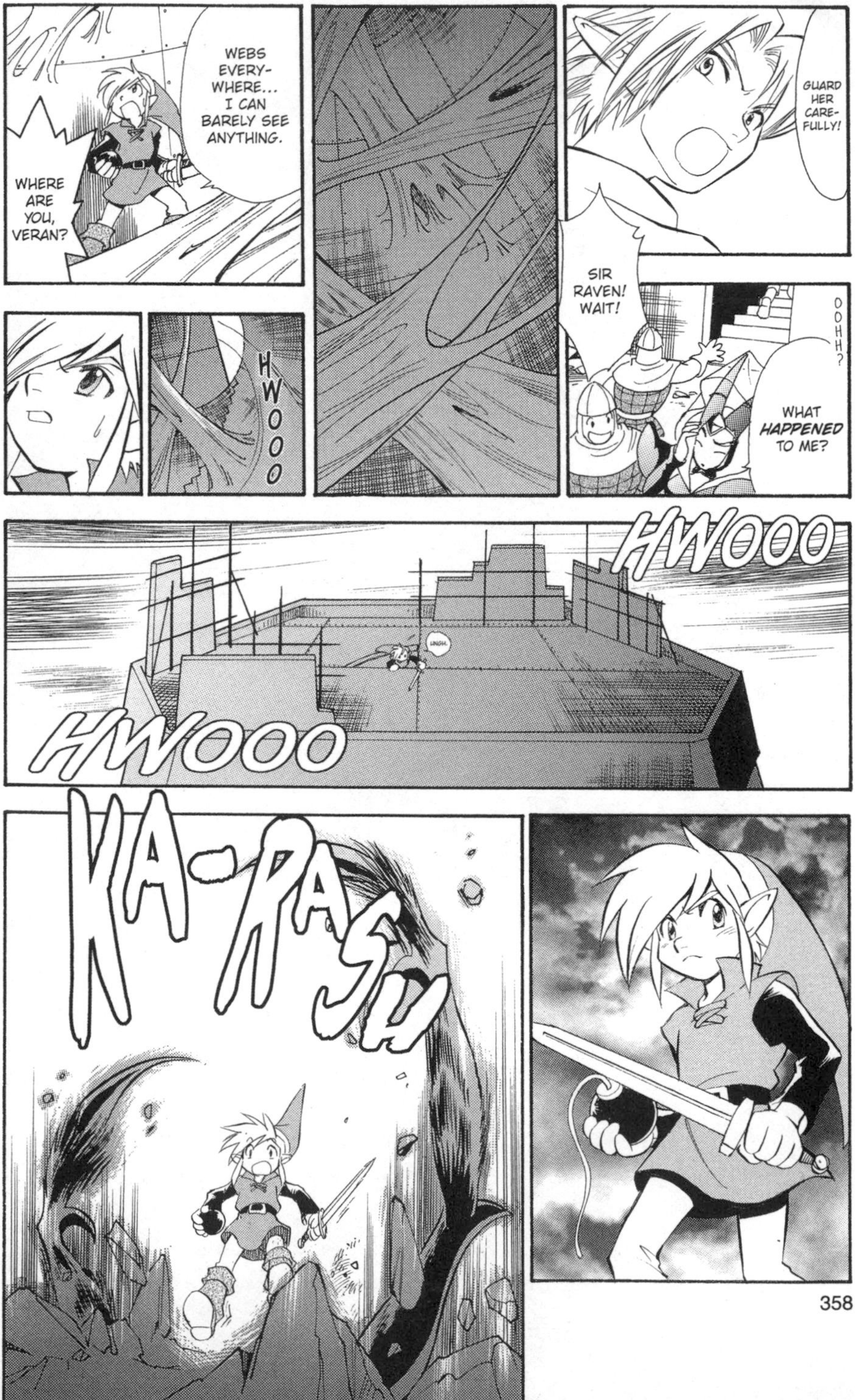

GUARD HER CARE-FULLY!
SIR RAVEN! WAIT!
OOHH?
WHAT *HAPPENED* TO ME?
WEBS EVERY-WHERE... I CAN BARELY SEE ANYTHING.
WHERE ARE YOU, VERAN?
HWOOO
HWOOO
UNGH.
HWOOO
KA-RASH

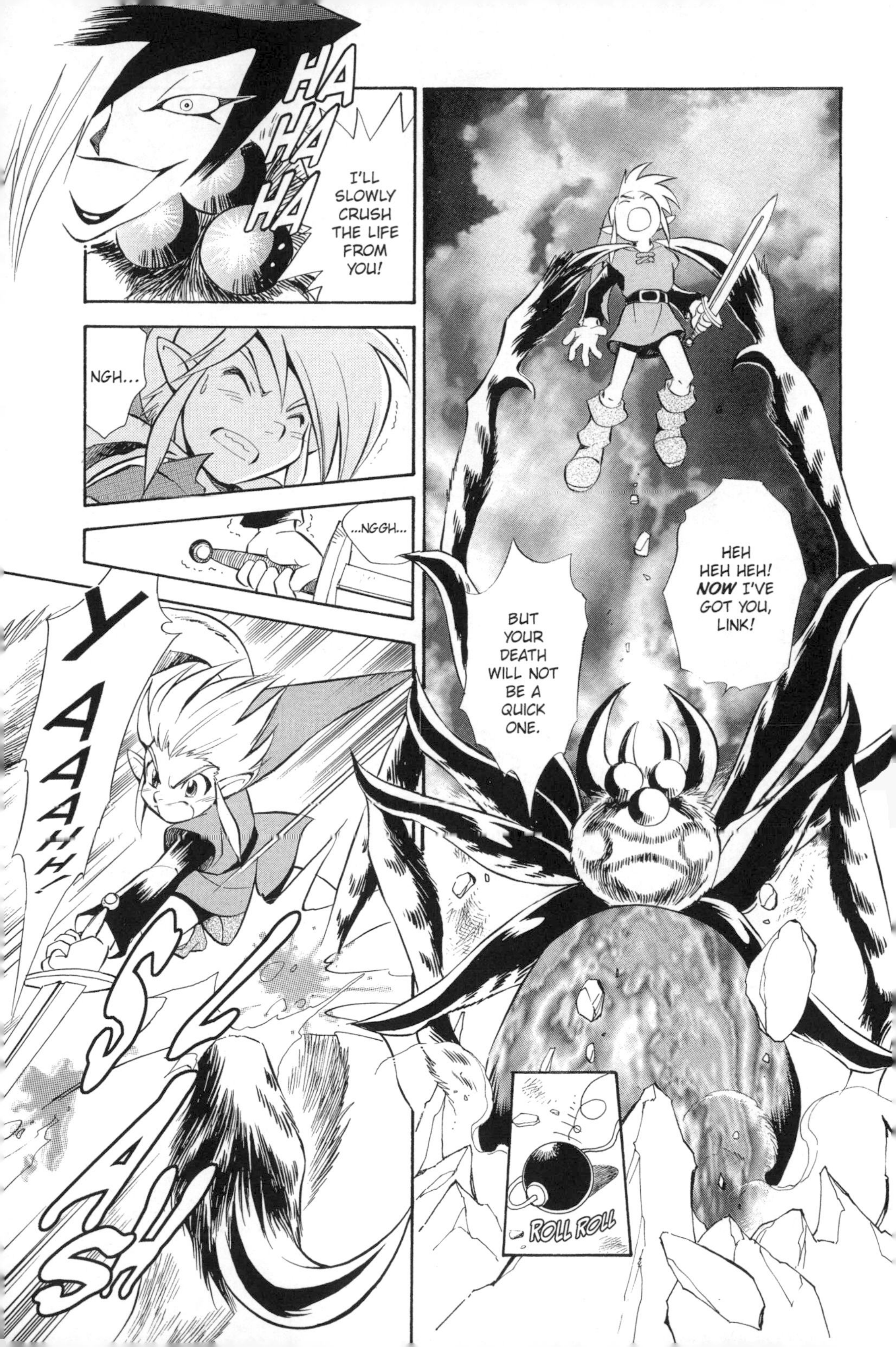
HEH HEH HEH! **NOW** I'VE GOT YOU, LINK!
BUT YOUR DEATH WILL NOT BE A QUICK ONE.
ROLL ROLL
HA HA HA HA
I'LL SLOWLY CRUSH THE LIFE FROM YOU!
NGH...
...NGGH...
YAAAAH!

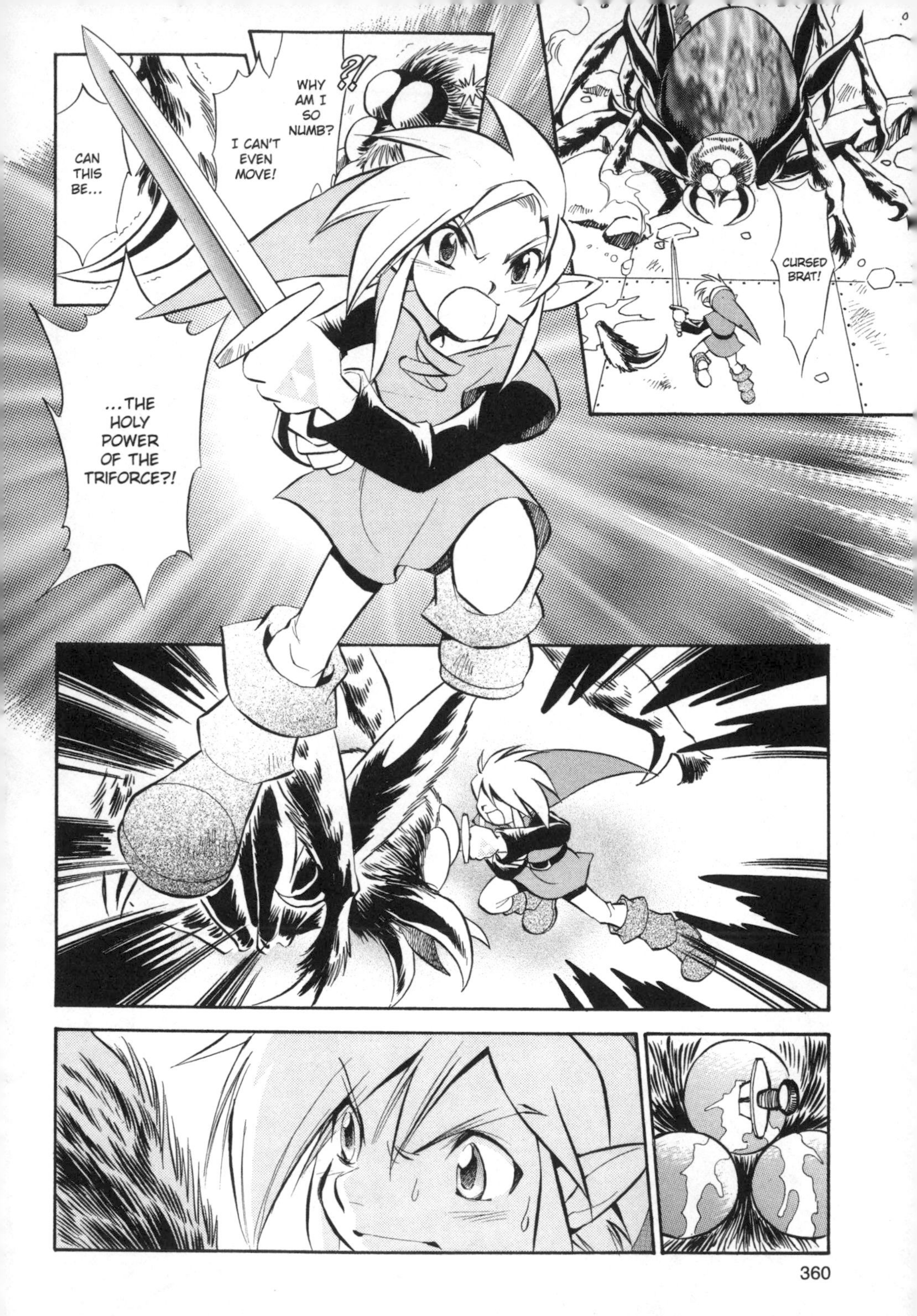
CURSED BRAT!
?!
WHY AM I SO NUMB?
I CAN'T EVEN MOVE!
CAN THIS BE...
...THE HOLY POWER OF THE TRIFORCE?!

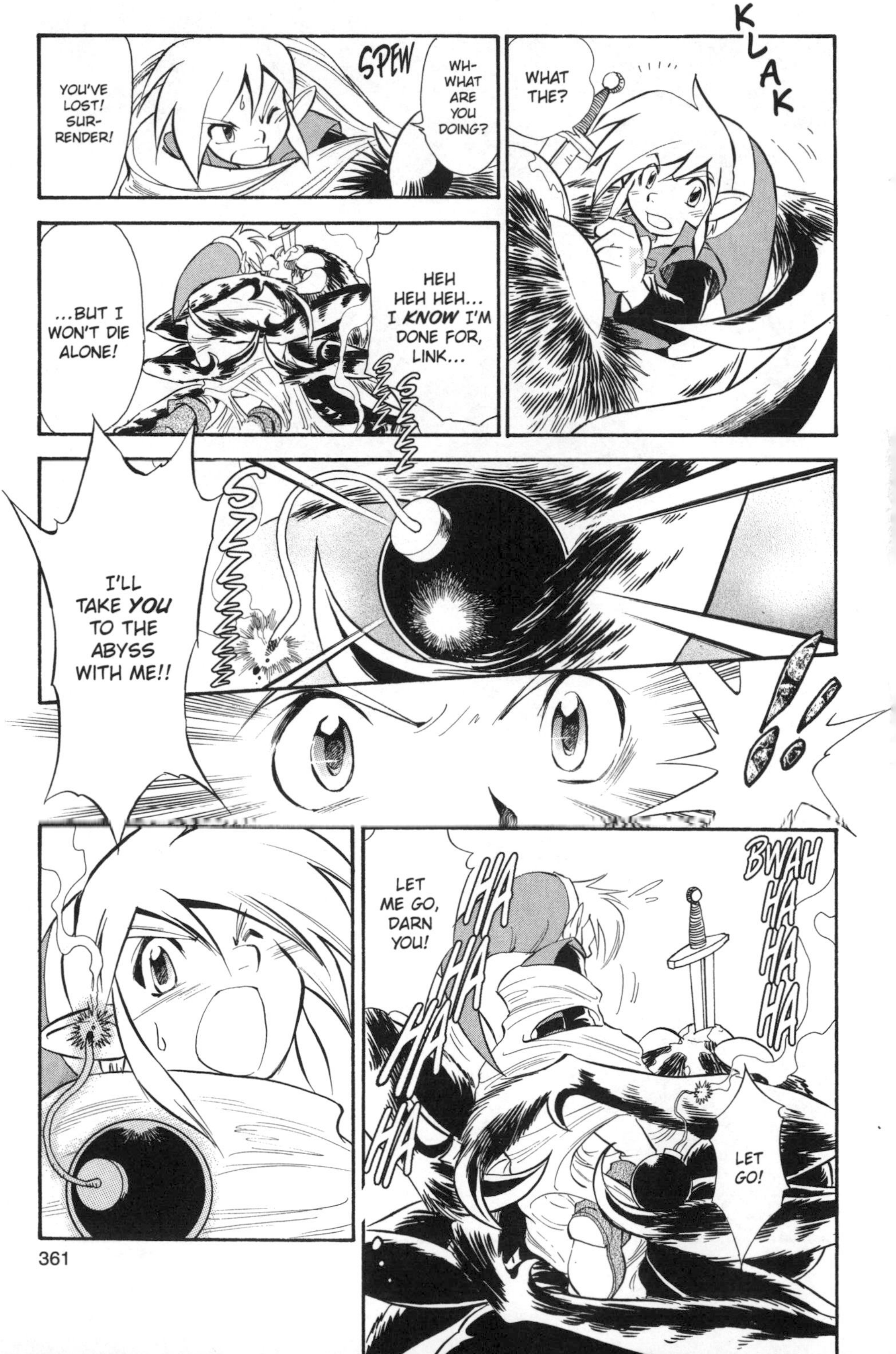
KLAK
WHAT THE?
WH- WHAT ARE YOU DOING?
SPEW
YOU'VE LOST! SUR- RENDER!
SZZZ
HEH HEH HEH... I **KNOW** I'M DONE FOR, LINK...
...BUT I WON'T DIE ALONE!
SZZZZZZZ
I'LL TAKE **YOU** TO THE ABYSS WITH ME!!
!!
BWAH HA HA HA HA
HA HA HA HA HA HA
LET ME GO, DARN YOU!
LET GO!

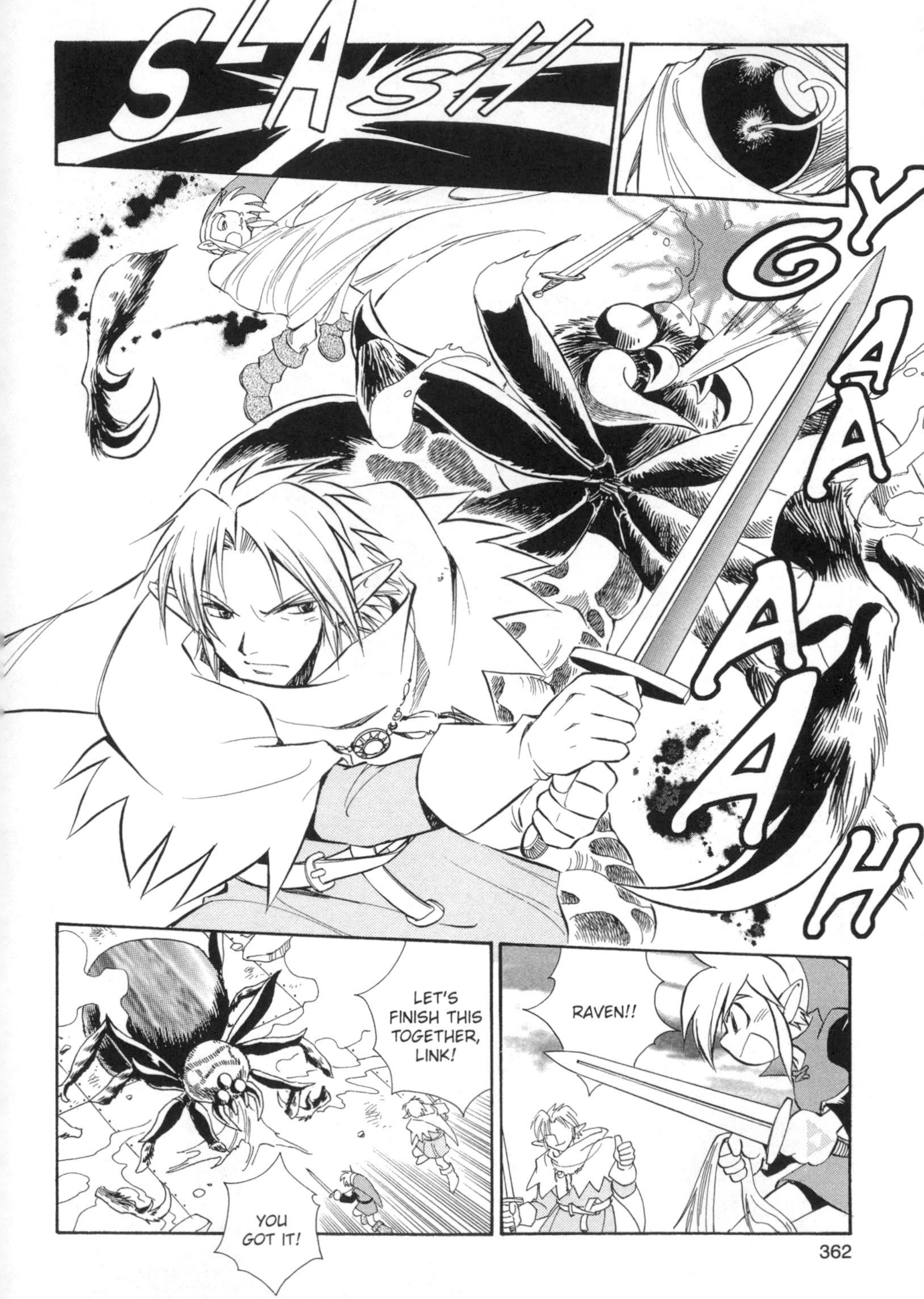
SLASH
GYAAAAH
RAVEN!!
LET'S FINISH THIS TOGETHER, LINK!
YOU GOT IT!

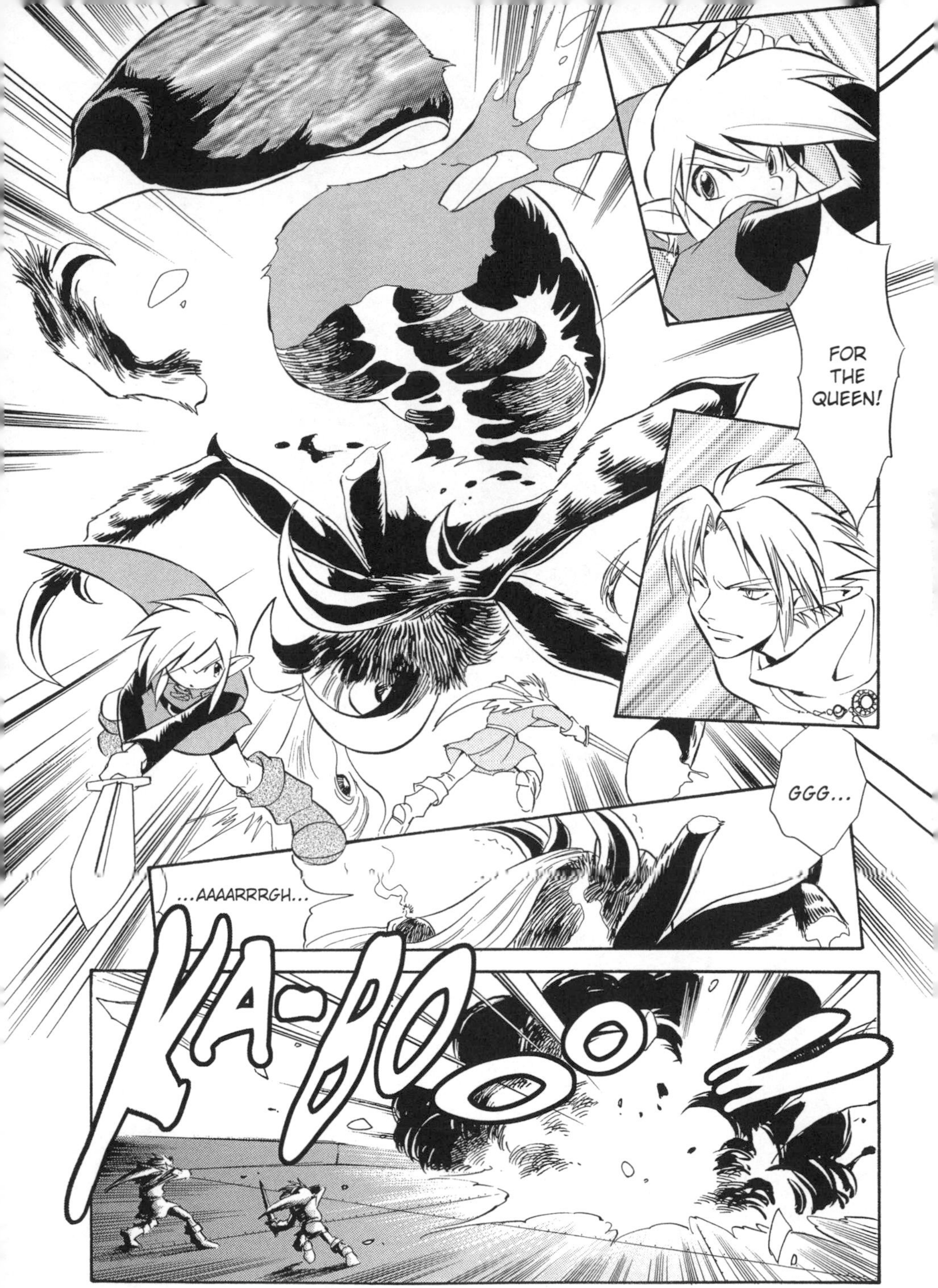
FOR THE QUEEN!
GGG...
...AAAARRRGH...
KA-BOOOOM!!

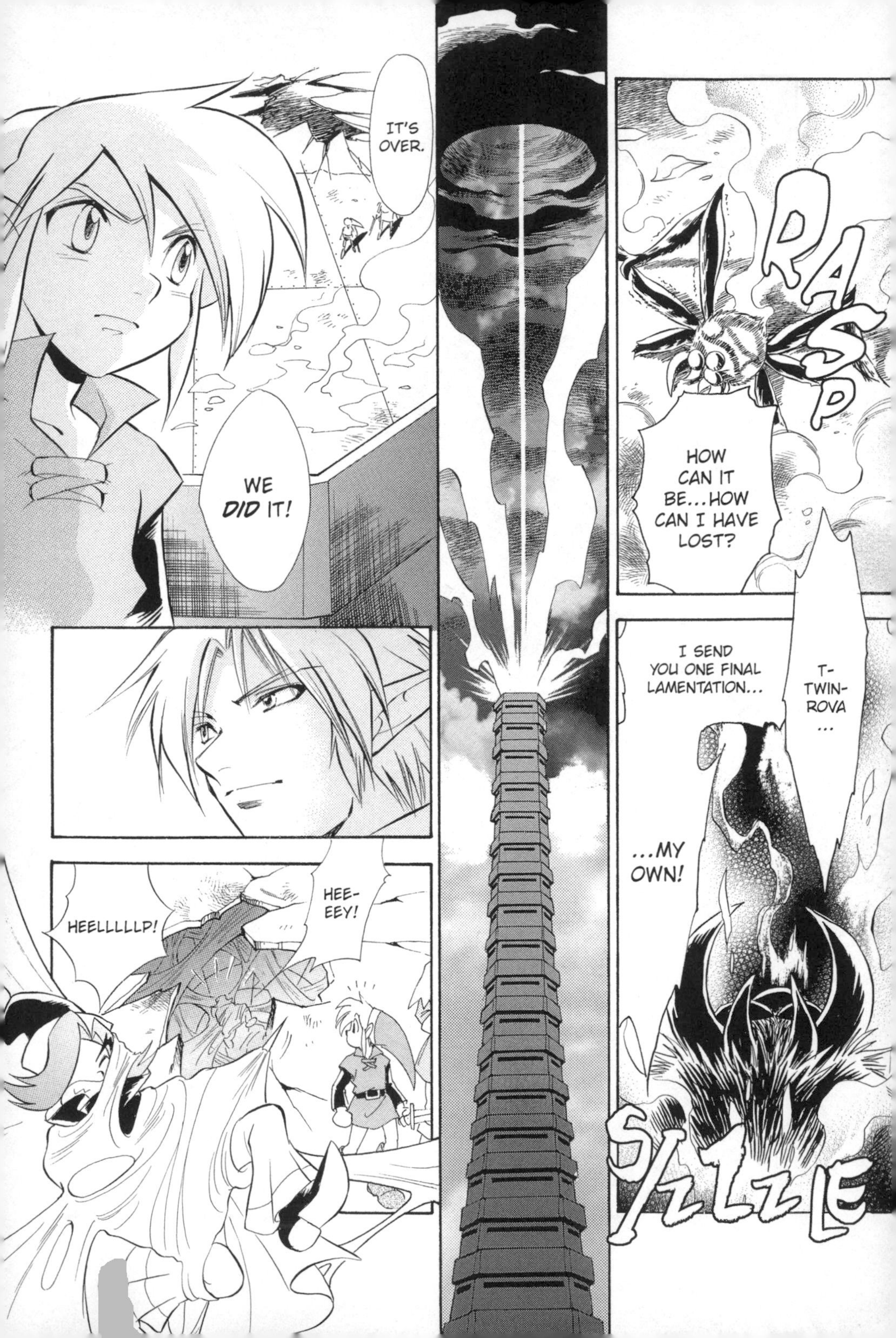
RASP
HOW CAN IT BE...HOW CAN I HAVE LOST?
T-TWINROVA...
I SEND YOU ONE FINAL LAMENTATION...
...MY OWN!
SIZZLE
IT'S OVER.
WE *DID* IT!
HEE-EEY!
HEELLLLLP!

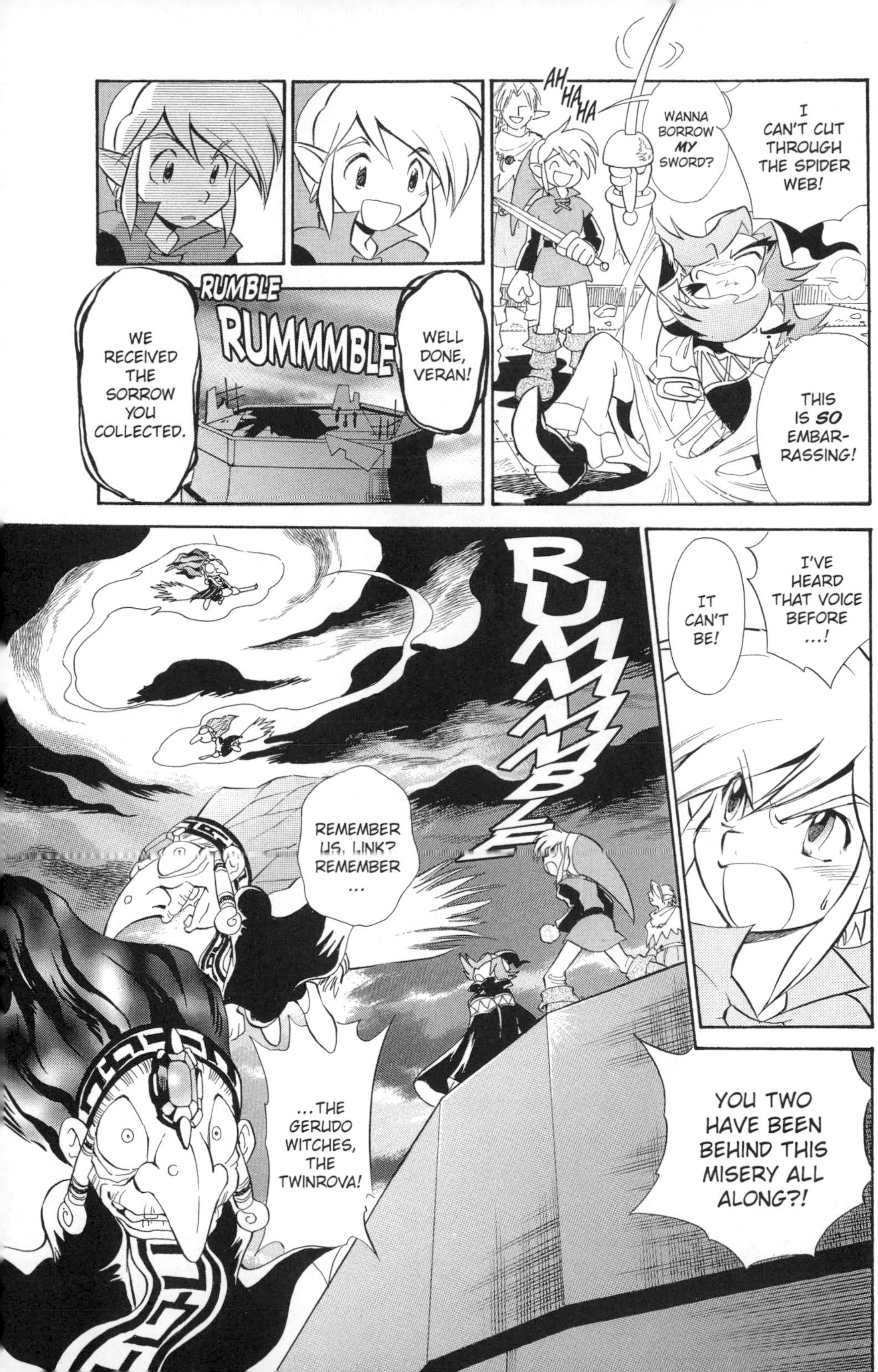
I CAN'T CUT THROUGH THE SPIDER WEB!
WANNA BORROW MY SWORD?
AH HA HA
THIS IS SO EMBARRASSING!
WELL DONE, VERAN!
RUMBLE RUMMMBLE
WE RECEIVED THE SORROW YOU COLLECTED.
I'VE HEARD THAT VOICE BEFORE ...!
IT CAN'T BE!
RUMMMBLE
REMEMBER US, LINK? REMEMBER ...
...THE GERUDO WITCHES, THE TWINROVA!
YOU TWO HAVE BEEN BEHIND THIS MISERY ALL ALONG?!

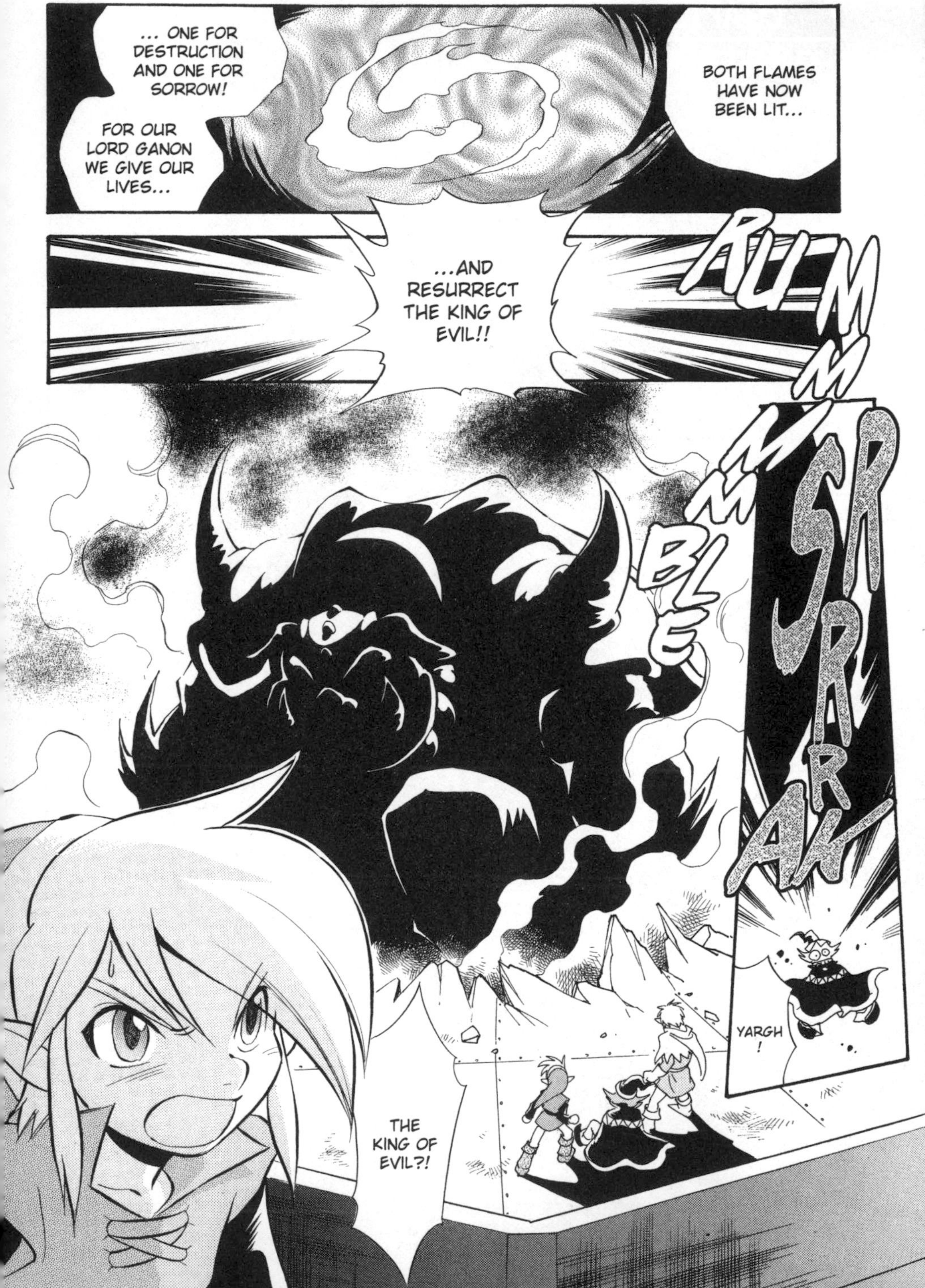
BOTH FLAMES HAVE NOW BEEN LIT...
... ONE FOR DESTRUCTION AND ONE FOR SORROW!
FOR OUR LORD GANON WE GIVE OUR LIVES...
...AND RESURRECT THE KING OF EVIL!!
RUMMMMMBLE
SRRRRAK
YARGH!
THE KING OF EVIL?!

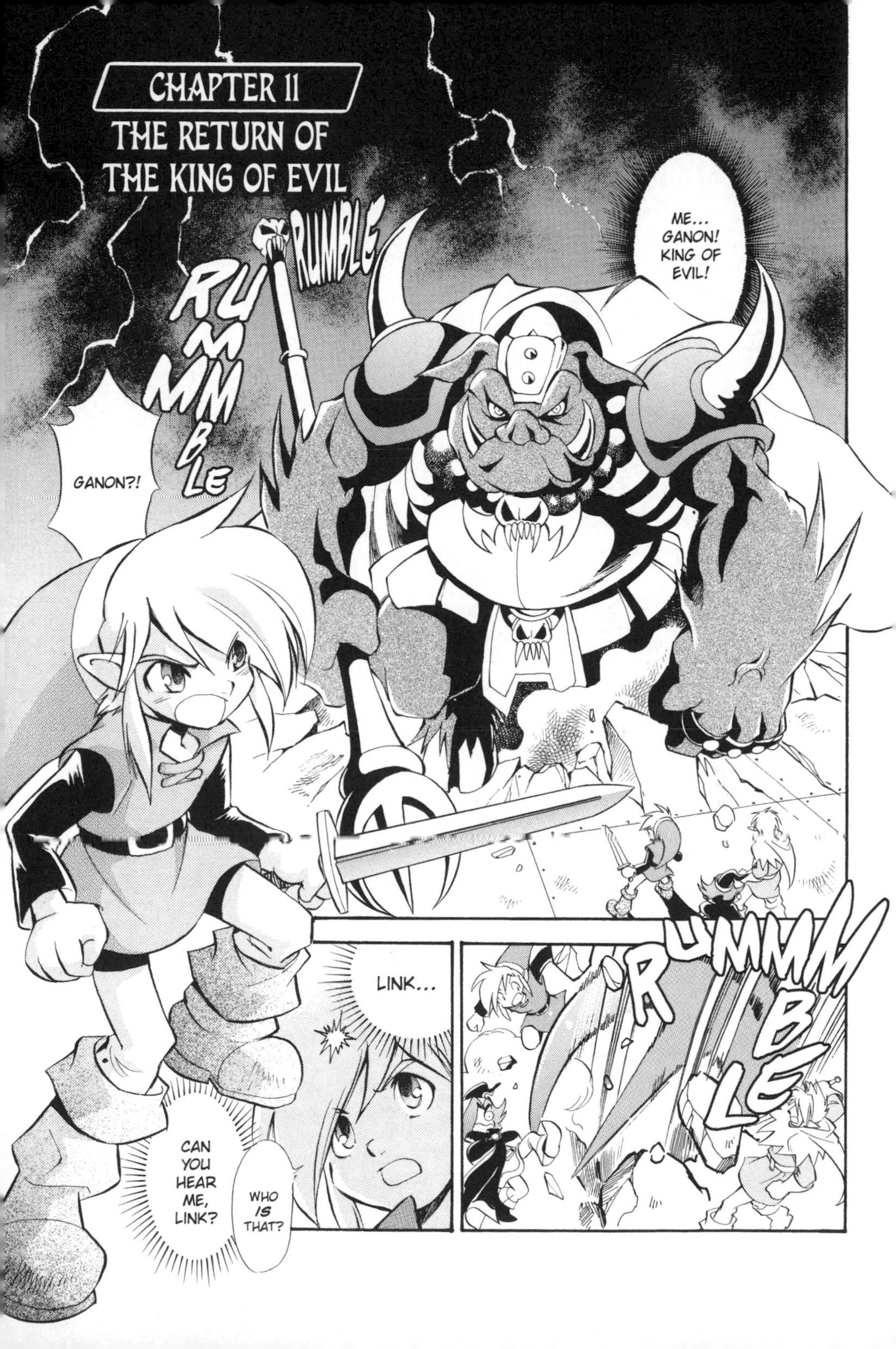
CHAPTER 11
THE RETURN OF THE KING OF EVIL
ME... GANON! KING OF EVIL!
RUMBLE
RUMMMBLE
GANON?!
RUMMMBLE
LINK...
CAN YOU HEAR ME, LINK?
WHO *IS* THAT?

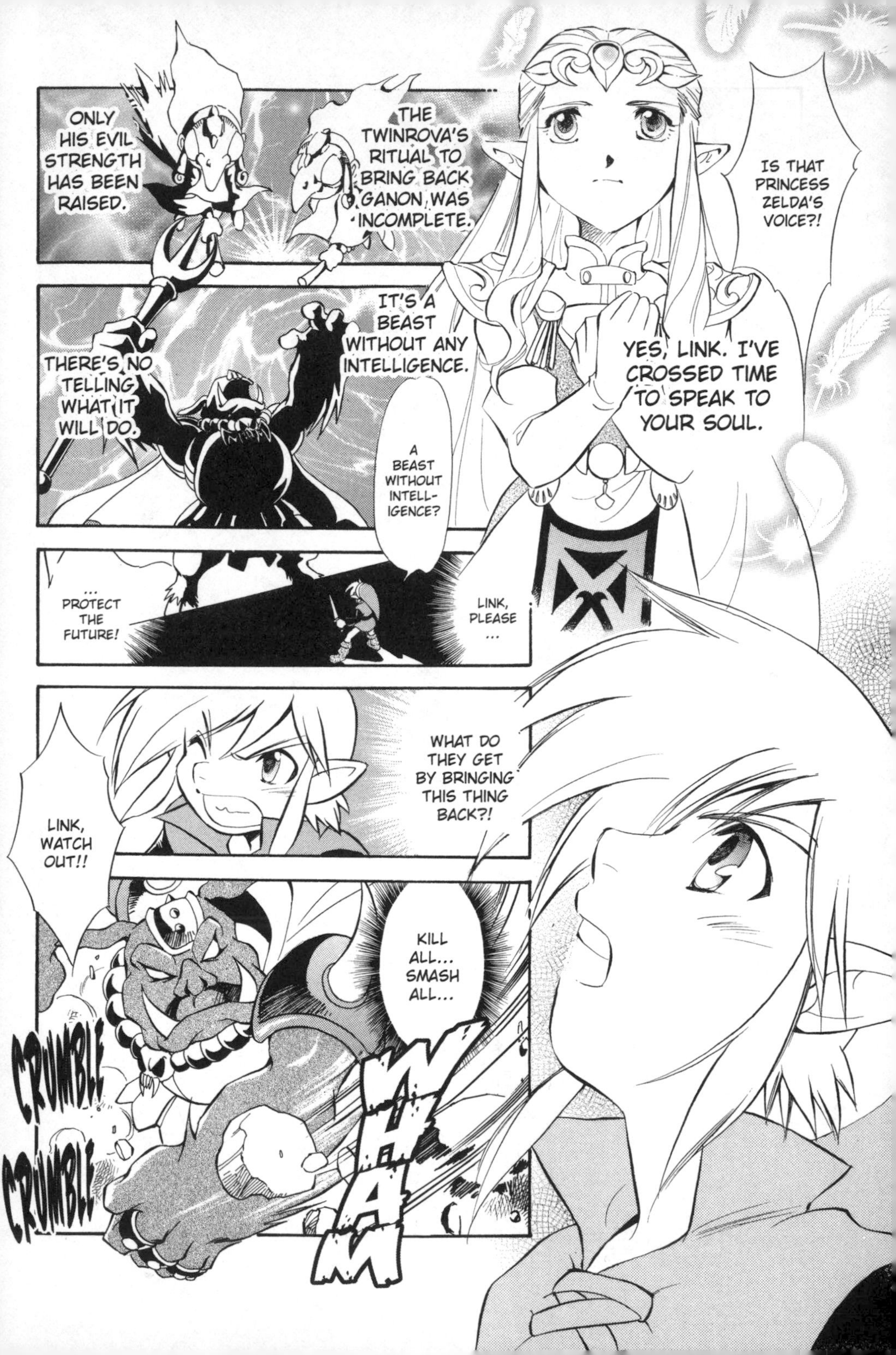

IS THAT PRINCESS ZELDA'S VOICE?!
YES, LINK. I'VE CROSSED TIME TO SPEAK TO YOUR SOUL.
THE TWINROVA'S RITUAL TO BRING BACK GANON WAS INCOMPLETE.
ONLY HIS EVIL STRENGTH HAS BEEN RAISED.
IT'S A BEAST WITHOUT ANY INTELLIGENCE.
THERE'S NO TELLING WHAT IT WILL DO.
A BEAST WITHOUT INTELL-IGENCE?
LINK, PLEASE ...
... PROTECT THE FUTURE!
WHAT DO THEY GET BY BRINGING THIS THING BACK?!
LINK, WATCH OUT!!
KILL ALL... SMASH ALL...
WHAM
CRUMBLE
CRUMBLE

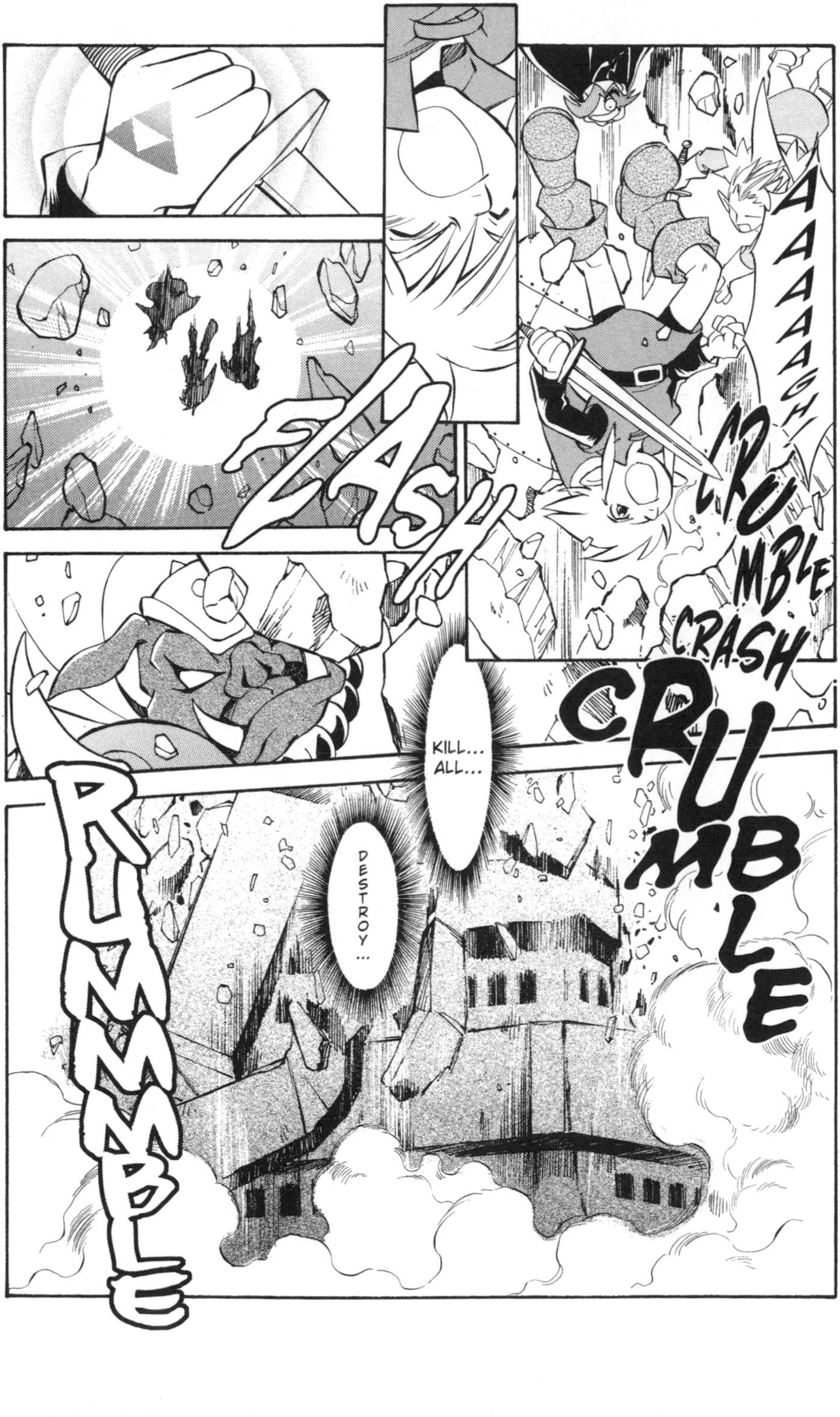
AAAAAAAGH!
CRUMBLE
CRASH
FLASH
CRUMBLE
KILL... ALL...
DESTROY...
RUMMMBLE

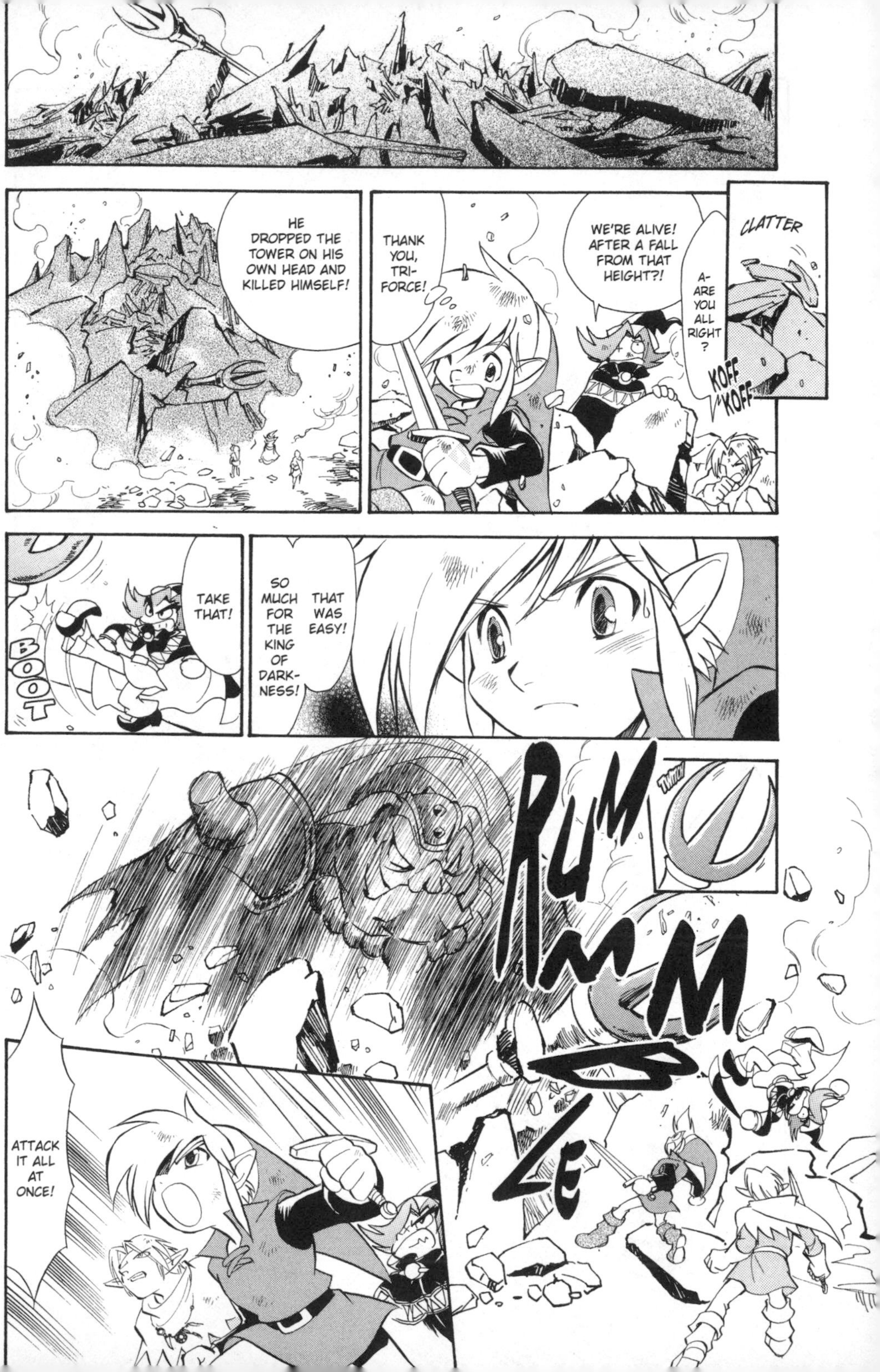
CLATTER
A-ARE YOU ALL RIGHT?
KOFF KOFF
WE'RE ALIVE! AFTER A FALL FROM THAT HEIGHT?!
THANK YOU, TRI-FORCE!
HE DROPPED THE TOWER ON HIS OWN HEAD AND KILLED HIMSELF!
THAT WAS EASY!
SO MUCH FOR THE KING OF DARKNESS!
TAKE THAT!
BOOT
TWITCH
RUMMMBLE
ATTACK IT ALL AT ONCE!

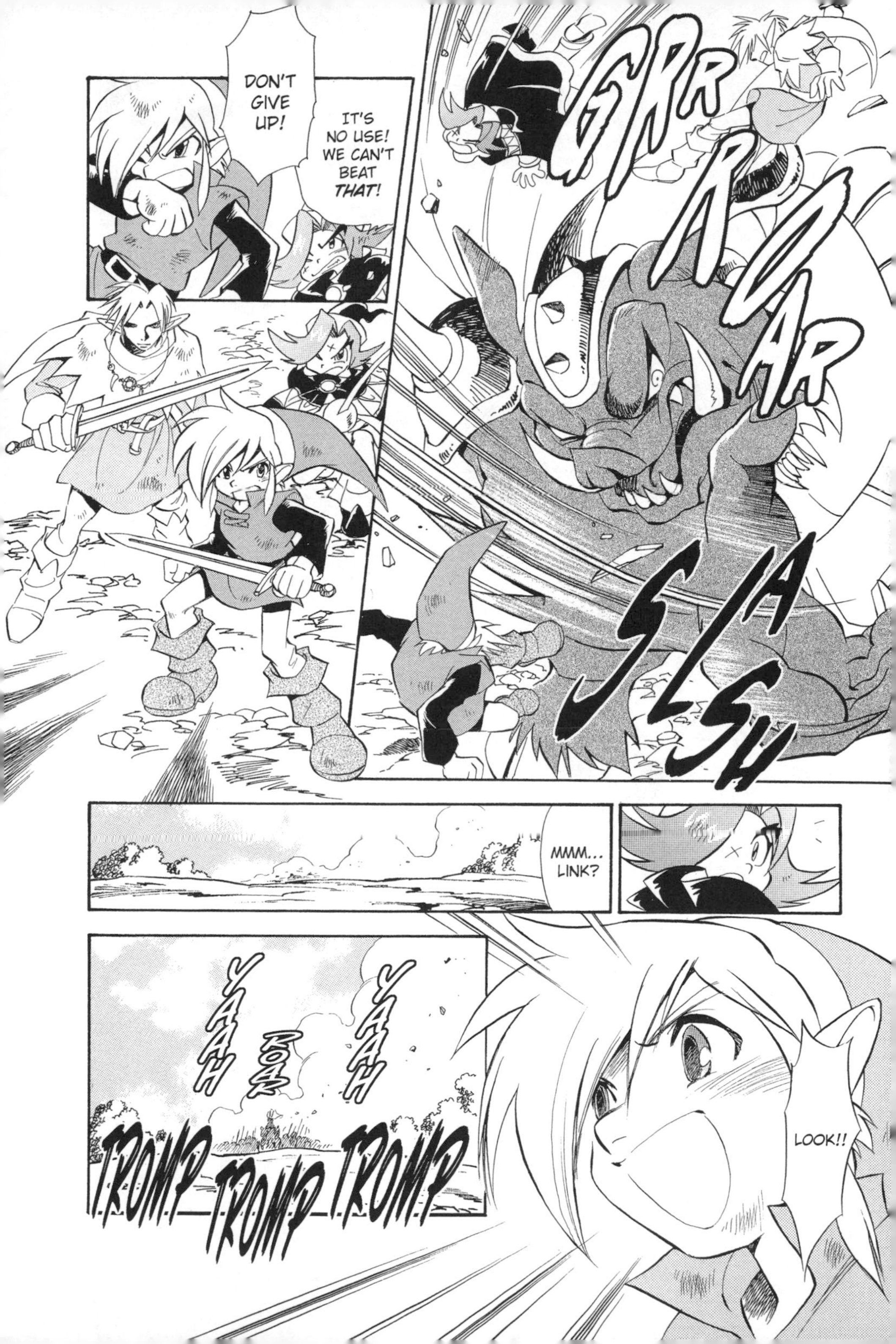
GRRROAR
SLASH
DON'T GIVE UP!
IT'S NO USE! WE CAN'T BEAT *THAT*!
MMM... LINK?
LOOK!!
YAAAH
ROAR
YAAAH
TROMP TROMP TROMP

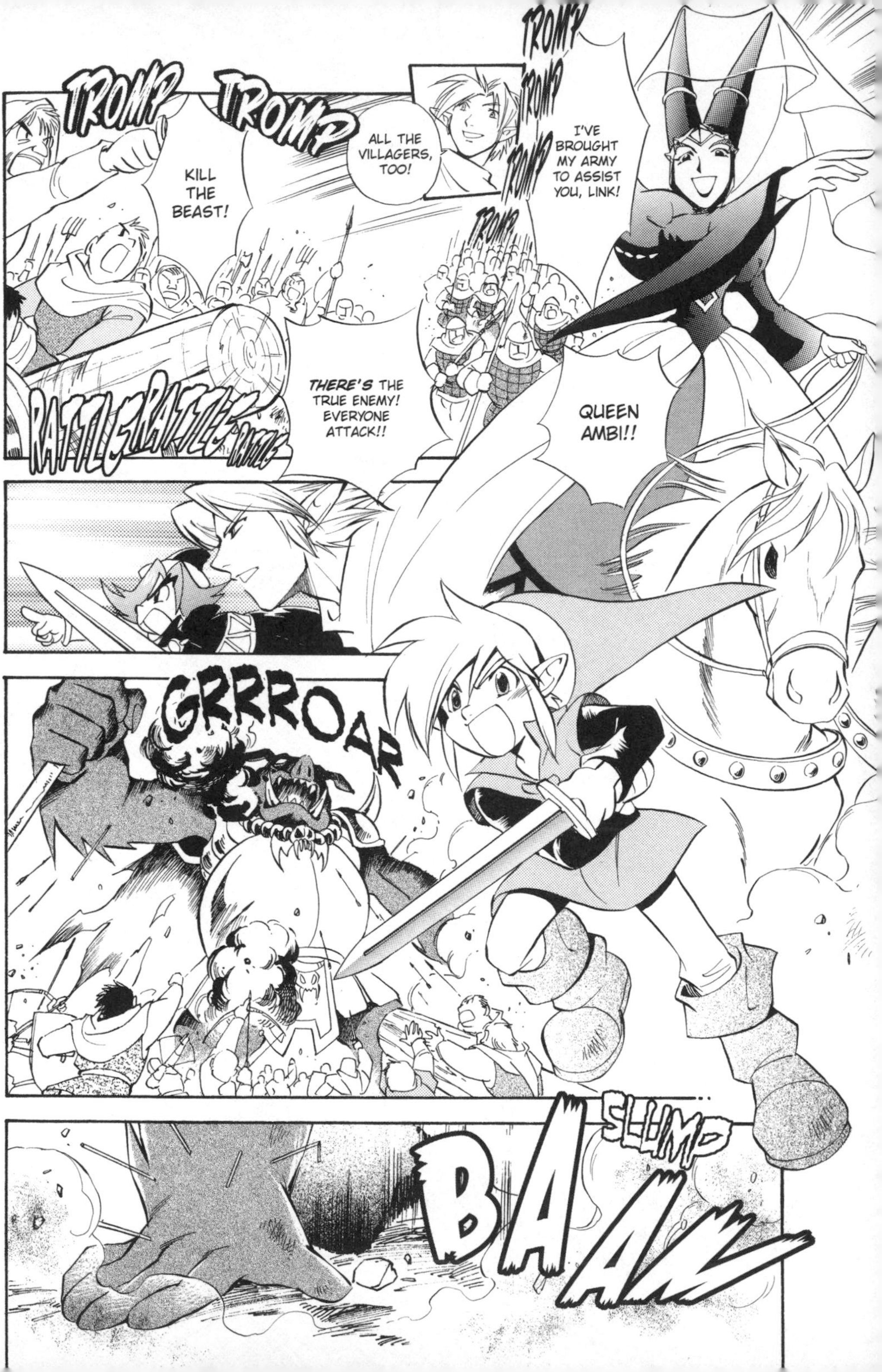
TROMP TROMP TROMP TROMP
I'VE BROUGHT MY ARMY TO ASSIST YOU, LINK!
ALL THE VILLAGERS, TOO!
TROMP
TROMP TROMP
KILL THE BEAST!
QUEEN AMBI!!
THERE'S THE TRUE ENEMY! EVERYONE ATTACK!!
RATTLE RATTLE RATTLE
GRRROAR
SLUMP
BAAM

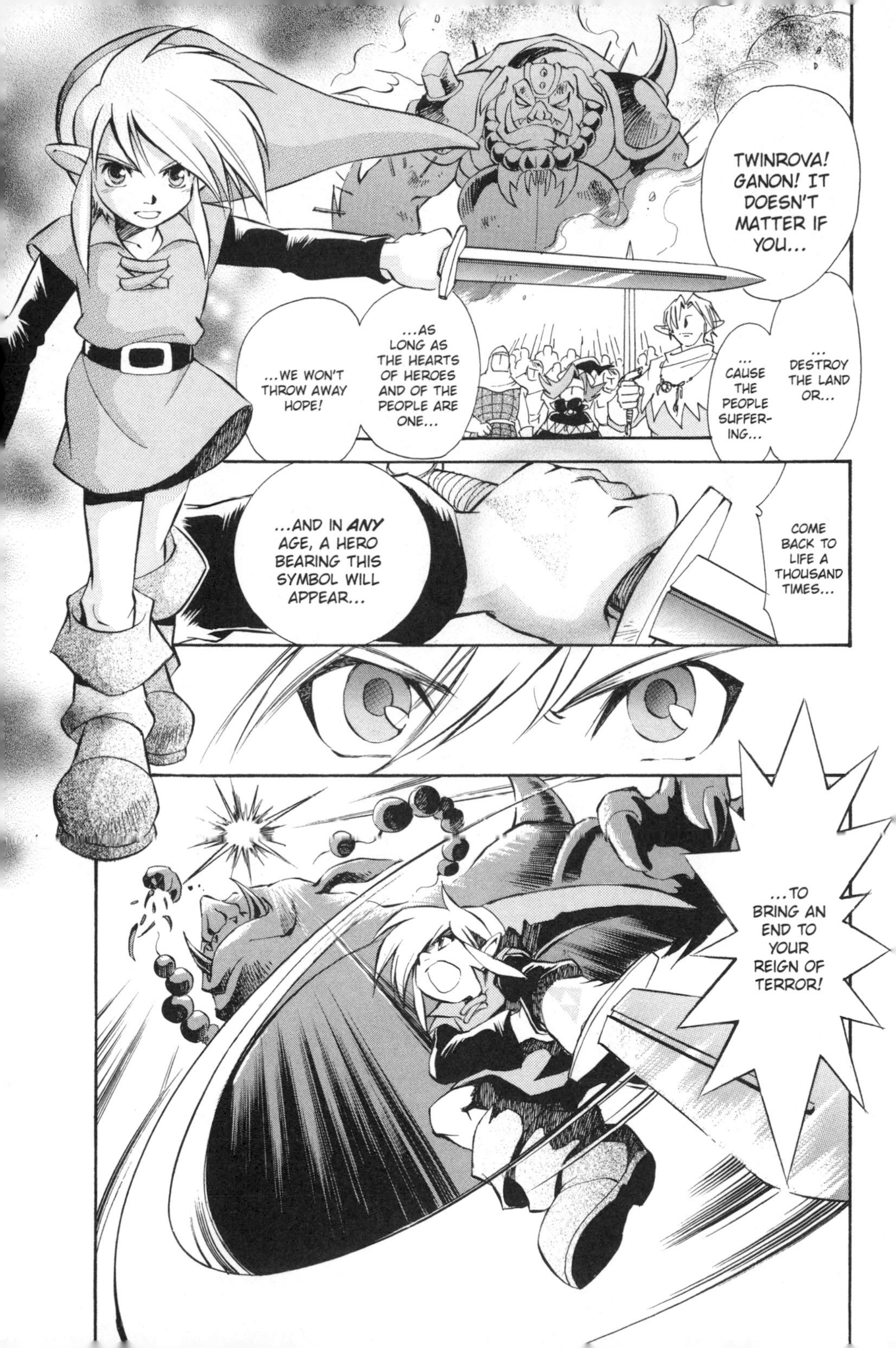
TWINROVA! GANON! IT DOESN'T MATTER IF YOU...
...DESTROY THE LAND OR...
...CAUSE THE PEOPLE SUFFERING...
COME BACK TO LIFE A THOUSAND TIMES...
...AS LONG AS THE HEARTS OF HEROES AND OF THE PEOPLE ARE ONE...
...WE WON'T THROW AWAY HOPE!
...AND IN *ANY* AGE, A HERO BEARING THIS SYMBOL WILL APPEAR...
...TO BRING AN END TO YOUR REIGN OF TERROR!

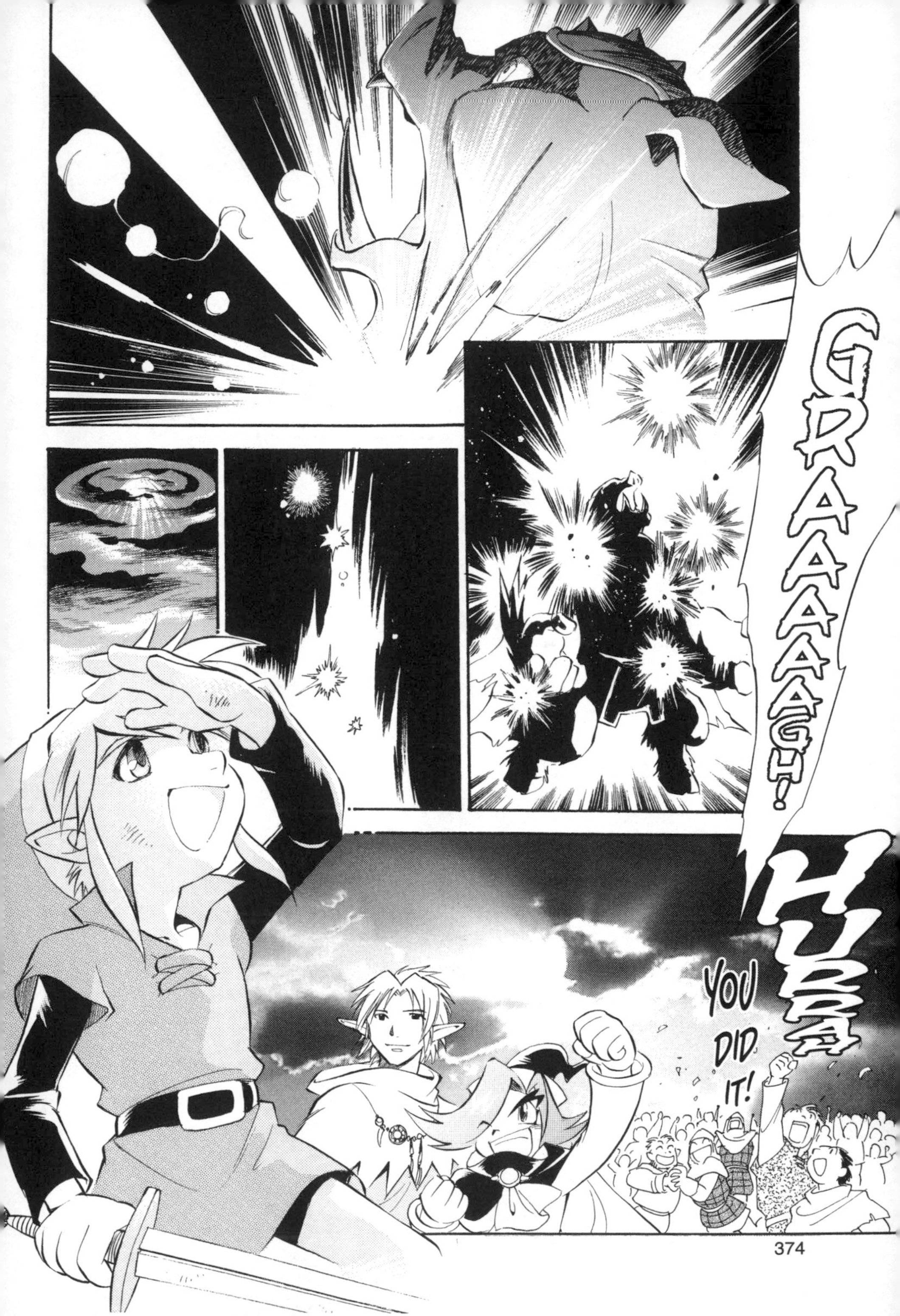
GRAAAAAGH!
HURRA
YOU DID IT!

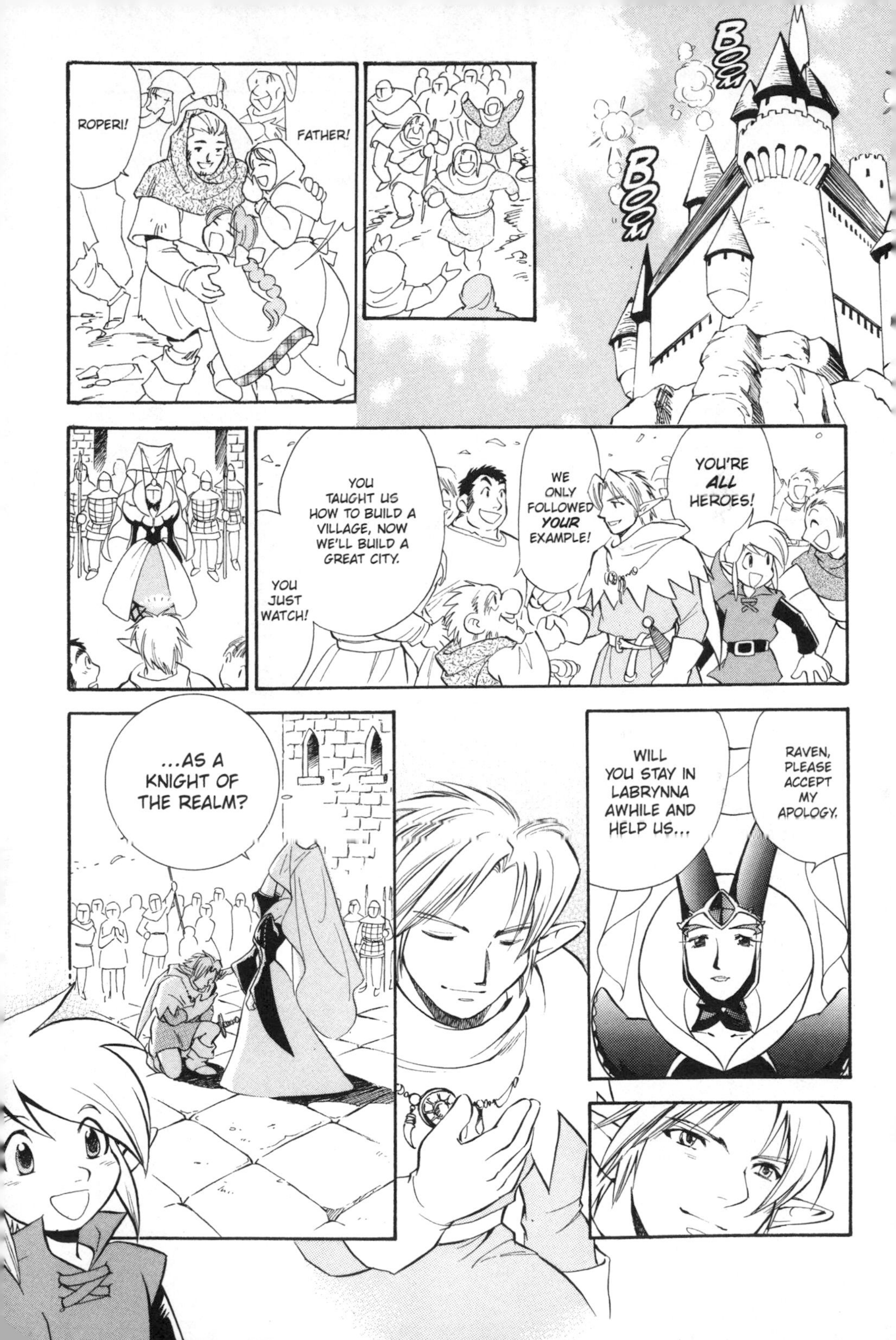

BOOM
BOOM
FATHER!
ROPERI!
YOU'RE ALL HEROES!
WE ONLY FOLLOWED YOUR EXAMPLE!
YOU TAUGHT US HOW TO BUILD A VILLAGE, NOW WE'LL BUILD A GREAT CITY.
YOU JUST WATCH!
RAVEN, PLEASE ACCEPT MY APOLOGY.
WILL YOU STAY IN LABRYNNA AWHILE AND HELP US...
...AS A KNIGHT OF THE REALM?

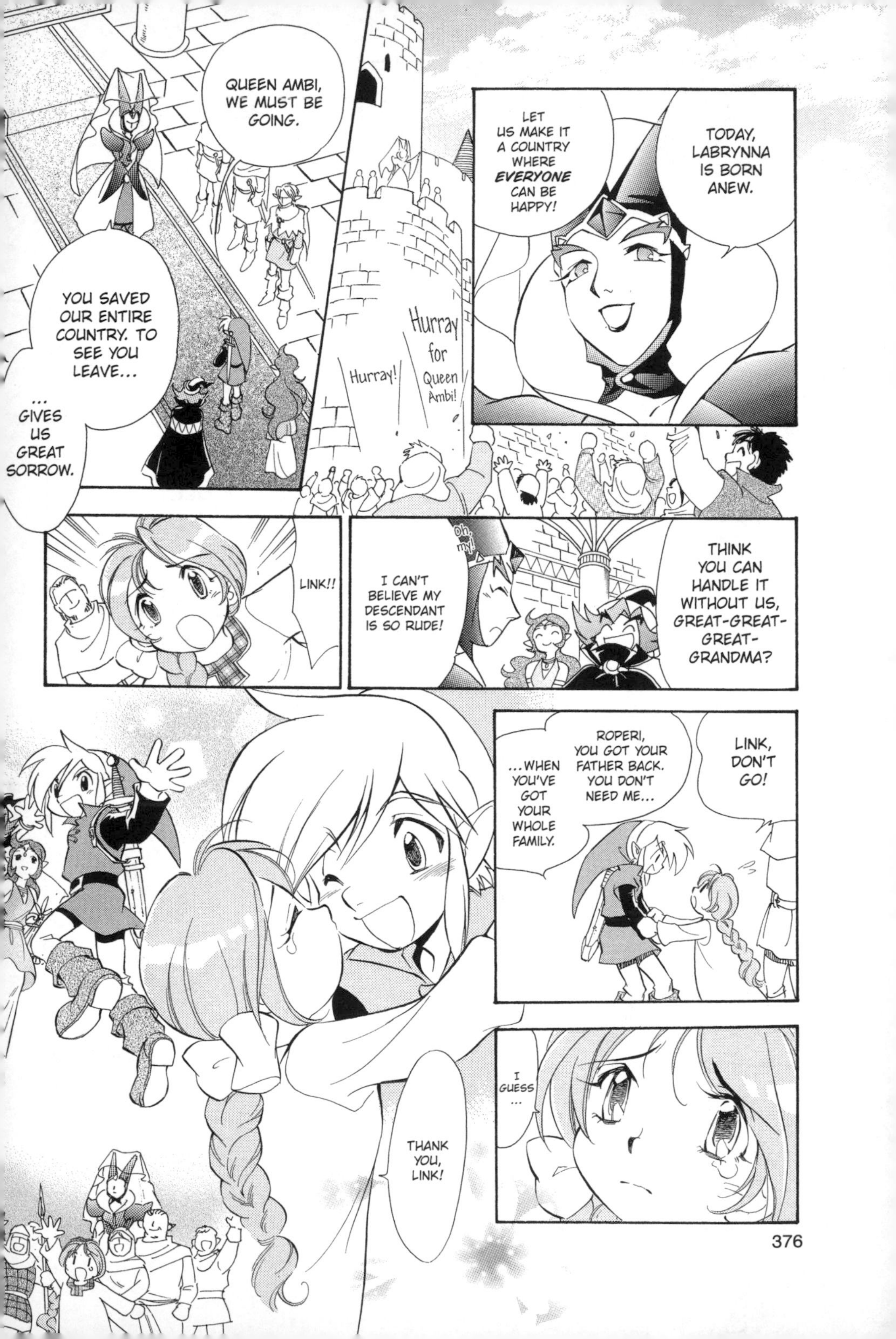
TODAY, LABRYNNA IS BORN ANEW.
LET US MAKE IT A COUNTRY WHERE ***EVERYONE*** CAN BE HAPPY!
Hurray for Queen Ambi!
Hurray!
QUEEN AMBI, WE MUST BE GOING.
YOU SAVED OUR ENTIRE COUNTRY. TO SEE YOU LEAVE...
...GIVES US GREAT SORROW.
THINK YOU CAN HANDLE IT WITHOUT US, GREAT-GREAT-GREAT-GRANDMA?
Oh, my!
I CAN'T BELIEVE MY DESCENDANT IS SO RUDE!
LINK!!
LINK, DON'T GO!
ROPERI, YOU GOT YOUR FATHER BACK. YOU DON'T NEED ME...
...WHEN YOU'VE GOT YOUR WHOLE FAMILY.
I GUESS...
THANK YOU, LINK!

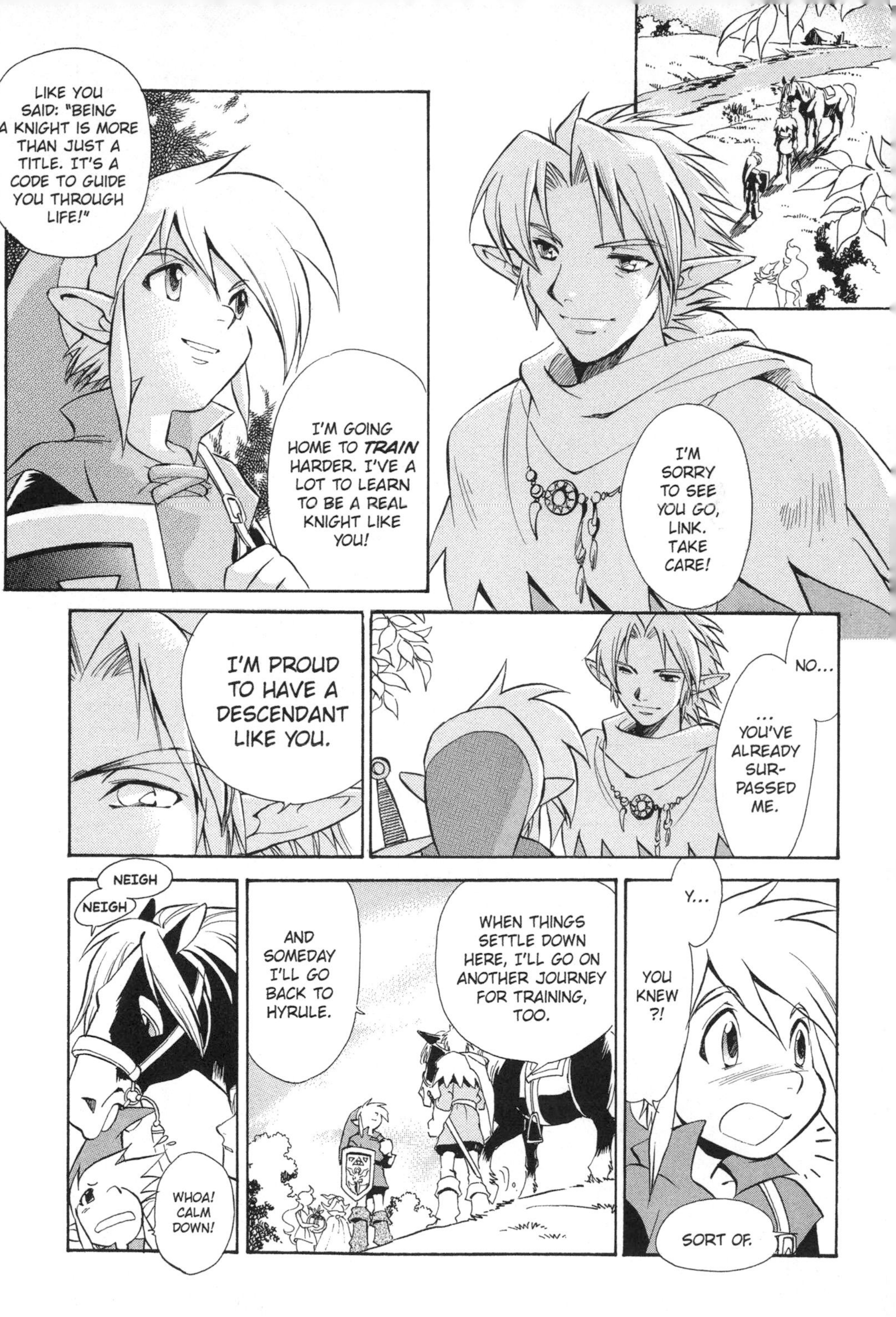
I'M SORRY TO SEE YOU GO, LINK. TAKE CARE!
LIKE YOU SAID: "BEING A KNIGHT IS MORE THAN JUST A TITLE. IT'S A CODE TO GUIDE YOU THROUGH LIFE!"
I'M GOING HOME TO TRAIN HARDER. I'VE A LOT TO LEARN TO BE A REAL KNIGHT LIKE YOU!
NO...
... YOU'VE ALREADY SUR-PASSED ME.
I'M PROUD TO HAVE A DESCENDANT LIKE YOU.
Y...
YOU KNEW ?!
SORT OF.
WHEN THINGS SETTLE DOWN HERE, I'LL GO ON ANOTHER JOURNEY FOR TRAINING, TOO.
AND SOMEDAY I'LL GO BACK TO HYRULE.
NEIGH
NEIGH
WHOA! CALM DOWN!

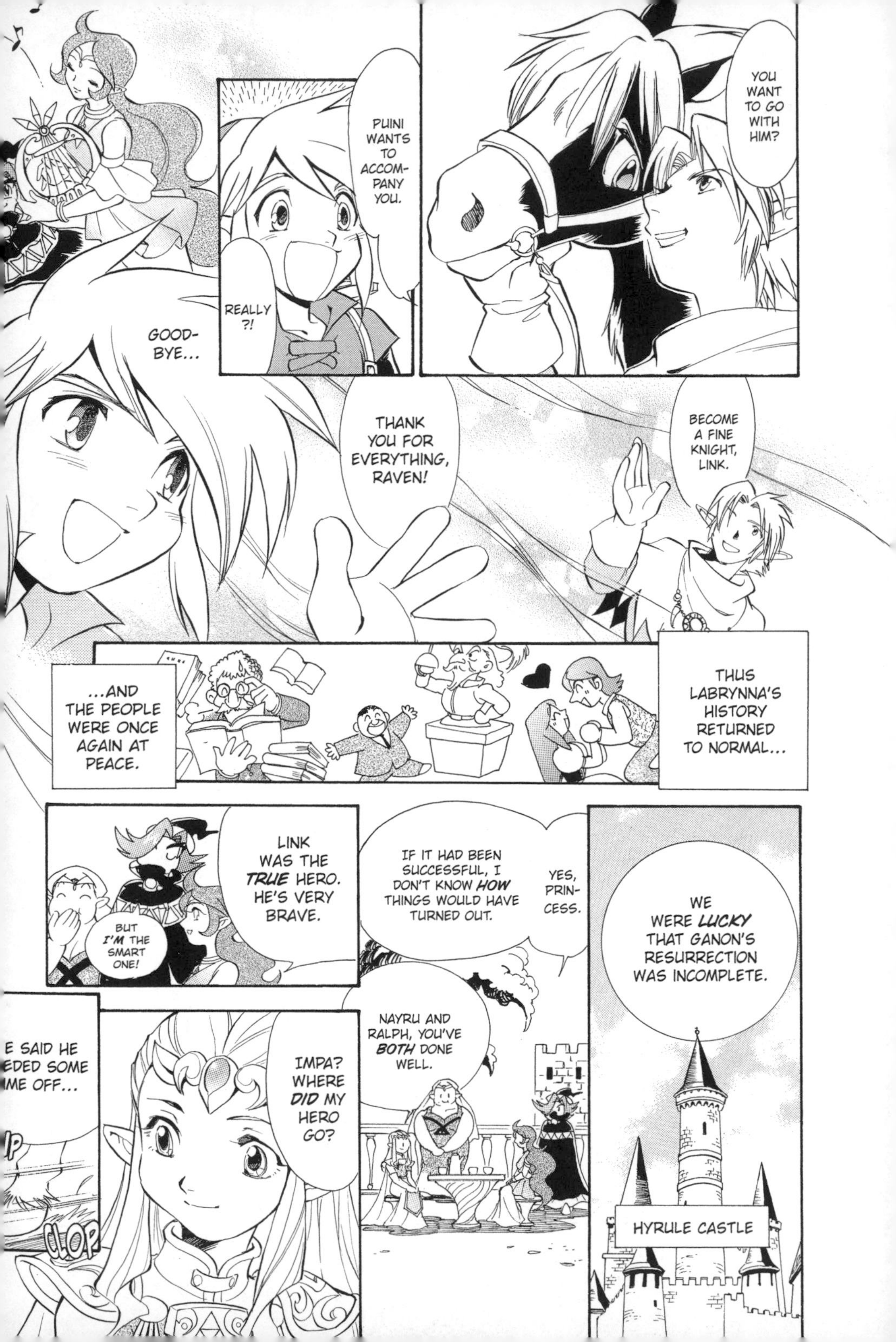
YOU WANT TO GO WITH HIM?
PUINI WANTS TO ACCOMPANY YOU.
REALLY ?!
BECOME A FINE KNIGHT, LINK.
THANK YOU FOR EVERYTHING, RAVEN!
GOOD-BYE...
THUS LABRYNNA'S HISTORY RETURNED TO NORMAL...
...AND THE PEOPLE WERE ONCE AGAIN AT PEACE.
HYRULE CASTLE
WE WERE *LUCKY* THAT GANON'S RESURRECTION WAS INCOMPLETE.
YES, PRINCESS.
IF IT HAD BEEN SUCCESSFUL, I DON'T KNOW *HOW* THINGS WOULD HAVE TURNED OUT.
LINK WAS THE *TRUE* HERO. HE'S VERY BRAVE.
BUT *I'M* THE SMART ONE!
NAYRU AND RALPH, YOU'VE *BOTH* DONE WELL.
IMPA? WHERE *DID* MY HERO GO?
E SAID HE EDED SOME ME OFF...
CLOP

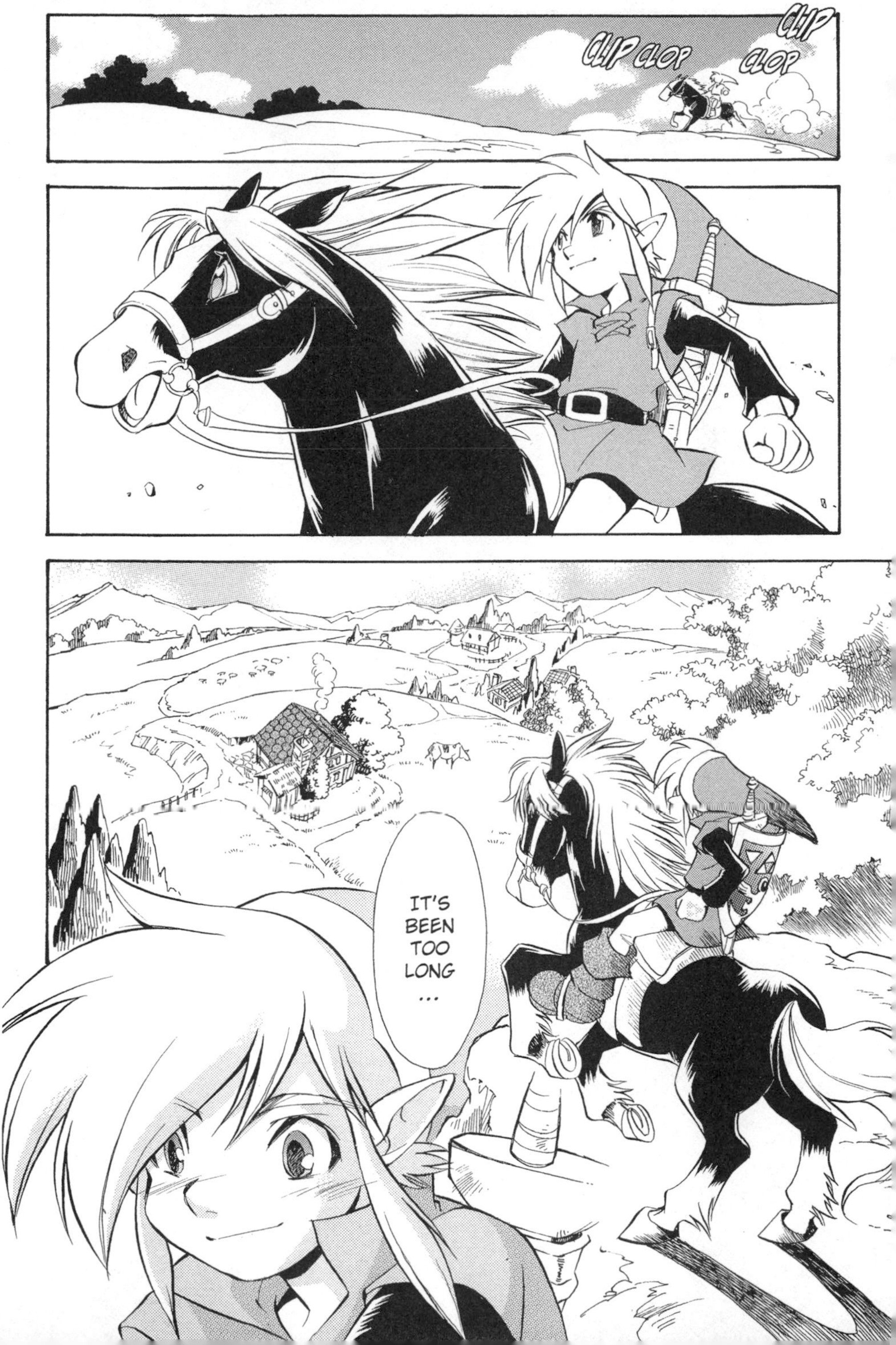

CLIP CLOP
CLIP CLOP
IT'S BEEN TOO LONG ...

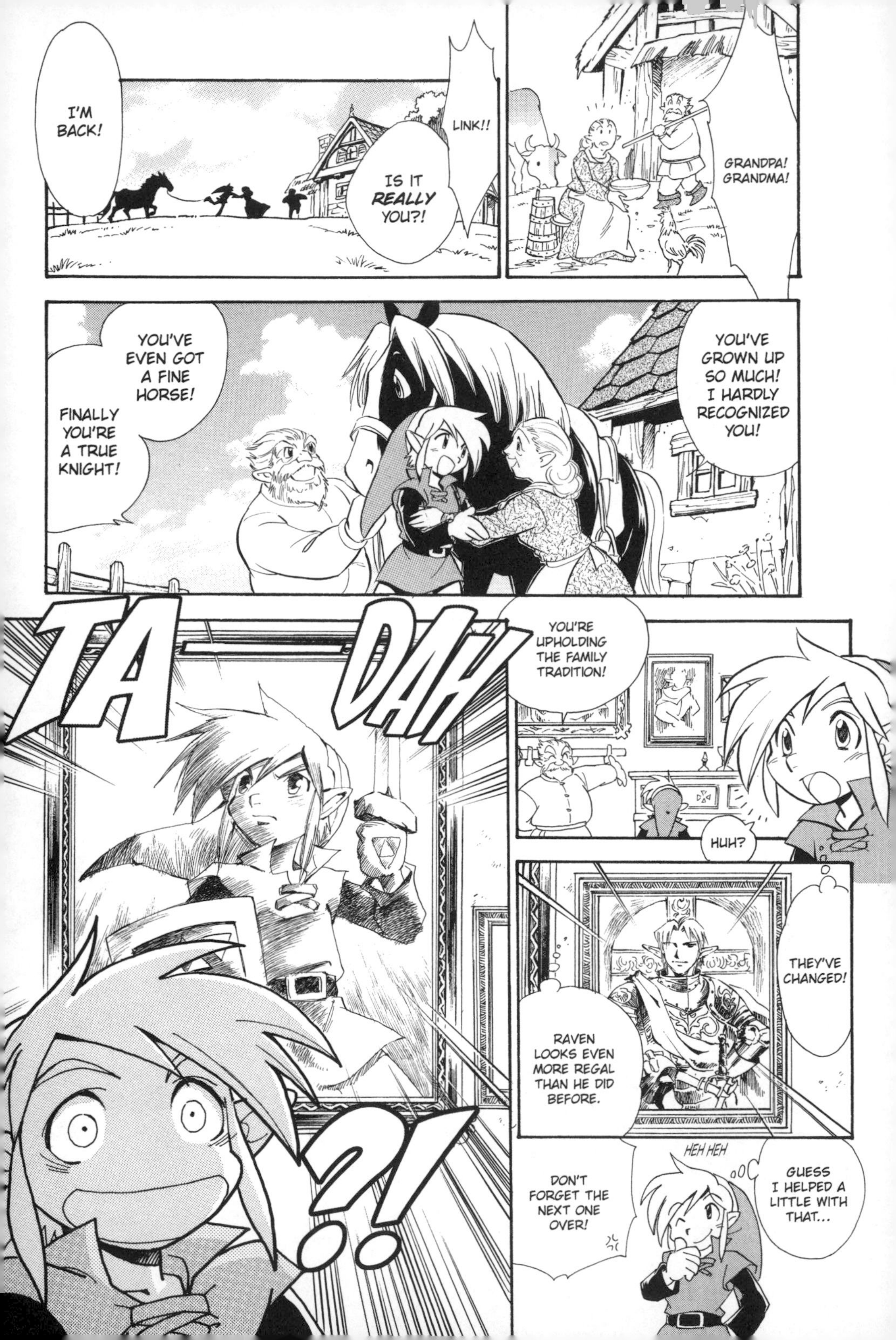
GRANDPA! GRANDMA!
LINK!!
IS IT REALLY YOU?!
I'M BACK!
YOU'VE GROWN UP SO MUCH! I HARDLY RECOGNIZED YOU!
YOU'VE EVEN GOT A FINE HORSE!
FINALLY YOU'RE A TRUE KNIGHT!
YOU'RE UPHOLDING THE FAMILY TRADITION!
HUH?
THEY'VE CHANGED!
RAVEN LOOKS EVEN MORE REGAL THAN HE DID BEFORE.
GUESS I HELPED A LITTLE WITH THAT...
HEH HEH
DON'T FORGET THE NEXT ONE OVER!
TA
DAH
?!

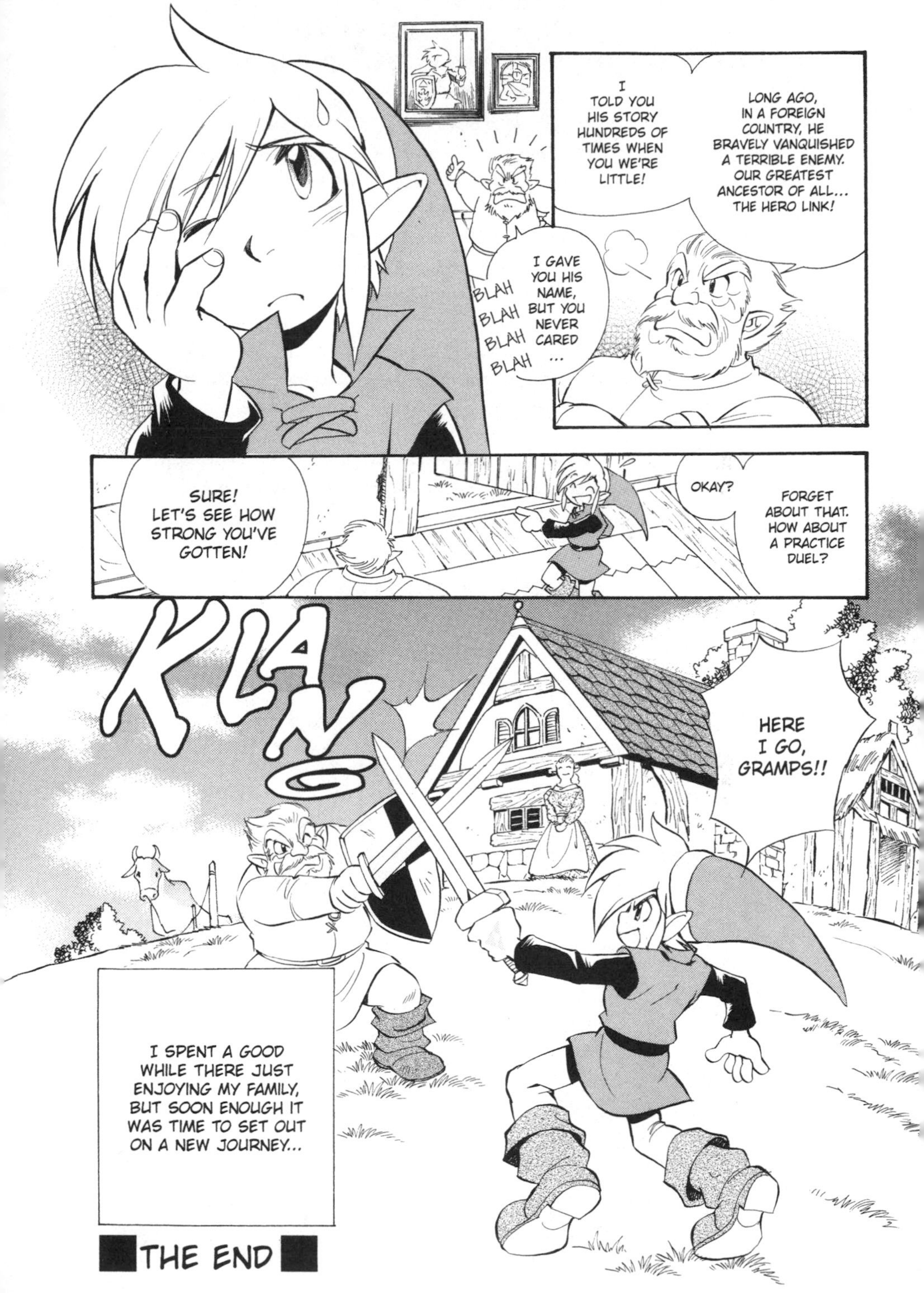
LONG AGO, IN A FOREIGN COUNTRY, HE BRAVELY VANQUISHED A TERRIBLE ENEMY. OUR GREATEST ANCESTOR OF ALL... THE HERO LINK!
I TOLD YOU HIS STORY HUNDREDS OF TIMES WHEN YOU WE'RE LITTLE!
I GAVE YOU HIS NAME, BUT YOU NEVER CARED ...
BLAH BLAH BLAH BLAH
FORGET ABOUT THAT. HOW ABOUT A PRACTICE DUEL?
OKAY?
SURE! LET'S SEE HOW STRONG YOU'VE GOTTEN!
HERE I GO, GRAMPS!!
KLANG
I SPENT A GOOD WHILE THERE JUST ENJOYING MY FAMILY, BUT SOON ENOUGH IT WAS TIME TO SET OUT ON A NEW JOURNEY...

THE END

THE STORY BEHIND ORACLE OF SEASONS: SHORT EDITION

The short edition of *Oracle of Seasons* that begins on the next page appeared in *Shogaku Ninensei* in February and March of 2001, but it's appearing in graphic novel format for the first time here. Seeing it for the first time in a long while, I was like, "Whoa! Did I do this?!" It was quite a jolt, but my memories gradually came back... *Oracle of Seasons* and *Oracle of Ages* were in serialization simultaneously. *Oracle of Seasons* began in a supplement to *Shogaku Gonensei* in March and had more pages, while *Oracle of Ages* began in *Shogaku Yonensei* in February. So when Parts 1 and 2 of this short edition overlapped those series, meeting my deadlines was awfully tough. I was just beginning the long version, but I had to include the story's conclusion and flashbacks and figure out a way for it to connect well with the graphic novels later. The format was rather distinctive of magazines for students, and now I remember it fondly. There aren't many pages, so it's basically a short summary, and the story is faithful to game strategy. What's more, some characters and items show up that aren't in the longer version. So, enjoy another take on *Oracle of Seasons*!

AKIRA HIMEKAWA

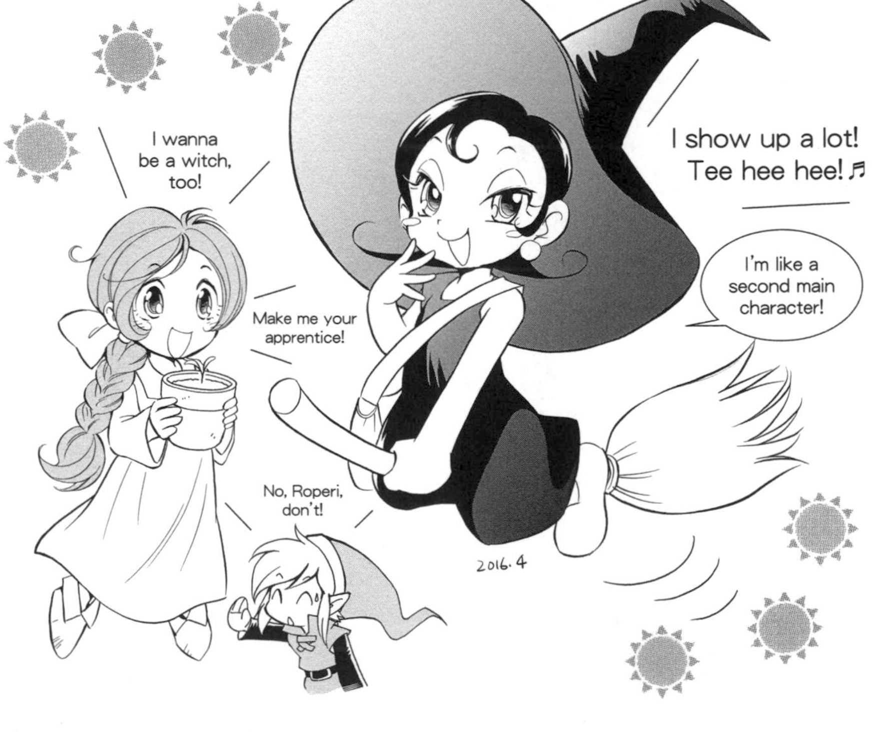
I show up a lot! Tee hee hee! ♬
I'm like a second main character!
I wanna be a witch, too!
Make me your apprentice!
No, Roperi, don't!
2016. 4

ORACLE OF SEASONS
SHORT EDITION PART 1

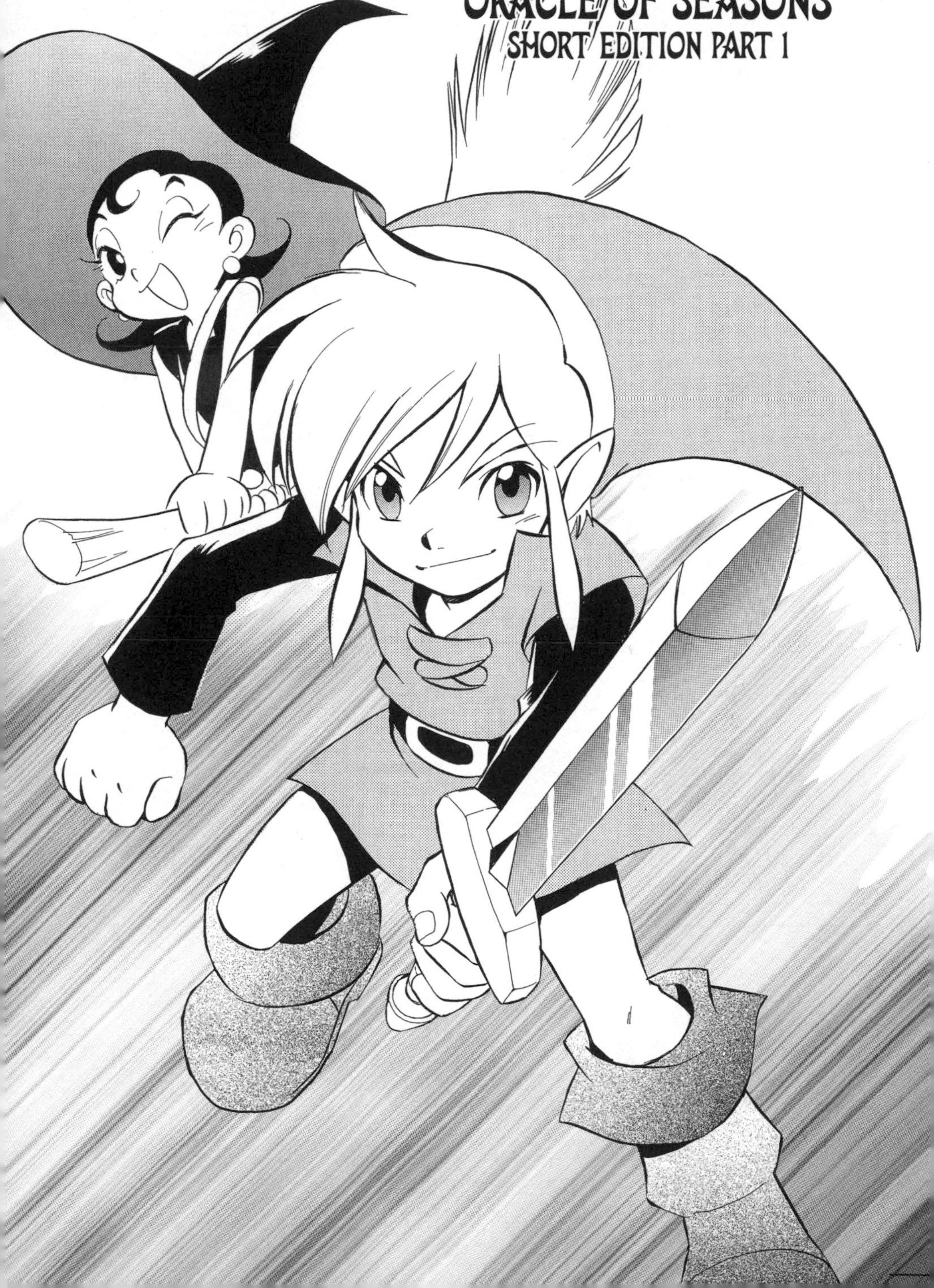

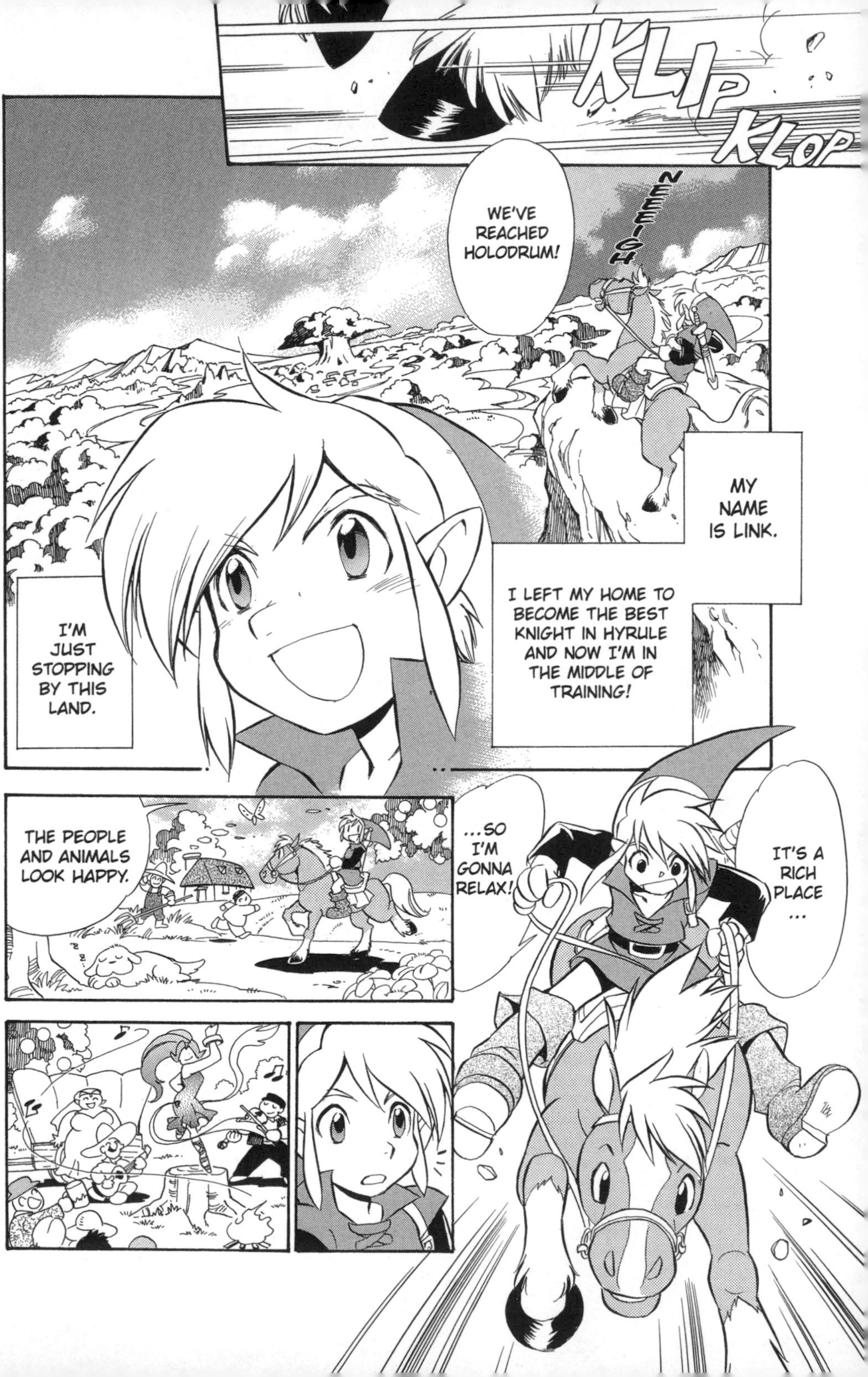
KLIP KLOP
NEEEIGH
WE'VE REACHED HOLODRUM!
MY NAME IS LINK.
I LEFT MY HOME TO BECOME THE BEST KNIGHT IN HYRULE AND NOW I'M IN THE MIDDLE OF TRAINING!
I'M JUST STOPPING BY THIS LAND.
IT'S A RICH PLACE ...
...SO I'M GONNA RELAX!
THE PEOPLE AND ANIMALS LOOK HAPPY.

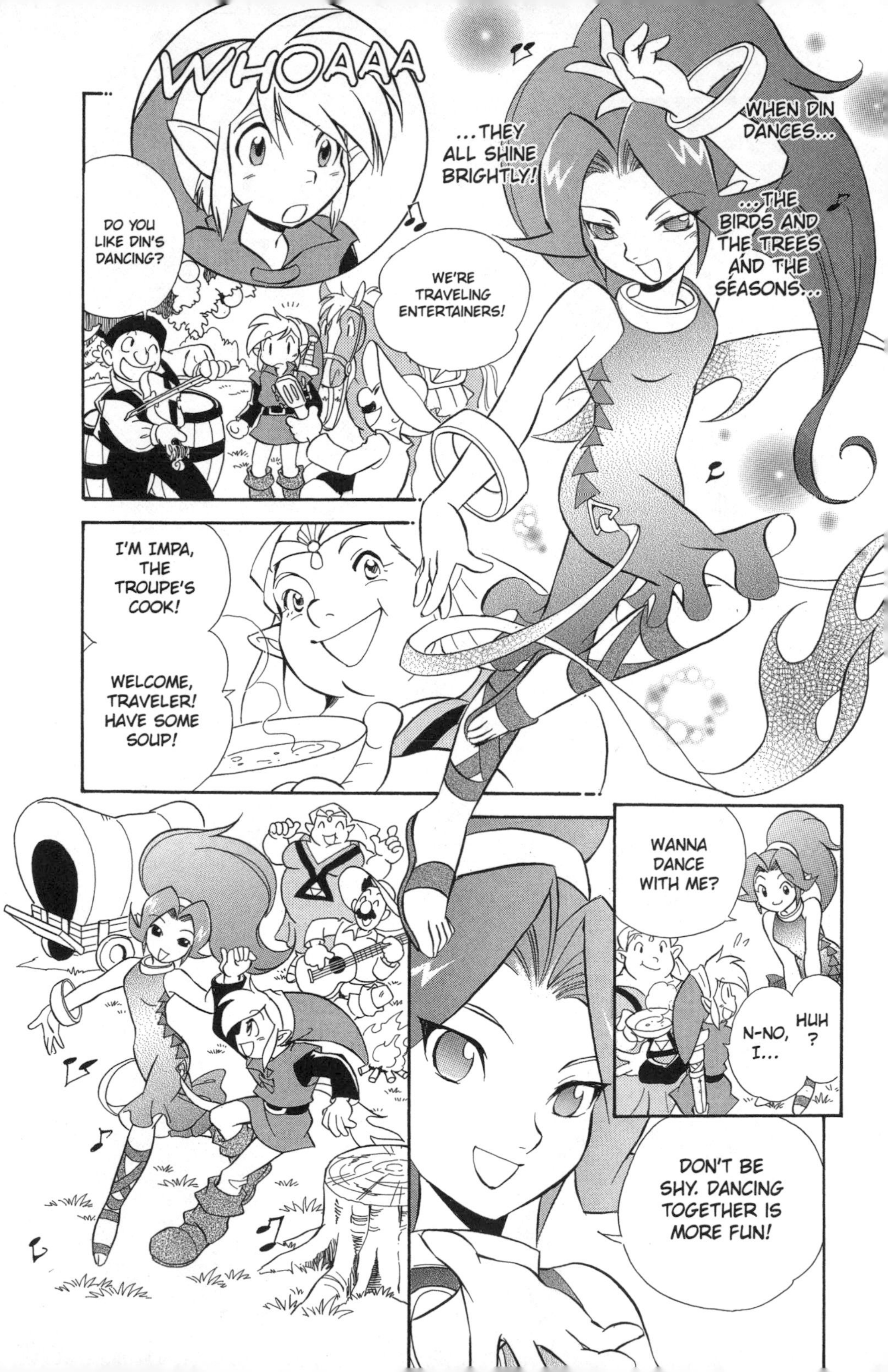
WHEN DIN DANCES...
...THE BIRDS AND THE TREES AND THE SEASONS...
...THEY ALL SHINE BRIGHTLY!
WHOAAA
WE'RE TRAVELING ENTERTAINERS!
DO YOU LIKE DIN'S DANCING?
I'M IMPA, THE TROUPE'S COOK!
WELCOME, TRAVELER! HAVE SOME SOUP!
WANNA DANCE WITH ME?
HUH?
N-NO, I...
DON'T BE SHY. DANCING TOGETHER IS MORE FUN!

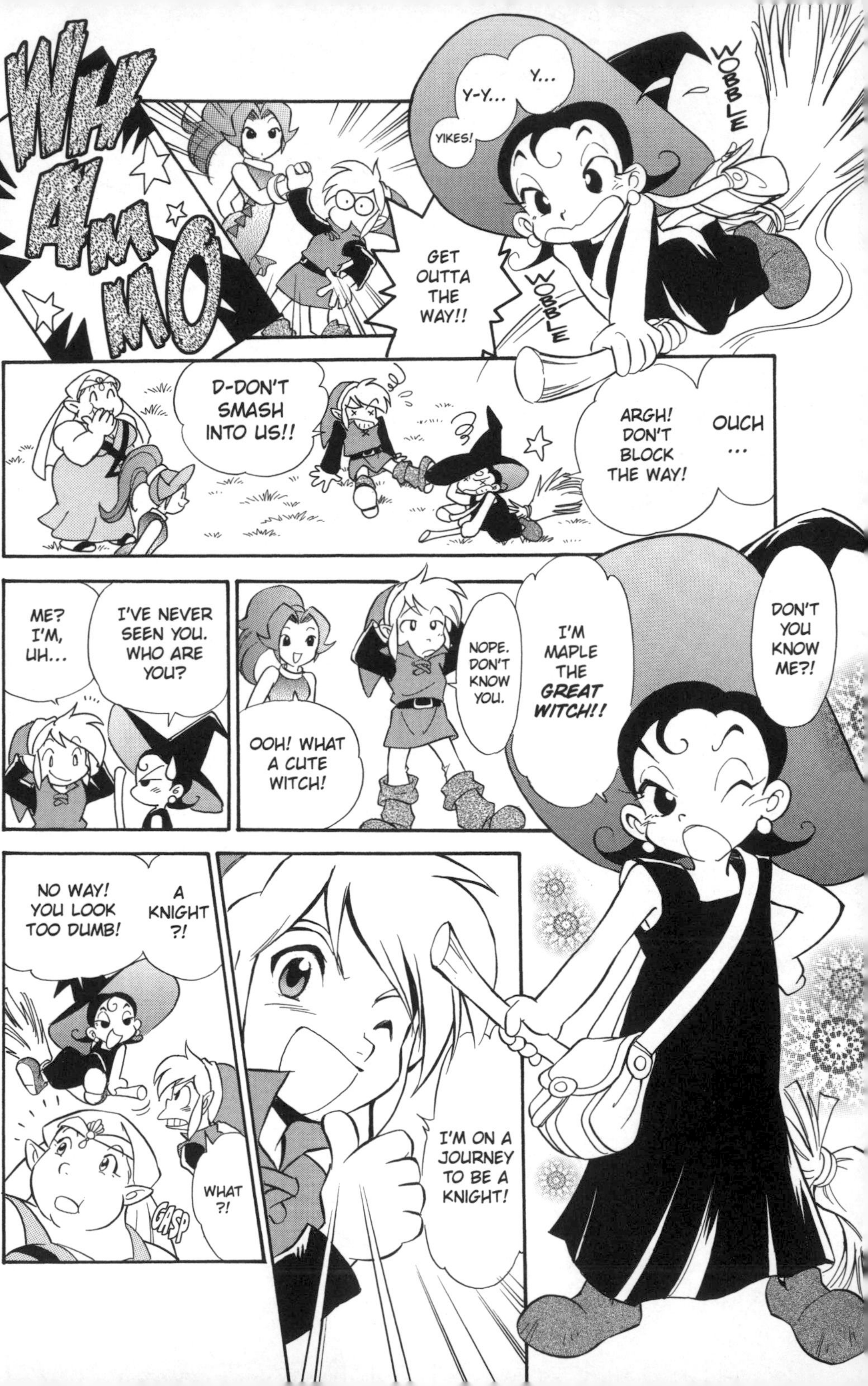

Y...
Y-Y...
YIKES!
WOBBLE
GET OUTTA THE WAY!!
WOBBLE
OUCH ...
ARGH! DON'T BLOCK THE WAY!
D-DON'T SMASH INTO US!!
DON'T YOU KNOW ME?!
I'M MAPLE THE GREAT WITCH!!
NOPE. DON'T KNOW YOU.
OOH! WHAT A CUTE WITCH!
I'VE NEVER SEEN YOU. WHO ARE YOU?
ME? I'M, UH...
I'M ON A JOURNEY TO BE A KNIGHT!
A KNIGHT ?!
NO WAY! YOU LOOK TOO DUMB!
WHAT ?!
GASP

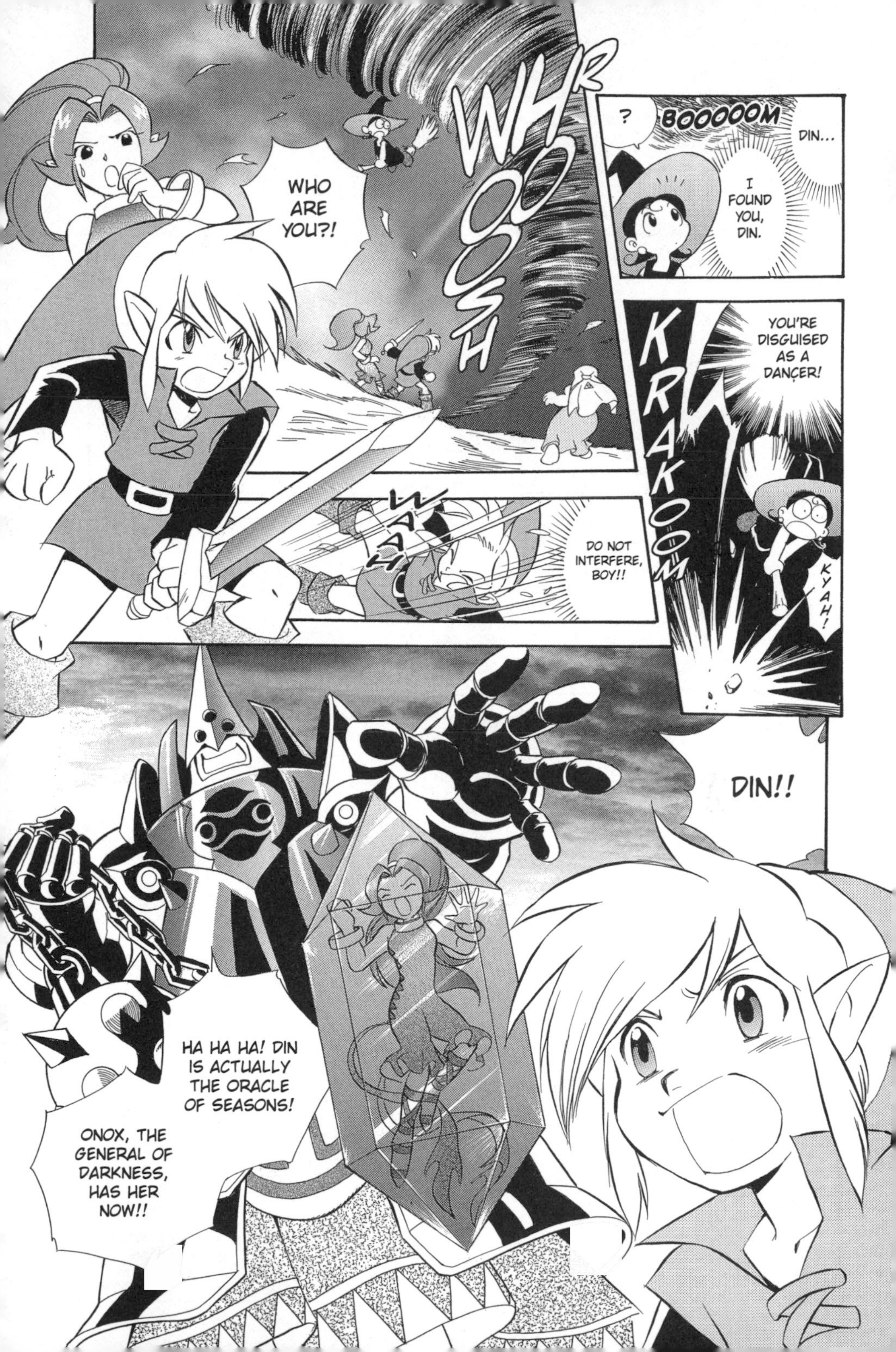
?
BOOOOOM
DIN...
I FOUND YOU, DIN.
KRAKOOOM
YOU'RE DISGUISED AS A DANCER!
KYAH!
WHROOOOSH
WHO ARE YOU?!
WAAH
DO NOT INTERFERE, BOY!!
DIN!!
HA HA HA! DIN IS ACTUALLY THE ORACLE OF SEASONS!
ONOX, THE GENERAL OF DARKNESS, HAS HER NOW!!

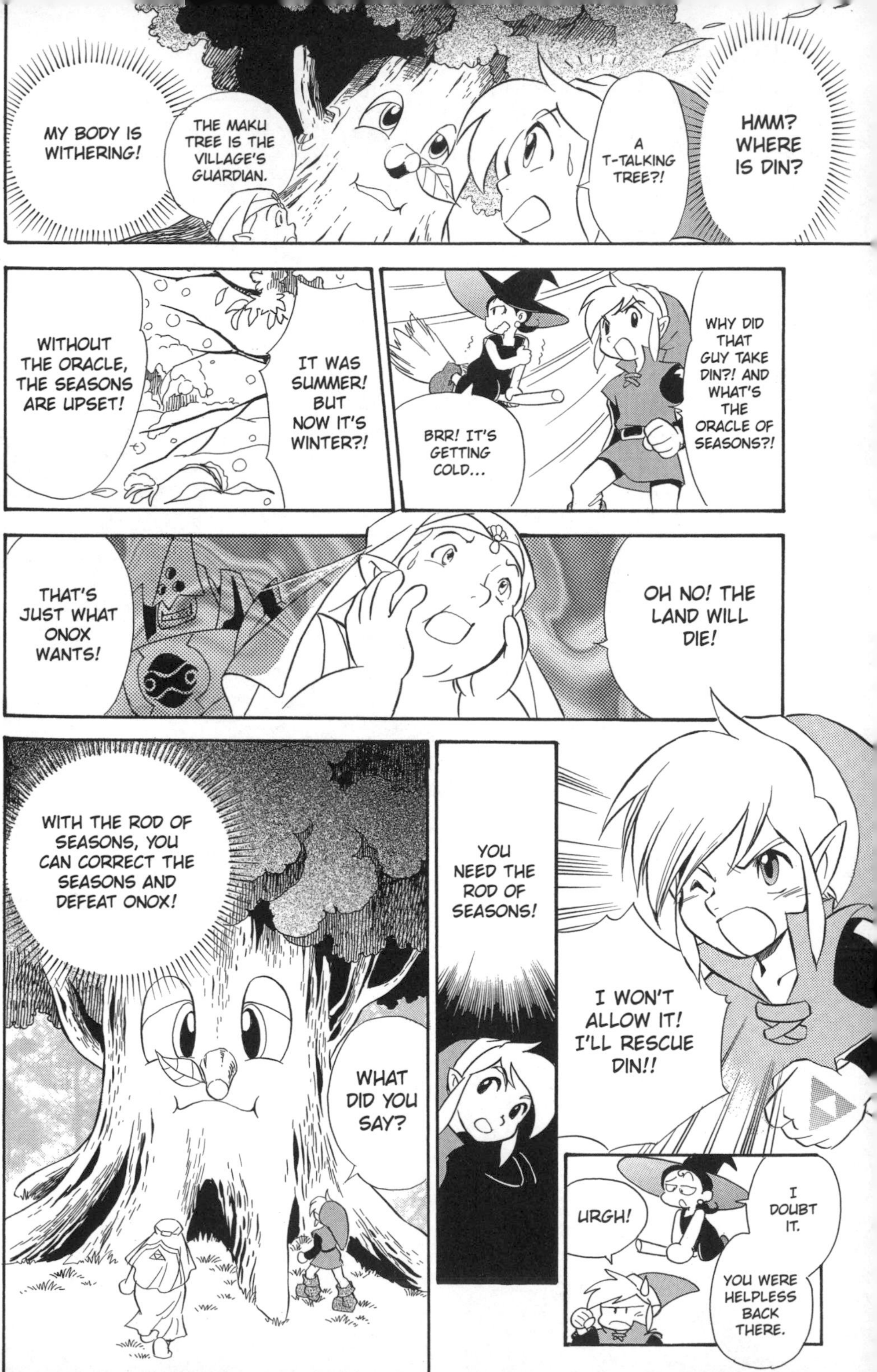
HMM? WHERE IS DIN?
A T-TALKING TREE?!
THE MAKU TREE IS THE VILLAGE'S GUARDIAN.
MY BODY IS WITHERING!
WHY DID THAT GUY TAKE DIN?! AND WHAT'S THE ORACLE OF SEASONS?!
BRR! IT'S GETTING COLD...
IT WAS SUMMER! BUT NOW IT'S WINTER?!
WITHOUT THE ORACLE, THE SEASONS ARE UPSET!
OH NO! THE LAND WILL DIE!
THAT'S JUST WHAT ONOX WANTS!
I WON'T ALLOW IT! I'LL RESCUE DIN!!
I DOUBT IT.
YOU WERE HELPLESS BACK THERE.
URGH!
YOU NEED THE ROD OF SEASONS!
WHAT DID YOU SAY?
WITH THE ROD OF SEASONS, YOU CAN CORRECT THE SEASONS AND DEFEAT ONOX!

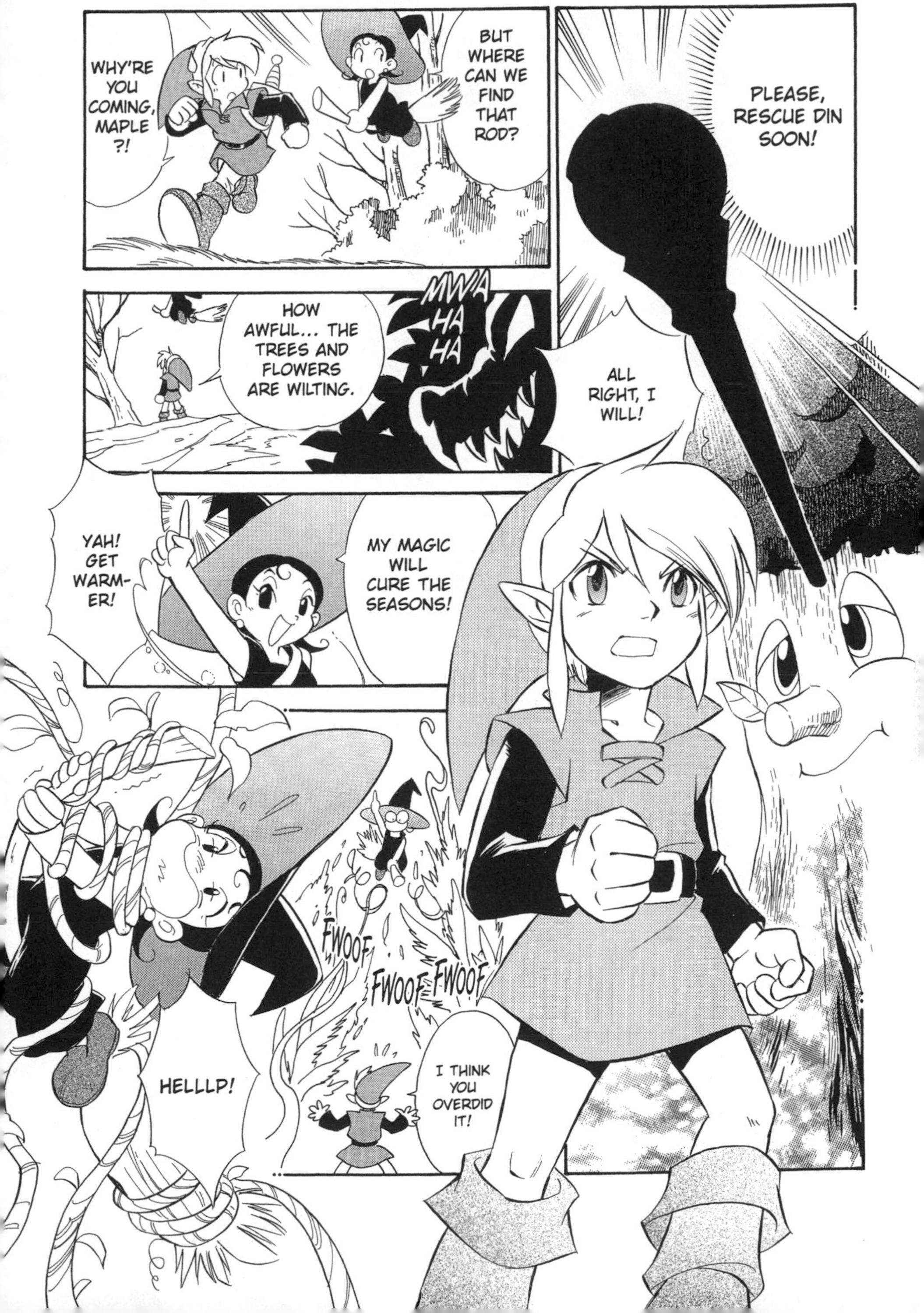
PLEASE, RESCUE DIN SOON!
ALL RIGHT, I WILL!
BUT WHERE CAN WE FIND THAT ROD?
WHY'RE YOU COMING, MAPLE?!
MWA HA HA
HOW AWFUL... THE TREES AND FLOWERS ARE WILTING.
MY MAGIC WILL CURE THE SEASONS!
YAH! GET WARMER!
FWOOF FWOOF FWOOF
I THINK YOU OVERDID IT!
HELLLP!

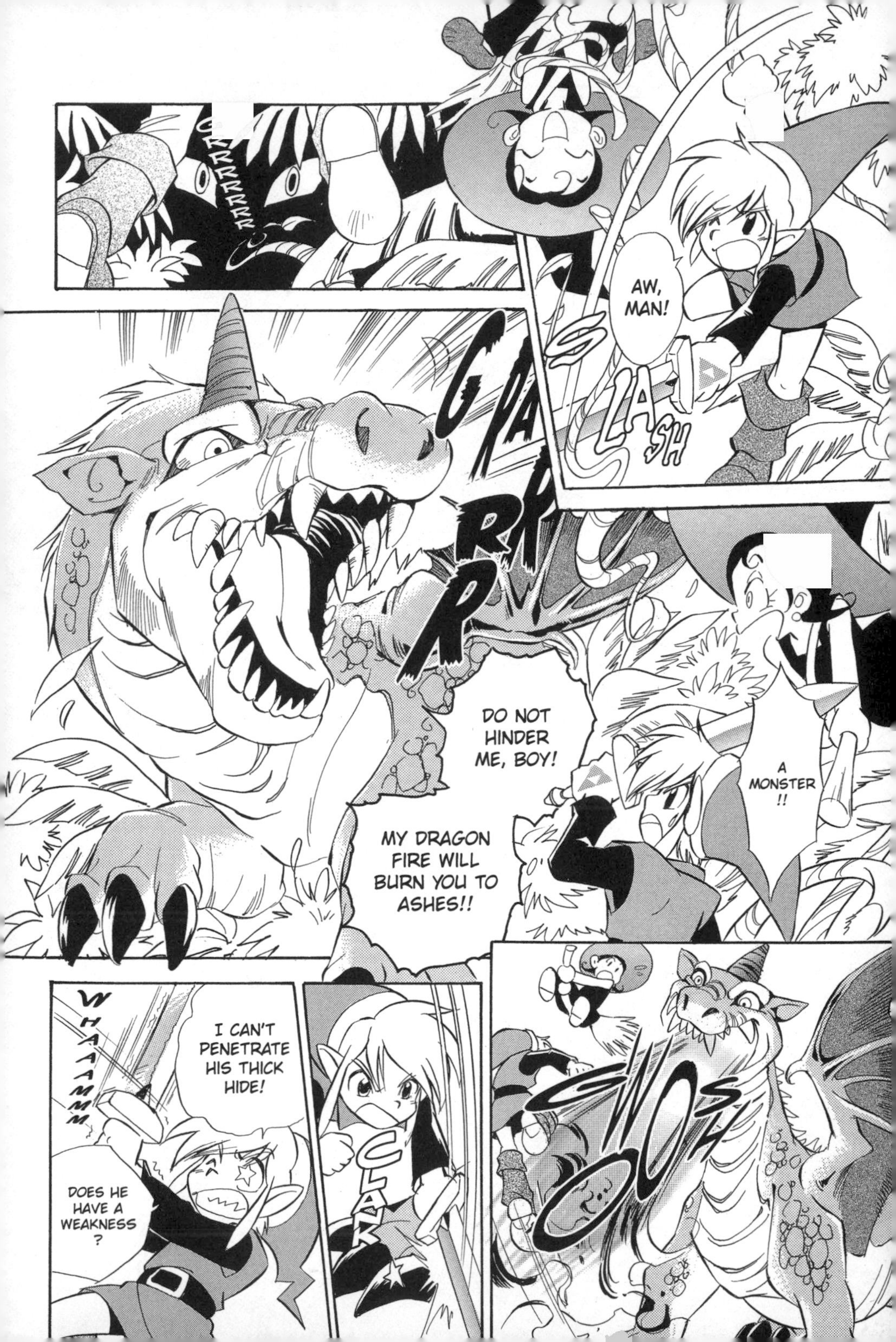

AW, MAN!
SLASH
GRRRRRRR
A MONSTER!!
GRRRR
DO NOT HINDER ME, BOY!
MY DRAGON FIRE WILL BURN YOU TO ASHES!!
SWOOSH
CLANK
I CAN'T PENETRATE HIS THICK HIDE!
WHAAAAMMM
DOES HE HAVE A WEAKNESS?

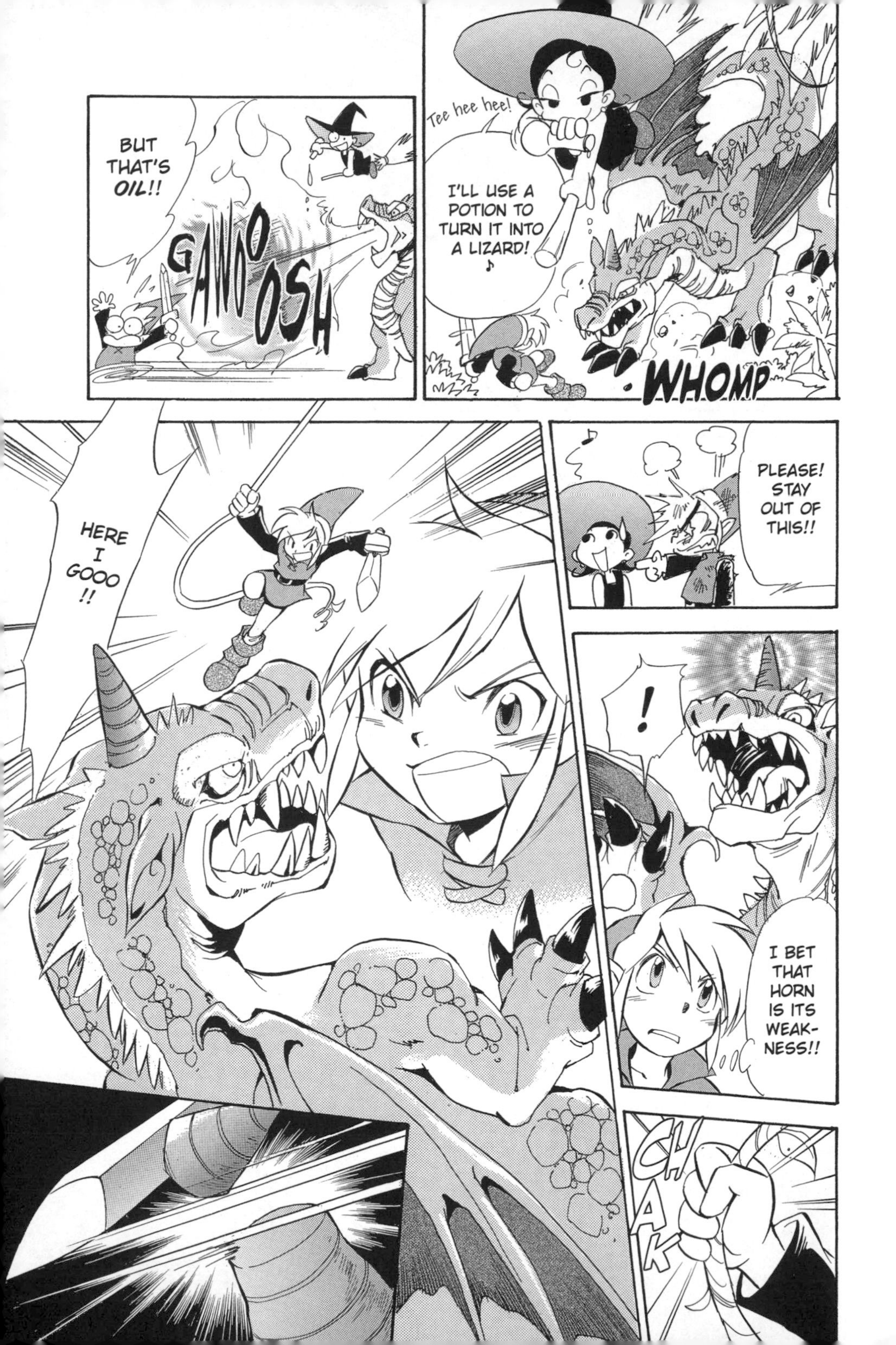
Tee hee hee!
I'LL USE A POTION TO TURN IT INTO A LIZARD! ♪
WHOMP
BUT THAT'S OIL!!
GAWOOOSH
PLEASE! STAY OUT OF THIS!!
!
I BET THAT HORN IS ITS WEAK-NESS!!
CHAK
HERE I GOOO!!

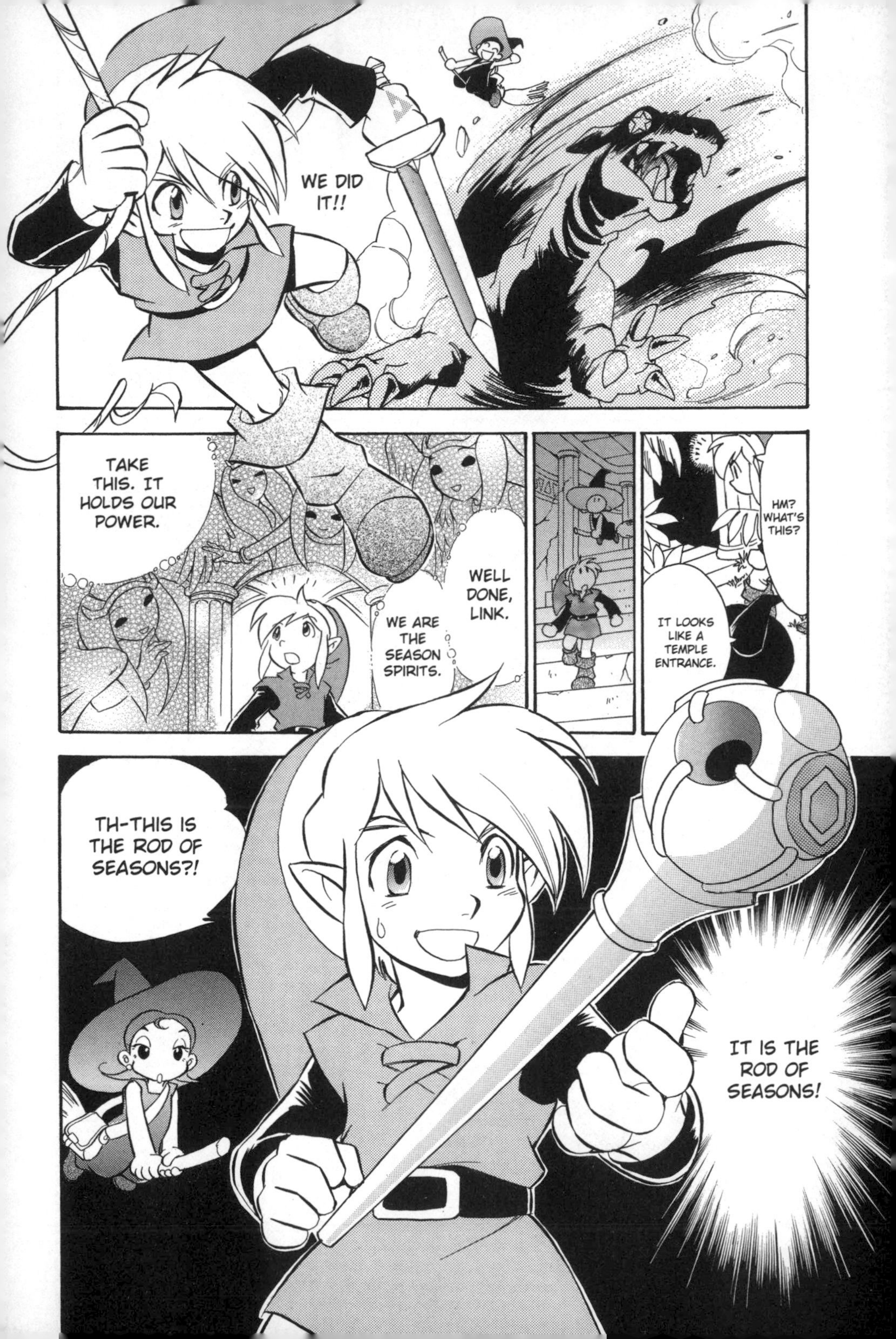
WE DID IT!!
HM? WHAT'S THIS?
IT LOOKS LIKE A TEMPLE ENTRANCE.
WELL DONE, LINK.
WE ARE THE SEASON SPIRITS.
TAKE THIS. IT HOLDS OUR POWER.
TH-THIS IS THE ROD OF SEASONS?!
IT IS THE ROD OF SEASONS!

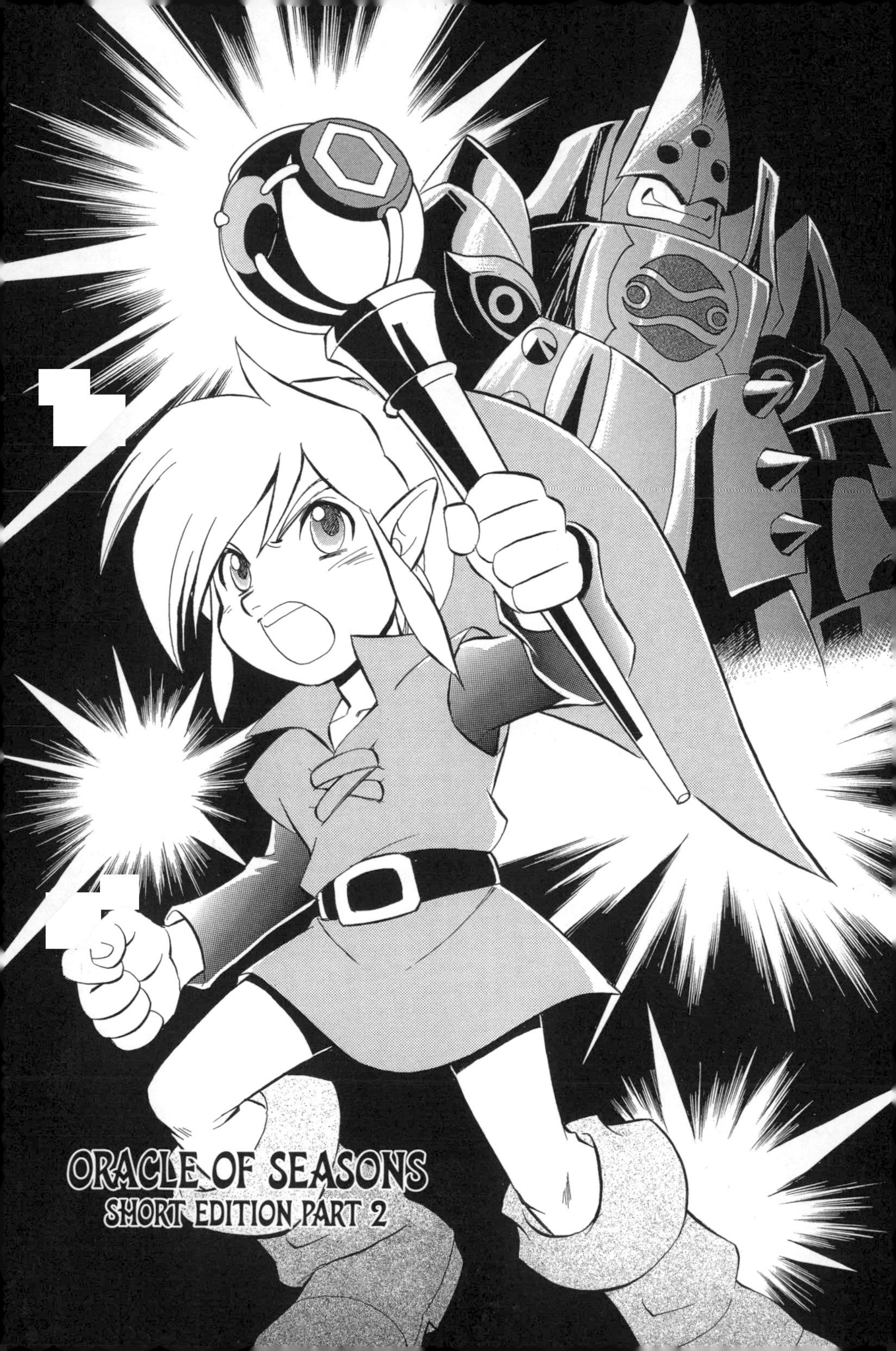
ORACLE OF SEASONS
SHORT EDITION PART 2

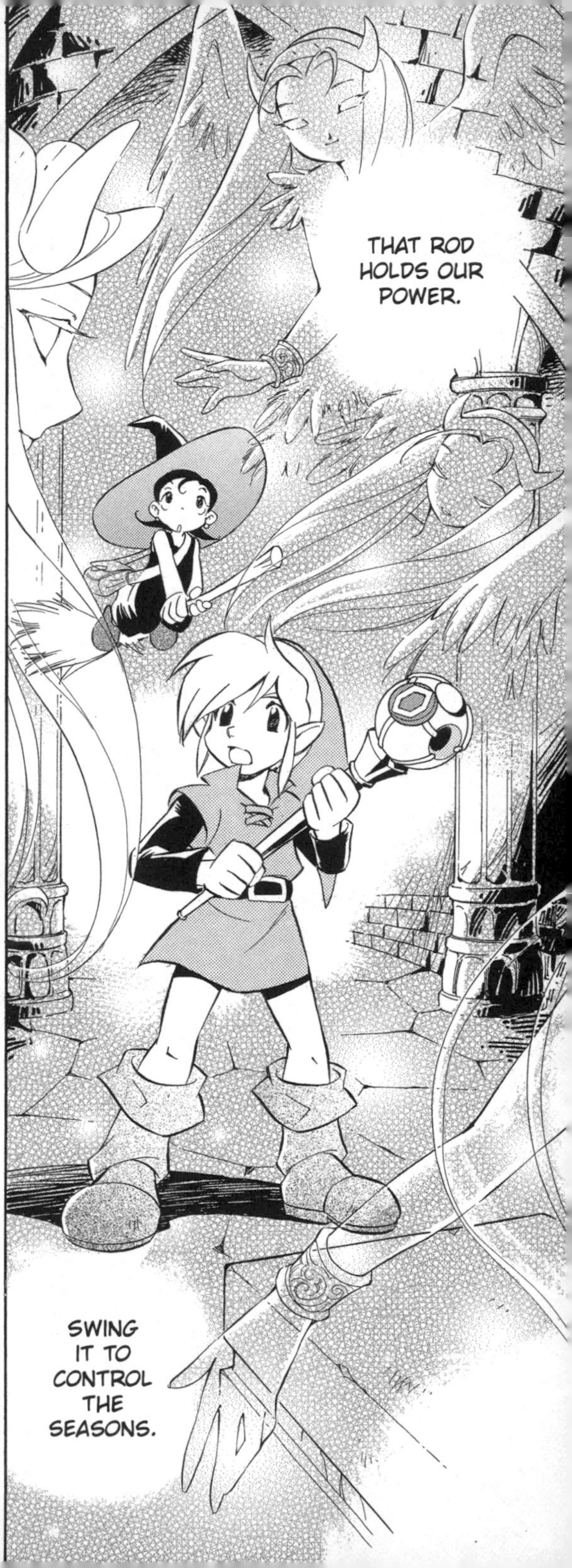
THAT ROD HOLDS OUR POWER.
SWING IT TO CONTROL THE SEASONS.

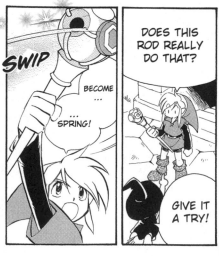

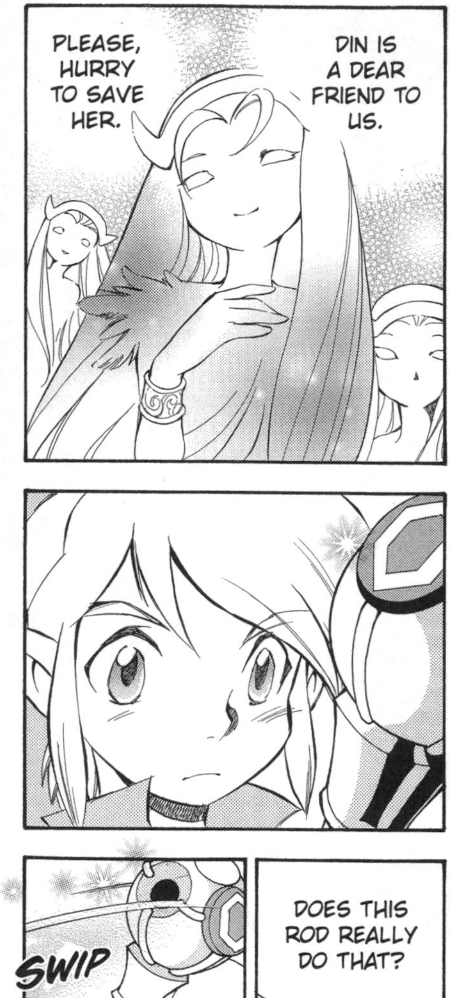
DIN IS A DEAR FRIEND TO US.
PLEASE, HURRY TO SAVE HER.
DOES THIS ROD REALLY DO THAT?
GIVE IT A TRY!
SWIP
BECOME ...
... SPRING!

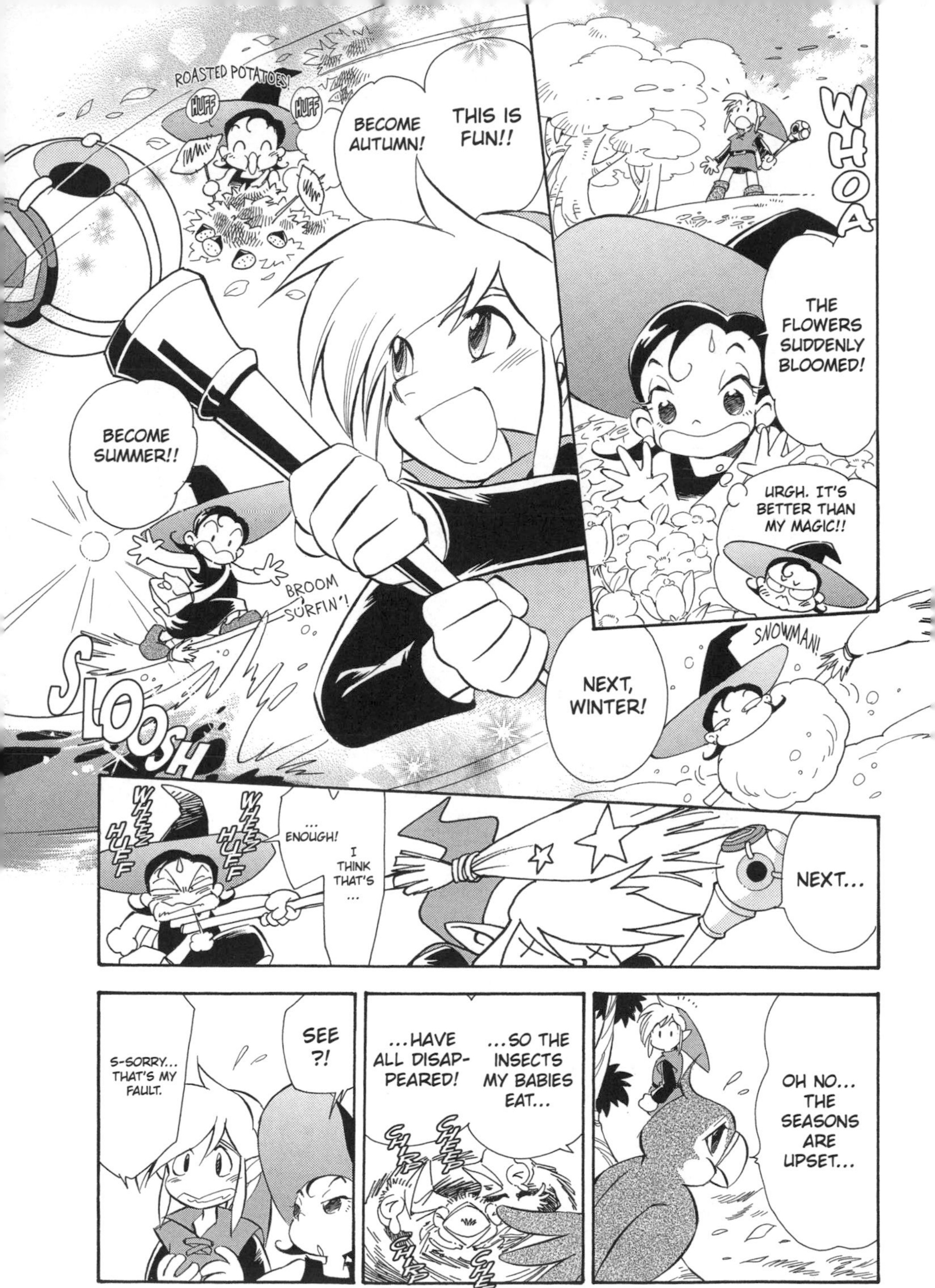
WHOA
THE FLOWERS SUDDENLY BLOOMED!
URGH. IT'S BETTER THAN MY MAGIC!!
THIS IS FUN!!
BECOME AUTUMN!
HUFF
HUFF
ROASTED POTATOES!
NEXT, WINTER!
SNOWMAN!
BECOME SUMMER!!
BROOM SURFIN'!
SLOOSH
NEXT...
... ENOUGH!
I THINK THAT'S ...
WHEEZ HUFF
WHEEZ HUFF
OH NO... THE SEASONS ARE UPSET...
...SO THE INSECTS MY BABIES EAT...
...HAVE ALL DISAP-PEARED!
CHEEP
CHEEP
SEE ?!
S-SORRY... THAT'S MY FAULT.

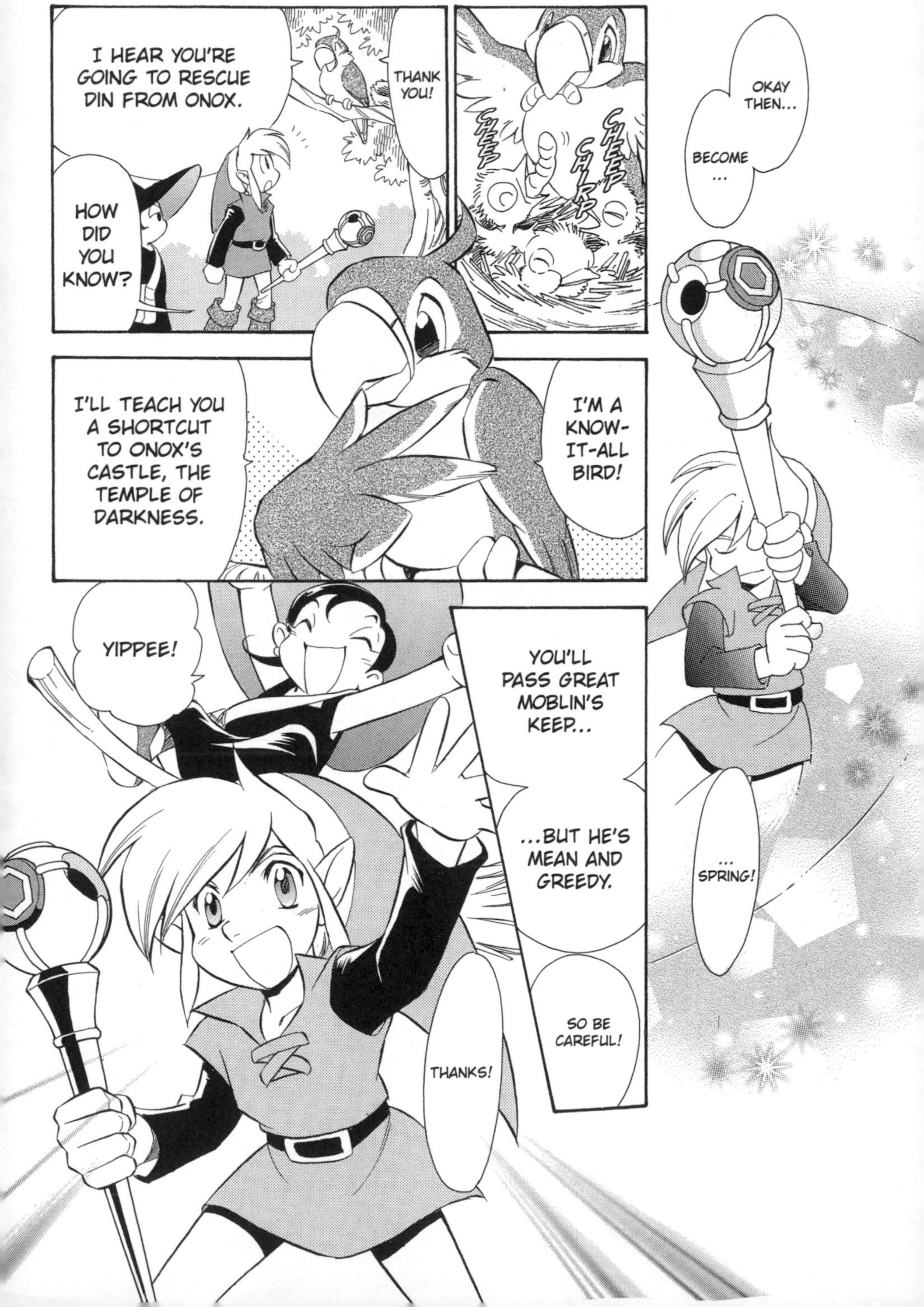
CHEEP
CHIRP
CHEEP
THANK YOU!
I HEAR YOU'RE GOING TO RESCUE DIN FROM ONOX.
HOW DID YOU KNOW?
I'M A KNOW-IT-ALL BIRD!
I'LL TEACH YOU A SHORTCUT TO ONOX'S CASTLE, THE TEMPLE OF DARKNESS.
YOU'LL PASS GREAT MOBLIN'S KEEP...
...BUT HE'S MEAN AND GREEDY.
SO BE CAREFUL!
YIPPEE!
THANKS!
OKAY THEN...
BECOME ...
... SPRING!

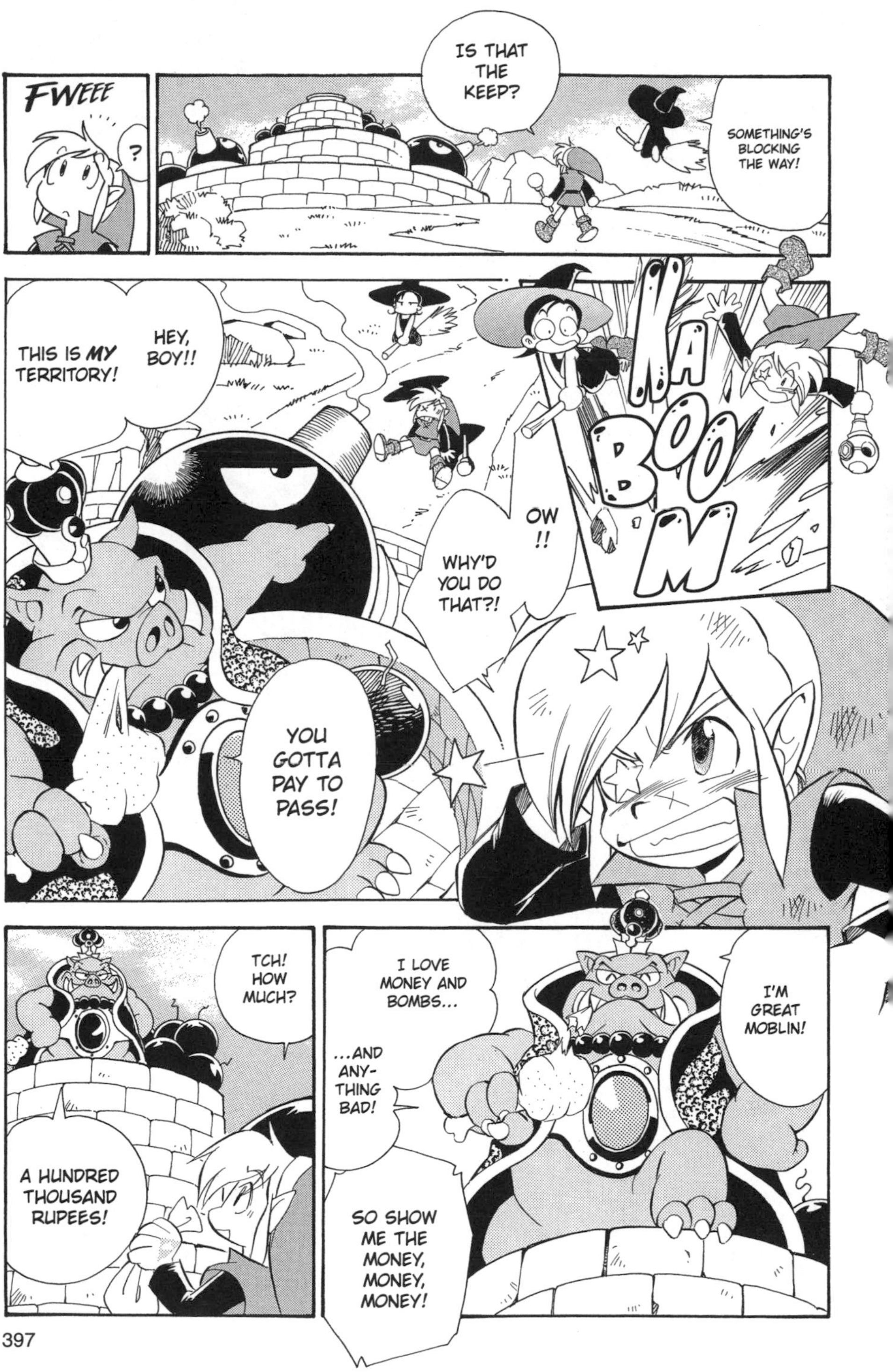
IS THAT THE KEEP?
SOMETHING'S BLOCKING THE WAY!
FWEEE
?
KA BOOM
OW!!
WHY'D YOU DO THAT?!
HEY, BOY!!
THIS IS *MY* TERRITORY!
YOU GOTTA PAY TO PASS!
I'M GREAT MOBLIN!
I LOVE MONEY AND BOMBS...
...AND ANY-THING BAD!
SO SHOW ME THE MONEY, MONEY, MONEY!
TCH! HOW MUCH?
A HUNDRED THOUSAND RUPEES!

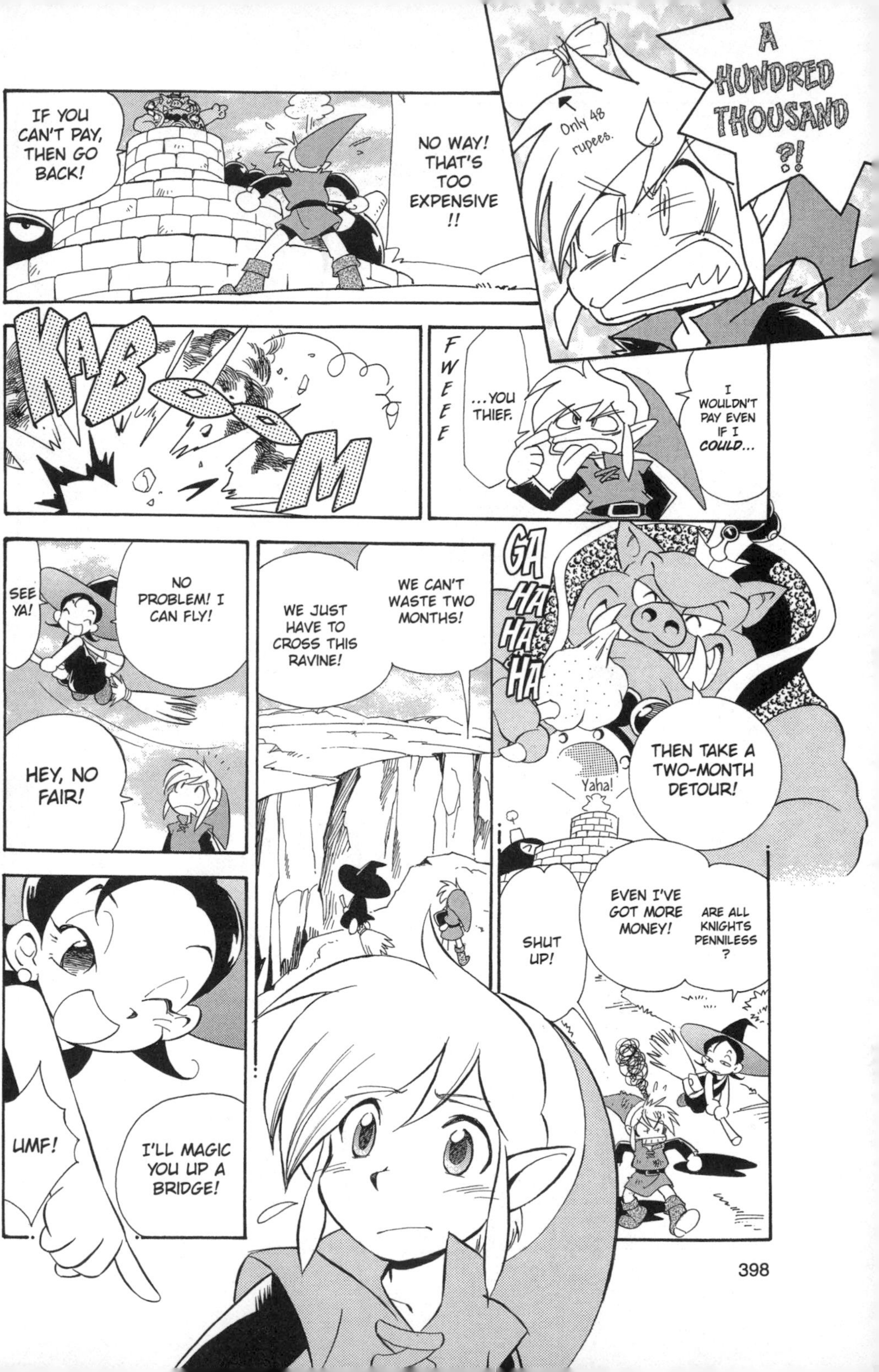
A HUNDRED THOUSAND ?!
Only 48 rupees.
NO WAY! THAT'S TOO EXPENSIVE !!
IF YOU CAN'T PAY, THEN GO BACK!
I WOULDN'T PAY EVEN IF I COULD...
...YOU THIEF.
FWEEE
KABOOM
GAHAHAHAHA
THEN TAKE A TWO-MONTH DETOUR!
Yaha!
ARE ALL KNIGHTS PENNILESS ?
EVEN I'VE GOT MORE MONEY!
SHUT UP!
WE CAN'T WASTE TWO MONTHS!
WE JUST HAVE TO CROSS THIS RAVINE!
NO PROBLEM! I CAN FLY!
SEE YA!
HEY, NO FAIR!
I'LL MAGIC YOU UP A BRIDGE!
UMF!

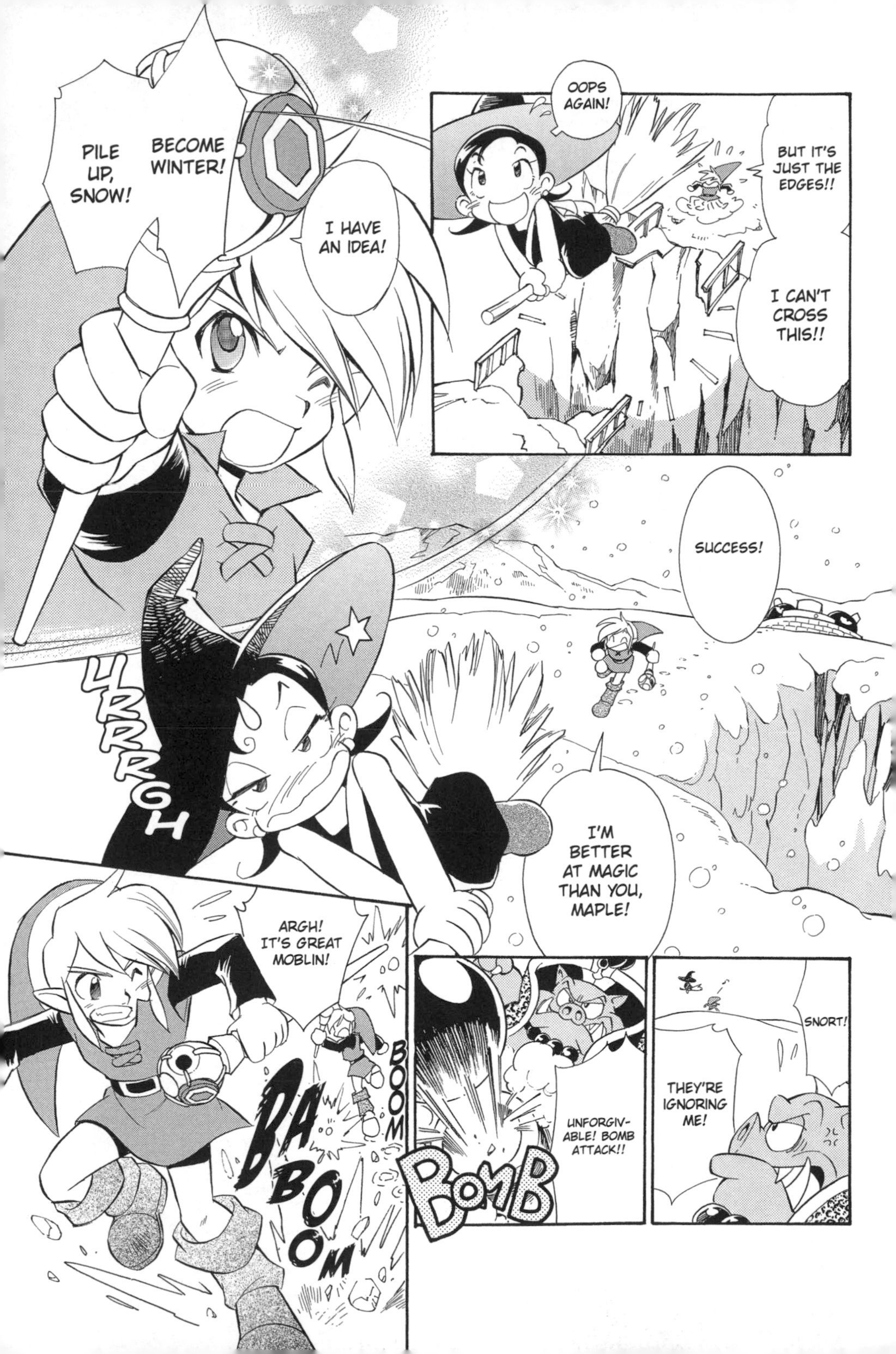
OOPS AGAIN!
BUT IT'S JUST THE EDGES!!
I CAN'T CROSS THIS!!
I HAVE AN IDEA!
BECOME WINTER!
PILE UP, SNOW!
SUCCESS!
URRRGH
I'M BETTER AT MAGIC THAN YOU, MAPLE!
SNORT!
THEY'RE IGNORING ME!
UNFORGIV-ABLE! BOMB ATTACK!!
BOMB
ARGH! IT'S GREAT MOBLIN!
BOOOM
BABOOM

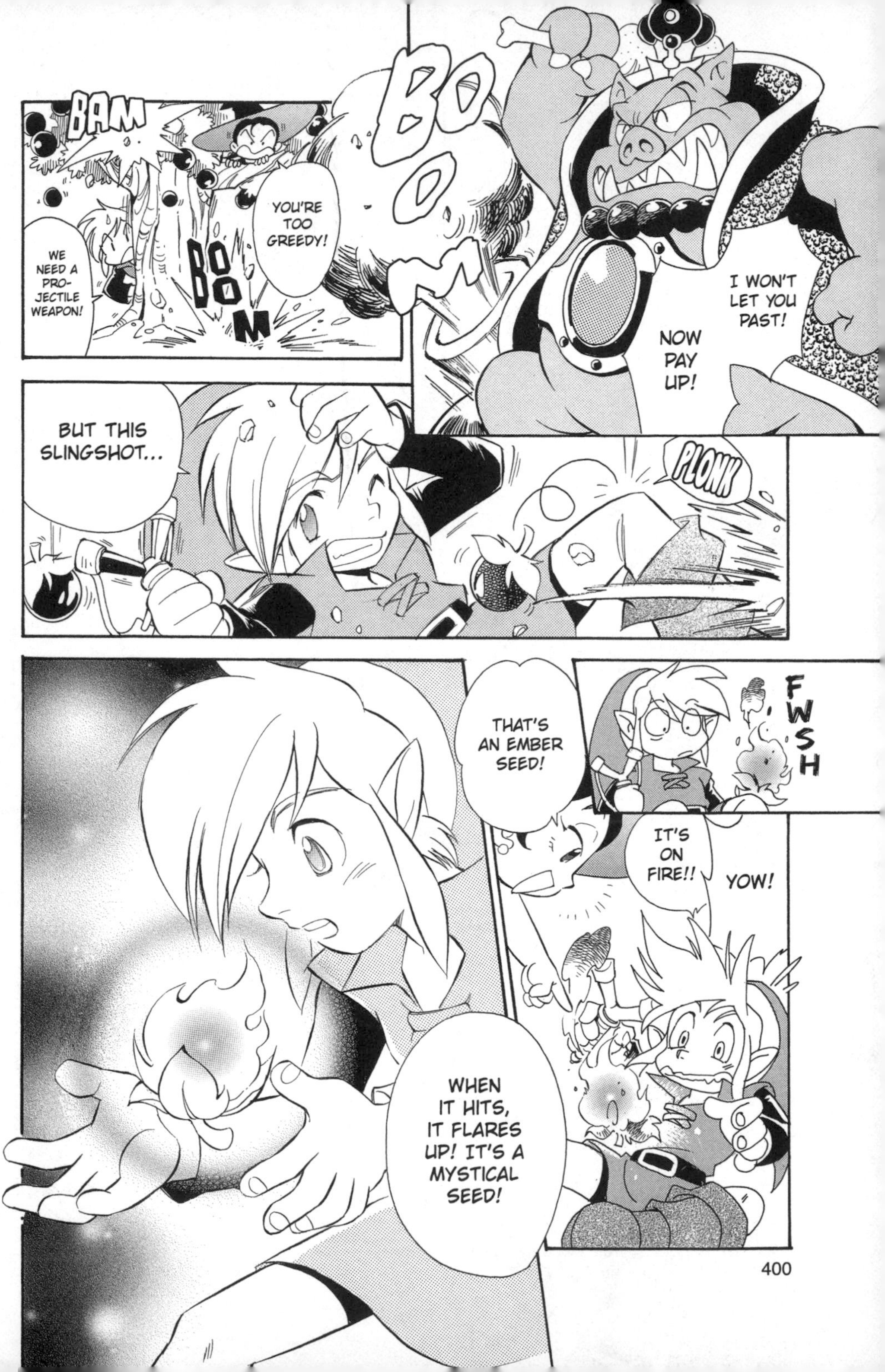
BOOM
I WON'T LET YOU PAST!
NOW PAY UP!
BAM
YOU'RE TOO GREEDY!
BOOM
WE NEED A PROJECTILE WEAPON!
PLONK
BUT THIS SLINGSHOT...
FWSH
IT'S ON FIRE!!
YOW!
THAT'S AN EMBER SEED!
WHEN IT HITS, IT FLARES UP! IT'S A MYSTICAL SEED!

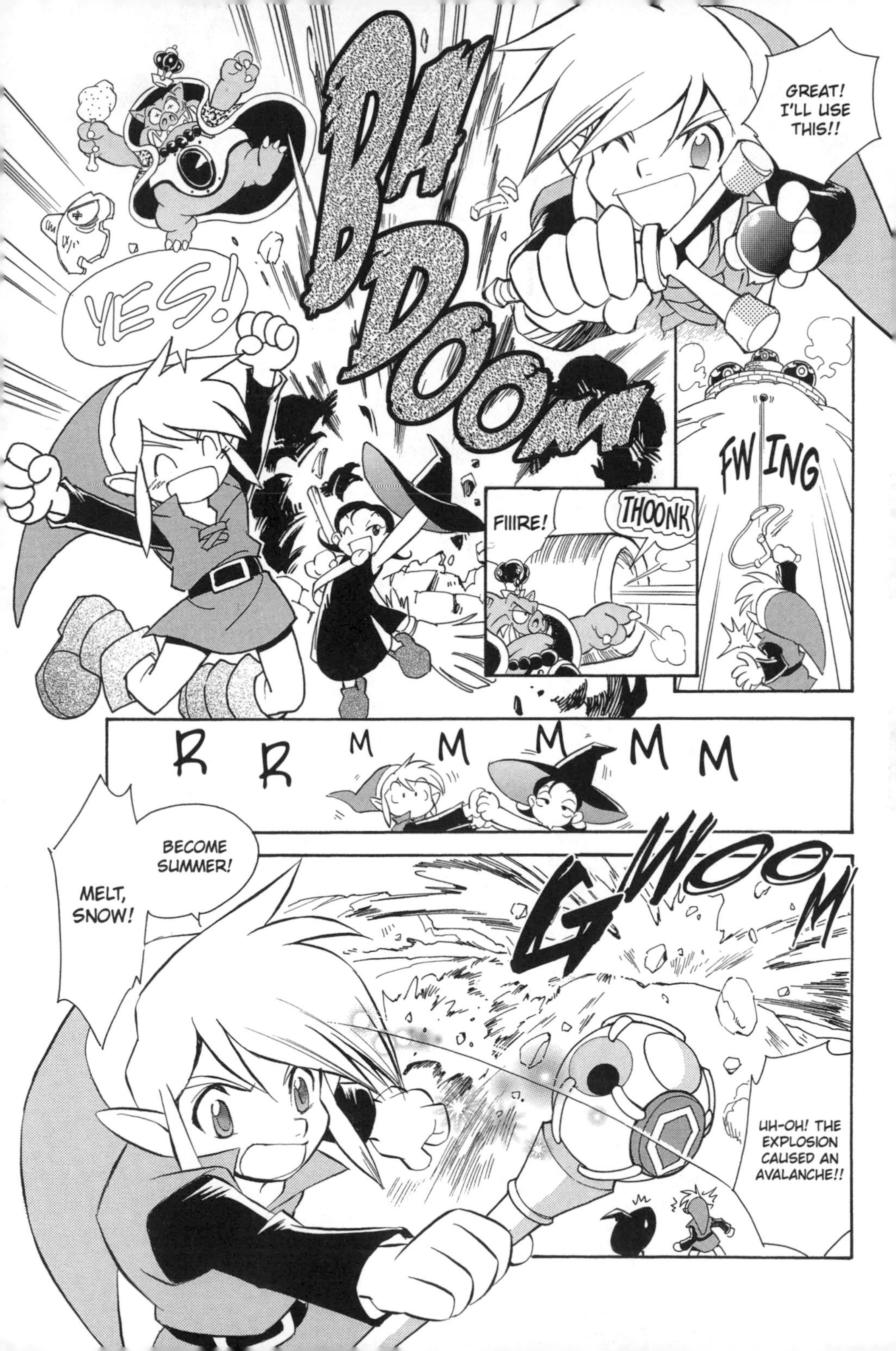
GREAT! I'LL USE THIS!!
FWING
FIIRE!
THOONK
DADOOM
YES!
RRMMMMM
BECOME SUMMER!
MELT, SNOW!
GWOOM
UH-OH! THE EXPLOSION CAUSED AN AVALANCHE!!

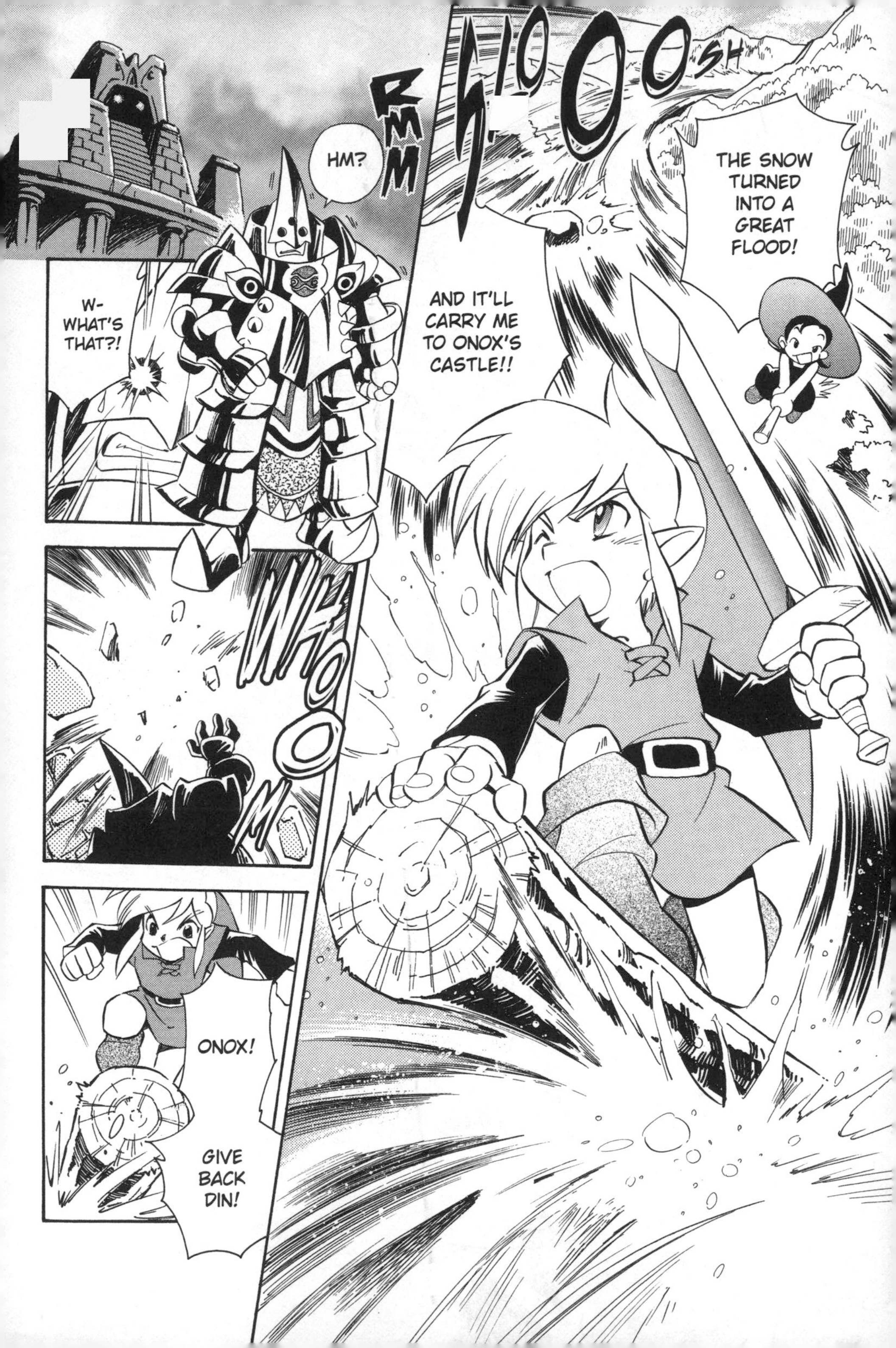
THE SNOW TURNED INTO A GREAT FLOOD!
AND IT'LL CARRY ME TO ONOX'S CASTLE!!
HM?
RMM
W-WHAT'S THAT?!
WHOOOM
ONOX!
GIVE BACK DIN!

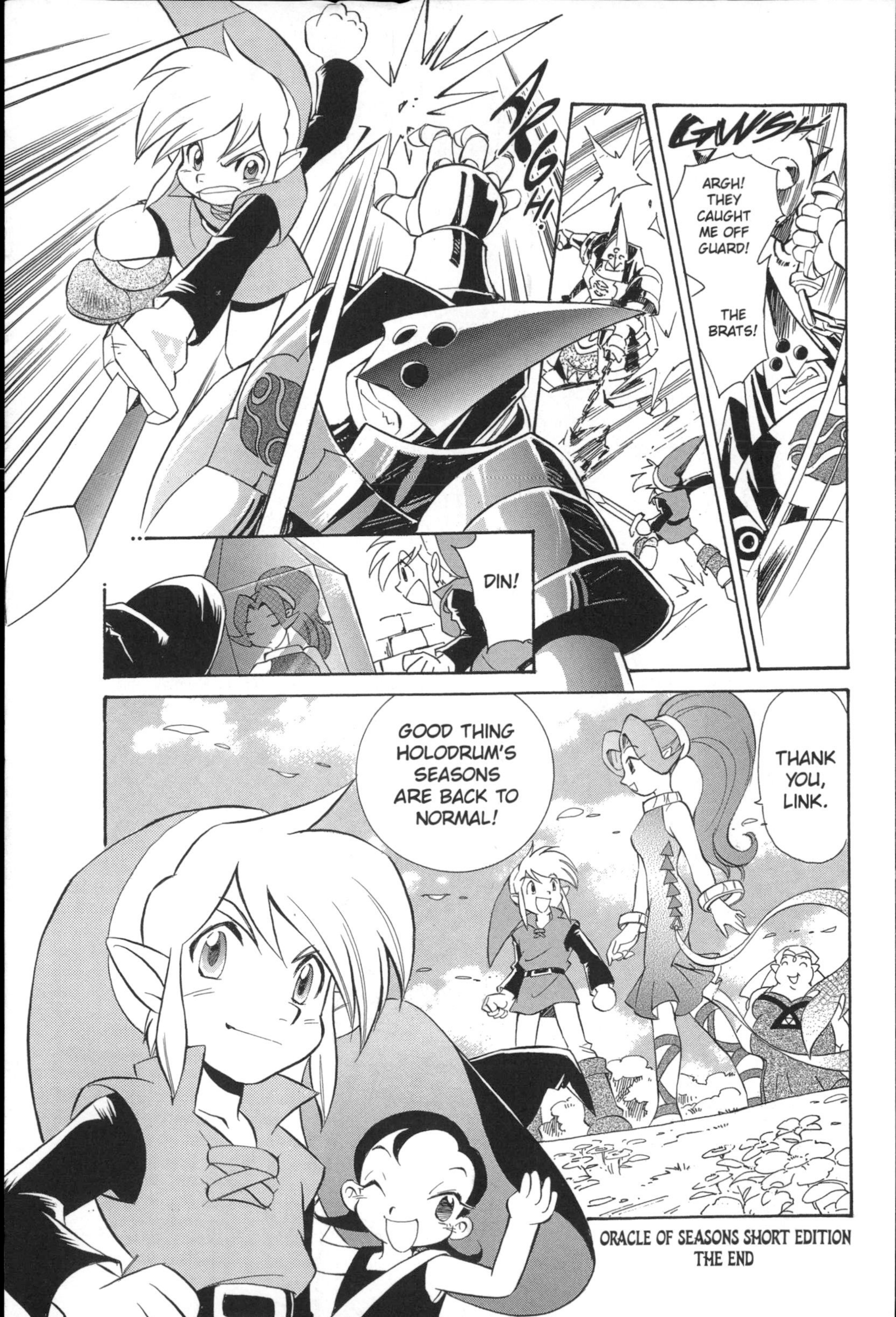
GWUSH
ARGH! THEY CAUGHT ME OFF GUARD!
THE BRATS!
ARGH!
DIN!
THANK YOU, LINK.
GOOD THING HOLODRUM'S SEASONS ARE BACK TO NORMAL!
ORACLE OF SEASONS SHORT EDITION
THE END

A MESSAGE FROM THE AUTHOR
FOR THE LEGENDARY EDITION

This story was divided into *Oracle of Seasons* and *Oracle of Ages*, so I designed the story and characters accordingly. The reason I wanted to have both themes underlying the stories is because one goal was to portray love without being embarassed. I hope everyone senses the simple love the characters around Link, including Piyoko, have for him. During serialization, I also did a version of *Oracle of Seasons* for younger readers in *Shogaku Ninensei*. It never appeared in the graphic novels, so it's appearing in graphic novel format here for the first time. Enjoy!

AKIRA HIMEKAWA

THE LEGEND OF
ZELDA™

ORACLE *of* SEASONS
ORACLE *of* AGES

LEGENDARY EDITION

TRANSLATION John Werry, Honyaku Center, Inc.

ENGLISH ADAPTATION Steven "Stan!" Brown

LETTERING John Hunt

ORIGINAL SERIES DESIGN Sean Lee

ORIGINAL SERIES EDITOR Mike Montesa

LEGENDARY EDITION DESIGN Shawn Carrico

LEGENDARY EDITION EDITOR Joel Enos

viz.com

PARENTAL ADVISORY
THE LEGEND OF ZELDA is rated A and is suitable for readers of all ages.

THE LEGEND OF ZELDA:
ORACLE OF SEASONS/ORACLE OF AGES
-LEGENDARY EDITION-

VIZ MEDIA EDITION

STORY AND ART BY **AKIRA HIMEKAWA**

The Legend of Zelda: Legendary Edition
- Oracle of Seasons/Oracle of Ages -
TM & © 2017 Nintendo. All Rights Reserved.

ZELDA NO DENSETSU FUSHIGI NO KINOMI
DAICHI NO SHO/JIKU NO SHO [KANZENBAN]
by Akira HIMEKAWA
© 2016 Akira HIMEKAWA
All rights reserved.
Original Japanese edition published by SHOGAKUKAN.
English translation rights in the United States of America,
Canada, the United Kingdom, Ireland, Australia
and New Zealand arranged with SHOGAKUKAN.

ORIGINAL DESIGN Kazutada YOKOYAMA

No portion of this book may be reproduced or transmitted in any form or by any means without written permission from the copyright holders.

Printed in the U.S.A.

Published by VIZ Media, LLC
P.O. Box 77010
San Francisco, CA 94107

10 9 8 7 6 5 4
First printing, January 2017
Fourth printing, April 2021